MEDIEVAL
LATIN

This mounted plate, from *Hieronymus, Epistolae*, Basel, 1492, shows Jerome, in characteristic garb and with his lion, perusing the texts of the *tres linguae sacrae*—Hebrew, Latin, and Greek. His work in those languages, mediated in his version of the Bible, called the Vulgate, made possible much of the literary activity of the Latin Middle Ages. The plate is collected in W.L. Schreiber, *Der Buchholzschnitt im 15. Jahrhundert in original-Beispielen*, Munich, 1929, p. 30, from which this photograph comes, by courtesy of Special Collections, John Hay Library, Brown University.

MEDIEVAL LATIN

SECOND EDITION

Edited by

K. P. HARRINGTON

Revised by

JOSEPH PUCCI

With a grammatical introduction by

ALISON GODDARD ELLIOTT

THE UNIVERSITY OF CHICAGO PRESS

Chicago & London

K. P. HARRINGTON (1861–1953) was professor of classics at Wesleyan University.
JOSEPH PUCCI is the William A. Dyer, Jr., Assistant Professor of the Humanities in the
Department of Classics and the Program in Medieval Studies at Brown University.

THE UNIVERSITY OF CHICAGO PRESS, CHICAGO 60637
THE UNIVERSITY OF CHICAGO PRESS, LTD., LONDON

Original edition published by Allyn and Bacon in 1925. Reissued by The University of
Chicago Press in 1962.

© 1997 by The University of Chicago
All rights reserved. Published 1997

Printed in the United States of America
06 05 04 03 02 01 00 99 98 97   1 2 3 4 5

ISBN: 0-226-31712-9 (cloth)
ISBN: 0-226-31713-7 (paper)

Library of Congress Cataloging-in-Publication Data

Medieval Latin / edited by K.P. Harrington ; revised by Joseph Pucci ; with a grammatical
introduction by Alison Goddard Elliott. — 2nd ed.
    p. cm.
  Rev. ed. of: Mediaeval Latin. 1962.
  Includes index.
  ISBN 0-226-31712-0 (cloth : alk. paper). — ISBN 0-226-31713-7
(pbk. : alk. paper)
    1. Latin language, Medieval and modern—Readers. 2. Civilization, Medieval—
Sources—Problems, exercises, etc. 3. Latin literature, Medieval and modern.
4. Readers—Civilization, Medieval.
  I. Harrington, Karl Pomeroy, 1861–1953. II. Pucci, Joseph Michael, 1957–   .
III. Mediaeval Latin.
PA2825.M43   1997
477—dc21   96-50254
                                                                           CIP

For
Winthrop Wetherbee
and in memory of
W. Braxton Ross, Jr.

CONTENTS

Part Two, 450–750
The Rise of Late Latin

PART FOUR, 900–1100
THE RISE OF MEDIEVAL LATIN

Contents

LIST OF ILLUSTRATIONS

PREFACE TO THE SECOND EDITION

K. P. Harrington aimed in *Mediaeval Latin* to expose as wide an audience as possible to the breadth and depth of post-Imperial Latin language and literature. He made no distinction between what we now call Late, Medieval, and Neo-Latin, choosing to allow the larger picture of his topic to dominate the details. My aim in revising *Mediaeval Latin* has been to play to the work's strengths. I have tried, therefore, to improve on the depth of coverage, adding selections from the fourth, ninth, and twelfth centuries; and I have more than doubled the selections by women writers. Fully one quarter of the selections have been expanded. I have played to the goal of depth also by eliminating those selections written after the thirteenth century. An anthology that stretches from the fourth to the seventeenth century was perhaps a good thing when *Mediaeval Latin* was published, in 1925. Today, however, at century's end, it only reinforces the notion that all of the Latin literature written after the "golden age" of early imperial Rome is easily categorized—and, therefore, dismissed. In any case, there is no need to justify the revision of a work that has not been remade since its original publication seventy-two years ago. Generations of students have learned what Medieval Latin they know out of Harrington and a revision on this score was long overdue, both as a service to its students and in order to make the book a competent witness to the vast and increasingly active fields of Late and Medieval Latin philology.

The book has been recast from top to bottom. A new grammatical introduction, written by the late Alison Goddard Elliott, has been included, which makes up in substance and detail for the brevity of the original grammatical notes. I have retained Harrington's organization, choosing to focus on authors and works, but I have divided my revision into five parts and have included a brief introductory essay for each, which establishes the wider context in which the authors and works function. The headnotes have been completely recast, with the aim of making each piece interconnected with neighboring ones, so that students can gain a sense of the coherence of the Latin tradition to which the selections at any given point speak. The headnotes are contextual and interpretive essays. They attempt to set the writer in his or her literary context, to state something of the life of the writer, so far as it is known, to comment specifically on the history, themes, and Latinity of the work in question, and to lead interested readers to further sources. To this end, I have recast Harrington's original bibliographic paragraphs, making his sometimes brief and obscure comments into more complete essays. But I have limited myself to an accounting of primary materials—editions, commentaries, concordances and, where applicable, standard English translations, citing secondary works, with the exception of standard surveys, only in rare instances. All the selections have been reprinted from the best modern editions. I have resisted the temptation to standardize orthography.

This revision has been written in the belief—surely accurate—that the study of Late and Medieval Latin begins from a classical base. Thus, I have tried to keep in mind the classically oriented student coming to Late and Medieval Latin for the first time. In the notes, therefore, I have assumed only a standard knowledge of classical grammar, syntax, and orthography. Hence many of the notes attend to divergences in Medieval Latin from classical norms, particularly where orthography is concerned. Any form, therefore, that is not classical has been glossed in its classical form. These glosses should not be understood to implicate me in an attempt to sanitize Medieval Latin into some approximate form of Classical Latin.

I have glossed all words that are not listed in John C. Traupman, *The New College Latin and English Dictionary* (New York, 1966, rev. 1995). I recommend this excellent paperback dictionary, recently updated, for students using this revision. It possesses the merits of compactness, affordability, and accuracy. Where a form does not appear in Traupman, I have cited at least one alternate lexical authority for the preferred usage. I have generally avoided in the notes scholarly commentary or controversy. Readers who wish to engage in such dialogues can refer to the bibliographic paragraphs for further reading on given authors and works.

The illustrations originally printed in *Mediaeval Latin*, which tended to be grainy and indistinct (and rarely helpful pedagogically), have been replaced with a fresh collection of plates focusing on medieval manuscript and book production. The plates speak to trends germane to the section in which they are placed. I hope they can function independently as a brief examination of a vital, and often overlooked, aspect of Late and Medieval Latin literary culture.

This book, far from being simply an anthology, has been compiled from the start with specific assumptions in mind, both about what we call literature in general, and about Late and Medieval Latin literature in particular. The introductions and headnotes have been written to function as overviews of a crucial epoch in the Western literary tradition for too long ignored, downplayed, or disparaged. As the twentieth century ends, it becomes increasingly clear that students of Latin have for too long worn blinders, inheriting and following the assumptions of scholars who, for the most part, constructed their views of the Latin Middle Ages in the bright glare of unfortunate biases. I hope this revision communicates a new sense of the urgency of the moment, suggesting anew that the time has come to work on the Latin materials of many centuries; that the narrow disciplinary protocols of the nineteenth century will no longer do on the eve of the twenty-first century; that there are good institutional and pedagogical reasons to expand our knowledge of, and interest in, the versions of Latin written between the fourth and the fourteenth centuries. If students can assent to these views after they use this revision, then I will feel that in some small way it has been received—and used—successfully.

ACKNOWLEDGMENTS

The notion that I might revise K. P. Harrington's *Mediaeval Latin* was first suggested to me by my colleague, William F. Wyatt, Jr., to whom I offer my first thanks. The proposal initiated by his comment, which he kindly critiqued, was warmly received at the University of Chicago Press by Penelope Kaiserlian, who has been my contact with the Press throughout and who, along with her assistant, Julee Tanner, gave every kind of good support when the project moved beyond the limits of the old page-frames into the more substantial revision ventured here. I know that Penny always had much more before her than my project, but she never made me feel that anything other than my work was her first concern. As the project proceeded, Carol Saller joined in the work in Chicago, and she has made a large-scale revision of this sort an easier task than it might otherwise have been.

Others helped in different ways. Janet Martin and Ian Thomson read and commented on my proposal. Sarah Spence and Michael Gleason read many of the headnotes and bibliographical essays, offering much improvement. Robert Mathiesen, William Crossgrove, and Michel-André Bossy answered questions, respectively, about Latin paleography, Old and Middle High German, and Occitan. Charles Segal retrieved a magnetic tape version of the grammar that forms the introduction to the revision and gave me permission to revise and publish it. I am particularly happy to bring out the grammar under the name of its author, Alison Goddard Elliott, my predecessor in Medieval Latin studies at Brown, whose memory has enriched my own time at the institution she served so well.

As the project proceeded, Samuel Streit put the treasures of the John Hay Library at my disposal, and John Stanley and Jean Rainwater opened up individual riches by allowing me ready access to literally hundreds of incunables, manuscripts, and books. The beauty of the plates that fill the pages of this revision is owed directly to their hard work, and to the expert photography of Brooke Hemerle. Sheila Blumstein and Kenneth Sacks, successive Deans of the College at Brown, awarded grants to me, respectively, in 1993 and 1996, to hire research assistants. Jesse Soodalter, my first assistant, plumbed the depths of the internet, on-line and standard bibliographies, and card catalogues, locating and in some cases securing the hundreds of works that have gone into producing this revision. Her hard work three summers ago started the project toward its completion.

Luckily for me, I had in Michael Costa a second research assistant equal to the task of helping me actually to finish the project. Mike took on the enormous task of proofing the Latin texts, and he also put his keen eye to work on other parts of the revision, as did Frances Yue. Both Jesse and Mike were helped in their work by Ruthann Whitten, who took on any task, including the typing of some of the Latin texts, amid other administrative burdens of her own. Peter T. Daniels was hired by the Press to bring the manuscript into some kind of final shape, and his devotion to it at times seemed even to rival my own. His efforts are equaled only by the work of Carole Cramer, who kept me on schedule, hunted down sources, smoothed arrangements, and served as a liaison throughout the project. Her name rightly belongs on the title page with mine. This revision would not exist without her. I owe thanks to my colleagues Sheila Bonde and James McIlwain, successive chairs of Medieval Studies at Brown, for permitting Carole to devote so much time to my project—and for the support they have given me over the years. My colleagues in Classics are incomparable, but I owe enormous debts in particular to Michael Putnam. I hope it is enough for the moment to thank him for allowing me to be his student, while remaining all the while my colleague.

Those who have used Harrington over the years know only too well the deficiencies of his anthology. Having worked through his collection now, I have come to a great admiration for the level and intensity of work that went into the production of *Mediaeval Latin*. My initial hope was to improve on a work that had grown long in tooth and claw. I hope now only that my revision is worthy of its predecessor. If it is, it will be due in no small way to the devotion of my wife and son—and of the two men who taught Medieval Latin to me, to whom this revision is dedicated.

J. P.

A BRIEF INTRODUCTION TO MEDIEVAL

LATIN GRAMMAR

Alison Goddard Elliott

Unlike a more traditional grammar of Classical Latin—such as AG, which will represent for us the standard of CL—no grammar of ML or VL can make any claim to completeness; the geographical and chronological boundaries are too great to be encompassed in a single chapter. What I have attempted to do here is to describe certain phenomena—changes from classical usage—which may cause difficulty. For this reason, I have focused on a few authors whose works offer interesting, if occasionally disconcerting, deviations from classical norms. Therefore this grammar is based primarily, but not exclusively, on a select number of VL texts—the pre-Vulgate translations of the Bible known as the *Vetus Latina*, the anonymous translation of Athanasius's *Vita Antonii* (= *VA*), the *Itinerarium* of Egeria (*Itin.*), the *Chronicon Salernitanum* (*Chron. Sal.*), the *Gospel of Nicodemus*, the *Gospel of Pseudo-Matthew*, the *Appendix Probi* (*App. P.*), and the *Histories of the Franks* of Gregory of Tours (Greg. T., *H.F.*). The student of CL will experience little trouble in reading the works of those writers whose works conform fairly closely to classical practice—writers of the Carolingian Renaissance such as Einhard, for example, or products of the Renaissance of the twelfth century such as John of Salisbury. But the others, users of so-called VL such as Egeria or Gregory of Tours, are a somewhat different story. Their writings, indeed, have sometimes been belittled or more often ignored by Classicists because of their "deviations" from more familiar grammar and syntax; or they have been studied with passionate interest by Romance philologists eager to discern the earliest traces of the modern national languages. Here I aim to strike a balance—describing deviations from classical practices, pointing to similarities with Romance vernaculars, but viewing neither as an end in itself. These texts, and their comprehension, are the goal. In addition to the abbreviations cited above, I use the standard forms for the various Romance languages: OFr., Old French; Fr., French; Sp., Spanish; It., Italian; Cat., Catalan; Port., Portuguese; Rom., Romanian. Classical works are cited by their standard abbreviations, as found in LS; medieval works other than those named above are cited in full.

1. ORTHOGRAPHY

One difficulty which the student of ML encounters is that familiar words may appear unfamiliar. Orthography was far from regular and was often influenced by

I

local pronunciation as well as by ignorance. As Mohrmann (409) has pointed out, Latin orthography, unlike that of modern English or French, closely followed the phonetic development of the language; the spelling of CL reflected with fair accuracy the contemporary pronunciation, and, in spite of the precepts of the grammarians, that spelling continued to evolve to reflect changing phonetic conditions. As Quintilian observed, *Orthographia quoque consuetudini servit ideoque saepe mutata est,* "Spelling is also subject to custom and therefore often changed" (*Inst. Or.* 1.7.11). For this reason, manuscript orthography often provides valuable evidence for the evolution of the Latin language and should not be altered or "regularized" to conform with artificial or "classical" norms, even if the unfamiliar spellings do make the student's task more difficult at first. Moreover, many of the seeming "changes" from classical norms can be documented from inscriptions on the walls at Pompeii (i.e., they were in use prior to 24 August 79 C.E.).

It is impossible here to offer anything like a full description of the phonetic and concomitant orthographic evolution of Latin over a period of more than a thousand years; for lengthy discussions of the subject, see the grammars of Löfstedt, Grandgent, and Norberg. Listed here are some of the more common changes from classical standards.

1.1 Accentuation

VL is generally believed to have had a stress accent which usually fell on the same syllable as in CL. There are, however, some exceptions:

> Falling diphthongs like -*ie*- in words like *paríetem,* where the semivowel became consonantal and the accent shifted to the following vowel, *paryétem.*

> Penultimate vowels before consonant groups ending in -*r* attracted the accent, and therefore CL *ténebrae* came to be pronounced *tenébrae; íntegrum* became *intégrum.*

1.1.1 SYNCOPATION

Unaccented vowels were frequently dropped:

> *coliclo* for *cauliculum,* "little cabbage"; *periclum* for *periculum,* "danger" (very frequent in CL poets, e.g. Plautus and Terence); numerous entries in the *Appendix Probi: speculum non speclum, masculus non masclus, vetulus non veclus,* etc. (*App. P.* 3, 4, 5); *domnae = dominae.*

1.2 Pronunciation

Orthography does not keep exact pace with pronunciation, and many of the so-called "mistakes" or departures from classical norms may be ascribed to this fact.

Wright maintains that prior to the Carolingian period there were not two languages, Latin and Romance vernacular, but one with a considerable gap between
pronunciation and spelling.

> In a single section (6) of the *Gospel of Nicodemus* (the manuscript dat-
> ing to the 10th century), the scribe wrote *misertus est mei* and *misertus
> est mihi*, "he had mercy on me." While *mihi* and *mei* look like two dif-
> ferent cases (and the first usage is technically "incorrect"), since *h* was
> not pronounced and short *e* and *i* not distinguished, both words would
> sound the same.

1.3 Vowels

E = I: short *i* commonly > *e*, from the 3d century on (Grandgent 84).

> *menus = minus; ille = illi.*

U = O: very common.

> *suppotatio = supputatio; deursum = deorsum; victuria = victoria;* this
> alteration is very frequent in Gregory of Tours.

Y = I

> *sydera = sidera; misterium = mysterium; presbiter = presbyter.*

1.3.1 REDUCTION OF DIPHTHONGS

AE > E; OE > E (the CL spellings did not reappear until they were introduced by
the humanists). In other cases, AE was used for E:

> *que = quae; Egyptus = Aegyptus; Phebus = Phoebus; cotidiae = coti-
> die; aeclesiae = ecclesiae; interpraetatum* (*Vetus Latina*, Itala, Matt.
> 1.23) = *interpretatum.*

1.3.2 PROTHETIC VOWELS

The tendency to put a vowel (*i*, and later *e*) before *sm, sp,* or *st,* or *z* in Greek
words was not uncommon (cf. Sp. *escuela,* Fr. *école* < SCHOLA); the reverse also
occurs:

> *esthomacho = stomacho* (Anthimus, *Pref.* 4.11); *stivis = aestivis* (ibid.
> 20.25); *exenium = xenium* (Greg. T., *H.F.* 5.46).

1.4 Consonants

Doubled consonants:

> *dicciones = ditiones; cottidie = cotidie.*

3

Consonant substitutions:

B = P

> scribturus = scripturus; optulit = obtulit.

C (K) = QU

> *eculeus* = *equuleus*, "torture rack"; *scalores* = *squalores*; *quirie* = *kyrie* (Mohrmann 413).

D = T

> *adque* = *atque*; *aput* = *apud*; *nequid* = *nequit*.

DI = Z

> *baptidiare* = *baptizare*.

F = PH

> *profetam* (*Vetus Latina*, Itala, Matt. 1.22), = *prophetam*.

S = X

> *elisos* = *elixos*; *mistus* = *mixtus*; *vis* = *vix*.

V = B: The confusion between these two sounds is today limited to certain areas of the Romance-speaking countries (e.g., the Auvergne, parts of the Iberian peninsula); it was, however, far more widespread in antiquity, especially in Spain.

> *baculus non vaclus* (*App. P.* 9); *sedabit* for *sedavit* (Greg. T., *H.F.* 2.10); *negabi* = *negavi* (Norberg 143).

V = F: intervocalic F may be voiced:

> *provano* = *profano* (Norberg 143).

1.4.1 PALATALIZATION

CI = TI: found in inscriptions from the 2d century on. The reverse also occurs occasionally:

> *precium* = *pretium*; *accio* = *actio*; *quociens* = *quotiens*; *nacio* = *natio* (cf. Sp. *nación* but Fr. *nation*); *pudititia* = *pudicitia*.

1.4.2 NASALS

-NT- = -NCT- (common in LL inscriptions from all regions).

> *santus* = *sanctus*; *(de)funtus* = *(de)functus* (cf. It. Sp. Port. *santo*, Cat. *sant*, Rom. *sînt*).

Loss of N before S (common from the earliest periods; cf. the epitaph of L. Cornelius Scipio, consul in 259 B.C.E.: L. CORNELIO L. F. SCIPIO AIDILES COSOL
CESOR (= *consul, censor; CIL* 1, 8.9).

> Cf. *App. P.: mensa non mesa* (Sp. *mesa* < MENSA); *ansa non asa* (ibid.
> 76); *ista = insta.*

> *thensauris = thesauris* (*Vetus Latina*): the epenthetic N is a hypercorrec-
> tion, following the general linguistic rule that one kind of error pro-
> vokes its opposite. *Formonsus* is also common for *formosus.*

1.4.3 REDUCTION OF CT > T

auctor non autor (*App. P.* 154).

1.5 Aspiration

The letter H was already weak in CL, and the Latin-speaker was likely to be
uncertain about where to use this sound (cf. Catullus 84). Internally, the H was
used to mark a syllable but was not pronounced (*mihi, nihil, prehendo*). In spite
of the pretensions of African orators who affected to pronounce an initial H at
the time of Saint Augustine (*Conf.* 1.18.19), there is no trace of Roman H in
Romance (the Fr. aspirate H is Germanic in origin, the H of Sp. *haber* a learnèd
spelling).

Greek loanwords: words borrowed early were pronounced and spelled without the H of their aspirated stops.

> *Feton = Pheton* (i.e., *Phaeton*); *Pithagoras = Phitagoras* (i.e., *Pythago-
> ras*); *spera = sphaera; Aprodite = Aphrodite* (*CIL* 4, 1589, from
> Pompeii).

Other:

> *habundare = abundare; habire = abire; asta = hasta; erba = herba;
> rhetor* and *rethoricus; hostium = ostium.*

MICHI = MIHI (etc.): after H lost all sound, scribes often wrote -CH- to indicate
a disyllable.

> *nichil* (in Spain *nicil*) = *nihil.* In Spain, also *mici, arcivum, macina.*

1.6 Proper Names

Proper names, especially biblical ones, may cause considerable difficulty for the
medieval scribe. In the *Vetus Latina*, for example, at Matt. 2.1 the following spellings for "Jerusalem" occur: *Hierosolyma, Hierusolima, Ierosolima, Hierosolima;*
for Israel: *Istrahel, Israhel, Isrl* (an abbreviation), *Sdrael, Istrael* (Matt. 2.6). The
Greek word "myrrh" is spelled *murra, myrra, mirra, smyrna* (Matt. 2.11).

2. Vocabulary Changes

Further difficulties of ML are that familiar words have changed their meaning, and that a perhaps less familiar word has replaced a better-known one. Löfstedt 1, 340, writes: "It is a characteristic feature of Latin in its later stages that a good many words well-known or seemingly well-known from earlier periods occur with new and surprising meanings. . . . The change is, in some cases, a natural and organic one due to special circumstances involving an inner change of meaning; in other cases it is more correct to consider it a sort of etymologizing new formation either learned or popular in origin or resting on ignorance (it is not always easy to decide which)."

Changes often involve the status of a word, as a term of humble origin replaces a more elevated one (i.e., CASA, "hut," replaces DOMUS, "house"). A phenomenon common to the development of all languages is the restriction of a word of general meaning to a specific use or the reverse (e.g., TESTIMONIUM, "evidence" becomes TESTIS, "witness" [Löfstedt 2, 151–52]). Another example of the specific replacing the general: MACHINA, "invention," "artifice" > "machine." Furthermore, seemingly irregular formations (e.g., verbs with reduplicated perfects) tend to be replaced by more regular (and first conjugation) forms (CANO, CANERE, CECINI is replaced by CANTO, CANTARE, CANTAVI).

By constant use, moreover, the meanings of words seem to erode. Simple verbs, e.g., DO, DARE, DEDI, with its monosyllabic forms and reduplicated perfect, were replaced by the frequentative, DONARE (cf. Fr. *donner*); frequentatives, moreover, had the additional advantage of seeming stronger than the simple forms (Löfstedt 2, 28). To give another example, AUSARE replaced AUDERE (It. *osare*, Fr. *oser*, Sp. *osar*).

Monosyllabic verb forms tended to be replaced—i.e., *is, it* from *ire* were replaced by compounds (*inire, exire*), or by other verbs such as *ambulare* and *vadere; fles, flet* (from *flere*) were replaced by forms of *ploro* or *plango; flas, flat* (from *flare*) were replaced by the compound *sufflare* (> Fr. *souffler*); *es, est* (from *edo*) were replaced by forms of *comedo* (or *manducare*). This process of compounding, moreover, was not limited to monosyllabic forms: cf. *expandere* replacing *pandere, adimplere* replacing *implere*.

For nouns, the fourth and fifth declensions disappeared from the spoken language, fourth declension nouns being assimilated to the second, and fifth to the third (see §§ 3.1 and 3.2). In addition, many diminutives, which belong to the first or second declension, replaced the customary CL form (e.g., SOLICULUM may replace SOL, SOLIS (cf. Fr. *soleil*, but It. *sole* < SOL).

Sound was yet another factor which influenced the vocabulary of Medieval Latin. It has been noted several times that words with similar sound clusters and adjacent senses influenced one another (Löfstedt and Norberg, cited by Westerbergh 289–90). For example, in the *Chronicon Salernitanum*, *expectare* (to expect) *aliquid ab aliquo* came to mean *expetere* (to demand) *aliquid ab aliquo*.

Finally, many Greek loanwords displaced the CL forms, as COLAPHUS replaced ICTUS (4th) (cf. It. *colpo*, Fr. *coup*, Sp. *golpe*); THIUS in Italy and Spain appears to have supplanted AVUNCULUS (It. *zio*, Sp. *tío*), while in France AVUNCULUS remained in use (*oncle*). C(H)ORDA replaced the deceptive FUNIS (3d).

2.1 Words Which Have Changed Meaning

ACER "sharp" (touch) > "bitter" (It. *agre*, Fr. *aigre*).

ADIUTARE replaces ADIUVO, ADIUVI (It. *aiuto*, Fr. *aider*, Sp. *ayudar*).

ALTER "one of two," assumes as well the meaning of ALIUS, "other," "different," which disappears (> Sp. *otro*, Fr. *autre*).

AMBULARE "to go about," "to walk" (with various shades of meaning in CL, replaces IRE (It. *andare*, Prov., Cat. *anar*, Sp. *andar*, Fr. *aller*).

APPREHENDERE "grasp" replaces DISCERE, DIDICI "learn" (Fr. *apprendre*).

AURICULA (ORICLA) the diminutive replaces AURIS "ear" (It. *orecchio*, Rom. *urechi*, Sp. *oreja*, Fr. *oreille*).

AVICELLUS (AUCELLUS) replaces AVIS (3d) "bird" (It. *ucello*, Fr. *oiseau*, Port. *augel*).

BELLUS "pretty," "nice," replaces PULCHER, "beautiful," which disappeared completely from Romance (It. *bello*, Fr. *bel*, etc).

BREVE, BREVIS "short" > "letter" (legal Eng. *brief*).

BUCCA "cheek," replaces OS, "mouth" (It. *bocca*, Fr. *bouche*, Sp. *boca*).

CABALLUS "nag," replaces EQUUS, "horse."

CAMERA (Greek) "vault" > "room" (It. *camera*, Fr. *chambre*).

CANTARE a frequentative form, replaces CANO, CECINI (3d) (Fr. *chanter*, Sp. *cantar*, etc.).

CASA "hut" replaces DOMUS (cf. It. Sp. *casa*).

CAUSA replaces RES, "thing" (It. *cosa*, Fr. *chose*). With a negative meaning, RES persists (Fr. *rien*, Cat. *res*).

CIVITAS replaces URBS and OPPIDUM, found first in Cic. *Ad Fam.* 9.9.3.

COLLOCARE "to put" > "to put (in bed)," "go to bed" (It. *coricare*, Fr. *coucher*, Cat. *colgar*).

COMEDO "eat up entirely," "waste," replaces EDO "eat" (Sp. *comer*).

COMES "companion" > "count" (Fr. *comte*).

COXA "hips," replaces FEMUR, "thigh" (Fr. *cuisse*).

CRIMEN "accusation" comes to mean "crime."

CULTELLUS the diminutive, replaces CULTER (It. *coltello*, Sp. *cuchillo*).

DIURNUS an adjective, replaces the 5th declension DIES (It. *giorno*, Fr. *jour*).

DOLUS "trickery" > DOLOR, "grief" (Löfstedt 2, 160f.; cf. It. *duolo*, OFr. *duel*, MFr. *deuil*, Sp. *duelo*).

Dux "leader" > "duke."

Ecclesia "assembly place" > "church building."

Expandere replaces pandere (It. *spandere*, Fr. *épandre*).

Fabulare (CL, *fabulor*) replaces loquor (Sp. *hablar*, Port. *falar*).

Flebilis "lamentable," by a transferral from the moral to the physical sphere, re-places debilis, "weak" (Fr. *faible*).

Focus "hearth," replaces ignis, "fire" (It. *fuoco*, Rom. Cat. *foc*, Sp. *fuego*, Fr. *feu*).

Geniculum this diminutive replaces genu (It. *ginocchio*, Fr. *genou*, OSp. *hinojo*).

Grandis "large" in size, "big," replaces magnus, "great" especially morally.

Hostis "enemy" > "expedition" > "army" (It. [poet.] *oste*, Rom. *oaste*, Sp. *hueste*, Ptg. *hoste*, OFr. Prov. *ost*).

Ingenium "wit, talent" > "strategem" > "siege engine" (Tertullian), "deceit"; *novaque semper ad laedendum populum ingenia perquaerebat*, "he was always seeking new tricks to injure the people" (Greg.T., *H.F.* 6.46) (Sp. *engaño*, Prov. *(en)genh*). (Note that Sp. *ingenio* [< *ingenium*] is a later borrowing which faithfully preserves the form and meaning of the Latin original.)

Irritare "annoy," "provoke" > "render void" (Löfstedt 2, 158–60).

Iterare "repeat" > *iter facere*, "journey" (cf. OFr. *errer*, "walk," "knight errant"; Löfstedt 2, 161).

Labor in addition to its customary meaning, "hard work," comes to mean "field" (= ager), and in particular "wheatfield" (= messis).

Ligare replaces vincio, vinxi (Fr. *lier*).

Manduca "chew," replaces edo (Fr. *manger*, It. *mangiare*).

Mansio "stay" > "stopping place," "inn" > "house" (OFr. *manoir* [Eng. *manor*], Fr. *maison*, but cf. Sp. *mesón*, "inn").

Mane, de mane replaces cras, "tomorrow" (Rom. *mîne*, It. *domani*, Fr. *demain*, Cat. *demà*).

Matutinum (adj.) replaces mane "morning" (It. *mattino*, Fr. *matin*); on parts of the Iberian penisula, maneana was used (Sp. *mañana*, Port. *manha*, but Cat. *matí*).

Memoria "tomb," "memorial"; in ecclesiastical Latin, especially a church erected to commemorate a saint or a martyr.

Miles "soldier" > "knight."

Mittere "send," replaces ponere, "put" (*nemo mittit vinum novum in utres veteres*, "No one puts new wine in old skins" (*Vetus Latina* and *Vulgate*, Matt. 2.22; cf. It. *mettere*, Fr. *mettre*).

Morosus "fretful," "capricious" > "slow," "long" (< mora, "delay").

Necare "kill" (Ovid, *Trist.* 1.2.36, *necaturas . . . aquas*) > "drown" (It. *annegare*, Fr. *noyer*, Prov. Cat. *negar*, Sp. Port. *anegar*).

Nepotem "grandson" > "nephew" (Fr. *neveu*; It. *nipote* < nepos).

NITIDUS "brilliant" > "clean" (It. *neto*, Fr. *net*).

ORARE "talk" (*orator*) > "ask" > "pray."

ORBUS "bereft of" (relations, children) > "blind" (Rom. *orb*, It. *orbo*, OFr. *orb*).

PACARE "pacify" > "pay" (It. *pagare*, Fr. *payer*, Sp. *pagar*).

PAGANUS "country dweller" (< PAGUS) > "civilian" > "pagan."

PARABOLARE replaces LOQUOR (It. *parlare*, Fr. *parler*, Cat. *parlar*).

PASSER "sparrow" > (little) "bird" (Sp. *pajaro*, Port. *pássaro*).

PARS "part" > "region," "place" (Sp. Port. *parte*).

PENSARE a frequentative, "to weigh carefully," replaces PENDO, PEPENDI (3d) (It. *pesare*, Fr. *peser*); it also came to mean "to weigh up mentally" > "to consider," "to think" (It., *pensare*, Fr. *penser*, Sp. *pensar*).

PLANGO "strike" > "wail aloud, wring hands" is one replacement for FLERE, "weep" (It. *piangere*). PLORARE, which classically means something like "bawl," "cry," also replaces the more poetic FLERE, which disappears (cf. Fr. *pleurer*, Sp. *llorar*, Cat. *plorar*).

(SE) PLICARE "fold" > "approach" (Sp. *llegar*, Port. *chegar*, but Rom. *pleca*, "leave"—where perhaps the simple verb has been used for the compound); *ut . . . sic plecaremus nos ad montem Dei*, "as we approached the mountain of God."

POENA "punishment" > "pain" (Fr. *peine*, and all Romance except Romanian where both meanings survive).

PORTARE displaces the highly irregular FERO, TULI, LATUM.

POTESTAS "power" > "one who has power" (Löfstedt 2, 154; cf. It. *podestà*).

PRAESTARE "show," offer" > "lend" (Fr. *prêter*, Sp. *prestar*).

PRAESUL "leading dancer" > LL "director" > ML "bishop."

PULLUS "young animal" (cf. the Eng. cognate, *foal*) > "chicken" (Hor. *Sat.* 1.3.92, 2.2.121, etc.) (It., Sp. *pollo*, Fr. *poulet*).

REGNUM "kingdom" may come to mean "king," or even more concretely, "crown."

SALTARE replaces SALIRE (Fr. *sauter*).

SATIS "enough" > "very".

SEDERE "be seated," > "be," "remain" (seated), a frequent replacement in Ibero-Romance for ESSE; *dum apud hostis sedimus*, "while we are in the presence of the enemy" (Plaut. *Amph.* 599); *illa valle . . . ubi sederant filii Israhel dum Moyses ascenderet in montem Dei*, "that valley where the sons of Israel remained [i.e., were] while Moses ascended the mountain of God" (*Itin.* 5.1) (Sp. *ser*, Cat. *ésser*, Port. *seer*).

SIC may mean "yes" (Sp. It. Cat. *si*), *quae sic professa*, "she said yes."

SPATULA "shovel" > "shoulder blade" (Fr. *épaule*, It. *spalla*, Sp. *espaldas*).

SPONSUS "betrothed" > "spouse" (It. *sposo*, Fr. *épouse*).

STARE "stand" > "be"; common in LL, e.g. Arnobius *in dubio stare*, "to be in doubt"; *itaque ergo stat semper presbyter qui . . . siriste interpretatur*, "there is always a priest who translates into Syriac" (It. *stare,* Fr. *être,* Sp., Prov., Cat., Port., *estar*).

Subinde adv. of succession, "thereafter," replaces saepe, "often" (*tragicum illud subinde iactabat,* "he often cited boastfully that familiar line from the tragic poet," Suet. *Calig.* 30) (Fr. *souvent,* Cat. *sovint*).

Tabula "plank," replaces mensa, "table," except in Spain (*mesa;* cf. Fr. *table,* It. *tavola*).

Testa "tile" > "shell" > "head" (It. *testa,* Fr. *tête*).

Testimonium "witnessing" > "witness" (Fr. *témoin*).

Toccare replaces tango, tetigi (3d) (It. *toccare,* Fr. *toucher,* Sp. *tocar*).

Totus replaces omnis in popular speech (It. *tutto,* Fr. *tout,* Cat. *tot,* Sp. *todo*). *Omnis* survives only in It. *ogni.* In the literary language cunctus, universus, etc., were used.

Vel "or" comes to mean "and."

Vetulus (2d) replaces vetus, veteris (3d) (Sp. *viejo*).

Virtus "strength" > "virtue" > "miracle" (in Christian contexts, the equivalent of *mirabilia*).

2.2 Doublets

Many words, indeed perhaps most, were common to both the literary language (which we know as "Latin") and the spoken language. This list of doublets is taken from Coseriu 57ff.:

Only Classical	Classical and "Vulgar"
aequor	mare
tellus	terra
sidus	stella
letum	mors
vulnus	plaga
cruor	sanguis
tergum	dorsum
alvus	venter
ager	campus
tuba	bucina
lorum	corrigia
formido	pavor, metus
pulcher	formosus, bellus
magnus	grandis
validus	fortis
alius	alter
omnis	totus
edere	manducare, comedere
potare	bibere
ludere	iocare
ferre	portare

Only Classical	Classical and "Vulgar"
vincire	ligare
equus	caballus
os	bucca
domus	casa, mansio, hospitale
aestus	calor
agere	facere
agna	spica
amittere	perdere
anguis	serpens
armilla	brachiale
ater	niger
balteus	cingulum
brassica	caulis
brevis	curtus
esurire	famam habere
fluere	currere
gramen	herba
imber	pluvia
ianua	porta
lapis	petra
linquere	laxare
plaustrum	carrus
sus	porcus
diu	longe, longum tempus
cum	quando
ob	pro, propter, per
sero	tarde
ut	quomodo
ab	de

Similarly, a whole series of functional elements (adverbs, prepositions, conjunctions) are exclusively classical (i.e., "dead" from the point of view of the spoken language): *an, at, autem, donec, enim, ergo, etiam, haud, igitur, ita, nam, postquam, quidem, quin, quoad, quoque, sed, sive, utrum, vel,* etc.

2.3 Suffixes and Prefixes

The vocabulary of ML is further enriched by a series of suffixes (following Coseriu 67ff.):

2.3.1 Nouns

-tor, -arius, form nouns of agent, the first from verbs and the second from substantives and adjectives: *salvator, auditor, argentarius, operarius, furnarius, cultellarius.*

-aculum, -torium, form instrumental nouns: *spiraculum, sufflatorium.*

-arium, forms nouns of place: *aerarium, granarium*, "granary," *apiarium.*

-etum, forms names of places derived from trees: *salpicetum*, "willow grove,"
 fraxinetum, "ash grove," *quercetum*, "oak grove," *fagetum*, "beech grove."

-ale, forms nouns of place or instrument.

-alia (pl. of *-ale*), *-men*, form collective nouns: *battalia, ossamen.*

-mentum, -tura, -sura, form abstract or collective nouns, names of actions, generally from verbs (as in CL *armatura, mensura*): *iuramentum, capillatura*
 (without the existence of a verb, *capillare*), *adventura* (> *aventure*), *arsura.*

-tio, -sio, -atio, -itio, -ntia, form abstract nouns derived from verbs: *demoratio,*
 custoditio, sufferentia, fragrantia (nouns in *-ntia*, in principle neuter plurals
 of present participles, were treated as feminine singulars).

-itas -itia, form abstract nouns derived from adjectives: *amicitatem, bellitatem*
 (cf. CL *bonitas, caritas*), *longitia, proditia* (cf. CL *pigritia, avaritia*).

-ata, forms nouns of quantity (matter or time): *diurnata* (Sp. *jornada*), *annata,*
 buccata (Sp. *bocada*).

-or or *-or/-ura*, form abstract nouns derived from verbs: *lucorem, laudorem* (Sp.
 loor); *fervor, fervura; rigor, rigura;* then, on the model of *strictura, directura*
 (future participles), were formed nouns in *-ura* from nonverbal adjectives:
 planura < planus.

-ulus, -iculus, -uculus, very frequent diminutive forms; the accented suffix *-ellus*
 was preferred to the unstressed -ulus: *rotulus–rotella*, > Sp. *rodilla; fibula–*
 fibella > Sp. *hebilla; anellus, vitellus, catellus*. In consequence, *-icellus* was
 preferred to *-iculus: avicellus, navicula–navicella, monticulus–monticellus.*

2.3.2 Adjectives

There are many adjective suffixes: *-bilis* (*amabilis, credibilis*); -alis, -ilis (*mortalis,*
hostilis); *-osus* (*montaniosus*, on the model of such CL forms as *herbosus, formo-*
sus); *-ivus* (*tardivus*, on the model of *captivus*); *-atus, -itus, -utus*, participial suffixes applied directly to substantival nouns, although there exists no corresponding verb—*barbatus, barbutus* (from *barba*), *crinitus* (from *crinis*), *cornutus* (from
cornu), *pilutus* (from *pilum*).

2.3.3 Verbs

-are, -ire, applied to the supine stem, also the present participle and substantives, and *-escere*, to form frequentative and inchoative verbs (cf. CL *plant-*
 are, vestire, flerescere): *cantare, adiutare, oblitare* (> Sp. *olvidar*), *ausare*
 (> Fr. *oser*, Sp. *osar*), *refusare, usare, expaventare* (> Sp. *espantar*), *calent-*
 are, levantare, crepantare (> Sp. *quebrantar*).

-iare, a new suffix formed on the basis of verbs in *-are*, on adjective stems in *-is*
 (like *molliare* from *mollis, alleviare* from *levis*), now used to form new verbs

from adjectives in *-us, -a, -um: altiare* (> Sp. *alzar, bassiare* (> Sp. *bajar*),
Cat. *baixar*), *directiare* (> Sp. *en-derezar,* Fr. *dresser,* It. *drizzare*).
-icare, to make verbs from adjectives or nouns: *amaricare* (> Sp. *amargar,*
< *amarus*), *follicare* (from *follis,* > Sp. *holgar*).
-izare, a suffix of Greek origin (cf. *-izein*), used frequently in medical and scientific terminology, and in the Christian vocabulary: *cauterizare, pulverizare,
baptizare, exorcizare, scandalizare.*
-itare, forms frequentative or iterative verbs: *vanitare* (> Fr. *vanter*), *taxitare*
(> It. *tastare*).
-ulare, also forms frequentative verbs: *ustulare, misculare* (> Sp. *mezclar*), *tremu-
lare* (> Sp. *temblar,* Fr. *trembler*), *turbulare* (> Fr. *troubler*).

2.3.4 Diminutives

Many diminutives lost all sense of smallness; in addition to the words cited above
(e.g. *auricula, avicellus, cultellus, geniculum*):
Corpusculum: *Nam ecce morbus invadit corpusculum,* "for behold disease in-
vades the body" (Norberg 143).
Loculus: "casket" (John 13.29, "bag").

2.3.5 Compounds

A fondness for compound forms is very typical of VL (Löfstedt 2, 92):

persubire; perexire; perdiscoprire; pertransire.

2.4 Periphrastic Locutions

The use of a noun (or adjective) in combination with a verb, usually either *habere*
or *facere,* to replace a single verb is characteristic of VL. Its use follows the general
tendency toward the breakup of synthetic structures and their replacement by
analytic forms (Weber 62; Bechtel 126).

2.4.1 Compounds consisting of a noun plus habere

concupiscentiam habere = concupiscere:

filii Israhel habuerunt concupiscentiam escarum, "the children of Israel
desired food" (*Itin.* 5.7).

timorem habere = timere (cf. Fr. *avoir peur*).

curam habere = curare:

habens curam domus et sororis suae, "being concerned for his house
and sister" (*VA* 2.1).

consuetudinem habere:

> *ad quos habebat consuetudinem eundi,* "those to whom he was accustomed to go" (*VA* 4.4).

odio habere = odisse:

> *unum odio habebit* (*Vulgate,* Matt. 6.24, where the *Vetus Latina* has *odiet* [for the future form, see § 7.6]).

habere potestatem = dominari, imperare:

> At Gen. 1.28, to translate the Greek ἄρχετε τῶν ἰχθύων, Jerome gave *dominamini piscibus,* while the variants of the *Vetus Latina* offer *habete potestatem piscium,* as well as *principamini, imperate,* and *dominamini.*

2.4.2 Compounds consisting of a noun or adjective (or participle) plus facere

coctos facere = coquere (Petronius 47.10).

interpositae fiunt = interponuntur (*Itin.* 35.3).

memoriam facere = memorare:

> *si tantum memoriam faciam Antonii,* "if only I commemorate Antony" (*VA* Prol. 3).

salvum facere = *salvare:*

> In the *Vetus Latina* at Matt. 9.22 the Itala reads *fides tua te salva fecit,* "your faith made you safe," while the Afra has *te salvavit.* At Matt. 14.30, the Itala reads *salvum me fac,* while one MS has the imperative *salva* and the Afra, *libera.*

2.4.3 Compounds consisting of a noun plus agere

In the *Vetus Latina* at Matt. 3.2, the Itala has *paenitentiam agite* while the Afra reads *penitemini.*

2.4.4 Compounds consisting of an adjective plus esse

salva ero (*Vetus Latina,* Matt. 9.21).

3. Nouns

3.1 Changes in Gender
3.1.1 Masculine and Feminine

In general masculine and feminine remained the same, with a few important exceptions: feminines of the second declension became masculine; feminines of the fourth declension were treated in various ways; in Gallia, abstract nouns ending in -or became feminine: *color, honor, dolor, timor* (Bonnet 503–4).

3.1.2 MASCULINE AND NEUTER

Even during the Classical period, certain neuter nouns became masculine: *balteum, caseum, cornu,* etc. In popular and Late Latin this tendency is pronounced (e.g., Plautus, *Miles Gloriosus,* 2.4, *guttur* and *dorsus,* masc.; in Petronius 75.10 the masc. *candelabrus* is found for *candelabrum;* see Grandgent 145).

Almost all neuter nouns became masculine:

hunc verbum (Greg. T., *H.F.* 1, Pref.); *hunc nefas* (ibid. 2.3), etc. (see Bonnet 386).

Mare, however, perhaps under the influence of *terra,* in general became feminine (Grandgent 146; but cf. Cat. *el mar* and *la mar*).

3.1.3 FEMININE AND NEUTER

Neuter plurals in -*a* came to be considered as feminine singulars (Grandgent 146–47; Norberg 58ff.):

In Gregory of Tours, *pro tantae pietatis gaudia,* "for joy at such piety" (*De virtutibus Martini* 3.19), according to Bonnet 351, *gaudia* is feminine singular, the ancestor of It. *gioia,* Fr. *joie.*

In other cases the difference between them is plainly blurred:

res mira . . . quod (*Chron. Sal.* 98.31).

Occasionally a neuter plural accusative did duty for a feminine ablative singular:

in disponsalia Mariae interfuimus, we were present at Mary's betrothal (*Gospel of Nicodemus* 2.4).

3.2 Changes in Declension

The tendency was to regularize seemingly "irregular" forms:

aper > aprus (*App. P.* 139).

litoris for *litoribus* (Greg. T.).

neptis (3d) > *neptilca* (1st) (*App. P.* 171).

nurus (4th) > *nura* (1st) (*App. P.* 169).

ossum for *os.*

In Gregory of Tours, and elsewhere, place names are treated as indeclinable nouns. Most Hebrew names are not declined.

> *Pectavus diregit,* "he directed his course toward Poitiers" (Greg. T.,
> H.F. 2.37); *et elegerunt VII viros, amicos Ioseph,* "and they chose seven
> men, friends of Joseph" (*Gospel of Nicodemus* 15.3).

3.3 Case Usage

Many seeming abnormalities may be explained by phonological developments which it is impossible to describe with thoroughness here, as they differed according to time and place; the Latin of Spain, for instance, was not necessarily that of southern Italy. To give only one example, by the time of the *Chronicon Salernitanum* (late 10th century), the nominative, accusative, and ablative singulars had merged into a single case, a fact which explains the vacillation in the Chronicle (and similar late Latin texts) between *-am, -us, -u, -o,* and *-um,* while the 3d declension underwent a different evolution (Westerbergh 235).

3.3.1 NOMINATIVE

Nominative Absolute. This construction, the so-called *nominativus pendens,* also existed in late Greek, a fact which may have influenced use of the nominative absolute in ML (the construction may also have arisen independently in Latin; see Bonnet 565).

> *Vox in Rama audita est, ploratus et ululatus multus,* "A voice was heard
> in Rama, weeping and loudly lamenting" (*Vetus Latina,* Itala, Matthew
> 2.18; *ploratio et fletus multus,* Afra); *benedicans nos episcopus, profecti
> sumus,* "when the bishop blessed us, we set forth" (*Itin.* 16.7).

3.3.2 VOCATIVE

In LL, participles are used in the vocative: *moriture. Meus* is used for *mi.*

3.3.3 GENITIVE

Genitive for Dative. The genitive may be found substituting for a dative; in this case the substantive, instead of being in the dative with the verb, is put in the genitive and made to depend on an other noun. Examples may be found in CL, but in LL the usage becomes much more widespread and freer. It is important to the development of the Romance languages as it explains how It. *loro,* Fr. *leur,* etc. (< ILLORU[M]) came to serve as both dative and genitive (see Löfstedt 125–28).

> *locum seditionis quaerere,* "to seek a place of (i.e., for) sedition" (Livy,
> 3.46.2); *ipsius urbis ferre subsidium gestiens,* "striving to bring aid for
> the city" (Jordanes, *De Orig.* 18.102).

Genitive for Accusative. In a similar fashion, the genitive may replace the accusative:

> *egressa est scentilla percuciens in oculo pincerne regis* (= *percutiens in oculo pincernam regis*), "a spark flew out, striking the king's butler in the eye" (Norberg 33).

Genitive for Ablative. In imitation of Greek, the genitive may replace the ablative (Nunn 26):

> With *egeo: Vulgate,* Apoc. 3.17.

> With *dignus* and *indignus: amplioris enim gloriae iste prae Mose dignus habitus est,* "for he thought he was worthy of a greater glory than Moses" (*Vulgate,* Heb. 3.3).

Objective and Subjective Genitive. The CL distinction between the use of the possessive pronoun for objective and partitive genitives and the possessive adjective for pure possession is not maintained:

> *hoc facite in meum commemorationem,* "do this in remembrance of me" (*Vulgate,* Luke 22.19); *elongati sunt ab auxilio meo,* "they are far removed from helping me" (Greg. T., *H.F.* 2.30).

Many genitives were replaced by DE and the ablative.

Possessive Genitive. The possessive genitive was frequently replaced by *de* plus the ablative (cf. the use of this preposition in Romance). Viellard 190 notes that the dative of possession replaces the genitive in many Merovingian diplomas.

> *carnales tribulationes de vita ista; hostia de basilica.*

Partitive Genitive. The partitive genitive also tends to be replaced by *de* and the ablative (classical examples can be found, although *ex* is more common):

> *summitates de ligno sancto,* "the extremities of the holy wood" (*Itin.* 37.2); *de ipsa re coclear plenum,* "a spoonful of the substance"; in the *Vetus Latina,* Matt. 8.21, the MSS offer all possibilities: *Alius autem discipulus; ex discipulis; de discipulis* (*Vulgate*); *discipulorum.*

Genitive of Quality. This construction becomes more common than the ablative:

> In place of *egregie* or *eximie sanctus,* Gregory of Tours, for example, preferred *egregiae, eximiae sanctitatis* (Bonnet 548).

SUMMITAS MONTIS: expressions such as *medius mons, summus mons,* where in CL the adjective agrees with the noun, came to be replaced by a noun and dependent genitive:

17

in summitatem montis, "on the top of the mountain" (*Itin.* 3.2); *in medio paradisi,* "in the middle of Paradise" (*Vetus Latina,* Gen. 3.8); at Gen. 1.6, translating ἐν μέσωι τοῦ ὕδατος, we find both the *Vetus Latina* and the *Vulgate in medio aquae.*

Elliptical Genitives. A considerable number of genitives are found where the noun on which the genitive depends has been omitted. These usually involve either *ecclesia* (cf. the English "at St. Paul's" (sc. "church"), or *liber* (cf. *in Regnorum,* "in the book of Kings"); see Löfstedt 133–35.

Augmentative Genitive. Although not unknown in CL (Plaut., *Trin.* 309, *victor victorum*), this construction becomes far more widespread in Christian Latin:

> *Dominus dominorum, rex regum,* "Lord of lords, king of kings" (*Vulgate,* Apoc. 17.14).

3.3.4 DATIVE

The dative was often replaced by *ad* and the accusative.

> *ad carnuficem dabo* (Plaut., *Capt.* 1019); *si pecunia ad id templum data erit,* "if money will be given to that temple" (*CIL* 9.3513, 57 B.C.E.); *et dixit serpens ad mulierem,* "and the serpent said to the woman" (*Vetus Latina,* Gen. 3.1, but cf. 3.4, *et dixit serpens mulieri*); *cum sanctus Moyses acciperet a Domino legem ad filios Israhel,* "when saint Moses received the law for the sons of Israel" (*Itin.* 4.4).

Rarely, a dative of agent may be used after a perfect participle:

> *et ecce nihil dignum morte actum est ei,* "and lo, nothing worthy of death has been done by him" (*Vulgate* Luke 23.15).

Dative of Interest. The use of the dative of interest was extended to mark the goal or direction; in Christian Latin it indicated that toward which the soul aspired (parallels can be found in Virgil and Tacitus; see Blaise 99).

> *psallam nomini tuo,* "I shall sing your name" (*Vulgate,* Ps. 7.18); *modo nati sunt Christo, qui prius nati fuerunt saeculo,* "now they are born for Christ who before were born for the world" (Aug., *Serm.* 228.1).

3.3.5 ACCUSATIVE

Forms. Apocope (cutting), or the loss of the final *-m,* was common (this sound disappeared early from the spoken language, as graffiti at Pompeii testify). It is, however, often difficult to determine whether an author has employed an ablative for an accusative or not.

adiuro te demon . . . agitatore Clarum et Felice et Primulum et Ro-manum ocidas, "I adjure you demon . . . that you kill the charioteer Clarus, and Felix, and Primulus, and Romanus"; *que ad modum = quem ad modum* (*Itin.* 5.3).

There was a tendency for the accusative to become a utility case, substituting for other inflections.

For the nominative, this substitution seems to be particularly common with the feminine accusative plural (cf. Weber 108; ET 31). According to Norberg 27, it was frequent in clauses involving passive or intransitive verbs:

Nam et usque ad reges famam Antonii, "For the fame of Anthony even reached as far as kings" (*VA* 81.1); *spatham illius contremuit,* "his sword trembled" (*Chron. Sal.* 23.20).

Duration of Time. In CL, duration of time is expressed by the accusative case. In ML, the ablative could be substituted, as could the preposition *per.*

per totos octo dies . . . is ornatus est, "it is adorned for eight whole days" (*Itin.* 25.12).

Accusative of Respect. The use of this construction was extended in imitation of Greek:

cum oculum graviter dolere coepisse, "when he began to suffer severe pain in his eye" (Sulpicius Severus, *Vita Martini* 193).

Accusative absolute. Not common until Gregory of Tours; it is not found in the *Itinerarium* (Bechtel 109).

Volebam quidem acceptam epistolam vestram mittere, "For I wanted, when I received your letter, to send to you. . . ." (*VA* 4). The construction is particularly frequent in Jordanes and Gregory of Tours, often in combination with the ablative absolute: *acceptam a nobis benedictionem purgatoque pectore,* "having received blessing from us and with a cleansed heart" (Greg. T., *H.F.* 5.43; see ET 32).

The accusative and ablative absolutes may be combined (see also § 7.4.6 [2]):

neminem alio praesente, "with no one else present" (*VA* 50.5); *collectam per chronicas vel historias anteriorum summam,* "all the facts having been gathered from previous chronicles and histories" (Greg. T., *H.F.* 1, Pref.).

Two Accusatives. A number of verbs are followed by two accusatives where CL would call for an accusative and, for example, an instrumental ablative. This construction appears to be due to contamination and analogy (Norberg 143ff.) Examples involving verbs of striking seem to be especially frequent.

> *unus elevata manu bipennem caerebrum eius inlisit,* "with an upraised hand, one struck his head with an axe" (Greg. T., *H.F.* 2.40); *baculum quem in manu gestabat liminarem nempe percussit (Chron. Sal.* 39.20; see the discussion of Westerbergh 246ff.).

Intransitive verbs with the accusative. Many formerly intransitive verbs become transitive, taking a direct object in the accusative case: e.g., *uti, frui, fungi, potiri, carere, nocere, benedicere; exire:*

> *exeunte autem illo ianuam,* "when he went out the door" (*Vulgate,* Matt. 26.71); *nec pulmentum aliquot utebatur* (Greg. T, *H.F.* 9.10); *metuemus nunc, ne et alius* (= *alios) . . . careamus,* "we fear now lest we lack others as well" (ibid. 7.47); *benedicerent deum* (ibid. 6.36).

3.3.6 Ablative

Forms. In the 3d declension the ablative singular frequently ends in *-i* (CB 62, 6, *etheri*).

The feminine dative and ablative plural may end in *-abus* (this also occurs in classical usage):

> To distinguish *filia* from *filius: filiabus* (Greg. T., *H.F.* 4.20, etc.).

> To distinguish *anima* from *animus: animabus* (*Vetus Latina,* Matt. 11.29, the Itala has *animis,* the Afra *animabus;* Greg. T., *De gloria confessorum* 62; Richard of Bury, *Philobib.* 1.21, 19.122).

> To distinguish *famula* from *famulus: famulabus* (Greg. T., *H.F.* 9.13).

> To distinguish *villa* from *villus: villabus* (Greg. T., *H.F.* 10.12).

By a form of hypercorrectness, *-ibus,* a form fallen into disuse in many periods, may be added to 2d declension nouns:

> *suffragibus, donibus.*

Ablative absolute. In CL, the ablative absolute is not normally employed if the epithet applies to a word which plays an integral part in the sentence. The "normal" Latin for "They hate Caesar as leader" is *Caesarem ducem oderunt,* not *Caesare duce, eum oderunt* (AG 419). In contrast to classical practice, ML allows the subject of the participial construction to be the same as that of the main verb, or its object:

> *huic se Christus . . . nasciturum . . . monstravit ipso in evangeliis dicente,* "Christ showed him that he would be born when he himself said

in the Gospels" (Greg. T., *H.F.* 1.7; Bonnet 559); in the *Vetus Latina*, at Matt. 8.34, the Itala reads *et viso eo, rogebant eum*, "and seeing him, they asked him," while the MS variants have constructions more in keeping with the norms of CL, *cum vidissent eum*, and *videntes eum*.

Even further from classical usage, the subject of the participial phrase may function as the (unexpressed) object of the main verb:

> *quo [equo] empto, negotiator adducit [eum] ad stabulam* (Fort., *Vit. Germ.* 22).

For the ablative and accusative absolutes combined, see § 3.5.4. For absolute participial constructions, see § 7.4.6.

Instrumental Ablative. The instrumental ablative ceases to be expressed by a pure ablative (without a preposition), or by OB or PROPTER and the accusative. Contrary to CL usage, PRO also comes to be used (cf. Sp. *por*). The instrumental ablative, moreover, was confused with the ablative of accompaniment (with CUM; cf. English "they killed him *with* a sword," which in CL would be *gladio*, without any preposition).

> *cum pinnis quando assantur tangatur*, "while being roasted they are touched with feathers" (Anthimus 9).

DE is also used for the instrumental ablative.

> *de laredo crudo Franci sanantur*, "the Franks are healed by raw bacon" (Anthimus 14).

Constructions with IN and PER also substitute for the instrumental ablative (Finaert 64).

Ablative of Material. In CL, the preposition EX is used to express the material out of which something is made (*ex animo constamus et corpore*, "we consist of mind and body," Cic. *Fin.* 4.8.19); with *fieri*, however, DE was used (*de templo carcerem fieri*, ibid. *Phil.* 5.7.18). In ML *de* with the ablative is common:

> *albumen de ovo*, "the white of an egg."

Ablative of origin. In CL, participles which signify birth take the ablative of origin, sometimes with the prepositions *ex* or *de*.

> *Oderunt natos de paelice* (Juv. 6.627), "they hate those born of a concubine."

In ML, the ablative of origin is usually replaced by *de:*

> *natus de parentibus nobilibus* (VA 1.1).

Ablative of price and value. May be expressed by a preposition:

> *libros . . . pro septuaginta duobus millibus sestertiis . . . emit,* "he bought books for 72,000 sesterces" (Richary of Bury, *Philobib.* 3.28).

Locative ablative. In CL, the locative ablative is maintained without a preposition with the names of towns (i.e., *Athenis* = at Athens"). In ML, a preposition may be used:

> *in Roma* (Richard of Bury, *Philobib.* 4. 35); *de Roma* (ibid. 4.41).

Ablative of time. In CL, "time when" is expressed by a locative ablative without a preposition; in ML, the prepositions *in* or *ad* may be used:

> In the *Vetus Latina* at Matt. 13.1, the Itala has *eodem die,* but the Afra reads *in illa die; ad horam sextam aguntur,* "they are performed at the sixth hour" (*Itin.* 44.3).

To express duration of time, the ablative may replace the accusative (see the long discussion of Löfstedt 2, 51–56). The ablative is used more frequently by Gregory of Tours than is the accusative. Duration of time may also be expressed by *per* and the accusative.

> *cum ieiunasset quandraginta diebus et quadraginta noctibus,* "when he had fasted for forty days and forty nights" (*Vetus Latina,* Matt. 4.2).

3.4 Gerund

It is common in LL to find the accusative of the gerund, especially with verbs of motion, denoting purpose (Norberg 225–28). This construction replaces the supine.

> *futurum esse enim ut Herodes quaerat puerum ad perdendum eum,* "it will come to pass that Herod seeks the boy to destroy him" (*Vulgate,* Matt. 2.13); *loca sunt grata ad videndum Christianis,* "the places are pleasing for Christians to see" (*Itin.* 19.5).

The ablative of the gerund might be used independently of the rest of the sentence, foreshadowing its use in Italian (for its use as present participle, see § 7.4.1). This construction is very common from the 4th century on.

> *et sic coquat lento foco agetando* (i.e., *agitando*) *ipsa olla frequenter,* "and let it cook on a slow fire, shaking the pot frequently."

3.5 Supine

The supine was weak, and from the 1st century on, it came to be replaced by various constructions; it is rare in Christian authors (Blaise 330, n.):

(1) by the infinitive of purpose: this construction occurs in early Latin:

> *reddere hoc, non perdere erus me misit,* "my master sent me to return
> this, not to lose it" (Plautus, *Ps.* 642); *erumpunt dicere,* "they burst into
> speech" (Tert., *Marc.* 1.17); *cum veneris ad bibere,* "since you have
> come to drink" (Aug. *Serm.* 225, 4; Grandgent 49).

(2) by *ad* plus an abstract noun:

> *presbiter loci misit puerum ad aliquorum hominum invitacionem,*
> "the priest of the place sent a servant to invite some men" (Greg. T.,
> *H.F.* 7.47).

(3) by *ad* plus the gerund:

> *quaerat puerum ad perdendum eum,* "he seeks the boy to destroy him"
> (*Vulgate* Matt. 2.13).

3.6 Comparison
3.6.1 FORMS

The synthetic forms in *-ior, -ius* disappeared and were replaced by analytic forms
employing *plus* or *magis* (also found in CL); *magis* was used in the peripheral
areas of the Roman empire (Romania and Iberia), while *plus* occurred in Italia
and Gallia (cf. Rom. *mai,* Sp. *más,* Cat. *més,* Port. *mais;* It. *più,* Fr. *plus,* and
OCat. *pus*).

3.6.2 DOUBLE COMPARISON

Double comparatives (and superlatives) are found, indicating that the synthetic
forms no longer were sufficient to convey the notion of comparison.

> *quanto magis melior est homo ove,* "how much better is a man than a
> sheep" (*Vetus Latina,* Matt. 12.12); *in superbia atque elacione plus ma-
> gis tumuit,* "he was even more swollen with pride" (*Chron. Sal.* 65.21;
> cf. Tuscan *più meglio*).

3.6.3 POSITIVE FOR COMPARATIVE

The positive may be used for the comparative:

> *bonum est tibi . . . in vitam intrare quam mitti in gehennam,* "it is bet-
> ter for you to enter into life than to be sent to hell" (*Vulgate,* Matt.
> 18.9).

3.6.4 REPLACEMENTS FOR QUAM WITH COMPARATIVES

AB may be used with the comparative instead of *quam* (also in Ovid and Pliny
the Elder):

quid enim peius a daemonibus, "what is worse than devils" (Aug., *Serm.* 12.3; cf. Finaert 58).

AD with the ablative: *ad* (*h*)*ora.*

DE becomes, perhaps after IN, the preposition par excellence, taking over for many other prepositions and replacing idiomatic constructions with the ablative and genitive (see Atzori).

de for *quam:* in comparisons, *de* might be substituted for *quam:*

> *Nullus inter nos fortior est de altero,* "No one of us is stronger than another."

3.6.5 SUPERLATIVES

The superlative forms in *-issimus* also fell into desuetude and were only reintroduced at a later period. They were replaced by *multum,* itself replacing *maxime* (It. *molto bene,* Sp. *muy bien,* Cat. *molt bé*). The 9th-century Reichenau glosses explain *valde bonum* as *optimum.* Comparative and superlative may also be confused; the same glosses equate *optimos* with *meliores.*

3.7 Changes in Case Construction

Many verbs or verbal constructions may be found taking a case different than the one normal in CL.

INTERROGARE plus the dative: frequent in Gregory of Tours: *cum uxori, quid sibi hoc vellit, interrogaret,* "when he asked his wife what she wanted" (Greg. T., *H.F.* 3.4). Similarly also ROGARE with the dative and, less frequently, *ad* and the accusative. For further discussion, see Löfstedt 129–31.

PERSUADERE plus the accusative (dative in CL): both are found in Petronius— with the dative in formal speech, *persuade gubernatori* (98.4); with the accusative in colloquial, *te persuadeam ut venias* (46.2).

PETERE plus the dative: *vicinis gentibus concubitum petierunt* (Jordanes, *De orig.* 8.56).

PRAEDITUS plus the genitive (CL ablative): *credo eos nullius esse potestatis praeditos,* "I believe that they are endowed with no power" (Greg. T., *H.F.* 2.30).

PRECARI plus dative (CL accusative of the person addressed): *veniam legentibus praecor,* "I ask my readers' pardon" (Greg. T., *H.F.* Pref.); cf. OFr. *prier* (Löfstedt 130).

QUAERERE plus dative (CL *ab, de,* or *ex*): *si nobis queratur,* "if we should be asked" (*Gesta Romanorum* 26). Cf. OFr. *querre: jo vus otri quanque m'avez ci quis* (*Chanson de Roland* 3202).

QUAERERE plus AD and accusative (on the confusion of *ad* and *ab,* see § 4.1.3): *sanitatem ad te, non tormenta quaesivi,* "we seek health from you, not tortures" (Greg. T., *De virtutibus Martini* 2.25). The same construction also occurs in OFr.: *quant a mei l'avez quis,* "since you have sought it from me." Verbs of remembering (*recordor, memini, obliviscor*) may be followed by the accusative.

DIGNUS: in CL *dignus* is followed by the ablative. In later usage other cases (i.e., genitive and dative) may be found: *dignum mortis* and *dignus est morti,* "worthy of death" (*Gospel of Nicodemus* 4.2).

3.7.1 SUBSTANTIVES AS ADJECTIVES

There was a tendency in Late Latin for substantives to function as adjectives (Löfstedt 120ff.).

Cum moderatione modo adducatur Iesus, "Let Jesus be led in in a restrained fashion" (*Gospel of Nicodemus* 1.2).

4. PREPOSITIONS AND ADVERBS

4.1 Prepositions

ML is characterized by an increasing reliance on prepositions, and a concomitant loss of the idiomatic use of cases or other, synthetic, modes of expression. This tendency is not necessarily a late one. For example, Virgil (granted, in poetry) wrote: *templum de marmore* (*Georg.* 3.13), where Cicero would have preferred *templum marmoreum* (Meillet 267). Furthermore, in his letters, Cicero, employing an idiom close to modern (Romance) usage, wrote that someone was *aptus ad aliquam rem,* while in his more formal orations he wrote *aptus alicui rei.* Hence one may find verbs which are used transitively in CL followed by a preposition in ML: *veritas vincens super omnia,* "truth conquers [i.e., "wins out over"] everything" (Richard of Bury, *Philobib.* 1.19).

4.1.1 WITH NAMES OF CITIES

In CL, a preposition was not used with the names of towns and small islands to mark the limit of motion; a simple accusative sufficed. In ML, a preposition may be used:

Venerunt magi ab oriente in Hierosolymam, "magi came from the east to Jerusalem" (*Gospel of Pseudo-Matthew,* 16).

4.1.2 CHANGE IN CONSTRUCTION

In CL, certain prepositions, notably *in* and *sub,* may be followed either by the accusative or the ablative. The distinction between rest and motion, however, was soon obscured, and already on the walls of Pompeii one may find the accusative following *ab, cum, sine,* and *pro* (ET 144). In Petronius, *prae* is used with the accusative (39.12, 46.1). One can also find *ante, apud, propter, ob,* and *per* taking the ablative. Bonnet (522) observes of Gregory of Tours that he was far from ignorant of the general difference in cases; it was in their specific use that he had his doubts. He functioned well when there was an absolute rule—i.e., *ad* and the accusative, *de* and the ablative—but when he had to decide whether motion or rest was involved, he hesitated. His case is far from atypical.

AB with the accusative:

> *ab ipsos audisse vos aestimate* (*VA* Prol. 1.3).
> (This source also uses *ab* with the ablative: *ab his,* Prol. 1.3.)

CUM with the accusative:

> *viderent infantem cum Mariam,* "they saw the baby with Mary" (*Vetus Latina,* Matt. 2.11, Afra); *cum dominam suam delectaretur,* "he was delighted with his mistress" (Petronius, 45.7); *cum Dei adiutorium,* "with God's help" (Greg. T., *H.F.* 2.37).

DE with the accusative: very common in the popular language from the 4th century (Mohrmann 417).

> *de illius vitam* (*VA,* Prol. 1.4); *omnes de sua sedilia surgant* (*Rule of St. Benedict* 9.21).

PER with the ablative:

> *Verbera iubet per membris inducere.*

POST with the ablative: very frequent, for example, in the *Itin.* (Mohrmann 417).

SINE with the accusative:

> *sine intermissionem* (*VA* 7.3)

4.1.3 Confusion in meaning

Clearcut distinctions in meaning between some pronouns tend to be obliterated; *ab, de,* and *ex,* for example, may be used indiscriminately. *Per, pre (prae),* and *pro* may be confused. A confusion of *ad* and *ab* is also characteristic of VL.

AD and AB:

> *Quaero, peto, obtineo ad aliquem* may replace (in seeming contradiction to classical usage) *ab aliquo; ad invicem* replaces *ab invicem* (*Chron. Sal* 8.12, 18.4); *ab bellum sunt preparati* replaces the more usual *ad bellum* (ibid. 168.15).

EX and DE:

> *de palatio exit,* "which went out of the palace" (*Itin.* 19.7); *egredere de terra tua,* "go out of your land" (*Vulgate,* Gen. 12.1); *unus de illis quattuor fluminibus,* "one of the four rivers" (Palladius, *Comm.* 1).

DE for AB:

> *et homo ille de Deo est,* "and that man is from God"; *et amicos meos de somno excitavi,* "and I awakened my friends from sleep" (Palladius, *Comm.* 4).

4.1.4 GENITIVE

AFORIS plus the genitive.

FORAS plus the genitive:

> *foras corporis,* "outside the body" (Apuleius, *Ap.* 50.2).

4.1.5 DATIVE

In Greek, unlike Latin, the dative is a prepositional case; in VL the dative may occur with prepositions.

AD with the dative:

> *ad superventurae claritate* (= *claritati; VA* 17.1).

4.1.6 ACCUSATIVE

AD may be used to mark proximity, *ad tumulum sancti* (Bonnet 582). Transferred to time, this construction marks the point at which an action occurred, replacing the ablative in CL.

> *ad oram tertiam,* "at the third hour" (Greg. T., *H.F.* 1.10).

AD with certain adjectives (*aptus, idoneus*) may replace the dative.

LOQUOR AD: classically, LOQUOR takes the dative or *cum* plus ablative, or is used absolutely.

> *beatus Paulus ad Antonium sic locutus est,* "Blessed Paul spoke thus to Antony" (Jer. *Vita Pauli* 11); cf. *quod ad Moysen dicit* (Greg. T., *H.F.* 1.10), *ad episcopum aiebat* (ibid. 2.3).

4.1.7 CHANGES IN MEANING AND USE

ABSQUE = *sine,* "without"; so used in Plautus and Terence, but only in conditional sentences. It is common in LL.

IUXTA in LL comes to mean "according to."

iuxta scripturas, "according to Scripture" (*Itin.* 1.1).

PRO may = PER.

sancti monachi pro diligentia sua arbusculas ponunt, "the holy monks with diligence planted bushes" (*Itin.*).

4.1.8 COMPOUND PREPOSITIONS

In LL (as also in Late Greek and elsewhere), we find a number of prepositions, adverbs, and particles used in combination, later forming inseparable compounds. The purpose was at first to add precision and exactness to an expression, but gradually the combination in question became purely a strengthened by-form, often giving rise to a new single word (Löfstedt 162). Grammarians often warned against the new compounds but to little avail, as many of them are the direct ancestors of prepositions and adverbs in use in the Romance languages.

The tendency to compound prepositions is, however, native to Latin, evident from the earliest days: cf. *propalam, inibi, abhinc, exinde, deinde,* etc. Unlike many features of later Latin, however, they are not common in Plautus, Petronius, or writers before Jerome. *Circumcirca* and *praeterpropter* can be documented in archaic Latin (Weber 105), and *derepente, desubito,* and *interibi* are found in Plautus. In many cases, the formation of compound prepositions may have been stimulated by the translations of the Bible as attempts to render literally the Greek sacred text (although their development may also have been independent).

AB ANTE (cf. Fr. *avant,* It. *avanti*)

et absconderunt se Adam et mulier eius abante faciem domini dei, "and Adam and his wife hid themselves from the face of the Lord God" (*Vetus Latina,* Gen., 3.8); *tollite fratres vestros abante faciem sanctorum,* "take your brothers away from the face of the saints" (*Vetus Latina,* Lev. 10.4).

A FORIS "without" (see AB INITUS).

AB INITUS

abintus autem sunt lupi rapaces, "within, however, they are ravaging wolves" (*Vetus Latina,* Matt. 7.15); *et bituminabis eam ab intus et a foris,* "you will caulk it [the ark] inside and out" (*Vetus Latina,* Gen. 6.14).

AD PROPE (> Prov. *aprop*)

aliquantola terra ad Uato ad prope casa nostra, "a little land at Uato(?) near our house" (Norberg 78).

On the model of the classical DEINDE, DESUPER, an important group of prepositions have *de* as their first term, denoting the point of departure.

DE AB (> It. *da*).

DE ANTE

> *ubi missa facta fuerit de ante Cruce,* "when the mass was completed before the Cross" (*Itin.* 37.8).

DE EX (> Fr. *dès,* Sp. *desde;* see Löfstedt 171)

> *vixit cum eo de ex die virginitatis suae,* "she lived with him since her virginity" (*CIL* 14.5210).

From DE EX POST comes the Spanish *después.*

DEFORIS (> It. *di fuori,* Fr. *dehors,* Prov. *defors,* Sp. *de fuera*)

> *sed sicut sum deforis, ita sum deintus,* "but as I am outside, so am I within" (*Vitae Patr.* 3.92); *si quis de foris venerit* (Jer. *Reg. Pach.* 146); *lumen autem de foris non affertur,* "the light is not brought outdoors" (*Itin.* 24.4).

DE INTER (> It. Sp. Port. *dentro*)

> *eduxisti populum hunc deinter illos,* "you have led this people out from among them" (*Vetus Latina,* Num. 14.13).

DE INTRO "behind, within": (> It. Sp. Port. *dentro,* Rom. *dîntru*)

> *Et de intro cancellos primum dicit orationem,* "and he said the first prayer from behind the grill" (*Itin.* 24.2).

DEINTUS (> Fr. *dans,* Prov. Cat. *dins*): (see DE FORIS).

DE POST (> It. *dopo,* Fr. *depuis,* Port. *depos*): from the 2d century, DE POST has a temporal value.

> *de post cuius morte,* "since his death" (*CIL* 8.9162).

DE RETRO (It. *dietro,* Fr. *derrière*).

4.1.9 NEW PREPOSITIONS

CATA (borrowed from Greek = κατά), has three uses:

(1) With the title of the Gospels = *secundum*

(2) in a temporal sense = *ad, iuxta*

(3) distributively; this latter use survived in Romance (cf. It. *caduno*, Cat. *cada*, Sp. *cada uno*)

> *evangelio in cata Mathaeo* (*Itin.* 33.2, where *cata Matheo* is treated as if it were a single word); *cata singulos ymnos* (*Itin.* 24.1); *faciet sacrificium super eo cata mane*, "he will make a sacrifice over it in the morning" (*Vulgate*, Ezek. 46.15); *cata mansiones monasteria sint cum militibus*, "at the stopping places there are posts with soldiers" (*Itin.* 7.2); *cata pascha*, "at Easter" (ibid. 15.5).

FORAS "outside of"

> with accusative: *foras civitatem* (*Itin.* 19.9);
>
> with genitive: *foras corporis* (Apul. *Ap.* 50.2).

FORIS with accusative and ablative: "outside of"

> *exiit foris pretorium Iesus*, "Jesus went out of the hall" (*Gospel of Nicodemus* 1.6).

IN GIRO (from the Greek loanword γύρος, circle) "round about" (= *circum*) with accusative and ablative (also *per giro* and *per girum*)

> *in giro parietes ecclesiae*, "around the walls of the church" (*Itin.* 3.8); *in giro colliculo isto*, "around that little hill" (ibid. 14.2); of a steep mountain ascent, *quoniam non eos subis lente et lente per girum, ut dicimus in cocleas*, "since you do not climb it slowly and circuitously, as we say 'in a spiral'" (ibid. 3.1).

LATUS and DE LATUS "beside"

> (*latus* > OFr. *lez*, still preserved in place names such as *Aix-les-Bains*).

RETRO, "behind" (in CL, RETRO is an adverb)

> *vade retro me*, "get behind me" (*Vetus Latina*, Matt. 4.10).

SECUS with accusative = *iuxta;* found only in ante- and post-classical Latin.

SUBTUS "beneath" (It. *sotto*, OFr. *soz*)

> *subtus me* (*Vulgate*, Ps. 17:40).

USQUE with ablative

> *usque hora nona* (*Rule of St. Benedict* 48.35; Mohrmann 423).

4.2 Adverbs
4.2.1 Forms

Adverbs ending in -*itus* become very popular (Löfstedt 2, 170):

e.g., *primitus, paenitus.*

In -*iter:*

granditer: first found in Ovid, *Heroides* 15.30; also in, for example, Sidonius, *Ep.* 7.4.

The ablative *mente* plus an adjective came to function as a normal adverb, replacing the forms in -*e* (2d declension) and -*iter.* Gradually the literal meaning of *mente* disappeared, leaving a pure adverb, the ancestor of adverbs in all Romance languages except Romanian. The glosses of Reichenau, for example, equate *singulariter* with *solamente.*

Sed obstinata mente perfer, obdura, "but obstinately persist, be resolute" (Catullus, 8.11); Virgil, *Aen.* 4.105: *sensit . . . simulata mente locutam,* "She [Venus] understood her [Juno] to speak with guile"; *res est apta iuventuti / laeta mente ludere,* "it is a suitable thing for youth to play happily" (CB 75, 7–8).

BENE may be used to strengthen an adjective (cf. Fr. *bien*):

melonis vero si bene maturi fuerint, "if the melons are really ripe" (Anthimus 58).

ET becomes very common as an adverb, = ETIAM, "even" (cf. the Greek καί).

4.2.2 Compound Adverbs

A similar process of compounding (and replacement of classical forms) occurs with adverbs as with prepositions. NUNC, for example, is replaced by *ad horam, hac hora* (> OSp. *agora,* MSp. *ahora,* Cat. *ara,* Fr. OFr. *or, ores, lor(e)s, alors, encore,* It. *allora*).

de lardo vero, qualiter melius comedatur, ad hora expono, "But now I am going to speak about bacon, how it is best eaten" (Anthimus 14).

AD SUBITO = *subito* (*Itin.* 16.4).

AD TUNC "then" (*Itin.* 16.6).

AFORIS "outside" (*TLL* 1. 1250, 33).

DE CONTRA "opposite," "facing"

Vidimus etiam de contra non solum Libiadam sed et Iericho, "We saw facing us not only Livias but also Jericho" (*Itin.* 12.4).

DE MAGIS (> Sp. *demás*).

DE UNDE (> Fr. *dont*, Sp. *donde*).

E CONTRA (or ECONTRA), "on the contrary," = CONTRA

aliis vero econtra videtur (Jer. *Ep.* 12).

INANTE

quanto denuo inante ibant, "as much as they went forward again" (*Itin.* 7.3); cf. Fr. *en avant*).

INDE as the equivalent of *ab, de, ex,* plus a pronoun was common in LL; traces of the usage occur in Livy and Tacitus (It. *ne,* Fr. *en*).

inde reddo rationem, "I [will] give a reason for it" (cf. the Fr. *j'en rends raison;* Weber 67).

IN HODIE

Nam et spelunca, ubi latuit Sanctus Helias in hodie ibi ostenditur ante hostium ecclesiae, "For the very cave in which St. Elijah hid is shown there even today before the door of the church" (*Itin.* 4.2).

IN TUNC (> Sp. *entonces*).

ITERATO "again," "a second time," post-classical for ITERUM:

Moyses, cum iterato ascendisset in montem Dei, "Moses, when he climbed God's mountain a second time" (*Itin.* 4.8).

PENITUS is used to strengthen negatives, replacing *omnino* and *prorsus* (Weber 82):

nulli paenitus nisi soli episcopi regnant, "really no one except bishops rule" (Greg. T., *H.F.* 6.46).

LOCO = IBI

gustavimus nobis loco in horto, "we ate there in the garden" (*Itin.* 3.7).

SUSUM, SUSO = SURSUM (reduction of RS > S after a long vowel).

4.2.3 Adverbs as substantives

The use of an adverb phrase as a substantive is essentially Greek:

et ipsorum ab intus, "and their inside."

5. Pronouns and Demonstratives

5.1 Forms

There was a tendency to regularize forms:

aliae for *alius*.

illum for *illud* (*VA* 11.20: *deficiebat illum vasculum*).

ipsus for *ipse* (*App. P.* 156).

A neuter *ipsud* (cf. *istud*), for *ipsum*, also found in Plautus and Terence (*ipsud martyrium; Itin.* 17.1).

The dative *illo* and *nullo* may replace *illi* and *nulli*.

ille for *illi* (nominative pl.), Greg. T., *H.F.* 2.7.

5.2 Demonstratives

The classical distinctions between *hic*, "this," what concerns the speaker, *iste*, "that (of yours)," what concerns the listener, and *ille*, "that," the more distant object or a known person or thing, tend to be obscured.

IS, EA, ID disappears on account of its brevity.

HIC gives way to ISTE.

> Only the neuter *hoc* survives in Romance (Prov. *oc;* It. *però* < PER HOC; ECCE HOC > OFr. *ço, ce;* It. *ciò*).

IPSE becomes a general demonstrative.

> *Ipse* replaces *idem* towards the end of the 2nd century C.E., in the compounds *hic ipse, ille ipse, iste ipse* (> It. *stesso*). It survives in It. *esso*, Cat. *eix*, Sp. *ese*.

5.2.1 Reflexive Uses

(1) *Ipse* can substitute for a reflexive pronoun, a use already found in Seneca (Blaise 155).

(2) In imitation of Greek, it can give a reflexive meaning to 1st and 2d person pronouns (Blaise 156).

> *tu de te ipso testimonium perhibes*, "you give testimony concerning yourself" (*Vulgate*, John 8.13, translating περί σεαυτοῦ).

ISTE is no longer restricted to a second person (and often somewhat derogatory) demonstrative.

de locis istis, "from these places."

ILLE becomes a general demonstrative, article, and personal pronoun.

As ISTE loses its demonstrative force, ECCE is added (ECCE ISTE, ILLE > It. *questo, quello;* Cat. *aquest, aquell;* Fr. *cette, quel;* Rom. *acest, acel*):

> *Nam ecce ista via quam videtis transire inter fluvium Iordanem et vi-cum istum,* "For this road which you see pass between the Jordan river and that village" (*Itin.* 14.3).

5.2.2 Indefinite pronouns

Many of the Latin indefinite pronouns are lost.

ANTEFATA, PRAEFATA, etc. = IDEM:

> *ecclesiam sancti Pancratii . . . eidem ecclesiae . . . antefatae ecclesiae . . . praefatae ecclesiae . . . in suprascriptae ecclesia . . . .* (Norberg 72).

CERTUS replaces QUIDAM

> *insolentiam certorum hominum,* "the insolence of certain [i.e., some] men" (Cic. *Pro Marc.* 16).

QUISQUE as a distributive was replaced by the Greek κατά, borrowed from ecclesiastical Latin.

> *cata singulos ymnos,* "at each hymn" (*Itin.* 24.1).

5.3 Possessive Pronouns

The CL distinction between the use of the possessive pronoun for objective and partitive genitives and the possessive adjective for pure possession is not maintained.

> *elongati sunt ab auxilio meo,* "they are far removed from helping me" (Greg. T., *H.F.* 2.30).

Similarly, the personal pronoun may substitute for the possessive adjective (Blaise 169).

> *mei membra,* "my limbs" (Cyprian, *Laps.* 4); *pro inpuritate et obscaenitate sui,* "by his impurity and immorality" (Rufinus, *Hist. Eccl.* 2).

5.3.1 Confusion of suus and eius

Confusion of reflexive and nonreflexive forms is common, and it was the reflexive forms which, in general, carried the day in the Romance languages (Fr. *son livre,*

Sp. *su libro*); in the plural, however, *illoru(m)* was maintained everywhere except in Spain (It. *loro*, Fr. *leur*, Cat. *llur*).

> *Cum autem vidisset inimicus se infirmari circa propositum Antonii et magis vinci eum a fortitudine illius,* "When, however, the enemy [the devil] saw that he was weak before the purpose of Anthony, and that he [the devil] was more likely to be conquered by the strength of that man" (*VA* 5.3).

5.4 Relative Pronouns

QUI and QUOD appear eventually to replace almost all other forms of the relative.

> *in custodia . . . qui.*

The genitive *cuius* survived in popular usage only in Spain (cf. *cuyo*).
Agreement between antecedent and relative pronoun is often loose.

> *in isdem diebus qua* (*Itin.* 12.9).

5.5 Reciprocal Pronouns

In CL, such expressions as *alius alium* or *inter se* were used to indicate reciprocal relations; in ML usually *invicem* (treated as an indeclinable pronoun) was used. *Alterutrum* was also employed in this fashion.

> *Estote autem invicem benigni,* "But be kind to one another" (*Vulgate,* Eph. 4.22); *Dicebant ad alterutrum,* "They were saying to one another" (*Vulgate,* Mark 4.40).

5.6 Articles
5.6.1 DEFINITE ARTICLE

Quintilian maintained: *Noster sermo articulos non desiderat,* "Our speech does not need articles" (1.4.19). Nevertheless, the absence of a definite article was felt in Latin (perhaps influenced by the translations of the Bible, since Greek has one). ILLE, ILLA, ILLUD soon came to supply that lack.

> *Est tamen ille daemon sodalis peccati,* "The devil is companion of sin" (*VA* 7.3); *sapiens illa apis,* "the wise bee" (translating Greek ἡ σοφὴ μέλισσα *VA* 3.4); *Ad vos nunc illam vos invitate puellam,* "You now invite the girl to you" (*Ruodlieb* 14.4).

In some regions, the indefinite article was supplied by IPSE.

> *per mediam vallem ipsam,* "through the middle of the valley" (*Itin.* 2.3; also 19.16; see Löfstedt 2, 64).

5.6.2 Indefinite article

QUIDAM and UNUS are used as in definite articles. Even in CL *unus* was used to mean "a certain" without numerical value.

> *cum uno gladiatore nequissimo,* "with an extremely base gladiator" (Cic. *Phil.* 2.3.7); *sicut unus paterfamilias his de rebus loquor,* "just as a head of the family do I speak about these matters" (Cic. *De Oratore* 1.29.132); *accessit ad eum una ancilla* (*Vulgate* Matt. 26.69); *et dictus unus psalmus aptus loco,* "and a psalm appropriate to the place was recited" (*Itin.* 4.4).

5.7 Changes in Meaning and New Pronouns

As the old demonstratives became degraded to the status of determiners, new words were used as demonstratives. This need explains the frequency of such legal borrowings as SUPRADICTUS, SUPRASCRIPTUS, PRAEDICTUS, in many medieval texts (see Norberg 70ff.). These words frequently mean little more than "this" or "that."

> *Erat autem eo tempore beatissimus Anianus in supradicta civitate episcopus,* "At that time the blessed Anianus was bishop in that city" (Greg. T., *H.F.* 2.7).

ALTER, "one of two," replaces ALIUS, "other" (Fr. *autre,* Sp. *otro*).

PROPRIUS is used as a possessive adjective.

> *Qua obtenta, ad propriam rediit,* (Greg. T., *H.F.* 4.14); *propriis se salutavere nominibus,* "they greeted each other by their names" (Jer. *Vita Pauli* 9).

Greek κατά may be compounded with UNUS > CATUNUS (It. *ciascuno,* Fr. *chacun*).

ID IPSUM replaces IDEM (> It. *desso,* the only Romance descendant of *is, ea, id*).

6. Conjunctions
6.1 Changes in Usage

AC SI = *tamquam*

> *tanti nitoris ac si de margarita esset,* "of such a polish as if it were of pearl" (*Itin.* 19.6).

AUT takes over for VEL (It. Sp. *o,* Fr. *ou*), which in its turn comes to mean "and" rather than "or." AUT may also mean "and."

> *quantum potuimus videntes aestimare aut ipsi dicebant,* "as we could judge by looking and they said" (*Itin.* 2.1).

DUM = CUM

dum non intellegebat, "since he did not understand" (Greg. T., *H.F.*
6.46; note as well the use of the indicative).

ET in VL may replace AC, ATQUE, and -QUE.

ETIAM may mean no more than *et.*

MAGIS wholly replaces SED, AT, VERUM, POTIUS (It. *ma,* Fr. *mais,* Sp. *más,* Port.
mais).

> Classical poets had often used MAGIS for POTIUS: *id non est turpe, ma-
> gis miserum est* (Catull. 68.30).

MOX = *postquam*

> *Non manducant nisi sabbato mane, mox communicaverint,* "they do
> not eat except on the Sabbath morning after they have taken commu-
> nion" (*Itin.* 27.9).

NAM: originally a particle of assurance (= Greek γάρ) *nam* came to be the equivalent of Greek δή in both its continuative and adversative senses (Weber 131).

NEC = NON found as early as Cato, and not uncommon in CL poetry.

> *pedibus me ascendere necesse erat, quia prorsus nec in sella ascendi pot-
> erat,* "I had to ascend by foot since really I could not ascend in the sad-
> dle" (*Itin.* 3.2; Löfstedt 2, 88f.).

NON entirely displaces other negatives such as HAUD. The double negative, moreover, becomes more common than in CL: *nihil respondit > non respondit nihil;
neminem vidi > non vidi neminem.* To strengthen negations, various negative particles were added: RES, GUTTA, MICA, PUNCTUM, PLUMA, PASSUS: e.g. *non video
rem, guttam, punctum* (cf. Fr. *rien, pas, point,* It. *mica,* Cat. *res, pas, mica*). This
pleonastic strengthening is very typical, and it testifies to a desire to stress a word
which is, by itself, considered worn out or inadequate. Many examples can be
found in all areas of Medieval Latin semantics.

QUARE: interrogative, becomes causal (Fr. *car*).

> *quare contra praeceptum evangelii iurare voluistis,* "since you wished to
> swear in contradiction to the Evangelist"; *et arguet Thomam, quare in-
> credulus fuisset,* "and he scolded Thomas because he was doubting"
> (*Itin.* 40.2).

QUATENUS may replace *ut* "in order that" (frequent in Ambrose and Augustine).

QUOD becomes a sort of universal conjunction (Herman 93). In CL, above all it is an explicative and causal conjunction; in VL, it does the job of UT, CUM, and SI.

Final QUOD (= UT): *non velle dici sanctum, antequam sit, sed prius esse, quod verius dicatur,* "he should not wish to be called a saint before being one, but he must be one first in order to receive the name more truly" (*Rule of St. Benedict* 4.42).

Consecutive QUOD (= ITA UT): *vulnus ita insanabile facit, quod totus pes amputandus sit,* "that produces a wound so incurable that the entire foot must be amputated" (Palladius, *Medicina pecorum* 31.4).

Comparative QUOD: *incedunt quaedam sine pedibus . . . quod angues,* "some approached without feet . . . like serpents" (Tertullian, *De anima* 10).

Temporal QUOD: *Tercia die, quod omnes Christiani celibrant pascha . . . ressurrexit de sepulchro,* "on the third day, while all the Christians were celebrating Easter, he arose from the grave" (*Dicta abbatis Priminii,* 9); *Mons autem ipse per giro quidem unus esse videtur; quod ingrederis, plures sunt,* "the mountain from the surroundings seems to be one; when you are on the inside, they are many" (*Itin.* 2.5). (See Bonnet 326; Löfstedt 2, 66–67).

For QUOD in indirect discourse, see § 7.10.

QUOMODO has a temporal aspect in addition to its CL uses.

vidi beatum Euphemiam per visionem et beatum Antonium; quomodo venerunt, sanaverunt me, "In a vision I saw the blessed Euphemia and the blessed Anthony; when they appeared, they healed me" (*Antonini Placentini itinerarium* 46, cited by Herman 94). QUOMODO > QUOMO > It. *come,* Fr. *comme,* Sp. *como,* Cat. *com,* Rom. *cum.*

SIC becomes a copulative:

benedicuntur cathecumini sic fideles, "the catechumens as well as the faithful received blessing" (*Itin.* 43.6). (Rom. *si* < SIC, "and").

UT disappears from spoken Latin, as does CUM. QUANDO replaces CUM temporal.

6.2 New Conjunctions

IAM UT "as soon as"

iam ut exiremus de ecclesia, dederunt nobis, "as soon as we came out of the church, they gave us . . ." (*Itin.* 3.6).

POST is used as a conjunction instead of *postquam*.

QUA becomes a temporal conjunction (Löfstedt 2, 125).

> *hic est locus Choreb, ubi fuit sanctus Helias propheta, qua fugit . . .,* "This place is Choreb, where Saint Elijah was when he fled . . ." (*Itin.* 4.2).

6.3 Pleonastic Compounds

The practice of pleonastic strengthening extended to conjunctions (see Löfstedt 175). Precedents can be found in CL, for example, the compounding of two synonyms, *itaque ergo* (Ter. *Eun.* 2.3.25; Livy 1.25.2):

> *singulis diebus cotidie (Itin.).*

ADHUC HACTENUS is less commonly found.

ETIAM ET is the most frequent of the pleonastic forms.

ITA SIC

> *non ita sic intelligendum est,* "it is not to be thus understood" (Epiphanius, *Interpr. Evangel.* 17.

NECNON ET (also found in CL).

> *Maxima pars Palestinae . . . inde videbatur, nec non et et omnis terra Iordanis,* "From there could be seen a great part of Palestine, and in particular the whole land of Jordan" (*Itin.* 12.5; also *Chron. Sal.* 65, 21.).

QUIA CUM, CUM QUANDO, DUM QUANDO

> *dissuria ideo appellatur, cum quando difficiliter urinam facit,* "it is called 'dysuria' when it is difficult to urinate."

7. VERBS

7.1 Forms
7.1.1 PRESENT TENSE

mittet = mittit; vivet = vivit: such forms may be due to phonetic changes, as long *e*, short *e*, and short *i* were pronounced similarly in final syllables, a fact which no doubt favored the use of analytic forms for the future tense of the 3d conjugation (Grandgent 243; Löfstedt 2, 133ff.).

> *qui rubus usque in hodie vivet et mittet virgultas,* "which bush even today is alive and puts out shoots" (*Itin.* 4.6).

7.1.2 Future

Third and fourth conjugation forms were sometimes confused.

> *periet* (*Vulgate*, Wisd. of Sol. 4:19); at Gen. 18:5 in the *Vetus Latina*, the Itala has *transietis*.

7.1.3 Imperfect

The imperfect in general survived without alteration. Occasionally anomolous forms occur:

> *erabamus* (*Chron. Sal.* 129.18); *quando nos erabamus iuvenculi,* "when we were youths" (Paul, *Hist. Lang.* 5.50; cf. It. *eravamo*).

7.1.4 Perfect

There was a marked tendency to replace 3d conjugation verbs, particularly those with irregular "strong" or reduplicated perfects, with first conjugation forms: e.g., *praestavi* for *praesteti*.

7.2 Periphrastic Verb Forms

The fondness for periphrasis and the preference for analytic over synthetic forms is particularly apparent in verb forms. The use of such pleonastic auxiliary verbs as *velle, posse, coepisse, videri, conari, dignari,* and *debere* is common (Löfstedt 2, 207; Weber 57).

> *sanitatem praestare debeant,* "they produce a healthy condition"; the *Vetus Latina*, at Gen. 18.17, to translate a Greek future gives *celabo,* while Jerome in the *Vulgate* translates *celare potero.* At Gen. 21.16 the *Vetus Latina* reads *sedere coepit,* and the *Vulgate, sedit.*

7.2.1 Compound Tenses

The synthetic verb forms of Classical Latin tend to be replaced by analytic forms whose descendants are the verbs of the Romance languages.

Compound present. In general, the present participle played a very limited role in periphrastic conjugations. It was only in the imperial epoch that this construction became widespread in the spoken language (see ET 274–75). It is, however, found in Plautus (*ut tu sis sciens, Poen.* 1038; *ille est cupiens, ibid.* 660).

> *non erit displicens* (*Itin.* 16.6); *invenerunt speluncam, quam sequentes fuerunt forsitan per passus centum,* "they found a cave which they followed for perhaps one hundred feet" (= *sequebantur,* or *secuti sunt; Itin.* 16.6; see Löfstedt 2, 245); *Is enim est et scientia pollens,* "for he is powerful even in knowledge" (Liutprand, *Antap.* 2.20).

Compound Imperfect.

Sanguine fluens eram, "I was flowing with blood" (Gospel of Nicodemus 7); *et ipse erat exspectans regnum Dei,* "and he was awaiting the kingdom of God" (Gospel of Nicodemus 11.3).

Compound future. In the Romance languages, there is no trace of the Latin future in *-bo* (*erit* survived in OFr. *ert*); in its place we find:

(1) analytic forms composed of the infinitive and forms of HABERE (cf. OCat. *seguir vos he = vos seguiré* [*Crònica* of Jaume I]). This separated form still survives in Portuguese (*dar-me-as,* "you will give me"; *dir-vos-emos,* "we will tell you"). For further discussion, see § 7.2.2.

admirari hominem habebitis, "you will admire the man" (*VA* Prol. 3).

The often-cited first example of the romance future is Fredegarius 85.27: *Et ille* [sc. the king Perses] *respondebat: Non dabo. Iustinianus dicebat: Daras,* "And he answered, 'I will not give,' and Justinian replied, 'Daras' (= *dare habes*)."

Wright 43, n. suggests that perhaps popular etymology considered -ABIT and HABET, pronounced identically, to be the same.

(2) a future participle plus ESSE.

habituri sumus munus, "we will have a reward" (Petronius 45.4); *sic et nos futuri sumus resurgere,* "we too will be resurrected" (Grandgent 57). At Gen. 18.17 in the *Vetus Latina* to translate the Greek future ποιήσω we find *non celabo Abraham puerum meum quae ego facturus sum,* "I shall not conceal from my child Abraham what I will do."

(3) periphrases with VELLE and POSSE plus an infinitive: (in Romanian, the future is derived from VOLO plus the infinitive).

(4) DEBERE plus an infinitive (retained in Sardinia).

(5) VADERE, IRE, VENIRE and an infinitive.

Compound Perfect. Parallel to the compound future, there evolved a compound perfect; the form already existed in CL: *satis habeo deliberatum* (Cic.); *Venit ad me pater. Quid habui facere?* (Seneca, *Contro.* 1.1.19).

Suspectamque habuit . . . pugnam, "He suspected a fight" (*Waltharius* 346; cf. Fr. *il a suspecté*); *ubi ipsi castra posita habebant,* "where they had placed camps" (*Itin.* 19.11); *causas pauperum exosas habebat,* "he hated things of the poor" (Greg. T., *H.F.* 6.46).

In medieval vernacular languages, the past participle agrees with the direct object: OCat. *nostro Senyor nos hauria dada aquesta victoria,* "Our Lord has given us this victory" (*Crònica* of Jaume I); OSp. *las armas avien presas,* "they captured the arms (*Poema de mio Cid* 1001). The agreement of the past participle continued in Spanish until the 14th century).

With the compound present and imperfect, compare also:

> *Hic non fuit consentiens uoluntatibus et accusationibus Iudaeorum,* "He was not in agreement with the desires and accusations of the Jews" (*Gospel of Nicodemus* 11.3).

7.2.2 Other uses of habeo and the Infinitive

To express ability and obligation. HABERE can express ability and then obligation—"to have something to do," "be able to do something."

> *habeo etiam dicere quem contra morem maiorum,* "I have to say [I can say] who, in contrast to the habit of our ancestors" (Cic. *Rosc. Am.* 35.100); *sed non ipsa parte exire habebamus qua intraveramus . . . quia necesse nos erat . . .,* "we were unable to leave by the way we had entered because it was necessary for us . . ." (*Itin.* 4.5).

This construction, with the infinitive or future passive participle is largely ante-classical and post-Augustan.

> *etiam Filius Dei mori habuit,* "even the Son of God had to die" (Tert., *Hab. Mul.* 1); *si inimicos iubemur diligere, quem habemus odisse,* "if we are ordered to love our enemies, whom must we hate?" (idem, *Apol.* 37); *ipsam ergo vallem traversare habebamus,* "therefore we had to cross the valley" (*Itin.* 2.1). (Cf., e.g., Cat. *he de dir,* "I have to say, I must say").

To represent a conditional. By a gradual weakening, the infinitive plus the imperfect, *habebam,* came to represent a modern conditional.

> *Sanare te habebat Deus . . ., si fatereris,* "God would heal you if you would confess" (Ps.-Aug. *Serm. app.* 253.4, Bourciez 257b).

7.3 Esse

When ESSE is used as a verb of motion, the verb implies at once the idea of going to a place and staying there (see Löfstedt 2, 171).

> *qua primitus ad Egyptum fueram,* "when I first went to [was in] Egypt" (*Itin.* 7.1; also 9.6, 20.2, 23.1).

7.4 Participles:
7.4.1 PRESENT

The present participle is replaced by the ablative of the gerund: *gratulando rediit,* "he returned rejoicing." This is the source of the present participle in Italian and Spanish.

> *ita miserrimus fui fugitando,* "I was so miserable fleeing" (Ter. *Eun.* 846–47); *redirent . . . dicendo psalmos vel antiphonas,* "they returned singing psalms and antiphons" (*Itin.* 15.5); *moriar stando,* "I shall die standing" (Amm. Marc. 24.3.7); *ad cellulam cum omni populo canendo rediit,* "singing, he returned to his cell with the whole people" (Greg. T., *De passione et virtutibus Iuliani* 7).

7.4.2 GERUNDIVE

By a similar weakening, the gerundive came to denote mere futurity (from the 3d or 4th century C.E.); with ESSE it supplied a future passive conjugation, devoid of the classical connotations of obligation or necessity.

> *Hannibal cum tradendus Romanis esset, venenum bibit,* "Hannibal, when he was to be handed over to the Romans, drank poison" (Flavius Eutropius 4.5); *filius hominis tradendus est,* "the son of man will be handed over" (Grandgent 49).

A gerundive plus the present tense of the verb "to be" may function as a compound present perfect.

> *de quali provincia vos estis oriundi?* "from what province have you originated? ("Life of Epictetus and Astion," *Vitae Patrum* 1, *PL* 73).

7.4.3 PRESENT FOR AORIST (PERFECT ACTIVE)

One problem of Latin, in comparison with Greek, is the absence for most verbs (i.e., all non-deponents) of a perfect *active* participle comparable to the Greek aorist. In Latin, the present participle should properly expresses action *contemporary* with the main verb, but even in CL there was a tendency for it to slip into the past tense:

> *eum primo incertis implicantes responsis . . . edocuerunt,* "at first trying to confuse him with uncertain replies, . . . they revealed" (Livy 27.43.3).

This lack was felt especially keenly by the translators of the *Vetus Latina,* eager to preserve as much as possible of the syntax of their Greek original. For example, at Matt. 2.10, to render the aorist participle ἰδόντες, "having seen," the Itala has *videntes,* which in CL properly expresses action contemporary with the main verb (*gavisi sunt*), not prior to it, as is required by the sense. Jerome followed the Itala, and in general present participles are very frequent in ML as a replacement for a perfect active participle.

7.4.4 Replacing a Finite Verb

In Greek, a very common construction is "participle plus verb" = "verb and verb." This is far more common in Greek than Latin due to the greater number of participles in both voices in Greek.

> *Nam Leo papa . . . ad eum accedens . . . ubi Mincius amnis transitur*,
> "For Pope Leo came to him where the Mincius river is crossed" (Jordanes, *De Orig.* 42); *quia rebellem, inquiens, ac sacrilegem celare quam militibus reddere maluisti,* "because you preferred, he said, to conceal a rebel and sacrilege than to hand him over to the soldiers" (Bede, *Hist. Eccl.* 1.7); in the *Vetus Latina* at Matt. 8.7, the Itala reads *Ego veniens, curabo eum.*

At Matt. 2.8, MSS of the Itala read *euntes requirite*, literally translating the Greek construction; the others read *ite et interrogate.*

7.4.5 Replacing an Infinitive in Indirect Discourse

With *audire* and *videre*, in imitation of Greek, a participle may replace the accusative and infinitive in indirect discourse (Nunn 65).

> *et vidit omnis populus eum ambulantem et laudantem Deum,* "and the entire people saw him walking and praising God" (*Vulgate*, Acts 3.9); *Cum ergo vidisset quidam de Iudaeis eum hoc facientem,* "When, therefore, one of the Jews saw him doing this" (*Gospel of Pseudo-Matthew* 27).

7.4.6 Absolute Participial Constructions

In addition to the ablative, nominative, and accusative absolute constructions, other, seemingly independent participial constructions are found in ML.

(1) When the substantive is an acting person, the substantive may be in the nominative and the participle in the ablative (Westerbergh 274).

(2) When the substantive functions as an object of the participle, the substantive is accusative and the participle ablative. This construction is known as the impersonal passive with an object (see Löfstedt 2, 290ff.; Westerbergh 275).

> *videntes autem Petri constantiam et Johannis, comperto quod homines essent sine litteris,* "seeing, however, the constancy of Peter and John,

having learned that they were uneducated men" (*Vulgate*, Acts 3.9); *Quidam autem de exercitu, invento cuiusque pauperis faenum, ait,* "One of the army, having found a poor man's hay, said" (Greg. T., *H.F.* 2.37); *apprehenso equi retinaculum, celeriter eum Beneventum ducebat,* "having grasped the rein of the horse, he quickly led him to Beneventum" (*Chron. Sal.* 83.5).

7.5 Transitive and Intransitive
7.5.1 TRANSITIVE VERBS BECOME INTRANSITIVE

REFICERE comes to mean "refresh oneself," "to eat a meal":

> *fratres reficiunt sexta hora,* "the brothers eat at the sixth hour" (*Rule of St. Benedict*).

7.5.2 PRONOMINAL FORMS

A reflexive form is often substituted for a passive (cf. the medio-passive of Greek); many of these words are reflexive in the Romance languages (*coangustare se,* cf. It. *angosciarsi; turbare* and *perturbare se,* cf. It. *turbarsi*). A few intransitive verbs may also be used reflexively (*credere se,* cf. It. *credersi; rebellare se,* cf. It. *ribellarsi;* see Westerbergh 272–73).

> *cum male sibi senserint,* "when they feel bad" (see Löfstedt 2, 140, and compare the French, *se sentir mal*).

7.6 Defective Verbs

In CL, *odi* is a defective verb with no present tense in use. In Christian writers, however, a present *odio* was in use.

> *benefacite his, qui odiunt vos,* "do good to those who hate you" (*Vetus Latina,* Matt. 5.44; Vulgate, *oderunt*); future, *odiet* (*Vetus Latina,* Matt. 6.4).

7.7 Tense
7.7.1 PRESENT FOR FUTURE

In CL, this usage (widespread in English) was used rarely, chiefly in compound sentences, and restricted by and large to certain verbs and phrases (e.g., *si vivo,* "if I live"). Its use was more general in ML.

> *non credo, nisi videro,* "I will not believe unless I see it" (*Itin.* 39.5, citing John 20.25 [doubting Thomas]; the *Vetus Latina* and *Vulgate* have *non credam*); *in illo . . . tempore cum illos gloria aeterna circumdat,* "at that time [the Last Judgment], when eternal glory surrounds [i.e., will surround] them" (Greg. T., *De virtutibus Martini* 106).

7.7.2 Tenses in Biblical Translations

In the Old Testament, the Hebrew use of tenses caused trouble for the translators, including Saint Jerome and the Greek translators of the Septuagint. Hebrew has only two "tenses," which express complete and incomplete aspect; either can be used for the present, past, or future. In the Septuagint, the perfective was treated as a past tense and the imperfective as a future. In the Latin texts, a past tense may be used for a present or a future (Blaise 226–33).

7.8 Mood

7.8.1 Indicative and Subjunctive

Classical rules concerning the use of the indicative and the subjunctive are relaxed, and the indicative may be found in all constructions which in CL require the subjunctive. Examples are too numerous to document with any thoroughness.

DUM = *cum* causal plus indicative: *dum non intellegebat,* "since he did not understand" (Greg. T., *H.F.* 6.46).

ITA UT = Greek ὥστε, often followed by the indicative, perhaps following the Greek construction (Weber 64).

7.8.2 Imperative

There were many ways of issuing negative commands in CL; since all imperatives refer to the future, the "tense" is purely aspectual:

ne audi (poetic)

ne audito (legal)

non audies (colloquial)

ne audias (chiefly ideal)

noli audire (common)

ne audiveris (correct but rare)

In ML, the most common method of issuing a negative command was *noli* plus the infinitive:

In the *Vetus Latina,* the MSS of the Itala offer at Matt. 1.20 *noli timere, ne timueris,* and *ne timeas.*

As *noli* passed out of use in popular speech, the word appears to have been understood as a negative (= *non*), and *non* plus the infinitive came into use. This use was limited to the 2d person singular negative (as in Italian and Old French).

si videris lassiorem esse, non tangere, "if you see [him] to be more tired, don't touch."

There was a general tendency in popular speech to eliminate constructions with *ne,* as the familiar *non audies* shows.

non . . . putet quis, "let no one think" (Reid 97).

7.9 Infinitive

Infinitives were widely used, replacing a number of classical constructions.

7.9.1 PURPOSE INFINITIVE

The use of the infinitive to express purpose (after verbs of motion) is found in very early Latin, and it continues in the colloquial language and in poetry (in literary Latin, the supine was used in this way).

venerat aurum petere, "he had come to seek gold" (Plaut. *Bacch.* 631); *non nos . . . Libycos populare Penates / venimus,* "we have not come to destroy the Libyan homes" (Virgil, *Aen.* 1.527–28).

The construction becomes common in VL.

futurum esse enim ut Herodes quaerat puerum istum perdere, "It will come to pass that Herod seeks the boy to destroy him" (*Vulgate* and *Vetus Latina,* Itala, Matt. 2.13; cf. the MS variant *ad perdendum eum*); *impetravit implere* (Tert., *Iei.* 7).

7.9.2 INFINITIVE OF THE GOAL

This construction is a Hellenism.

dare ad manducare (*Vetus Latina,* John 6.52); *sedit manducare* (*Vulgate,* Exod. 32.16).

7.9.3 INFINITIVE FOR RESULT CLAUSE

tum filios . . . more Francorum equitare fecit, "he made his sons ride in the Frankish fashion" (Einhard, *Vita Karoli* 19); *quo audito, Decius Caesar fecit eum sibi praesentari,* "having heard this, Decius Caesar had him presented" (Notker Balbulus, *Martyrologium,* Saint Lawrence).

7.9.4 INDIRECT QUESTION

In VL and ML, the subjunctive in an indirect question came to be replaced by a complement (and an infinitive). *Nescio quid dicam,* "I do not know what to say," came to be expressed *nescio quid dicere; nescio quo eam,* "I do not know where to go," came to be *nescio ubi ire.*

Rogo vos . . . ut adtentius cogitemus quare christiani sumus, "I ask you
. . . that we consider carefully why we are Christians" (Norberg 94).

7.9.5 CLAUSES OF FEARING

In clauses of fearing, the infinitive may replace *ut* or *ne* and the subjunctive.

> *noli timere accipere Mariam coniugem,* "do not fear to accept Mary as
> your wife" (*Vulgate,* Matt. 1.20); *timuit illuc ire,* "he feared to go
> there" (*Vulgate,* Matt. 2.20).

7.10 Indirect Discourse

The classical construction with infinitive and subject accusative died out, replaced
by a clause introduced by QUIA, QUOD, or QUONIAM. This construction had existed side by side with the more learned construction in popular usage, and spo-
radic examples can be found from all periods. It does not, however, become common until the postclassical period.

> *scio iam filius quod amet meus istanc meretricem,* "I know that my son
> is in love with that prostitute" (Plaut. *Asinaria* 52–53); *dixi quia mus-
> tela comedit,* "I said that he ate the lamprey" (Petronius 46.4).

> *Tunc Herodes, ut vidit quoniam (quia,* MS d; *quod* MSS fl) *delusus est,*
> "Then Herod, when he saw that he was tricked" (*Vetus Latina,* Matt.
> 2.16). The three MS variants of the Itala here preserve the three possible
> solutions to the problem of translating here the Greek ὅτι; *fateor quod
> perfectus non sit,* "I admit that he is not perfect" (Aug., *C. Acad.* 1.9);
> *ut intellegamus quia Deus semper iustus fuit,* "so that we may under-
> stand that God was always just" (Aug., *De ordine* 2.22).

In biblical translations, another problem arose with respect to translating ὅτι: in
Greek this conjunction introduces direct quotations. In Latin, *quod, quia,*
and *quoniam* were used in the same ways, and should not here be translated
(Nunn 64).

> *et mulieri dicebant: Quia iam non propter tuam loquellam credimus,*
> "and they were saying to the woman, 'We believe, not because of your
> talking'" (*Vulgate,* John 4.42); *si quis dixerit quoniam diligo Deum, et
> fratrem suum oderit, mendax est,* "if anyone says, 'I love God' and
> hates his brother, he is a liar" (*Vulgate,* 1 John 4.20).

7.10.1 MOOD IN INDIRECT DISCOURSE

Greek ὅτι is followed by the indicative. *Quia* and *quod* may be followed by either
the indicative or the subjunctive; *quod* tends to take the subjunctive, *quia* the
indicative.

7.10.2 SUBORDINATE CLAUSES IN INDIRECT DISCOURSE

Classical usage demands the subjunctive in such clauses; in ML the indicative may be found in a subordinate clause.

At Gen. 1.7 in the *Vetus Latina* the Itala reads, *et vidit Deus quia bonum est*, "and God saw that it is good."

7.11 Indirect Question

Archaic Latin often used the indicative mood in indirect questions; this construction is found in ML. For the infinitive in an indirect question, see § 7.9.4.

miror cur . . . visa sunt, "I wonder why they seem . . ." (Aug., *Solil.* 2.18).

UTRUM . . . AN and the subjunctive was replaced by SI with the indicative (perhaps under the influence of the Greek εἰ): *nescio utrum Romanus an barbarus sit* became *nescio si Romanus aut barbarus est*.

Visam si domi est, "I shall see whether he is at home" (Ter. *Heaut.* 170); *dic mihi si Romanus es*, "tell me if you are a Roman citizen" (*Vulgate*, Acts 22.27; for CL *dic mihi an Romanus sis*); *quaerite ergo si vera est ista divinitas Christi*, "seek therefore whether Christ's divinity is a true one" (Tertullian, *Apol.* 21).

7.12 Sequence of Tenses

Classical rules concerning the sequence of tenses are frequently violated (indeed, medieval tense structures in all situations frequently conform to norms other than those of classical or modern usage—mixtures are frequent).

Latinam ita didicit ut aeque illa ac patria lingua orare sit solitus, "He learned Latin so well that he was equally accustomed to pray in it or in his native tongue" (Einhard, *Vita Karoli* 25).

7.13 Voice
7.13.1 ANALYTIC FORMS

On the model of *carus est, amatus est* came to mean "he is loved" (= *amatur*), not "he was loved." The precise date at which this change occurred is, however, a matter of controversy. In Gen. 1.9, the *Vetus Latina*, however, translates the Greek present passive ἀφορίζεται by *dividitur*, but one MS of the Itala offers the analytic form *divisum est*.

Invocavi enim deos meos, sed, ut experior, elongati sunt ab auxilio meo, "I have called upon my gods, but, as I am finding out, they are far removed from helping me" (Greg. T., *H.F.* 2.30).

In compound tenses, *fueram* and *fuero* became popular replacements for *eram* and *ero*. This use can be paralleled in CL.

> *Non, hodie si / exclusus fuero, desistam,* "I shall not cease, even if I am shut out today" (Hor., *Sat.* 1.9.57–58); *fuerunt impediti* (*Itin.* 3.4) = *impediti sunt.*

7.13.2 The pronomial passive

Pronomial forms are often reflexive, replacing a medio-passive form (*me excrucio* = *excrucior;* see ET 214). In the late period, this usage was extended to purely intransitive verbs:

> *recipit se episcopus et vadent* [e.g. *vadunt*] *se unusquisque . . . ut se resumant,* "the bishop withdrew and everyone departed . . . to rest" (*Itin.* 25.7).

The reflexive verb forms may, indeed, come so close to a passive as to be substituted for them, especially in the third person:

> *Myrinam quae Sebastopolim se vocat,* "Myrina, which is called Sebastopol" (Pliny, *N.H.* 5.121); cf. the use in the Romance languages, e.g., French, where *cela se dit* = *dicitur,* or *dici solet;* It. *si chiama,* Fr. *il s'appelle,* Sp. *se llama; haec ergo dum aguntur, facit se hora quinta,* "While these things were taking place, it came to be the fifth hour" (= *fit; Itin.* 27.3); cf. It. *si fa* (*notte, sera*), Fr. *il se fait* (*tard*), Sp. *se hace* (*tarde*).

7.13.3 Active for Deponent Forms

The loss of deponent forms occurred early in popular Latin. In Plautus, for example, the following active forms occur: *horto, lucto, partio, sortio, auspicavi,* etc. In Petronius *loquere* is found for *loqui* (46.1), also *amplexare* (63.8).

ADGREDERE for *adgredior: cum Chuni in exercitu contra gentem qualibet* [for *quamlibet?*] *adgrediebant,* "when the Huns went out in an army against any people" (Fredegarius, 4.48).

OPERARE for *operior: VA* 28.25; also in Commodian and Cassiodorus.

7.14 Impersonal Constructions

(1) HABET, used intransitively, comes to mean "there is," "there are" (Fr. *il y a,* Sp. *hay*); examples can be found in Roman comedy (e.g. Terence, *Phormio* 419).

> *Habebat autem de eo loco ad montem Dei forsitan quattuor milia,* "there were, moreover, from that place to the mountain of God perhaps

four miles" (*Itin.* 1.2); *habebat autem ante se ipse fons,* "there was, moreover, before it a spring" (*Itin.* 15.2); *Et quoniam inde ad sanctam Teclam . . . habebat de civitate forsitan mille quingentos passus* (*Itin.* 23.2).

(2) The use of HOMO for an impersonal subject (cf. Fr. *on*).

Cf. *Vetus Latina,* Gen. 11.3, where the Itala has *et dixit homo proximo* but one manuscript reads, *ait unusquisque. Quomodo potest se homo mortificare?* "how can one (a man) mortify himself?"

(3) Extended use of the impersonal passive (very common, for example, in the *Itin.*).

in eo ergo loco cum venitur, "when we came to that place" (*Itin.* 1.2); *O quam beata civitas / In qua redemptor venitur,* "O how blessed is the city in which the redeemer comes" (Bede, *Martyrdom of the Holy Innocents*).

7.14.1 Impersonal Verbs used Personally

The use of impersonal verbs in personal constructions is rare but classical; it is commoner in LL and VL.

paenituit eum quod hominem fecisset in terra (*Vulgate,* Gen. 6:6); *et cogitavit deus quia fecit hominem super terram et paenituit,* "and God knew that he had made man on earth, and regretted it" (*Vetus Latina*).

7.15 Concessive Clauses

May be introduced by *esto, fac, pone*:

Fac tot annos in penitentia expleam, dimittantur omnia, restet hoc unum, "Even though I should complete many years of penance, and though all was forgiven, this one thing would remain" (Rather of Verona, *Conf.* 21.410C; Reid 103).

ABBREVIATIONS

§	Introduces references to the numbered sections of the Brief Introduction to Medieval Latin Grammar, pp. 1–51.
Adcock	F. Adcock, trans. and ed., *Hugh Primas and the Archpoet*, Cambridge Medieval Classics 2, Cambridge, 1994.
AG	J. B. Greenough, G. L. Kittredge, A. A. Howard, B. L. D'Ooge, eds., *Allen and Greenough's New Latin Grammar*, New York, 1983 (cited by section number).
Anderson and Kennen	J. D. Anderson and E. T. Kennan, trans., *Five Books on Consideration: Advice to a Pope*, Cistercian Fathers Series 37, Kalamazoo, Mich., 1976.
Atzori	M. T. Atzori, *La Preposizione "de" nel latino volgare*, Florence, 1939.
Bechtel	E. A. Bechtel, *Sanctae Silviae Peregrinatio: The Text and a Study of the Latinity*, Chicago, 1902.
Becker	J. Becker, ed., *Die Werke Liudprans von Cremona*, Hanover, 1915.
Beeson	C. H. Beeson, ed., *A Primer of Medieval Latin: An Anthology of Prose and Poetry*, Washington, D.C., 1953.
Bertini/Dronke	F. Bertini and P. Dronke, eds., *Rosvita Dialoghi Drammatici*, Milan, 1986.
Blaise	A. Blaise, *Manuel du latin chrétien*, Turnhout, 1955, trans. by G. C. Roti as *A Handbook of Christian Latin: Style, Morphology, and Syntax*, Washington, D.C., 1994 (cited by section number).
Blaise/Chirat	A. Blaise and H. Chirat, eds., *Dictionnaire latin–français des auteurs chrétiens*, Turnhout, 1954.
Bonnet	M. Bonnet, *Le Latin de Grégoire de Tours*, Paris, 1890.
Bourciez	E. Bourciez, *Eléments de linguistique romane*, Paris, 1956.
Browne	R. A. Browne, ed., *British Latin Selections: 500–1400*, Oxford, 1954.
CB	*Carmina Burana*
CIL	*Corpus Inscriptionum Latinarum*
CL	Classical Latin
Colgrave/ Mynors	R. A. B. Mynors and B. Colgrave, eds. and trans., *Bede's Ecclesiastical History of the English People*, Oxford, 1969.
Coseriu	E. Coseriu, *El Llamado "latin vulgar" y las primeras diferenci-*

	aciones romances: Breve introducción a la lingüística ro-mánica, Montevideo, 1954.
Curley	M. J. Curley, *Geoffrey of Monmouth*, Twayne's English Authors Series, New York, 1994.
Dronke 1	P. Dronke, ed. and trans., *Nine Medieval Latin Plays*, Cambridge Medieval Classics 1, Cambridge, 1993.
Dronke 2	P. Dronke, ed., *Bernardus Silvestris, Cosmographia*, Leiden, 1978.
Du Cange	C. Du Fresne Du Cange, ed., *Glossarium mediae et infimae aetatis*, 6 vols., Paris, 1733–36.
EL	Ecclesiastical Latin
ET	A. Ernout and F. Thomas, *Syntaxe latine*, Paris, 1951.
Finaert	J. Finaert, *L'Evolution littéraire de Saint-Augustin*, Paris, 1939.
Foulke	W. D. Foulke, trans., *The History of the Lombards of Paul the Deacon*, New York, 1907.
Godman	P. Godman, ed. and trans., *Poetry of the Carolingian Renaissance*, Norman, Okla., 1985.
Goffart	W. Goffart, *The Narrators of Barbarian History (A.D. 550–800): Jordanes, Gregory of Tours, Bede, and Paul the Deacon*, Princeton, N.J., 1988.
Grandgent	C. H. Grandgent, *An Introduction to Vulgar Latin*, Boston, 1907.
Habel/Gröbel	E. Habel and F. Gröbel, eds., *Mittellateinisches Glossar*, Paderborn, 1989.
Haefele	H. Haefele, ed., *Ekkehard IV, St. Galler Klostergeschichten*, Darmstadt, 1980.
Hagenmeyer	H. Hagenmeyer, ed., *Fulcheri Carnotensis Historia Hierosolymitana (1095–1127)*, Heidelberg, 1913.
Halphen	L. Halphen, ed., *Éginhard, Vie de Charlemagne*, Paris, 1947.
Henshaw	M. Henshaw, *The Latinity of the Poems of Hrabanus Maurus*, Chicago, 1936.
Herman	J. Herman, *Le Latin vulgaire*, Paris, 1967.
Hill and Hill	J. H. Hill and L. L. Hill, eds., *Le Liber de Raymond d'Aguilers*, in "Documents relatifs à l'histoire des croisades," Académie des Inscriptions et Belles-Lettres, Paris, 1969.
James	M. R. James, ed., *Walter Map, De nugis curialium*, Oxford, 1914.
LL	Late Latin
Latham	R. E. Latham, ed., *Revised Medieval Latin Word List from British and Irish Sources*, Oxford, 1965.
Latouche	R. Latouche, ed., *Richer, Histoire de France (888–995)*, Paris, 1930.

Löfstedt	E. Löfstedt, *Late Latin*, Oslo, 1959.
Löfstedt 1	E. Löfstedt, "Some Changes of Sense in Late and Medieval Latin," *Eranos* 44 (1946): 340–54.
Löfstedt 2	E. Löfstedt, *Philologischer Kommentar zur Peregrinatio Aetheriae*, Uppsala, 1936.
Lokrantz	M. Lokrantz, ed., *L'opera poetica di S. Pier Damiani*, Studia Latina Stockholmiensia, Stockholm, 1964.
LS	C. Lewis and C. Short, eds., *A Latin Dictionary*, Oxford, 1879.
Meillet	A. Meillet, *Esquisse d'une histoire de la langue latine*, Paris, 1928.
ML	Medieval Latin
Mohrmann	C. Mohrmann, *Etudes sur le latin des chrétiens*, Rome, 1958.
Mozley/Raymo	J. H. Mozley and R. R. Raymo, eds., *Nigel de Longchamps, Speculum Stultorum*, Berkeley and Los Angeles, 1960.
MW	O. Prinz, ed, *Mittellateinisches Wörterbuch bis zum ausgehenden 13. Jahrhundert*, Munich, 1967.
Muckle	J. T. Muckle, "Abelard's Letter of Consolation to a Friend (*Historia Calamitatum*)," *Medieval Studies* 12 (1950): 163–213.
Nelson and Shirk	L. H. Nelson and M. V. Shirk, trans., *Liudprand of Cremona: Mission to Constantinople (968 A.D.)*, Lawrence, Kans., 1972.
Newman	B. Newman, ed. and trans., *Saint Hildegard of Bingen: Symphonia: A Critical Edition of the Symphonia armonie celestium revelationum [Symphony of the Harmony of Celestial Revelations]*, Ithaca, N. Y., 1988.
Niermeyer	J. F. Niermeyer, ed., *Mediae latinitatis lexicon minus*, Leiden, 1976, repr., 1993.
Norberg	Dag Norberg, *Manuel pratique de latin médiéval*, Paris, 1968.
Nunn	H. P. V. Nunn, *An Introduction to Ecclesiastical Latin*, Eton, 1952.
OED	*Oxford English Dictionary.*
Pertz	G. Pertz, ed., *Widikundi Res Gestae Saxonicae*, Hanover, 1839.
PL	J.-P. Migne, ed., *Patrologia cursus completus, Series latina*, 221 vols., Paris, 1844–55.
Plummer	C. Plummer, ed., *Venerabilis Bedae Opera Historica*, 2 vols., Oxford, 1896.
Pritchard	R. T. Pritchard, trans., *Walter of Châtillon, The Alexandreis*, Mediaeval Sources in Translation 29, Toronto, 1986.
Raby 1	F. J. E. Raby, *A History of Christian Latin Poetry from the Beginnings to the Close of the Middle Ages*, Oxford, 1927.

Raby 2   F. J. E. Raby, *A History of Secular Latin Poetry in the Middle Ages*, 2 vols., Oxford, 1934.

Reid   P. L. D. Reid, *Tenth Century Latinity: Rather of Verona*, Malibu, 1981.

Riché   P. Riché, ed. and trans., *Dhuoda, Manuel pour mon fils*, Sources chrétiennes, vol. 225, Paris, 1991.

Ryan   F. R. Ryan, trans., *Fulcher of Chartres, A History of the Expedition to Jerusalem, 1095–1127*, Knoxville, Tenn., 1969.

Schmeidler B. Schmeidler, ed., *Adam von Bremen, Hamburgische Kirchengeschichte*, Hanover, 1917.

Sheridan 1 J. J. Sheridan, trans., *Alan of Lille, The Plaint of Nature*, Mediaeval Sources in Translation 26, New York, 1980.

Sheridan 2 J. J. Sheridan, trans., *Alan of Lille, Anticlaudianus or the Good and Perfect Man*, Toronto, 1973.

Sidwell   K. Sidwell, ed., *Reading Medieval Latin*, Cambridge, 1995.

Sleumer   A. Sleumer, *Kirchenlateinisches Wörterbuch*, Limburg a. d. Lahn, 1926, repr. Hildesheim, 1990.

Souter   A. Souter, comp., *A Glossary of Later Latin to 600 A.D.*, Oxford, 1949.

TLL   *Thesaurus Linguae Latinae.*

Vielliard   J. Vielliard, *Le Latin des diplômes royaux et chartres privées de l'époque mérovingienne*, Paris, 1927.

VL   Vulgar Latin

Walsh   P. Walsh, ed. and trans., *Love Lyrics from the Carmina Burana*, Chapel Hill, 1993.

Weber   S. Weber, *Anthimus, De observatione ciborum: Text, Commentary, and Glossary with a Study of the Latinity*, Leiden, 1924.

Westerbergh U. Westerbergh, *Chronicon Salernitanum*, Stockholm, 1956.

Wetherbee 1 W. Wetherbee, *Platonism and Poetry in the Twelfth Century: The Literary Influence of the School of Chartres*, Princeton, 1972.

Wetherbee 2 W. Wetherbee, trans., *The Cosmographia of Bernardus Silvestris*, New York, 1973.

Wetherbee 3 W. Wetherbee, ed. and trans., *Johannes de Hauvilla, Architrenius*, Cambridge Medieval Classics 3, Cambridge, 1994.

Wright   F. A. Wright, trans., *The Works of Liudprand of Cremona*, London, 1930.

Ziolkowski J. Ziolkowski, ed. and trans., *The Cambridge Songs (Carmina Cantabrigiensia)*, New York and London, 1994.

Classical authors and works are cited in accordance with standard abbreviations found at LS vii–xi.

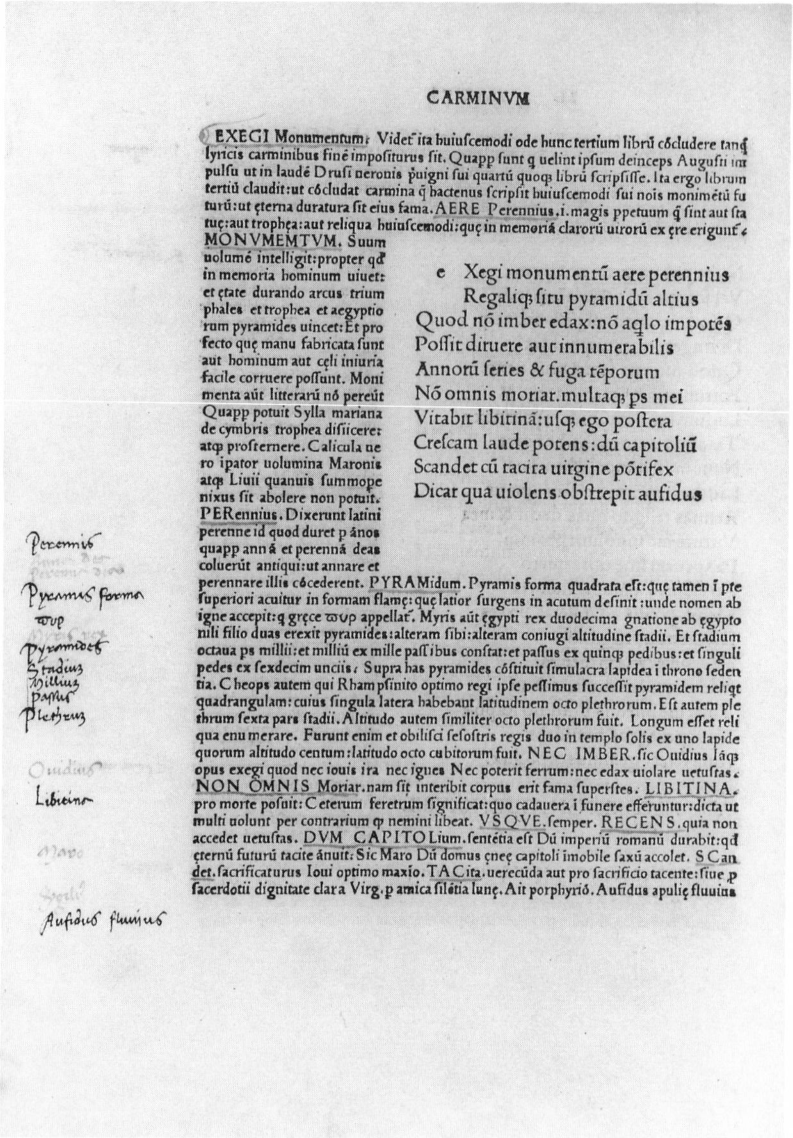

EXEGI Monumentum; Videt ita huiufcemodi ode hunc tertium librū cōcludere tanq̓ lyricis carminibus finē impofiturus fit. Quapp̓ funt q̓ uelint ipfum deinceps Augufti in pulfu ut in laudē Drufi neronis p̓uigni fui quartū quoq̓ librū fcripfiffe. Ita ergo librum tertiū claudit:ut cōcludat carmina q̓ hactenus fcripfit huiufcemodi fui nois monimētū fu turū:ut ęterna duratura fit eius fama. AERE Perennius.i. magis ppetuum q̓ fint aut fta tuę:aut trophęa:aut reliqua huiufcemodi:quę in memoria clarorū uirorū ex ęre eriguntꞓ MONVMEMTVM. Suum

uolumē intelligit:propter qd̓ in memoria hominum uiuet: et ętate durando arcus trium phalē et trophea et aegyptio rum pyramides uincet:Et pro fecto quę manu fabricata funt aut hominum aut cęli iniuria facile corruere poffunt. Moni menta aūt litterarū nō pereūt Quapp̓ potuit Sylla mariana de cymbris trophea diffiicere: atq̓ profternere. Caligula ue ro ipator uolumina Maronis atq̓ Liuii quanuis fummope nixus fit abolere non potuit. PERennius. Dixerunt latini perenne id quod duret p̓ ānos quapp̓ annā et perennā deas coluerūt antiqui:ut annare et perennare illis cōcederent. PYRAMidum. Pyramis forma quadrata eft:quę tamen ī pte fuperiori acuitur in formam flamę:quę latior furgens in acutum definit:unde nomen ab igne accepit:q̓ gręce τυρ appellat. Myris aūt ęgypti rex duodecima gnatione ab egypto nili filio duas erexit pyramides:alteram fibi:alteram coniugi altitudine ftadii. Et ftadium octaua ps millii:et milliū ex mille paffibus confrat:et paffus ex quinq̓ pedibus:et finguli pedes ex fexdecim unciis̓ Supra has pyramides cōftituit fimulacra lapidea ī throno feden tia. Cheops autem qui Rham pfinito optimo regi ipfe peffimus fucceffit pyramidem reliq̓t quadrangulam:cuius fingula latera habebant latitudinem octo plethrorum. Eft autem ple thrum fexta pars ftadii. Altitudo autem fimiliter octo plethrorum fuit. Longum effet reli qua enumerare. Furunt enim et obilifci fefoftris regis duo in templo folis ex uno lapide quorum altitudo centum:latitudo octo cubitorum fuit. NEC IMBER. fic Ouidius Iaq̓s opus exegi quod nec iouis ira nec ignes Nec poterit ferrum:nec edax uiolare uetuftas̓ NON OMNIS Moriar. nam fit interibit corpus erit fama fuperftes. LIBITINA. pro morte pofuit:Ceterum feretrum fignificat:quo cadauera ī funere efferuntur:dicta ut multi uolunt per contrarium q̓ nemini libeat. VSQVE. femper. RECENS. quia non accedet uetuftas. DVM CAPITO Lium. fentētia eft Dū imperiū romanū durabit:qd̓ ęternū futurū tacite ānuit. Sic Maro Dū domus cnęę capitoli imobile faxū accolet. SCan det. facrificaturus Ioui optimo maxio. TACita. uerecūda aut pro facrificio tacente:fiue p̓ facerdotii dignitate clara Virg. p̓ amica fidētia lunę. Ait porphyrió. Aufidus apulię fluuius

e Xegi monumentū aere perennius
Regaliq̓ fitu pyramidū altius
Quod nō imber edax:nō aqlo impotēs
Poffit diruere aut innumerabilis
Annorū series & fuga tēporum
Nō omnis moriar.multaq̓ ps mei
Vitabit libitinā:ufq̓ ego poftera
Crefcam laude potens:dū capitoliū
Scandet cū tacita uirgine pōtifex
Dicar qua uiolens obftrepit aufidus

[Marginal handwritten annotations:]
Peremis
Pyramis forma
τυρ
Pyramides
ftadius
miliius
paffus
plethrus

Ouidius

Libitina

Maro

Aufidus fluuius

PLATE 1. A page from Landino's edition of Horace, showing the opening lines of *Odes* 3.30, with marginal and interlinear annotations and markings by Torquato Tasso.

PLATE 1

Cristoforo Landino, ed., Horace, *Opera*, Florence, 1482, p. 243.
Foster Horace Collection
John Hay Library, Brown University

Cristoforo Landino published his edition of and commentary on the works of Horace in 1482 in Florence, with a dedication to Guidobaldo di Montefeltro. The printer was Antonio di Bartolommeo Miscomini. This copy eventually became the property of Torquato Tasso (1544–1595), whose numerous annotations line the margins of its pages. Like his contemporaries, Tasso was steeped in the Latin classics, which he used as a foundation to his own poetic output, and which he studied carefully. It was, however, a result of the medieval preservation of antiquity's best works that Renaissance poets like Tasso, not to mention printers such as Miscomini, were able to find legible, accurate copies of the masterworks of Latin antiquity to analyze and print.

Landino's Horace represents the sort of early printing produced in Italy in the late fifteenth century. Printing arose in the mid fifteenth century in Mainz with Gutenberg and spread throughout Germany, then to Italy through the craft of Conrad Sweynheym and Arnold Pannartz, who worked at the abbey of St. Scholastica at Subiaco. Printing, of course, revolutionized the production of classical works, making obsolete the old process of copying out manuscripts by hand. But the care evinced in bringing Latin manuscripts to publication after the mid fifteenth century speaks to the crucial work of cultural preservation accomplished by medieval scriptoria, as subsequent plates suggest.

PART ONE: 350–450
THE FORMATION OF
LATE LATIN

EGERIA (fl. c. 385)

SULPICIUS SEVERUS (c. 400)

AUSONIUS (c. 310–c. 395)

PAULINUS OF NOLA (c. 350–431)

PRUDENTIUS (fl. c. 400)

PROBA (fl. c. 360)

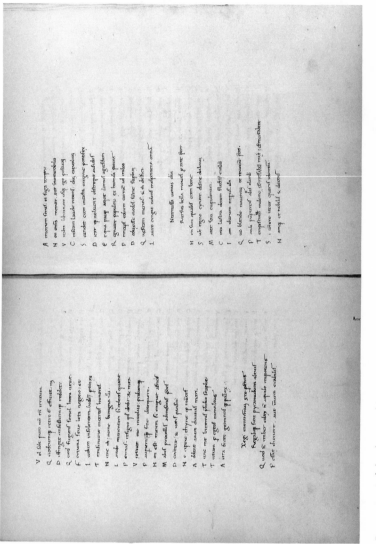

PLATE 2. A folio from a fifteenth-century manuscript of Horace's complete works, showing the poet's most famous declaration of poetic glory, *Odes* 3.30, *Exegi monumentum aere perennius*, with the first word spelled "Xegi" and a space left for the omitted rubrication.

PLATE 2

Horace, *Opera*, Latin manuscript on paper, 1466, fols. 50 verso and 51 recto.
Foster Horace Collection
John Hay Library, Brown University

The poetry of Horace circulated widely throughout the Latin Middle Ages in manuscripts not unlike this one, and medieval writers turned often to this most exemplary of antique Latin poets for spiritual and artistic direction. *Odes* 3.30, depicted here, is the poet's most famous declaration of poetic immortality, which closed off his three-book collection of *Odes*, published in 23 B.C.E. Horace evinces a clear sense of the insuperability of his monumental project and of his own long-lasting fame. His accomplishments in lyric were to be superseded in the coming centuries, however, by comparable innovations in late and medieval lyric forms, most notably the hymn, and eventually the sequence, as we will see. Students of antique Latin tend, however, to share the superior attitude suggested in Horace's boasts in this ode. Poetry—and Latin—marched on, nonetheless, as the following pages suggest.

This manuscript is of unknown origin, though its semi-Gothic script might suggest a German provenance. It records all the works of Horace, and it is bound in calfskin over wooden boards. Later hands have added some rubrics and marginal glosses. The spine is lettered "Q. Horatii Flacci Carmina." A colophon records only the year in which the manuscript was copied.

INTRODUCTION

The publication, late in the first century B.C.E., of a cohort of Latin literary masterpieces—Horace's fourth book of *Odes*, Virgil's *Aeneid*, the elegies of Propertius and Tibullus, Livy's history—endures in the Western literary tradition as a permanent monument to the cultural aspirations of Imperial Rome. The care evinced in preserving and studying those masterpieces, points to the worth assigned to these and other works like them by succeeding generations, who considered Latin antiquity a superb foundation for their own literary productions, even after the empire which had sponsored their creation had changed in profound and permanent ways. In the monastery, the cathedral school, and, later, the university, these works were central to the curriculum, to the wider development of Latin literature, indeed, to culture-production of every sort in the Latin Middle Ages. Nor were the early imperial writers oblivious to their accomplishments. As Horace concluded his career late in the first century B.C.E., those accomplishments must have seemed secure—and insuperable. He could hardly have anticipated the kinds or the rates of change that would overtake Latin in succeeding centuries.

The imperial achievement in letters was deeply imprinted with the accoutrements of empire—in topic, outlook, and vocabulary—as it was written in an elite Latin, circumscribed by rigid rules of grammar, syntax, prosody, and *cursus* and cut off from the common discourse of life. But the characteristics of that achievement were already in flux within the lifetime of the emperor Augustus. Barely two decades after Horace's death, Ovid had produced a monumental poem, the *Metamorphoses*—destined to become canonical to the Latin Middle Ages—that merged the lyric affect of Horace's *Odes* with the epic sweep of Virgil's *Aeneid*. In the process, this craftiest of ancient Latin poets destabilized both the lyric and the epic genres, for the affect of his stories did not depend (as in the *Odes*) on the fierce visions of independent spirit, but rather on the contingent power of fickle gods, whose worst habits and predilections became the focus of Ovid's vision (as they were not in the *Aeneid*). At the same time, the elite Latin of the Empire was altered by Ovid, who created in his new epic a more natural language by limiting his use of dependent clauses and the participle and by making the coincidence of ictus and accent more prominent.

Ovid's reshaping of generic and linguistic assumptions has an analogue in his treatment of the givens informing imperial culture. Virgil's insistence on the fundamental order of the epic world, for example, was abandoned by Ovid, replaced by a pantheon of gods prone to the worst fits of envy, pride, and violence. At the same time, the private spaces of Horace's best lyric moments were transformed to the stage of epic contest, where victimized humans acted out their private emotions in a cosmic context. As if to highlight his own worries about divinity, Ovid had begun his epic with three creation stories, implicitly calling into question antique cosmological assumptions. Lucan, writing forty years after Ovid, in an epic style also much altered since Virgil's masterpiece, took this sentiment one step further in his *De bello civili,* questioning the very premises of divinity by declaring that the gods in fact no longer existed.

Lucan's affirmation of the death of the gods points to a fundamental ingredient in the development of Late Latin: the shifting spiritual landscape of the later Empire. By the time that Tacitus was producing his ironic, bitter versions of the imperial past, Christianity was already a flourishing Jewish sect; and by the time Pliny the Younger was posted as imperial legate to Bithynia, some time after the turn of the second century C.E., Christians were numerous enough to draw his attention away from other matters, their presence problematic enough for him to raise the issue of their status with the emperor, Trajan, directly. When, several generations later, Tertullian wrote his famous apology in defense of the now regularly persecuted Christians, the spiritual stakes that Pliny had raised had become hardened into cultural norms. The strains of unbelief evinced in Lucan had been transformed into a new passion for Christian monotheism, a passion portended in the opening of Ovid's *Metamorphoses* and whose necessity was adumbrated in his depictions of the Roman pantheon.

As Christianity gained adherents, however, it did more than simply meet the spiritual needs of a large segment of the Empire. It also increasingly became a cultural force that put new challenges to Latin that had the effect of liberating the language from the rigid strictures of classical diction, syntax, and grammar, and allowing it to give expression to the kinds of (new) experiences demanded by this new faith. The rise of the Second Sophistic in the second century, for example, though pagan in origin, had an important effect on the development of theological discourse written in Latin, as the work of Tertullian suggests. So, too, did the independent development of ecclesiastical Latin expand and widen the language, creating new forms of expression, a new lexicon of ecclesiastical meanings, and a fresh semantics, which had the effect of freeing the language even further from its classical guises. Two ingredients especially helped in this liberation. First, the place made in Christian writing for popular, or vulgar, discourse, especially in the construction of the various versions of the Latin Bible, had the effect of opening up Late Latin in general to much simpler and more concrete modes of expression.

Especially because the Bible needed to make its appeal to the widest possible audience, consisting mainly of listeners (for whom it was a recited document), it was important that it not be written in the elite language of the Empire. At the same time, the centuries-old inclination on the part of Roman littérateurs to keep Latin separated from the syntactic, semantic, and lexical influences of Greek was, under the aegis of Christianity, abandoned, as Latin readily adopted Greek vocabulary, idiom, and syntax in order to accommodate the language to theological speculation and abstract expression.

The combination of features specific to Vulgar Latin and Ecclesiastical Latin had the effect, then, of transforming the language by the fourth century into something of extraordinary vigor. Ecclesiastical themes had dominated the output of Latin writers in the second and third centuries, as the works of Lactantius, Arnobius, Minucius Felix, Tertullian, and Cyprian, among others, attest. But by the fourth century, under the growing prestige of Christianity's enfranchisement as a licit religion in the Empire, a profusion of literary forms and artists arose, in part sponsored by the growing position of the institutional Church but owing also to changes in the Latin language itself as it responded to the new spiritual demands made on it by large segments of the Empire. Among the important achievements of this century, apart from the glory of Jerome's version of the Bible, were Augustine's foray into self-reflection and autobiography in the *Confessions* and Ambrose's mediation of the lyrical rhetoric and tonal intensity of Horace into his hymns on the divinity of Christ. But these monumental achievements were accompanied by other important accomplishments, as the selections in this part reflect.

Under the impetus of the Church's need to proselytize, Vulgar Latin retained an important place in the development of Late Latin. The Christian sermon especially became a venue for the inculcation of the racy, direct, simplified diction of the largest segment of the Empire's peoples and in Egeria's *Itinerarium*, the influence of Vulgar Latin is witnessed through Egeria's own simple learning and in the fact that she places much of the record of her journey to the Holy Land against the background of Scripture, itself written in a style that owed much to popular speech. At the same time, the old genres gave way to fresh forms, one of the most popular being the saint's life, of which Sulpicius Severus's life of Saint Martin is an early example. In this new form, the best features of antique history were merged with an emphasis on exemplarism, moral instruction, and a syntax and diction that delivered its message in different registers—now in a common style, now in a style more beholden to older standards of Classical Latin prose.

But the old genres were not entirely abandoned, as the enormous output of Ausonius demonstrates. In fact, since all the Christian littérateurs of the fourth century were raised in the pagan schools (and since many of them had been pagan at some point in their lives), there is throughout the works of these pioneering artists a familiarity—even a warm intimacy—with the literary traditions of the early Empire. Ausonius is perhaps the boldest Christian poet of the fourth century to engage these traditions fully in order to rework them to fresh purposes. But his student, Paulinus of Nola, attempted much the same aim in his poetic work, though with the goal of turning his readers away from classical material entirely, an aim Ausonius never shared—and never understood.

In the main, however, Christian littérateurs tried for new forms and in so doing exemplified Goethe's maxim that the power of a language lies in its being able to devour what is foreign. In the work of Prudentius, clearly, Christian poetry was put on firm footing as the meters of classical Latin lyric were made to sing the praises of Christ. Those praises were sung by Proba also, but from a more substantially classical base, in the cento form. Here half-lines of Virgil's *Aeneid* were cut and pasted into a new poetic product, wherein Virgil's old words were made to say new, Christian, things. In these works, with their obvious bows to the formalism of Imperial Latin, the Latin language was made to say new things by devouring the old. In being able to do this, however, Christian littérateurs exposed their exotic and visionary talents, as they struggled, successfully, to invent a culture and a language to support it. Their songs are various, the forms they invent and assume numerous, but the visions and voices which emerge from the fourth century are as clear as any managed by the Imperial writers, and brimming with the vigor of belief, the rhetoric of a language feeling the first pangs of a long and sweet liberation from the rigors of Classicism's domination. When the balance between classical meters and vocabulary, and Christian belief and function, was achieved, the result, as in Ambrose's deceptively simple hymns, was incomparable:

> Splendor paternae gloriae,
> de luce lucem proferens,
> lux lucis et fons luminis,
> dies dierum illuminans.

It was a sentiment, a form, an expressiveness in language that was to prove remarkably resilient in the coming centuries, as Hopkins, a more recent inheritor of much from the Latin Middle Ages, proves:

> The world is charged with the grandeur of God.
>> It will flame out, like shining from shook foil;
>> It gathers to a greatness, like the ooze of oil

Crushed. Why do men then now not reck his rod?
Generations have trod, have trod, have trod;
    And all is seared with trade; bleared, smeared with toil;
    And wears man's smudge and shares man's smell: the soil
Is bare now, nor can foot feel, being shod.

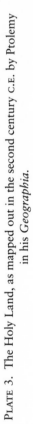

PLATE 3. The Holy Land, as mapped out in the second century C.E. by Ptolemy in his *Geographia*.

PLATE 3

Claudius Ptolemaeus [=Ptolemy], *Geographia,* Rome, 1490, fols. 134 verso
and 135 recto.
Annmary Brown Memorial Collection
John Hay Library, Brown University.

When Egeria left for the Holy Land, the maps drawn up by Claudius Ptolemy formed the standard by which the known world was viewed. Indeed, much of the work done on astronomy and cartography in the Latin Middle Ages was owed to earlier work produced in Roman, and in some instances Greek, antiquity. Ptolemy lived in the second century C.E. in Alexandria, where he worked on projects in astronomy and cartography, the results of which were published in Greek over the course of several decades. Arabic translations of most of his works were made in the ninth century and retranslation into Latin followed in the twelfth and thirteenth centuries in Spain. Ptolemy is most famous for his observation that the earth was the center of the universe, a view that held sway until the seventeenth century. His cartography was equally important because he made use of measurements of latitude and longitude, as this plate shows.

The translation of the *Geographia* from which this plate comes was made by Jacobus Angelus Florentinus, early in the fifteenth century. It contains twenty-seven maps (one of the world, ten of Europe, four of Africa, and twelve of Asia). It was printed by Petrus de Turre at Rome in 1490 (one of only four books ascribed to his press). The maps had been engraved on copper by Conrad Sweynheym for an edition completed after his death and brought out in 1478 by Arnold Buckink, which was the earliest attempt at copperplate printing.

EGERIA

The Journey
(*Itinerarium*; c. 385)

When she arrived at Edessa, some time in the mid 380s, on one leg of a
lengthy journey throughout the Holy Land, Egeria was met by the
Bishop of that city, who said that it was clear to him that she had come
"from the very ends of the earth" (19.5). The contrasts between the erudite bishop and the simple nun—in education, social status, and spirituality—must have been stark. But Egeria's account of her journey to the
Holy Land itself is a work of marked contrasts, representing the intersec-
tion of cultural, linguistic, and spiritual traditions resident in the West
in the fourth century. Most importantly, perhaps, the *Itinerarium* speaks
to the ways in which post-Imperial Latin threw to the side the limitations
of elite diction, genre, and syntax imposed from on high during the imperial period. More specifically, the coexistence of VL and EL in Egeria's
work renders the Latin of the *Itinerarium* representative of the living
language of the fourth century, a language mostly spoken and constantly
in flux.

That flux is important to the development of LL in general, for it
includes features common to the older version of the language but configured in new ways, including more freedom in the application of CL
syntax and orthography and, in some instances, the appropriation of entirely new rules. Egeria is a witness to these trends in several ways. For
example, she is more liberal in the ways she construes prepositions with
specific cases: she writes *per giro, per girum, per valle illa*, and, for the
place to which construction, *in eo loco*. Nor are these constructions
simply the result of ignorance, for Egeria knows and uses the CL idioms.
Instead, her syntactic changes often reflect the simplifying influence of
EL, which Egeria knew through the Latin translations of the Bible. EL is
responsible, for example, for Egeria's preference for a succession of short
clauses and the repetition of transitional particles. And when grammatical change does not announce a simplicity owed to EL, then Egeria's style
more often than not reflects VL usage, in a way as revealing as the earlier
texts of Plautus, Catullus, or Petronius are in measuring out the characteristics of popular Latin of the Republic and Empire. In this regard, the
wider presence in the *Itinerarium* of pleonasm and Egeria's tendency to

end sentences with anacolutha reveal Latin in perhaps its most vigorous guise—as a living and changing language.

Egeria's *Journey* also offers a perspective on the place of women in the fourth-century church. The work was written for the benefit, and presumably under the sponsorship, of Egeria's religious community; and her assiduous attention to the instruction of her fellow sisters in her work speaks revealingly of the vibrancy of the group (though we are ignorant of its origins) and of Egeria's place in it (though we know nothing of her status in this regard either). That her community was somehow involved in sponsoring her trip confirms the place that women would seem to have carved for themselves in the growing monastic movements of the fourth century, for the journey involved much planning and mustering of resources reflective of a well-established foundation.

Egeria comes from a community, but she travels as an individual and it is as an individual that she fashions her record in the *Journey*. That fashioning has something specific to say about the experiences of individual women in the context of fourth-century spiritual habits; and the generous reception accorded to her throughout her travels reflects, beyond general attitudes, a specific disposition toward female religious on the part of people at disparate social, economic, and political strata. Egeria is taken seriously by bishops, locals, and other religious. Her faith cuts across lines of economic status, gender, and education and puts her on a level plane with the simplest hermit or the bishop of superior educational and social background.

On a literary level, Egeria's task was to record her experiences of the Holy Land for her fellow sisters. But she does so rarely, if ever, as personal reminiscences. Indeed, rather than act as a modern traveler reporting private adventures, she turns to Scripture—the one text that all her sisters would know—to frame her record, thus filtering most of what she sees through the prism of God's word. This tendency is not unique to Egeria, to be sure, but rather is a measure of cultural assumptions. One of the chief means by which Christianity solidified its power, in both an institutional and a cultural sense, was to insist on the authority of Scripture as the single source by which Christian life could be articulated, and to claim sole responsibility for producing and disseminating authoritative versions of that life. In turning to Scripture in this way, Egeria assumes a role akin to that of exegete, filling out in vivid detail the words of the Bible for her sisters, but yoking her own experience, and theirs, to the authority of God's word, not her own.

The manuscript preserving what remains of Egeria's *Journey* (along with an account of the liturgical year at Jerusalem) was copied out sometime in the eleventh century, probably at Monte Cassino. It was discovered late in the nineteenth century by J. F. Gamurrini, who prepared successive editions in 1887 and 1888. Of Egeria herself we know only those things that can be conjectured from the text, viz., that she was associated with a religious community in the West, that she journeyed widely over the Holy Land, and that she stayed there, visiting sites and numerous religious, for at least several years.

Various attempts have been made at identifying her. Gamurrini thought she was the well-connected Silvia Aquitana of Gaul, mentioned by Palladius. Subsequently, on the authority of external evidence, she has been identified as Egeria (the preferred spelling of a name that exists in some five other forms). She may indeed hail from Gaul, but the place of her birth remains unknown. The exact date of Egeria's journey is impossible to determine. A rough date of around 385 is now widely accepted, based on a careful analysis of whom Egeria visited and when.

Apart from Gamurrini's two early editions (*Biblioteca della Accademia storico-giuridica*, vol. 4, Rome, 1887; *Studi e documenti di storia e diritto* 9, 1888: 97–174), the *Itinerarium* has been edited by P. Geyer (*Corpus Scriptorum Ecclesiasticorum Latinorum*, vol. 39, Vienna, 1898, pp. 35–101), W. Heraeus (Heidelberg, 1929, 1939), H. Pétré (*Sources chrétiennes*, vol. 21, Paris, 1948), O. Prinz (Heidelberg, 1960), and E. Franceschini and R. Weber (*Corpus Christianorum, Series Latina*, vol. 175, Turnhout, 1965, pp. 27–90). E. Bechtel's edition (*Chicago Studies in Classical Philology*, vol. 4, 1902) contains an exhaustive analysis of language and style. D. R. Blackman and G. G. Betts have prepared a concordance (*Concordantia in Itinerarium Egeriae*, Hildesheim, 1989). J. P. Wilkinson has produced an English translation for the Society for Promoting Christian Knowledge (*Egeria's Travels*, London, 1971), which includes an extensive discussion of social and ecclesiastical issues, and full notes and bibliography. M. Starowieyski has prepared a bibliography on Egeria up to the late 1960s ("Bibliografia Egeriana," *Augustinianum* 19 (1970): 297–318).

The excerpt reprinted here picks up Egeria's story several lines into the text as we have it, at the moment when her entourage finally enters into view of Mount Sinai. Though Egeria is often faulted for her intellectual naivety, not to mention linguistic decadence, one cannot help but experience in these lines the vigorous spirituality that informed much Christian activity in the fourth century. In addition to an attention to detail that suggests a steadfast, if not prodigious, intellect, there is a rhetorical consistency to Egeria's narrative. The reporting of what is seen or heard by Egeria is generally rendered, as here, in VL, while the reminiscences about sacred history are articulated in a simpler style more closely approximating the characteristics of EL. In this way the immediacy of the present moment is contrasted rhetorically with the austerity of the history whose details constantly influence what Egeria sees and how she sees it, rendering the *Journey* something more than a mere collection or travelogue, something bordering on a literary work of art of its own shape and kind. The text of Franceschini and Weber is reprinted here with some minor formatting changes.

A Pilgrimage to Mount Sinai

In eo ergo loco cum venitur, ut tamen commonuerunt deductores sancti illi, qui nobiscum erant, dicentes: "Consuetudo est, ut fiat hic oratio ab his qui veniunt, quando de eo loco primitus videtur mons Dei": sicut et nos fecimus. Habebat autem de eo loco ad montem Dei forsitan quattuor milia totum per valle illa, quam dixi ingens.   5

1. **in eo . . . loco** = CL *in eum locum,* accusative of place to which (cf. AG 426.2) but here = LL/ML ablative of place to which (cf. Löfstedt 41). It is common in LL/ML for *is, ea, id* to be used as adjectives (cf. Beeson 19).   **cum:** temporal conjunction with indicative.   **venitur:** impersonal passive of *venire* (cf. Cic. *Verr.* 2.5.54, e.g.); the person of the verb in CL is fluid in the present tense. When the perfect passive form, *ventum est,* is used, it usually refers to a singular subject (cf. Cic. *Verr.* 2.5.141: *ad me ventum est,* "it has fallen to me"). If Egeria is using first person plural for singular (*nobiscum*), then *venitur* may equal *ventum est,* "when I came to this place." If not, then *venitur* can stand for the first person plural and refer to the group with which she is traveling, "when we came to this place" (LS 1969, s. v. *venio,* I β, II B; cf. AG 208d and cf. the nearly identical phrase in Caesar, *BG* 6.43: *in eum locum ventum est,* "it came to pass"). Egeria's phrase is governed by *cum* in a more literal construction that presumably reflects the norms of spoken Latin.   **ut tamen commonuerunt:** *ut* = temporal conjunction with indicative, correlative with *cum; tamen* = a particle of transition (Souter 412); *commonere* takes an understood *nos* as object here, whereas in CL *commonere* usually takes an undefined object (LS 382, s. v. *commoneo,* a–d). 2. **ut fiat** = CL clause of result expressing necessity or obligation (AG 568).   **hic** = adverb. 3. **mons Dei** = Sinai; in Egeria's reckoning, *Syna;* the more common LL/ML spelling = *Sina* or *Syna* (Sleumer 728).   **sicut** = *ita.* 4. **habebat** = CL impersonal *fuit; habere* is often used impersonally in LL/ML; § 7.14. 5. **totum** = CL *omnino.*   **per valle illa** = CL *per vallem illam.*   **quam dixi ingens** = CL *quam dixi ingentem.* The valley is the psychological subject of this clause, so Egeria conceives of it in terms of the nominative, though it properly belongs in the accusative. This tendency is probably strengthened by assimilation, since *vallis,* in the

Vallis autem ipsa ingens est valde, iacens subter latus montis Dei, quae habet forsitan, quantum potuimus videntes estimare aut ipsi dicebant, in longo milia passos forsitan sedecim, in lato autem quattuor milia esse appellabant. Ipsam ergo vallem nos traversare habebamus, ut possimus
5 montem ingredi. Haec est autem vallis ingens et planissima, in qua filii Israhel commorati sunt his diebus, quod sanctus Moyses ascendit in montem Domini et fuit ibi quadraginta diebus et quadraginta noctibus. Haec est autem vallis, in qua factus est vitulus, qui locus usque in hodie ostenditur: nam lapis grandis ibi fixus stat in ipso loco.

10 Haec ergo vallis ipsa est, in cuius capite ille locus est, ubi sanctus Moyses, cum pasceret pecora soceri sui, iterum locutus est ei Deus de rubo in igne. Et quoniam nobis ita erat iter, ut prius montem Dei ascenderemus, qui hinc paret, quia unde veniebamus melior ascensus erat, et illinc denuo ad illud caput vallis descenderemus, id est ubi rubus erat,
15 quia melior descensus montis Dei erat inde: itaque ergo hoc placuit ut, visis omnibus quae desiderabamus, descendentes a monte Dei, ubi est rubus veniremus, et inde totum per mediam vallem ipsam, qua iacet in longo, rediremus ad iter cum hominibus Dei, qui nobis singula loca, quae scripta sunt, per ipsam vallem ostendebant, sicut et factum est. Nobis
20 ergo euntibus ab eo loco, ubi venientes a Faran feceramus orationem, iter

---

nominative, is the very next word, and also the noun which *ingens* describes, though in a discrete clause; cf. Löfstedt 18–19.   1. **valde** = exclamatory and emphatic adverb.   2. **habet** = CL *est;* § 7.14.   **quantum potuimus** = CL *quantum* + *posse* = "as much as. . . ."   3. **forsitan:** pleonastic, given the prior phrase *"quae habet forsitan."*   **milia passos sedecim** = CL *milia sedecim passuum;* cf. AG 135c.   4. **appellabant** = CL *dicebant; esse appellabant* is pleonastic; the sentence ends with an anacoluthon.   **traversare habebamus** = CL *nobis traversandum erat;* LL/ML regularly uses *habere* to express obligation, akin to CL *debere.*   6. **Israhel:** indeclinable noun, here construed in the genitive, dependent on *filii* (cf. Sleumer 450).   **his diebus quod** = CL *his diebus cum.*   7. **quadraginta diebus et quadraginta noctibus** = CL *quadraginta dies et quadraginta noctes,* accusative of extent of time (cf. AG 424b), but here = LL/ML ablative of extent of time; § 3.3.5. On the story recounted here, cf. Exod. 24.18.   8. **vitulus:** the golden calf; cf. Exod. 32.   **usque in hodie:** in CL *hodie* is an adverb; here it functions as an indeclinable noun governed by *in.*   10. **ille:** functions here as the definite article, as often in LL/ML; § 5.6.1.   12. **de rubo in igne:** cf. Exod. 3.1.   **ita erat iter** = CL *tale erat iter;* the alliteration (which also verges on punning) is a good instance of VL expressiveness.   15. **hoc placuit ut** = CL *hoc placitum est,* impersonal construction with *ut* = "and thus we decided to. . . ."   17. **veniremus . . . rediremus:** subjunctives with *ut,* expressing purpose.   20. **Faran:** or Paran, indeclinable place name, governed by the preposition *a.*

sic fuit, ut per medium transversaremus caput ipsius vallis et sic plecaremus nos ad montem Dei.

Mons autem ipse per giro quidem unus esse videtur; intus autem quod ingrederis, plures sunt, sed totum mons Dei appellatur; specialis autem ille, in cuius summitate est hic locus, ubi descendit maiestas Dei, sicut 5
scriptum est, in medio illorum omnium est. Et cum hi omnes, qui per girum sunt, tam excelsi sint quam nunquam me puto vidisse, tamen ipse ille medianus, in quo descendit maiestas Dei, tanto altior est omnibus illis ut, cum subissemus in illo, prorsus toti illi montes, quos excelsos videramus, ita infra nos essent ac si colliculi permodici essent. Illud sane satis 10
admirabile est et sine Dei gratia puto illud non esse ut, cum omnibus altior sit ille medianus, qui specialis Syna dicitur, id est in quo descendit maiestas Domini, tamen videri non possit, nisi ad propriam radicem illius veneris, ante tamen quam eum subeas; nam posteaquam completo desiderio descenderis inde, et de contra illum vides, quod, antequam subeas, facere 15
non potest. Hoc autem, antequam perveniremus ad montem Dei, iam referentibus fratribus cognoveram, et postquam ibi perveni, ita esse manifeste cognovi.

—It. Eg. 1–2.

1. **transversaremus:** from *transversare,* "to travel across" (Blaise/Chirat 827). **plecaremus** = CL *plicaremus,* but with LL/ML meaning = "to approach" (Blaise/Chirat 630, s. v. *plico* 2); § 2.1. 3. **per giro** = CL *per gyrum;* in LL/ML orthography, often i = y. The strict association of case with preposition is loosened in VL, LL/ML, but not abandoned, as the correct phrase, *per girum,* in line 11 suggests (if it is not simply the result of scribal correction). *Per giro* means the opposite of the phrase *intus autem quod ingrederis,* i.e., "to walk around," as against "to enter into." In VL, though not in Egeria, *in giro* comes to have the force of a preposition, governing the accusative or ablative (see Löfstedt 111; § 4.1.9). 4. **quod ingrederis** = CL *cum ingrederis; quod* is a universal conjunction in LL/ML, akin to English *that* or French *que;* § 6.1. 5. **descendit maiestas Dei:** cf. Exod. 19.18, 20. 7. **tamen** = CL *sed;* in LL/ML = particle of transition used with more freedom. 10. **colliculi permodici:** "very small little hills"; an example of pleonastic strengthening, a common tendency in VL and LL/ML (cf. Löfstedt 21f.). 11. **admirabile** = CL *mirabile.* 15. **de contra** = CL *contra* or *coram;* here = LL/ML adverb *decontra,* "face to face," "front-face" (Blaise/Chirat 243); § 4.2.2.

SULPICIUS SEVERUS

The Life of Saint Martin
(*Vita Sancti Martini;* c. 400)

geria represents one strain of spiritual activity in the fourth century, Sulpicius Severus quite another. Egeria's aims are broader, centering on the presentation of personal experience filtered through the prism of Scripture, with instruction the ultimate goal. The presence of competing prose styles in her account, gathered from the best traditions of LL, VL, and EL, suggests an emphasis on communicating the immediacy of experience without any special regard for literary tradition.

Sulpicius Severus' aims are less general, more beholden to the dictates of CL. He writes, presumably, for a wider and better educated audience than did Egeria, as the classical standards of his Latinity attest, and he is—his disclaimers notwithstanding—aware of those standards as an important measure of the respect owed his subject. That subject—Saint Martin—points to the further development in the fourth century of an important literary genre, hagiography, and the association of CL with saints' lives suggests the ways in which CL was taken over by Christianity. Christianity's appropriation of CL also represents the importance attached to this genre by its practitioners, for only the oldest language, the language possessing the most *gravitas*, would do. And, of course, the elevation implicit to hagiography reveals now an emphasis not so much on personal experience filtered through scripture, as on the exemplariness of a special life that mediates the human and divine natures of God.

The presentation of Martin's life is carefully framed by Sulpicius. Martin's earthly existence is consistently viewed, for example, as a channel for miraculous occurrences, and their potency speaks to an exemplarism of transcendence, ratifying the ways in which this special life was used by God to further the privileged faith. In turn, the simplicity of his life matters—the ways in which Martin always kept to the course at hand, either as a pious believer pursuing the monastic life, as a more aggressive proselytizer of the faith, or even as an important bishop working hard for the success of the Church as an institution. In the details of Martin's quotidian habits, where often enough the roles of monastic piety, conversion, and administration were bridged, an earthly exemplariness arises, a modeling in which the most important feature is to live in imitation of Christ.

Sulpicius affirms the bold exemplariness of his subject rhetorically also. As one of the first hagiographers in the Latin West, he wrote with virtually no Christian models to speak of for formal or contextual guidance. He turns, therefore, to two fundaments of CL prose for assistance, following thematically the oratorical model of Cicero, and formally the prototype of Sallust, especially with respect to word-choice. Yet one also finds a divergence from CL prose style in the periphrastic constructions and the borrowing of poetic expressions more common in Pliny the Younger or Apuleius.

Little is known of the life of Sulpicius. He was born of a noble family native to Aquitaine, but the dates of his birth and death have never been established with authority. We know on external evidence that he was younger than his frequent correspondent and good friend, Paulinus of Nola. A birthdate of around 360 C.E. is plausible. On the evidence of Sulpicius's flirtation with the Pelagian controversy specific to southern Gaul, we can estimate that he was still alive in 420, usually cited, roughly, as the year of his death.

Sulpicius acquired an education commensurate with his social standing and, like many well-known figures of his century, he was a zealous student who quickly made a career for himself as an advocate. His natural talents were bolstered when he married into a family of the senatorial rank, entering by all accounts a happy marriage that ended tragically when Sulpicius's wife died suddenly. At this juncture in his life, Sulpicius seems to have taken a keener interest in his faith, particularly in the ascetic life that was also drawing favor with other intellectuals in the West, including Paulinus of Nola (see pp. 94–100). Eventually, and perhaps under the influence of Paulinus, Sulpicius made a pilgrimage to Tours to meet Saint Martin, who by this time had gained a wide reputation in the West as a devout man with special powers, and who was practicing the new and attractive way of life as a hermit. This visit preceded by several years the death of Saint Martin, in November 397.

Sulpicius was favorably impressed by his meeting with the famous monk and bishop and, after taking up the ascetic life, devoted his talents exclusively to writing and to the pursuits of the spirit. In turn, Martin became for Sulpicius a spiritual and intellectual model, for which reason most of Sulpicius's writings deal in some way with him. In addition to the *Life,* the *Epistles* help to flesh out certain aspects of Martin's career, while the *Dialogues* sing the praises of Martin's particular brand of asceticism. Only Sulpicius' *Chronicle* avoids a focus on Martin, dealing instead with the details of sacred history as a means of instructing those ignorant of Christian teachings, and functioning as a compendium of world history from creation down to 400. But in moving from this more historical work back to the *Life*, one cannot help but be struck by the spiritual intensity informing so much of Sulpicius's work, a feature of his output grounded, as he himself said of Saint Martin's life, in the conviction that "not he who reads, but he who believes" (as Saint Mark taught) shall have the full measure of God's reward (cf. *Vita* 27.7). In this sense, the tender devotion of Sulpicius' life is itself equal in its own way to the exemplary qualities of St. Martin's career, both pointing to higher, grander things.

Sulpicius's collected works have been edited by K. Halm (*Sulpicius Severus Libri qui supersunt* in *Corpus Scriptorum Ecclesiasticorum Latinorum*, vol. 1, Vienna, 1866, repr. 1983 (*Vita S. Martini*, pp. 109–37)). The *Vita S. Martini* has been edited, with an exhaustive introduction and magisterial commentary (in French), by J. Fontaine (*Sources chrétiennes*, vols. 133–35, Paris, 1967–69). A. Roberts has translated all of Sulpicius's works into English (*The Works of Sulpitius Severus* in *A Select Library of Nicene and Post-Nicene Fathers of the Christian Church*, 2d ser., vol. 11, New York, 1894, repr. Ann Arbor, Mich., 1964). F. R. Hoare has translated the works relating to Martin into English (*The Western Fathers: Being the Lives of SS. Martin of Tours, Ambrose, Augustine of Hippo, Honoratus of Arles, and Germanus of Auxerre*, New York, 1954). There is an English translation of the *Life* also by B. Peebles (in *The Fathers of the Church*, vol. 7, New York, 1949, pp. 101–40). A comprehensive introduction to Martin and Sulpicius has been written by C. Stancliffe (*St. Martin and His Hagiographer: History and Miracle in Sulpicius Severus*, Oxford, 1983). On hagiography in late antiquity in general, see A. G. Elliott, *Roads to Paradise* (New York, 1985).

The excerpt from the *Life* reprinted here focuses on the miraculous element of Martin's activities in relation more specifically to proselytizing. The narrative is structured so that the presence of God, evinced at a distance early on, becomes dominant as the narrative proceeds. At the same time, the steadfastness of Martin, his humility and common sense, are contrasted with the bold pagan who challenges his faith and those who follow him. Their faith evanesces as Martin's power increases, pointing to the verity of Martin's position, the staying power of his faith, and the veracity of his God. The symbolism of the tree works to good effect here, finally, suggesting in its pagan associations the dark and potentially sinister vestiges of antique spirituality, which are supplanted ultimately by the Tree of Life. Fontaine's text is reprinted with some minor formatting changes and "u" and "v" distinguished.

SAINT MARTIN AND THE PINE TREE

Item, cum in vico quodam templum antiquissimum diruisset et arborem pinum, quae fano erat proxima, esset adgressus excidere, tum vero antistes loci illius ceteraque gentilium turba coepit obsistere. Et cum idem illi, dum templum evertitur, imperante Domino quievissent, succidi arborem non patiebantur. Ille eos sedulo commonere nihil esse religionis in 5 stipite; Deum potius, cui serviret ipse, sequerentur; arborem illam excidi oportere, quia esset daemoni dedicata. Tum unus ex illis, qui erat audacior ceteris: si habes, inquit, aliquam de Duo tuo, quem dicis te colere, fiduciam, nosmet ipsi succidemus hanc arborem, tu ruentem excipe; et si tecum est tuus, ut dicis, Dominus, evades. Tum ille, intrepide confisus in 10 Domino, facturum se pollicetur. Hic vero ad istius modi condicionem omnis illa gentilium turba consensit, facilemque arboris suae habuere iacturam, si inimicum sacrorum suorum casu illius obruissent. Itaque, cum unam in partem pinus illa esset adclinis, ut non esset dubium quam

---

2. **arborem pinum:** object of *excidere.* **fano** = *templo.* **adgressus:** perfect participle of *aggredi,* with infinitive *excidere* = "to begin to cut down." The "i" in *excidere* is long. 3. **obsistere:** dependent on *coepit* = "began to oppose (Martin)." 4. **imperante Domino:** ablative absolute, modifying *quievissent.* **cum . . . quievissent:** *cum* concessive with subjunctive, with subject *illi.* 5. **commonere:** historical infinitive, with subject *ille,* used frequently in CL prose as an alternate form for the imperfect or present indicative (AG 463). 7. **oportere:** historical infinitive, used impersonally as the verb of an infinitive clause. 8. **ceteris:** ablative of comparison. **aliquam:** modifies *fiduciam.* **quem . . . colere:** indirect discourse. 9. **nosmet** = *nos* + enclitic emphatic suffix "*met.*" **ipsi:** demonstrative adjective, modifying *nosmet* = "we ourselves." **excipe:** imperative, with object *ruentem.* 10. **tuus:** modifies *Dominus.* 11. **facturum** = *facturum esse,* future active infinitive, with subject accusative *se* in indirect discourse, dependent on *pollicetur:* "he promised that he would do it." **pollicetur:** historical present, often used in historical writing for effect; it can be translated in the present or the perfect (AG 469). **ad istius modi condicionem:** prepositional phrase, with *ad* governing *condicionem,* and *istius modi* dependent on *condicionem* (= lit. "of this kind"). The phrase is the object of *consensit.* In English idiom it means something like "to the condition agreed to by Martin and his antagonist." 12. **habuere:** alternate third person plural, perfect active indicative = *habuerunt;* this sense of *habere* is "to consider," "to judge," "to decide," etc. 13. **iacturam:** from *iactura, ae,* object of *habuere,* modified by *facilemque.* 14. **unam in partem:** i.e., "leaning in one direction."

in partem succisa corrueret, eo loci vinctus statuitur pro arbitrio rusticorum, quo arborem esse casuram nemo dubitabat. Succidere igitur ipsi suam pinum cum ingenti gaudio laetitiaque coeperunt. Aderat eminus turba mirantium. Iamque paulatim nutare pinus et ruinam suam casura
5 minitari. Pallebant eminus monachi et periculo iam propiore conterriti spem omnem fidemque perdiderant, solam Martini mortem expectantes. At ille confisus in Domino, intrepidus opperiens, cum iam fragorem sui pinus concidens edidisset, iam cadenti, iam super se ruenti, elevata obviam manu, signum salutis opponit. Tum vero,—velut turbinis modo
10 retro actam putares,—diversam in patrem ruit, adeo ut rusticos, qui tuto in loco steterant, paene prostraverit. Tum vero, in caelum clamore sublato, gentiles stupere miraculo, monachi flere prae gaudio, Christi nomen in commune ab omnibus praedicari; satisque constitit eo die salutem illi venisse regioni.

—*Vita S. Mart.* 13.1–9.4.

1. **quam in partem:** "in which direction . . . ." **succisa:** perfect passive participle of *succidere,* here modifying an understood *arbor pinus* = "the felled tree." **ut . . . corrueret:** result clause. **eo:** adverb modifying *vinctus* = "there." **loci:** dependent on *vinctus* = "bound at the spot" (lit. "of the spot"). **vinctus:** perfect passive participle of *vincire* = "bound," i.e., Martin has been tied up for purposes of the test. 2. **quo:** adverb = "where," i.e., "the spot where. . . ." **casuram:** future active participle of *cadere,* modifying *arborem.* 4. **nutare:** historical infinitive. **suam:** modifies *ruinam,* i.e., "threatened its own ruin"; or, perhaps *suam* = *eius,* as often in LL/ML, i.e., "threatened [Martin's] ruin"; § 5.3.1. 5. **minitari:** historical infinitive. 7. **fragorem:** i.e., the sound of the tree as it snaps and begins to fall. **sui** = CL *suum,* a common usage in LL/ML. 9. **signum salutis** = *signum crucis.* **velut turbinis modo:** i.e., "just as if in the manner of a coil." 10. **retro actam putares:** i.e., "you would have thought it thrown in the opposite direction." 11. **prostraverit:** from *prosternere.* 13. **praedicari:** historical infinitive. **satisque constitit:** "and it is well established . . .," governing indirect discourse.

AUSONIUS

About Bissula; Crucified Cupid
(*De Bissula,* c. 375; *Cupido Cruciatur,* c. 385)

For all their differences, Egeria and Sulpicius Severus are writers of an early moment. Although trained in the classical tradition, Sulpicius made classicism perform fresh tasks, consciously forging into the uncharted terrain of hagiography. Egeria, too, though unselfconscious about her literary aims, reflects a growing tendency in the fourth century to express faith through writing, to fashion a permanent record of belief for the edification of others, a tendency that found a more permanent place in EL writing in succeeding centuries. By distinction, Ausonius is a poet of a late moment, standing at the end of the long and varied classical literary tradition which forms the backdrop of all his work. His poetry engages the classical tradition comprehensively as to meter, theme, and genre, and there is no Late Latin poet who is more adept at handling classical material, or as facile in shaping it to newer forms.

Part of the burden of being late, of course, is to feel the weight of what appears to be a ceaseless literary discourse anterior to one's own work that must be accounted for if one's work is to be authentic. One senses Ausonius's understanding of this aspect of his place in literary culture, especially if his views on language are any barometer. Ausonius is always aware of the fact that language works as a system. Yet he seems always determined, perhaps owing to this awareness, to undermine or to call into question the stable ground implied by language's system, highlighting his own unstable position as a verbal artist at the same time that he articulates that instability in language itself.

In the *De Bissula,* for example, this instability is highlighted in a consideration of the ability of any mimetic form to copy, to recreate, beauty. In his poem the poet promises verses written about his slave girl, Bissula, and he uses no uncertain terms to praise her insuperability. But the details of her primacy never materialize; readers are told only that she is an unrivaled figure and that her beauty cannot be mimetically reproduced. Though he holds out painting as especially unsuited to the task of recreating the beauty of his lover, it cannot go unnoticed that verbal mimesis, that is, the poem about Bissula itself, must also be included in the group of mimetic forms that fail at the task of proffering Bissula's beauty. This is why the poem ends abruptly, and without ever achieving the task of recreating Bissula's beauty. It is a task, as it turns out, that is impossible.

In the *Cupido cruciatur,* much the same point is made from a different perspective. Now the stable referential ground of the poem itself is called into question, so that, at the poem's end, the reader is not sure what he has experienced or where he stands in terms of the poem's situation of discourse. The poem takes up the dual themes of verbal and pictorial mimesis and love gone awry, beginning as an extended ecphrasis of a painting of Cupid being crucified, but concluding as a nightmare that takes place in the mind of Cupid himself. In between, readers enter the fields of mourning as they are verbally brought into the underworld of Virgil's *Aeneid* 6. They enter a terrain of demented lovers and vividly cast scenes of suffering, torment, and guilt, all caused by the arrows of Cupid—for which reason he is to be crucified by these lovelorn figures. But the convergence of competing imitative forms—painting, poetry, dreamscape—gives fullest shape to Ausonius' larger concern with the limits and even the dangers of verbal mimesis.

Ausonius was born around 310 in Bordeaux. He was educated there and at Toulouse, where his uncle, Aemilius Magnus, an important teacher, took him under his wing. After these studies, some time in the early 330s, Ausonius quickly established himself as an accomplished *grammaticus,* and teaching consumed the next three decades so successfully that in the mid 360s, when he was already past middle age, Ausonius was appointed imperial tutor to Gratian, the son of the emperor, Valentinian I. This appointment effectively established for Ausonius a second career, where his talents as a teacher, put to good use in the private lessons owed to Gratian, were supplemented by new, public demands for his poetry.

This second, more public, career saw for Ausonius the accrual of many honors and a growing political influence, culminating in his appointment as consul for the year 379. Maximius's revolt, in 383, temporarily choked Ausonius's fortunes. Gratian, his old pupil, was murdered, and Valentinian II, his successor, was eventually routed. Ausonius was already an old man whose eagerness for the public life must have been waning when he found himself embroiled in these political turmoils. In the event, Maximius's successes effectively ended Ausonius's public career and launched the poet on his third and final career, his retirement, which proved to be perhaps the most active period in the poet's life relative to the writing and publication of fresh work. The poet continued at his writing until his death, some time in the mid 390s.

The poetry of Ausonius, comprising some twenty-seven works and ranging in length from two to several hundred lines, is written strictly in classical quantities and displays a keen sense of prosody sharpened in years of instruction and practice. The poet varies widely in his themes and moods, showing a full mastery of classical genres but also a willingness to experiment generically.

The many editions of Ausonius's poetry include those by R. Peiper (Leipzig, 1886), S. Prete (Leipzig, 1978), and R. P. H. Green (Oxford, 1991). There is also a concordance (L. J. Bolchazy and J. M. Sweeney, with M. G. Antonetti, *Concordantia in Ausonium*, Hildesheim, 1982). Green's edition also contains a commentary on the poetry, together with an introduction and bibliography. There is an English translation by H. G. Evelyn White in the Loeb Classical Library (2 vols.; London and Cambridge, Mass., vol. 1, 1919; vol. 2, 1921). For the literary context of Ausonius's poetry see C. Witke, *Numen Litterarum: The Old and the New In Latin Poetry from Constantine to Gregory the Great* (Leiden and Cologne, 1971), pp. 3–74, and Raby 1, pp. 73ff. Peiper's text is reprinted here with the following changes: *De Biss.* 1, *tandem* for *tamen; De Biss.* 6 supplying *laterent*, following Evelyn White; *De Biss.* II.5, *aut* for *haut; De Biss.* III.5–6 and Cup. Cruc. 1 and 25 following Evelyn White; with some minor changes in punctuation and capitalization throughout and with "u" and "v" distinguished.

ABOUT BISSULA

Ausonius Paulo suo S.D.

Pervincis tandem et operta musarum mearum, quae initiorum velabat obscuritas, quamquam non profanus, irrumpis, Paule carissime. Quamvis enim te non eius vulgi existimem, quod Horatius arcet ingressu, tamen sua cuique sacra, neque idem Cereri, quod Libero, etiam sub isdem cultoribus. Poematia, quae in alumnam meam luseram rudia et incohata ad domesticae solacium cantilenae, cum sine metu [laterent] et arcana securitate fruerentur, proferre ad lucem caligantia coegisti. Verecundiae meae scilicet spolium concupisti, aut, quantum tibi in me iuris esset, ab invito   5

---

1. **operta musarum mearum:** object of *irrumpis.*   2. **Paule:** the addressee of the introduction and a close friend of Ausonius.   4. **sua cuique sacra:** supply an understood *sunt.*   6. **arcana securitate:** object of *fruerentur.*   7. **cum sine metu . . . fruerentur:** *cum* temporal + subjunctive.   **proferre:** dependent on *coegisti,* with *ad lucem* as direct object.   **caligantia:** present active participle, modifying *poematia,* object of *coegisti.*   8. **quantum tibi in me iuris esset:** i.e., "how much respect there is in me for you."   **ab invito:** lit., "away from unwillingness"; i.e., "apart from my hesitation."

indicari. Ne tu Alexandri Macedonis pervicaciam supergressus, qui, fatalis iugi lora cum solvere non posset, abscidit et Pythiae specum, quo die
fas non erat patere, penetravit.

Utere igitur ut tuis, pari iure, sed fiducia dispari: quippe tua possunt
5 populum non timere; meis etiam intra me erubesco. Vale.

I. PRAEFATIO

Ut voluisti, Paule, cunctos Bissulae versus habes,
lusimus quos in Suebae gratiam virgunculae,
otium magis foventes, quam studentes gloriae.
Tu molestus flagitator lege molesta carmina.
5 Tibi, quod intristi, exedendum est: sic vetus verbum iubet,
compedes, quas ipse fecit, ipsus ut gestet faber.

II. AD LECTOREM HUIUS LIBELLI

Carminis incompti tenuem lecture libellum,
pone supercilium.
Seria contractis expende poemata rugis:
nos Thymelen sequimur.

1. **ne tu:** *ne* + pronoun or demonstrative = "indeed," "to be sure." Although joined
to the negative particle, *tu* still functions as the subject of the sentence.   **qui:** i.e.,
Alexander of Macedon.   2. **fatalis iugi lora:** *fatalis iugi* depends on *lora,* which is the
object of *non posset solvere* and *abscidit.*   **solvere:** "to untie," referring to the Gordian
knot, which, instead of untying, Alexander cut with his sword.   3. **penetravit:** the
main verb of the relative clause with subject *qui* and object *Pythiae specum,* i.e., the
cave of the Pythia, or the Delphic oracle. Alexander wished to consult the oracle before
beginning his Persian campaign. Arriving on a day when the Pythia, the priestess of the
temple, was not available, he nevertheless dragged her into the temple for the desired
"consultation."   4. **utere:** present active imperative.   **ut:** "as."   **tuis:** ablative object of *utere,* modifying an understood *poematiis.*   **pari iure . . . fiducia dispari:** ablatives of specification.   **tua:** i.e., *poematia.*   5. **meis:** i.e., *poematiis,* the object of *erubesco.*

I. Written in trochaic tetrameters.   2. **in . . . gratiam:** *in* + *gratia* with the genitive = "for the sake of wooing," with the genitive governing the object being wooed
(i.e., *Suebae virgunculae*).   3. **otium . . . foventes . . . studentes:** both participles, co-
ordinated by *magis quam,* modify the subject of the verb *lusimus,* with *otium* as their
object; *foventes* = "pampering," "amusing"; *studentes* + dative object = "seeking."
5. **verbum:** lit. "word," but here = "saying," modified by *vetus.*   6. **compedes . . . ut
gestet faber:** result clause.

II. Written in First Archilochian meter (see AG 422).   1. **lecture:** future active
participle, vocative case, from *legere.*   4. **Thymelen:** a celebrated Greek dancer (cf.
Juv. 1.36, 8.197; Mart. 1.5,5), here in accusative singular.

Bissula in hoc scedio cantabitur, aut Erasinus: 5
   admoneo, ante bibas.
Ieiunis nil scribo; meum post pocula si quis
   legerit, hic sapiet.
Sed magis hic sapiet, si dormiet et putet ista
   somnia missa sibi.   10

III. Ubi Nata Sit Bissula et Quomodo in Manus Domini Venerit

Bissula, trans gelidum stirpe et lare prosata Rhenum,
   conscia nascentis Bissula Danuvii,
capta manu, sed missa manu dominatur in eius
   deliciis, cuius bellica praeda fuit.
Matre carens, nutricis egens, [quae] nescit herai   5
   imperium, [domini quae regit ipsa domum,]
fortunae ac patriae quae nulla obprobia sensit,
   illico inexperto libera servitio,
sic Latiis mutata bonis, Germana maneret
   ut facies, oculos caerula, flava comas.   10
Ambiguam modo lingua facit, modo forma puellam:
   haec Rheno genitam praedicat, haec Latio.

IV. De Eadem Bissula

Delicium, blanditiae, ludus, amor, voluptas,
barbara, sed quae Latias vincis alumna pupas,

5. **Erasinus:** a river; cf. Ovid, *Met.* 15.276.   6. **ante** = adverb, "beforehand," modifying *bibas*.   **bibas:** present active subjunctive in jussive construction.   7. **ieiunis:** lit., "for dry ones," i.e., for ones who do not drink.   **meum:** modifies an understood *carmen*.

III. Written in elegiac couplets.   1. **stirpe et lare:** ablatives of specification.   **prosata:** perfect passive participle, from *prosere* (the third principal part of this verb is *prosevi*), modifying *Bissula*.   4. **dominatur in eius deliciis:** *dominari* + *in* + ablative *deliciis* (always in the plural) = "to tyrannize," "to lord over someone"; here, with *eius* = "she lords it over him whose pet she is. . . ."   **cuius . . . fuit:** "whose wartime booty she was."   5. **carens . . . egens:** both take ablative objects.   **herai:** archaic genitive singular of *herae* or *erae*.   9. **sic:** correlative conjunction = "while."   10. **ut:** correlative conjunction with *sic* = "yet."   **facies, caerula, flava:** substantives modified by *Germana*.   11. **modo . . . modo:** "sometimes . . . sometimes."   12. **genitam:** perfect passive participle of *gignere*.   **haec . . . haec:** "the latter . . . the former."

IV. Written in Fifth Asclepiadean meter (see AG 422).

Bissula, nomen tenerae rusticulum puellae,
horridulum non solitis, sed domino venustum.

V. AD PICTOREM DE BISSULAE IMAGINE

Bissula nec ceris nec fuco imitabilis ullo
naturale decus fictae non commodat arti.
Sandyx et cerusa, alias simulate puellas:
temperiem hanc vultus nescit manus. Ergo age, pictor,
5   puniceas confunde rosas et lilia misce,
quique erit ex illis color aeris, ipse sit oris.

VI. AD PICTOREM DE BISSULA PINGENDA

Pingere si nostram, pictor, meditaris alumnam,
   aemula Cecropias ars imitetur apes.

—De Biss.

CRUCIFIED CUPID

Ausonius Gregorio Filio Sal.

En umquam vidisti tabulam pictam in pariete? Vidisti utique et memi-
nisti. Treveris quippe in triclinio Zoili fucata est pictura haec: Cupidinem
cruci adfigunt mulieres amatrices, non istae de nostro saeculo, quae
5   sponte peccant, sed illae heroicae, quae sibi ignoscunt et plectunt deum.
Quarum partem in lugentibus campis Maro noster enumerat. Hanc ego

---

4. **horridulum . . . venustum:** both adjectives modify *nomen.*
    V. Written in dactylic hexameter. 2. **naturale decus:** object of *non commodat.*
fictae: modifies *arti,* a phrase in the dative of indirect object. 3. **sandyx et cerusa:**
vocative. **simulate:** imperative. 4. **vultus:** genitive singular, dependent on *temperiem hanc.* **age:** imperative, with the sense of "go away." **pictor:** vocative.
5. **confunde . . . misce:** imperatives. 6. **ex illis:** i.e., *ex illis pictoribus.* **oris:** from
os, oris.
    VI. An elegiac couplet. 1. **meditaris:** from *meditari,* with *pingere* dependent on
it. 2. **imitetur:** jussive subjuntive.
    2. **en umquam:** sometimes in CL written *enumquam* = "ever indeed." **utique:**
restrictive adverbial particle of confirmation = "of course." 3. **Treveris:** Treves, locative plural (*Treveris* is declined in the plural only). **Zoili:** *Zoilus,* an otherwise unknown figure. 4. **mulieres amatrices:** asyndeton = "wives and lovers." 5. **ignoscunt:** "to excuse"; the normal construction with *ignoscere* is for those being excused
to take the dative case (= *sibi*) and for the thing being exused to take the accusative.
6. **in lugentibus campis:** cf. Virgil, *Aen.* 6. 440 ff. **Maro noster** = Publius Virgilius
Maro (Virgil).

imaginem specie et argumento miratus sum. Deinde mirandi stuporem
transtuli ad ineptiam poetandi. Mihi praeter lemma nihil placet; sed commendo tibi errorem meum: naevos nostros et cicatrices amamus. Nec soli
nostro vitio peccasse contenti adfectamus, ut amentur. Verum quid ego
huic eclogae studiose patrocinor? Certus sum, quodcumque meum   5
scieris, amabis; quod magis spero, quam ut laudes. Vale et dilige par-
entem.

Aeris in campis, memorat quos musa Maronis,
myrteus amentes ubi lucus opacat amantes,
orgia ducebant heroides et sua quaeque,   10
ut quondam occiderant, leti argumenta gerebant,
errantes silva in magna et sub luce maligna
inter harundineasque comas gravidumque papaver
et tacitos sine labe lacus, sine murmure rivos:
quorum per ripas nebuloso lumine marcent   15
fleti, olim regum et puerorum nomina, flores
mirator Narcissus et Oebalides Hyacinthus
et Crocus auricomans et murice pictus Adonis
et tragico scriptus gemitu Salaminius Aeas;
omnia quae lacrimis et amoribus anxia maestis

1. **specie et argumento:** ablatives of specification, the words should be translated as
opposites here, i.e., "appearance and content." **deinde:** here used as an adverb of
time = "hereafter." 2. **lemma:** from the Greek, λέμμα = "theme," "story," or more
likely here, "title." 3. **nec soli:** predicate adjective with *peccasse contenti*. 4. **peccasse:** syncopated perfect active infinitive of *peccare* = *peccavisse.* **ut amentur:** purpose clause with *adfectamus;* the subject here is understood to be *vitia* (from *nostro
vitio,* a restatement of *naevos nostros et cicatrices*). 5. **eclogae:** from the Greek,
ἔκλογη = "selection" or "piece of writing." **patrocinor:** "to serve as patron"; a dative
object (*huic eclogae*) specifies the thing being patronized. 6. **scieris:** future passive
indicative of *scire.* 11. **argumenta:** "the details" or "the story," with *leti* dependent
on it. 17. **Narcissus:** though loved by Echo, he fell in love with his own reflection
and, not being able to possess himself, wasted away to death from lovesickness. **Oebalides:** lit., *Hyacinthus Oebalides* = Hyacinth, son of Oebalus (or Oebalidean Hyacinth). Hyacinth was loved by Apollo and by Zephyrus, but only returned the affection
of Apollo. Zephyrus, in anger, killed Hyacinth with a discus and a flower grew where
Hyacinth's body fell. 18. **Crocus:** a youth metamorphosed into a flower. **Adonis:**
beloved of Venus, he was killed by a wild boar sent against him out of jealousy by
Mars (or Diana); he was made a flower by Venus. 19. **Salaminius Aeas:** lit., Sala-
minian Ajax = Ajax of Salamis, the so-called "great Ajax," as against "lesser Ajax,"
both figures in Homer. Ajax of Salamis contended for the arms of Achilles and lost to
Odysseus. He was grief-stricken (in Ovid he commits suicide) and the blood from his
tomb was said to give life to a flower.

exercent memores obita iam morte dolores:
rursus in amissum revocant heroidas aevum.
Fulmineos Semele decepta puerpera partus
deflet et ambustas lacerans per inania cunas
5   ventilat ignavum simulati fulguris ignem.
Irrita dona querens, sexu gavisa virili,
maeret in antiquam Caenis revocata figuram.
Vulnera siccat adhuc Procris Cephalique cruentam
diligit et percussa manum. Fert fumida testae
10   lumina Sestiaca praeceps de turre puella.
Et de nimboso saltum Leucate minatur
[mascula Lesbiacis Sappho peritura sagittis.]
Harmoniae cultus Eriphyle maesta recusat,
infelix nato nec fortunata marito.
15   Tota quoque aeriae Minoia fabula Cretae
picturarum instar tenui sub imagine vibrat.
Pasiphae nivei sequitur vestigia tauri.
Licia fert glomerata manu deserta Ariadne.
Respicit abiectas desperans Phaedra tabellas.
20   Haec laqueum gerit, haec vanae simulacra coronae:

1. **iam:** "even though." 3. **decepta:** perfect passive participle of *decipere*. **Semele puerpera:** "pregnant Semele," who was tricked by Hera into asking Zeus to reveal his full divinity to her, resulting in her death. Before she died, however, she gave birth to Bacchus (Dionysus)—the story recounted here by Ausonius—who later fetched her from Hades and brought her to Olympus. **partus:** masculine singular (objective) genitive, with *decepta*. 4. **lacerans:** "rends," "picks." 6. **gavisa:** perfect passive participle of *gaudere*. 7. **Caenis:** here nominative feminine, Caenis was changed into a man (afterward called Caeneus) by Poseidon, who gifted him with great strength. 8. **Procris:** hid in some thickets to spy on her husband and was shot with an arrow by Caephalus. Here Procris is nominative singular. **cruentam:** present active participle of *cruere*, here used as a substantive meaning "the hand that drew blood." 9. **percussa:** perfect passive participle of *percutere*, modifying Procris. 10. **Sestiaca puella:** lit., "the Sestiacan girl," = "the girl of Sestos," i.e., Hero, who used to guide her lover, Leander, across the channel that separated them for nightly romps. One night her lamp went out and Leander was lost. 12. **Lesbiacis sagitiis:** ablative of means. 13. **Eriphyle:** plotted against her husband under the influence of a bribe—the necklace of Harmonia. 14. **nato ... marito:** ablatives of specification. 15. **Minoia:** from *Minoius, a, um*, modifying *fabula*, i.e., the story of King Minos of Crete. The history of his daughters is told in these lines. 17. **Pasiphae:** nominative singular; Pasiphae fell in love with a bull after being hexed by Poseidon. 18. **Ariadne** = CL *Ariadna* (but cf. Ovid, *A.A.* 3.35); she used to ball of thread to guide Theseus from the Labyrinth but was deserted by him later. 19. **Phaedra:** another daughter of Minos, who married Theseus but fell hopelessly in love with Hippolytus, over whom she killed herself. The word *tabellas* here makes reference to a letter in which she betrayed to Hippolytus her love for him. 20. **haec ... haec:** the first *haec* refers to Pasiphae, who is depicted

Daedaliae pudet hanc latebras subiisse iuvencae.
Praereptas queritur per inania gaudia noctes
Laudamia duas, vivi functique mariti.
Parte truces alia strictis mucronibus omnes
et Thisbe et Canace et Sidonis horret Elissa.   5
Coniugis haec, haec patris et haec gerit hospitis ensem.
Errat et ipsa, olim qualis per Latmia saxa
Endymioneos solita adfectare sopores,
cum face et astrigero diademate Luna bicornis.
Centum aliae veterum recolentes vulnera amorum   10
dulcibus et maestis refovent tormenta querellis.
Quas inter medias furvae caliginis umbram
dispulit inconsultus Amor stridentibus alis.
Agnovere omnes puerum memorique recursu
communem sensere reum, quamquam umida circum   15
nubila et auratis fulgentia cingula bullis
et pharetram et rutilae fuscarent lampados ignem:
agnoscunt tamen et vanum vibrare vigorem
occipiunt hostemque unum loca non sua nanctum,

---

here with a snare (*laqueum*), by which she might catch the bull that she loves. The second *haec* refers to Ariadne, who might have been queen with Theseus had he not deserted her. **1. pudet:** takes an accusative of person (= *hanc,* i.e., Pasiphae) and a genitive or ablative of the cause of the feeling (= here genitive, *Daedaliae iuvencae*). **3. Laudamia:** her husband, Protesilaus, died at Troy after being married to Laudamia for but a single day. She was permitted by the gods to see him one final time after his death, hence the *duas noctes* mentioned here by Ausonius, the one refering to the marriage night, the other the night on which the couple was permitted one final time to see each other. **4. parte . . . alia** = *in parte . . . alia,* i.e., "in another part of this imaginary landscape." **5. Thisbe, Canace, Sidonis Elissa** (lit., Sidonian Elissa, Elissa of Sidon = Dido): each of these figures suffered at the hands of love. **6. haec, haec . . . haec:** Thisbe, Canace, Elissa, respectively; Thisbe killed herself with her husband's (Pyramus) sword after he had killed himself (thinking mistakenly that she had died). Canace lived incestuously with her brother and bore him a son, whom her father ordered her to kill. Dido killed herself after her guest, Aeneas, whom she loved passionately, left her to sail for Italy. **8. olim quasi solita:** "as she was inclined to do before." **9. Luna:** fell in love with Endymion, who, after having fallen in love himself with Juno, was condemned by Jupiter to eternal sleep. **14. agnovere:** alternate perfect active indicative, third person plural of *agnoscere* = *agnoverunt.* **memorique recursu:** "with their minds turned to the past." **15. sensere:** alternate perfect active indicative, third person plural of *sentire* = *senserunt.* **17. lampados:** governs *rutilae* (both genitive), dependent on *ignem,* the object of *fuscarent,* subjunctive with *quamquam* (= *etsi*) in a simple condition. **18. vibrare:** complementary infinitive of *occipiunt.* **19. nanctum:** from *nancisci,* "to get by accident"; here modifying *unum hostem* (i.e., Amor [or Cupid]) and dependent on *agnoscunt.*

cum pigros ageret densa sub nocte volatus,
facta nube premunt. Trepidantem et cassa parantem
suffugia in coetum mediae traxere catervae.
Eligitur maesto myrtus notissima luco,
5   invidiosa deum poenis. Cruciaverat illic
spreta olim memorem Veneris Proserpina Adonin.
Huius in excelso suspensum stipite Amorem
devinctum post terga manus substrictaque plantis
vincula maerentem nullo moderamine poenae
10   adficiunt. Reus est sine crimine, iudice nullo
accusatur Amor. Se quisque absolvere gestit,
transferat ut proprias aliena in crimina culpas.
Cunctae exprobrantes tolerati insignia leti
expediunt: haec arma putant, haec ultio dulcis,
15   ut, quo quaeque perit, studeat punire dolorem.
Haec laqueum tenet, haec speciem mucronis inanem
ingerit, illa cavos amnes rupemque fragosam
insanique metum pelagi et sine fluctibus aequor.
Nonnullae flammas quatiunt trepidaeque minantur
20   stridentes nullo igne faces. Rescindit adultum
Myrrha uterum lacrimis lucentibus inque paventem
gemmea fletiferi iaculatur sucina trunci.
Quaedam ignoscentum specie ludibria tantum
sola volunt, stilus ut tenuis sub acumine puncti
25   eliciat tenerum, de quo rosa nata, cruorem
aut pubi admoveant petulantia lumina lychni.
Ipsa etiam simili gentrix obnoxia culpae
alma Venus tantos penetrat secura tumultus.

1. **cum:** temporal conjunction with subjunctive.   2. **facta:** subject of *premunt* (from *premere*) + *nube* as ablative of specification.   3. **traxere:** alternate perfect active indicative, third person plural of *trahere* = *traxerunt*.   5. **deum** = *dei*; the construction is an accusative of specification, used on the model of Greek, for the purposes of meter. **illic:** refers to *maesto luco*.   6. **Adonin:** masculine singular accusative of *Adonis, is*; this is a typical accusative ending for a noun brought over from the Greek.   8. **manus:** is the object of *devinctum* (from *devincire*).   12. **transferat ut** = *ut transferat*. 21. **inque paventem:** *paventem* modifies Amor (understood) and functions in a prepositional phrase with *iaculatur*: "Myrrha throws . . . at trembling Amor." Myrrha was changed into a myrrh tree, to which *trunci* (v. 74) refers.   25. **quaedam . . . cruorem:** *quaedam ignoscentum* is the subject of *volunt*, *ludibria* is the object, with adverbial *tantum* and *specie sola* specifiying the subject: "a few of those inclined to forgive in appearance alone wish to mock Amor"; the *ut* clause (result) reveals what these false-forgivers really desire to do: "that the thin stylus might draw his youthful blood under the point of its head." 27. **ipsa:** anticipates Venus in v. 80.

Nec circumvento properans suffragia nato
terrorem ingeminat stimulisque accendit amaris
ancipites furias natique in crimina confert
dedecus ipsa suum, quod vincula caeca mariti
deprenso Mavorte tulit, quod pube pudenda   5
Hellespontiaci ridetur forma Priapi,
quod crudelis Eryx, quod semivir Hermaphroditus.
Nec satis in verbis: roseo Venus aurea serto
maerentem pulsat puerum et graviora paventem.
Olli purpureum mulcato corpore rorem   10
sutilis expressit crebro rosa verbere, quae iam
tincta prius traxit rutilum magis ignea fucum.
Inde truces cecidere minae vindictaque maior
crimine visa suo, Venerem factura nocentem.
Ipsae intercedunt heroides et sua quaeque   15
funera crudeli malunt adscribere fato.
Tum grates pia mater agit cessisse dolentes
et condonatas puero dimittere culpas.
    Talia nocturnis olim simulacra figuris
exercent trepidam casso terrore quietem.   20
Quae postquam multa perpessus nocte Cupido
effugit, pulsa tandem caligine somni
evolat ad superos portaque evadit eburna.

—*Cup. Cruc.*

3. **natique:** from *natus, i.* 5. **deprenso** = CL *deprehenso.* **pube pudenda:** *forma* is
the subject modified by *pudenda* (*pudere*) in passive periphrastic construction. *Pudere,*
"to be embarrassed," takes an ablative of the cause of embarassment (= *pube*). Priapis
(here called Hellespontine Priapis because he was born in the Hellespont, near the
Dardanelles) was the god of procreation, and his form would have made that fact
abundantly clear. 9. **maerentem . . . paventem:** modify *puerum* = Amor, with *graviora* as object of *paventem*, "weeping and fearing worse." 10. **olli** = archaic form of
illo; read with *mulcato corpore.* 13. **cecidere:** alternate perfect active indicative,
third person plural of *caedere* = *ceciderunt.* 14. **Venerem factura nocentem:** *factura,*
future active participle of *esse,* modifies *vindictaque* in v. 93, "about to make Venus the
guilty party." 17. **agit:** historical present tense which can be translated as a perfect.
cessisse: perfect active infitive of *cedere.* 21. **quae postquam:** *postquam* = "when";
quae (referring back to *simulacra,* v. 99) is the object of the perfect passive participle,
perpessus (from *perpeti*): "when Cupid has endured these visions for much of the
night."

Paulinus of Nola

The Poems
(*Carmen* 10, vv. 19–102; c. 390)

There is no little irony in the fact that Paulinus of Nola, who worked so assiduously to discredit the saliency of classical culture, was trained by Ausonius, the most gifted classicist of the Late Latin tradition. Perhaps more than any other Christian writer, however, Paulinus took as his task the articulation of a specifically Christian literary culture that, while making full linguistic use of CL, consciously rejected the literary culture associated with it. Paulinus's treatment of classical literary culture renders him a radical separatist.

Some of the details of this radicalism are evinced in poem 15, where Paulinus takes up the symbol of the cithara, the classical instrument of lyric that betokens a production inspired both by private experience and the Muses. In his handling of this loaded symbol, however, classical resonances evanesce as the cithara is yoked to a new symbolic habitat that speaks exclusively to a Christian theme. Now the cithara is associated with the precious Christian soul; and its sounds, formerly the hallmark of antiquity's greatest lyric singers, now evoke the innate music of the soul as it stretches to accommodate God's love. Paulinus articulates this new vision of the classical cithara in a language beholden to the best standards of classical poetry, going even so far as to use parallel phrasing in his poems. Still the verbal engagement of CL is severely proscribed by the thematics of his poetry's topics. The point in all of Paulinus's work is to depict cultural divorcement, old from new, pagan from Christian, even if, as it had to, linguistic continuity remains for this poet a given.

Divorcement of a literary and cultural kind has an analogue in social and personal detachment, for once Paulinus began to attend fully to his faith, sometime in the 390s, he put to the side not only the literary traditions on which he had been raised but also the man responsible for teaching them to him. Ausonius, much the older figure, had enjoyed a sophisticated banter with his most talented pupil for many years, and the tone and flavor of this exchange has been in part preserved in a series of poetic epistles—one of which, poem 10, is excerpted here. Increasingly, however, as poem 10 makes clear, Ausonius came to represent in Paulinus's mind the classical tradition itself, the very thing that had to be rejected if Christian literary culture was to proceed in bold and fresh ways.

Poem 10 records, then, the social fissures of culture construction. At the same time it is a witness to the ways in which CL was appropriated and made to serve fresh purposes of a Christian kind. This appropriation is most easily heard in the shifting loyalties of vocabulary, as Paulinus' articulation of Christian norms builds onto the structure of ancient words new connotations. *Pater* is a case in point (vv. 32, 90 and 96). Paulinus claims at the end of his poem that Ausonius is still "father" to him, is still the source of all that is praiseworthy in him. Yet this seemingly earnest declaration of filial piety, grounded in a sure history of paternal devotion, is undercut by the articulation earlier in the poem of God as *pater*. Ausonius's paternity, in kind, pales when compared, as it must be, to God's, whose strength and sustenance are the new measures of paternal devotion, and whose nurturance stands in direct and unflattering contrast to the praises of Ausonius offered by Paulinus in vv. 93 ff.

In much the same way, the function of *pietas* in vv. 84–85 and 87 sets into high relief the fact that the piety owed by the disciple to his master has been replaced by a higher, more sublime piety owed by the faithful Christian to his creator. The impiety of which Ausonius has accused Paulinus (v. 84) for not answering prior letters, therefore, cannot be impiety in the sense that Paulinus now understands the term (which is not how Ausonius intends the term anyway), for the poet is not impious toward his "father" God, although he has in fact turned his back on his earthly father, Ausonius. This fact is brought home directly in the lines that announce Paulinus's innocence, as their brutal irony declares the process by which Latin words with ancient pedigrees were transformed into fresh terms with Christian connotations.

The earlier friendship of Ausonius and Paulinus can be likened to a variety of factors. Both poets hailed from Bordeaux, where Paulinus most likely was born around 350. Both came from distinguished families. Both received excellent educations, befitting the status their families enjoyed, and both held political office. It was as governor of Campania that Paulinus initially came into contact with Nola, the city which was to have so important a place in his later life. The happy marriage of Paulinus to a Spaniard, Therasia, a woman of means whose especial influence on her husband came in spiritual, not worldly, gifts, also mirrors Ausonius's happy marriage.

Politics did not hold Paulinus for long, nor did the profits of his extensive holdings of land in Gaul. After a series of personal setbacks in the late 380s, Paulinus and Therasia moved first to Spain and then, in 395, to Nola. By this time, both he and Therasia had given away their considerable wealth, choosing to lead ascetic lives dedicated in particular to Saint Felix of Nola. Paulinus's life was far from reclusive, however. He struck up a correspondence with Saint Jerome around 395 and was even able to meet Saint Martin of Tours (perhaps more than once) before that important figure died near the close of the century. The administrative and institutional duties assumed by Paulinus after the turn of the century also ensured his active involvement in the wider world. Ordained a priest in 393, Paulinus was made bishop of Nola in 409. He died there in 431.

While much of the poetry of Paulinus articulates the theme of divorcement of classical from Christian literary culture, Paulinus was a committed student of CL. Perhaps more sharply than any other writer of his age, Paulinus caricatures the dilemmas attending to the articulation of a new culture in an old and venerable language, for, while it is true that Paulinus consistently speaks of the need to banish the Muses and hearken back to the purer, interior songs of God, it is also true that the poet found himself in the position of articulating this necessity in an old way, and, in doing this, implicitly affirming the very culture being explicitly rejected.

Other writers faced the identical dilemma with a variety of responses. Prudentius, as we will see, is unselfconscious in his deployment of CL; Augustine announces divorcement from classical norms but practices them just the same. Paulinus is different from these exemplary contemporaries, then, both in the severity of his pronouncements of divorcement and in the extent to which he goes out of his way to dramatize them in personal terms, as a vocational rejection of the Muses for Christ, or, more severely, as a rejection of one father, Ausonius, for another, God. In this way, through a consistent and personalized voicing of the theme of cultural and literary divorcement as well as through the careful yoking of old words to new Christian meanings, one is able to sense Paulinus's higher aim—a sanitization of CL as it became part of the growing fabric of LL. To say that Paulinus does not fully succeed in divorcing CL from its centuries-old foundation is to take nothing away from the efforts he made to do so, or our ability so many centuries later still to sense the deep fervor of the attempt.

Paulinus's poetry has been edited by W. von Hartel (*Corpus Scriptorum Ecclesiasticorum Latinorum,* vol. 30, Vienna, 1894). The poems have been translated into English by P. G. Walsh (*The Poems of St. Pauli-*

nus of Nola, Ancient Christian Writers Series, vol. 40, New York, 1975). For an overview of Paulinus's life and career, see Raby 1, pp. 101ff. An exhaustive analysis of Paulinus's Latinity has been published by R. P. H. Green (*The Poetry of Paulinus of Nola: A Study of His Latinity,* Collection Latomus, vol. 120, Brussels, 1971).

The excerpt reprinted here comprises vv. 19–102 of Poem 10, itself some 331 lines in length. Verses 1–18 are written in elegiac couplets; vv. 19–102, excerpted here, in iambics; and vv. 103–331, in hexameters. Von Hartel's text is reprinted with some minor changes in capitalization.

WHY DO YOU ORDER THE DEPOSED MUSES TO RETURN?

Quid abdicatas in meam curam, pater,
  redire Musas praecipis?   20
Negant Camenis nec patent Apollini
  dicata Christo pectora.
Fuit ista quondam non ope, sed studio pari
  tecum mihi concordia
ciere surdum Delphica Phoebum specu,   25
  vocare Musas numina
fandique munus munere indultum dei
  petere e nemoribus aut iugis.
Nunc alia mentem vis agit, maior deus,
  aliosque mores postulat,   30
sibi reposcens ab homine munus suum,
  vivamus ut vitae patri.
Vacare vanis, otio aut negotio,
  et fabulosis litteris
vetat, suis ut pareamus legibus   35
  lucemque cernamus suam,
quam vis sophorum callida arsque rhetorum et
  figmenta vatum nubilant,
qui corda falsis atque vanis imbuunt

---

23. **ope ... studio:** ablatives of specification, with *pari* modifying both.   25. **specu:** ablative of separation without a preposition (AG 402), modified by *Delphica.*   26. **numina:** i.e., "to call the Muses Gods."   27. **fandique munus:** object of *petere.* **indultum:** perfect passive participle of *indulgere,* modifying *munus* with *munere dei,* ablative of means, modifying it.   33. **vacare:** complementary infinitive dependent on *vetat,* with dative objects.   **otio aut negotio:** ablatives of specification with *vacare,* i.e., "to have time, either at work or play...."   35. **pareamus** + dative object.   39. **qui:** i.e., *vates.*

40   tantumque linguas instruunt,
       nihil ferentes, ut salutem conferant
          aut veritate nos tegant.
       Quod enim tenere vel bonum aut verum queunt
          qui non tenent summae caput,
45   veri bonique fomitem et fontem deum,
          quem nemo nisi in Christo videt?
       Hic veritatis lumen est, vitae via,
          vis mens manus virtus patris,
       sol aequitatis, fons bonorum, flos dei,
50   natus deo, mundi sator,
       mortalitatis vita nostrae et mors necis,
          magister hic virtutium;
       deusque nobis atque pro nobis homo
          nos induendo se exuit,
55   aeterna iungens homines inter et deum
          in utroque se commercia.
       Hic ergo nostris ut suum praecordiis
          vibraverit caelo iubar,
       absterget aegrum corporis pigri situm
60   habitumque mentis innovat;
       exhaurit omne quod iuvabat antea
          castae voluptatis vice
       totusque nostra iure domini vindicat
          et corda et ora et tempora;
65   se cogitari intellegi credi legi,
          se vult timeri et diligi.
       Aestus inanes, quos movet vitae labor
          praesentis aevi tramite,
       abolet futurae cum deo vitae fides.
70   Quae quas videmur spernere

40. **tantumque:** adverb = "alone," "only."   44. **summae caput:** the head of the summit, i.e., God.   52. **virtutium** = CL *virtutum.*   54. **nos induendo:** i.e., "in the assumption of our form that he had to take. . . ."   55. **aeterna:** modifies *commercia.* 56. **in utroque se:** i.e., "in which he himself is of both parts."   57. **ut** = temporal conjunction, equivalent to *cum.*   58. **vibraverit:** future perfect active indicative. 62. **vice** + genitives *castae voluptatis* = "in return for a chaste desire."   68. **tramite:** i.e., "in the course of. . . ."   70. **quae:** i.e., *fides.* **quas:** proleptic of *opes,* the object of *abicit,* and modified by *profanas* and *viles.*

non ut profanas abicit aut viles opes,
  sed ut magis caras monet
caelo reponi creditas Christo deo,
  qui plura promisit datis,
contempta praesens vel mage deposita sibi   75
  multo ut rependat fenore.
Sine fraude custos aucta creditoribus
  bonus aera reddet debitor
multaque spretam largior pecuniam
  restituet usura deus.   80
Huic vacantem vel studentem et deditum,
  in hoc reponentem omnia
ne, quaeso, segnem neve perversum putes
  nec crimineris inpium.
Pietas abesse christiano qui potest?   85
  namque argumentum mutuum est
pietatis, esse christianum, et inpii,
  non esse Christo subditum.
Hanc cum tenere discimus, possum tibi
  non exhibere id est patri,   90
cui cuncta sancta iura, cara nomina
  debere me voluit deus?
Tibi disciplinas dignitatem litteras,
  linguae togae famae decus
provectus altus institutus debeo,   95
  patrone praeceptor pater.

---

71. **ut ... aut:** "either as ... or as. ..."   74. **datis:** ablative of comparison, i.e., "who has promised more than has been given."   75. **praesens** adverb = "at once," "immediately."   76. **ut rependat:** result clause.   77. **sine fraude custos:** i.e., God, who is also described in the next verse as *bonus debitor;* both are subjects of *reddet*, with object *aucta aera.* **aucta:** perfect passive participle of *augere*, " to increase."   78. **aera:** from *aes, aeris,* here in the specific sense of "money."   80. **multaque ... largior ... usura:** i.e., "with much greater interest. ..."   81. **vacantem ... studentem ... deditum:** each modify an understood *me.*   82. **huic ... in hoc** i.e., to God ... in God.   83. **ne ... putes:** negative purpose clause functioning as a negative imperative.   86. **argumentum:** i.e., "sign."   89. **hanc** = *pietatem.*   90. **patri:** i.e., to Ausonius, the "father" to whom this poetic epistle is written.   93. **disciplinas ... litteras:** asyndeton.   94. **decus:** governing the genitives of this line.   95. **provectus ... institutus:** three perfect passive participles modifying the subject named in the verb *debeo*, i.e., Paulinus himself.   96. **patrone** = *patronus;* the form *patrone* shows affection and respect (if only in the past).

Sed cur remotus tamdiu degam arguis
    pioque motu irasceris?
Conducit istud aut necesse est aut placet,
100   veniale quicquid horum inest.
Ignosce, amans, mi si geram quod expedit;
    gratare, si vivam ut libet.

—*Carm.* 10.19–102.

99. **istud:** i.e., that Paulinus has not written and has been away for so long.   101. **ignosce:** imperative.   **amans:** i.e., Ausonius, "dear one."   102. **gratare:** imperative.

Prudentius

Preface to the Collected Works; Hymn at the Song of the Rooster
(*Praefatio,* c. 405; *Hymnus ad Galli Cantum* = *Liber Cathemerinon* I, c. 395)

The immanence of God is a fundamental construct of Christian culture, informing at its most basic level the theology of Christ as mediator between ideal and real space. Prudentius deals often with this theme in his large body of poetry. His treatment, however, is unique among fourth-century writers, for he regularly takes the view that the world is laden with accessible and sustained experience of the divine in day-to-day life. In Hymn 1, printed here, this quotidian immanence is specified by focusing on the singing of the rooster, whose identity gently coalesces with Christ's. In the first stanza, symmetry effects a delicate balance between bird and Christ. The rooster, the "winged messenger of the day," is introduced in v. 1 and Christ, who calls Christians to life, concludes the stanza in v. 4. Two intervening lines specify the two figures. The bird, in v. 2, is described as "predicting the approach of the light," while Christ, in v. 3, is called the "exciter of minds."

This delicate balance of identity evanesces in the second stanza, to be replaced by a bolder declaration that merges the bird and Christ into a single identity. Unlike in the first stanza, no overt subject is named in vv. 5–8. The stanza begins crisply with the subject implied in the verb *clamat,* presumably the same subject who is the speaker of the phrase *iam sum proximus,* in v. 8. But both the bird and Christ easily function in a logical sense as the subjects of the stanza. It is not necessary to choose one over the other. In this way, Prudentius merges the identities of a real event, the singing of the rooster at dawn, and a transcendent God who created the scene and set it into motion.

When Prudentius affirms in v. 16, then, that the voice of the bird "is a *figura* of our judge [i.e., Christ]," importance attaches to the meaning of *figura* as a way to explain more thoroughly this merging of identities. Given the ways in which the hymn presents its temporal and transcendent characters, as somehow intimately connected each to the other, it is well to move beyond the denotations of *figura* as "symbol" and to understand the word to embody the joining of ideal with real experience. In this way, the singing of the rooster is a temporal event that yet points beyond temporal limits to the ideal space where God abides.

That pointing does not diminish the quality or the worth of the temporal material—here, the singing of the rooster. Nor does the singing point beyond itself as if to symbolize or draw attention to God at its own expense. On the contrary, the thrust here is to affirm the balance of temporal and transcendent, in the same way that the hymn affirms the equality of both in the symmetry of the first stanza. The singing of the rooster, then, *is* the presence of Christ; and that presence, emanating from beyond time, yet makes human experience sensible by grounding it objectively. This perspective on human experience renders the function of symbol impotent in this hymn, therefore, for the voice of the rooster does not symbolize anything: it is not one thing standing for something else, not a signifier operating in a strictly literary orbit, yoked to a fabricated situation in order to instruct or to praise. Rather, as Prudentius himself declares at v. 92, in a phrase calculated to herald the equality of Christ and the rooster, "it is the truth which is *here.*"

Freedom resonates in Prudentius's notion of immanence. Poetry has much to offer, it turns out, in attaining this freedom, as the conclusion to his *Preface* makes clear. As a poem, the *Preface* can be read as a preliminary statement of Prudentius's poetic aims, which take shape from the clear ground of moral action. He offers in the first half of the poem, in stanzas that rely to a large extent on the poetic traditions and vocabulary of Horace's *Odes,* the failings of his life, whose limits are cast in a moral question: "of what use has my life been?" (*quid utile,* v. 6). That question is recast in Christian terms in v. 30, where the poet declares that "death shall abolish whatever you have been" (*quod fueram, mors aboleverit*).

A concern with the things of this world is replaced in vv. 34ff., however, with a strict focus on the soul as the only source by which the worldly stains of human life can be lifted. The focal point now is Christian identity forged by the soul's abandonment of worldly things, its turning away from the foolishness of vanities to those things that are not frivolous. But this is not simply a moral procedure. Part of the process of abandonment is accomplished through writing itself, as the catalogue of the poet's own works that follows makes clear. It is no coincidence that after this catalogue has been articulated, the poet is able (vv. 43–45) to announce his own freedom from the chains of worldly things. But being free, *liber* pronounced with a long "i," is also a freedom evinced through writing, through the book, as *liber,* when pronounced with a short "i," also means. This play on the pronunciation of *liber,* then, which equates freedom with book, much like the equation of Christ and the rooster in the first hymn, does away with mediation and affirms, through the poet's craft as through the simple living of one's daily life, the sure presence of God in this world, a presence that ratifies the promise of the next.

The *Preface* in which Prudentius declares his liberation is the only source we have pertaining to the poet's life. He tells us he was born in 348 (probably in Spain, though he does not say where). It is assumed that the poet was raised a Christian, though his early life seems hardly devout if it was lived in the faith, as the first half of the *Preface* makes clear. Prudentius was, if not morally superior, in any case a hard-working student. His course of study included the arts of rhetoric and oratory, which he mastered, so he tells us, vehemently and with a stubborn passion for victory. Although vague as to location and exact duties, Prudentius tells us also that he pursued a public career, a path which led him to achieve high posts in the administration of justice. He distinguished himself in this capacity, for he was promoted by imperial directive, in his words, to a higher order, usually taken to indicate the rank of *comes primi ordinis*. But he seems to have abandoned worldly power and pursuits for a career devoted to intense writing, which presumably consumed the last years of his life. The date of Prudentius' death is not known, but having the year of his birth enables one to speculate that the poet probably did not live much past 420.

As the selections indicate, Prudentius is an exacting CL prosodist. He is more often praised in the context of his conservative beliefs, expressed in the high style of Horatian and Virgilian Latin. But the polish of his language and the apparent uniformity of his (Christian) topics ought not to deflect interest from the bold experimentations of his output. His reworking of Christian hymnody in the *Liber Cathemerinon*, for example, functions in the expansion of generic distinction, so that lyric, epic, and elegiac diction are merged into a hybrid form of personal poetry. But while Ambrose, say, or Hilary had also used Horatian and Virgilian language to sing their praises of God, Prudentius goes the next step in downplaying the performative aspect of hymnody, opting instead to emphasize the literary quality of his project. Theology, in this way, while still central to the function of Prudentius's hymns, is made to serve on equal footing with literary tradition.

Prudentius's innovations are in evidence in the *Peristephanon* also, where the full range of classical allusion and mythography is made to inform Christian stories of martyrdom, a literary procedure seemingly in place also in the *Hamartigenia*, where Roman mythology is especially put to the service of a consideration of Christian sin, sometimes with bold results that devolve onto the function of Prudentius himself as a

poet. Most famous, perhaps, is Prudentius's *Psychomachia,* an allegory
of the vices and the virtues that invigorated allegoresis in Latin poetry for
a millennium and which poses as many questions about virtue as answers
about vice. Prudentius also put his poetry to the service of politics, writing the *Contra Symmachum,* in support of the removal of the Altar of
Victory from the Roman senate house, a controversy that embroiled secular and ecclesiastical leaders of many stripes in 384. Prudentius also
wrote the *Apotheosis,* on heresy, and the *Dittochaeon* (sometimes called
the *Tituli historiarum*), a collection of inscriptions inspired by, and
written to explain, biblical scenes that were depicted on the wall of a
church.

Numerous editions of the poetry of Prudentius exist, including those
by J. Bergman (*Corpus Scriptorum Ecclesiasticorum Latinorum,* vol. 61,
Vienna, 1926); M. Lavarenne (Paris, 1945–51); M. P. Cunningham (*Corpus Christianorum, Series Latina,* Turnhout, 1966). There is an English
translation in the Loeb Classical Library (*Prudentius,* H. J. Thomson, ed.
and trans., 2 vols., London and Cambridge, Mass., vol. 1, 1949; vol. 2.,
1953). There is also a concordance (R. J. Deferrari and J. M. Campbell,
A Concordance to Prudentius, Cambridge, Mass., 1932). Raby 1, pp.
44–71, devotes an entire chapter to Prudentius. The poet has received
much recent critical attention also. In addition to the chapter by C. Witke
(*Numen Litterarum: The Old and the New in Latin Poetry from Constantine to Gregory the Great,* Leiden, 1971, pp. 102–44) are the studies
by S. G. Nugent (*Allegory and Poetics: The Structure and Imagery of
Prudentius'* Psychomachia, Frankfurt a. M., 1985); M. Malamud (*A Poetics of Transformation: Prudentius and Classical Mythology,* Ithaca,
N. Y., 1989); A.-M. Palmer (*Prudentius on the Martyrs,* Oxford, 1989);
and M. Roberts (*Poetry and the Cult of the Martyrs: The* Liber Peristephanon *of Prudentius,* Ann Arbor, Mich., 1993). Cunningham's text is reprinted here without change.

PREFACE TO THE COLLECTED WORKS

Per quinquennia iam decem,
ni fallor, fuimus; septimus insuper
annum cardo rotat, dum fruimur sole volubili.
    Instat terminus et diem
5   vicinum senio iam deus adplicat.

---

1. **decem:** indeclinable adjective functioning as if in the accusative with *per quinquennia.*   5. **adplicat** = CL *applicat*

Quid nos utile tanti spatio temporis egimus?
    Aetas prima crepantibus
flevit sub ferulis, mox docuit toga
infectum vitiis falsa loqui non sine crimine.
    Tum lasciva protervitas   10
et luxus petulans (heu pudet ac piget)
foedavit iuvenem nequitiae sordibus et luto.
    Exim iurgia turbidos
armarunt animos et male pertinax
vincendi studium subiacuit casibus asperis.   15
    Bis legum moderamine
frenos nobilium reximus urbium;
ius civile bonis reddidimus, terruimus reos.
    Tandem militiae gradu
evectum pietas principis extulit   20
adsumptum propius stare iubens ordine proximo.
    Haec dum vita volans agit,
inrepsit subito canities seni,
oblitum veteris me Saliae consulis arguens.
    Sub quo prima dies mihi   25
quam multas hiemes volverit, et rosas
pratis post glaciem reddiderit, nix capitis probat.
    Numquid talia proderunt
carnis post obitum vel bona vel mala,

---

9. **infectum:** perfect passive participle of *inficere*, modifying an understood *me,* with *vitiis* modifying it. **loqui:** infinitive of purpose with *falsa* as its object. 12. **iuvenem:** in CL = "young man," but here used abstractly, akin to CL *adulescentia.* **sordibus et luto:** ablatives of means, with *nequitiae* dependent on them. 14. **male pertinax:** modifies (*vincendi*) *studium* in v. 15. 15. **subiacuit** + dative = "was coupled with. . . ." 20. **evectum:** perfect passive participle of *evehere,* modifying an understood *me,* and functioning as the object of *extulit.* With *militiae gradu* dependent on it, it has the sense of "promoted." 21. **adsumptum:** perfect passive participle of *assumere,* object of *iubens;* modifying an understood *me.* **stare:** completes the meaning of *iubens adsumptum,* with *proprius . . . ordine proximo* dependent on it. 23. **inrepsit** = CL *irrepsit.* 24. **oblitum:** perfect participle of *oblivisci,* modifying *me,* both objects of *arguens.* 25. The line functions as a complete thought: "under whom [i.e., the consul Salia] I was born (literally, "there were first days for me"). 26. **quam:** adverb. 27. **volverit . . . reddiderit:** perfect subjunctives in indirect question. 28. This phrase has the sense of "did such things mean anything?" [literally, "beget anything"). 29. **obitum:** perfect passive participle of *obire,* here used as a substantive governed by *post* and with dependent *carnis.* **bona . . . mala:** both modify *talia.*

30   cum iam quidquid id est quod fueram mors aboleverit?
      Dicendum mihi: "Quisquis es,
      mundum quem coluit mens tua perdidit;
      non sunt illa dei quae studuit cuius habeberis."
        Atqui fine sub ultimo
35   peccatrix anima stultitiam exuat;
      saltem voce deum concelebret, si meritis nequit.
        Hymnis continuet dies
      nec nox ulla vacet quin dominum canat;
      pugnet contra hereses, catholicam discutiat fidem,
40   conculcet sacra gentium,
      labem, Roma, tuis inferat idolis,
      carmen martyribus devoveat, laudet apostolos.
        Haec dum scribo vel eloquor,
      vinclis o utinam corporis emicem
45   liber quo tulerit lingua sono mobilis ultimo!

—Praef.

Hymn at the Song of the Rooster

    Ales diei nuntius
lucem propinquam praecinit,
nos excitator mentium
iam Christus ad vitam vocat.
5   "Auferte" clamat "lectulos
aegros soporos desides,
castique recti ac sobrii
vigilate; iam sum proximus."
    Post solis ortum fulgidi
10 serum est cubile spernere,
ni parte noctis addita
tempus labori adieceris.

30. **quidquid id est quod fueram:** these two clauses together form the object of *aboleverit*. 33. **quae:** antecedent = *illa*, which stands as a substantive in neuter plural. **studuit:** the subject is *mens tua*. **cuius habeberis:** "whose [i.e., God] you shall be." 37. **continuet:** the verbs in vv. 37–42, all jussive subjunctives, take as their subject *peccatrix anima*. 38. **quin** = *ut*.

    4. **Christus:** in apposition with *excitator mentium*. 9. **ortum:** perfect participle of *oriri*, used here as a substantive. 10. **spernere:** complementary infinitive of *serum est*, with *cubile* as object. 11. **parte . . . addita:** ablative absolute. 12. **adieceris:** perfect subjunctive in simple condition with *ni* = *si non*, "unless."

Vox ista, qua strepunt aves
stantes sub ipso culmine
paulo ante quam lux emicet,   15
nostri figura est iudicis.
    Tectos tenebris horridis
stratisque opertos segnibus
suadet quietem linquere
iam iamque venturo die,   20
    ut, cum coruscis flatibus
aurora caelum sparserit,
omnes labore exercitos
confirmet ad spem luminis.
    Hic somnus ad tempus datus   25
est forma mortis perpetis;
peccata, ceu nox horrida,
cogunt iacere ac stertere.
    Sed vox ab alto culmine
Christi docentis praemonet   30
adesse iam lucem prope,
ne mens sopori serviat,
    ne somnus usque ad terminos
vitae socordis opprimat
pectus sepultum crimine   35
et lucis oblitum suae.
    Ferunt vagantes daemonas,
laetos tenebris noctium,

15. **paulo ante quam:** adverbial phrase modifying *emicit*, "a little while before. . . ."
17. **tectos:** perfect passive participle of *tegere*, here modifying an understood *eos*.
18. **opertos:** perfect passive participle of *operire*, parallel with *tectos* and modifying
an understood *eos*.   20. **venturo:** future active participle of *venire*, modifying *die* in
ablative of time.   21. **ut:** introduces the purpose clause governed by *confirmet*.
23. **exercitos:** perfect passive participle of *exercere*, modifying *omnes* with *labore* dependent on it; the entire phrase is the object of *confirmet*.   25. **datus:** perfect passive
participle of *dare*, modifying *somnus* with *ad tempus* dependent on it.   28. **cogunt**
+ infinitives *iacere* and *stertere* = "to compel [us] to lie and to snore."   30. **Christi
docentis:** genitives dependent on *vox*.   **praemonet:** here governs indirect statement.
32. **ne . . . serviat:** negative purpose clause; *servire* takes a dative object.   34. **ne . . .
opprimat:** negative purpose clause, parallel with *ne serviat*.   35. **pectus:** object of *opprimat*.   **sepultum:** perfect passive participle of *sepelire*, modifying *pectus* with *crimine* dependent on it.   36. **oblitum:** from *oblivisci*, here modifying *pectus*.   37. **ferunt** = *dicunt*, governing indirect discourse with *timere* and *cedere*.   **vagantes:**
predicate adjective with *laetos* as object.

40
gallo canente exterritos
sparsim timere et cedere.
Invisa nam vicinitas
lucis salutis numinis
rupto tenebrarum situ
noctis fugat satellites.

45
Hoc esse signum praescii
norunt repromissae spei,
qua nos soporis liberi
speramus adventum dei.

50
Quae vis sit huius alitis
salvator ostendit Petro
ter antequam gallus canat
sese negandum praedicans.

Fit namque peccatum prius
quam praeco lucis proximae
55
inlustret humanum genus
finemque peccandi ferat.

Flevit negator denique
ex ore prolapsum nefas,
cum mens maneret innocens
60
animusque servaret fidem.

Nec tale quidquam postea
linguae locutus lubrico est
cantuque galli cognito
peccare iustus destitit.

65
Inde est quod omnes credimus
illo quietis tempore
quo gallus exultans canit
Christum redisse ex inferis.

43. **rupto . . . situ:** ablative absolute. 45. **praescii:** subject of *norunt.* 46. **norunt:** alternate present active indicative, third person plural of *noscere,* here governing indirect discourse. 49. **quae . . . sit:** indirect question. 50. **Salvator** = *Christus.* 51. **canat:** cf. *Matt.* 26.34. 52. **praedicans:** modifies *Salvator* and governs indirect discourse: "predicting that he himself would be denied." *Negandum* is in passive periphrastic construction. 54. **quam:** read with *prius* in v. 53 = *priusquam.* 55. **inlustret** = CL *illustret.* 57. **negator:** i.e., *Petrus.* 58. **nefas:** object of *flevit,* with *prolapsum,* perfect participle of *prolabi,* modifying it. 59. **cum . . . maneret . . . servaret:** *cum* concessive + subjunctive = "since." 61. **nec tale quidquam:** "no such thing." 62. **locutus . . . est** = *locutus est,* from *loqui.* 63. **cantuque . . . cognito:** ablative absolute. 65. **Inde est quod:** i.e., "so it is that. . . ."

Tunc mortis oppressus vigor,
tunc lex subacta est tartari,   70
tunc vis diei fortior
noctem coegit cedere.
   Iam iam quiescant inproba,
iam culpa furva obdormiat,
iam noxa letalis suum   75
perpessa somnum marceat.
   Vigil vicissim spiritus,
quodcumque restat temporis
dum meta noctis clauditur,
stans ac laborans excubet.   80
   Hisum ciamus vocibus
flentes precantes sobrii;
intenta supplicatio
dormire cor mundum vetat.
   Sat convolutis artubus   85
sensum profunda oblivio
pressit gravavit obruit
vanis vagantem somniis.
   Sunt nempe falsa et frivola
quae mundiali gloria   90
ceu dormientes egimus;
vigilemus, hic est veritas.
   Aurum voluptas gaudium
opes honores prospera
quaecumque nos inflant mala,   95
fit mane, nil sunt omnia.

---

69. **oppressus:** perfect passive participle of *opprimere.*   70. **subacta:** perfect passive participle of *subigere,* modifying *lex.*   **tartari:** i.e., *Tartarus* = Hell.   73. **quiescant:** jussive subjunctive, as are all the verbs in this stanza.   **inproba** = CL *improba,* subject of *quiescant.*   76. **perpessa:** perfect participle of *perpeti,* modifying *noxa letalis,* with *suum somnum* as object   77. **spiritus:** subject of *excubet* in v. 80.   81. **Hisum** = *Jesum* (cf. Sleumer 405).   **ciamus:** jussive subjunctive.   83. **supplicatio:** subject of *vetat,* with *intenta* modifying it.   84. **dormire . . . vetat:** i.e., "forbids the pure heart to sleep."   85. **sat:** adverb = "long enough."   **convolutis artubus:** ablative absolute. 87. **pressit . . . obruit:** all three verbs take *profunda oblivia* as subject and *sensum* as object.   88. **vagantem:** present active participle of *vagare,* modifying *sensum.* 90. **mundiali gloria:** ablative of specification with *egimus* = "things we did for worldly glory."   96. **fit mane:** i.e., "becomes morning. . . ."

Tu, Christe, somnum dissice,
tu rumpe noctis vincula,
tu solve peccatum vetus
100 novumque lumen ingere.

—*Liber Cath.* 1.

97. **dissice:** imperative mood, like the remaining verbs in this stanza.

PROBA

The Cento
(*Probae Cento;* c. 360)

Cento means literally a "garment stitched together," "a patchwork," but in literary terms it denotes a work entirely comprising "pieces"—lines, half-lines, phrases—derived from earlier works. There are numerous examples of the cento form surviving from Greek antiquity, usually comprising Homeric tags strung together for fresh purposes. Though less appealing to Roman tastes, Latin centos date to the early second century and normally attend to a variety of new themes by recasting the Latin phraseology of Virgil.

Proba, who makes Virgil retell the story of creation and the life of Christ, is one of the first poets in the West to put to the cento a Christian task. That she is not alone in doing this, however, is attested to by Jerome, who, in a letter to Paulinus of Nola, written around 395, condemns centoists as useless to the larger purposes of spiritual instruction (*Ep.* 53). Though, as he notes, centoists present biblical themes in the guise of Virgil's Latin, Jerome finds it ludicrous even to suggest, as the form of a cento would, that Virgil can somehow be considered a useful source for spiritual fullness. From Jerome's view, the greatest threat the cento poses is to substitute for a close engagement of sacred history an inordinate study of Virgil. Needless to say, Jerome's condemnation did not fall on deaf ears. Paulinus of Nola would be the first to agree that a command of rhetoric does not imply a fullness of belief.

Yet clearly Christian writers had been pursuing the balancing act between Virgilian rhetoric and Christian belief for several decades prior to Jerome's harangue. The attention he lavishes on centoists suggests a body of cento poetry in circulation, posing the sorts of risks that make Jerome uneasy. His unease is in any case ironic to witness. After all, a chief means by which Christian literary culture acclimated itself to its antique origins was to put to fresh uses the words of pagan authors, as Jerome well understood by virtue of his own long practice of this brand of acclimation—of which his famous Ciceronian dream is but one example.

The cento tradition has a famous exemplar in Ausonius, who stitched together a quilt of Virgilian lines in order to recreate the goings-on of a bride and groom on their wedding night. In his *Cento nuptialis,* written

probably after Proba's cento, Ausonius makes Virgil's weighty and solemn hexameters announce what is perhaps the lewdest, brashest seduc-
tion scene in Latin writing. But Ausonius's cento is pagan in theme and
content. Proba's work is forcefully Christian, and her shaping of Christian themes in Virgilian rhetoric is notable in several respects. Proba's
consideration of the Genesis account and the life of Christ is highly original. She is no mere copier of sacred history: she omits, adds, embellishes.
She contrasts important points of sacred history by framing them in
words bound to strike the memory of Virgil's readers. Often, she will
stitch together lines whose Virgilian contexts are strikingly at odds (cf.
vv. 85–86, e.g.), but whose Christian setting renders them consonant and
sensible. Apart from the aesthetic value of this strategy of composition,
such moments in Proba's *Cento* speak directly to the ways in which Christians took up the task of unifying knowledge, of making coherent, both
from within their tradition and without, the vast repertoire of human
conduct bequeathed to them from antiquity. One of the boldest features
of Proba's poem, in fact, is the way that moments such as these put to the
lie the idea of the inevitability of a conflict between pagan and Christian
cultures, a position confirmed in the opening lines of the poem, where
the poet declares that she will sing about Virgil's versification of Christ.

Faltonia Betitia Proba, a member of the distinguished Petronii, was a
wife and mother as well as the first woman poet of the Christian tradition
whose major work survives. The year of her birth, based on the relative
ages of her sons, who all reached high positions attested to in extant
evidence, is around 320. She died around 370. She may have been a con-
vert to Christianity. She seems to have converted her husband, Adelphius,
to the faith. Her high station in life assured her access to an education
few others attained, an education put to good use in her cento, which
evinces a full knowledge of the Virgilian corpus. In addition to her *Cento*,
which we have complete, there is an earlier poem, perhaps written when
Proba was still a pagan, in which she takes up the topic of war, possibly
the rebellion of Magnentius of 353.

Proba's *Cento* has been edited by K. Schenkl (*Poetae Christiani Mi-
nores, Corpus Scriptorum Ecclesasticorum Latinorum,* vol. 16, Vienna,
1888), which also includes a line-by-line indication of the Virgilian
sources of Proba's language. The American Academy of Religion has published an English translation of the *Cento,* along with Schenkl's text,
short notes, and a full discussion of the social and literary contexts of the
poem in its Texts and Translations series (E. A. Clark and D. F. Hatch,

The Golden Bough, The Oaken Cross: The Virgilian Cento of Faltonia Betitia Proba, Ann Arbor, Mich., 1981).

The excerpt here, reprinted from Schenkl's text as given in Clark and Hatch, takes up the narrative at the point in the Genesis account where God is instructing Adam and Eve, describing life in Eden, and proffering a warning about the forbidden tree. These verses, written in dactylic hexameter, conclude with Eve's temptation of Adam and God's discovery and rebuke of their transgression. I have changed consonantal "u" to "v" throughout and made some minor formatting changes.

THE SCENE OF TEMPTATION IN EDEN

'Est in conspectu ramis felicibus arbos,
quam neque fas igni cuiquam nec sternere ferro,
religione sacra numquam concessa moveri.
Hac quicumque sacros decerpserit arbore fetus,
morte luet merita: nec me sententia vertit.   5
nec tibi tam prudens quisquam persuadeat auctor
conmaculare manus—liceat te voce moneri—,
femina, nec te ullius violentia vincat,
si te digna manet divini gloria ruris.'
postquam cuncta pater, caeli cui sidera parent,   10
conposuit, legesque dedit camposque nitentis
desuper ostentat, tantarum gloria rerum.
ecce autem primi sub limina solis et ortus
devenere locos, ubi mollis amaracus illos

---

1. **arbos** = *arbor.* 3. **religione sacra:** ablative of means. **concessa:** perfect passive participle of *concedere*, modifying *arbos*, meaning something like "granted" or "permitted." 4. **decerpserit:** from *decerpere.* **hac ... arbore:** ablatives of separation without preposition. **fetus:** object of *decerpserit*, modified by *sacros.* 5. **luet:** the subject is *quicumque* of the previous line; here the verb is used intransitively, i.e., "that one will pay . . .," with ablative of means *morte merita* completing the thought. 6. **tibi:** dative object of *persuadeat.* **tam:** adverb modifying *prudens*, which itself, along with *quisquam*, modifies *auctor.* The four words mean something like "any bold one, however wise . . ." 7. **conmaculare** = CL *commaculare*, infinitive of purpose with *manus* as object. 8. **femina:** ablative of accompaniment without the expected *cum*, bringing Eve into the series of commands articulated to Adam by God in these lines. 10. **parent** + dative object = "to obey"; *caeli* is genitive singular, dependent on the subject of the clause, *sidera.* 11. **nitentis:** alternate accusative plural of *nitens*, modifying *campos.* 14. **devenere:** alternate perfect active indicative, third person plural of *devenire* = *devenerunt.*

15 floribus et dulci adspirans conplectitur umbra.
Hic ver purpureum atque alienis mensibus aestas,
hic liquidi fontes, hic caeli tempore certo
dulcia mella premunt, hic candida populus antro
inminet et lentae texunt umbracula vites.
20 Invitant croceis halantes floribus horti
inter odoratum lauri nemus ipsaque tellus
omnia liberius nullo poscente ferebat.
Fortunati ambo, si mens non laeva fuisset
coniugis infandae: docuit post exitus ingens.
25 Iamque dies infanda aderat: per florea rura
ecce inimicus atrox inmensis orbibus anguis
septem ingens gyros, septena volumina versans
nec visu facilis nec dictu affabilis ulli
obliqua invidia ramo frondente pependit,
30 vipeream spirans animam, cui tristia bella
iraeque insidiaeque et crimina noxia cordi.
Odit et ipse pater: tot sese vertit in ora
arrectisque horret squamis, et, ne quid inausum
aut intemptatum scelerisve dolive relinquat,
35 sic prior adgreditur dictis seque obtulit ultro:
'dic' ait, 'o virgo—lucis habitamus opacis
riparumque toros et prata recentia rivis
incolimus—, quae tanta animis ignavia venit?
Strata iacent passim sua quaeque sub arbore poma,

---

15. **floribus:** dative object of *adspirans*. **adspirans** = CL *aspirans*. **conplectitur** = CL *complectitur*. 18. **populus:** the initial "o" in this (feminine) word is long. 19. **inminet** = CL *imminet*. 20. **invitant:** the understood object is Adam and Eve. 22. **nullo poscente:** lit., "with no demanding," i.e., "without request." 24. **post:** adverb of time = "afterward." 26. **inmensis** = CL *immensis*. **orbibus:** used to describe the coils of the *inimicus atrox . . . anguis*. 27. **septem ingens gyros:** *septem* (indeclinable) and *ingens* modify *gyros*, the object of *versans*; *gyros* means something like "coils." **volumina:** means something like "twists." 29. **obliqua invidia:** i.e., "with enmity hidden. . . ." 30. **animam:** i.e., "breath." **cui:** modifies *cordi*: "for whom at heart there were. . . ." The idiom is *cordi sunt*. 32. **vertit in ora:** *vertere* + *in* + *accusative* = "to change something into something else"; here the serpent changes his faces. 34. **scelerisve dolive:** "either of wickedness or of deceit"; these genitives depend on *ne quid*, "nothing," which is, in turn, modified by the perfect passive participles *inausum* (*inaudere*) and *intemptatum* (*intemptare*). 35. **prior:** functions as an adverb = "first." **obtulit:** from *offerre*. **ultro:** adverb = "of his own accord." 37. **recentia:** adjective modifying *prata*, with ablative of means *rivis*. 39. **strata:** perfect passive participle from *sternere*, modifying *poma*.

pocula sunt fontes liquidi: caelestia dona   40
adtractare nefas: id rebus defuit unum.
Quid prohibet causas penitus temptare latentes?
Vana superstitio. Rerum pars altera adempta est.
Quo vitam dedit aeternam? Cur mortis adempta est
condicio? Mea si non inrita dicta putaris,   45
auctor ego audendi sacrata resolvere iura.
Tu coniunx, tibi fas animum temptare precando.
Dux ego vester ero: tua si mihi certa voluntas,
extruimusque toros dapibusque epulamur opimis.'
Sic ait, et dicto citius, quod lege tenetur,   50
subiciunt epulis olim venerabile lignum
instituuntque dapes contactuque omnia foedant.
Praecipue infelix pesti devota futurae
mirataque novas frondes et non sua poma,
causa mali tanti, summo tenus attigit ore.   55
Maius adorta nefas maioremque orsa furorem
heu misero coniunx aliena ex arbore germen
obicit atque animum subita dulcedine movit.
Continuo nova lux oculis effulsit; at illi
terrentur visu subito nec plura morati   60
corpora sub ramis obtentu frondis inumbrant:
consertum tegumen: nec spes opis ulla dabatur.
At non haec nullis hominum rerumque repertor
observans oculis caedes et facta tyranni

---

41. adtractare = CL *attrectare*. 42. **Quid prohibet** . . . **temptare:** i.e., "what stops you from trying. . . ." 43. **adempta est:** from *adimere*. 45. inrita = CL *irrita*, modifying *mea dicta*. 47. **tu coniunx:** i.e., "you are a wife. . . ." **precando:** i.e., "by prayer." 49. **extruimusque** = CL *exstruimusque*. 50. **dicto:** ablative of comparison with *citius*. **quod:** refers to *venerabile ignum*. **tenetur:** lit., "is held," but here with the sense of "is prohibted." 51. **subiciunt:** the subjects are Eve and the serpent. 52. **contactuque:** ablative of means; the word means both "touch" and "infection," and both senses apply here. 53. **praecipue** = adverb. **pesti** . . . **futurae:** datives with *devota*, perfect passive participle of *devovere*, which modifies *infelix* = Eve. 54. **mirataque:** perfect participle of *mirari*, modifying Eve (*infelix*). 55. **summo tenus** = CL adverb *summotenus* = "all the way up to. . . ." **ore:** i.e., "with her lips." 56. **adorta:** from *adoriri*, modifying Eve. **orsa:** from *ordiri*, modifying Eve. 57. **misero:** dative object of *obicit*, standing for Adam. **aliena:** in the sense of "forbidden." 58. **subita:** perfect passive participle from *subere*, modifying *dulcedine*. 59. **continuo:** adverb. 60. **nec plura morati:** i.e., "no longer as they were before." 63. **nullis** . . . **oculis:** "with unseeing eyes"; *non* is construed with *observans*, whose object is *haec*.

65   praesensit: notumque furens quid femina posset.
Continuo invadit: 'procul, o procul este profani'
conclamat, caelum ac terras qui numine firmat.
Atque illi longe gradientem ac dira frementem
ut videre, metu versi retroque ruentes
70   diffugiunt silvasque et sicubi concava furtim
saxa petunt. Piget incepti lucisque, neque auras
dispiciunt: taedet caeli convexa tueri.

—*Prob. Cen.* 148–219.

69. **ut:** "when."   **videre:** alternate perfect active indicative, third person plural of *videre* = *viderunt;* its objects are the present active participles *gradientem* (with *longe* modifying it) and *frementem* (with *dira* as its object).   **versi:** perfect passive participle of *vertere,* referring to Adam and Eve, with *metu* dependent on it.   **ruentes:** i.e., Adam and Eve.   71. **piget incepti lucisque:** impersonal *piget* takes a genitive of the thing which causes embarrassment.   72. **taedet . . . tueri:** impersonal *taedet* takes the infinitive *tueri,* whose object is *(caeli) convexa.*

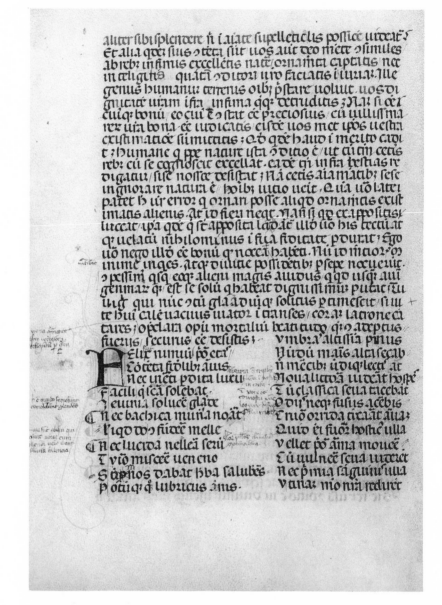

PLATE 4. A folio from a manuscript of Boethius's *De consolatione philosophiae* from c. 1350.

PLATE 4

Boethius, *De consolatione philosophiae*
Latin manuscript on parchment, Italy, c. 1350, fol. 3 verso
Boethius Manuscript, Lownes Collection
John Hay Library, Brown University

Boethius's *Consolation of Philosophy*, like so many works of the fifth, sixth, and seventh centuries, is a mixture of tradition and innovation. Its author was steeped in both Greek and Latin learning, much of which he drew on to compose this famous work. He put that learning to fresh purpose, however, by asking new questions of ancient philosophy, and by articulating those questions in an ancient (and unphilosophical) genre, the Menippean form. The result was a new mode of expression that became central to the philosophical and literary output of the Latin Middle Ages, as the selections from Dhuoda in part 3 and Bernardus Silvestris in part 5 demonstrate.

This manuscript of the *Consolation* begins at 2 pr. 3.4 with the words *nam qu[a]e in profundum sese*. It is written on parchment, with 32 leaves. There are two notable ink drawings, one of Lady Philosophy at folio 9 verso (presumably by the scribe), the other of the head of a Roman woman, on the flyleaf (from a later hand and date). The scribe, Gilbertus de Salustris, produced this copy in a round, Gothic, Bolognese hand, datable to c. 1350. It contains initials in blue and red, marginal scrollwork, and penwork flourishes. It is bound in calfskin.

THE RISE OF LATE LATIN

Jordanes (fl. 554)
Boethius (480–c. 525)
Avitus (c. 450–c. 518)
Gregory of Tours (539–594)
Venantius Fortunatus (c. 535–c. 600)
Gregory I (c. 540–604)
Isidore of Seville (c. 565–636)
Bede (672–735)

INTRODUCTION

Because Roman literary culture was the domain of an elite group of patronized writers, there remain from antiquity, with the possible exceptions of those by Plautus, Terence, and Petronius, few works that speak to literary concerns apart from those canonized by the imperial system. This is perhaps the chief reason that Late Latin has been—practically since the Renaissance—scorned by readers, who have taken their measure of the literary remains of post-Imperial Latin on the old Roman model of the economies of Cicero's prose style, or on the symmetries and novelties of the prosody of Virgil or of Horace. But that measure is faulty, because the categories are incomparable. Late Latin literary activity reflects a dizzying array of cultural moments, the result of the burgeoning of Christian culture in general. These betoken not a restricted, privately patronized elite of writers, but a vibrant engagement on the part of Late Latin litterateurs of the whole gamut of literary possibilities, ranging from Classicism's elite traditions to the new music of Christian song to the cadences of sermons, prayers, hymns, mime, and performance.

In several discrete genres, Late Latin contributions are perhaps most significant. Historical prose is one notable example. This genre developed at a much more rapid pace in the several hundred years between the transformation of the western Roman empire, in the fifth century, into smaller geopolitical units, and its reemergence, late in the eighth century, under Charlemagne. Nor can the political shifts from empire to nation-states and back be downplayed. Christianity, of course, had a salutary effect on the writing of history, because it offered up, as it revealed, a systematic temporal and spatial scheme in which to make sense of human events. This system, stressing discrete beginning and ending points for history, and emphasizing the imperfection of contemporary events, encompassed both sacred and imperial Roman history. But an increased awareness of local and national identities, based on ethnic and linguistic differences, also had the effect of creating a need for historical works that pressed not only the broad temporal and spatial claims of Christianity, but also the ethnographic concerns of the various barbarian successor states. Selections from three of the so-called barbarian historians—Jordanes, Gregory of Tours, and Bede—are included in this part.

These historians are never in lockstep, however, for an examination of their histories reveals divergent pedigrees. The personal background of Jordanes, the earliest of the barbarian historians, for example, suggests the sorts of social and ethnic varieties common to the late antique period—and that help account for its intellectual and linguistic vibrancy. Jordanes was ethnically a Goth, yet he lived all his life (so far as we know) in Constantinople, where a substantial Gothic population had resided for at least a century. In his *History*, therefore, one finds the sentiments of an (eastern) Roman as much as one finds a partisan of Gothic nationalism. More to the point, Jordanes' history reflects the multinationalism of its origins. Its Latin is a mixture of classical and vulgar forms, its expressiveness beholden to Classical and Late Latin syntax and grammar.

Of the barbarian historians as a group, Gregory of Tours is perhaps the most original. He turned his back on classical historiographic models, both as sources of information and as linguistic exemplars, and he tends in his *Histories* to experiment with prose styles as a ballast to his reporting. He is perhaps the best example of a historian who used Christian models of time and space to best effect, for his narrative is introduced by sacred history, which leads naturally (via the Crucifixion) to Roman history, and in turn to the more specific local concerns of Gregory's Frankish homeland. There is a strategic balance, therefore, between the cosmic implications of Scripture itself, which serves as an introduction to Gregory's narrative, and the more immediate national and ethnic concerns that always take shape against the backdrop of sacred history. In much the same way, sacred cosmology and local exemplarism are the mainstays of Bede's history also; but he configures those concerns differently than Gregory of Tours, using a simplified Classical Latin style to shape his version of British national history, concentrating not on experimental prose styles but on giving best shape to the moral and spiritual harvests of his homeland.

Prose functioned in two other key venues in the late antique period: philosophy and ecclesiology. Latin had been specifically and radically sanitized of Grecisms in the Republic, and the tendency had always been to keep the languages apart. The sturdy, straightforward syntax of Latin—with its defective participle and impoverished vocabulary—could only be harmed, so the practitioners of Imperial Latin thought, by Greek. And so, philosophical and, until the second century, theological speculation was next to impossible in the language. By the sixth century, however, Late Latin had received fresh doses of Greek semantics, syntax, and vocabulary, which, when coupled with the extraordinary talents of writers like Tertullian, Augustine, and Boethius, made the language available for abstract theological speculation.

But the sort of straightforward prose writing that had dominated philosophical and even theological discourse for centuries in Greek and, to a much lesser extent, in Latin was challenged by Late Latin writers of the so-called mixed style, like Boethius, who put to the test the old allegiances of a rational prose set against a poetry grounded in the passions of the heart. In part, the extreme position in which Boethius found himself—he wrote his *Consolation* while awaiting execution for treason—accounts for the rise of this new mode of discourse (or better, the maturation of what was an ancient form never much developed in antiquity). But the tendency in Boethius and his successors to blur the distinctions between prose and poetry, between reason and emotion, had an analogue in Scripture itself, which was so supremely a book of rational passion, and impassioned rationality. The Christian outlook, then, privileged a view of the world that discounted, at least by antique terms, hard and fast categories of reason and emotion—a view championed by Boethius and carried forward in several later works of the Medieval Latin tradition.

At the same time, ecclesiastical discourse expanded in the Late Latin tradition from its earlier domains—sermons, apologies, and theological tracts. Now, given the institutional growth of the church, a bureaucratic discourse came of age in the sixth century, and in the letters of Pope Gregory I, this prose style is shown to its best advantages. Gregory's prose does not conform to the familiar epistolary style of Cicero's, but accords more closely with the fourth-century epistolography of Jerome and Augustine. But even here, the formality and distance of Jerome and Augustine renders them less suited to a comparison with Gregory, for Gregory's letters are real, not literary, and they evince the full range of style, perspective, and form. At the same time, the more serious of them portend the slowly growing bureaucracy of the church, whose institutional influence became so great by the twelfth century as to bring about a fresh Medieval Latin prose style owed specifically to its influence.

If the rise of Late Latin heralded new forms and writers of varying background, training, and social status, so too did it take cognizance of antique formalism, as the works of Avitus and Fortunatus best represent. Avitus, long neglected in the history of Latin literature, is perhaps most responsible for mediating the antique epic tradition to future centuries. He did this, as many Late Latin epicists did, through a hexametric version of the Pentateuch that was much indebted to the epic model of Virgil. Less beholden to Classical formalism is the enormous body of writing produced over several decades by Venantius Fortunatus. Fortunatus worked in myriad genres: he produced two important and long-lived hymns, epithalamia, pastoral pieces, short epics, and metrical saints' lives. But much of his verse is occasional and lyric, and mostly the poet chose the elegiac couplet to display the wealth of emotions, situations, and perspectives to which his poetry gives vent. Above the fresh affirmations of his vision and voice, Fortunatus stands as a bold formal experimenter, configuring the elite genres and meters of Latin antiquity to newer tasks and shapes and mediating his own versions of pastoral and lyric to the Carolingian poets who read him assiduously.

Again and again in working through the literary remains that mark the rise of Late Latin literary culture, one is struck by the importance attached to language. All the authors excerpted in this part overtly discuss their attitudes toward language at some point (or points) in their work. This is not surprising, for the very premises of Christian culture were founded on the reading of and writing about Scripture itself. More to the point, Augustine had made language the touchstone of Christian culture in general by analogizing Christian reading in the *De doctrina christiana* to the Crucifixion—wherein the dissonant passages of Scripture, like wounds on the body of Christ, required the soothing salve of Christian interpretation to be healed, that is, to be made to mean.

Isidore of Seville represents the tendency of Late Latin literary culture to attend to the details of linguistic function. Education in the West in the centuries in question focused on the reading and interpretation of key texts, but from a larger view, too, language was understood to embody a strategic relationship to truth. As Isidore suggests in his etymological work, there is a necessary connection between the conventions by which we name things and the position of those things in nature. This means that the symbols of language are not arbitrary but bear an authentic relationship to what they signify. Words mediate, much like Christ, from the impure, fallen world of humanity to a higher reality embedded within the logic implicit in their function. Like Christ as Word, words themselves are mediatory and authentic and can lead to salvation.

A culture of the book slowly emerged from the rise of monasticism, the edifices of education in the West, and in the cultural norms attending to Christianity's solidification of authority and power. Isidore represents one strain of this development. The Carolingian rapprochement with the Church would mark another advance of this development, with the book, the word, and reading made even more central to the configuration of culture in the West. But always the central paradox remained: that language was supremely a function of original sin, that to use it was to wallow in the unfathomable gulf separating divinity from humanity. Yet one needed to use it if, as Augustine hoped, one were to become truly united with God; if one were truly to transcend this world of darkness and inestimable pain; if one were to be able, with Hopkins, to say:

Shape nothing, lips; be lovely-dumb:
It is the shut, the curfew sent
From there where all surrenders come
Which only makes you eloquent.

JORDANES

The History of the Goths
(*De origine actibusque Getarum;* c. 554)

The Latin poetry written by early Christians such as Prudentius or Proba exemplifies a tendency to engage the generic, metrical, and thematic models of CL without blush. Christian Latin historical writing displays no such tendency. It developed as a genre more slowly than did Christian poetry, and substantially in isolation from classical models. This is in part due to Christian notions about the aims of historical writing that were alien to antique conceptions, and also to fresh assumptions about the broader architecture of time and space—both of which led to a more circumscribed, but by no means less sophisticated, conception of what could be articulated about the past.

But in part, too, as Jordanes' *History* suggests, the relative isolation of late antique and early medieval Christian historiography is due to a shift in perspective and subject matter. Geographic, linguistic, and ethnic topics never before treated from the viewpoint of Roman history now took center stage. Not only had the architecture of time and space changed, with a God of creation carefully controlling the flowing forth of time. So, too, had the players themselves changed. History was tending to its final end, to be sure, but Goths, Franks, Britons, Angles, and Huns, among dozens of other ethnic and linguistic groups, were now important to that end. And if, on the Roman view, many of the most liminal places and peoples on earth were now suddenly important players in the march of God's time, then clearly their history had to be articulated in the larger fabric of that time, but in a new way, for the old way—based on biography, moral judgment, and the details of personality—would no longer do.

If the so-called four great barbarian historians—Jordanes, Gregory of Tours, Bede, and Paul the Deacon—reach out in fresh directions, each in his own way, all of them are alike in their insistence on contextualizing their story from a wider view. Jordanes' *History*, for example, forms the third part of a trilogy devoted to a general treatment of world history. The first and second parts of the trilogy deal with the broader course of events: part one offers a chronology of world history while part two deals with Roman history down to Jordanes' own time. These two parts are given the collective title *Romana*. Part three of the trilogy, excerpts of which follow, then focuses on Gothic history in particular.

Jordanes' account of Gothic history makes no pretense to originality in the normal sense. Jordanes himself advertises the fact that his work is an epitome of a monumental, twelve-volume history of the Goths written several decades earlier by Cassiodorus and now, unfortunately, lost except for a few meager lines. This does not mean, on the other hand, that the *History* is simply a slavish copy of its larger predecessor. On the contrary, though he is deeply indebted to his exemplar, the temperaments, historical situations, and innate biases of both authors conspire to suggest that much in the *History* is original to Jordanes.

That originality is resident, for example, in the ways that Jordanes emphasizes the larger, political aspirations of the eastern Roman empire, as against the more localized and particular aims of the Goths as a people ruled by their own king, not the Roman emperor. More to the point, it is difficult to imagine that Cassiodorus would have cottoned to the ending of the *History*, which assists in articulating Justinian's aims for more peaceful relations between the Goths and the eastern empire. This is especially true given the fact that Cassiodorus wrote his history for Theodoric, the Ostrogoth king. More than Cassiodorus must have, Jordanes attempts to balance the competing interpretive demands placed on him by the historical weight of ancient Rome and the modern Gothic kingdom so recently at the height of its powers.

Although a Romanized Goth, Jordanes is less than successful in mediating the rift between his race and his adopted home, for he seems to have felt himself more an eastern Roman than a Goth. When he treats the Justinianic reconquest of the West, for example, in which the Goths as a people were essentially obliterated as a political and military power, Jordanes seems almost pleased at Justinian's success. And many of the *History*'s lines are avidly given over to a recapitulation of Roman history as a logical and important buttress to the Gothic material. But this is perhaps to say too much, to place too much emphasis on the political context in which Jordanes wrote, for though he would seem to expend much historical currency on Rome, his *History* nonetheless concludes with the Goths, who are placed in direct descent of the glorious peoples and kingdoms he recounts in his *Romana*.

Jordanes was himself a Goth, but he presumably hailed from a Romanized family that formed part of the substantial population of Goths who had lived in the eastern empire for several generations. The dates of his birth and death are unknown. A *floruit* of around 554 C.E. is based on evidence internal to the *History*, which allows one to date it to that year. Jordanes seems to have lived all his life in Constantinople.

The Latinity of Jordanes is difficult to classify, both because of its variety and owing to the lack of a context in which to assess it. In this regard, too, he stands apart from his exemplar Cassiodorus. Where the latter was in full command of his language in its classical guise, Jordanes is much looser in his approximation of CL. In spelling and syntax, there is already in place in the east, as in the west, a liberation from CL. Jordanes is at once colloquial and austere, polished and vulgar. Oftentimes, this *variatio* seems merely to reflect the deficiencies of Jordanes' knowledge of Latin or the changes infiltrating written Latin from the speech of everyday life. Often, however, this loosening seems calculated. For example, at several points in the *History* the colloquial *quia* introduces indirect discourse in Jordanes' reporting of gossip about Attila, which reflects VL and suggests a lack of rhetorical control on Jordanes' part. But since Jordanes is perfectly able to construct indirect discourse in the mode of CL, with a subject accusative and infinitive, the idea that he suddenly slips into colloquial usage for no reason other than ignorance seems hard to accept. Rather than affirming linguistic degeneration, the use of *quia* is one way for Jordanes to qualify the kinds of information he is using at certain points in his *History*. Gossip, after all, is colloquial. This stylistic freedom perhaps speaks to a deeper acuity of historical imagination than Jordanes has heretofore been credited with, in which language accords with theme, mood, source. In any case, as with much LL prose, the form of Jordanes' *History* needs to be assessed in conjunction with its content.

The *History* has been edited by T. Mommsen (*Monumenta Germaniae Historica, Auctores Antiquissimi*, vol. 5, Berlin, 1882). The English translation is by C. Mierow (*The Gothic History of Jordanes in English Version*, Princeton, N.J., 2d ed., 1915, repr. New York, 1960). Goffart 20–111 is a comprehensive treatment of Jordanes with full bibliography.

The excerpts reprinted here, from Mommsen's edition with some changes in capitalization and formatting, focus on the life of Attila the Hun, who ravaged the Gothic peoples and figured prominently in the psychology of Gothic nationalism. While moving the narrative of the *History* away from a direct consideration of the Goths, these passages and others like them assist Jordanes in authenticating the centrality of the Gothic race, who had direct dealings with the Huns as well as the Romans, among other important peoples.

ATTILA, KING OF THE HUNS

Is namque Attila patre genitus Mundzuco, cuius fuere germani Octar et Roas, qui ante Attilam regnum tenuisse narrantur, quamvis non omnino cunctorum quorum ipse. Post quorum obitum cum Bleda germano Hunnorum successit in regno, et, ut ante expeditionis quam parabat, par
5   foret, augmentum virium parricidio quaerit, tendens ad discrimen omnium nece suorum. Sed librante iustitia detestabili remedio crescens deformes exitus suae crudelitatis invenit. Bleda enim fratre fraudibus interempto, qui magnae parti regnabat Hunnorum, universum sibi populum adunavit, aliarumque gentium quas tunc in dicione tenebat, numerositate
10 collecta, primas mundi gentes Romanos Vesegothasque subdere praeoptabat. Cuius exercitus quingentorum milium esse numero ferebatur. Vir in concussione gentium natus in mundo, terrarum omnium metus, qui, nescio qua sorte, terrebat cuncta formidabili de se opinione vulgata. Erat namque superbus incessu, huc atque illuc circumferens oculos, ut elati
15 potentia ipso quoque motu corporis appareret; bellorum quidem amator, sed ipse manu temperans, consilio validissimus, supplicantium exorabilis, propitius autem in fide semel susceptis; forma brevis, lato pectore, capite grandiore, minutis oculis, rarus barba, canis aspersus, semo nasu, teter colore, origenis suae signa restituens. Qui quamvis huius esset naturae,
20 ut semper magna confideret, addebat ei tamen confidentia gladius Martis

1. **genitus** = *genitus est*, from *gignere*, here with ablative of source (AG 403.2a). **Mundzuco:** from *Mundzucus, i,* here in the ablative = Attila's father. **fuere:** alternate perfect active indicative, third person plural of *sum* = *fuerunt*. **germani:** here used as a substantive in the nominative plural. 2. **Octar et Roas:** i.e., Attila's uncles; both names are in the nominative singular. **narrantur:** i.e., "it is reported . . ."; this verb governs indirect statement here. 3. **non omnino cunctorum quorum ipse:** ellipsis for *non omnino cunctorum regnum tenuerunt quorum regnum ipse tenuit.* The phrase reads something like: "although his uncles did not hold entirely all of the tribes over which Attila held sway." **quorum:** i.e., Octar and Roas. **obitum:** from *obire,* used as a substantive. **Bleda:** here in the ablative singular = Attila's brother. 4. **ante** = adverb. **expeditionis:** genitive of specification with *par* (AG 349). 6. **librante iustitia:** ablative absolute with causal sense (AG 420; cf. 540). **crescens:** participial phrase expressing concession (AG 496). 8. **parti** = *partis.* 9. **numerositate** = CL *multitudine.* 12. **in concussione** = CL *in concussionem,* an example of apocope; §3.3.5. 13. **formidabili . . . opinione vulgata:** ablative of means; *vulgata* has the sense of "bandied about." 14. **elati:** i.e., *spiritus.* 16. **supplicantium** = CL *supplicantibus.* 17. **susceptis:** perfect passive participle of *suscipere,* standing as a substantive in the dative plural. 18. **barba:** masculine here (but feminine in CL). **semo** = CL *simo.* **teter** = CL *taeter.* 19. **origenis** = CL *originis.* 20. **confidentia** = *confidentiam.*

inventus, sacer apud Scytharum reges semper habitus, quem Priscus istoricus tali refert occasione detectum. Cum pastor, inquiens, quidam gregis unam boculam conspiceret claudicantem nec causam tanti vulneris inveniret, sollicitus vestigia cruoris insequitur tandemque venit ad gladium, quem depascens herbas incauta calcaverat, effossumque protinus ad Atti- 5
lam defert. Quo ille munere gratulatus, ut erat magnanimis, arbitratur se mundi totius principem constitutum et per Martis gladium potestatem sibi concessam esse bellorum.

—*De Orig. 35.*

ATTILA IS HALTED BY POPE LEO IN ITALY

Attila vero nancta occasione de secessu Vesegotharum, et, quod saepe optaverat, cernens hostium solutione per partes, mox iam securus ad oppressionem Romanorum movit procinctum, primaque adgressione Aquileiensem obsidet civitatem, quae est metropolis Venetiarum, in mucrone vel lingua Atriatici posita sinus, cuius ab oriente murus Natissa amnis 5
fluens a monte Piccis elambit. Ibique cum diu multumque obsidens nihil paenitus praevaleret, fortissimis intrinsecus Romanorum militibus resistentibus, exercitu iam murmurante et discedere cupiente, Attila deambulans circa muros, dum, utrum solveret castra an adhuc remoraretur, deliberat, animadvertit candidas aves, id est ciconias, qui in fastigia domorum 10
nidificant, de civitate foetos suos trahere atque contra morem per rura

1. **Priscus istoricus** = *Priscus historicus,* i.e., Priscus, the author of the *Byzantine History* (now only fragmentary), especially rich in details about Attila since its author accompanied the Emperor Maximinus on an embassy to the Hunnish leader in the mid fifth century.   2. **inquiens** = CL *inquit.*   3. **boculam** = CL *buculam.*   5. **effossumque:** from *effodere,* modifying *gladium* and the object of *defert.*   6. **magnanimis** = CL *magnanimus.*   8. **concessam esse:** perfect passive infinitive of *concedere* in indirect discourse with *arbitratur.*

2. **quod saepe optaverat:** this phrase modifies the clause introduced by *cernens.* **solutione** = CL *solutionem,* here with *hostium* dependent on it.   3. **procinctum:** here meaning something like "armies." As often in LL/ML, abstract nouns from CL are given a more concrete meaning.   4. **Aquileiensem:** from *Aquileiensis, e,* modifies *civitatem* and refers to Aquileia, in northeastern Italy (Sleumer 121).   **metropolis Venetiarum:** *metropolis, is* = a term of imperial and ecclesiastical organization (LS 1141); *Venetiae, arum* = Venetia (Sleumer 814); the phrase is translated "the metropolis of Venetia."   5. **in mucrone . . . sinus:** "positioned [i.e., Aquileia] on the point or slip of the fold of the Adriatic" [*Atriatici* = CL *Hadriatici*].   **murus** = CL *muros.*   6. **Piccis:** i.e., Mount Piccis.   7. **paenitus** = CL *penitus;* the phrase *nihil paentius praevaleret* has the sense of "was thoroughly unsuccessful."   10. **fastigia:** more properly *fastigiis.*   11. **foetos** = CL *fetus.*

forinsecus conportare. Et ut erat sagacissimus inquisitor, presensit et ad suos: "Respicite," inquid, "aves futurarum rerum providas perituram relinquere civitatem casurasque arces periculo imminente deserere. Non hoc vacuum, non hoc credatur incertum; rebus presciis consuetudinem
5 mutat ventura formido." Quid plura? Animos suorum rursus ad oppugnandam Aquileiam inflammat. Qui machinis constructis omniaque genera tormentorum adhibita, nec mora et invadunt civitatem, spoliant, dividunt vastantque crudeliter, ita ut vix eius vestigia ut appareat reliquerunt. Exhinc iam audaciores et necdum Romanorum sanguine satiati, per reli-
10 quas Venetum civitates Hunni bacchantur. Mediolanum quoque Liguriae metropolim et quondam regiam urbem pari tenore devastant nec non et Ticinum aequali sorte deiciunt vicinaque loca saevientes allidunt demoliuntque pene totam Italiam. Cumque ad Romam animus fuisset eius adtentus accedere, sui eum, ut Priscus istoricus refert, removerunt, non urbi,
15 cui inimici erant, consulentes, sed Alarici quondam Vesegotharum regis obicientes exemplo, veriti regis sui fortunam, quia ille post fractam Romam non diu supervixerit, sed protinus rebus humanis excessit. Igitur

1. **forinsecus:** properly an adverb = "outside," Jordanes gives this word the force of a prepositional phrase, making it mean something like "into the country." **conportare:** dependent, along with *trahere*, on *animadvertit*, in indirect discourse. 2. **Respicite:** this imperative governs indirect statement, with *relinquere* and *deserere* dependent on it. **inquid** = CL *inquit;* the substitution of mutes ("d" for "t") is common in LL/ML orthography; § 1.4. **providas:** modifies *aves*, with *futurarum rerum* dependent on it. 3. **civitatem:** modified by *perituram*, and the object of *relinquere*. 7. **omniaque genera tormentorum adhibita:** although functioning on the model of an ablative absolute, this phrase is nominative (or accusative) absolute, common in LL/ML (Blaise 67); §§ 3.3.1, 3.3.5. 8 **appareat** = *appareant*. 10. **Venetum** = *Venetorum*, from *Veneti, orum*, i.e., in the area of Venice (Sleumer 814). **Mediolanum:** i.e., Milan; the subsequent reference to this city as *quondam regiam urbem* is a reference to the fact that the city was one of the four capitals designated in Diocletian's reorganization. 11. **Liguriae metropolim:** *Liguria, ae* = Liguria (Sleumer 475); *metropolis, e* = "metropolis," a term of imperial and ecclesiastical urban organization. The phrase is translated "the metropolis of Liguria." 12. **Ticinum:** from *Ticinum, i* = Pavia (Sleumer 782). 13. **pene** = CL *paene*. **cumque:** *cum* concessive + subjunctive; a concessive adverb such as *tamen* needs to be supplied. 14. **adtentus** = CL *attentus*, governing *accedere*. **sui:** lit., "his own," referring to Attila's troops; *sui* is the subject of *removerunt*. 15. **consulentes:** modifies *sui*, means something like "out of consideration," and takes as its (dative) object *urbi*. 16. **obicientes:** i.e., "exposing," "remembering," etc. **exemplo** = CL *exemplum*, the object of *obicientes*. **veriti:** perfect participle of *vereri*, modifying *sui*. 17. **excessit:** one might expect, with *supervixerit, excesserit*.

dum eius animus ancipiti negotio inter ire et non ire fluctuaret secumque
deliberans tardaret, placida ei legatio a Roma advenit. Nam Leo papa
per se ad eum accedens in agro Venetum Ambuleio, ubi Mincius amnis
commeantium frequentatione transitur. Qui mox deposuit exercitatu furore et rediens, quo venerat, iter ultra Danubium promissa pace discessit,   5
illud pre omnibus denuntians atque interminando decernens, graviora se
in Italia inlaturum, nisi ad se Honoriam Valentiniani principis germanam,
filiam Placidiae Augustae, cum portione sibi regalium opum debita mit-
terent. Ferebatur enim, quia haec Honoria, dum propter aulae decus ad
castitatem teneretur nutu fratris inclusa, clam eunucho misso Attilam invi-   10
tasse, ut contra fratris potentiam eius patrociniis uteretur: prorsus indignum facinus, ut licentiam libidinis malo publico conpararet.

—*De Orig.* 42.

1. **ancipiti negotio:** this phrase is a periphrastic way of suggesting doubt on the part
of Attila. It literally means something like "two-headed matter." **inter ire et non ire** =
CL *inter eundum et non eundum;* here, the present active infintive functions in the
accusative; in CL the infinitive would function only as the nominative form of the
gerund. 2. **secumque deliberans:** lit., "pondering it with himself," i.e., "thinking it
over." **placida:** modifies *legatio* but describes the mission, not the temperament, of
the delegation from Rome. The CL construction = *causa pacis petendae.* **Leo papa:**
Pope Leo the Great, reigned 440–461, an important figure in political and temporal
affairs of the church in the fifth century. 3. **accedens** = CL *accedit.* **in agro Venetum Ambuleio:** i.e., "in the Ambuleian district in the area of Venice"; *Ambuleio* is
ablative singular with *in agro; Venetum* is a false form for *Venetorum,* i.e., "in the area
of Venice" (cf. Sleumer 814; LS 1968). 4. **commeantium frequentatione:** locative
ablative without *in;* "at the well-frequented ford" of the Mincius River (now the Min-
cio, a tributary of the Po). **exercitatu furore:** this looks to be an ablative construction
but must function as the object of *deposuit;* in CL = *exercitatum furorem.* 5. **promissa pace:** i.e., left "with peace promised." 6. **pre** = CL *prae.* 7. **in Italia** = CL
in Italiam. **inlaturum** = CL *inlaturum esse,* from *inferre,* here in indirect discourse
governed by *denuntians* and *decernens;* i.e., "Attila announced and made clear one
thing above all else, viz., that he (*se*) would bear forth harsher things. . . ." 9. **quia:**
commonly in LL/ML, *quia* introduces indirect statement and means something like
"that." This construction came to prominence chiefly through the influence of EL,
especially the Vulgate. The infinitive in CL is replaced now with a clause, in the subjunctive or indicative, portending the continued simplificaton of syntax that will become the hallmark of ML; § 7.10 (cf. Blaise 241–45). 10. **clam:** "secretly." **invitasse:** the syncopated form of the perfect active infinitive *invitavisse.* Here there would
seem to be some confusion on Jordanes' part as to how exactly to put indirect discourse, for he introduces the construction with *ferebatur enim quia,* but, after the
dum clause, concludes it with the infinitive *invitasse.* 11. **eius:** i.e., Attila; modifies
patrociniis, which is the object of *uteretur.*

The Death of Attila

Qui, ut Priscus istoricus refert, exitus sui tempore puellam Ildico nomine decoram valde sibi in matrimonio post innumerabiles uxores, ut
mos erat gentis illius, socians eiusque in nuptiis hilaritate nimia resolutus,
vino somnoque gravatus resupinus iaceret, redundans sanguis, qui ei sol-
5   ite de naribus effluebat, dum consuetis meatibus impeditur, itinere ferali
faucibus illapsus extinxit. Ita glorioso per bella regi temulentia pudendos
exitos dedit. Sequenti vero luce cum magna pars diei fuisset exempta,
ministri regii triste aliquid suspicantes post clamores maximos fores ef-
fringunt inveniuntque Attilae sine ullo vulnere necem sanguinis effusione
10   peractam puellamque demisso vultu sub velamine lacrimantem. Tunc, ut
gentis illius mos est, crinium parte truncata, informes facies cavis turpavere vulneribus, ut proeliator eximius non femineis lamentationibus et lacrimis, sed sanguine lugeretur virile. De quo id accessit mirabile, ut Marciano principi Orientis de tam feroci hoste sollicito in somnis divinitas
15   adsistens arcum Attilae in eadem nocte fractum ostenderet, quasi quod
gens ipsa eo telo multum praesumat. Hoc Priscus istoricus vera se dicit
adtestatione probare. Nam in tantum magnis imperiis Attila terribilis
habitus est, ut eius mortem in locum muneris superna regnantibus indi-
carent.

—*De Orig.* 49 (excerpts).

1. **exitus sui tempore:** i.e., "at the end of his days." 3. **socians eiusque . . . resolutus:**
nominative absolute; § 3.3.1 (cf. Blaise 67). 4. **iaceret:** *cum* is understood. **solite:**
i.e., "normally." 5. **itinere ferali:** i.e., "on a lethal journey. 6. **illapsus:** from *illabor,*
modifying *sanguis.* **extinxit** = *exstinxit,* with Attila the understood object. 7. **exitos** = CL *exitus.* 11. **truncata:** from *truncare,* standing here as the object of *turpavere,* with *crinium* dependent on it. **cavis:** modifies *vulneribus* and means "deep."
turpavere: alternate third person plural, perfect active indicative of *turpare* = *turpav-
erunt.* 13. **virile** = CL *virili.* **Marciano:** Marcian, eastern Emperor. 14. **sollicito:**
modifies *Marciano.* **divinitas:** i.e., "a godly form." 15. **in eadem nocte:** i.e., on the
same night that Attila died. 17. **in tantum:** i.e., "to such an extent." 18. **habitus
est:** i.e., "was constituted," "was set up," "was thought." **superna** = CL *superi.*

PLATE 5. A folio from a late fourteenth–century manuscript, showing Boethius's
De arithmetica.

PLATE 5

Boethius, *De Arithmetica*
Latin manuscript on paper, Italy, c. 1390, fol. 34 recto
Boethius, Grosseteste, Fibonacci Manuscript; J. G. Bergart Deposit
John Hay Library, Brown University

Boethius's work in philosophy was augmented by his wide-ranging interests in other intellectual areas, including music, theology, logic, and arithmetic. Those interests were indulged both in original works and in adaptations and translations of earlier treatises of Greek and Latin antiquity. Much of the work he produced in this vein became central to the curriculum of the Latin Middle Ages. This is true for the *De arithmetica,* shown here, which Boethius adapted around 520 from Nicomachus's *Introductio arithmetica;* and also for his *De musica,* which held much the same place in the medieval curriculum, both in the monastic schools that arose quickly in the West in the Carolingian period, and in the later cathedral schools and nascent universities of the twelfth and thirteenth centuries.

The manuscript shown here is itself a witness to medieval pedagogy, for Boethius' work is joined in it to a copy of the *Computus* of Robert Grosseteste (discussed at plate 30). Both works were copied together for the sake of pedagogical convenience around 1390. They are written on paper, in dark brown ink, in a Gothic hand. The manuscript is double-columned and rubricated. The watermark on the paper—a crossbow in a circle—localizes the manuscript to Italy. The *De arithmetica* runs to fol. 64a recto; the *Computus,* from 65a verso to 93a recto. In the nineteenth century a third manuscript of several works of Fibonacci was bound to it, forming a unique compendium of medieval mathematical texts. The Fibonacci manuscript is discussed at plate 31.

BOETHIUS

The Consolation of Philosophy
(*De consolatione philosophiae*; c. 525)

The face of Western culture would be different had Boethius lived to complete the prodigious series of projects he set for himself. Probably no other scholar of his age could have made similar plans, or made good on their completion, for Boethius aimed to translate into Latin and to comment on the Platonic dialogues and all of Aristotle. Before his untimely death, Boethius managed to translate and comment on Porphyry's *Introduction to the Categories of Aristotle* and Aristotle's logical works. He also produced a commentary on Cicero's *Topics*. Boethius was not merely a translator, however. He also wrote original works on music and theology, and, most notably, *De consolatione philosophiae*, excerpted here. Lacking these important original works, however, it would still be difficult to deny the importance of Boethius's translations from the Greek, for, particularly with regard to Aristotle's logical works, these translations served as the single conduit of Western knowledge of Aristotle for nearly six hundred years. Moreover, Boethius helped to establish for posterity a philosophical vocabulary in Latin that could support the nuances and subtleties of Greek speculative thought.

Boethius was a member of the illustrious Anicii, an ancient and distinguished family that traced its lineage back to the Republic. When Boethius was born into it in 480 C.E., the Anicii could claim as its own at least two emperors and, more recently, a pope. Boethius's father died when he was young, and the boy was brought up at Rome in the household of another eminent family, the Symmachi, into which Boethius eventually married. Boethius's obvious talents earned for him the best education available and eventually brought him in the prime of his life to the attention of Theodoric, king of the Ostrogoths, who made Boethius, in short order, *consul* and then *magister officiorum*, a position that allowed him access to the inner circle of Theodoric's government. Close dealings with this government, in the end, led to Boethius's downfall, for he was embroiled in the early 520s in a controversy in which the Senate was accused of attempting to usurp some of Theodoric's power for its own in the calming days following the Acacian schism. Boethius was implicated in this treasonous act, so he says, on false charges. He was exiled to Pavia, tortured, and bludgeoned to death around 525.

The excerpts reprinted here are taken from the conclusion of the first book of the *Consolation*, written while Boethius was awaiting execution at Pavia. As the excerpts show, the *Consolation* is composed in the Menippean style (sometimes called the "mixed form"), with alternating sections of prose and poetry. The prose section excerpted here takes up Lady Philosophy's musings about the "illness" afflicting Boethius, her "student," who has, so she says, forgotten his true nature and thus the true source of all happiness. While preparing to give the first moderate doses of medicine to cure her patient, Lady Philosophy's reasoned discourse gives way to *metron* 1.7, written in adonics (see AG 625.3), in which the cares of Boethius's mind and heart are ramified in terms of the natural world. Here, the theme of the prose extends to the poetry also, but the simplicity of the prose, when read against the compression of the poetry, suggests the underlying emotional trauma of the moment, which reason's discourse cannot expunge completely, if at all. Here the beauty of Boethius' form carefully refracts the harsher realities underlying the work's content.

Boethius's Latinity is simple and compressed. Like Augustine's, his prose style is clearly not classical, but neither is it so far removed from CL standards as to be considered a fundamentally altered language, as is the case with Egeria or, to a lesser extent, Jordanes. The poetry is accomplished thematically and metrically, with a variety of classical meters employed. The more fundamental stylistic question inheres in the relationship of the work's form to its content. What, for example, is the relationship of the poetry to the prose; and, more specifically, from a formally philosophical point of view, what function does poetry—irrational, emotive, spontaneous—play in a work of rational discourse? Stylistic changes attend to these questions—the assumption and abandonment of rhetorical polish, the severe compression of poetic language (as in *metron* 1.7 below) as against more fluent pieces that sometimes detail important philosophical points (*metron* 3.9, e.g.), the merging of poetic and prose themes as measured against those moments in the *Consolation* when either level of discourse would seem to be working at cross purposes. The *Consolation* in this way attends to a fundamental question about the kinds of knowledge humans possess and to a consideration of the relationship and relative values of these competing kinds of knowledge. In this regard, the work's form speaks to an issue as enduring as, and perhaps more important than, its content.

The *Consolation* has been edited by R. Peiper (Leipzig, 1871); W. Weinberger (*Corpus Scriptorum Ecclesiasticorum Latinorum*, vol. 67, Vienna and Leipzig, 1934); K. Büchner (Heidelberg, 1947, 3d ed., 1977); and L. Bieler (*Corpus Christianorum, Series Latina*, vol. 94, Turnhout, 1957). There are two English translations in the Loeb Classical Library, and the more recent, by S. J. Tester (*Boethius: The Consolation of Philosophy*, London and Cambridge, Mass., 1973), is the better. There is also an English translation by V. E. Watts in the Penguin Classics (*Boethius: The Consolation of Philosophy*, Harmondsworth, 1969). A concordance has been prepared by L. Cooper (*A Concordance to Boethius: The Five Theological Tractates and the Consolation of Philosophy*, Cambridge, Mass., 1928). A grammatical commentary has been prepared by J. J. O'Donnell for the Bryn Mawr Latin Commentaries series (*Boethius: Consolatio Philosophiae*, Bryn Mawr, Pa., 1984). Important recent works on the *Consolation* have been written by S. Lerer (*Boethius and Dialogue: Literary Method in* The Consolation of Philosophy, Princeton, N.J., 1985) and G. O'Daly (*The Poetry of Boethius*, Chapel Hill, N.C., 1991). P. Dronke's book on the Menippean form (*Verse with Prose from Petronius to Dante: The Art and Scope of the Mixed Form*, Cambridge, Mass., 1994) contains a substantial discussion of Boethius. Bieler's text is reprinted with "u" and "v" distinguished.

PHILOSOPHY TALKS TO BOETHIUS

Iam scio, inquit, morbi tui aliam vel maximam causam; quid ipse sis nosse desisti. Quare plenissime vel aegritudinis tuae rationem vel aditum reconciliandae sospitatis inveni. Nam quoniam tui oblivione confunderis, et exsulem te et exspoliatum propriis bonis esse doluisti; quoniam vero quis sit rerum finis ignoras, nequam homines atque nefarios potentes felicesque arbitraris; quoniam vero quibus gubernaculis mundus regatur oblitus es, has fortunarum vices aestimas sine rectore fluitare: magnae non ad morbum modo, verum ad interitum quoque causae. Sed sospitatis auctori grates quod te nondum totum natura destituit. Habemus maxi-

---

1. **inquit:** i.e., Lady Philosophy. **quid ipse sis:** this clause, an indirect question, is the object of *nosse desisti.* 2. **nosse** = *gnoscere.* **vel ... vel:** "both ... and." 3. **tui oblivione** = *tua oblivione.* 5. **ignoras:** the object is *quis sit rerum finis.* **nequam:** indeclinable adjective = "evil," "wicked," modifying *homines.* 7. **oblitus es:** the object is the preceding relative clause governed by *quibus.* **fluitare:** infinitive in indirect discourse, governed by *aestimas,* with *has ... vices* as subject accusative. 9. **grates** + dative = "give thanks to . . .," with the force of an imperative. **totum:** adverb.

mum tuae fomitem salutis veram de mundi gubernatione sententiam, quod eam non casuum temeritati sed divinae rationi subditam credis; nihil igitur pertimescas, iam tibi ex hac minima scintillula vitalis calor illuxerit. Sed quoniam firmioribus remediis nondum tempus est, et eam mentium constat esse naturam ut quotiens abiecerint veras, falsis opinionibus   5
induantur, ex quibus orta perturbationum caligo verum illum confundit intuitum, hanc paulisper lenibus mediocribusque fomentis attenuare temptabo, ut dimotis fallacium affectionum tenebris splendorem verae lucis possis agnoscere.

—*Cons. Phil.* 1 pr. 6.17–21 (excerpts).

Metron 1.7

Nubibus atris
condita nullum
fundere possunt
sidera lumen.
Si mare volvens   5
turbidus Auster
misceat aestum,
vitrea dudum
parque serenis
unda diebus   10
mox resoluto
sordida caeno
visibus obstat,
quique vagatur
montibus altis   15
defluus amnis
saepe resistit
rupe soluti
obice saxi.
Tu quoque si vis   20
lumine claro
cernere verum,
tramite recto

---

1. **fomitem:** i.e., *maximam spem.* **veram . . . sententiam:** in apposition with *maximum . . . salutis.* 2. **eam,** i.e., *gubernatio mundi.* 8. **dimotis:** from *dimovere.*

2. **condita:** i.e., "hidden." 7. **aestum:** i.e., "surge," "storm." 13. **visibus obstat:** i.e., "stand in the way of sight."

carpere callem:
25   gaudia pelle,
pelle timorem
spemque fugato
nec dolor adsit.
Nubila mens est
30   vinctaque frenis
haec ubi regnant.

—*Cons. Phil.* 1 met. 7.

31. **haec:** i.e., *gaudia, timor, spes, dolor.*

Avitus

A Poem on the Events of Mosaic History
(*De spiritalis historiae gestis*; c. 500)

Unlike Christian and classical historiography, classical and Christian epic formed an easy and long-lived partnership. The depiction in classical epic of glorious exploits focused on an individual hero well suited the literary aims of Christian poets whose chief goal was to glorify God and extol his earthly activity. Beyond the tradition exemplified by Proba, who was able to use Virgilian language to frame a fresh version of Scripture, Christian Latin epicists, Avitus chief among them, were able to recast sacred material in the guise of an epic story rivaling the best epic moments of Virgil and his Aeneas.

In Avitus's hands, moreover, the treatment of Scripture reaches beyond the epical confines of Virgil's greatest poem to broader themes, attending to the role of the poet and his topic in Christian culture. The narrative of Avitus's epic and the development of its plot and theme move in a straightforward enough way, sometimes relying on Scripture itself, sometimes working out from sacred events to press typological themes. But other resources are marshaled by the poet in the service of his art. In the first book of his poem, for example, the poet describes the Garden of Eden in terms that recall the best habitats of Virgil's bucolic landscapes. When the poet arrives at a precise description of the choice smells of his Eden, however, he includes in his catalogue the attractions of cinnamon, the material from which the phoenix fashions its nest. Mention of this exotic bird brings to focus the function of the Christian soul symbolized by it and readers have good right to see in Avitus's description of the phoenix's death and rebirth a figuration of Christ's death and rebirth. But given the lack of a Christian context for the phoenix, readers are also invited to view this bird in a classical guise, as a symbol of the poet. In this context, one senses the presence of Avitus himself highlighting his own role as a Christian artist, climbing, or attempting to climb, to Eden, being burned in the process, but ultimately attaining redemption for the effort.

Little has been made of this or similar moments in Avitus's masterpiece, his poem on the events of Mosaic history. The poem itself enjoyed an illustrious career after it was written, culminating in John Milton's close reliance on it in parts of *Paradise Lost*. The modern career of the poem has been less happy, and Avitus has fallen into obscurity. Of the life of Alcimius Ecdicius Avitus we know next to nothing. His date of birth is conjectured to be c. 450. We know that he was bishop of Vienne in Burgundy from around 490 until around 518, the approximate year of his death. He came from a noble family, for he was almost surely related to the emperor Avitus. As bishop, he seems to have been an active opponent of Arianism, then rampant in the West, as his letters attest (of which some eighty are still extant). His greatest accomplishment as bishop was undoubtedly his conversion of Sigismun, heir to the Burgundian throne, from Arianism to Catholicism. We possess from his pen homilies and another poem, the *De consolatoria castitatis laude*.

The *De spiritalis* is a poem in five books. Excerpts from books one and two follow here, which deal with the creation of the world and original sin. The other parts of the poem deal successively with the judgment of God and the expulsion from Paradise, the Deluge, and the passage through the Red Sea. Avitus's Latin is classical. His aim in his lengthy poem would seem to be to adapt to the dictates of classical epic style and diction the themes of the Old Testament. In doing this, Avitus joined a growing rank of poets in the sixth century who took as their task the epicization of Scripture. Avitus's is perhaps the most accomplished of the several poems that attempted this task, but the poetic benefits of such an undertaking seem to have been outweighed by the moral issue at stake in daring to make grand epic out of so venerable a story. The sixth century is the apogee of Scriptural epic. Avitus awaits a critic who can read him as a poet of original daring and bold vision, at the forefront of this important movement in LL/ML literary history.

The works of Avitus have been edited by R. Peiper (*Monumenta Germaniae Historica, Auctores Antiquissimi,* vol. 6, Berlin, 1883) and U. Chevalier (*Oeuvres complètes de Saint Avit, Évêque de Vienne,* Lyon, 1890). There is an edition of book one alone (A. Schippers, ed., *De mundi initio, Book 1,* Amsterdam, 1945); and, most recently, an edition of books 1–3, brought out by D. J. Nodes in the Toronto Medieval Latin Texts series (*Avitus: The Fall of Man: De Spiritalis Historiae Gestis Libri I–III,* Toronto, 1985). Avitus's Latinity is analyzed by H. Goelzer (*Le Latin de Saint Avit,* Paris, 1909). There is a concordance also (J. Ramminger, *Concordantiae in Alcimi Ecdicii Aviti Carmina,* Hildesheim, 1990). Raby 1, pp. 77ff., discusses Avitus, as does C. Witke (*Numen Litterarum: The Old and the New in Latin Poetry from Constantine to Gregory the Great,* Leiden, 1971, pp. 179–90). Nodes's text is reprinted here, reading at line 6 *revulsus* for *revulsis;* consonantal "u" has been changed throughout to "v."

PARADISE

Ergo ubi transmissis mundi caput incipit Indis,
quo perhibent terram confinia iungere caelo,
lucus inaccessa cunctis mortalibus archae
permanet aeterno conclusus limite, postquam
decidit expulsus primevi criminis auctor,   5
atque reis digne felici ab sede revulsus,
caelestis haec sancta capit nunc terra ministros.
Non hic alterni succedit temporis umquam
bruma, nec aestivi redeunt post frigora soles,
sic celsus calidum cum reddit circulus annum,   10
vel densente gelu canescunt arva pruinis.
Hic ver adsiduum caeli clementia servat,
turbidus auster abest, semperque sub aere sudo
nubila diffugiunt iugi cessura sereno.
Nec poscit natura loci, quos non habet, imbres,   15
sed contenta suo dotantur germina rore.
Perpetuo viret omne solum, terraeque tepentis
blanda nitet facies; stant semper collibus herbae
arboribusque come, quae cum se flore frequenti
diffundunt, celeri confortant sua germina suco.   20
Nam quicquid nobis toto tunc nascitur anno,
menstrua maturo dant illic tempora fructu.
Lilia perlucent nullo flaccentia sole,
nec tactus violat violas, roseumque ruborem
servans perpetuo suffundit gratia vultu.   25
Sic cum desit hiems nec torrida ferveat aestas,

1. **transmissis . . . Indis:** ablative absolute; the *Indi* (from *Indus, a, um*) are inhabitants of India, used here to evoke the most distant of places. 2. **perhibent:** i.e., "they say"; this verb governs indirect discourse. 3. **archae** = *arce*, i.e., "on a height, bluff, summit, etc."; ablative of place where, without a preposition (AG 421). In LL, *ae* often = *e*; § 1.3. 4. **postquam:** causal, as often in CL poetry (LS, p. 1406, s. v. *postquam*, II), introducing the reason why the *arx* and *lucus* are inaccessible to mortals. 7. **caelestis** = *caelestes*. 8. **hic:** adverb. **alterni . . . temporis:** dependent on *bruma*. 9. **bruma:** here means something like winter solstice, an individual day heralding the advent of other seasons (*alternus tempus*). 12. **adsiduum** = *assiduum*, modifying *ver*. 14. **iugi:** from *iugis, e*. **cessura:** future active participle of *cedere*, modifying *nubila*. 17. **perpetuo:** adverb. 19. **come** = CL *comae*; § 1.3.

fructibus autumnus, ver floribus occupat annum.
Hic, que donari mentitur fama Sabeis,
cinnama nascuntur, vivax que colligit alis,

30 natali cum fine perit nidoque perusta
succedens sibimet quaesita morte resurgit;
nec contenta suo tantum semel ordine nasci,
longa veternosi renovatur corporis aetas,
incensamque levant exordia crebra senectam.

35 Illic desudans fragrantia balsama ramus
perpetuum pingui promit de stipite fluxum.
Tum si forte levis movit spiramina ventus,
flatibus exiguis lenique inpulsa susurro
divis silva tremit foliis et flore salubri,

40 qui sparsus terris suaves dispensat odores.
Hic fons perspicuo resplendens gurgite surgit:
talis in argento non fulgit gratia, tantam
nec cristalla dabunt nitido de frigore lucem.
Margine riparum virides micuere lapilli

45 et, quas miratur mundi iactantia gemmas,
illic saxa iacent; varios dant arva colores
et naturali campos diademate pingunt.

—*De Spir. His. Ges.* 1.211–57.

THE JEALOUSY OF THE SERPENT

Vidit ut iste novos homines in sede quieta
ducere felicem nullo discrimine vitam,

---

28. **que** = CL *quae*; i.e., *cinnama*. **mentitur**: "reports"; this verb always connotes deceit or lying, but Avitus uses it here more because of *fama* than owing to any sense of the *Sabaei* as liars. **Sabeis**: from *Sabaei, orum* = the inhabitants of Saba (Greek Σάβα), a region in Arabia famous for its spices (LS 1609); by synecdoche for Arabians. 29. **alis** = *ales*, the phoenix. 30. **perusta**: perfect passive participle of *perurere*, modifies *alis*. 31. **quaesita**: perfect passive participle of *quaerere*, modifies *morte* in ablative of means. **resurgit**: intransitive. 32. **tantum semel**: i.e., "only once." **suo . . . ordine**: i.e., "at the right time"; "in the right order." 37. **spiramina**: here means something like "breath," but, taken with *movit*, could simply be translated as "blows." 38. **inpulsa**: from *impellere*, modifies *silva* in the next line. 39. **divis** = *dives*. 41. **perspicuo . . . gurgite**: means something like "evident depth." 42. **fulgit** = *fulget*. 44. **micuere**: alternate perfect active indicative, third person plural of *micare* = *micuerunt*.

1. **vidit**: the subject is Satan, who is about to take the form of the serpent.

lege sub accepta famulo dominarier orbi,
subiectisque frui placida inter gaudia rebus,
commovit subitum zeli scintilla vaporem,   5
excrevitque calens in saeva incendia livor.
Vicinus tunc forte fuit, quo concidit alto,
lapsus, et innexam traxit per prona catervam.
Hoc recolens casumque premens in corde recentem,
plus doluit periisse sibi quod possidet alter.   10
Tum mixtus cum felle pudor sic pectore quaestus
explicat et tali suspiria voce relaxat:
   "Pro dolor, hoc nobis subitum consurgere plasma
invisumque genus nostra crevisse ruina!
Me celsum virtus habuit, nunc ecce reiectus   15
pellor et angelico limus succedit honori.
Caelum terra tenet, vili conpage levata
regnat humus nobisque perit translata potestas.
Non tamen in totum periit: pars magna retentat
vim propriam summaque cluit virtute nocendi.   20
Nec differre iuvat; iam nunc certamine blando
congrediar, dum prima salus experta nec ullos
simplicitas ignava dolos ad tela patebit;
et melius soli capientur fraude priusquam
fecundam mittant aeterna in saecula prolem.   25
Inmortale nihil terra prodire sinendum est;

3. **dominarier:** (archaic) present infinitive, parallel with *ducere* and *frui*, each of them being a verb in indirect statement, governed by *vidit iste*.   4. **subiectisque . . . rebus:** ablative objects of *frui*.   11. **quaestus** = CL *questus*, object of *explicat*.   13. **consurgere:** exclamatory infinitive, with *subitum plasma* as subject.   **plasma:** in LL/ML = "creature" (Niermeyer 806), modified by *subitum*, from *subire*, with the sense of "fallen."   14. **crevisse:** exclamatory infinitive, with *invisum genus* as subject.   **nostra . . . ruina:** ablative of means.   16. **limus:** here a masculine noun = "mud."   17. **conpage** = CL *compage*, modified here by *vili*, meaning "vile body."   **levata:** from *levare*, modifies *humus* in the next line.   19. **non . . . periit:** *potestas* is understood.   20. **summaque . . . nocendi:** *cluit* means something like "it [i.e., *magna pars*] attends to," with ablative of manner; *summa* is probably best translated adverbially = "chiefly" (as often with LL adjectives); *virtute* is used ironically, since it describes the "strength" of Satan's power to harm others. The whole phrase reads something like "and chiefly attends (so it is said) to the power to do harm."   22. **experta:** from *experiri*, modifying both *prima salus* and *simplicitas ignava*, and taking *nec ullos dolos* as its object; *ad tela patebit* completes the thought ("will endure [my] weapons").   26. **terra:** ablative of separation.   **prodire:** complementary infinitive with *sinendum est*.   **sinendum est:** from *sinere*, with *immortale nihil* as subject.

fons generis pereat; capitis deiectio victi
semen mortis erit. Pariat discrimina laeti
vitae principium; cuncti feriantur in uno.
30   Non faciet vivum radix occisa cacumen.
Haec mihi deiecto tantum solatia restant:
si nequeo clausos iterum conscendere caelos,
his quoque claudantur. Levius cecidisse putandum est,
si nova perdatur simili substantia casu.
35   Sit comis excidii, subeat consortia poenae
et, quos praevideo, nobiscum dividat ignes.
Sed ne difficilis fallendi causa petetur:
haec monstranda via est dudum quam sponte cucurri
in pronum lapsus; quae me iactantia regno
40   depulit, haec hominem paradisi limine pellet."
Sic ait et gemitus vocem clausere dolentis.

                                   —*De Spir. His. Ges.* 2.77–117.

28. **laeti** = CL *leti.*   29. **in uno:** Adam is understood here.   31. **solatia** = CL *so-lacia.*   35. **consortia:** Eve is understood here. **poenae:** dative with *subeat;* "let Eve join in the penalty."   36. **dividat:** the sense is "share," with the subject *consortia;* "let Eve share the fires with us which I forsee."   39. **regno:** ablative of separation without a preposition.   40. **haec:** *iactantia* is understood.   41. **clausere:** alternate perfect active indicative, third person plural of *claudere* = *clauserunt.*

GREGORY OF TOURS

The Histories
(*Historiae*; 594)

O do of Cluny, writing in the tenth century, tells us that Gregory of Tours was of such small stature that he had to fend off the quizzical stare of Pope Gregory I with the reminder of the words of the Psalmist: "It is God who has made us, and not we ourselves." Never has physical stature been more at odds with literary importance. Gregory's *Histories* is a work strikingly original in conception and equally bold in execution. It is comprehensive in perspective, recording the history of the world from Creation down to the fall of the Roman empire (before taking up its prized topic, Frankish history), but it is also truly a local and ethnocentric history, brimming with insights into the details of the Frankish kingdoms in the sixth century. It is also a history grounded in a discrete sense of time and space, for Gregory's narrative is organized around the principles of Christian teleology, an order affirmed in the presence of so much sacred material at the start of the *Histories*. Though he relies much on prior historical writing, not to mention Scripture, as sources of evidence, Gregory is novel also in the independence he displays from those writers, for there is no obvious modeling of style, approach, method, or vocabulary in the *Histories*—indeed, there are few if any verbal borrowings to indicate what earlier sources, apart from the ones he cites, were read by, or influential on, Gregory.

Gregory strikes out in new ways as a prose stylist also. With no obvious models inhibiting him, he asserts his own narrative principles in manifold ways. He is prodigiously eclectic. His Latin reflects now the dictates of EL, now the discourse of VL, now the higher style, now an idiosyncratic mix of styles. Gregory seems always to be aware of the intricate, sometimes even delicate, linkages of style and sense, form and content. Much has been made of Gregory's naivety, his deficiencies of composition, temperament, intellect, of his humility masking ignorance. But these monolithic characterizations, surely each applicable in part to Gregory (as to every writer), fail to qualify the *Histories* as a whole. He writes not only as he speaks, nor only as he was taught, but according to the demands of his theme. There are, then, as many prose styles in the *Histories* as stories told, and Gregory is never a slave to any of them. He has no peer as a prose stylist in the Latin Middle Ages.

Georgius Florentius Gregorius was born at Clermont-Ferrand in Auvergne in 539. Both his parents hailed from distinguished families long prominent in the Church and in Frankish politics in Gaul. The early death of his father and his mother's subsequent retirement to Burgundy meant that Gregory spent much of his boyhood with an uncle, Gallus, Bishop of Clermont-Ferrand. Given the close connection of his family to the affairs of Church and state in Gaul and the upbringing secured for him under the protection of so prominent a figure, coupled with his obvious talents, it is not surprising that Gregory soon made a place for himself especially in the service of the Church. He rose to the bishopric of Tours in 573 and held it until his death in 594.

It is hard to know how Gregory managed to guide his flock as bishop of Tours for nearly two decades while producing the prodigious amount of writing that he did. The tasks he would have performed as bishop would hardly have ended with the affairs of the Church, and those tasks alone were considerable. But the bishops of Tours—indeed, any bishop in Gaul in the sixth century—also shouldered enormous moral, political, and economic burdens. The bishop was a moral teacher and needed to instruct by example as well as precept. This sometimes proved difficult, owing to the need for bishops also to be astute politicians in the ever-shifting sands of Merovingian politics. At the same time, when not attempting to keep a foothold on those sands, the bishop had to be a clever and careful administrator of the many economic interests at stake in his diocese. And, often enough, bishops were expected to find time for reading, writing, and reflecting. At this Gregory excelled. He seems to have had two interests: in addition to the *Historiae*, which alone would have ensured his reputation, Gregory devoted much time to hagiography and treatises on the miracles of several saints, including *Liber de miraculis Beati Andreae apostoli* and the *Libri octo miraculorum*, which includes well-known treatises on Saint Martin of Tours and the Fathers.

The excerpts show a range of literary styles and historical aims. Gregory modestly tells us in the first passage that he is not well-versed in classical literature and is more a rustic speaker than a philosophizing rhetor. Whether rhetor or rustic, he manages to accomplish a careful balance between competing modes of expression. He can be straightforward, as in the passage on Attila; or dramatic and direct, as in the passage on Clovis. The shifts of his Latin style reflect equally important historical goals. The larger context of the *Historiae* is world history, and initially much attention is paid to the ways in which events have developed since creation. But, as the passage on Clovis makes clear, Frankish history is both important in its own right, but also sensible only within this larger context. Larger-than-life figures such as Attila are made to play on the same historical field as Frankish saints and kings; and when Gregory wants to summarize his narrative on Clovis, he easily calls this important Frankish king a new Constantine.

The *Historiae* has been edited by B. Krusch and W. Levison (*Monumenta Germaniae Historica, Scriptores Rerum Merovingicarum,* vol. 1, Hanover, 1885, repr. 1951); and H. Omont and G. Collon (*Grégoire de Tours: Histoire des Francs,* Paris, 1886–93). There is an excellent English translation in the Penguin Classics by L. Thorpe (*Gregory of Tours: The History of the Franks,* Harmondsworth, 1974) and an older translation by O. M. Dalton also (*The History of the Franks by Gregory of Tours,* 2 vols., Oxford, 1927, repr. 1971). Gregory's Latinity has been exhaustively analyzed by M. Bonnet (*Le Latin de Grégoire de Tours,* Paris, 1890). E. Auerbach has treated the prose style of Gregory (*Literary Language and Its Public in Late Latin Antiquity and in the Middle Ages,* trans. R. Manheim, New York, 1965, chap. 2, pp. 85–179). Goffart 112–234 reconsiders the aims and merits of Gregory's *Historiae,* with full bibliography. The text of Krusch and Levison is reprinted here with minor changes.

Gregory Explains Why He Writes History

Decedente atque immo potius pereunte ab urbibus Gallicanis liberalium cultura litterarum, cum nonnullae res gererentur vel rectae vel inprobae, ac feretas gentium desaeviret, regum furor acueretur, eclesiae inpugnarentur ab hereticis, a catholicis tegerentur, ferveret Christi fides in plurimis, tepisceret in nonnullis, ipsae quoque eclesiae vel ditarentur a   5
devotis vel nudarentur a perfides, nec repperire possit quisquam peritus dialectica in arte grammaticus, qui haec aut stilo prosaico aut metrico depingeret versu: ingemescebant saepius plerique, dicentes: "Vae diebus nostris, quia periit studium litterarum a nobis, nec reperitur rethor in po-

2. **decedente . . . litterarum:** ablative absolute.   3. **feretas** = CL *feritas.*   5. **tepisceret** = CL *tepesceret.*   6. **perfides** = CL *perfidis;* the change from "i" to "e" is common in LL/ML orthography; cf. *repperire* below; § 1.3.   **repperire** = *reperiri,* complementary infinitive of *possit.*   7. **grammaticus:** modified both by *quisquam* and *peritus,* which is a predicate adjective here.   **haec:** neuter plural object of *depingeret.*   9. **rethor** = CL *rhetor.*

pulis, qui gesta praesentia promulgare possit in paginis." Ista etenim atque et his similia iugiter intuens dici pro commemoratione praeteritorum, ut notitiam adtingerint venientum, etsi incultu effatu, nequivi tamen obtegere vel certamena flagitiosorum vel vitam recte viventium; et

5 praesertim his inlicitus stimulis, quod a nostris fari plerumque miratus sum, quia: "Philosophantem rethorem intellegunt pauci, loquentem rusticum multi." Libuit etiam animo, ut pro suppotatione annorum ab ipso mundi principio libri primi poniretur initium, cuius capitula deursum subieci.

—*Hist.* Praef.

Gregory Confesses His Faith and Deplores His Ignorance

Scripturus bella regum cum gentibus adversis, martyrum cum paganis, eclesiarum cum hereticis, prius fidem meam proferre cupio, ut qui ligirit me non dubitet esse catholicum. Illud etiam placuit propter eos, qui adpropinquantem finem mundi disperant, ut, collectam per chronicas vel

5 historias anteriorum annorum summam, explanitur aperte, quanti ab exordio mundi sint anni. Sed prius veniam legentibus praecor, si aut in lit-

2. **et:** superfluous, as often in LL/ML. **dici** = CL *scripsi.* 3. **adtingerint** = CL *attingerent.* **venientum:** i.e., "those yet to come." **incultu** = CL *inculto.* **effatu** = CL *affatu.* 4. **obtegere:** lit., "to hide," "to keep secret"; here, complementary infinitive of *nequivi* = "I have not been able to ignore . . ." **certamena** = CL *certamina.* **vitam:** object of *viventium.* 5. **inlicitus:** false form for *illectus,* perfect passive participle of *illicere;* here in perfect passive indicative, first person singular, without *sum,* meaning something like "I am encouraged . . ." 6. **miratus sum:** governs indirect statement with *quod,* but here, with normal CL construction of verb of perception (*miratus sum*), subject accusative (*plerumque*) and infinitive (*fari*). The sentence is colloquial, an example of VL, and Gregory undoubtedly means to suggest rhetorically the distinction pressed in this sentence between a rustical and a philosophical speaker. **quia** + verb in the indicative (*intellegunt*) = indirect statement, as often in LL/ML (Blaise 261–62); § 7.10. 7. **libuit:** takes a dative object, here *animo,* lit., "It has pleased me . . ." **suppotatione** = CL *supputatione.* 8. **poniretur** = CL *poneretur;* governs *ut* in a purpose clause dependent on *libuit animo.* **deursum** = CL *deorsum.*

1. **martyrum:** *martyr, martyris;* of common gender, this form is genitive plural, parallel with *eclesiarum* and *regum,* all of which depend on *bella.* 3. **ligirit** = CL *legerit;* the substitution of "i" for "e" is common in LL/ML orthography. **placuit:** impersonal verb with *illud* as its subject = "it is important . . ." 4. **adpropinquantem** = CL *appropinquantem.* 5. **collectam . . . summam:** accusative absolute; § 3.3.5 (cf. Blaise 76). **explanitur** = CL *explanetur;* the change of "e" to "i" is common in LL/ML orthography. This is present passive subjunctive with *ut* in a statement of purpose, with impersonal force, "so that it might be explained. . . ." 6. **sint:** subjunctive in indirect question, "how many years there are from the beginning of the world."

teris aut in sillabis grammaticam artem excessero, de qua adplene non sum inbutus; illud tantum studens, ut quod in eclesia credi praedicatur sine aliquo fuco aut cordis hesitatione reteneam, quia scio, peccatis obnoxium per credulitatem puram obtenire posse veniam apud Deum.

—*Hist.* 1 Praef. (excerpts).

THE FOUNDING OF LYONS

Post hos imperator primus Iulius Caesar fuit, qui tutius imperii obtenuit monarchiam; secundus Octavianus, Iulii Caesaris nepus, quem Augustum vocant, a quo et mensis Agustus est vocitatus. Cuius nono decimo imperii anno Lugdunum Galliarum conditam manefestissime repperimus; quae postea, inlustrata martyrum sanguine, nobilissima nuncupatur. 5

—*Hist.* 1.18.

ATTILA THE HUN IN GAUL

Attela vero Chunorum rex a Mittense urbe egrediens, cum multas Galliarum civitates oppraemeret, Aurilianis adgreditur eamque maximo arietum inpulsu nititur expugnare. Erat autem eo tempore beatissimus

1. **sillabis** = CL *syllabis;* the substitution of "i" for "y" is common in LL/ML orthography. **adplene:** "fully," "completely" (Blaise/Chirat 57). 2. **credi:** present passive infinitive of *credere.* 3. **fuco:** from *fucus, i,* "dye," "rouge," from which arises the connotation of "deceit," "stain," "blemish," suggested here.

1. **tutius** = CL *totius;* the substitution of "u" for "o" is common in LL/ML orthography, as with *nepos,* below; § 1.3. 2. **nepus** = CL *nepos.* 3. **Agustus** = CL *Augustus;* the loss of "u" may reflect the orthography of the source from which Gregory was copying his information at this point, Jerome's translation of the chronicle of Eusebius. 4. **conditam:** with understood *esse,* = perfect active infinitive governed by *repperimus,* with subject accusative *Lugdunum. Conditam* is properly neuter singular accusative here, but is feminine either due to a confusion of gender for *Lugdunum,* or by attraction to the idea that it is an *urbs* or a *civitas.* **repperimus:** the subject of the verb is Gregory himself; "and I have been clearly informed that. . . ." 5. **inlustrata** = CL *illustrata,* from *illustrare.* **nobilissima:** agrees with *quae,* modifying an understood *urbs* or *civitas.*

1. **Chunorum** = *Hunorum,* from *Hunni, orum,* the Huns (Sleumer 393). **Mittense:** i.e., Metz. 2. **oppraemeret** = CL *opprimeret,* from *opprimere* here with *cum* causal in the subjunctive. **Aurilianis:** the better spelling is *Aurelianis* = Orleans; Gregory seems to consider this an indeclinable feminine noun, here in the ablative expressing place to which without a preposition (Beeson 19), though *Aurelianis,* from *Aurelianus, a, um,* is technically the adjectival form of *Aurelia, ae,* the better form for Orleans (see Sleumer 140, s. v. *Aurelia*). As often in LL/ML, this construction replaces CL accusative of place to which with *ad* or *in* (cf. AG 426.2). **adgreditur** = CL *aggreditur.* **eamque** = Aurilianis.

Annianus in supradicta urbe episcopus, vir eximiae prudentiae ac laudabilis sanctitatis, cuius virtutum gesta nobiscum fideliter retenentur. Cumque inclusi populi suo pontefice, quid agerent, adclamarent, ille confisus in Deo, monet omnes in oratione prosterni et cum lacrimis praesentem
5 semper in necessitatibus Domini auxilium inplorare. Denique his ut praeciperat depraecantibus, ait sacerdus: "Aspicite de muro civitatis, si Dei miseratio iam succurrat." Suspicabatur enim per Domini misericordiam Aetium advenire, ad quem et Arelate abierat prius suspectus futuri. Aspicientes autem de muro, niminem viderunt. Et ille: "Orate," inquid,
10 "fideliter; Dominus enim liberavit vos hodie!" Orantibus autem illis, ait: "Aspicite iterum!". Et cum aspexissent, niminem viderunt qui ferret auxilium. Ait eis tertio: "Si fideliter petitis, Dominus velociter adest." Ad ille cum fletu et heiulatu magno Domini misericordiam inplorabant. Exactam quoque orationem, tertio iuxta senis imperium aspicientes de muro, viderunt
15 unt a longe quasi nebolam de terra consurgere. Quod renuntiantes, ait sacerdus: "Domini auxilium est." Interea iam trementibus ab impetu arietum muris iamque ruituris, ecce! Aetius et Theodor Gothorum rex ac Thorismodus, filius eius, cum exercitibus suis ad civitatem adcurrunt adversumque hostem eiciunt repelluntque. Itaque liberatam obtentu beati ante-
20 stites civitatem, Attilanem fugant. Qui Mauriacum campum adiens, se praecingit ad bellum. Quod hi audientes, se contra eum viriliter praeparant.

---

2. **virtutum gesta** = *miracula*.   **retenentur** = CL *retinentur*.   3. **pontefice** = CL *pontifice*, synonymous in this passage with *episcopus* = "bishop" and modified by *suo* as the object of *adclamarent*.   **quid agerent**: indirect question with *adclamarent*.   **adclamarent** = CL *acclamarent*, with dative object.   4. **prosterni**: present passive infinitive of *prosternere*, parallel with *inplorare*, both dependent on *monet* in indirect statement. **praesentem**: more properly *praesens*, modifying *auxilium*.   5. **inplorare** = CL *implorare*.   6. **depraecantibus** = CL *deprecantibus*, with *his* in ablative absolute.   **sacerdus** = CL *sacerdos;* the form shows the characteristic substitution of "u" for "o" in LL/ML orthography; § 1.3.   8. **Arelate**: from *Arelate, is* = Arles (Sleumer 124). 9. **niminem** = CL *neminem*, showing a characteristic vowel change in LL/ML orthography.   **ille** = Annianus.   **inquid** = CL *inquit*.   12. **Ad ille** = CL *At illi*.   13. **heiulatu** = CL *eiulatu* from *eiulare*, here in supine as ablative of specification.   **inplorabant** = CL *implorabant*.   **exactam . . . orationem**: accusative absolute; § 3.3.5 (Blaise 76).   15. **nebolam** = CL *nebulam*, here the subject accusative of *consurgere*, dependent on *viderunt*.   **quod** = CL *cum* in temporal construction: "when they reported this to Annianus. . . ."   19. **eiciunt** = CL *eiiciunt*.   **obtentu**: ablative of means = "by the intercession of. . . ."   **antestites** = CL *antistitis*.   **liberatam . . . civitatem**: accusative absolute; § 3.3.5 (Blaise 76).   20. **Attilanem**: the best spelling of Attila's name is *Attila, ae* (Sleumer 136), but the forms are various, even within these passages.   **Mauriacum**: i.e., the plain of Moirey.

Igitur Aetius cum Gothis Francisque coniunctus adversus Attilanem confligit. At ille ad internitionem vastari suum cernens exercitum, fuga delabitur. Theodor vero Gothorum rex huic certamine subcubuit. Nam nullus ambigat, Chunorum exercitum obtentu memorati antestites fuisse fugatum. Verum Aetius patritius cum Thorismodo victuriam obtinuit hostesque delivit. Expletoque bello, ait Aetius Thorismodo: "Festina velociter redire in patriam, ne insistente germano a patris regno priveris." Haec ille audiens, cum velocitate discessit, quasi antecipaturus fratrem et prior patris cathedram adepturus. Simili et Francorum regem dolo fugavit. Illis autem recedentibus, Aetius, spoliato campo, victor in patriam cum grande est reversus spolia. Attila vero cum paucis reversus est, nec multo post Aquileia a Chunis capta, incensa atque deruta, Italia pervagata atque subversa est. Thorismodus cui supra meminimus, Alanos bello edomuit, ipse deinceps post multas lites et bella a fratribus oppraessus ac iugulatus interiit. 5

10

15

—*Hist.* 2.7 (excerpts).

CLOVIS DEFEATS THE ALAMANNI AND
ACCEPTS CHRISTIANITY

Regina vero non cessabat praedicare, ut Deum verum cognusceret et idola neglegerit. Sed nullo modo ad haec credenda poterat commoveri, donec tandem aliquando bellum contra Alamannos conmoveretur, in quo conpulsus est confiteri necessitate, quod prius voluntate negaverat. Fac-

---

2. **ille:** i.e., Attila. **vastari:** present passive infinitive of *vastare,* takes *suum exercitum* as its subject and depends on *cernens* in indirect statement. 3. **Theodor:** the better spelling is *Theodoricus, i* = Theodoric, King of the Ostrogoths (Sleumer 778), but the forms are various in these passages. **huic certamine:** *certamine* may be a false form for *certamini,* which is the simplest construction with the verb, meaning something like "Theodoric succumbed to this battle." It is possible, however, that *certamine* is ablative of place where, with *huic* referring to Attila (i.e., "Theodoric succumbed to Attila in this battle"). **subcubuit** = CL *succumbuit;* the omission of the parasitic consonant "m" is common in LL/ML. 4. **memorati:** i.e., "of the aforementioned. . . ." 5. **patritius** = CL *patricius.* **victuriam** = CL *victoriam.* 6. **delivit** = CL *delevit.* 7. **insistente** = CL *insistenti.* 8. **antecipaturus** = CL *antecepturus.* 9. **fugavit:** the subject here is once again Aetius. 11. **spolia:** with *cum grande* the CL form = *spolio.* **nec multo post:** i.e., "not much time later. . . ." 12. **Chunis:** from *Hunni, orum* = the Huns (Sleumer 393), here in ablative plural governed by the preposition *a.* **deruta** = CL *diruta,* from *diruere.* 13. **cui supra meminimus:** CL would have *quem memoratus sum.* 14. **oppraessus** = CL *oppressus,* from *opprimere.*

1. **Regina:** i.e., Queen Clotilda. **praedicare:** i.e., "praying." **cognusceret** = CL *cognosceret.* 4. **conpulsus** = CL *compulsus.*

tum est autem, ut confligente utroque exercitu vehementer caederentur, atque exercitus Chlodovechi valde ad internitionem ruere coepit. Quod ille videns, elevatis ad caelum oculis, conpunctus corde, commotus in lacrimis, ait: "Iesu Christi, quem Chrotchildis praedicat esse filium Dei vivi,
5 qui dare auxilium laborantibus victuriamque in te sperantibus tribuere diceris, tuae opis gloriam devotus efflagito, ut, si mihi victuriam super hos hostes indulseris et expertus fuero illam virtutem, quam de te populus tuo nomine dicatus probasse se praedicat, credam tibi et in nomine tuo baptizer. Invocavi enim deos meos, sed, ut experior, elongati sunt ab auxi-
10 lio meo; unde credo, eos nullius esse potestatis praeditos, qui sibi oboedientibus non occurrunt. Te nunc invoco, tibi credere desidero, tantum ut eruar ab adversariis meis." Cumque haec diceret, Alamanni terga vertentes, in fugam labi coeperunt. Cumque regem suum cernirent interemptum, Chlodovechi se ditionibus subdunt, dicentes: "Ne amplius, quaesu-
15 mus, pereat populus, iam tui sumus." Ad ille, prohibito bello, cohortato populo cum pace regressus, narravit reginae, qualiter per invocationem nominis Christi victuriam meruit obtenire. Actum anno 15 regni sui.

Tunc regina arcessire clam sanctum Remedium Remensis urbis episcopum iubet, depraecans, ut regi verbum salutis insinuaret. Quem sac-
20 erdos arcessitum secritius coepit ei insinuare, ut Deum verum, factorem caeli ac terrae, crederit, idola neglegerit, quae neque sibi neque aliis prodesse possunt. At ille ait: "Libenter te, sanctissime pater, audiebam; sed restat unum, quod populus, qui me sequitur, non patitur relinquere deus suos; sed vado et loquor eis iuxta verbum tuum." Conveniens autem cum
25 suis, priusquam ille loqueretur, praecurrente potentia Dei, omnes populus pariter adclamavit: "Mortalis deus abigimus, pie rex, et Deum quem Re-

2. **Chlodovechi:** from *Chlodovechus, i* = King Clovis.   4. **Chrotchildis:** from *Chrot-childis, is* = Queen Clotilda.   5. **victuriamque** = CL *victoriamque,* as in the subsequent line.   9. **baptizer:** present passive subjunctive, with *credam,* in future more vivid construction.   13. **cernirent** = CL *cernerent.* **interemptum:** from *interimere.* 14. **quaesumus** = CL *quaesimus.*   15. **ad** = CL *at.*   18. **Remedium:** from *Remedius, i* = Remigius, bishop of Rheims.   **Remensis:** the better spelling is *Rhemensis, e* = Rheims; the form used here by Gregory is actually the adjectival form; the substantive = *Rhemi, orum* (cf. Sleumer 675 on these forms).   19. **depraecans** = CL *deprecans,* from *deprecari.*   20. **arcessitum:** from *arcessere.* **secritius** = CL *secretius,* comparative adverb modifying *arcessitum.*   21. **crederit** = CL *crederet.* **neglegerit** = CL *neglegeret.* **sibi** = *ei.*   22. **ille:** i.e., Clovis.   23. **deus** = CL *deos.*   24. **vado et loquor:** both *vado* (*vadere*) and *loquor,* though in the present indicative here, have the force of future tense, as often in CL (AG 468).   25. **omnes** = CL *omnis.*   26. **adclamavit** = CL *acclamavit.* **Remegius:** Gregory is not consistent in the spelling of Remigius's name, perhaps a reflection of the different orthographies of his sources or, more likely, a result of scribal error.

megius praedicat inmortalem sequi parati sumus." Nuntiantur haec ante-
stiti, qui gaudio magno repletus, iussit lavacrum praeparari. Velis depictis
adumbrantur plateae, eclesiae curtinis albentibus adurnantur, baptistirium conponitur, balsama difunduntur, micant flagrantes odorem cerei,
totumque templum baptistirii divino respergetur ab odore, talemque ibi   5
gratiam adstantibus Deus tribuit, ut aestimarent se paradisi odoribus col-
locari. Rex ergo prior poposcit, se a pontifeci baptizare. Procedit novos
Constantinus ad lavacrum, deleturus leprae veteris morbum sordentesque
maculas gestas antiquitus recenti latice deleturus. Cui ingresso ad bap-
tismum sanctus Dei sic infit ore facundo: "Mitis depone colla, Sigamber;   10
adora quod incendisti, incende quod adorasti." Erat autem sanctus Remegius episcopus egregiae scientiae et rethoricis adprimum inbutus studiis, sed et sanctitate ita praelatus, ut sancti Silvestri virtutebus equaretur.
Est enim nunc liber vitae eius, qui eum narrat mortuum suscitasse. Igitur
rex omnipotentem Deum in Trinitate confessus, baptizatus in nomine   15
Patris et Filii et Spiritus sancti delebutusque sacro crismate cum signaculo
crucis Christi. De exercito vero eius baptizati sunt amplius tria milia.

—*Hist.* 2.30–31 (excerpts).

1. **inmortalem** = CL *immortalem.* 2. **lavacrum:** i.e., baptismal font. 3. **curtinis** =
CL *cortinis,* "curtain." **adurnantur** = CL *adornantur.* **baptistirium** = CL *baptister-*
ium. 4. **conponitur** = CL *componitur.* **cerei:** the subject of *micant,* with *flagrantes*
odorem dependent on it. 5. **respergetur** = CL *respergitur.* **ab:** superfluous.
6. **paradisi:** dependent on *odoribus.* Gregory may mean to summon the CL idiom *se*
collocare "to settle in a place," making this phrase read something like "so that they
judged themselves settled in sweet-smelling paradise." 7. **pontifeci** = CL *pontifice.*
novos = CL *novus.* 9. **gestas:** from *gerere,* here a predicate adjective modified by the
adverb *antiquitus.* 10. **mitis:** with adverbial force = *mite,* "meekly." **Sigamber:** the
general title taken by the Merovingian kings, indicating their mythic origins from the
Sigambri, an ancient German people. 11. **adorasti:** syncopated perfect active indicative, second person singular of *adorare* = *adoravisti.* 12. **adprimum** = CL *apprime,*
"chiefly." 13. **Silvestri:** from *Silvester, tri* = Saint Sylvester, pope 314–335, cured
Constantine of leprosy, and received power over the western church and empire in
return from a thankful emperor. This story is the basis of the so-called Donation of
Constantine, a document of the Carolingian period claiming to be in Constantine's
hand, which granted to the pope supreme political power in the West. **virtutebus** =
CL *virtutibus.* **equaretur** = CL *aequaretur.* 14. **liber:** Gregory probably refers here
to the life of Remigius written by the contemporary poet and hagiographer, Venantius
Fortunatus (see the next section). **suscitasse:** syncopated perfect active infinitive =
suscitavisse. 16. **delebutusque** = CL *delibutusque.* **crismate:** the better spelling is
chrismate, from *chrisma, atis* = "anointing" (Niermeyer 177), dependent on *delibutus*
and modified by *sacro* = "he was baptized."

VENANTIUS FORTUNATUS

Hymns; Poems to Gogo, Agnes, and Radegund
(*Carmina;* c. 575–595)

Venantius Honorius Clementianus Fortunatus was born at Duplavis, near Treviso around 535 and spent his childhood there, before moving to Ravenna to further his education. Ravenna was still an important city when Fortunatus came to it, in the mid 550s, having benefited from the patronage of Theodoric the Ostrogoth, who had made it his capital city in the late fifth century. The Ostrogothic legacy lived on in the city in the contacts enjoyed with the Greek East, in the architecture and literary culture fostered by the Church, and in the opportunities, even in the decades of the Justinianic wars, for advancement and betterment.

Fortunatus presumably took a full course of studies in Ravenna, which included work in the Latin classics and in Greek. He remained in Ravenna until the mid 560s. He reports that he left Italy for parts north and west to make good a vow to Saint Martin to make a pilgrimage to Tours if the saint would intercede on his behalf and restore his failing eyesight, a restoration which occurred soon thereafter. Another reason for Fortunatus's departure may have been the continually deteriorating political situation in northern Italy—although that situation had never been anything but bad in the poet's lifetime. A third reason may ring truest of all: the poet left in search of adventure.

Whatever the reasons, the poet traveled over the Alps and arrived first at Mainz and then at Cologne, duly celebrating his visits to these important cities with accomplished poems. He then made his way to Treves. At Metz, Fortunatus lingered for over a year, becoming intimate with Sigibert, king of the Austrasian Franks, for whose marriage to Brunhilde the poet composed an epithalamium. While at Metz, too, Fortunatus made the acquaintance of Gogo, Sigibert's aide-de-camp, a friendship which lasted a considerable time and which the poet celebrates in erotic terms in several poems. Fortunatus eventually left Metz for Paris and then made his way southward to Tours. In 567 he arrived in Poitiers after making good on his vow to visit Saint Martin's tomb at Tours. At Poitiers, Fortunatus met Agnes and Radegund, the two remarkable women with whom he spent a good portion of the rest of his life. Agnes was abbess at the religious community founded by Radegund, who had fled from her husband, Clothar, the Frankish chieftain (after he had murdered her brother) in order to pursue a life of spiritual devotion and solitude. Radegund and Agnes seem both to have died by 590, for early in that decade Fortunatus became a priest. In 597 he was elected bishop of Poitiers. He died around 600.

The poetry of Fortunatus is varied as to theme, topic, meter, and style, and the poems excerpted here give a sense of that variety. Among the more interesting are the poems written to Agnes (11.5, 11.6), where spiritual concerns are kept carefully in balance by the erotic undertones of the poet's language. No less impressive for verbal and tonal authority are the two hymns reprinted here (2.2, 2.6), justly praised for the careful ways they portray their topic and the vivid personalization of the Crucifixion in time and place.

The poetry of Fortunatus has been edited by F. Leo (*Monumenta Germaniae Historica, Auctores Antiquissimi*, vol. 4, Berlin, 1881) and, most recently, by M. Reydellet in the Budé series (*Venance Fortunat, Poèmes*, 4 vols., Paris, 1994; with facing French translation and Latin text). G. Cook has translated a few of the poems into English (*From the Miscellanea of Venantius Fortunatus: A Basket of Chestnuts*, Rhinebeck, N. Y., 1981). Raby 1, pp. 86ff., discusses much of the poetry of Fortunatus. J. George has written an extensive consideration of the secular and occasional poetry, with a full bibliography and an up-to-date consideration of the social, political, and personal aspects of Fortunatus's poetry (*Venantius Fortunatus: A Latin Poet in Merovingian Gaul*, Oxford, 1992). Leo's text is reprinted without change.

To Radegund in Retreat

Regali de stirpe potens Radegundis in orbe,
    altera cui caelis regna tenenda manent,
despiciens mundum meruisti adquirere Christum,
    et dum clausa lates, hinc super astra vides.
gaudia terreni conculcas noxia regni,   5

The poem is written in elegiac couplets. 1. **Radegundis:** from *Radegundis, is* = Radegund, daughter of King Berthar of Thuringia and formerly queen of Clothar I (who won her as booty), she founded the Convent of the Holy Cross at Poitiers, to which Fortunatus became attached, though not in a religious capacity, in the 570s. Radegund and Fortunatus were close friends, as this poem attests. Note that the first letters of each line of the poem spell out Radegund's name. 2. **caelis:** ablative of place where, without a preposition. **manent:** the thought in this couplet is concessive. 3. **adquirere** = CL *acquirere*. 4. **dum . . . hinc:** "as long as" . . . "from there. . . ." 5. **regni:** notice the chiastic structure of this line.

ut placeas regi laeta favente polo.
nunc angusta tenes, quo caelos largior intres:
   diffundens lacrimas gaudia vera metes.
et corpus crucias, animam ieiunia pascunt,
10   solo quam dominus servat amore suus.

—Carm. 8.5.

To Radegund: On Violets

Tempora si solito mihi candida lilia ferrent
   aut speciosa foret suave rubore rosa,
haec ego rure legens aut caespite pauperis horti
   misissem magnis munera parva libens.
5   sed quia prima mihi desunt, vel solvo secunda:
      profert qui vicias, ferret amore rosas.
inter odoriferas tamen has quas misimus herbas
   purpureae violae nobile germen habent.
respirant pariter regali murice tinctae
10   et saturat foliis hinc odor, inde decor.
hae quod utrumque gerunt pariter habeatis utraque,
   et sit mercis odor flore perenne decus.

—Carm. 8.6.

6. **regi:** i.e., Deo. **favente polo:** i.e., "in the favor of God" (lit., "with heaven inclined"). 7. **nunc angusta tenes:** i.e., "now you are close-confined" (lit., "now you are holding narrow places"); as this and other verses make clear, Radegund is in cloistered retreat, probably for Lent. **largior:** i.e., "fuller," "richer." **quo . . . intres:** Fortunatus follows here the CL construction which deploys a relative clause of purpose introduced by *quo* (= *quo eo*) with a comparative (AG 531.2a).

The poem is written in elegiac couplets. 1. **tempora:** i.e., Spring. **solito:** adverb, "normally." **ferrent:** imperfect active subjunctive in contrary-to-fact condition, with *foret* in v. 2. 2. **speciosa:** predicate adjective with *rosa*. **foret** = alternate form for *esset*. 4. **misissem:** apodosis of the condition in pluperfect subjunctive, expressing time past relative to the imperfect verbs of the protasis, "I would have sent. . . ." **magnis:** i.e., *muneribus;* presumably this poem is sent, with violets, in thanks for some "greater" gifts. 5. **prima:** i.e., *candida lilia.* **vel . . . secunda:** *vel* is an intensive particle with no alternative force here, meaning something like "even"; *solvo* (*solvere*) means something like "lost" or "lack"; *secunda* = *speciosa rosa.* 8. **germen:** i.e., "bud," "shoot." The idea is that the violet is not as obviously beautiful as the rose or the lily because it is smaller. But, as vv. 9–10 suggest, its smell (*odor*) compensates for its stature. 10. **foliis:** i.e., *viciae*, object of *saturat;* the idea is that among the *viciae* he has sent are violets. 11. **hae:** i.e., *viciae* and *violae.* **utrumque:** modifies *odor*, i.e., the *viciae* and *violae* bear the odor of each other equally (*pariter*). **habeatis utraque:** "what you have with either"; an indirect question. The line is difficult: "For both bear the odor equally which you have with either." 12. **mercis:** from *merx, mercis,*

To Radegund at Lent

Mens fecunda deo, Radegundis, vita sororum,
　quae ut foveas animam membra domando cremas:
annua vota colens hodie claudenda recurris:
　errabunt animi te repetendo mei.
lumina quam citius nostris abscondis ocellis!　　　　　　　5
　nam sine te nimium nube premente gravor.
omnibus exclusis uno retineberis antro:
　nos magis includis, quos facis esse foris.
et licet huc lateas brevibus fugitiva diebus,
　longior hic mensis quam celer annus erit.　　　　　　　10
tempora subducis, ceu non videaris amanti,
　cum vos dum cerno hoc mihi credo parum.
sed tamen ex voto tecum veniemus in unum
　et sequor huc animo quo vetat ire locus.
hoc precor, incolumem referant te gaudia paschae,　　　　15
　et nobis pariter lux geminata redit.

—Carm. 8.9.

To Radegund on Her Return

Unde mihi rediit radianti lumine vultus?
　quae nimis absentem te tenuere morae?
abstuleras tecum, revocas mea gaudia tecum,

---

here meaning something like the *munera* of v. 4. Picking up the theme of the worthiness of the violets suggested in v. 10 (*inde decor*), here the poet enjoins the recipient of his gift to consider its smell (*odor mercis*) worthy (*sit decus*) because its flower is perennial (*flore perenne*)—this is a gift that will last for the seasons, a thought that returns the reader to the first word of the poem, *tempora*.

The poem is written in elegiac couplets. 2. **domando:** i.e., "by fasting" (lit., "by conquering," "subduing," "vanquishing"). 3. **annua vota:** i.e., Lent. **claudenda recurris:** i.e., "you return to your cloistered retreat" (lit., "you return to places that must be enclosed, cut off, etc. (*claudere*)"; *claudenda*, in passive periphrastic construction, suggests the necessity of retreat attending to the observances of Lent. 8. **foris:** adverb. 9. **licet:** with a subjunctive verb (*lateas*) = "although." **huc:** i.e., "in this place of retreat." 10. **hic:** parallel with *huc*, "here where we are. . . ." 11. **ceu:** i.e., "as if." 15. **paschae:** from *paschae, ae* = Easter (LS 1311), here dependent on *gaudia*.

The poem is written in elegiac couplets. 2. **quae:** modifies *morae*, the subject of *tenuere*. **tenuere:** alternate perfect active indicative, third person plural of *tenere* = *tenuerunt*. 3. **abstuleras:** from *afferre*.

paschalemque facis bis celebrare diem.
5   quamvis incipiant modo surgere semina sulcis,
         hic egomet hodie te revidendo meto.
colligo iam fruges, placidos conpono maniplos:
         quod solet Augustus mensis, Aprilis agit;
et licet in primis modo gemma et pampinus exit,
10   iam meus autumnus venit et uva simul.
malus et alta pirus gratos modo fundit odores,
         sed cum flore novo iam mihi poma ferunt.
quamvis nudus ager nullis ornetur aristis,
         omnia plena tamen te redeunte nitent.

—*Carm.* 8.10.

To Absent Agnes

Dulce decus nostrum, Christi sanctissima virgo,
         Agnes quae meritis inmaculata manes:
sic tibi conplacuit hodiernum ducere tempus,
         ut mihi nec solitam distribuisses opem?
5   nec dare nunc dominae modulamina dulcia linguae,
         cui dum verba refers pascitur ore tuo?
abstinuisse cibis etiam vos ipse probavi
         et quasi pro vobis est mihi facta fames.
audio, somnus iners radiantes pressit ocellos;
10   an nimias noctes anticipare volis?
cui non sufficiant haec tempora longa quietis,

4. **paschalemque:** from *paschalis, e* = "pertaining to Easter" (LS 1311). 5. **incipiant:** present subjunctive with *quamvis,* in hortatory construction expressing concession (AG 440). 6. **meto:** *semina* is the understood object. 7. **placidos:** i.e., "ripe." **conpono** = CL *compono.* **maniplos** = CL *manipulos* (from *manipulus, i*). 9. **licet:** conjunction = "even if." **in primis modo:** i.e., "just now, in the first weeks of Spring. . . ." **exit:** though *gemma* and *pampinus* are a plural subject, the number of the verb is singular. 11. **malus:** the "a" of this form is long. 12. **ferunt:** the subjects are *malus et alta pirus.* 13. **ornetur:** present subjunctive with *quamvis* in hortatory construction expressing concession, as in v. 5. 14. **plena:** predicate adjective.

    The poem is written in elegiac couplets. 2. **Agnes:** abbess of the convent of the Holy Cross at Poitiers and close friend and confidante of Radegund, she was also, as this poem attests, well known to Fortunatus. **inmaculata** = CL *immaculata.* 5. **dominae:** i.e., Radegund. **modulamina dulcia linguae:** i.e., poems. 6. **cui:** i.e., Radegund (*domina*). 7. **cibis:** ablative of separation. **probavi:** i.e., "I have heard"; governs indirect statement here. 8. **fames:** i.e., "a fast," taking up the idea of v. 7. 10. **volis:** false form for *vultis,* sometimes spelled *voltis.*

cum prope nox teneat quod duplicata dies?
nubila cuncta tegunt, nec luna nec astra videntur;
si sis laeta animo, me nebulae fugiunt.
gaudia vera colat quae nos haec scribere iussit   15
et tecum faveat ducta sub arce poli.

—*Carm.* 11.5.

ON THE POET'S LOVE FOR AGNES

Mater honore mihi, soror autem dulcis amore,
   quam pietate fide pectore corde colo,
caelesti affectu, non crimine corporis ullo:
   non caro, sed hoc quod spiritus optat amo.
testis adest Christus, Petro Pauloque ministris,   5
   cumque piis sociis sancta Maria videt,
te mihi non aliis oculis animoque fuisse,
   quam soror ex utero tu Titiana fores,
ac si uno partu mater Radegundis utrosque,
   visceribus castis progenuisset, eram,   10
et tamquam pariter nos ubera cara beatae
   pavissent uno lacte fluente duos.
heu mea damna gemo, tenui ne forte susurro
   impediant sensum noxia verba meum;
sed tamen est animus simili me vivere voto,   15
   si vos me dulci vultis amore coli.

—*Carm.* 11.6.

15. **quae:** i.e., Radegund.
The poem is written in elegiac couplets. 1. **honore . . . amore:** ablatives of specification. 7. **fuisse:** the idiom is *esse in oculis*, i.e., "to be loved," negated here and dependent on *videt* in indirect statement: "holy Mary sees that you were not loved by me in other ways (*aliis*) in my heart. . . ." 8. **Titiana:** from *Titiana, ae,* apparently the real sister of Fortunatus. **quam . . . fores:** i.e., "than were you . . ." (or, "than if you were . . ."); *fores = esses*. 9. **Radegundis:** nominative singular feminine, in apposition with *mater*. 10. **progenuisset:** pluperfect active subjunctive in a contrary-to-fact condition. **eram:** the apodosis of the condition begun in v. 9, "thus I was to you. . . ." In the apodosis of a contrary-to-fact condition, the past tenses of the indicative may be used to express actual intention (AG 517b). 11. **beatae:** i.e., "of blessed Radegund." 12. **duos:** modifies *nos* in the previous line. 13. **tenui:** *tenuis, e,* modifying *susurro.* **ne:** with *impediant* = a negative purpose clause qualifying the main clause, *heu mea damna gemo.* 15. **est animus:** this idiom means "it is my intention," and governs indirect statement. 16. **coli:** present passive infinitive of *colere*, in indirect statement governed by *vultis.*

A POEM TO ABSENT FRIENDS

Quae carae matri, quae dulci verba sorori
solus in absenti cordis amore loquar?
quas locus excludit mens anxia voce requirit
et simul ut videat per pia vota rogat.
5   te peto, cara soror, matri pietate benigna
quod minus inpendi tu famulare velis.
illa decens tecum longo mihi vivat in aevo
et tribus in Christo sit precor una salus.
nos neque nunc praesens nec vita futura sequestret,
10   sed tegat una salus et ferat una dies.
hic tamen, ut cupio, vos tempora longa reservent,
ut soror et mater sit mihi certa quies.

—*Carm.* 11.7.

TO GOGO OF METZ

Nectar vina cibus vestis doctrina facultas —
muneribus largis tu mihi, Gogo, sat es;
tu refluus Cicero, tu noster Apicius extas:
hinc satias verbis, pascis et inde cibis.
5   sed modo da veniam: bubla turgente quiesco,
nam fit lis uteri, si caro mixta fremat.
hic, ubi bos recubat, fugiet puto pullus et anser:
cornibus et pinnis non furor aequus erit.
et modo iam somno languentia lumina claudo:
10   nam dormire meum carmina lenta probant.

—*Carm.* 7.2.

The poem is written in elegiac couplets. 6. **inpendi** = CL *impendi*. **famulare** = CL *famulari*; the complementary infinitive of *velis*, with *matri* the dative object. LL/ML has the form *famulare*, which has the specialized meaning "to enslave" (cf. Blaise/Chirat 345, s. v. *famulo* 2), but the more common meaning, as here, is "to serve."

The poem is written in elegiac couplets. 1. **nectar . . . facultas:** nominatives in apposition with Gogo, the addressee of the poem, a close friend and official in the court of Sigibert of Metz, whom the poet met when he was at Metz in the 560s. 3. **Apicius:** a famous gourmand in the Augustan period, whose name is given to a lengthy imperial cookbook. **extas** = CL *exstas*, but here, as often in LL/ML = *es*. 5. **bubla** = CL *bubula*. 10. **dormire:** here used as a noun, with *meum* modifying it.

TO RADEGUND: ON FLOWERS

O regina potens, aurum cui et purpura vile est,
    floribus ex parvis te veneratur amans.
et si non res est, color est tamen ipsa per herbas:
    purpura per violas, aurea forma crocus.
dives amore dei vitasti praemia mundi: 5
    illas contemnens has retinebis opes.
suscipe missa tibi variorum munera florum,
    ad quos te potius vita beata vocat.
quae modo te crucias, recreanda in luce futura,
    aspicis hinc qualis te retinebit ager.   10
per ramos fragiles quos nunc praebemus olentes
    perpende hinc quantus te refovebit odor.
haec cui debentur precor ut, cum veneris illuc,
    meque tuis meritis dextera blanda trahat.
quamvis te expectet paradisi gratia florum,   15
    isti vos cupiunt iam revidere foris.
et licet egregio videantur odore placere,
    plus ornant proprias te redeunte comas.

—Carm. 8.8.

THE POET SENDS CHESTNUTS

Ista meis manibus fiscella est vimine texta:
    credite mi, carae, mater et alma soror;
et quae rura ferunt, hic rustica dona ministro,
    castaneas molles, quas dedit arbor agris.

—Carm. 11.13.

The poem is written in elegiac couplets. 1. **regina:** i.e., Radegund. 2. **amans:** i.e., Fortunatus. 5. **vitasti:** syncopated perfect active indicative, second person singular of *vitare* = *vitavisti.* 7. **missa:** predicate adjective, modifying *munera.* 13. **illuc:** i.e., "to that place"; the antecedent of the preceding *cui.* 14. **trahat:** read with *ut* in a result clause. 15. **expectet** = CL *exspectet.* 16. **isti:** i.e., *flores;* the idea is that Radegund is in retreat, concentrating on heavenly and spiritual beauties, while she ignores the beauty of the world, a reflection, in Fortunatus's view, of the world yet to come. 17. **videantur:** i.e., *isti.*
    The poem is written in elegiac couplets. 2. **mater . . . soror:** the poem is written to Radegund (*mater*) and Agnes (*soror*); hence the vocative plural, *carae. Mi* is the alternate dative singular form of *ego.*

VEXILLA REGIS PRODEUNT

Vexilla regis prodeunt,
fulget crucis mysterium,
quo carne carnis conditor
suspensus est patibulo.
5 Confixa clavis viscera
tendens manus, vestigia
redemptionis gratia
hic inmolata est hostia.
Quo vulneratus insuper
10 mucrone diro lanceae,
ut nos lavaret crimine,
manavit unda et sanguine.
Inpleta sunt quae concinit
David fideli carmine,
15 dicendo nationibus:
regnavit a ligno deus.
Arbor decora et fulgida,
ornata regis purpura,
electa digno stipite
20 tam sancta membra tangere!
Beata cuius brachiis
pretium pependit saeculi!
statera facta est corporis
praedam tulitque Tartari.

This hymn is in iambic dimeter. 1. **Vexilla:** appropriately for an Easter hymn, the *vexillum* was the red flag placed on the general's tent as a signal for marching to battle (LS 1984). 3. **quo:** modifies *patibulo,* in v. 4. **carne:** ablative of specification with *suspensus est.* 5. **clavis:** the "i" is long. 6. **tendens:** i.e., *crux.* 8. **inmolata** = CL *immolata.* 9. **quo:** modifies *mucrone diro* in v. 10 and is parallel with *quo* in v. 3. 13. **inpleta** = CL *impleta.* **quae:** i.e., "the things which David sang. . . ." 16. **a ligno:** cf. Ps. 95.10, which, in the early Latin versions based on the Greek Septuagint, added these two words to the verse. 18. **regis purpura:** both the blood of Christ apropos of the real cross, and also a reference to the veiling of the cross in deep red or purple during the two weeks before Easter. 19. **digno stipite:** "by your worthy lineage"; Christians believed that the cross on which Christ was crucified came from a tree descended from the Tree of Knowledge. The story is treated more fully by Fortunatus in his other Easter hymn, "Pange, lingua," below. 20. **tangere:** infinitive of purpose with *electa,* with *tam sancta membra* the object. 23. **statera:** literally "a balance" or "goldsmith's scales," here it means something more like "value." 24. **Tartari:** from *Tartarus, i;* in CL = the lower reaches of Hades, but here, as is common in LL/ML = Hell.

Fundis aroma cortice,   25
vincis sapore nectare,
iucunda fructu fertili
plaudis triumpho nobili.
Salve ara, salve victima
de passionis gloria,   30
qua vita mortem pertulit
et morte vitam reddidit.

—*Carm.* 2.6.

PANGE, LINGUA, GLORIOSI

Pange, lingua, gloriosi proelium certaminis
et super crucis tropaeo dic triumphum nobilem,
qualiter redemptor orbis immolatus vicerit.
De parentis protoplasti fraude factor condolens,
quando pomi noxialis morte morsu conruit,   5
ipse lignum tunc notavit, damna ligni ut solveret.
Hoc opus nostrae salutis ordo depoposcerat,
multiformis perditoris arte ut artem falleret
et medellam ferret inde, hostis unde laeserat.
Quando venit ergo sacri plenitudo temporis,   10

25. **aroma:** neuter accusative singular, object of *fundis.*   26. **vincis . . . nectare:** *vincis* here has the sense of "outdo," with *nectare* its object in neuter accusative singular. 27. **iucunda:** i.e., *arbor.*   28. **plaudis:** takes a dative object.   31. **qua:** refers to *passio* in v. 30.   **vita:** "life" in the literal sense, but also more specifically a reference to Christ, who is characterized as *vita* at John 11.25.

This hymn is written in trochaic septenarii. 1. **proelium certaminis:** the two words are virtually synonymous. *Certamen* is perhaps more abstract; in post-Augustan historians it invariably means "war" (cf. Eutropius 1.16, e.g.). *Proelium* is perhaps more concrete, suggestive of a military campaign. The modifier *gloriosi* affirms these senses, linked as it is to *certamen,* which suggests the wider and more abstract battles of heart, mind, soul. 2. **super:** here a preposition + ablative. 4. **protoplasti:** *protoplastus, a, um,* from the Greek, προτοπλαστὸς, "first-formed," here modifying *parentis;* the phrase refers to Adam. 5. **morte:** ablative of specification with *conruit.* **morsu:** ablative of means, with *pomi noxialis* dependent on it. **conruit** = CL *corruit.* 6. **lignum:** i.e., the Tree of Knowledge. 7. **hoc opus:** object of *depoposcerat,* referring to the Crucifixion; in EL it has the meaning of "miracle" (cf. John 5.36, 7.21, 14.10; Cyprian *Ep.* 18.2; Matt. 5.16). 8. **arte:** ablative of means. **artem:** object of *falleret,* with *multiformis perditoris* dependent on it. **falleret:** the subject is *factor condolens* from v. 4. 9. **inde:** i.e., "from there"; the reference is to the Tree of Knowledge in the Garden of Eden. **hostis:** i.e., Satan, the subject of this clause. **unde:** i.e., "from which."

missus est ab arce patris natus orbis conditor
atque ventre virginali carne factus prodiit.
Vagit infans inter arta conditus praesepia,
    membra pannis involuta virgo mater adligat
15   et pedes manusque, crura stricta pingit fascia.
Lustra sex qui iam peracta tempus inplens corporis,
    se volente natus ad hoc, passioni deditus
    agnus in crucis levatur immolandus stipite.
Hic acetum fel harundo sputa clavi lancea,
20   mite corpus perforatur, sanguis, unda profluit,
    terra pontus astra mundus quo lavantur flumine.
Crux fidelis, inter omnes arbor una nobilis
    (nulla talem silva profert flore fronde germine),
    dulce lignum, dulce clavo dulce pondus sustinens!
25 Flecte ramos, arbor alta, tensa laxa viscera,
    et rigor lentescat ille quem dedit nativitas,
    ut superni membra regis mite tendas stipite.
Sola digna tu fuisti ferre pretium saeculi
    atque portum praeparare nauta mundo naufrago
30   quem sacer cruor perunxit fusus agni corpore.

—Carm. 2.2.

11. **natus:** predicate adjective. 12. **ventre virginali:** ablative of separation with *prodiit.* **carne:** ablative of specification with *factus.* 13. **arta:** i.e., "small." 14. **pannis involuta:** i.e., "wrapped in rags." **adligat** = CL *alligat.* 16. **qui:** i.e., *agnus.* **lustra . . . peracta:** nominative absolute; § 3.3.1 (cf. Blaise 67). 17. **se volente:** referring ablative absolute which refers, as often in LL/ML, to the subject of the main clause. 24. **dulce** = CL *dulci,* although this form could also be an adverb. 25. **laxa:** imperative. 26. **nativitas:** "nature." 29. **praeparare:** complementary infinitive with *fuisti.* **nauta:** in apposition with *tu* in v. 28. The image of the Church as a ship, with the Cross as mast, and the world represented by the stormy seas, is common in EL.

GREGORY I

Letters
(*Registrum epistolarum* 4.30; June 594)

In the initial chapter of the second book of the *Historia ecclesiastica gentis Anglorum,* Bede offers a biography of Gregory I. He frames his narrative, which contains a wealth of information about Gregory's career as papal legate, abbot, and pope of the western church, with the details of Gregory's life as a monk, for it was the monastic life that spoke most directly to Bede, as to Gregory himself. Though he went far in the world, Bede remembers, Gregory's vision was focused always on salvation.

Gregory was born of noble parents in Rome, probably in the early 540s. He received an excellent education that prepared him for the public career he had easily assumed by the early 570s, having become by that time prefect of Rome, the highest civil office of the city. But Gregory was attracted to the life of the soul even as he achieved the full measure of secular success, and not long after he attained it he renounced the prefectship of Rome for the monastic habit of Saint Benedict. He rose almost as quickly through the ranks of the church hierarchy as he had through the secular offices, becoming an abbot, deacon, and then papal ambassador, and finally (so he said), against his will, pope in 590, an office he held until his death in 604.

Gregory's papacy marked two important shifts from earlier pontificates: a recognition of the importance of the Frankish kingdoms in the success of the church, and an alignment of the church with the fortunes of those kingdoms, and away from the influence of the Byzantine east. Both shifts had the effect of increasing the power of the papacy which they helped to announce. Gregory worked hard to bolster the physical security of the papacy in Italy also, increasing the patrimony of Saint Peter and attending to the details of the papal revenues in order to strengthen his treasury.

Much like Gregory of Tours, Pope Gregory was able to write prodigiously and widely while attending to his many duties. He was a constant letter-writer, as nearly 900 extant letters attest. They witness the full range of human issues: the rooting out of heresy, the propagation of the faith in heathen lands, moral and ethical instruction, censure, the pronouncement of papal ideology, or, as in our selection, answering requests, in this case from the Byzantine empress, for apostolic relics. Gregory's prose style strikes a balance between sophistication and function. His aims are much more limited than those of his contemporary, Gregory of Tours, so his letters do not so much reflect literary as professional concerns. Predictably, he assumes the more obtuse style of the bureaucrat when attending to the business at hand, as at the start of the letter excerpted here. But he abandons that style when the topics turn to saints, other popes, or matters of the heart, as here, in those lines that recount his predecessors' use of relics. In addition to the letters, there are, among some minor writings, homilies on the prophet Ezekiel and on the evangelists, the *Dialogi*, the *Moralia in Iob*, and the *Regula pastoralis*, the last three of which are fundamental works of the LL/ML tradition.

The letters of Gregory have been edited by P. Ewald and L. Hartmann (*Monumenta Germaniae Historica, Epistolae*, 2 vols., Berlin, 1887–99) and by D. Norberg (*Corpus Christianorum, Series Latina*, vols. 140 and 140A, Turnholt, 1982). Books 1 and 2 of the *Registrum* have been edited by P. Minard (*Sources chrétiennes*, vols. 370–71, Paris, 1991). The premises of Gregory's thought and spirituality have been analyzed by C. Straw (*Gregory the Great: Perfection in Imperfection*, Berkeley and Los Angeles, 1988). Norberg's text is reprinted here with minor punctuation changes and "u" and "v" distinguished.

A LETTER TO EMPRESS CONSTANTINA AUGUSTA OF BYZANTIUM ON RELICS

Serenitas vestrae pietatis religionis studio et sanctitatis amore conspicua, propter eam quae in honore sancti Pauli apostoli in palatio aedificatur ecclesiam, caput eiusdem sancti Pauli, aut aliud quid de corpore ipsius, suis ad se iussionibus a me praecepit debere transmitti. Et dum illa

---

1. **Serenitas:** governs *vestrae pietatis;* it is an honorific referring to Constantina Augusta, the addressee of this letter, written in June 594. She was the daughter of Tiberius Constantine and the wife of Mauricius, the Byzantine Emperor from 582 to 602. **conspicua:** predicate adjective modifying *serenitas* and governing *studio* and *amore.* 2. **propter eam:** proleptic of *ecclesiam,* i.e., "for the sake of that church. . . ." **quae:** i.e., *ecclesia,* the subject of *aedificatur.* 3. **caput:** accusative singular neuter. **eiusdem sancti Pauli:** i.e., "of the same St. Paul" who was mentioned in the previous line. **aliud quid:** i.e., "anything." 4. **ad se:** lit., "to herself," but with the sense of "to her Highness," picking up the nuance of *Serenitas.* **praecepit:** the subject is *Serenitas,* i.e., Constantina Augusta; this verb governs indirect statement, with *caput* and *aliud quid* the subjects accusative, *debere* the verb of indirect statement, and *transmitti* its complementary infinitive. **illa:** accusative of the thing demanded (i.e., *caput* and *aliud quid de corpore*) with *imperari.*

mihi desiderarem imperari de quibus facillimam oboedientiam exhibens, vestram erga me amplius potuissem gratiam provocare, maior me maestitia tenuit, quod illa praecipitis quae facere nec possum nec audeo. Nam corpora sanctorum Petri et Pauli apostolorum tantis in ecclesiis suis coruscant miraculis atque terroribus, ut neque ad orandum sine magno illic 5 timore possit accedi. Denique dum beatae recordationis decessor meus, quia argentum quod supra sacratissimum corpus sancti Petri apostoli erat, longe tamen ab eodem corpore fere quindecim pedibus mutare voluit, signum ei non parvi terroris apparuit. Sed et ego aliquid similiter ad sacratissimum corpus sancti Pauli apostoli meliorare volui, et quia necesse 10 erat ut iuxta sepulchrum eiusmodi effodiri altius debuisset, praepositus loci ipsius ossa aliqua non quidem eidem sepulchro coniuncta repperit. Quae quoniam levare praesumpsit atque in alio loco transponere, apparentibus quibusdam tristibus signis, subita morte defunctus est.

Praeter haec autem sanctae memoriae decessor meus idem ad corpus 15 sancti Laurentii martyris quaedam meliorare desiderans, dum nescitur ubi corpus esset venerabile collocatum, effoditur exquirendo. Subito sepulchrum ipsius ignoranter apertum est, et hi qui praesentes erant atque laborabant monachi et mansionarii, quia corpus eiusdem martyris viderunt, quod quidem minime tangere praesumpserunt, omnes intra decem 20 dies defuncti sunt, ita ut nullus vitae superesse potuisset, qui semiustum corpus illius viderat.

Cognoscat autem tranquillissima domina quia Romanis consuetudo

---

1. **mihi:** dative of the source of the demand (Gregory himself) with *imperari.* **quibus:** i.e., *illa.* 2. **gratiam:** i.e., "thanks." 3. **quod:** conjunction. **illa praecipitis quae:** i.e., "those things you ordered"; this relative clause is the object of *facere,* the complementary infinitive of *possum* and *audeo.* 6. **dum:** i.e., "when." **decessor:** i.e., Pelagius II, who reigned from 579 to 590. 8. **longe tamen:** i.e., "at a distance." **fere:** i.e., "approximately." 9. **non parvi terroris:** litotes. **aliquid:** i.e., "to some extent." 10. **meliorare:** i.e., "to improve." 11. **eiusmodi:** indeclinable adjective, equivalent to *talis,* "such," "of this sort." The sense here demands that the word refer back to Saint Paul, i.e., "next to the tomb of that one." **praepositus:** a noun, meaning something like "prefect," with *loci ipsius* depending on it. 12. **coniuncta:** modifies *ossa aliqua* with *eidem sepulchro* dependent on it. 13. **quae:** i.e., *ossa aliqua.* **quoniam** = CL *cum,* as often in LL/ML. 16. **Laurentii:** from *Laurentius, i* = Saint Laurence (Sleumer 465); martyred in 258, he was first scourged and then roasted on a gridiron, with which he is commonly depicted in Christian iconography (see below, pp. 300–306). 19. **mansionarii:** from *mansionarius, i,* a widely used noun in LL/ML, here refers to servants of the papal household (Niermeyer 640–41). 21. **superesse** + dative (*vitae*) = "to remain alive." **semiustum** = CL *semustum.* Saint Lawrence was burned alive.

non est, quando sanctorum reliquias dant, ut quicquam tangere praesumant de corpore. Sed tantummodo in buxide brandeum mittitur atque ad sacratissima corpora sanctorum ponitur. Quod levatum in ecclesia quae est dedicanda debita cum veneratione reconditur, et tantae per hoc ibidem
5   virtutes fiunt, acsi illic specialiter eorum corpora deferantur. Unde contigit ut beatae recordationis Leonis papae tempore, sicut a maioribus traditur, dum quidam Graeci de talibus reliquiis dubitarent, praedictus pontifex hoc ipsum brandeum allatis forficibus incidit, et ex ipsa incisione sanguis effluxit. In Romanis namque vel totius Occidentis partibus
10   omnino intolerabile est atque sacrilegum, si sanctorum corpora tangere quisquam fortasse voluerit. Quod si praesumpserit, certum est quia haec temeritas impunita nullomodo remanebit. Pro qua re de Graecorum consuetudine, qui ossa levare sanctorum se asserunt, vehementer miramur et vix credimus. Nam quidam Graeci monachi hic ante biennium venientes,
15   nocturno silentio iuxta ecclesiam sancti Pauli corpora mortuorum in campo iacentia effodiebant, atque eorum ossa recondebant, servantes sibi dum recederent. Qui cum tenti et cur hoc facerent diligenter fuissent discussi, confessi sunt quod illa ossa ad Graecias essent tamquam sanctorum reliquias portaturi. Ex quorum exemplo, sicut praedictum est, maior no-
20   bis dubietas nata est, utrum verum sit quod levari veraciter ossa sanctorum dicuntur.

De corporibus vero beatorum apostolorum quid ego dicturus sum, dum constet quia eo tempore quo passi sunt ex Oriente fideles venerunt, qui eorum corpora sicut civium suorum repeterent? Quae ducta usque ad
25   secundum urbis milliarium, in loco qui dicitur Catacumbas collocata

---

1. **quicquam** = *quisquam*.   2. **buxide** = CL *pyxis, pyxidis*, from Greek πυξίς, "box." **brandeum:** i.e., "linen cloth," sometimes used in ML to designate the altarcloth (Niermeyer 104). Gregory carefully delineates Roman practice here; the body of the saint is inviolate but the linen cloth that at one point touched the saint's body can be used as a holy relic.   3. **levatum:** i.e., *corpus*, but referring to the elevation of relics in general also (Niermeyer 599–600, s. v. *levare*, 4).   8. **allatis:** from *afferre*, i.e., "that he had brought with him," modifies *forficibus*, from *forfex, forficis*.   11. **quia** = CL *ut*. 17. **tenti:** from *tenere*, "detained," dependent on *fuissent*, modifies *qui*.   **discussi:** from *discutere*, "examined," dependent on *fuissent*, modifies *qui*. This verb in ML is used to designate trial by ordeal also (Niermeyer 339, s. v. *discutere*, 1, 2).   20. **nata est:** from *nasci*.   **quod** = CL *cum*.   22. **dicturus sum:** future active participle with *sum* forms the active periphrastic construction (AG 194–95); with *quid* = "what am I going to say . . .?"   23. **dum constet quia:** i.e., "since it is well known that . . ."; *quia* = CL *ut*.   **eo tempore:** ablative of time when.   **passi sunt:** from *pati*, referring here to Christian martyrs, i.e., "those who suffered," "endured."   25. **secundum . . . milliarium:** the second milestone, one of many markers set up by Augustus for better use of military roads. **Catacumbas:** from *catacumba, ae* = "the catacombs" (LS 300), ancient Christian under-

sunt. Sed dum ea exinde levare omnis eorum multitudo conveniens niteretur, ita eos vis tonitrui atque fulguris nimio metu terruit ac dispersit, ut talia denuo nullatenus temptare praesumerent. Tunc autem exeuntes Romani eorum corpora, qui hoc ex Domini pietate meruerunt, levaverunt, et in locis quibus nunc sunt condita posuerunt. 5

Quis ergo, serenissima domina, tam temerarius possit exsistere, ut haec sciens eorum corpora non dico tangere, sed vel aliquatenus praesumat inspicere? Dum igitur talia mihi a vobis praecepta sunt, de quibus parere nullatenus potuissem, quantum invenio, non vestrum est. Sed quidam homines contra me pietatem vestram excitare voluerunt, ut mihi, 10
quod absit, voluntatis vestrae gratiam subtraherent, et propterea quaesiverunt capitulum, de quo vobis quasi inoboediens invenirer. Sed in omnipotente Domino confido quia nullomodo benignissimae voluntati subripitur, et sanctorum apostolorum virtutem, quos toto corde et mente diligitis, non ex corporali praesentia sed ex protectione semper habebitis. 15

Sudarium vero, quod similiter transmitti iussistis, cum corpore eius est. Quod ita tangi non potest, sicut nec ad corpus illius accedi. Sed quia serenissimae dominae tam religiosum desiderium esse vacuum non debet, de catenis, quas ipse sanctus Paulus apostolus in collo et in manibus gestavit, ex quibus multa miracula in populo demonstrantur, partem vobis 20
aliquam transmittere festinabo, si tamen hanc tollere limando praevaluero. Quia dum frequentur ex catenis eisdem multi veniunt et benedictionem petunt, ut parum quid ex limatura accipiant, assistit sacerdos cum lima, et aliquibus petentibus ita concite aliquid de catenis ipsis excutitur, ut mora nulla sit. Quibusdam vero petentibus diu per catenas ipsas lima 25
ducitur, et tamen ut aliquid exinde exeat non obtinetur.

—Reg. Ep. 4.30.

---

ground burial sites. 1. **niteretur**: normally intransitive in CL, here it takes *levare* as complementary infinitive and means something like "endeavoring," "striving." 6. **exsistere** = *esse,* as often in LL/ML. 13. **subripitur**: the understood subject is *gratia; subripere* with the dative = "to take something away from. . . ." 16. **transmitti**: present passive infinitive, complement of *iussistis.* **eius**: i.e., Paul. 21. **hanc**: i.e., *catena.* **limando**: i.e., "by filing." 23. **quid** = CL *aliquid.* **limatura**: "filings" from the chains. 24. **concite** = CL *concitate.*

ISIDORE OF SEVILLE

The Etymologies
(*Etymologiarum sive originum libri XX*; c. 630)

Much like his older contemporaries Gregory of Tours and Gregory the Great, Isidore of Seville balanced the competing demands of the lives of contemplation and of action. Much like his Roman and Gaulish counterparts, too, he seems to have been of an old and established family, with roots in North Africa, but with closer ties to Cartagena, in Spain. Though there is some evidence that Isidore was born there, it seems likely that his family had already left Cartagena for Seville in the early 560s. Isidore was more than likely born, between 565 and 570, in the city which would form the backdrop of his manifold career.

Isidore received a monastic education and immediately took to the life of scholarship and spirituality. He seems to have been interested early on in the affairs of the Church, an interest encouraged perhaps by close contact with his older brother, Leander, during Leander's tenure as bishop of Seville. Among other accomplishments, Leander was especially active in rooting out Arianism in Seville. Isidore succeeded him as bishop some time around 600 and continued the strain of activism for which his brother had been known, working at the affairs of his bishopric until his death in 636. He convened and presided at councils, promulgated directives on liturgical, theological, and practical matters, promoted education and culture, and cultivated the support and friendship of the Visigothic kings, especially Sisebut.

Indeed, Isidore's most famous work, the *Etymologies*, excerpts of which are presented here, was commissioned by Sisebut. Clearly the king did not mean for it to become his favorite text, for it is not an intrinsically readable work. But it does throw considerable light on the intellectual interests of its author and of early medieval culture in general. As its title suggests, this work is a compendium of the sources of words, explicated, as in the excerpts, in sometimes lengthy narratives that oftentimes attend to the social, cultural, and anthropological issues pertinent to individual words. At the same time, however, Isidore did not live and work in a vacuum. His interest in authenticating meaning through etymological narratives suggests a basic approach to the world that is language-centered and that privileges allegory, symbol, association, and the weight

174

of tradition. Though it clearly represents Isidore's intellectual predilections, which tend to center on the compilation of information, the *Etymologies* also reveals a Christian emphasis on the importance of language as the means to attain authentic knowledge. In addition to the *Etymologies*, the largest and most ambitious of his projects, Isidore wrote a history of the Goths, Vandals, and Sueves; a chronicle of world history; *On the Nature of Things; On the Differences and Meaning of Words; Lamentations of a Sinful Soul; On Famous Men; On the Christian Faith, Against the Jews;* and letters.

Isidore's Latin is much like Gregory the Great's in terms of style, syntax, and vocabulary. Expectedly, given his topic, he does not range widely, but many of the anthropological excursuses, like the one given here on the development of glass, take an open and direct tone reflective of their author's deep engagement with his topic.

The *Etymologies* has been edited by W. M. Lindsay (*Isidori Hispalensis Episcopi Etymologiarum sive Originum Libri XX*, 2 vols., Oxford, 1911, repr. 1985). J. Fontaine offers a comprehensive treatment of Isidore in his classical context, with attention paid to his Latinity (*Isidore de Séville et la culture classique dans l'Espagne wisigothique*, 2 vols., Paris, 1959). K. B. Wolf has a useful essay on Isidore together with a translation of Isidore's *History of the Kings of the Goths* (*Conquerors and Chroniclers of Early Medieval Spain*, Liverpool, 1990, pp. 12–27, 81–110). Lindsay's text is reprinted here without change.

NIGHT

DE NOCTE. Nox a nocendo dicta, eo quod oculis noceat. Quae idcirco lunae ac siderum lucem habet, ne indecora esset, et ut consolaretur omnes nocte operantes, et ut quibusdam animantibus, quae lucem solis ferre non possunt, ad sufficientiam temperaretur. Noctis autem et diei alternatio propter vicissitudinem dormiendi vigilandique effecta est, et ut operis diurni laborem noctis requies temperet. Noctem autem fieri, aut quia longo itinere lassatur sol, et cum ad ultimum caeli spatium pervenit, elanguescit ac tabefactus efflat suos ignes; aut quia eadem vi sub terras cogitur qua super terras pertulit lumen, et sic umbra terrae noctem facit. Unde et Vergilius: 5

---

1. **eo quod . . . noceat:** the subjunctive with *eo quod* indicates that the reason given is on the authority of another; hence the sense of this clause is "because it is said that night harms the eyes" (cf. AG 540, 592.3; and Blaise 275). 6. **fieri:** impersonal use of the infinitive, with *noctem* as object: "it becomes night. . . ."

Ruit Oceano nox,
involvens umbra magna terramque polumque.

Noctis partes septem sunt, id est vesper, crepusculum, conticinium, intempestum, gallicinium, matutinum, diluculum. Vesperum ab stella occi-
5 dentali vocatum, quae solem occiduum sequitur et tenebras sequentes
praecedit. De qua Vergilius:

Ante diem clauso conponit vesper Olympo.

Tenebras autem dictas, quod teneant umbras. Crepusculum est dubia lux.
Nam creperum dubium dicimus, hoc est inter lucem et tenebras. Contici-
10 nium est quando omnes silent. Conticescere enim silere est. Intempestum
est medium et inactuosum noctis tempus, quando agi nihil potest et omnia sopore quieta sunt. Nam tempus per se non intellegitur, nisi per actus
humanos. Medium autem noctis actum caret. Ergo intempesta inactuosa,
quasi sine tempore, hoc est sine actu, per quem dinoscitur tempus; unde
15 est: "Intempestive venisti." Ergo intempesta dicitur quia caret tempora,
id est actum. Gallicinium propter gallos lucis praenuntios dictum. Matutinum est inter abscessum tenebrarum et aurorae adventum; et dictum matutinum quod hoc tempus inchoante mane sit. Diluculum quasi iam incipiens parva diei lux. Haec et aurora, quae solem praecedit. Est autem
20 aurora diei clarescentis exordium et primus splendor aeris, qui Graece
ἠώς dicitur; quam nos per derivationem auroram vocamus, quasi eor-
oram. Unde est illud:

et laetus Eoos
Eurus equis.

25 et:

Eoasque acies.

—*Ety.* 5.31.

2. *Aen.* 2. 250. 3. **septem:** indeclinable. **vesper . . . diluculum:** these are not precise distinctions, as the first three mean roughly the same thing ("evening"), as do the
last two ("morning"); only *intempestum*, "dead of night," and *gallicinium*, "the time
of the rooster's crowing," are distinctive. Nevertheless, Isidore goes on to make distinctions of his own. 4. **vesperum** = *vesper*, but neuter in gender. 7. *Aen.* 1.374.
9. **creperum:** used as a substantive here = "darkness." 14. **dinoscitur** = CL *dignos-
citur.* **unde est:** i.e., "whence comes the saying . . ." 15. **caret:** transitive here, with
tempora as object. 18. **inchoante** = *incohante*, from *incohare.* **mane:** indeclinable
mane is modified by *inchoante* in an ablative of time construction, i.e., "when the
morning begins." 24. Virgil, *Aen.* 2.417. 26. *Aen.* 1.489.

GLASS

DE VITRO. Vitrum dictum quod visui perspicuitate transluceat. In aliis enim metallis quidquid intrinsecus continetur absconditur; in vitro vero quilibet liquor vel species qualis est interius talis exterius declaratur, et quodammodo clausus patet. Cuius origo haec fuit. In parte Syriae, quae Phoenice vocatur, finitima Iudaeae circa radices montis Carmeli palus est, ex qua nascitur Belus amnis, quinque milium passuum spatio in mare fluens iuxta Ptolomaidem, cuius arenae de torrente fluctu sordibus eluuntur. Hic fama est pulsa nave mercatorum nitri, cum sparsim per litus epulas pararent, nec essent pro adtollendis vasis lapides, glebas nitri e nave subdiderunt; quibus accensis permixta arena litoris, translucentes novi liquoris fluxisse rivos: et hanc fuisse originem vitri. Mox, ut est ingeniosa sollertia, non fuit contenta solo nitro sed et aliis mixturis hanc artem [condire] studuit. Levibus enim aridisque lignis coquitur, adiecto cypro ac nitro continuisque fornacibus ut aes liquatur, massaeque fiunt. Postea ex massis rursus funditur in officinis, et aliud flatu figuratur, aliud torno teritur, aliud argenti modo caelatur. Tinguitur etiam multis modis, ita ut iacinthos sapphirosque et virides imitetur et onyches vel aliarum gemmarum colores; neque est alia speculis aptior materia vel picturae adcommodatior. Maximus tamen honor in candido vitro, proximoque in crystalli similitudine; unde et ad potandum argenti metalla et auri pepulit vitrum. Olim fiebat et in Italia, et per Gallias et Hispaniam arena alba mollissima pila molaque terebatur. Dehinc miscebatur tribus partibus, nitri pondere vel mensura, ac liquata in alias fornaces transfundebatur, quae massa vocabatur ammonitrum; atque haec recocta fiebat vitrum purum et candidum. In genere vitri et obsianus lapis adnumeratur. Est autem

5

10

15

20

25

---

5. **finitima** + dative = "bordering on. . . ." **Carmeli:** from *Carmelus, i* = Mount Carmel (Sleumer 190). **palus:** from *palus, paludis.* 6. **Belus amnis:** presumably the brook Kishon, at which Elijah ordered slain the prophets of Baal after the so-called conflict on Mount Carmel (cf. 1 Kings 18.17–40). *Beel, Bel,* and *Belus* are forms of *Baal* (see Sleumer 144, s. v. *Baal*). 7. **Ptolomaidem** = CL *Ptolemaidem,* modifies *mare.* **arenae** = CL *harenae.* 8. **pulsa nave:** ablative absolute. **mercatorum nitri:** dependent on *pulsa nave,* i.e., "the ship of the natron sellers having been stranded on the rocks. . . ." 9. **adtollendis** = CL *attollendis,* governed by *pro* and modifying *vasis,* the phrase means something like "that could be used for preparing meals. . . ." 11. **fluxisse . . . fuisse:** perfect active infinitives dependent on *fama est.* 14. **massaeque:** i.e., "a mass." 15. **funditur in officinis:** i.e., "it was melted down again in workshops. . . ." 17. **iacinthos** = CL *hyacinthos.* 18. **adcommodatior** = CL *accommodatior.* 20. **pepulit:** the sense is "outdoes," "surpasses." 22. **mollissima . . . molaque:** ablative of means. 24. **recocta:** from *recoquere.* 25. **obsianus lapis:** a kind of glass, named after its discoverer, Obsius. **adnumeratur** = CL *annumeratur.*

virens interdum et niger aliquando et translucidus, crassiore visu et in speculis parietum pro imagine umbras reddente; gemmas multi ex eo faciunt. Hunc lapidem et in India et in Italia et ad Oceanum in Hispania nasci tradunt. Ferunt autem sub Tiberio Caesare quendam artificem excogi-
5 tasse vitri temperamentum, ut flexibile esset et ductile. Qui dum admissus fuisset ad Caesarem, porrexit phialam Caesari, quam ille indignatus in pavimentum proiecit. Artifex autem sustulit phialam de pavimento, quae conplicaverat se tamquam vas aeneum; deinde marculum de sinu protulit et phialam correxit. Hoc facto Caesar dixit artifici: "Numquid alius scit
10 hanc condituram vitrorum?" Postquam ille iurans negavit alterum hoc scire, iussit illum Caesar decollari, ne dum hoc cognitum fieret, aurum pro luto haberetur et omnium metallorum pretia abstraherentur; et revera, quia si vasa vitrea non frangerentur, melius essent quam aurum et argentum.

—*Ety.* 16.16.

4. **tradunt:** i.e.,"they say"; also the meaning of "*ferunt*," the next word. 5. **temperamentum:** in CL = "moderation" but here, with *vitri*, it must mean something like "moderate sort of glass . . .," with the idea being that the texture of this glass makes it less inclined to break. 8. **conplicaverat** = CL *complicaverat*, here meaning "picked up." 10. **condituram:** i.e., "making." 13. **quia si** = CL *cum* in a causal construction with the subjunctive: i.e., "since glass dishes didn't break, they were better than gold or silver."

BEDE

The Ecclesiastical History of the English People
(*Historia ecclesiastica gentis Anglorum;* 731)

The simplicity of his chosen life belies the intellectual vigor, spiritual certainty, and artistic pride that inform the voluminous writings of Bede. Of his life we know very little beyond what he tells us. He was born in 672 in Northumbria, not far from the monastic communities of Wearmouth and Jarrow, dedicated to Saints Peter and Paul. He was sent to these communities, which owing to their proximity functioned essentially as a single institution, as an oblate some time in the late 670s. He became a deacon and then a priest and remained for the rest of his life at Jarrow, working at his various intellectual pursuits, including the compilation and writing of his masterpiece, excerpted here, the *Ecclesiastical History of the English People*. He died just after finishing this monumental work, in 735.

Bede's interests were wide and eclectic. He was an aficionado of Old English poetry and enjoyed translating from Latin into this language, his mother tongue. He devoted many years to the reading of Scripture and to the writing of commentaries on it. But he trained himself also as an expert chronologer and metrician, grammarian, and martyrologist. There are treatises also on orthography and on the nature of poetry.

If all Bede had written was his *Historia,* his reputation would be assured. In it a variety of his talents coalesce: his ability to communicate in a deceptively direct Latin style, built on the foundation of a CL embellished as need be by Christian vocabulary and sentiment; a scrupulous fairness; a wide and eclectic vision that enabled him to see importance in the small as well as the great figures and events; a keen intellect that was able to manipulate material to best effect without being duplicitous. Above all, Bede was a teacher, and the *Historia* speaks most clearly to that predilection in him and the aims it implies. The words he wrote of Caedmon might well apply to Bede himself: "He was singularly touched by the grace of God; he served God with a simple and pure mind, and with a tranquil devotion; he was a man of much religion, and willingly gave himself over to regular learning; his life ended sweetly."

The *Historia* is a complex work. Its organization is chronological, moving from Bede's unique version of creation, based on Pliny's *Natural*

History, to a consideration of Roman history, which in turn leads to the proselytizing of the British under the aegis of Pope Gregory—thence to the local histories of the seven kingdoms of Anglo-Saxon England. Bede takes his history down to his own time, as the increasing detail of the successive books indicates. Apart from preaching the understood unity of creation and human events within God's masterly universe, however, Bede's aim is to suggest the continuity of spiritual authenticity and vigor in the British Isles in the centuries after the giants—Augustine of Canterbury, Gregory the Great, Edwin, or Alban, some of whose important biography is reprinted below—had shaped it. The *History* is, therefore, carefully written to focus on biography and hagiography in the first two books, culminating in lengthy treatments of Edwin in book 3. The fourth and fifth books are dominated, however, by remembrances of simpler folk—the nuns at Barking, Caedmon, the miracles wrought by a nameless boy. In this way, Bede's history affirms the worthiness of Britain's Christian past, but uses that past as a mirror to reflect contemporary events. The hard work of Edwin, Alban, Gregory, or Augustine lives on in the functions of the church in the eighth century, now fully routinized, as Bede's life itself (and the writing of his *History*) attests. In this, as in so many ways, Bede strikes his twentieth-century readers as very much akin to his favorite figure, Caedmon; both were visionaries.

The *Historia* has been edited, with commentary, by C. Plummer (*Venerabilis Bedae Opera Historica,* 2 vols., Oxford, 1896) and by R. A. B. Mynors and B. Colgrave (*Bede's Ecclesiastical History of the English People,* Oxford, 1969). Colgrave and Mynors have Latin text facing an English translation. The Penguin Classics also has a translation into English by L. Sherley-Price with an introduction and notes by D. H. Farmer (*Bede: Ecclesiastical History of the English People,* Harmondsworth, 1955; rev. ed., 1990). A concordance to the *Historia* has been prepared by P. F. Jones (*A Concordance to the Historia Ecclesiastica of Bede,* Cambridge, Mass., 1929), and J. M. Wallace-Hadrill has published a commentary (*Bede's Ecclesiastical History of the English Nation: A Historical Commentary,* Oxford, 1988). Bede has been most recently studied by Goffart 295ff., with full bibliography. The text of Colgrave and Mynors is reprinted here with "u" and "v" distinguished.

The Martyrdom of Saint Alban

Siquidem in ea passus est sanctus Albanus, de quo presbyter Fortunatus in Laude Virginum, cum beatorum martyrum qui de toto orbe ad
Dominum venirent mentionem facit, ait:

> Albanum egregium fecunda Britania profert.

Qui videlicet Albanus paganus adhuc, cum perfidorum principum man-   5
data adversum Christianos saevirent, clericum quendam persecutores fugientem hospitio recepit. Quem dum orationibus continuis ac vigiliis die
noctuque studere conspiceret, subito divina gratia respectus exemplum
fidei ac pietatis illius coepit aemulari, ac salutaribus eius exhortationibus
paulatim edoctus relictis idolatriae tenebris Christianus integro ex corde   10
factus est. Cumque praefatus clericus aliquot diebus apud eum hospitare-
tur, pervenit ad aures nefandi principis confessorem Christi, cui necdum
fuerat locus martyrii deputatus, penes Albanum latere; unde statim iussit
milites eum diligentius inquirere. Qui cum ad tugurium martyris prevenis-
sent, mox se sanctus Albanus pro hospite ac magistro suo ipsius habitu, id   15
est caracalla qua vestiebatur, indutus militibus exhibuit, atque ad iudicem
vinctus perductus est.

Contigit autem iudicem ea hora, qua ad eum Albanus adducebatur,
aris adsistere ac daemonibus hostias offerre. Cumque vidisset Albanum,
mox ira succensus nimia quod se ille ultro pro hospite quem susceperat   20
militibus offerre ac discrimini dare praesumsisset, ad simulacra daemo-

1. **ea:** i.e., *persecutione;* the previous chapter leaves off with a discussion of the persecutions of the Emperor Diocletian (284–305). Despite what Bede says in this passage,
it is not established fact that these persecutions, which were widespread and severe,
reached Britain. **presbyter:** from *presbyter, teris* = "priest" (Blaise/Chirat 661); on
Fortunatus' life and for selections of his poetry, of which Bede was a careful reader,
see pp. 158–68. 4. Fortunatus, *Carmen* 8.3.155. 5. **perfidorum:** *perfidus* and *perfidia* are used by Bede and other LL writers as opposites of *fides* and *fidelis* (cf. Plummer 2.18). Thus *perfidorum principum mandata* are "mandates of the unbelieving
rulers." 8. **respectus:** from *respicere,* with *divina gratia* = "Alban was visited by divine grace. . . ." 10. **integro ex corde:** lit., "from a whole heart," but with adverbial
force = "wholeheartedly." 12. **pervenit . . . principis:** this phrase effectively introduces an indirect statement, with *confessorem Christi* the subject of *latere,* whose object, in turn, is *penes Albanum.* 13. **deputatus:** i.e., "reckoned." 16. **caracalla:**
from *caracalla, ae* = "monk's tunic" (Blaise/Chirat 132). 19. **aris:** from *ara, ae,*
"altars." **adsistere** = CL *assistere.* **daemonibus:** from *daemon, daemonis* =
"demons," "impure spirits" (Blaise/Chirat 237). 20. **ille:** i.e., Saint Alban. 21. **discrimini:** *offerre se discrimini* is the thought. **quod . . . praesumsisset** = CL *praesump-
sisset,* i.e., "since he had presumed"; *dare* and *offerre* both depend on *praesumsisset,*
with *se* the object of both.

181

num quibus adsistebat eum iussit pertrahi, "Quia rebellem" inquiens "ac
sacrilegum celare quam militibus reddere maluisti, ut contemtor divum
meritam blasfemiae suae poenam lueret, quaecumque illi debebantur supplicia tu solvere habes, si a cultu nostrae religionis discedere temtas." At
5 sanctus Albanus, qui se ultro persecutoribus fidei Christianum esse pro-
diderat, nequaquam minas principis metuit, sed accinctus armis militiae
spiritalis palam se iussis illius parere nolle pronuntiabat. Tum iudex "Cuius" inquit "familiae vel generis es?" Albanus respondit: "Quid ad te per-
tinet qua stirpe sim genitus? Sed si veritatem religionis audire desideras,
10 Christianum iam me esse Christianisque officiis vacare cognosce." Ait iudex: "Nomen tuum quaero, quod sine mora mihi insinua." At ille: "Albanus" inquit "a parentibus vocor, et Deum verum ac vivum, qui universa
creavit, adoro semper et colo." Tum iudex repletus iracundia dixit: "Si vis
perennis vitae felicitate perfrui, diis magnis sacrificare ne differas." Alba-
15 nus respondit: "Sacrificia haec, quae a vobis redduntur daemonibus, nec
auxiliari subiectis possunt nec supplicantium sibi desideria vel vota conplere. Quin immo quicumque his sacrificia simulacris obtulerit, aeternas
inferni poenas pro mercede recipiet." His auditis iudex nimio furore commotus, caedi sanctum Dei confessorem a tortoribus praecepit, autumans
20 se verberibus, quam verbis non poterat, cordis eius emollire constantiam.
Qui cum tormentis afficeretur acerrimis, patienter haec pro Domino,
immo gaudenter ferebat. At ubi iudex illum tormentis superari vel a cultu

1. **inquiens** = CL *inquit.* 2. **reddere**: the thought is *"quia maluisti celare . . . quam
militibus reddere;* here, *quam* means "rather than." **contemtor** = CL *contemptor;* it
is common in LL/ML for the parasitic consonant to be omitted. **divum** = alternate
genitive plural of *deus.* 3. **blasfemiae suae**: the better spelling is *blasphemiae,* from
blasphemia, ae (Blaise/Chirat 117); the phrase depends on *meritam,* which modifies
poenam, the object of *lueret.* 4. **solvere habes**: i.e., "you have to undergo. . . ." The
infinitive with *habere* expresses obligation in LL/ML; § 7.2.2. **temtas** = CL *temptas*
or *tentas.* 7. **parere**: takes a dative object, here *iussis (illius),* i.e., the orders of the
judge." 10. **vacare** + dative = "to have time for something," i.e., "I am prepared to
do my Christian duties." 11. **insinua**: i.e., "tell," "inform," etc., with *mihi.*
13. **colo**: *colere* has the primary sense of "to worship" or "to be devoted" in LL/ML
but it can also be used to represent emotional longing. **vis**: from *velle,* with the infinitive *perfrui* dependent on it. 14. **perfrui**: takes an ablative object. **ne differas** = a
negative hortatory subjunctive construction: "do not postpone," with *sacrificare* as
complement. 16. **subiectis**: i.e., "to those who perform them." **supplicantium**: genitive plural, dependent on *desideria vel vota.* **conplere** = CL *complere.* 17. **quin
immo**: i.e., "on the contrary." 19. **caedi**: present passive infinitive of *caedere,* dependent on *praecepit* = "the judge ordered . . . to be killed." **autumans**: i.e., "saying,"
"declaring."

Christianae religionis revocari non posse persensit, capite eum plecti iussit.

Cumque ad mortem duceretur, pervenit ad flumen quod muro et harena, ubi feriendus erat, meatu rapidissimo dividebatur; viditque ibi non parvam hominum multitudinem utriusque sexus, condicionis diversae et aetatis, quae sine dubio divinitatis instinctu ad obsequium beatissimi confessoris ac martyris vocabatur, et ita fluminis ipsius occupabat pontem, ut intra vesperam transire vix posset. Denique cunctis pene egressis iudex sine obsequio in civitate substiterat. Igitur sanctus Albanus, cui ardens inerat devotio mentis ad martyrium ocius pervenire, accessit ad torrentem, et dirigens ad caelum oculos, illico siccato alveo, vidit undam suis cessisse ac viam dedisse vestigiis. Quod cum inter alios etiam ipse carnifex, qui eum percussurus erat, vidisset, festinavit ei, ubi ad locum destinatum morti venerat, occurrere, divino nimirum admonitus instinctu, proiectoque ense quem strictum tenuerat, pedibus eius advolvitur, multum desiderans ut cum martyre vel pro martyre, quem percutere iubebatur, ipse potius mereretur percuti.

Dum ergo is ex persecutore factus esset collega veritatis et fidei, ac iacente ferro esset inter carnifices iusta cunctatio, montem cum turbis reverentissimus Dei confessor ascendit, qui oportune laetus gratia decentissima quingentis fere passibus ab harena situs est, variis herbarum floribus depictus, immo usquequaque vestitus; in quo nihil repente arduum, nihil praeceps, nihil abruptum, quem lateribus longe lateque deductum in modum aequoris Natura conplanat, dignum videlicet eum pro insita sibi spe-

5

10

15

20

---

1. **plecti:** present passive infinitive. 3. **quod muro et harena:** i.e., *flumen quo murus ab harena . . . dividebatur* (cf. Plummer 2.19 and Colgrave/Mynors 30.a.) The passage is corrupt, but Bede apparently was copying from a manuscript of the *Passio sancti Albani* which has this troublesome wording. The established text of the *Passio* has *quo murus; harena* refers here to the "arena" in which Alban was ordered to die. 5. **non parvam . . . multitudinem:** litotes. 6. **obsequium:** although the word can mean "death" or "obsequies," it is probably best to render it here as "escort," to pick up the ironic contrast in the next sentence, where the *iudex* is left in the city *sine obsequio* (cf. LS 1242). 8. **intra vesperam:** i.e., "within the course of the evening." **pene** = CL *paene*. 12. **suis . . . vestigiis:** lit., "for his own footsteps," but with *viam* = "for him to walk in." 13. **percussurus:** future active participle of *percutere*. 14. **occurrere:** complementary infinitive with *festinavit*. 15. **multum:** adverb. 20. **qui:** i.e., *mons*. **oportune** = CL *opportune*. 22. **usquequaque** = CL *usque quaque*, i.e., "everywhere." **vestitus:** an emphatic correction of *depictus*, introduced by *immo*, for purposes of stressing the incomparable beauty of this *mons*. 24. **aequoris:** i.e., "of a level surface." **conplanat** = CL *complanat*.

cie venustatis iam olim reddens, qui beati martyris cruore dicaretur. In huius ergo vertice sanctus Albanus dari sibi a Deo aquam rogavit, statimque incluso meatu ante pedes eius fons perennis exortus est, ut omnes agnoscerent etiam torrentem martyri obsequium detulisse; neque enim
5 fieri poterat ut in arduo montis cacumine martyr aquam, quam in fluvio non reliquerat, peteret, si hoc oportunum esse non videret. Qui videlicet fluvius ministerio persoluto, devotione conpleta officii testimonium relinquens reversus est ad naturam. Decollatus itaque martyr fortissimus ibidem accepit coronam vitae, quam repromisit Deus diligentibus se. Sed
10 ille, qui piis cervicibus impias intulit manus, gaudere super mortuum non est permissus; namque oculi eius in terram una cum beati martyris capite deciderunt.

Decollatus est ibi etiam tum miles ille, qui antea superno nutu correptus sanctum Dei confessorem ferire recusavit; de quo nimirum constat
15 quia, etsi fonte baptismatis non est ablutus, sui tamen est sanguinis lavacro mundatus ac regni caelestis dignus factus ingressu. Tum iudex, tanta miraculorum caelestium novitate perculsus, cessari mox a persecutione praecepit, honorem referre incipiens caedi sanctorum, per quam eos opinabatur prius a Christianae fidei posse devotione cessare.

—*Hist. Eccl.* 1.7 (excerpts).

1. **pro . . . venustatis:** i.e., "by virtue of the innate form of its own beauty. . . ." **reddens:** with *dignum . . . eum* its object = "rendering this a worthy place. . . ." 3. **incluso meatu:** i.e., "enclosed in its own channel"; *incluso* is from *includere.* **exortus est:** from *exoriri.* 5. **neque enim fieri poterat ut:** impersonal construction = "for it would not have been able to happen that. . . ." 6. **si . . . videret:** i.e., "if he did not see that this was the right thing to do." 7. **conpleta** = CL *completa;* the phrases *ministerio persoluto* and *devotione conpleta* are ablative absolutes. 11. **una:** adverb. 13. **correptus:** from *corripere,* governs *superno nutu* and modifies *miles.* 15. **quia** = CL *ut,* with *constat* = "it is established that. . . ." 18. **cessari . . . praecepit:** "he ordered a respite from persecution"; the present passive infinitive, *cessari,* acts as the object of *praecepit,* with *a persecutione* dependent on it. **caedi:** from *caedes, caedis.* **quam:** i.e., *persecutio.*

syon sca suscepit. in quo credens pmanet.
mnis illa deo sacra et dilecta cuitas ple
na mcdulis inlaude. et canore iubilo in
num dni uincunq; cum fauore pdicat.
oc in templum summe ds. euiat ad
uem et eterna bonitate pcium uotam uo
ta suscipe. largam benedictionem. hic in
sunde uigit. te pnciantur onis pec
ta adquirere. 7 adepta possroe. cum
plennit. padisium intione canssa in
requiem. la 7 honor deo usq; quo aint
simo una patri filioq; cum in clito pari
elito cuilaus est potestas. per eterna scla

Os creator omnium poliq; rector ne
stiens diem decoro lumine noctē
soporis gra. rt solutos ut quies red
dat laboris usui mentesq; fessas alleuet
luctusq; soluat anxios. rates pacto iā
die 7 nochs exortu pces uoti reos ut
adiuues ymnū canentes solum. e
condis ima geinant te uox canora con
crepet te diligat castus amor te mens

PLATE 6

Hymnary (with Ambrose, "Deus Creator Omnium," at lines 15–23)
Single folio on parchment, after 1100
Specimen leaf 129, Koopman Collection
John Hay Library, Brown University

Monastic culture was well established in the West by the seventh century, including a particularly literate strain in Ireland, whose traditions of learning (including copying and illuminating manuscripts) was influential in England for several centuries (and directly important to Bede). Part of the work of the monastery collectively was to pray, that is, to keep the divine office, to pursue, as Saint Benedict called it, the *opus Dei*—the work of God. The office consisted of eight periods of formal, communal, oral prayer, comprising mainly psalms and hymns, with supplemental readings from Scripture. Each of these periods was called an *hora*. These *horae* were Vigils (2:00 A.M.), or the night office; then, the first of the day offices, called Lauds because it usually included the singing of the praise psalms; then, spaced throughout the day at roughly 6:00 A.M., 9:00 A.M., 12 noon, and 3:00 P.M. four other hours, called Prime, Terce, Sext, and None. The seventh hour, Vespers, was prayed in the hour before sundown; the eighth hour was Compline, timed to end with the full arrival of the night's darkness. The divine office was constructed so as to fit, along with the Mass itself, into the larger liturgical practices for the year, which were controlled by the three great feasts, Easter, Pentecost, and Christmas. Originally there was a standard set of hymns, psalms, and readings associated with the office, but as monasticism grew as an institution and spread throughout western Europe, newly composed hymns and observances were added. Ambrose's "Deus Creator Omnium," which was written in the late fourth century, was an established hymn from the inception of the divine office in the *Regula* of Saint Benedict (c. 480–543).

This parchment folio was cut out of its original codex in the twelfth century and recycled as the backing for a new codex. It remains in good condition, however, retaining its original dimensions—17 cm. × 24 cm.—with holes from pricking clearly visible in the verso left margin (and the recto right margin). Its 23 lines are ruled, as are the margins. The left margin is 2.5 cm.; the right, a bit smaller, is 2 cm.—as befits a verso folio. The top margin is 1 cm.; the bottom 3.25 cm. The Ambrosian hymn is copied in a much darker black ink and decorated with green and red initials, and is preceded by a notation indicating its use at Vespers, while the material preceding it is written in a neat late Carolingian bookhand of brown ink with some red initials.

PART THREE: 750–900
FROM LATE TO
MEDIEVAL LATIN

PAUL THE DEACON (c. 730–799)
ALCUIN (735–804)
THEODULF (c. 750–821)
EINHARD (c. 775–840)
ERMOLDUS NIGELLUS (fl. c. 826)
HRABANUS MAURUS (c. 780–856)
WALAHFRID STRABO (c. 809–849)
JOHN SCOTTUS ERIUGENA (c. 810–c. 880)
DHUODA (c. 800–c.850)
SEDULIUS SCOTTUS (fl. c. 855)

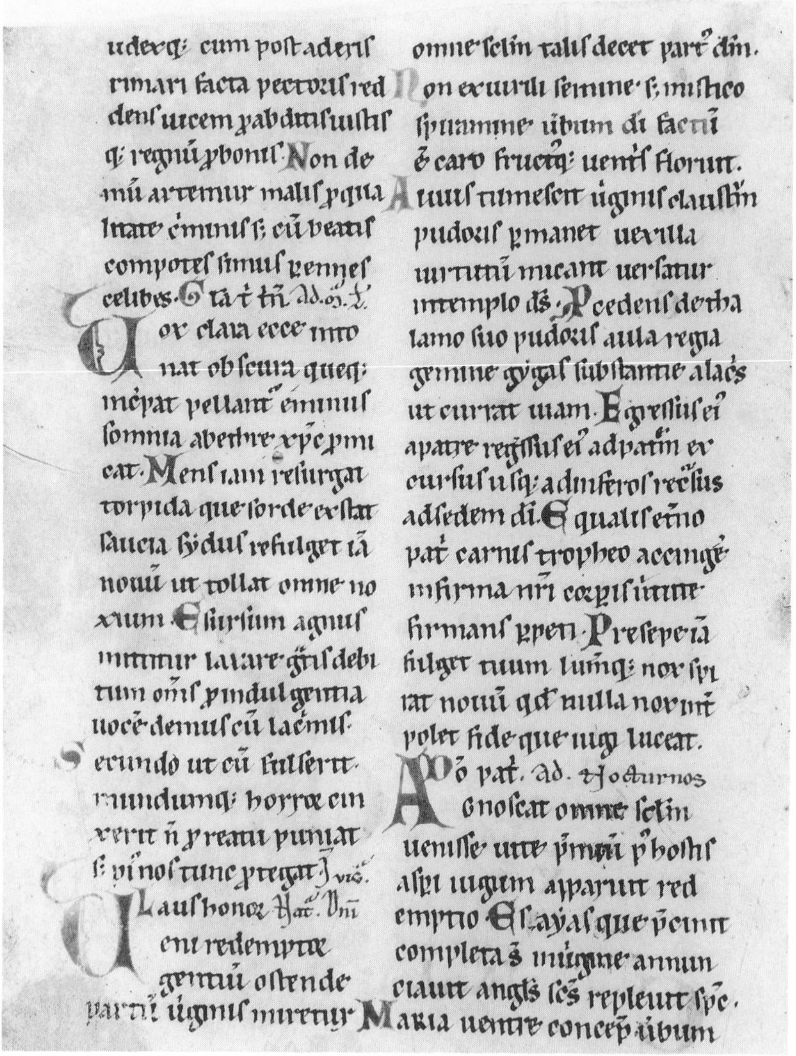

PLATE 7. A loose folio from a hymnary.

Plate 7

Hymnary, single folio on parchment, after 1100
AMB ms. 4.1; Annmary Brown Memorial Collection
John Hay Library, Brown University

Book production increased astronomically in the Carolingian period, owing to the work of culture formation undertaken by the scholars entrusted with this task by Charlemagne. In addition to normalizing orthography and reforming scripts, establishing a better foundation for monastic schools, and making classical and patristic authors equally canonical in them, these scholars gathered together the first formal libraries of the Latin Middle Ages and saw to the production of good copies of those works deemed important to the monastery and to education more generally.

Some books were scarce—copies of, say, Plautus. Other books, such as the Gospels, hymnals, antiphonaries, and psalters, were more plentiful. As books circulated throughout Europe, sometimes by request, more often by luck, accident, or chance, monasteries sometimes got the opportunity to copy out a famous work. Sometimes, too, as the centuries proceeded, the pangs of expansion were felt, as the body of written knowledge increased. In this case, works that were more plentiful could be recycled in order to accommodate this expansion— a practice common in the twelfth and thirteenth centuries especially.

The plate shown here is a witness to both trends, viz., to the growth of book production after the Carolingian period and to the pressures monasteries felt in the twelfth and thirteenth centuries to expand their canon. Presumably, this single folio, along with two other fragments preserved with it, formed part of a larger hymnary dating to the twelfth century. Of the three pieces that form AMB ms. 4.1, this is the only one that is in good shape. It appears to be intact, though with some of its top cut in order to make it usable in the later medieval codex of which it formed the backing. Written on parchment, in brown ink and in a late Carolingian hand, it has red initials. There are no visible rulings for lines or margins, though both are observed. The left and right margins are 2 cm., the bottom is 3 cm.; the top margin has been cut down, but must have been around 1.5 cm. It has 28 lines.

INTRODUCTION

When the western Roman empire reconstituted itself in the fifth century into smaller geographic, ethnic, and political units, there occurred a liberation of the Latin language from the earlier prescriptions of Imperial prose and poetry. These new-found freedoms were ballasted by the simultaneous rise of the Christian church, whose spiritual goals were matched by a set of cultural aspirations grounded in literary activities—reading, writing, the interpretation of Scripture. No longer the domain of private, patronized elites, literary culture after the fifth century was peopled now by writers of wider social rank and of diverse literary interests. In their hands, a host of innovations were managed, from the metrical and generic experiments of Fortunatus and Boethius, to the new forms of historical prose attempted by Bede, Jordanes, or Gregory of Tours, to the ecclesiastical prose style practiced by Gregory I.

At the same time, both in the schools, where it formed the basis of the curriculum, and in pockets throughout Italy, Spain, and Gaul, classical literary forms remained intact not as a vestige of empire but as an unbroken conduit to the past. This past became increasingly important, in turn, as the old model of *Romanitas* and the myths attending to empire were resuscitated in the West in the eighth century. By the 750s, the old Merovingian kingdoms of which Gregory of Tours had written were losing their identities as their royal lines died, or were snuffed, out. In the Austrasian kingdom, the mayor of the palace, Pepin the Short, had grown tired of being only *de facto* king and had usurped the throne for himself. His usurpation was legitimated not long afterward when, in 754, Pope Stephen found himself threatened by the armies of Lombards in Italy. Stephen found in Pepin what he required on short notice, a military leader with a ready-to-hand army. An easy deal was struck. In order to gain Pepin's support against the Lombards, Stephen agreed to anoint Pepin as king of the Austrasian Franks and to bind the Franks to Pepin's heirs. In return, Pepin agreed to rout the Lombards and return order to Rome and the surrounding countryside. Both sides kept their word. The Lombards were routed, while in one simple act Pepin's power was made *de jure*. Pepin's adroit manipulation of the authority of the church was a lesson his son, Charlemagne, never forgot.

In anointing Pepin, Stephen granted to him the title *Patricius Romanorum*, thus extending to the newly empowered king the accoutrements of the old empire.

The logical extension of this ceremony occurred on Christmas day, 800, when Charlemagne was crowned Holy Roman Emperor by Pope Leo III, thus joining in the figure of one ruler the spiritual assumptions of the Christian church and the imperial aspirations of the Carolingian line. Those aspirations had a long pedigree, dating back to the mayoralty of Charlemagne's grandfather, Charles Martel, early in the eighth century. But under Charlemagne they were most fully realized. The old empire was translated and the accoutrements of imperial culture were not long in coming.

The Carolingians were conscious imperialists in both abstract and concrete ways, drawing on the idea of Rome to support their continental aspirations, while attending to the renovation of Rome itself as the tangible symbol of their ideology. Part and parcel of this cultivation of all things Roman was a veneration of Roman cultural monuments, especially a nostalgia for Latin antiquity. This predilection had the effect of canonizing antiquity's best Latin works, but it also coincided with the cultural assumptions of Christianity, which privileged the book, writing, order, unity, as positive qualities of the best Christian culture. We can see vestiges of these qualities in the Carolingian love of the book, in the introduction of new forms of handwriting, in the copying out of antique manuscripts for fresh circulation and pleasure. Angilbert has recorded a sense of that pleasure in his poem on Charlemagne's court, in which, he tells us, Charlemagne was the glory of the poets, and the poets were the glory of Charlemagne (see Godman 112–18).

In pursuing the march of empire, Carolingian literary culture became more consciously devoted to classical models, effecting a fundamental shift from the literary assumptions of the fifth, sixth, and seventh centuries. Many of the more important literary figures of this age were contemporaries, and many worked together at the various movable courts visited by Charlemagne on his incessant imperial travels, where they sought his continued patronage, wrote for him, and constructed a privileged and rarefied literary culture in which to work and play. The court poets called each other by pseudonyms meant to conjure up antique associations—Pindar (Theodulf), Homer (Angilbert), Flaccus (Alcuin), and Naso (Modoin). More than this, they worked hard in their verse to bring the old genres of Latin antiquity down to their new golden age.

One can measure this attempt especially in the work of Alcuin, one of the most important figures of the age. While it is true that there is a line of influence in Alcuin's work that leads back to Fortunatus, especially in terms of metrical and thematic associations, it is also true that, unlike Fortunatus, Alcuin seems to have taken a special interest in revivifying antique pastoral and in carrying on the antique epic tradition in Christian terms on the model of the work of Avitus. The Carolingian interest in pastoral or, more generally, nature poetry is evinced also in Walahfrid Strabo's work, where the classical *locus amoenus* frames the struggle of the brutal forces of nature against the beneficence of their bounty and their seemingly innocuous charms. Like Alcuin and Walahfrid, Ermoldus Nigellus participates also in the classicizing tendencies of the age; but Ermoldus's topic is contemporary history, which, in his hands, is given the form of a classical epic. Historical prose, so well developed by this time apart from classicizing tendencies, nonetheless comes under the influence of those tendencies, in Paul the Deacon's historical account of the Lombards and in Einhard's biography of Charlemagne. For Paul, this means a return to a classicizing prose style, while for Einhard, this translates into a reliance on Suetonius's biographies of the Caesars for stylistic and organizational principles.

Though it is an age dominated by a deep nostalgia for classicism, the Carolingian period also had its share of litterateurs who looked elsewhere for models. Owing mostly to the increased status accorded to the Church once Charlemagne gave it the task of educating his empire, there arose from within its ranks a cohort of literary figures who were less susceptible to imperial nostalgia. Theodulf, for example, evinces in his work two strains of thought: a tendency to denigrate writing and reading, and an interest in the relationship of verbal to visual arts. In a culture of the book, the latter interest seems natural. Less expected is the negative view of the fundaments of Christian rhetoric that inform his poem on the books he was accustomed to reading. Sedulius, too, is less directly classical in the aesthetic goals set for his work, seeking to establish in his verse the social context of his art, where the dictates of faith and private devotion dovetail with the abilities of political power to sustain spiritual needs. Already in Sedulius's work one can see a movement toward a more personal perspective, albeit one framed by classical models and meters.

The poetry of Hrabanus Maurus witnesses this slow movement of Latin into the cloister most directly. Hrabanus focuses on simple topics in his verse—faithfulness to God, love of friends, purity of soul, unity of spirit—but he refracts these topics under the organizing rubric of his own personality. And, as his own personality becomes more important in his verse, the old classicizing augments of meter, diction, word-choice evanesce, replaced now by the personal expression of immediate feeling. Nor is this fading away from the older traditions of courtly poetry unique to Hrabanus's output. Indeed, it is not wrong to say that Hrabanus's work marks the rise of a new literary standard, medieval in sentiment because it is post-Imperial, a harbinger of the literary innovations of the next several centuries.

The literary work of the Carolingian period had the effect of making Latin once again a privileged language. In the simple expressiveness of Dhuoda, perhaps, one could still hear the strains of Egeria, and the varying social registers represented by the Carolingian authors—including the lowly and elites—embodied the wide compass granted to literary activity in this period. But the almost severe classicizing of this age's best authors had the effect of divorcing the language from its vulgar or popular roots. By the time Hrabanus Maurus was writing, vernacular languages had already supplanted Latin as the medium for everyday speech, cultivating a gamut of literary traditions, oral and eventually written, that spoke most directly to the experiences of the greatest number of people.

In the meantime, Latin retired to the cloister, a victim of its own success at remembering its classical pedigree. Over the course of the next several centuries, the language would experience its boldest innovations of genre, theme, and topic precisely in those areas—the sequence, beast poetry, drama, devotional poetry, folk lyric—untouched by classical hands. In the event, classicism, when it returned substantively to literary culture in the twelfth century, was no longer the force its had been at the court of Charlemagne. There, it had represented a living literary tradition. By 1100, it was little more than one aspect of tradition, a repertoire, but by no means the only repertoire, of Western literary experience.

Charlemagne had brought about the collusion of Christian and Roman culture. But only Christianity survived him. *Romanitas* lived on only in the fiction of the Holy Roman Empire. Medieval culture emerged in the ethnic, linguistic, and social currents of France, Germany, Spain, Italy, and England. The new unifying force was Christianity itself, announcing the rise of the Latin Middle Ages. The golden age that Modoin proclaimed in his poem on the power of imperial poetry was in fact the final chapter of the long story of empire—an end, not a beginning. Already the cloister, in Hopkins's words, was shaping, molding, the rise of Medieval Latin itself:

> I have desired to go
>   Where springs not fail,
> To fields where flies no sharp and sided hail
>   And a few lilies blow.
>
> And I have asked to be
>   Where no storms come,
> Where the green swell is in the havens dumb,
>   And out of the swing of the sea.

Paul the Deacon

History of the Lombards; The Poems
(*Historia Langobardorum*, c. 785; *Carmina* 4, 5, c. 775; *Carmina* 12, 19, c. 783)

Paul the Deacon is usually remembered as the author of the *Historia Langobardorum*, his most venturesome work, which established his reputation and which was left unfinished at his death. He is also a poet of some power and the author, too, of an earlier historical work, the *Historia Romana*, a continuation of the *Breviarium* of Eutropius. Paul has left us also a history of the bishops of Metz, an abridgment of the epitome of Festus, the *De verborum significatu*, and some letters, hymns, and sermons. The exact date of his birth is unknown. A reasonable conjecture, based on his known death date, 799, is around 730.

Paul was a Lombard by birth and received an exceptional education, presumably at Friuli, where he was born, and also at the court of the Lombard kings at Pavia. He was well read in the Latin classics and had a command of Greek unusual for his day but clearly available to him in Benevento, a city in which he also studied, then under the influence of the Byzantine east. By the early 760s, Paul was established at the Lombard court, and he presumably stayed there, receiving the patronage necessary to support his historical and poetical interests. Paul's fortunes were tied to a kingdom that increasingly drew the ire of Charlemagne, however, who invaded Lombardy in the 770s. At this point, Paul holed up in the illustrious Benedictine monastery at Monte Cassino. The "Angustae Vitae," reprinted here, almost certainly dates from this period. In the meantime, Paul's brother, Arichis, had been captured by Charlemagne's forces and imprisoned. Paul wrote an impassioned and successful plea for his brother's release, which seems to have brought him to the attention of Charlemagne. In any case, he was invited to join the court circle of intellectuals not long afterward, an invitation he accepted in 783. His verse epistle in response to a welcoming poem by Peter of Pisa, doyen of the court circle, reprinted here, speaks clearly to the larger issues of intellectual control and geographic isolation that colored official life at the various movable courts that served Charlemagne. Paul remained at Charlemagne's court for about five years. He retired to Monte Cassino around 786, where he spent the remainder of his life in scholarly pursuits, especially fleshing out the *Historia Langobardorum*.

The *Historia Langobardorum,* excerpted here, was exceptionally popular in the Middle Ages. It is a storehouse of information that would otherwise be lost, but it is also a coherent and strategically written consideration of the Lombard past in the context of Christian history, constructed carefully with literary and pedagogical aims in mind. Paul's poetry, on the other hand, evinces a sound knowledge of the classical poetical tradition but at the same time a willingness to forge ahead into new poetical practices that center on the liberation of genre, meter, and diction from rigid classical norms. In this regard, especially, Paul stands as one of the key figures in the development of ML verse.

The poetry of Paul the Deacon has been edited by E. Duemmler (*Monumenta Germaniae Historica, Poetae Latini Aevi Carolini,* vol. 1, Berlin, 1881, pp. 35–86); and by K. Neff (*Die Gedichte des Paulus Diaconus,* Munich, 1908). The *Historia Langobardorum* has been edited by G. Waitz (*Monumenta Germaniae Historica, Scriptores Rerum Langobardicarum et Italicarum,* Hanover, 1878, repr. 1978). The *Historia* has been translated by R. J. Deferarri et al. (*The Fathers of the Church,* New York, 1953) and by W. D. Foulke (*The History of the Lombards of Paul the Deacon,* New York, 1907). Raby 1, 162ff. discusses Paul's poetry in some detail. Goffart 329–431 offers a full and up-to-date treatment of the *Historia* and of Paul's intellectual world. Godman 86–89 translates *Carm.* 12. The text of Waitz is reprinted here for the *Historia,* Duemmler's for the poetry, both without change.

THE SEVEN SLEEPERS

Haut ab re esse arbitror, paulisper narrandi ordinem postponere, et quia adhuc stilus in Germania vertitur, miraculum, quod illic apud omnes celebre habetur, seu et quaedam alia breviter intimare. In extremis circium versus Germaniae finibus, in ipso oceani littore, antrum sub eminenti 5 rupe conspicitur, ubi septem viri, incertum ex quo tempore, longo sopiti sopore quiescunt, ita inlaesis non solum corporibus, sed etiam vestimentis, ut ex hoc ipso, quod sine ulla per tot annorum curricula corruptione perdurant, apud indociles easdem et barbaras nationes veneratione habeantur. Hi denique, quantum ad habitum spectat, Romani esse cer-

---

1. **haut** = CL *haud.* **ab re:** idiomatic phrase meaning "contrary to interests," here with the negative adverb *haut* and *esse arbitror* = "I do not think it to be contrary to my purposes. . . ." The infinitives *postponere* and *intimare* are dependent on *arbitror.* 2. **illic:** i.e., *in Germania.* 3. **circium versus:** i.e., "toward the northwest." 7. **ut ex hoc ipso:** lit., "that from this fact itself," proleptic of the subsequent *quod* clause. 9. **quantum . . . spectat:** lit., "how much attends to their dress."

nuntur. E quibus dum unum quidam cupiditate stimulatus vellet exuere, mox eius, ut dicitur, brachia aruerunt, poenaque sua ceteros perterruit, ne quis eos ulterius contingere auderet. Videres ad quod eos profectum per tot tempora providentia divina conservet. Fortasse horum quando- que, quia non aliter nisi christiani esse putantur, gentes illae praedicatione   5
salvandae sunt.

—Hist Lang. 1.4.

THE MAELSTROM

Nec satis procul ab hoc de quo praemisimus litore, contra occidenta- lem partem, qua sine fine oceanum pelagus patet, profundissima aquarum illa vorago est, quam usitato nomine maris umbilicum vocamus. Quae bis in die fluctus absorbere et rursum evomere dicitur, sicut per uni- versa illa litora accedentibus et recedentibus fluctibus celeritate nimia fieri   5
conprobatur. Huiusmodi vorago sive vertigo a poeta Virgilio Caribdis ap- pellatur; quam ille in freto Siculo esse suo in carmine loquitur, hoc modo dicens:

Dextrum Scilla latus, laevum inplacata Caribdis
Obsidet, atque imo baratri ter gurgite vastos   10
Sorbet in abruptum fluctus, rursusque sub auras
Erigit alternos, et sidera verberat unda.

Ab hac sane de qua diximus vertigine saepe naves raptim cursimque ad- trahi adfirmantur tanta celeritate, ut sagittarum per aera lapsus imitari videantur; et nonnumquam in illo baratro horrendo nimis exitu pereunt.   15
Saepe cum iam iamque mergendae sint, subitis undarum molibus retroac- tae, tanta rursus agilitate exinde elongantur, quanta prius adtractae sunt.

Adfirmant, esse et aliam huiusmodi voraginem inter Brittaniam insu-

---

3. **Videres ad quod . . . profectum:** potential subjunctive, "you will perhaps see for what purpose. . . ;" *quod* = CL *quem,* since *profectum* is masculine; *profectum* = perfect passive participle of *proficere,* but also a fourth declension masculine substan- tive, as here (LS 1457, s. v. 3 *profectus*).

1. **praemisimus:** the meaning of *praemittere* is "to send out word in advance," but Paul simply means here that he has mentioned this "shore" before. 2. **oceanum pelagus:** an example of pleonastic strengthening, common in LL/ML/VL, comparable to an English phrase such as "ocean sea." (cf. Löfstedt 21–24). 6. **conprobatur** = CL *comprobatur; fieri* is dependent on it. 9. *Aen.* 7.420. 13. **adtrahi** = CL *at- trahi,* present passive infinitive, complement of *adfirmantur.* 14. **adfirmantur** = CL *affirmantur;* the subject is *naves.* 16. **retroactae:** from *retroagere.* 17. **adtractae sunt** = CL *attractae sunt.* 18. **adfirmant** = CL *affirmant;* here as elsewhere Paul uses this verb to mean "they say," "they tell," etc.

Iam Galliciamque provinciam; cui etiam rei adstipulantur Sequanicae Aquitaniaeque litora; quae bis in die tam subitis inundationibus opplentur, ut, qui fortasse aliquantulum introrsus a litore repertus fuerit, evadere vix possit. Videas earum regionum flumina fontem versus cursu velocis-
5   simo relabi ac per multorum milium spatia dulces fluminum limphas in amaritudinem verti. Triginta ferme a Sequanico litore Evodia insula milibus distat. In qua, sicut ab illius incolis adseveratur, vergentium in eandem Caribdin aquarum garrulitas auditur.

Audivi quendam nobilissimum Gallorum referentem, quod ali-
10   quantae naves prius tempestate convulsae, postmodum ab hac eadem Caribdi voratae sunt. Unus autem solummodo ex omnibus viris qui in navibus illis fuerant, morientibus ceteris, dum adhuc spirans fluctibus supernataret, vi aquarum labentium abductus, ad oram usque inmanissimi illius baratri pervenit. Qui cum iam profundissimum et sine fine patens
15   chaos adspiceret, ipsoque pavore praemortuus se illuc ruiturum exspectaret, subito, quod sperare non poterat, saxo quodam superiectus insedit. Decursis siquidem iam omnibus quae sorbendae erant aquis, orae illius fuerant margines denudati; dumque ibi inter tot angustias anxius vix ob metum palpitans resederet, dilatamque ad modicum mortem nihilominus
20   operiret, conspicit ecce subito quasi magnos aquarum montes de profundo resilire navesque, quae absortae fuerant, primas emergere. Cumque una ex illis ei contigua fieret, ad eam se nisu quo potuit adprehendit; nec mora, celeri volatu prope litus advectus, metuendae necis casus evasit, proprii postmodum periculi relator existens. Nostrum quoque, id est
25   Adriaticum, mare, quod licet minus, similiter tamen Venetiarum Histri-

1. **Galliciamque:** the better spelling is *Gallaecia, ae* = Galicia, in the northwestern part of Spain (Sleumer 350). Paul could very easily have written *Galliamque* or *Gallicamque*, as some MSS record, but either Spain or Gaul makes sense here. **adstipulantur** = CL *astipulantur*. **Sequanicae Aquitaniaeque:** *Sequanicae* is from *Sequanica, ae* = Seine (Sleumer 716); *Aquitaniae* is from *Aquitania, ae* = Aquitaine (Sleumer 121); with *litora* = "the shores of Aquitaine and of the region of the Seine." 4. **flumina:** subject accusative in indirect statement introduced by *videas*. **versus** = CL *versus ad* + accusative = "to flow toward. . . ." 5. **relabi:** present infinitive in indirect statement. **limphas** = CL *lymphas*. 6. **ferme:** alternate form of the adverb *fere*. **Evodia:** the island of Alderney (Foulke 10). 7. **adseveratur** = CL *asseveratur*. 8. **Caribdin** = CL *Charybdin*, from *Charybdis, is*, here in the accusative in the prepositional phrase *in eandem. . . .* 13. **labentium:** present participle, from *labi* = "receding." 15. **adspiceret** = CL *aspiceret*. 22. **se nisu quo potuit:** lit., "by his own effort, to the extent he was able. . . ." **adprehendit** = CL *apprehendit*. 25. **quod licet minus:** "though with less violence. . . ." **Venetiarum Histriaeque litora:** *Venetiarum* is from *Venetiae, arum* (Sleumer 814); *Histriae* is from *Istria, ae* (Sleumer 450); the phrase = "the shores of Venetia and Istria . . ." on the eastern Adriatic Sea.

aeque litora pervadit, credibile est, parvos huiusmodi occultosque habere
meatus, quibus et recedentes aquae sorbeantur et rursum invasurae litora
revomantur. His ita praelibatis, ad coeptam narrandi seriem redeamus.

—*Hist. Lang.* 1.6.

ALBOIN, THE HUNS, AND THE GEPIDAE (c. 567)

Igitur Audoin, de quo praemiseramus, Langobardorum rex Rodelin-
dam in matrimonio habuit; quae ei Alboin, virum bellis aptum et per omnia strenuum, peperit. Mortuus itaque est Audoin, ac deinde regum iam
decimus Alboin ad regendam patriam cunctorum votis accessit. Qui cum
famosissimum et viribus clarum ubique nomen haberet, Chlotarius rex   5
Francorum Chlotsuindam ei suam filiam in matrimonio sociavit. De qua
unam tantum filiam Alpsuindam nomine genuit. Obiit interea Turisindus
rex Gepidorum; cui successit Cunimundus in regno. Qui vindicare veteres
Gepidorum iniurias cupiens, inrupto cum Langobardis foedere, bellum
potius quam pacem elegit. Alboin vero cum Avaribus, qui primum Hunni,   10
postea de regis proprii nomine Avares appellati sunt, foedus perpetuum
iniit. Dehinc ad praeparatum a Gepidis bellum profectus est. Qui cum
adversus eum e diverso properarent, Avares, ut cum Alboin statuerant,
eorum patriam invaserunt. Tristis ad Cunimundum nuntius veniens, in-
vasisse Avares eius terminos edicit. Qui prostratus animo et utrimque in   15
angustiis positus, hortatur tamen suos primum cum Langobardis con-
fligere; quos si superare valerent, demum Hunnorum exercitum e patria

1. **credibile est . . . habere:** the subject is [*n*]*ostrum mare*, with *habere:* "it is believed
that our sea has. . . ." 3. **redeamus:** Paul prepares now to take up the narrative he
abandoned at 1.4, with the story of the seven sleepers.
    1. **Rodelindam:** from *Rodelinda, ae* = Rodelinda; here in the accusative singular;
on the names in the passage, see Foulke 49–51. 2. **Alboin:** this name is indeclinable;
here it is in the accusative case. 3. **peperit:** from *parere,* with direct and indirect objects. 5. **Chlotarius:** from *Chlotarius, i* = Chlotar, here in the nominative. 6. **Chlotsuindam:** from *Chlotsuinda, ae* = Chlotsuinda, here in the accusative. 7. **Alpsuindam:** from *Alpsuinda, ae* = Alpsuinda, here in the accusative. 8. **Gepidorum:** from
Gepidae, arum = the Gepidae, ethnically a Gothic people who lived traditionally in the
areas beyond the Black Sea (LS 811). **Turisindus . . . Cunimundus:** *Turisindus* is from
Turisindus, i = Turisind; and *Cunimundus* is from *Cunimundus, i* = Cunimund.
9. **inrupto** = CL *irrupto.* 11. **Avares:** a form of *Avari, orum* = Avars (Sleumer 142);
generally declined in the second declension, but here it is used as a third declension
noun. 12. **ad praeparatum a Gepidis bellum:** lit., "for a war prepared by the Gepidae." 13. **properarent:** i.e., the Gepidae. **Avares, ut cum Alboin statuerant:** "as the
Avars had arranged with Alboin. . . ." 14. **eorum patriam invaserunt:** i.e., "the Avars
invaded the country of the Gepidae." 15. **eius:** i.e., Cunimund's. **in angustiis positus:** the idiom means something like "and placed in a tight spot."

pellerent. Committitur ergo proelium. Pugnatum est totis viribus. Langobardi victores effecti sunt, tanta in Gepidos ira saevientes, ut eos ad
internitionem usque delerent atque ex copiosa multitudine vix nuntius
superesset.

5   In eo proelio Alboin Cunimundum occidit, caputque illius sublatum,
ad bibendum ex eo poculum fecit. Quod genus poculi apud eos "scala"
dicitur, lingua vero Latina patera vocitatur. Cuius filiam nomine Rosi-
mundam cum magna simul multitudine diversi sexus et aetatis duxit cap-
tivam; quam, quia Chlotsuinda obierat, in suam, ut post patuit, perni-
10   ciem, duxit uxorem. Tunc Langobardi tantam adepti sunt praedam, ut
iam ad amplissimas pervenirent divitias. Gepidorum vero ita genus est
deminutum, ut ex illo iam tempore ultra non habuerint regem. Sed uni-
versi qui superesse bello poterant aut Langobardis subiecti sunt, aut usque hodie, Hunnis eorum patriam possidentibus, duro imperio subiecti
15   gemunt. Alboin vero ita praeclarum longe lateque nomen percrebuit, ut
hactenus etiam tam aput Baioariorum gentem quamque et Saxonum, sed
et alios eiusdem linguae homines eius liberalitas et gloria bellorumque
felicitas et virtus in eorum carminibus celebretur. Arma quoque praecipua
sub eo fabricata fuisse, a multis hucusque narratur.

—Hist. Lang. 1.27.

HOW THE LOMBARDS CAME TO ITALY

Igitur deleta, ut dictum est, vel superata Narsis omni Gothorum
gente, his quoque de quibus diximus pari modo devictis, dum multum
auri sive argenti seu ceterarum specierum divitias adquisisset, magnam a
Romanis, pro quibus multa contra eorum hostes laboraverat, invidiam
5   pertulit. Qui contra eum Iustiniano augusto et eius coniugi Sophiae in
haec verba suggesserunt, dicentes quia: "Expedierat Romanis, Gothis

---

3. **internitionem** = CL *internecionem*. 5. **sublatum:** from *tollere*. 7. **Rosimun-
dam:** from *Rosimunda, ae* = Rosemund, here in the accusative. 9. **ut post patuit:**
"as was afterwards made plain." **in suam . . . perniciem:** idiomatic phrase meaning
"at his own peril." **quam . . . duxit uxorem:** "whom he made his wife" (i.e., Rosem-
und). 13. **superesse bello:** *superesse* is the complement of *poterant;* with a dative
object, *bello*, it means "to survive the war." 16. **aput** = CL *apud*. **Baioariorum:**
more properly *Baiuvariorum*, from *Baiuvarii, orum* = Bavarians (Sluemmer 146).

1. **Narsis:** from *Narsis, is* = Narses, the famous general of Justinian; the subject
of *pertulit*. **deleta . . . superata . . . gente:** ablative absolute. 2. **his . . . devictis:** ablative absolute, parallel with *deleta . . . gente*. 3. **adquisisset** = CL *acquisisset*, syncopated form of *acquisivisset*. **magnam:** modifies *invidiam* in the next line.
4. **quibus:** i.e., the Romans. **contra eorum hostes:** i.e., "against the enemies of the
Romans." 5. **qui:** i.e., "the Romans." 6. **expedierat Romanis:** impersonal use of

potius servire quam Grecis, ubi Narsis eunuchus imperat et nos servitio premit; et haec noster piissimus princeps ignorat. Aut libera nos de manu eius, aut certe et civitatem Romanam et nosmet ipsos gentibus tradimus."
  Cumque hoc Narsis audisset, haec breviter retulit verba: "Si male feci cum Romanis, male inveniam." Tunc augustus in tantum adversus Narse- 5
tem commotus est, ut statim in Italiam Longinum praefectum mitteret, qui Narsetis locum obtineret. Narsis vero, his cognitis, valde pertimuit; et in tantum maxime ab eadem Sophia augusta territus est, ut regredi ultra Constantinopolim non auderet. Cui illa inter cetera, quia eunuchus erat, haec fertur mandasse, ut eum puellis in genicio lanarum faceret 10
pensa dividere. Ad quae verba Narsis dicitur haec responsa dedisse: talem se eidem telam orditurum, qualem ipsa, dum viveret, deponere non possit.
Itaque odio metuque exagitatus in Neapolim Campaniae civitatem se-
cedens, legatos mox ad Langobardorum gentem dirigit, mandans, ut pau-
pertina Pannoniae rura desererent et ad Italiam cunctis refertam divitiis 15
possidendam venirent. Simulque multimoda pomorum genera aliar-
umque rerum species, quarum Italia ferax est, mittit, quatenus eorum ad veniendum animos possit inlicere. Langobardi laeta nuntia et quae ipsi praeobtabant gratanter suscipiunt deque futuris commodis animos adtollunt. Continuo aput Italiam terribilia noctu signa visa sunt, hoc et igneae 20
acies in caelo apparuerunt, eum scilicet qui postea effusus est sanguinem coruscantes.

—Hist. Lang. 2.5.

the verb with dative object, *Romanis* = "it would be better for the Romans. . . ."
1. **servire:** complementary infinitive with *Romanis,* it takes a dative object, *Gothis,* and means, with modifying *potius* "rather to serve the Goths. . . ." 2. **libera:** impera-
tive. 3. **gentibus:** i.e., the Goths. 6. **praefectum:** "prefect." 9. **cui:** i.e., "to Narses." **illa:** i.e., Sophia. 10. **mandasse** = *mandavisse,* syncopated perfect active infinitive of *mandare.* 12. **orditurum** = *orditurum esse.* **deponere:** i.e., Sophia would not be able to find the end of the thread. 13. **Neapolim:** from *Neapolis, is* = Naples, this form is accusative singular (Sleumer 540). **Campaniae civitatem:** "a city of Campania," in apposition with *Neapolim.* One perhaps expects *urbem,* but in LL/
ML *civitas* = *urbs.* 15. **refertam:** from *refercire,* i.e., "teeming with. . . ." 16. **pos-
sidendam:** the gerundive of *possidere,* in agreement with the object of a verb expressing the act of undertaking something, signifies purpose, i.e., "he suggested that they come to Italy, teeming with all manner of riches, for the purpose of possessing it" (AG 500.4). 17. **quatenus** = CL *ut;* in LL/ML *quatenus* introduces both purpose and result clauses, usually with the subjunctive, though result clauses with *quatenus* and the indicative are found in LL/ML; § 6.1 (cf. Blaise 285, 290, 291). 19. **praeobtabant** = CL *praeoptabant;* the interchange of labial consonants is common in LL/ML orthography. **adtollunt** = CL *attolunt.* 21. **eum:** emphatic use of *is,* where one would expect in CL *illum.*

A FATAL JEST

Qui rex postquam in Italia tres annos et sex menses regnavit, insidiis suae coniugis interemptus est. Causa autem interfectionis eius fuit. Cum in convivio ultra quam oportuerat aput Veronam laetus resederet, cum poculo quod de capite Cunimundi regis sui soceris fecerat reginae ad
5 bibendum vinum dari praecepit atque eam ut cum patre suo laetanter biberet invitavit. Hoc ne cui videatur inpossibile, veritatem in Christo loquor: ego hoc poculum vidi in quodam die festo Ratchis principem ut illut convivis suis ostentaret manu tenentem. Igitur Rosemunda ubi rem animadvertit, altum concipiens in corde dolorem, quem conpescere non
10 valens, mox in mariti necem patris funus vindicatura exarsit, consiliumque mox cum Helmechis, qui regis scilpor, hoc est armiger, et conlactaneus erat, ut regem interficeret, iniit. . . .

Tunc Rosemunda, dum se Alboin in meridie sopori dedisset, magnum in palatio silentium fieri praecipiens, omnia alia arma subtrahens,
15 spatham illius ad lectuli caput, ne tolli aut evaginari possit, fortiter conligavit, et iuxta consilium Peredeo Helmechis interfectorem omni bestia crudelior introduxit. Alboin subito de sopore experrectus, malum quod imminebat intellegens, manum citius ad spatham porrexit; quam strictius religatam abstrahere non valens, adprehenso tamen scabello subpedaneo,
20 se cum eo per aliquod spatium defendit. Sed heu pro dolor! vir bellicosis-

---

1. **rex:** i.e., Alboin, whom Paul treats in the third excerpt above. 3. **ultra quam oportuerat:** lit., "beyond which it had been deemed appropriate. . . ." 4. **soceris** = *soceri;* the subtle difference between the two forms, consisting of the addition of a single consonant, suggests, to the extent that orthography reflects it, the ways in which inflection was changing in LL. 6. The details of the death of Cunimund and the marriage of Alboin to Rosemund are given in the third excerpt above. **inpossibile** = CL *impossibile.* 7. **Ratchis:** from *Ratchis, is* = Ratchis, accusative singular here, modified by *principem* (cf. Foulke 81). 8. **illut** = CL *illud,* i.e., *poculum;* the interchange of dentals is common in LL/ML orthography. **convivis:** in the plural = "dinner guests." 9. **conpescere** = CL *compescere.* 10. **vindicatura:** from *vindicare;* it is common in LL for the future active participle to be used to express purpose, intention, or readiness; § 7.4 (cf. AG 499.1, 2). **exarsit:** from *exardescere.* 11. **scilpor:** not a Latin word, hence Paul's explanation in the next clause. **conlactaneus** = CL *collactaneus,* i.e., "foster brother." 15. **evaginari:** from *evaginare,* "to be unsheathed." **conligavit** = CL *colligavit.* 16. **Peredeo:** another of the conspirators; the phrase *iuxta consilium Peredeo* means something like "following the advice of Peredeo"; cf. Foulke 82. **Helmechis:** from *Helmechis, is* = Helmechis, accusative singular here, in apposition with *interfectorem.* 19. **adprehenso** = CL *apprehenso.* **scabello subpedaneo:** pleonastic strengthening: *scabellum* and *subpedaneum* (CL *suppedaneum*) both mean "footstool." 20. **cum eo:** this typically LL/ML phrase makes sense to English readers, but CL would express the thought with ablative of means or accompaniment.

simus et summae audaciae nihil contra hostem praevalens, quasi unus de inertibus interfectus est, uniusque mulierculae consilio periit, qui per tot hostium strages bello famosissimus extitit.

—*Hist. Lang.* 2.28 (excerpts).

Emperor Tiberius Constantinus and the Treasure of Narses

Mortuo igitur Iustino, Tiberius Constantinus, Romanorum regum quinquagesimus, sumpsit imperium. Hic cum, ut superius diximus, sub Iustino adhuc caesar palatium regeret et multas cottidie elimosinas faceret, magnam ei Dominus auri copiam subministravit. Nam deambulans per palatium vidit in pavimento domus tabulam marmoream, in qua erat 5 crux dominica sculpta, et ait: "Crucem Domini frontem nostram et pectora munire debemus, et ecce eam sub pedibus conculeamus." Et dicto citius iussit eandem tabulam auferri. Defossamque tabulam atque erectam, inveniunt subter et aliam hoc signum habentem. Qui et ipsam iussit auferri. Qua amota, repperiunt et tertiam. Iussumque eius cum et 10 haec fuisset ablata, inveniunt magnum thesaurum habentem supra mille auri centenaria. Sublatumque aurum, pauperibus adhuc habundantius quam consueverat largitur. Narsis quoque patricius Italiae cum in quadam civitate intra Italiam domum magnam haberet, cum multis thesauris ad supra memoratam urbem advenit; ibique in domo sua occulte 15 cisternam magnam fodit, in qua multa milia centenariorum auri argentique reposuit. Interfectisque omnibus consciis, uni tantummodo seni haec per iuramentum ab eo exigens commendavit. Defuncto vero Narsete, supradictus senex ad caesarem Tiberium veniens, dixit: "Si," inquid, "mihi aliquid prodest, magnam rem tibi, caesarem, dicam." Cui ille: 20

1. Justin died in 578.   3. **caesar:** not in the ancient Roman sense but equivalent now to "king," a more generic term.   **elimosinas** = *eleemosynas*, from *eleemosyna, ae,* derived from the Greek ἐλεημοσύνη = "alms" (Blaise/Chirat 303).   6. **Crucem . . . debemus:** the thought is elliptical; Paul seems to say "we ought to wear the Lord's Cross on our forehead and chest, whereas, lo, we trample it under foot."   10. **iussumque** = *iussuque;* in CL *iussu* occurs only in the ablative; here, though in the accusative, it should be read with *eius* = "by his command."   11. **supra . . . centenaria:** a *centenarium* is 100 pounds of gold; this phrase thus means that they found "more than 100,000 pounds of gold."   12. **sublatumque aurum:** nominative absolute construction; § 3.3.1 (cf. Blaise 67).   **habundantius:** the addition of aspirates is common in LL/ML.   **habundantius . . . consueverat:** an adverbial clause modifying *largitur*, "it was distributed . . . more abundantly than was usual."   17. **per iuramentum . . . exigens:** lit = "demanding from him through an oath . . ." but with the sense simply of "demanding of him an oath."   18. **Narsete:** the ablative of Narsis.   19. **inquid** = CL *inquit.*   20. **caesarem:** assimilation of the vocative *caesar* into the accusative case,

"Dic," ait, "quod vis; proderit enim tibi, si quid nobis profuturum esse narraveris." "Thesaurum," inquid, "Narsis reconditum habeo, quod in extremo vitae positus celare non possum." Tunc caesar Tiberius gavisus mittit usque ad locum pueros suos. Recedente vero sene, hi secuntur at-

5 toniti; pervenientesque ad cisternam, deopertamque ingrediuntur. In qua tantum auri vel argenti repertum est, ut per multos dies vix a deportanti-bus potuisset evacuari. Quae ille pene omnia secundum suum morem ero-gatione largiflua dispensavit egenis.

—*Hist. Lang.* 3.12 (excerpts).

A Royal Wooing

Flavius vero rex Authari legatos post haec ad Baioariam misit, qui Garibaldi eorum regis filiam sibi in matrimonium peterent. Quod ille be-nigne suscipiens, Theudelindam suam filiam Authari se daturum pro-misit. Qui legati revertentes cum haec Authari nuntiassent, ille per semet

5 ipsum suam sponsam videre cupiens, paucis secum sed expeditis ex Lan-gobardis adhibitis, unumque sibi fidelissimum et quasi seniorem secum ducens, sine mora ad Baioariam perrexit. Qui cum in conspectum Gari-baldi regis iuxta morem legatorum introducti essent, et his qui cum Auth-ari quasi senior venerat post salutationem verba, ut moris est, intulisset:

10 Authari, cum a nullo illius gentis cognosceretur, ad regem Garibaldum propinquius accedens ait: "Dominus meus Authari rex me proprie ob hoc direxit, ut vestram filiam, ipsius sponsam, quae nostra domina futura est,

---

though with vocative force still (on assimilation in LL see Löfstedt 19). **1. profutu-rum:** future active participle of *prodesse*. **si quid . . . narraveris:** lit., "if you report that there is something that will be of benefit to us"; technically, *narraveris* introduces indirect statement, with *si quid* the subject accusative, modified by *nobis profuturum,* and *esse* the infinitive of the construction. **3. gavisus:** from *gaudere*. **4. secuntur** = CL *sequntur*. **5. deopertamque:** from *deoperire,* "disclosed," modifies *cisternam.* **7. pene** = CL *paene*.

1. Authari: this form, which in Paul's usage is indeclinable, is in the nominative here; read with *Flavius rex*. **post haec:** i.e., after those events recounted in the previ-ous chapter. **Baioariam:** from *Baioaria, ae* (the better spelling; cf. Sleumer 146) = Bavaria. **qui . . . peterent:** the thought is somewhat elliptical: "who [i.e., *legatos*] were to seek for him [*sibi,* i.e., Flavius Authari] in marriage the daughter of their [*eorum,* i.e. the Bavarians] king, Garibaldi." **4. nuntiassent:** syncopated pluperfect active subjunctive, third person plural of *nuntiare* = *nutiavissent.* **per semet:** i.e., "for his very self." **6. seniorem:** the sense is "chief" or "leader," a meaning *senior* has in LL/ML through EL (Blaise/Chirat 751 s. v. *senior* 3, 5, 6). **9. ut moris est:** CL id-iom = "as it was the custom." **11. Authari:** the king is pretending to be the *senior* in order to get a closer look at his prospective bride.

debeam conspicere, ut, qualis eius forma sit, meo valeam domino certius nuntiare." Cumque rex haec audiens filiam venire iussisset, eamque Authari, ut erat satis eleganti forma, tacito nutu contemplatus esset, eique satis per omnia complacuisset, ait ad regem: "Quia talem filiae vestrae personam cernimus, ut eam merito nostram reginam fieri optemus, si placet 5 vestrae potestati, de eius manu, sicut nobis postea factura est, vini poculum sumere praeoptamus." Cumque rex id, ut fieri deberet, annuisset, illa, accepto vini poculo, ei prius qui senior esse videbatur propinavit. Deinde cum Authari, quem suum esse sponsum nesciebat, porrexisset, ille, postquam bibit, ac poculum redderet, eius manu, nemine animadvertente, dig- 10 ito tetigit dexteramque suam sibi a fronte per nasum ac faciem produxit. Illa hoc suae nutrici rubore perfusa nuntiavit. Cui nutrix sua ait: "Iste nisi ipse rex et sponsus tuus esset, te omnino tangere non auderet. Sed interim sileamus, ne hoc patri tuo fiat cognitum. Re enim vera digna persona est, quae tenere debeat regnum et tuo sociari coniugio." Erat autem 15 tunc Authari iuvenali aetate floridus, statura decens, candido crine perfusus et satis decorus aspectu. Qui mox, a rege comeatu accepto, iter patriam reversuri arripiunt deque Noricorum finibus festinanter abscedunt. Noricorum siquidem provinica, quam Baioariorum populus inhabitat, habet ab oriente Pannoniam, ab occidente Suaviam, a meridie Italiam, ab 20 aquilonis vero parte Danuvii fluenta. Igitur Authari cum iam prope Italiae fines venisset secumque adhuc qui eum deducebant Baioarios haberet, erexit se quantum super equum cui praesidebat potuit et toto adnisu securiculam, qua manu gestabat, in arborem quae proximior aderat fixit eamque fixam reliquit, adiciens haec insuper verbis: "Talem Authari feri- 25 tam facere solet." Cumque haec dixisset, tunc intellexerunt Baioarii qui cum eo comitabantur, eum ipsum regem Authari esse. Denique post aliquod tempus, cum propter Francorum adventum perturbatio Garibaldo regi advenisset, Theudelinda, eius filia, cum suo germano nomine Gundoald ad Italiam confugiit seque adventare Authari suo sponso nuntiavit. 30

---

1. **qualis . . . sit:** indirect question functioning as a noun clause, the object of *nuntiare*. 6. **de** = CL *ex,* as is common in LL/ML. 9. **Authari:** dative case. 10. **eius:** i.e., "her." **manu:** apocope for *manum,* the object of *tetigit* (although it may be that Paul thinks the ablative case is in order here with verbs of motion). 12. **nutrici:** from *nutrix, nutricis.* 14. **re . . . vera:** "for in fact. . . ." 17. **comeatu** = CL *commeatu.* 20. **Pannoniam:** Pannonia, the Roman name for the land generally lying south of the Danube. **Suaviam:** i.e., Swabia. 22. **qui . . . deducebant:** modifies *Baioarios,* the object of *haberet.* 23. **cui praesidebat:** *praesidere* + dative object = "to ride." **adnisu** = CL *annisu* (*annisus*), with modifying *toto* = lit., "complete exertion," i.e., "with all his strength." 30. **Authari:** dative case, in apposition with *suo sponso.*

Cui statim ille obviam cum magno apparatu nuptias celebraturus in campum Sardis, qui super Veronam est, occurrens, eandem cunctis laetanti-
bus in coniugium Idus Maias accepit.

—Hist. Lang. 3.30 (excerpts).

A Remarkable Tale

Interea Authari rex legationem verbis pacificis ad Gunthramnum regem Francorum, patruum scilicet Childeperti regis, direxit. A quo legati
idem iocunde suscepti, sed ad Childepertum, qui ei nepus ex fratre erat,
directi sunt, ut per eius notum pax cum gente Langobardorum firmaretur.
5 Erat autem Gunthramnus iste, de quo diximus, rex pacificus et omni bonitate conspicuus. Cuius unum factum satis ammirabile libet nos huic
nostrae historiae breviter inserere, praesertim cum hoc Francorum historia noverimus minime contineri. Is cum venatum quodam tempore in
silvam isset, et, ut adsolet fieri, hac illacque discurrentibus sociis, ipse cum
10 uno fidelissimo tantum suo remansisset, gravissimo somno depressus, caput in genibus eiusdem fidelis sui reclinans, obdormivit. De cuius ore parvum animal in modum reptilis egressum, tenuem rivulum, qui propter
discurrebat, ut transire possit, satagere coepit. Tunc isdem in cuius gremio
quiescebat spatham suam vagina exemptam super eundem rivulum po-
15 suit; super quam illud reptile, de quo diximus, ad partem aliam transmea-
vit. Quod cum non longe exinde in quoddam foramen montis ingressum
fuisset, et post aliquantum spatii regressum super eandem spatham prae-
fatum rivulum transmeasset, rursum in os Gunthramni, de quo exierat,
introivit. Gunthramnus post haec de somno expergefactus, mirificam se
20 visionem vidisse narravit. Retulit enim, paruisse sibi in somnis, quod
fluvium quendam per pontem ferreum transisset et sub montem quoddam
introisset, ubi multos auri pondus aspexisset. Is vero in cuius gremio caput tenuerat, cum dormisset, quid de eo viderat, ei per ordinem retulit.
Quid plura? Effossus est locus ille, et inaestimabiles thesauri, qui ibidem
25 antiquitus positi fuerant, sunt reperti. De quo auro ipse rex postmodum

1. **cui** + *obviam* = "in order to meet her. . . ."
    1. **Gunthramnum:** from *Gunthramnus, i* = King Gunthram of Burgundy.
3. **nepus** = CL *nepos*, "nephew." 6. **ammirabile** = CL *admirabile*. 8. **noverimus:**
from *noscere* (*gnoscere*), in perfect active subjunctive, first person plural with *cum*.
minime contineri: i.e., "not contained." 9. **isset:** syncopated (but more common)
pluperfect active subjunctive, third person singular of *ire* = *ivisset*. **adsolet** = CL
assolet. 11. **genibus:** from *genu, genus*. 12. **propter:** adverb. 14. **quiescebat:**
i.e., King Authari. 23. **de eo:** i.e., "concerning the matter [just related by the King]."
per ordinem: i.e., "in the order [that those events happened which he had seen]."
24. **effossus:** from *effodere*. 25. **antiquitus:** adverb.

cyborium solidum mirae magnitudinis et magni ponderis fecit, multisque illud preciosissimis gemmis decoratum ad sepulchrum Domini Hierosolimam transmittere voluit. Sed cum minime potuisset, eodem supra corpus beati Marcelli martyris, quod in civitate Cavallono sepultum est, ubi sedes regni illius erat, poni fecit; et est ibi usque in praesentem diem. Nec   5
est usquam ullum opus ex auro effectum, quod ei valeat conparari. Sed nos, his breviter quae relatu digna erant contactis, ad historiam revertamur.

—*Hist. Lang.* 3.34.

PAUL'S GENEALOGY

Exigit vero nunc locus, postposita generali historia, pauca etiam privatim de mea, qui haec scribo, genealogia retexere, et quia res ita postolat paulo superius narrationis ordinem replicare. Eo denique tempore quo Langobardorum gens de Pannoniis ad Italiam venit Leupchis meus abavus ex eodem Langobardorum genere cum eis pariter adventavit. Qui post-   5
quam aliquod annos in Italia vixit, diem claudens extremum, quinque ex se genitos filios adhuc parvulos reliquit; quos tempestas ista captivitatis, de qua nunc diximus, conprehendens, omnes ex castro Foroiulensi in Avarorum patriam exsoles deduxit. Qui cum per multos annos in eadem regione captivitatis miseriam sustinuissent et iam ad virilem pervenissent   10
aetatem, ceteris quattuor, quorum nomina non retinemus, in captivitatis angustia persistentibus, quintus eorum germanus nomine Lopichis, qui noster postea proavus extitit, inspirante sibi, ut credimus, misericordiae auctore, captivitatis iugum abicere statuit et ad Italiam, quo gentem Langobardorum residere meminerat, tendere atque ad libertatis iura studuit   15

1. **cyborium:** (sometimes *ciborium* or *ciburium;* cf. Blaise/Chirat 149), not with the CL meaning that Horace gives it of "drinking cup" on the model of the Greek κιβ-ώριον, but rather "canopy" (cf. Sleumer 209). 2. **Hierosolimam:** more properly *Hierosolymam* (cf. Sleumer, p. 385, s. v. *Hierosolyma*), here in accusative of place to which construction. 3. **eodem** = CL *idem.* 4. **Cavallono:** Chalon-sur-Saône, Gunthram's capital.

   2. **postolat** = CL *postulat.* 3. **paulo superius:** i.e., "a little bit earlier. . . ." 4. **Leupchis:** nominative singular, in apposition with *meus abavus.* 6. **aliquod** = CL *aliquot.* **diem claudens extremum:** periphrasis for *mori.* 7. **tempestas:** used figuratively here. 8. **de qua nunc diximus:** Paul has related some of the details of *tempestas ista captivitatis* earlier in the *Hist. Lang.* **conprehendens** = CL *comprehendens,* has the sense of "including. . . ." **Foroiulensi:** i.e., the Forum Julii. 9. **exsoles** = CL *exules.* 12. **Lopichis:** from *Lopichis, is* = Lopichis, in the nominative case here in apposition with *germanus.* 13. **misericordiae auctore:** periphrasis for *Deo,* read with *inspirante sibi.* 15. **tendere:** governed by *statuit* (parallel with *abicere*), with *ad Italiam* as object.

reppedare. Qui cum adgressus fugam adripuisset, faretram tantum et arcum et aliquantulum cibi propter viaticum gerens, nesciretque omnino
quo pergeret, ei lupus adveniens comes itineris et ductor effectus est. Qui
cum ante eum pergeret et frequenter post se respiceret et cum stante sub-
5   sisteret atque cum pergente praeiret, intellexit, sibi eum divinitus datum
esse, ut ei iter, quod nesciebat, ostenderet. Cum per aliquod dies per montium solitudines hoc modo pergerent, panis eidem viatori, quem exiguum
habuerat, omnino defecit. Qui cum ieiunans iter carperet et iam fame
tabefactus defecisset, tetendit arcum suum et eundem lupum, ut eum in
10 cibum sumere possit, sagitta interficere voluit. Sed lupus idem ictum ferientis praecavens, sic ab eius visione elapsus est. Ipse autem, recedente
eodem lupo, nesciens quo pergeret, insuper famis penuria nimium debilis
effectus, cum iam de vita desperaret, sese in terram proiciens, obdormivit;
viditque quendam virum in somnis talia sibi verba dicentem: "Surge!
15 Quid dormis? Arripe viam in hanc partem contra quam pedes tenes; illac
etenim est Italia, ad quam tendis." Qui statim surgens, in illam partem
quam in somnis audierat pergere coepit; nec mora, ad habitaculum hominum pervenit. Erat enim Sclavorum habitatio in illis locis. Quem cum una
mulier iam vetula vidisset, statim intellexit, eum fugitivum esse et famis
20 penuria laborare. Ducta autem misericordia super eum, abscondit eum in
domo sua et secreto paulatim ei victum minsitravit, ne, si ei usque ad
saturitatem alimoniam praeberet, eius vitam funditus extingueret. Denique sic conpetenter ei pastum praebuit, quousque ipse recuperatus vires
accipere potuisset. Cumque eum iam validum ad iter faciendum vidisset,
25 datis ei cibariis, ad quam partem tendere deberet, admonuit. Qui post
aliquod dies Italiam ingressus, ad domum in qua ortus fuerat pervenit;
quae ita deserta erat, ut non solum tectum non haberet, sed etiam rubis

---

1. **reppedare** = CL *repedare,* governed by *studuit* with the prepositional phrase *ad
libertatis iura* its object. **adgressus** = CL *aggressus.* **adripuisset** = CL *arripuisset.*
faretram = CL *pharetram.* 5. **eum:** i.e., *lupum.* **divinitus:** adverb. 9. **tabefactus:**
lit., "melting," "dissolving," but used here figuratively with *fame* to mean something
like "dying of hunger." 10. **ferientis:** from *ferire,* lit., "the one striking," referring
presumably to Lopichis but perhaps to the arrow itself. 12. **famis penuria:** "by the
want of famine." 15. **contra . . . tenes:** i..e, "contrary to the part you hold your feet
to now." 17. **habitaculum:** "dwelling-place." 18. **Sclavorum:** from *Sclavi, orum* =
Slavs (Sleumer 702). 20. **laborare** + *penuria famis* = "laboring under the want of
famine," the phrase is governed by *intellexit,* with *eum* the subject accusative.
21. **victum:** *victus, victus,* lit., "livelihood," "way of life," but here meaning something
like "food," "sustinence." 22. **funditus:** adverb. 23. **conpetenter** = CL *compet-
enter.* 25. **ad quam . . . deberet:** a noun clause functioning as the object of *admonuit:*
"she showed him in which direction he ought to head."

et sentibus plena esset. Quibus ille succisis intra eosdem parietes vastam
hornum repperiens, in ea sua faretra suspendit. Qui postea consan-
guineorum et amicorum suorum muneribus dotatus, et domum reaedi-
ficavit et uxorem duxit; sed nihil de rebus quas genitor suus habuerat,
exclusus iam ab his qui eas invaserant longa et diuturna possessione, con-　5
quirere potuit. Iste, ut iam superius praemisi, extitit meus proavus. Hic
etenim genuit avum meum Arichis, Arichis vero patrem meum Warnefrit,
Warnefrit autem ex Theudelinda coniuge genuit me Paulum meumque
germanum Arichis, qui nostrum avum cognomine retulit. Haec paucis de
propriae genealogiae serie delibatis, nunc generalis historiae revertamur　10
ad tramitem.

—Hist. Lang. 4.37 (excerpts).

THE COMO POEM

Ordiar unde tuas laudes, O maxime Lari?
　Munificas dotes ordiar unde tuas?
Cornua panda tibi sunt instar vertice tauri;
　Dant quoque sic nomen cornua panda tibi.
Munera magna vehis divinis dives asylis,　　　　　　　　　　5
　Regificis mensis munera magna vehis.
Ver tibi semper inest, viridi dum cespite polles;
　Frigora dum superas, ver tibi semper inest.
Cinctus oliviferis utroque es margine silvis;
　Numquam fronde cares cinctus oliviferis.　　　　　　　　　10
Punica mala rubent laetos hinc inde per hortos;

2. **hornum** = CL *ornum,* "mountain ash tree"; the addition of aspirates in LL/ML is
common. **faretra** = CL *pharetra; as object of *suspendit,* the correct form is *pharetram,* but through attraction to *in ea* it has become *pharetra.* 5. **conquirere potuit:**
the object is *nihil,* modified by a prepositional phrase and relative clause.

　1. **Lari:** *Larius* is Como's Latin name, here in the vocative. 2. **dotes:** from *dos,
dotis.* 3. **tauri:** Lake Como has two branches which proceed southward from it,
making it appear as if it has horns. 4. **cornua panda:** Paul implies the richness of the
land surrounding Lake Como, quite apart from its shape, in a pun on Como's Latin
name, *Larius,* akin to the Roman tutelary gods of the hearth and harvest, the *Lares,*
who were represented as pouring forth their wealth from cornucopiae—thus the reference to *nomen* here. 5. **dives:** vocative case. **asylis:** Paul uses this word, which has
the meaning in CL of "sanctuary" or "refuge" (on the model of the Greek ἄσυλον, cf.
LS 185), to designate churches in the vicinity of Lake Como. 7. **dum:** in LL/ML
dum loses the explanatory force it has in CL ("while") and commonly means "since,"
as here; § 6.1 (cf. Blaise 281). **cespite** = CL *caespite,* modified by *viridi (viridis)* in
ablative of specification with *polles.* 9. **cinctus:** perfect passive participle of *cingere.*
11. **Punica mala:** the pomegranate. **hinc inde:** "here and there."

Mixta simul lauris Punica mala rubent.
Myrtea virga suis redolet de more corimbis,
   Apta est et foliis myrtea virga suis.
15   Vincit odore suo delatum Perside malum,
   Citreon has omnes vincit odore suo.
Cedat et ipse tibi me iudice furvus Avernus,
   Epyrique lacus cedat et ipse tibi.
Cedat et ipse tibi vitrea qui Fucinus unda est,
20   Lucrinusque potens cedat et ipse tibi.
Vinceres omne fretum, si te calcasset Iesus,
   Si Galilaeus eras, vinceres omne fretum.
Fluctibus ergo cave tremulis submergere lintres;
   Ne perdas homines fluctibus ergo cave.
25   Si scelus hoc fugias, semper laudabere cunctis;
   Semper amandus eris, si scelus hoc fugias.
Sit tibi laus et honor, trinitas inmensa, per aevum;
   Quae tam mira facis, sit tibi laus et honor.
Qui legis ista, precor, "Paulo" dic "parce, redemptor,"
30   Spernere neve velis, qui legis ista, precor.

                         —*Carm.* 4.

THE CLOISTERED LIFE

Angustae vitae fugiunt consortia Musae,
Claustrorum septis nec habitare volunt,
Per rosulenta magis cupiunt sed ludere prata,
Pauperiem fugiunt, deliciasque colunt:

15. **delatum:** from *deferre*. **Perside malum:** "the peach," here in the nominative singular. 16. **Citreon:** "the citrus tree." 17. **me iudice:** lit., "with me as judge." **Avernus:** the lake famous in classical lore as the marker of the entrance to the underworld, it was thus considered, owing to the fumes exhaled from it, noxious enough to kill even birds flying overhead. 18. **Epyrique lacus:** "the lake of Epirus"; the province of Epirus (in ancient times part of northern Greece) was famous for its own lake that served as a conduit to the underworld. The CL spelling is *Epirus, i.* 19. **Fucinus:** Lake Fucinus, mentioned by Virgil in the story of the priest Umbro in *Aen.* 7.759ff. 20. **Lucrinusque:** the Lucrine lake, in Campania. 21. **calcasset:** syncopated pluperfect active subjunctive, third person singular of *calcare* = *calcavisset.* 22. **Galilaeus:** the Sea of Galilee. 23. **lintres:** from *linter, lintris.* 25. **laudabere** = *laudaberis,* alternate future passive indicative, second person singular, "you will be praised."

    2. **septis** = CL *saeptis;* the phrase *claustrorum septis* means something like "in the gardens of the monasteries" (*claustrum* regularly means "cloister" or "monastery" in LL/ML [Sleumer 214]).

Quapropter nobis aversae terga dederunt,   5
    Et comitem spernunt me vocitare suum.
Inde est quod vobis inculta poemata mitto,
    Suscipe sed libens qualiacumque tamen.
Inmodico flagrat de vestro pectus amore,
    Crede pater, nostrum, semper amande mihi.   10
Et peream, si non tecum captare per aevum
    Per domini munus regna beata volo.
Hoc mihi est votum, hoc fido pectore spero,
    Hoc licet indignus nocte dieque precor.
Tu quoque, si felix vigeas de munere Christi,—   15
    Namque potes—misero redde, beate, vicem.
Ante potest flavos Hrenus repedare Suavos,
    Ad fontem et versis pergere Tibris aquis,
Quam tuus e nostro labatur pectore vultus
    Ore colende mihi tempus in omne pater!   20
                                        —*Carm. 5.*

PAUL RESPONDS TO PETER OF PISA

Sensi, cuius verba cepi exarata paginis,
nam a magno sunt directa, quae pusillus detulit;

5. **aversae:** the subject of *dederunt,* with dependent *nobis* = "those averse to us."
terga + *do* = "to turn their backs. . . ."   9. **inmodico** = CL *immodico* + *de vestro
amore* = "from immoderate love of you."   10. **nostrum:** modifies *pectus* in the previous line.   **amande mihi:** passive periphrastic construction in the vocative case, with
mihi in dative of reference: "[pater] who must be loved by me always."   11. **captare:**
alternate present passive indicative, second person singular = *captaris,* "you are captured," "seized," etc.   16. **vicem:** this adverb means "in turn" and refers to the author's hope that his *pater* will send back to him a response to this poem.
17. **Hrenus** = CL *Rhenus,* the Rhine River.   **Suavos** = CL *Suebi, orum:* the Swabians,
a Germanic people who lived near to the mouth of the Rhine, hence, *repedare* must
mean "to turn back away from. . . ."   19. **quam:** the construction is *ante . . . quam,*
on the famous model of Virgil, *Ecl.* 1.63ff.   20. **colende:** passive periphrastic construction, vocative case, with dative of reference *mihi.*   **tempus in omne** = *semper.*
    1. **sensi:** the perfect active indicative, first person singular, corresponds to a per-
fect definitive = "I have known"; thus it can be rendered "I know" (AG 161).   **cuius
verba:** Paul refers to the verse epistle sent to him earlier by Peter of Pisa, welcoming
him to the court of Charlemagne and praising his wide knowledge of the *tres linguae
sacrae.* That letter was written as if by Charlemagne, hence the play in v. 2 between
magno and *pusillus.*   **cepi:** from *capere,* lit. "I seized," but with the idea of compre-
hending through reading, i.e., "I have read."   **exarata:** from *exarare.*   **cuius . . . paginis:** this relative clause stands as the object of *sensi.*

fortes me lacerti pulsant, non inbellis pueri.

Magnus dicor poetarum vatumque doctissimus,
5   omniumque preminere gentium eloquio,
cordis et replere rura fecundis seminibus.

Totum hoc in meam cerno prolatum miseriam;
totum hoc in meum caput dictum per hyroniam;
eheu, laudibus deridor et cacinnis obprimor.

10   Dicor similis Homero, Flacco et Vergilio,
similor Tertullo sive Philoni Memphitico,
tibi quoque, Veronensis o Tibulle, conferor.

Peream, si quenquam horum imitari cupio,
avia qui sunt sequuti pergentes per invium;
15   potius sed istos ego conparabo canibus.

Graiam nescio loquellam, ignoror Hebraicam;
Tres aut quattuor in scolis quas didici syllabas,
ex his mihi est ferendus maniplus ad aream.

Nulla mihi aut flaventis est metalli copia
20   aut argenti sive opum, desunt et marsuppia;

4. dicor: present passive indicative, first person singular, lit., "I am called," "I am said [to be] . . ." **7. prolatum** = *prolatum esse,* with *cerno* and subject accusative *totum hoc:* "I see that all of this is done to make me miserable. . . ." **8. dictum** = *dictum esse.* **hyroniam** = CL *ironiam;* the addition of aspirates in common in LL/ML orthography. **9. obprimor** = CL *opprimor.* **10. Homero:** *Homerus,* i.e., Homer, the Greek epic poet of the 8th c. B.C.E., whose works were read only in translation at the court of Charlemagne. **Flacco:** (*Quintus Horatius) Flaccus,* i.e., Horace, the Roman lyric poet who died in 8 B.C.E. **Vergilio:** (*Publius) Vergilius (Maro),* i.e., Virgil, the Roman epic poet, famous for the *Aeneid,* who died in 19 B.C.E. **11. Tertullo:** *Tertullus,* otherwise unknown, but perhaps the orator of Acts 24. **Philoni:** *Philo, Philonis,* the Jewish philosopher. **Memphitico:** *Memphiticus, a, um* = "Egyptian," referring to Philo's birth at Alexandria. **12. Veronensis:** "of Verona"; Catullus, not Tibullus, is from Verona, but Paul may be reflecting a tradition about Tibullus that has receded from our sources. **Tibulle:** vocative case. **13. quenquam:** from *quisquam,* with *horum* = "any one of them." **14. avia:** object of *sequuti,* the initial "a" is long. **sequuti** = CL *secuti,* perfect participle of *sequi.* **15. canibus:** from *canis, canis.* **16. Graiam:** *Graius, a, um,* modifies *loquellam,* and refers to written, not spoken, Greek. **Hebraicam:** *Hebraicus, a, um,* modifies *loquellam* and refers to written, not spoken Hebrew. **17. scolis** = CL *scholis.* **18. maniplus:** in CL poetry this is the syncopated form of *manipulus.* The thought of this somewhat difficult line is "and from these [syllables] is the handful that I must carry to the threshing floor." **19. mihi:** dative of reference. **aut . . . aut . . . sive:** "neither . . ., nor . . ., nor. . . ."

vitam litteris ni emam, nihil est quod tribuam.

Pretiosa quaeque vobis dona ferant divites;
alii conportant gemmas Indicosque lapides;
meo pura tribuetur voluntas in munere.

Anchora me sola vestri hic amoris detinet,   25
nectar omne quod precellit quodque flagrat optime;
non de litteris captamus vanae laudem gloriae.

Nec me latet, sed exulto, quod pergat trans maria
vestra, rector, et capessat sceptrum pulchra filia,
ut per natam regni vires tendantur in Asiam.   30

Si non amplius in illa regione clerici
Graece proferunt loquellae, quam a me didicerint,
Vestri, mutis similati deridentur statuis.

Sed omnino ne linguarum dicam esse nescius,
pauca mihi quae fuerunt tradita puerulo   35
dicam; cetera fugerunt iam gravante senio:

De puero qui in glacie extinctus est

Trax puer adstricto glacie dum ludit in Hebro,
   Frigore concretas pondere rupit aquas.
Dumque imae partes rapido traherentur ab amni,
   Presecuit tenerum lubrica testa caput.   40
Orba quod inventum mater dum conderet urna,
   "Hoc peperi flammis, cetera," dixit, "aquis."

                              —*Carm.* 12.

22. **divites:** the adjective *dives, divitis,* used substantively as the subject of this line.
23. **conportant** = CL *comportant.*   25. **anchora** = CL *ancora.*   26. **quod** = *qui,*
referring to *amor.*   28. **Nec me latet:** lit., "Nor is it hidden to me . . .," i.e., "Nor am I
blind to the fact that (*quod*). . . ."   29. **rector:** i.e., Charlemagne; although this poetic
epistle is written as a response-in-kind to Peter of Pisa, both letters function under the
convention of being from, and for, the king.   **capessat:** from *capessere.*   30. **natam:**
i.e., Charlemagne's daughter Rothrud, who had recently been betrothed to the young
Constantine VI of Byzantium; the wedding never took place, however.   32. **Graece**
. . . **loquellae:** dependent on *non amplius . . . quam* = "no more of the Greek language
. . . than. . . ."   **didicerint:** from *discere.*   33. **vestri:** modifies *clerici.*   35. **tradita:**
from *tradere,* modifying *pauca.*   37. **Trax** = CL *Thrax, acis,* "Thracian," modifies
puer.   **adstricto** = CL *astricto,* from *astringere,* here meaning "hard."   **Hebro:** i.e.,
Hebrus, i, the Hebrus, the chief river in Thrace.   40. **presecuit:** from *praesecare,* i.e.,
"cut off."   42. **peperi:** from *parere.*

AN EPITAPH FOR THE TOMB OF FORTUNATUS

Ingenio clarus, sensu celer, ore suavis,
  Cuius dulce melos pagina multa canit,
Fortunatus, apex vatum, venerabilis actu,
  Ausonia genitus hac tumulatur humo.
5 Cuius ab ore sacro sanctorum gesta priorum
  Discimus: haec monstrant carpere lucis iter.
Felix, quae tantis decoraris, Gallia, gemmis,
  Lumine de quarum nox tibi tetra fugit.
Hos modicos prompsi plebeio carmine versus,
10 Ne tuus in populis, sancte, lateret honor.
Redde vicem misero: ne iudice spernar ab aequo,
  Eximiis meritis posce, beate, precor.

—*Carm.* 19.

See part 2 on Fortunatus; Paul composed this epitaph at the request of Aper, abbot of the monastery of Saint Hilary in Poitiers, c. 785.   **8. tetra** = CL *taetra,* modifying *nox.*   **9. prompsi:** from *promere,* "to bring out."   **11. Redde vicem misero:** lit., "return like honors to me, in need of them."

ALCUIN

Poems and Letters
(*Carmina; Epistulae;* c. 775–796)

It is difficult to think of Western culture configured in the same terms absent the vigorous presence of Alcuin, so influential and various are his accomplishments. He was born in York around 735 and educated at the cathedral school there, where he began his scholarly and intellectual pursuits, eventually becoming, in 778, head of the school, a position he held until 782. Alcuin had already achieved an international reputation for learning when, returning from a trip to Rome in 781, at a stopover in Parma, he attracted the attention of Charlemagne, who made inquiries as to his willingness to organize a palace school at Aix-la-Chapelle. Alcuin moved from England to the continent soon thereafter to pursue the work of culture-building for Charlemagne.

Alcuin's work at the court was wide and eclectic. He concentrated on the development of the *schola palatina,* which became the intellectual center of the Carolingian empire. At the school, studies were organized carefully around the seven liberal arts, whose division into the quadrivium and trivium is probably owed to Alcuin. Education did not dominate his interests, however, as the extant output of Alcuin's writings attests. Alcuin wrote hundreds of epistles, of which some 310 survive, one of which is reprinted here, biographies of several saints, including a lengthy epic poem on the bishops, kings, and saints of York; theological treatises; commentaries on the Bible; dialogues on education, grammar, rhetoric, philology, and dialectic; and a large amount of poetry, examples of which follow. He also produced a revision of the Vulgate (no longer extant) and a new version of the Gregorian sacramentary, which became the basis of the Latin Missal of the Western church. Alcuin remained at Charlemagne's court for fourteen years, influencing scores of students while pursuing his own fundamental work in so many key areas of western Christian culture. He took his leave of the bustle of court life in 796, when Charlemagne conferred on him the abbacy of Saint Martin of Tours. His residence there, from 796 until his death in 804, raised the status of the monastery inestimably. Predictably, Alcuin founded what would become an important library and school at the abbey, whose care became his sole concern for the remainder of his life.

The poetry excerpted here displays the wide range of mood, emotion, and form that characterizes Alcuin's verse. The poems are constructed with a sure knowledge of CL, but the more formal qualities of diction and meter, while ostensibly classical, are put to new tasks, as in the cell poem, where, in classical terms, a pastoral topic adduces epic vocabulary in elegiac meter to talk about a lyrical moment. The blend nevertheless is successful because the balance between the classical elements is informed by an honesty of vision and a deftness of voice that render Alcuin, in addition to his many other talents, one of the key players in the development of Medieval Latin poetry in the Western tradition. Those talents are in evidence especially in the poetry of monastic friendship reprinted here. In these complex and allusive works, Alcuin keys into various traditions—CL pastoral, Hiberno-Latin debate poetry, Christian bird poetry—in order to render his relationship with his monastic students and friends more palpable. In the relationships recalled in these poems, with their warm intimacy and playfulness, there is both an intensely personal voice singing to readers, but also a voice whose very consonance with its materials and traditions affirms the wider symmetries of God's creation. Like the nightingale in the poem he wrote in honor of this dull and drab bird, Alcuin himself could let loose the emotion of his desire—for friendship, for God, for learning—knowing that the surface polish of his learning would not prove too much an obstacle to understanding. When he turns from poetry to writing admonitions to King Aethelred in the letter reprinted here, on the other hand, the tone is direct, simple, crisp. The pedagogue wants to ensure that his student, even though he is king of Northumbria, understands his points. At the same time, the clarity of style and presentation, much like Bede's in his *Historia,* speaks to the important moral topics at hand. The stakes are high but the choices clear.

The poetry of Alcuin has been edited by E. Duemmler (*Monumenta Germaniae Historica, Poetae Latini Aevi Carolini,* vol. 1, Berlin, 1881, pp. 160–351). Godman 118–49 translates several of the poems and offers a historical and literary introduction at 16–22. Raby 1, 159ff., discusses Alcuin's poetry at some length. The letters have also been edited by E. Duemmler (*Monumenta Germaniae Historica, Epistolae,* vol. 4, Berlin, 1895). C. Chase has more recently edited a selection of letters (*Two Alcuin Letter-Books,* Toronto, 1975). Duemmler's text of the poetry and Chase's edition of the letter are reprinted here without change.

POEM TO CORYDON

En tuus Albinus, saevis ereptus ab undis,
    Venerat, altithrono nunc miserante deo,
Te cupiens apel—peregrinis—lare camenis,
    O Corydon, Corydon, dulcis amice satis.
Quicquid tu volitas per magna palatia regum,   5
    Ut ludens pelago aliger undisono:
Qui sophiae libros primis lac ore sub annis
    Suxisti et labris ubera sacra tuis.
Dum tibi, dum maior per tempora creverat aetas,
    Tunc solidos sueras sumere corde cibos,   10
Fortia de gazis veterum et potare Falerna;
    Sensibus et fuerant pervia cuncta tuis.
Quicquid ab antiquo invenerunt tempore patres,
    Nobile cuncta tibi pandit et ingenium,
Ac divina tuis patuit scriptura loquelis,   15
    Aedibus in sacris dum tua vox resonat.
Quid tua nunc memorem scolastica carmina, vatis,
    Qui cunctos poteras tu superare senes?
Viscera tota tibi cecinerunt atque capilli,
    Nunc tua lingua tacet; cur tua lingua tacet?   20
Nec tua lingua valet forsan cantare camenas,
    Atque, reor, dormit lingua tibi, Corydon?
Dormit et ipse meus Corydon, scolasticus olim,
    Sopitus Bacho. Ve tibi, Bache pater!

This poem is written in elegiac couplets. 1. **Albinus** = Alcuin. 2. **altithrono** = *altus* + *thronus*. 3. **apel-lare:** tmesis. **camenis:** from *Camena, ae,* often used by metonymy for poetry. 4. **Corydon:** a pastoral figure prominent in the *Eclogues* of Virgil, to which this line alludes (2.69), Alcuin uses this name as a pseudonymn for the addressee of this poem, a former student. It is indeclinable. 5. **quicquid:** "wherever." 7. **lac:** along with *libros* and *ubera sacra,* the objects of *suxisti; lac* and *ubera sacra* are appositional to *libros:* "you sucked the milk which is the books of holy wisdom with your mouth . . . and the sacred breasts which are those same books with your lips." **ore:** "with your mouth." 8. **Suxisti:** from *sugere.* **labris:** from *labrum, i;* the "a" is short. 9. **dum tibi:** "until you"; *tibi* is dative of reference; the phrase introduces *tunc . . . sueras sumere . . .* in the next line. **dum** = CL *cum* temporal, as often in LL/ML; § 6.1 (Blaise 311). **creverat:** from *crescere.* 10. **sueras:** *suere* + infinitive = "to be or grow accustomed to . . ." 11. **Falerna:** i.e., Falernian wine. 13. **patres:** i.e., Alcuin and the other teachers of "Corydon." 17. **scolastica** = CL *scholastica.* **vatis:** vocative, i.e., Cordyon. 18. **senes:** i.e., *patres.* 19. **cecinerunt:** from *canere.* 24. **Sopitus:** from *sopire.* **Bacho** = CL *Baccho,* i.e., Bacchus, the god of wine, used here by metonymy for wine and drunkenness. Alcuin fears that his prized student no longer writes the beautiful poetry to which he had grown accustomed owing to

25   Ve, quia tu quaeris sensus subvertere sacros,
       Atque meum Corydon ore tacere facis.
    Ebrius in tectis Corydon aulensibus errat,
       Nec memor Albini, nec memor ipse sui.
    Obvia non misit venienti carmina patri,
30   Ut canerent "salve:" tu tamen, ecce, vale!
    Rusticus est Corydon, dixit hoc forte propheta
       Virgilius quondam: "Rusticus es Corydon."
    Dixerat ast alter, melius sed, Naso poeta:
       "Presbyter est Corydon," sit cui semper ave.

                                        —*Carm.* 32.

DAFNIS AND MENALCAS MOURN THE CUCKOO

    Plangamus cuculum, Dafnin dulcissime, nostrum,
       Quem subito rapuit saeva noverca suis.
    Plangamus pariter querulosis vocibus illum,
       Incipe tu senior, quaeso, Menalca prior.
5   "Heu, cuculus nobis fuerat cantare suetus,
       Quae te nunc rapuit hora nefanda tuis?
    Heu, cuculus, cuculus, qua te regione reliqui,
       Infelix nobis illa dies fuerat.
    Omne genus hominum, volucrum simul atque ferarum
10   Conveniat nostrum querere nunc cuculum.

---

his drunkenness. **Ve** = CL *vae* + dative = "woe to . . ." **26. ore tacere facis:** lit., "you make silent with respect to mouth"; *facere* in a causative sense commonly governs the accusative and infinitive in LL/ML (Browne xxvii). **27. in tectis . . . aulensibus:** *aulensis* is a LL/ML neologism meaning "of or for a hall," derived from *aula*. Here, Alcuin says that Corydon wanders "under hall-like roofs," suggesting that he may be with some secular official or with a royal entourage. **29. patri:** Alcuin himself. **30. canerent:** i.e., *carmina*. **31. propheta:** in apposition with *Virgilius*, this first declension noun is masculine. **32. Rusticus es Corydon:** cf. Virgil, *Ecl.* 2.56.

    1. The poem is a pastoral dialogue between Daphnis and Manalcas, both of whom lament the loss of their close friend, the "*cuculus*." Menalcas speaks the opening couplet, then Daphnis responds with a couplet, and so the poem proceeds antiphonally to its conclusion. It is written in elegiac couplets. **cuculum:** a friend lost to Daphnis and Menalcas for reasons that are made clear later, this loss is the context in which this elegiac pastoral takes shape. **Dafnin** = CL *Daphnis*, the mythical inventor of pastoral song, son of Mercury, and a shepherd in Sicily. He appears in several *Eclogues* of Virgil and in other ancient verse, both Greek and Roman. *Daphnin* is vocative here, though, as a Greek noun of the third declension, the form should be *Daphnis*. **4. Menalca:** *Menalcas*, the name of a shepherd in Virgil's fifth *Eclogue*. Greek nouns of the first declension have an "a" in the vocative singular, as here. **10. querere:** present active infinitive = CL *quaerere*, dependent on *conveniat*.

Omne genus hominum cuculum conplangat ubique,
    Perditus est, cuculus, heu, perit ecce meus.
Non pereat cuculus, veniet sub tempore veris.
    Et nobis veniens carmina laeta ciet.
Quis scit, si veniat; timeo, est summersus in undis,   15
    Vorticibus raptus atque necatus aquis.
Heu mihi, si cuculum Bachus dimersit in undis,
    Qui rapiet iuvenes vortice pestifero.
Si vivat, redeat, nidosque recurrat ad almos,
    Nec corvus cuculum dissecet ungue fero.   20
Heu quis te, cuculus, nido rapit ecce paterno?
    Heu rapuit, rapuit, nescio si venias.
Carmina si curas, cuculus, citus ecce venito,
    Ecce venito, precor, ecce venito citus.
Non tardare, precor, cuculus, dum currere possis,   25
    Te Dafnin iuvenis optat habere tuus.
Tempus adest veris, cuculus modo rumpe soporem,
    Te cupit, en, senior atque Menalca pater.
En tondent nostri librorum prata iuvenci,
    Solus abest cuculus, quis, rogo, pascit eum?   30
Heu, male pascit eum Bachus, reor, impius ille,
    Qui sub cuncta cupit vertere corda male.
Plangite nunc cuculum, cuculum nunc plangite cuncti,
    Ille recessit ovans, flens redit ille, puto.
Opto tamen, flentem cuculum habeamus ut illum,   35
    Et nos plangamus cum cuculo pariter.
Plange tuos casus lacrimis, puer inclite, plange:
    Et casus plangunt viscera tota tuos.
Si non dura silex genuit te, plange, precamur,
    Te memorans ipsum plangere forte potes.   40
    Dulcis amor nati cogit deflere parentem,

---

11. **conplangat:** "to mourn together."   15. **timeo . . . undis** = CL *timeo ne summersus in undis sit.*   17. **Bachus** = CL *Bacchus.*   21. **cuculus:** vocative.   23. **Carmina si curas:** i.e., "if you care about poetry. . . ."   **venito:** future active imperative, singular, best translated here in the present tense.   25. **tardare:** present passive imperative, singular, with *non* = "do not be late."   29. **iuvenci:** in the masculine, *iuvencus, a, um* = "bullock," here modified by *nostri* and the subject of *tondent.*   32. **sub** + accusative = "approaching," governs *cuncta corda:* "approaching all hearts, desires to turn them wickedly."   37. **puer inclite:** the cuckoo is now called a "noble boy."   41. **nati:** perfect passive participle of *nasci,* the masculine form *natus, i* = "son," here governed by *dulcis amor.*

Natus ab amplexu dum rapitur subito.
Dum frater fratrem germanum perdit amatum,
Quid nisi iam faciat, semper et ipse fleat.
45   Tres olim fuimus, iunxit quos spiritus unus,
Vix duo nunc pariter, tertius ille fugit.
Heu fugiet, fugiet, planctus quapropter amarus
Nunc nobis restat, carus abit cuculus.
Carmina post illum mittamus, carmina luctus,
50   Carmina deducunt forte, reor, cuculum.
Sis semper felix utinam, quocumque recedas,
Sis memor et nostri semper ubique vale."

—Carm. 57.

POEM TO THE STUDENTS AT YORK

Nunc cuculus ramis etiam resonavit in altis;
Florea versicolor pariet nunc germina tellus.
Vinea bachiferas trudit de palmite gemmas,
Suscitat et vario nostras modulamine mentes
5   Indefessa satis rutilis luscinia ruscis.
Et sol signiferi medium transcendit in orbem,
Et Phoebus vicit tenebrarum regna refulgens;
Atque natans ad vos pelagi trans aequora magni
Albini patris deportat carta salutem,
10   Moenibus Euboricae habitans tu sacra iuventus.
Fas idcirco, reor, comprehendere plectra Maronis,
Somnigeras subito te nunc excire camenas,

44. **fleat:** *nisi* is more properly read with this verb: "what might he do now except always cry." 49. **luctus:** from *luctus, us.* 52. **Sis memor et nostri:** i.e., "may you be mindful of us" (i.e., Daphnis and Menalcas).

This poem is written in dactylic hexameters. 6. **signiferi:** as a noun *signifer, i =* "standard bearer," "leader," but here it means something more like "sky," dependent on *medium in orbem.* 8. **aequora:** this noun can be a synonym for *pelagus* but here, governing *pelagus* in a prepositional phrase with *trans,* it means "surface." 9. **Albini:** Alcuin. **carta:** i.e., this poem itself, conceived of as a letter traveling the seas to send greetings from Alcuin to the students at York (*ad vos*), where Alcuin had taught before leaving for the continent. 10. **Moenibus Euboricae:** i.e., "at the walls of York"; with formal names, place where is expressed by the locative (AG 427.3). **iuventus:** this word can have the collective sense of "youths," a meaning indicated here by the *vos* of v. 8. 11. **fas idcirco:** with subject accusative *te* in the next line = "it is therefore right that you . . ."; read with the subsequent infinitives *comprehendere, excire,* and *implere.* **Maronis:** i.e., Virgil.

Carminibusque sacris naves implere Fresonum,
Talia namque placent vestro quia munera patri,
Qui nunc egregias regalibus insonat artes   15
Auribus et patrum ducit per prata sequentem
Praepulchro sophiae regnantem stemmate celsae.
Tu quoque, tu patri nimium dilecta iuventus,
Tu sobolis vitae, patriae laus et decus omne,
Aetheriis sophiae feliciter utere donis,   20
Ut tibi permaneat merces et gloria semper.
Ebrius initiat vobis neu vincula Bachus,
Mentibus inscriptas deleat neu noxius artes.
Nec vos Cretensis depellat ab arce salutis
Improbus ille puer, stimulis armatus acutis.   25
Nec vos luxivagus raptet per inania mundus,
Vertice submergens vitalia pectora nigro:
Sed praecepta sacrae memores retinete salutis,
Dulcisono Christum resonantes semper in ore.
Ille cibus, potus, carmen, laus, gloria vobis   30
Sit, rogo, qui vobis tribuat felicia regna
Atque suis sanctis iungat super aethera semper.
                                                —*Carm.* 59.

The Conflict of Winter and Spring

Conveniunt subito cuncti de montibus altis
Pastores pecudum vernali luce sub umbra
Arborea, pariter laetas celebrare Camenas.
Adfuit et iuvenis Dafnis seniorque Palemon;
Omnes hi cuculo laudes cantare parabant.   5
Ver quoque florigero succinctus stemmate venit,

---

13. **Fresonum** = *Germanorum;* Alcuin uses *Fresones* (from *Friso, Frisones* in the plural only; see Sleumer 344 for the various forms) to designate the people with whom he is now living, though Frisia pertains technically only to northern Germany between the Rhine and Ems (modern West Friesland); *Fresonum* depends here on *naves*.   14. **patri:** Alcuin.   16. **Auribus:** modified by *regalibus* in the previous line.   **patrum:** i.e., the Church fathers; depends on *per prata*.   **sequentem:** i.e., "the next generation."   17. **regnantem:** modifies *sequentem*.   18. **iuventus:** now Charlemagne's son and heir, Charles, is presumably meant, hence the *patri* of this line is not Alcuin, but Charlemagne himself.   20. **utere:** present active imperative, *utor* takes an ablative object.   24. **Cretensis:** i.e., Cretans, known for their skill with arrows; modifies *puer* in the next line.   28. **memores:** in apposition with *praecepta*.   32. **iungat:** the object is *vobis*.
    This poem is written in dactylic hexameters.   2. **pecudum:** from *pecus, pecudis*.

Frigida venit Hiems, rigidis hirsuta capillis.
His certamen erat cuculi de carmine grande.
Ver prior adlusit ternos modulamine versus:
VER

5   "Opto meus veniat cuculus, carissimus ales.
Omnibus iste solet fieri gratissimus hospes
In tectis, modulans rutilo bona carmina rostro."
HIEMS

Tum glacialis hiems respondit voce severa:
10   "Non veniat cuculus, nigris sed dormiat antris.
Iste famem secum semper portare suescit."
VER

"Opto meus veniat cuculus cum germine laeto,
Frigora depellat, Phoebo comes almus in aevum.
15   Phoebus amat cuculum crescenti luce serena."
HIEMS

"Non veniat cuculus, generat quia forte labores,
Proelia congeminat, requiem disiungit amatam,
Omnia disturbat: pelagi terraeque laborant."
20   VER

"Quid tu, tarda Hiems, cuculo convitia cantas?
Qui torpore gravi tenebrosis tectus in antris
Post epulas Veneris, post stulti pocula Bacchi."
HIEMS

25   "Sunt mihi divitiae, sunt et convivia laeta,
Est requies dulcis, calidus est ignis in aede.
Haec cuculus nescit, sed perfidus ille laborat."
VER

"Ore feret flores cuculus et mella ministrat,
30   Aedificatque domus, placidas et navigat undas,
Et generat soboles, laetos et vestiet agros."
HIEMS

"Haec inimica mihi sunt, quae tibi laeta videntur.
Sed placet optatas gazas numerare per arcas
35   Et gaudere cibis simul et requiescere semper."

---

3. **adlusit** = CL *allusit*. **modulamine:** from *modulamen, inis*, "melody." 6. **iste** = CL *ille:* the restrictions of person and the pejorative sense associated with this pronoun in CL are not observed in LL/ML; § 5.2.1 (cf. Blaise 164ff.). 21. **convitia** = CL *convicia*, "abuses." 26. **aede** = *domus.* 29. **mella:** from *mel, mellis*. 34. **placet:** impersonal verb governing the three infinitives that follow. 35. **gaudere** + ablative = "to enjoy. . . ."

VER

"Quis tibi, tarda Hiems, semper dormire parata,
Divitias cumulat, gazas vel congregat ullas,
Si ver vel aestas ante tibi nulla laborant?"

HIEMS   5

"Vera refers: illi, quoniam mihi multa laborant,
Sunt etiam servi nostra ditione subacti,
Iam mihi servantes domino, quaecumque laborant?"

VER

"Non illis dominus, sed pauper inopsque superbus,   10
Nec te iam poteris per te tu pascere tantum,
Ni tibi qui veniet cuculus alimonia praestet."

PALEMON

Tum respondit ovans sublimi e sede Palemon
Et Dafnis pariter, pastorum et turba piorum: 15
"Desine plura, Hiems; rerum tu prodigus, atrox.
Et veniat cuculus, pastorum dulcis amicus.
Collibus in nostris erumpant germina laeta,
Pascua sint pecori, requies et dulcis in arvis,
Et virides rami praestent umbracula fessis,   20
Uberibus plenis veniantque ad mulctra capellae,
Et volucres varia Phoebum sub voce salutent.
Quapropter citius cuculus nunc ecce venito!
Tu iam dulcis amor, cunctis gratissimus hospes:
Omnia te expectant, pelagus tellusque polusque,   25
Salve, dulce decus, cuculus, per saecula salve!"

—*Carm.* 58.

The Cell Poem

O mea cella, mihi habitatio dulcis, amata,
    Semper in aeternum, o mea cella, vale.
Undique te cingit ramis resonantibus arbos,
    Silvula florigeris semper onusta comis.
Prata salutiferis florebunt omnia et herbis,   5

---

4. **nulla laborant:** lit., "worked nothing," but more accurately "produced nothing."
7. **ditione** = CL *dicione.*   19. **Pascua:** the object of *sint,* with *pecori* (*pecus, pecoris*)
the indirect object.

This poem is written in elegiac couplets.   1. **cella:** lit., "monastic cell," but Alcuin
uses it to designate the palace school at Aix-la-Chapelle, from which he had retired in
796.   3. **arbos** = *arbor.*

Quas medici quaerit dextra salutis ope.
　　Flumina te cingunt florentibus undique ripis,
　　　　Retia piscator qua sua tendit ovans.
　　Pomiferis redolent ramis tua claustra per hortos,
10　　　　Lilia cum rosulis candida mixta rubris.
　　Omne genus volucrum matutinas personat odas,
　　　　Atque creatorem laudat in ore deum.
　　In te personuit quondam vox alma magistri,
　　　　Quae sacro sophiae tradidit ore libros.
15　　In te temporibus certis laus sancta tonantis
　　　　Pacificis sonuit vocibus atque animis.
　　Te, mea cella, modo lacrimosis plango camaenis,
　　　　Atque gemens casus pectore plango tuos.
　　Tu subito quoniam fugisti carmina vatum,
20　　　　Atque ignota manus te modo tota tenet.
　　Te modo nec Flaccus nec vatis Homerus habebit,
　　　　Nec pueri musas per tua tecta canunt.
　　Vertitur omne decus secli sic namque repente,
　　　　Omnia mutantur ordinibus variis.
25　　Nil manet aeternum, nihil immutabile vere est,
　　　　Obscurat sacrum nox tenebrosa diem.
　　Decutit et flores subito hiems frigida pulcros,
　　　　Perturbat placidum et tristior aura mare.
　　Qua campis cervos agitabat sacra iuventus,
30　　　　Incumbit fessus nunc baculo senior.
　　Nos miseri, cur te fugitivum, mundus, amamus?
　　　　Tu fugis a nobis semper ubique ruens.
　　Tu fugiens fugias, Christum nos semper amemus,

6. **medici . . . dextra salutis:** lit., "the hand of medical help," i.e., "the doctor's hand." **ope:** ablative of specification, lit., "for help," i.e., "for healing." 8. **qua:** adverb. 9. **claustra:** "enclosures." 12. **creatorem . . . deum:** double object, with *creatorem* in apposition with *deum.* 13. **magistri:** i.e., Alcuin, Angilbert, and the other intellectuals associated with the palace school. 15. **tonantis** = *Dei.* 17. **camaenis** = CL *camenis.* 18. **casus:** modified by *tuos.* 20. **tota:** as in CL, *totus, a, um,* modifies the subject, *ignota manus,* but has adverbial force, "wholly" (LS 1882, s. v. 1 *totus* I B). 21. **Flaccus** = Alcuin; it was common at Charlemagne's court for the intellectuals gathered there to take pseudonyms. *Homerus* is the poet Angilbert (d. 814). 22. **musas:** lit., "Muses," but, as often = "poetry," by metonymy. 23. **secli** = CL *saecli.* **repente:** adverb. 27. **pulcros** = CL *pulchros.* 29. **qua campis:** "in the fields where. . . ." **iuventus:** although this can mean a single "youth," it also has a collective sense of "young people," as here. 31. **mundus:** vocative case.

Semper amor teneat pectora nostra dei.
Ille pius famulos diro defendat ab hoste,   35
   Ad caelum rapiens pectora nostra, suos;
Pectore quem pariter toto laudemus, amemus;
   Nostra est ille pius gloria, vita, salus.

—*Carm.* 23.

ALCUIN TO KING AETHELRED

Domino dilectissimo Aethelredo regi Alchuine diaconus salutem.

Propter familiaritatem dilectionis familiares tibi soli litteras scribere curavi, et quia semper te amabo semper te ammonere non cessabo, ut Dei voluntati subditus Dei protectione dignus efficiaris et nobilitas regiae dignitatis magna morum nobilitate honorificetur.   5

Non est liber vel nobilis qui peccatis serviet, dicente Domino, "Omnis qui facit peccatum servus est peccati." Non decet te in solio sedentem regni rusticis vivere moribus. Ira tibi non dominetur sed ratio. Misericordia te amabilem faciat, non crudelitas odibilem. Veritas audiatur ex ore tuo, non falsitas. Kastitatis tibi conscius esto, non libidinis, continentie   10 non luxurie, sobrietatis non ebrietatis. Noli notabilis esse in aliquo peccato, sed laudabilis in omni opere bono, largus in dando, non avarus in rapiendo.

Iustitia omnes tuos exornet actus. Esto forma honestatis omnibus te videntibus. Noli, noli rapere aliena ne et propria perdas. Deum time, qui   15 dixit, "In quo enim iudicio iudicabitis, iudicabitur de vobis."

Ama Deum Christum et eius oboedire mandatis, quatenus illius misericordia tibi tuisque filiis et amicis in benedictione conservet regnum

---

36. **suos:** the masculine plural form of *suus, a, um* = "one's own people"; this line means something like "snatching us and our hearts to heaven." 37. **toto:** modifies *pectore* but has adverbial force, as often is the case with *totus, a, um.*

1. **Aethelredo:** King of Northumbria, 774–788. **salutem:** i.e., *dat.* 6. **serviet** + dative = "to be a slave to . . ." 7. **non decet te:** in CL *decet* takes a dative of the person affected; here the accusative is used; *decet* is impersonally used only in the third person, normally with an infinitive, here *vivere;* the phrase means "it is not fitting for you to live. . . ." 9. **non:** i.e., *non faciat.* 10. **tibi:** *conscius* + genitive or dative = "aware of. . . ." **esto:** present active imperative of *sum.* **continentie** = CL *continentiae.* 11. **luxurie** = CL *luxuriae.* **Noli:** present imperative of *nolle;* as in CL, *noli* + infinitive is a standard way to express prohibition in LL/ML. 12. **dando . . . rapiendo:** gerunds which mean, respectively, something like "giving" and "taking." **te:** the object of *videntibus,* which itself modifies *omnibus.* 17. **oboedire:** present passive imperative = "be obedient," with dative object. **illius:** i.e., *Dei.* **quatenus . . . misericordia tibi . . . conservet regnum:** i.e., "and let however much of God's mercy there is for you . . . preserve your kingdom. . . ."

quod te habere voluit et gloriam future beatitudinis concedere dignetur.

Deus omnipotens regni felicitate, morum dignitate, longeva prosperitate te florere faciat, dilectissime fili.

—*Ep.* 2.5 (Chase = Duemmler 30).

1. **future** = CL *futurae*.   3. **faciat:** as often in LL/ML, *facere* is used with the infinitive, here *florere*, which, with the ablative = "flourish in. . . ." The phrase means "May all-powerful God make you flourish in. . . ."

PLATE 8. A loose folio (Pseudo-Theodulf), dating from after the year 900.

PLATE 8

Carolingian manuscript (Pseudo-Theodulf)
Single folio on parchment, after 900
Specimen leaf 131; Koopman Collection
John Hay Library, Brown University

What remains of this folio, which comes from an otherwise unknown abridgment of Theodulf's *De ordine baptismi*, was cut down to 30 cm. × 21 cm. in order to form the backing of a fourteenth-century English codex. It is clearly cut off at the top, the bottom, and at right side; the left margin remains intact, at 4 cm. The manuscript originally had 2 columns: the left column is 11 cm. wide, and what remains of the right column is 4 cm. wide, with a 2 cm. margin separating them. This folio is in good shape, written on parchment in brown ink in a clean, clear Carolingian minuscule. There are no illuminations, marginalia, penwork, or decorations.

THEODULF

"The Books I Used to Read"; "Why I Don't Write Poetry" (*Carmina* 44 & 45; c. 800)

Theodulf lived a life of extraordinary range and activity. He was a prominent and powerful political figure in his own right, yet was considered by his peers to have such a deftness of touch as a poet that he was given the pseudonym Pindar. By nationality, Theodulf was a Visigoth, born in northern Spain around 750. We know virtually nothing about his upbringing or education, although his intellectual training must have been of a sufficiently high order to allow him to make his way to the court of Charlemagne at a relatively young age. He was there in the early 780s already, composing poetry and writing on theological matters.

In 787 Theodulf was appointed bishop of Orleans, an assignment he carried out with his inordinate energy. Under his leadership, his bishopric experienced a building program and an increased acquisition of land. He took as one of his chief goals also the establishment of chapel schools. But his success in these endeavors took him away from the affairs of the Church when, in 798, Theodulf was appointed *missi* by Charlemagne, a delicate position in Carolingian administration fundamental to the exercise of Charlemagne's central authority. This appointment at once raised the power and prestige of Theodulf as an individual but it also speaks to the high esteem in which he was held by Charlemagne. Theodulf remained bishop of Orleans during his tenure as *missi*.

Charlemagne died in 814 and was succeeded by his son, Louis the Pious, who did not command as much authority or respect as had his father. An example of this decline in the royal authority, unfortunately, had negative implications for Theodulf. In 817 Bernhard of Italy, nephew of Louis the Pious, revolted against his uncle's rule. For unknown reasons, Theodulf was implicated in this revolt. Louis eventually captured Bernhard and had his eyes put out. He was kinder to Theodulf, banishing him to Angers, where Theodulf wrote much of his personal poetry. His exile was not inordinately lengthy—he was released in 821—but Theodulf did not long survive afterward, dying later in the year.

The output of Theodulf is enormous and varied as to genre, style, and aim. He is now generally credited with the composition of the so-called *Libri Carolini*, which stated the official Carolingian position on the iconoclastic controversy. He also produced a version of the Vulgate and a large collection of poems, some serious, some satirical, some based on his experiences as *missi*. Theodulf's style, especially in his verse, is grounded in a thorough knowledge of CL, yet imbued with his own distinctive nuances. One can sense his interest in the topic of verbal mimesis in the poems excerpted here. In the first, on the books Theodulf used to read, the poet works into a sustained—and increasingly strident—allegorization of Cupid. His claims are complementary, viz., that he no longer reads (he says, after all, that "these are the books I used to read," at the start of the poem) and that reading, especially in the Christian tradition, leads to allegory and to a perversion of intent and meaning. The second poem, by distinction, places writing in the context of work and duty, arguing for a better separation of the two, owing to the incompatibility of either.

The poetry has been edited by, among others, K. Liersch (Halle, 1880) and E. Duemmler (*Monumenta Germaniae Historica, Poetae Latini Aevi Carolini*, vol. 1, Berlin, 1881, pp. 437–581). L. Nees analyzes the relationship of verbal and visual materials in Theodulf and other court poets (*A Tainted Mantle: Hercules and the Classical Tradition at the Carolingian Court*, Philadelphia, 1991). Raby 1, 171ff., analyzes Theodulf's poetry. *Carmen* 44 has been translated at Godman 169–71. Duemmler's text is reprinted here; at *Carm.* 45.59, *oculus* is printed for Duemmler's *oculis*, following Godman 171.

THE BOOKS I USED TO READ

Namque ego suetus eram hos libros legisse frequenter,
  Extitit ille mihi nocte dieque labor.
Saepe et Gregorium, Augustinum perlego saepe,
  Et dicta Hilarii seu tua, papa Leo.
Hieronymum, Ambrosium, Isidorum, fulvo ore Iohannem, 5
  Inclyte seu martyr te, Cypriane pater.

This poem is written in elegiac couplets. 2. **Extitit** = CL *exstitit*. 3. **Gregorium:** from *Gregorius, i* = Pope Gregory I (Sleumer 366), on whom see pp. 169–73. **Augustinum:** from *Augustinus, i* = Saint Augustine (354–430) (Sleumer 139). 4. **Hilarii:** from *Hilarius, i* = Saint Hilary of Poitiers (c. 315–c.367) (Sleumer 386). 5. **Hieronymum:** from *Hieronymus, i* = Saint Jerome (c. 341–420) (Sleumer 385). **Ambrosium:** from *Ambrosius, i* = Saint Ambrose (c. 339–397) (Sleumer 103). **Isidorum:** see pp. 174–78. **Iohannem:** from *Ioannes, is* = Saint John Chrysostom (c. 347–407) (Sleumer 438 ff.) known for his "golden mouth," i.e., his mastery of Greek. Theodulf presumably read John not in the original Greek but in the Latin translations made some time in the fifth century. 6. **Cypriane:** from *Cyprianus, i* = Saint Cyprian

Sive alios, quorum describere nomina longum est,
  Quos bene doctrinae vexit ad alta decus.
Legimus et crebro gentilia scripta sophorum,
10   Rebus qui in variis eminuere satis.
Cura decens patrum nec erat postrema piorum,
  Quorum sunt subter nomina scripta, vide:
Sedulius rutilus, Paulinus, Arator, Avitus,
  Et Fortunatus, tuque, Iuvence tonans;
15 Diversoque potens prudenter promere plura
  Metro, o Prudenti, noster et ipse parens.
Et modo Pompeium, modo te, Donate, legebam,
  Et modo Virgilium, te modo, Naso loquax.
In quorum dictis quamquam sint frivola multa,
20   Plurima sub falso tegmine vera latent.
Falsa poetarum stilus affert, vera sophorum,
  Falsa horum in verum vertere saepe solent.
Sic Proteus verum, sic iustum Virgo repingit,
  Virtutem Alcides, furtaque Cacus inops.
25 Verum ut fallatur, mendacia mille patescunt,
  Firmiter hoc stricto pristina forma redit,
Virginis in morem vis iusti inlaesa renidet,
  Quam nequit iniusti conmaculare lues.
Gressibus it furum fallentum insania versis,

(d. 257) (Sleumer 255). 8. **ad alta:** "to the heights." **doctrinae . . . decus:** "a worthiness of/for learning," this is the subject of *vexit*. 9. **gentilia:** i.e., "pagan"; transferred epithet = "the writings of the pagan philosophers." 10. **eminuere:** alternate perfect active indicative, third person plural of *eminere* = *eminuerunt*. 13. **Sedulius:** from *Sedulius, i* = Sedulius, fl. last quarter of the fifth century. **Paulinus:** i.e., Paulinus of Nola, on whom see pp. 94–100. **Arator:** fl. middle of the sixth century. **Avitus:** c. 450–c.518; see pp. 143–48. 14. **Fortunatus:** d. c. 600; see pp. 158–68. **Iuvence:** from *Iuvencus, i* = Juvencus (Sleumer 456), fl. first quarter of the fourth century. 16. **metro:** modified by *diversoque*. **Prudenti:** from *Prudentius, i,* d. c. 405; see pp. 101–10. 17. **Pompeium:** from *Pompeius, i* = Pompeius, fl. later fifth century, the author of a commentary on Donatus, the next figure named. **Donate:** from *Donatus, i* = Donatus, fl. after 350, the author of a grammar much used in the Middle Ages. 18. **Virgilium . . . Naso:** Publius Virgilius Maro, i.e., Virgil, the author of, most famously, the *Aeneid;* and Publius Ovidius Naso, the author of, among other works, the *Metamorphoses.* 22. **horum:** i.e., *poetarum.* **solent:** the subject is *sophii.* 25. **mille:** indeclinable adjective modifying *mendacia.* 26. **hoc stricto:** "when the truth has been cut back to its essential. . . ." 28. **conmaculare** = CL *commaculare.* 29. **furum fallentum:** dependent on *gressibus it,* "(*insania*) goes with the backward steps of deceiving thieves." **versis:** with *gressibus* = "with backward steps."

Ore vomunt fumum probra negando tetrum. 30
Vis sed eos mentis retegit, perimitque, quatitque,
    Nequitia illorum sic manifesta patet.
Fingitur alatus, nudus, puer esse Cupido,
    Ferre arcum et pharetram, toxica, tela, facem.
Quod levis, alatus, quod aperto est crimine, nudus, 35
    Sollertique caret quod ratione, puer.
Mens prava in pharetra, insidiae signantur in arcu,
    Tela, puer, virus, fax tuus ardor, Amor.
Mobilius, levius quid enim vel amantibus esse
    Quit, vaga mens quorum seu leve corpus inest? 40
Quis facinus celare potest quod Amor gerit acer,
    Cuius semper erunt gesta retecta mala?
Quis rationis eum spiris vincire valebit,
    Qui est puer effrenis et ratione carens?
Quis pharetrae latebras poterit penetrare malignas, 45
    Tela latent utero quot truculenta malo?
Quo face coniunctus virosus prosilit ictus,
    Qui volat, et perimens vulnerat, urit, agit?
Est sceleratus enim moechiae daemon et atrox,
    Ad luxus miseros saeva barathra trahens. 50
Decipere est promptus, semperque nocere paratus,
    Daemonis est quoniam vis, opus, usus, ei.
Somnus habet geminas, referunt ut carmina, portas,
    Altera vera gerit, altera falsa tamen.
Cornea vera trahit, producit eburnea falsa, 55
    Vera vident oculi, falsa per ora meant.
Rasile nam cornu, tener et translucet ocellus,

---

30. **tetrum** = CL *taetrum*.   31. **eos:** i.e., *insania* and *probra*.   34. **ferre:** like *esse*, dependent on *fingitur*.   35. **est:** this *est* is understood with the other *quod* clauses here and in the next verse.   36. **caret:** takes an ablative object.   38. **Tela . . . virus** = *Tela tua vira sunt*.   **fax . . . ardor:** *est* is understood here.   **puer . . . Amor:** Theodulf suddenly addresses Cupid directly, hence these vocatives.   39. **amantibus:** ablative of comparison.   40. **quit:** from *quire*.   **inest** = *est*.   44. **effrenis:** alternate nominative singular masculine of *effrenus*.   47. **quo:** conjunction.   **face:** from *fax, facis*, dependent on *coniunctus*.   49. **moechiae daemon:** i.e., "the demon of fornication."   50. **barathra:** read with *ad saeva*, with *luxus* (genitive singular) dependent and *miseros trahens* governing it.   52. **ei:** i.e., Cupid.   55. **cornea . . . eburnea:** respectively the "horn" and "ivory" gates of sleep bear truth and falsehood; horn bears truth because, like the eye, it is transluscent, whereas ivory bears falsehood because it is like the teeth of the mouth that speaks falsely. Theodulf explains this in the next line (cf. Godman 171).

Obtunsumque vehit oris hiatus ebur.
Non splendorem oculus, non sentit frigora cornu,
60   Par denti atque ebori visque colorque manet.
Est portis istis virtus non una duabus,
    Os fert falsa, oculus nil nisi vera videt.
Pauca haec de multis brevibus constricta catenis
    Exempli causa sit posuisse satis.

—Carm. 45.

Why I Don't Write Poetry

Carmina saepe mihi, fratres, pergrata tulistis,
    Et nunc quae fertis, credite, valde placent.
His delector enim, vestri studiumque laboris
    Conlaudo, et moneo vos potiora sequi.
5   Crescitis in melius, nobis hinc gaudia crescunt,
    Ut magis atque magis id faciatis, amo.
Qui ex facili pridem poteram depromere versus,
    Aestuo, nec condo, ut volo, dulce melos.
Quaeritis hoc, quando novus hic successit habendus
10   Usus, nostram Erato qui reticere facit.
Sunt mihi nunc lacrimis potius deflenda piacla,
    Carmina quam lyrico nempe boanda pede.
Non amor ipse meus Christus mea carmina quaeret,

---

58. **obtunsumque:** perfect passive participle from *obtundere,* meaning something like "hard," "impenetrable," here modifying *ebur,* both the objects of *vehit.* 61. **duabus:** modifies *portis istis.*

This poem is written in elegiac couplets. 1. **tulistis** = *scripsistis.* 3. **delector:** passive forms of *delectare* + ablative = "to be delighted by . . ." 7. **ex facili:** adverbial force = "easily." 8. **Aestuo:** intransitive here, with the sense of "hesitate," rather than "burn." **melos:** from *melos, i,* modified by *dulce,* the object of *condo.* 9. **hoc:** the object of *quaeritis* = "you ask this. . . ." **habendus:** modifies *novus hic usus* and means something like "this new habit that must be followed." 10. **Erato:** the Muse of lyric and erotic poetry, this is the only form (nominative singular feminine) in CL; here, however, Theodulf makes it accusative by modifying it with *nostram.* The phrase *nostram Erato,* as object of *reticere facit,* means something like "which makes us keep silent about Erato," i.e., "which keeps us from writing poetry." **qui:** i.e., *usus.* 11. **Sunt mihi . . . potius deflenda piacla:** Theodulf had become bishop of Orleans in 787 and refers here to the fact that he must now cry for the sins of his flock, rather than compose poems. This is the context of the reference to *grandia lucra gregis* in v. 14 also. **potius . . . quam:** the idiom is "more . . . rather than." 12. **boanda:** from *boare.* **pede:** from *pes, pedis,* i.e., meter. 13. **meus Christus:** in apposition with *amor ipse.*

Sed mage commissi grandia lucra gregis.
Pro quo proque meis orare erratibus opto,   15
  Carmina ni pangam, crimina nulla gero.
Ludite vos pueri, metrica sat lusimus arte,
  Praemia, quae cupitis, iam mihi parta manent.
Discite sic fratres, docti ut possitis haberi,
  Et fieri socii civibus aethereis.   20
En veneranda piis tanti sollemnia festi,
  Nos modo non multum versificare sinunt.
His ita praemissis, festum hoc celebremus ovantes,
  Aptius edendi carmina tempus erit.
Annua sic etiam veneranter festa colamus,   25
  Continua ut nobis det sine fine deus.
Nam, Vulfine, tibi debentur praemia laudum,
  Cuius ab amne fluunt metrica docta bene.
Hinc tibi multiplices agimus, carissime, grates,
  Praemia pro meritis rex deus ipse dabit.   30

—*Carm.* 44.

14. **gregis:** *grex, gregis,* i.e., the flock of Christians over whom Theodulf watches as bishop of Orleans.   18. **parta:** perfect passive participle of *parere,* modifying *praemia,* with *iam mihi* dependent on it; the line means something like "the rewards which you seek, obtained by me already, remain." In this and the previous lines, Theodulf is making the case for his withdrawal from poetry writing, though he encourages his monastic brethren here and at the start of the poem to continue writing verses. 19. **docti . . . haberi:** "so that you might be able to be considered learned."   23. **his:** i.e., "these lines of poetry"; modified by *praemissis.*   24. **edendi:** from *edere,* "to publish," here in the genitive, with *carmina* its object, dependent on *tempus.* The line means something like "there will be a better time for publishing poems."   26. **continua:** i.e., *festa,* "unbroken celebrations."   27. **Vulfine:** from *Vulfinus, i* = Vulfinus, in the vocative case here, a well-known grammarian from Orleans, whose learning Theodulf goes on to praise.

EINHARD

The Life of Charlemagne
(*Vita Karoli Magni;* c. 820)

The variety of Late and Medieval Latin prose styles is a function of the wide compass put to prose in the early Middle Ages, as it is also a witness to the talents of those writers working in prose. We have seen this variety in the prose style of Sulpicius Severus in his treatment of Saint Martin's life, where the function of the narrative impinged on the style employed. And, more widely, we have seen Gregory of Tours marshal a panoply of styles to augment his thematic concerns, a tack Bede reverses in his *History,* where prose variety is replaced by stylistic conformity, reflecting the larger tone of the *Historia,* viz., to celebrate unity, wholeness, and continuity. Einhard draws on the traditions of several of his predecessors in this regard, fashioning a tightly woven narrative devoted to a single individual, the style of which, reaching back to Latin antiquity and to more recent exemplars, has much to say about thematic concerns and also about Carolingian prose stylistics.

Einhard was born of a noble family in the valley of the River Main, around 775. He was sent as a boy to be educated under Abbot Baugulfus at the monastery at Fulda, the great center of intellectual activity in the Frankish kingdom in the eighth and ninth centuries. Einhard brought to his training at Fulda important gifts of intellect and innate talent, so much so that in 791 he was selected by Baugulfus to study at the palace school of Charlemagne, which, by this time, had experienced extraordinary growth under the leadership of Alcuin of York. While at the *schola palatina,* Einhard became well acquainted with Charlemagne, who made him his emissary and sent him on several political missions.

Not long after Charlemagne's death, in 814, Einhard was made private secretary to Louis the Pious, the old king's son and successor, who bestowed on him the full benefits of imperial favor, including a cohort of estates, abbacies, and court honors. The scholarly strain in Einhard grew stronger as the reign of Louis the Pious proceeded, however, especially when the political turmoils so common in it increased. Those turmoils, involving as they did the intrigues of the sons of Louis the Pious against their father, soured Einhard for good on the public life and led him, despite his prized position at court, to retire around 830 to Seligenstadt.

He spent his final decade in peaceful retirement there, dying on 14 March 840.

Of the several works of Einhard, the most famous is the *Vita Karoli Magni*, excerpted here. The work was written at some point between 814, the year in which Charlemagne died, and 821, the year in which, for the first time, the work is listed in the inventory of a monastic library. The work takes as its model Suetonius's *Lives of the Caesars*, and many of Suetonius's phrases and much of his vocabulary are used freely by Einhard. The point is obvious that Einhard means for Charlemagne's life to be considered in the context of (and to be seen ultimately as far superior to) the lives of the Roman emperors. The skeleton of the *Vita Karoli* may be classical, but the factual material is Carolingian, deriving from the royal archives, the *annales royales* (chronicles of events, year-by-year), and, most importantly, Einhard's own memory. Einhard's history is strikingly different from its equally famous cousin, the *Gesta Karoli Magni* of Notker, written nearly a century later, as it is different from Bede's *Historia* and Gregory of Tours's *Histories*. Where Notker's treatment is anecdotal and personal, Einhard's tends more toward veneration of its topic, merged always with the larger view of his accomplishments. And Einhard's focus, unlike Bede's or Gregory's, is on biography and the attendant details of a single life. Both Bede and Gregory use biography, but in Einhard's hands the life of a historical figure reaches a new, medieval form, apart from national and ethnocentric histories but also not quite hagiography either. The Latinity of the *Vita Karoli* is classical, due not only to the model provided by Suetonius but also to the literary learning of Einhard himself.

The *Vita Karoli Magni* has been edited by, among others, G. H. Pertz (*Monumenta Germaniae Historica, Scriptores,* vol. 2, Berlin, 1829, pp. 443–65); P. Jaffé (*Bibliotheca Rerum Germanicarum,* vol. 4, pp. 487–541, in *Monumenta Carolina,* Berlin, 1867), L. Halphen (*Éginhard, Vie de Charlemagne,* Paris, 1923, rev. 1947), and H. W. Garrod and R. B. Mowat (*Einhard's Life of Charlemagne,* Oxford, 1925, with nearly 40 pages of notes). Sidney Painter has translated the *Vita* into English (*The Life of Charlemagne by Einhard,* Ann Arbor, Mich., 1960), as has L. Thorpe for the Penguin Classics (*Einhard and Notker the Stammerer: Two Lives of Charlemagne,* Harmondsworth, 1969). The text of Garrod and Mowat is reprinted here with some minor formatting changes.

THE SAXONS

Post cuius finem Saxonicum, quod quasi intermissum videbatur, re-
petitum est. Quo nullum neque prolixius neque atrocius Francorumque
populo laboriosius susceptum est, quia Saxones, sicut omnes fere Germaniam incolentes nationes, et natura feroces et cultui daemonum dediti
5 nostraeque religioni contrarii neque divina neque humana iura vel pol-
luere vel transgredi inhonestum arbitrabantur. Suberant et causae quae
cotidie pacem conturbare poterant, termini videlicet nostri et illorum
pene ubique in plano contigui, praeter pauca loca in quibus vel silvae
maiores vel montium iuga interiecta utrorumque agros certo limite dister-
10 minant, in quibus caedes et rapinae et incendia vicissim fieri non cessabant. Quibus adeo Franci sunt inritati ut non iam vicissitudinem reddere,
sed apertum contra eos bellum suscipere dignum iudicarent. Susceptum
est igitur adversus eos bellum, quod magna utrimque animositate, tamen
maiore Saxonum quam Francorum damno, per continuos triginta tres an-
15 nos gerebatur. Poterat siquidem citius finiri, si Saxonum hoc perfidia pateretur. Difficile dictu est quoties superati ac supplices regi se dediderunt,
imperata facturos polliciti sunt, obsides qui imperabantur absque dilatione dederunt, legatos qui mittebantur susceperunt, aliquoties ita domiti
et emolliti ut etiam cultum daemonum dimittere et christianae religioni
20 se subdere velle promitterent; sed, sicut ad haec facienda aliquoties proni,
sic ad eadem pervertenda semper fuere praecipites, ut non sit satis aesti-

1. **cuius finem:** i.e., the end of the struggle against the Lombards, with a description
of which Einhard concludes the previous chapter. **Saxonicum:** from *Saxonicus, a,*
um = Saxon; supply *bellum*. The Saxon wars were waged from 772 to 804. 2. **nul-**
lum: modifies an understood *bellum*. 3. **Germaniam:** the object of *incolentes*, which
itself modifies *omnes nationes*. 4. **feroces . . . dediti . . . contrarii:** each modifies *Sax-*
ones, with corresponding adjectives in the oblique cases. 6. **arbitrabantur:** i.e., *Sax-*
ones. **suberant et causae:** i.e., "the causes were at hand. . . ." 8. **pene** = CL *paene*.
contigui: *erant* is understood here. 11. **non iam vicissitudinem reddere:** dependent
on the result clause governed by *ut iudicarent* (and parallel with *bellum suscipere dig-*
num), this phrase has the sense of "they decided not to return attacks in kind. . . ."
15. **siquidem:** in CL = "if in fact"; in LL/ML it loses its conditional force and means
"accordingly." **perfidia:** this is a word commonly used of the Saxons; the *Royal*
Frankish Annals ascribe perfidy to the Saxons no less than seven times. See Halphen
23, n. 4. **pateretur:** i.e., "were not inclined." 16. **regi:** i.e., "to Charlemagne."
17. **imperata facturos polliciti sunt:** i.e., "promised to do the things they had been
ordered to do. . . ." **absque dilatione:** i.e., "without hesitation"; *abs* = CL *sine*, as
often in LL/ML. 20. **subdere velle promitterent:** i.e., "they promised to be open to
submitting themselves [to the Christian religion]." 21. **fuere** = *fuerunt*. **praecip-**
ites: i.e., "swift." **non sit satis aestimare:** i.e., "so that it is not possible to know. . . ."

mare ad utrum horum faciliores verius dici possint; quippe cum post inchoatum cum eis bellum vix ullus annus exactus sit quo non ab eis huiuscemodi facta sit permutatio.

Sed magnanimitas regis ac perpetua tam in adversis quam in prosperis mentis constantia nulla eorum mutabilitate vel vinci poterat vel ab his 5 quae agere coeperat defatigari. Nam numquam eos huiuscemodi aliquid perpetrantes inpune ferre passus est, quin aut ipse per se ducto aut per comites suos misso exercitu perfidiam eorum ulcisceretur et dignam ab eis poenam exigeret, usque dum, omnibus qui resistere solebant profligatis et in suam potestatem redactis, decem milia hominum ex his qui utrasque 10 ripas Albis fluminis incolebant cum uxoribus et parvulis sublatos transtulit et huc atque illuc per Galliam et Germaniam multimoda divisione distribuit. Eaque conditione a rege proposita et ab illis suscepta, tractum per tot annos bellum constat esse finitum ut, abiecto daemonum cultu et relictis patriis caerimoniis, christianae fidei atque religionis sacra- 15 menta susciperent et Francis adunati unus cum eis populus efficerentur.

—Vita Kar. 7.

How the King Brought Up His Chidren

Liberos suos ita censuit instituendos ut tam filii quam filiae primo liberalibus studiis, quibus et ipse operam dabat, erudirentur; tum filios, cum primum aetas patiebatur, more Francorum equitare, armis ac venatibus exerceri fecit, filias vero lanificio adsuescere coloque ac fuso, ne per otium torperent, operam inpendere atque ad omnem honestatem erudiri 5 iussit.

Ex his omnibus duos tantum filios et unam filiam priusquam moreretur

1. **ad utrum horum:** lit., "respecting either of them," i.e., promising to surrender or reverting to their former ways.   **faciliores ... possint:** the subject of *aestimare,* but modifying the idea of *utrum horum,* i.e., "which of these was able to be spoken more easily and more truthfully."   4. **tam ... quam:** coordinating conjunctions = "as ... so."   5. **ab his:** i.e., *rebus;* the understood antecedent of *quae.*   7. **inpune** = CL *impune.*   **passus est:** from *pati,* negated by *numquam.*   **quin** = CL *ut,* with *ulcisceretur.*   11. **Albis fluminis:** from *Albis, is* = the Elbe (Sleumer 94).   14. **tractum:** from *trahere,* modifying *bellum,* and governing *per tot annos.*

2. **operam dabat:** Charlemagne could draw his monogram, but could not write; he could, it seems, however, read.   3. **venatibus** = CL *venationibus.*   4. **fecit:** governs the infinitives *equitare* and *exerceri; facere* with the infinitive is common in LL/ML, though not unknown in CL (Browne xxvii).   **adsuescere** = CL *assuescere* + dative = "to become familiar with...."   5. **inpendere** = CL *impendere.*   7. **moreretur:** from *morior;* the subject of this verb is Charlemagne.

amisit, Karolum, qui natu maior erat, et Pippinum, quem regem Italiae praefecerat, et Hruodthrudem quae filiarum eius primogenita et a Constantino Grecorum imperatore desponsata erat. Quorum Pippinus unum filium suum Bernhardum, filias autem quinque, Adalhaidem, Atulam,
5 Gundradam, Berhthaidem ac Theoderadam, superstites reliquit. In quibus rex pietatis suae praecipuum documentum ostendit, cum, filio defuncto, nepotem patri succedere et neptes inter filias suas educari fecisset. Mortes filiorum ac filiae pro magnanimitate, qua excellebat, minus patienter tulit, pietate videlicet, qua non minus insignis erat, conpulsus ad lacrimas.
10 Nuntiato etiam sibi Hadriani Romani pontificis obitu, quem in amicis praecipuum habebat, sic flevit ac si fratrem aut carissimum filium amisisset. Erat enim in amicitiis optime temperatus, ut eas et facile admitteret et constantissime retineret, colebatque sanctissime quoscumque hac adfinitate sibi coniunxerat.
15 Filiorum ac filiarum tantam in educando curam habuit, ut numquam domi positus sine ipsis caenaret, numquam iter sine illis faceret. Adequitabant ei filii, filiae vero pone sequebantur, quarum agmen extremum ex satellitum numero ad hoc ordinati tuebantur.
Quae cum pulcherrimae essent et ab eo plurimum diligerentur, mirum
20 dictu quod nullam earum cuiquam aut suorum aut exterorum nuptum dare voluit, sed omnes secum usque ad obitum suum in domo sua retenuit, dicens se earum contubernio carere non posse.
—*Vita Kar.* 19 (excerpts).

1. **Karolum** = Charles, who died on 4 December 811. **Pippinum:** from *Pippinus, i* = Pippin (or Pepin), who died on 8 July 810 (Sleumer 610).   2. **Hruodthrudem:** from *Hruodthrudis, is* = Rotrud, betrothed, but never married, to the Byzantine emperor, Constantine VI (780–802), died on 6 June 810. To Roderick, Count of Maine, she bore a son, Louis, who later became Abbot of Saint Denis (d. 867).   3. **desponsata erat:** from *despondere*, "to be promised," i.e., "betrothed."   4. **Bernhardum:** from *Bernardus, i* = Bernhard, King of Italy, 813–817 (Sleumer 160).   5. **superstites:** i.e., "as survivors"; this word stands in apposition to the names of the six children of Pippin.   7. **succedere ... educari fecisset:** *facere* with the infinitive in a causal construction.   8. **pro:** in LL/ML, *pro* often has a causal sense, "because of . . ." (Browne, xxiv), but here is more akin to CL usage = "in comparison with. . . ."   10. **Hadriani ... pontificis:** from *Hadrianus, i* = Pope Hadrian I (772–795) (Sleumer 371).   13. **sanctissime:** i.e., "most conscientiously."   **adfinitate** = CL *affinitate*, with modifying *hac*.   16. **caenaret** = CL *cenaret*.   **Adequitabant** + dative in CL = "to ride up to"; Einhard means something like "to ride with."   17. **quarum agmen extremum:** i.e., "whose rear flank. . . ."   **ex satellitum numero:** i.e., "by a number of attendants. . . ."   18. **ad hoc:** the purpose meant here is implied in the verb.   19. **mirum dictu quod:** i.e., "it is strange to say that. . . ."   20. **nuptum dare:** "to be married."   22. **contubernio:** the ablative object of *carere*, it means something like "company."

CHARLEMAGNE'S PHYSIQUE, EXERCISING, BATHING

Corpore fuit amplo atque robusto, statura eminenti, quae tamen iustam non excederet—nam septem suorum pedum proceritatem eius constat habuisse mensuram—, apice capitis rotundo, oculis praegrandibus ac
vegetis, naso paululum mediocritatem excedenti, canitie pulchra, facie
laeta et hilari; unde formae auctoritas ac dignitas tam stanti quam sedenti   5
plurima adquirebatur; quamquam cervix obesa et brevior venterque pro-
iectior videretur, tamen haec caeterorum membrorum celabat aequalitas.
Incessu firmo totaque corporis habitudine virili; voce clara quidem, sed
quae minus corporis formae conveniret; valitudine prospera, praeter
quod, antequam decederet, per quattuor annos crebro febribus corripie-   10
batur, ad extremum etiam uno pede claudicaret. Et tunc quidem plura
suo arbitratu quam medicorum consilio faciebat, quos pene exosos habebat, quod ei in cibis assa, quibus adsuetus erat, dimittere et elixis adsuescere suadebant.

Exercebatur adsidue equitando ac venando; quod illi gentilicium erat,   15
quia vix ulla in terris natio invenitur quae in hac arte Francis possit ae-
quari. Delectabatur etiam vaporibus aquarum naturaliter calentium, frequenti natatu corpus exercens; cuius adeo peritus fuit ut nullus ei iuste
valeat anteferri. Ob hoc etiam Aquisgrani regiam exstruxit ibique extremis vitae annis usque ad obitum perpetim habitavit. Et non solum filios   20
ad balneum, verum optimates et amicos, aliquando etiam satellitum et
custodum corporis turbam invitavit, ita ut nonnumquam centum vel eo
amplius homines una lavarentur.

—Vita Kar. 22.

7. **haec:** object of *celabat.* **caeterorum** = CL *ceterorum.* **aequalitas:** governs *caeterorum membrorum.* 12. **quos . . . habebat:** i.e., *medici.* 13. **assa:** from *assum, i* =
"roast"; in CL *assum, i* = "roast" and *assa, orum* = "sudatory" (LS 182); Einhard de-
clines *assum* as a first declension feminine, but he means *praeter assum.* **adsuetus
erat** = CL *assuetus erat.* **elixis:** lit., "wet," "soaked through," but here meaning something like "boiled," the opposite of *assa,* "roasted" meat. 15. **adsidue** = CL *assidue.*
quod illi gentilicium erat: "for there was for him an inborn attraction" i.e., in pursuing
riding and hunting; *gentilicium* also can mean something like "specific to a family or
clan," so the phrase might be understood to refer to the Frankish inclination to hunting
and riding, in which Charlemagne is an eager participant. Since Einhard goes on to mention the Franks in the next clause, the latter reading might be preferable. 17. **delectabatur** + ablative object = " to take delight in. . . ." 18. **cuius:** the antecedent is *corpus.*
19. **anteferri:** "to be preferred," dependent on *valeat,* with *ei* the object. **Aquisgrani:**
from *Aquisgranum, i* = Aix-la-Chapelle, or Aachen, where Charlemagne built his capital city (Sleumer 121). 22. **vel eo amplius** = "or more"; the adverb *eo* expresses measure or degree with *amplius* (LS 649 s. v. 2 *eo,* I C); the conjunction *vel* = "or"; the
phrase means something like "so that several hundred or more men bathed together."

His Habits in Daily Life

In cibo et potu temperans, sed in potu temperantior, quippe qui ebrietatem in qualicumque homine, nedum in se ac suis, plurimum abominabatur. Cibo enim non adeo abstinere poterat, ut saepe quereretur noxia corpori suo esse ieiunia.

5   Convivabatur rarissime, et hoc praecipuis tantum festivitatibus, tunc tamen cum magno hominum numero. Caena cotidiana quaternis tantum ferculis praebebatur, praeter assam, quam venatores veribus inferre solebant, qua ille libentius quam ullo alio cibo vescebatur. Inter caenandum aut aliquod acroama aut lectorem audiebat. Legebantur ei historiae et

10   antiquorum res gestae. Delectabatur et libris sancti Augustini, praecipueque his qui *De Civitate Dei* praetitulati sunt.

Vini et omnis potus adeo parcus in bibendo erat ut super caenam raro plus quam ter biberet. Aestate post cibum meridianum pomorum aliquid sumens ac semel bibens, depositis vestibus et calciamentis velut noctu sol-

15   itus erat, duabus aut tribus horis quiescebat. Noctibus sic dormiebat ut somnum quater aut quinquies non solum expergescendo, sed etiam desurgendo interrumperet.

Cum calciaretur et amiciretur, non tantum amicos admittebat, verum etiam, si comes palatii litem aliquam esse diceret quae sine eius iussu de-

20   finiri non posset, statim litigantes introducere iussit et, velut pro tribunali sederet, lite cognita sententiam dixit; nec hoc tantum eo tempore, sed etiam quicquid ea die cuiuslibet officii agendum aut cuiquam ministrorum iniungendum erat expediebat.

—Vita Kar. 24.

1. **qui:** i.e., Charlemagne. 2. **plurimum:** adverb. 3. **quereretur:** from *queri*. 5. **hoc:** lit., "with respect to this," referring to those times when Charlemagne did, in fact, hold large gatherings; *tantum* = "only." 6. **caena** = CL *cena*. 7. **veribus:** from the defective fourth declension noun, *veru, verus*. 8. **qua:** i.e., *assa*. **caenandum** = CL *cenandum*. 9. **acroama:** lit., "things that gratify the ear," but here referring to a singer or a jester (LS 24). 10. **res gestae:** collective noun = "deeds," governing *antiquorum* here. 12. **super caenam** = CL *cenam*, with *super* + accusative in a temporal construction = "at." In CL, temporal *super* is normally expressed with the ablative. 13. **aestate:** ablative of time. **meridianum:** modifies *cibum*, referring to the midday meal. 14. **calciamentis** = CL *calceamentis;* the substitution of "i" for "e" is common in LL/ML orthography, though the CL form is also regularly found; § 1.3 (cf. Blaise/Chirat 123). 19. **comes palatii** = "count of the palace," a high-ranking official in the government of Charlemagne. **eius** = CL *ipsius;* the use of *is* for *ipse* is common in LL/ML. 21. **nec hoc tantum eo tempore:** i.e., "he did not do this only at that time [i.e., when dressing]. . . ." 22. **quicquid . . . agendum:** i.e., "whatever matter of any official had to be done on that day. . . ." **cuiquam . . . iniungendum erat:** passive periphrastic construction with dative of agency = "or what-

His Studies and Educational Ambitions

Erat eloquentia copiosus et exuberans poteratque quicquid vellet apertissime exprimere. Nec patrio tantum sermone contentus, etiam peregrinis linguis ediscendis operam inpendit; in quibus Latinam ita didicit ut aeque illa ac patria lingua orare sit solitus, Graecam vero melius intellegere quam pronuntiare poterat. Adeo quidem facundus erat ut etiam diaculus appareret.

Artes liberales studiosissime coluit, earumque doctores plurimum veneratus magnis adficiebat honoribus. In discenda grammatica Petrum Pisanum diaconem senem audivit; in caeteris disciplinis Alcoinum cognomento Albinum, item diaconem, de Brittannia Saxonici generis hominem, virum undecumque doctissimum, praeceptorem habuit; apud quem et rhetoricae et dialecticae, praecipue tamen astronomiae ediscendae plurimum et temporis et laboris inpertivit. Discebat artem conputandi et intentione sagaci siderum cursum curiosissime rimabatur. Temptabat et scribere tabulasque et codicellos ad hoc in lecto sub cervicalibus circumferre solebat, ut cum vacuum tempus esset manum litteris effigiendis adsuesceret; sed parum successit labor praeposterus ac sero inchoatus.

—*Vita Kar.* 25.

5

10

15

---

ever matter was to be attended to by whomever of his ministers"; *iniungere* takes the dative object *cuiquam,* with *ministrorum* dependent on it.   23. **expediebat:** the main verb of this complex sentence, with *quicquid* and *iniungendum* the objects.

2. **peregrinis linguis ediscendis:** object of *operam inpendit* = lit., "to foreign language learning."   3. **inpendit** = CL *impendit;* with *operam* = "gave attention to. . . ." 4. **orare** = *dicere;* cf. Suetonius, *Titus* 3, on which this passage is modeled.   5. **pronuntiare** = *dicere,* as against the more concrete "to pronounce."   8. **Petrum Pisanum** = Peter of Pisa; in 774, Charlemagne captured Pavia, the Lombard capital, and found Peter of Pisa teaching there. Famous for his linguistic learning, Charlemagne compelled Peter to return northward with him, where he became a central figure in the establishment of a court circle of intellectuals. Little is known of him apart from what contemporaries tell; we do not even know his birth or death date. Alcuin reports that Peter and the poet Paul the Deacon, who were colleagues at court for a time, were rivals.   9. **caeteris** = CL *ceteris.*   **Alcoinum . . . Albinum:** Alcuin, the chief intellectual of Carolingian Europe, on whom see pp. 217–28.   11. **praeceptorem:** modifies *Alcoinum.*   13. **inpertivit** = CL *impertivit;* the object is *plurimum et temporis et laboris* = "he devoted much time," with indirect object *ediscendae* = "for the learning of. . . ."   15. **ad hoc:** i.e., "for the purpose of writing."   **circumferre:** in LL/ML can have the sense, as here, of "keep," "hold" (Blaise/Chirat 153).   17. **praeposterus:** modifies *labor,* and means "out of order"; i.e., he tried learning to write much later than was normal.   **inchoatus** = CL *incohatus* = "begun," modifies *labor.*

HIS DEVOTION TO THE CHURCH

Religionem Christianam, qua ab infantia fuerat inbutus, sanctissime et cum summa pietate coluit; ac propter hoc plurimae pulchritudinis basilicam Aquisgrani exstruxit auroque et argento et luminaribus atque ex aere solido cancellis et ianuis adornavit. Ad cuius structuram cum col-
5 umnas et marmora aliunde habere non posset, Roma atque Ravenna devehenda curavit.

Ecclesiam et mane et vespere, item nocturnis horis et sacrificii tempore, quoad eum valitudo permiserat, inpigre frequentabat curabatque magnopere ut omnia quae in ea gerebantur cum quam maxima fierent
10 honestate, aedituos creberrime commonens ne quid indecens aut sordidum aut inferri aut in ea remanere permitterent. Sacrorum vasorum ex auro et argento vestimentorumque sacerdotalium tantam in ea copiam procuravit, ut in sacrificiis celebrandis ne ianitoribus quidem, qui ultimi ecclesiastici ordinis sunt, privato habitu ministrare necesse fuisset.
15 Legendi atque psallendi disciplinam diligentissime emendavit. Erat enim utriusque admodum eruditus, quamquam ipse nec publice legeret nec nisi submissim et in commune cantaret.

—Vita Kar. 26.

2. **plurimae:** Einhard uses the concrete *plurimus, a, um,* in place of the abstract *magnus.* **basilicam:** i.e., the Chapel of the Virgin, to which Aix-la-Chapelle owes part of its name, dedicated 6 January 805 and modelled on the Church of St. Vitalis in Vienna. 3. **Aquisgrani:** locative. **luminaribus:** i.e., "candelabra," "lamps." 4. **cancellis:** from *cancelli, orum;* occurs only in the plural. 5. **aliunde:** i.e., "from elsewhere." 6. **curavit:** lit., "he took care that Rome and Ravenna were plundered"; *devehenda* is probably too strong; as a letter written in 787 from Pope Hadrian I to Charlemagne suggests, the king sought and gained permission from the Pope to take back to Aix-la-Chapelle the materials he sought from the palace at Ravenna. 8. **valitudo** = CL *valetudo.* **inpigre** = CL *impigre.* 9. **omnia:** i.e., "all the services." **cum . . . honestate** = CL *maxima cum honestate;* Einhard conflates the idiom *quam maxime* and the form he seems to mean, *cum maxima honestate.* 13. **in sacrificiis celebrandis:** i.e., celebrating the Eucharist. **ianitoribus** = CL *ostiariis.* **ne . . . necesse fuisset:** result clause whose idiom in the indicative = *non necesse est:* "it is not necessary."

Ermoldus Nigellus

In Honor of Louis the Pious
(*In Honorem Hludowici Christianissimi Caesaris Augusti*; 826)

The life of Ermoldus Nigellus is known to us mostly through the lengthy poem he wrote to Louis the Pious, excerpted here. He was probably a secular official, not merely because of his obviously wide knowledge of worldly affairs, but also owing to the kinds of activities he pursued for his patrons, Louis the Pious and Louis's son, Pepin. He tells us, for example, that he took up arms, or attempted to, but with little success on campaign with Pepin in 824; and that, when Louis removed him from court, he was sent to Strasbourg to run surveillance on that city's bishop. These are hardly activities one would expect someone who had taken orders to pursue. His education, too, while implying training for the church, does not exclude a secular career, and though it is not known where or when Ermoldus acquired it, one can surmise from his poetry an education of the first order. It seems likely that he hailed from Aquitaine, for he was attached to the court of Louis the Pious when that future emperor was in residence there as king before the death of his father, Charlemagne. And when Charlemagne's death made Louis emperor in 814, Ermoldus remained attached to the imperial court, though more closely associated after that time with Pepin, Louis's son. A *floruit* of 826 is based on the events he records in the poem to Louis.

Although Ermoldus seems to have long been in the favor of Louis the Pious and Pepin, the political tensions of Carolingian Europe in the 820s—arising from dynastic claims mostly between Louis and his sons—put to the test the most enduring of friendships. Ermoldus, unfortunately, became caught up in these tensions. Initially, he was placed under a mild form of house arrest on the grounds that he was exerting a negative influence on Pepin, Louis's son and Ermoldus's close friend. But by the time Ermoldus found himself in Strasbourg, watching over that city's bishop, it was clear that the poet had in fact been exiled. The political instability of the worlds in which he lived suggests that Ermoldus was probably innocent of the charges leveled against him, making his poem to Louis, written in response to his exile, all the more compelling for its earnestness. The poem was meant to do Ermoldus's bidding, praising Louis in order to regain his favor and end the poet's exile, an outcome it failed to accomplish for its author.

Ermoldus is an important Latin poet. Like his older contemporaries, Alcuin, Paul the Deacon, and Theodulf, he turns to his Latin predecessors for his poetic materials, affirming the currency of the classical literary tradition in the choices he makes as to theme, vocabulary, and meter. More reflective of his own poetic workings are the fresh tasks he puts to his inherited materials. For example, though he frequently alludes to CL poetry in his poem in praise of Louis, he balances the older verbal texture those allusions create with a narrative that relies in part on a contemporary (and now anonymous) poem, the *Karolus Magnus et Leo Papa*. Yet he departs both from this poem and his older exemplars in the ways he exploits meter and theme. There is no clearer indication of Ermoldus's poetic vision than his merging of epic diction with the elegiac couplet— a melding of poetic materials that, together with the poem's shifts of tone and vision, reveals a bold and innovative poet engaging his tradition fully. In this regard especially, Ermoldus helps to reconfigure epic to the personal level, where elegy helps to cement the personal and doleful qualities that support the poet's purposes and mood. In this way, Ermoldus represents in the development of Latin literature a continuation of the bold experimentation of the Carolingian poets, for his reconfiguration of his poetic materials accords with the work pursued earlier by Alcuin, Paul the Deacon, and other of the court poets.

The poetry of Ermoldus has been edited by E. Duemmler (*Monumenta Germaniae Historica, Poetae Latini Aevi Carolini*, vol. 2, Berlin, 1884, pp. 4–93) and by E. Faral (*Ermold le Noir, Poème sur Louis le Pieux et Épitres au Roi Pépin*, Paris, 1932). Portions of the poem (though not those reprinted here) have been translated by Godman 250–57, with excellent introductory comments at 45–47. Cf. Raby 1, 178ff.

The excerpts recount the exploits of Datus, a Frankish hero, and Zado, a Moorish chieftain, in the siege of Barcelona by the Franks, which was launched from Aquitaine, in 800–801, while Louis the Pious was king there. Faral's text is given, with consonantal "i" printed for "j" (note that his line numbers, because he includes the prefatory acrostic in his count, do not accord with Duemmler's).

THE SIEGE OF BARCELONA

Tempore vernali, cum rus tepefacta virescit,
  Brumaque sidereo sole fugante fugit,
Pristinus ablatos remeans fert annus odores,
  Atque humore novo fluctuat herba recens,
Regni iura movent renovantque solentia reges,   5
  Quisque suos fines, ut tueantur, adit.
Nec minus accitu Francorum more vetusto
  Iam satus a Carolo agmina nota vocat,
Scilicet electos populi, seu culmina regni,
  Quorum consiliis res peragenda manet.   10
Occurrunt celeres primi parentque volendo,
  Quos sequitur propius vulgus inorme satis.
Considunt moniti; solium rex scandit avitum;
  Caetera turba foris congrua dona parat,
Incipiunt fari, cepit tunc sic Carolides,   15
  Haec quoque de proprio pectore verba dedit:
"Magnanimi proceres, meritis pro munere digni,
  Limina quos patriae praeposuit Carolus,
Ob hoc Cunctipotens apicem concessit honoris
  Nobis, ut populo rite feramus opem.   20
Annuus ordo redit, cum gentes gentibus instant
  Et vice partita Martis in arma ruunt.
Vobis nota satis res haec, incognita nobis:
  Dicite consilium, quo peragamus iter."

The poem is written in dactylic hexameters. **1. tepefacta** = *tepefactum*. **5. solentia** = CL *sollemnia*, modifying *iura*. **reges:** the subject of this line. **8. satus:** perfect passive participle of *serere;* in the masculine = "son," governing *a Carolo,* i.e., Louis the Pious. **agmina:** as *nota,* and the next several verses, imply, *agmen* has a civil as well as military connotation, here referring to the most illustrious figures of the kingdom. **9. scilicet:** explanatory particle. **11. volendo:** gerund, in the ablative, with the force of the present participle *volentes,* § 3.4 (cf. Blaise 341–42), functioning on the model of the Greek participle. However, *parere* + dative has the meaning of "to satisfy . . ."; an alternate meaning is something like "they satisfy their desire [to help the king]." **12. inorme** = CL *enorme*. **13. moniti:** lit., "those who have been advised [to gather together]," i.e., "the king's council." **14. caetera** = CL *cetera*. **congrua dona:** i.e., "gifts suitable [for the king]." **15. incipiunt fari:** lit., "they begin to speak," i.e., "the council begins." **cepit** = CL *coepit*. **Carolides:** patronymic = Louis the Pious. **18. Carolus** = Charlemagne, father of Louis the Pious. **19. Cunctipotens:** an ecclesiastical neologism = *omnipotens*. **20. populo . . . feramus opem:** the idiom is *opem ferre,* "to bring help" + dative.

25   Datus, ut agnovit propriam matremque domumque
       Direptam, varium pectore versat onus.
     Prorsus equum faleris ornans, se nec minus armis
       Coniunctis sociis adparat ire sequax.
     Forte fuit castrum, vallo seu marmore firmum,
30   Quo reduces Mauri cum spoliis remeant.
     Huc celer et socii, Datus cunctusque popellus,
       Certatim coeunt, frangere claustra parant.
     Ac velut accipiter pennis per nubila lapsus
       Ungue rapit volucrem notaque ad antra fugit;
35   At sociae crocitant raucasque per aethera voces
       Nequicquam recinunt atque sequuntur avem;
     Ipse sedens tutus praedam stringitque feritque,
       Versat et in partes quas sibi cumque placet:
     Non aliter Mauri, vallo praedaque potiti,
40   Dati bella timent, spicula sive minas.
     Tum iuvenem muri quidam conpellat ab arce,
       Voce cacinnosa dicta nefanda dabat:
     "Date sagax, nostras modo quae res vexit ad arces
       Te sociosque tuos, dicito, namque precor.
45   Si modo, quo resides, tali pro munere nobis
       Dedere mavis equum, quo faleratus abis,
     Nunc tibi mater eat sospes seu caetera praeda;
       Sin autem, ante oculos funera matris habes."
     Reddidit orsa sibi Datus non digna relatu:
50   "Funera matris age; nec mihi cura satis.
     Nam quem poscis equum, non unquam dedere dignor,

25. **Datus:** from *Datus, i* = Datus, abbot of the monastery at Conches, and as these lines suggest, one of the key figures at the siege of Barcelona. 26. **direptam:** perfect passive participle of *diripere.* 27. **faleris** = CL *phaleris.* 28. **adparat** = CL *apparat.* 30. **Mauri:** the Moors, here in nominative plural; Barcelona, like much of Spain, was under Muslim control by the late eighth century. 38. **cumque:** adverb. 39. **vallo:** ablative of place where, without *in,* as often in LL/ML (Blaise 108). **potiti:** from *potiri* + ablative = "to be in possession of . . .," i.e., "The Moors were in possession of their booty. . . ." 40. **minas:** LL/ML neologism = "war cries" (Blaise/Chirat 531, s. v. II *mina*). 41. **iuvenem:** i.e., Datus. **muri:** i.e., *ab arce muri,* "from the top of the wall." **conpellat** = CL *compellat.* 42. **cacinnosa** = CL *cachinnosa,* lit., "given over to loud laughter," i.e., "with a loud, laughing voice . . .," but the sense is that there is sarcasm in his voice. 44. **dicito:** future active imperative, "you will tell me." 46. **mavis:** present active indicative, second person singular of the irregular verb *malle.* **faleratus** = CL *phaleratus,* "adorned." 49. **orsa:** perfect passive participle of *ordior,* the neuter plural form = "words," "utterances."

Inprobe, haud equidem ad tua frena decet."
Nec mora: crudelis matrem consistit in arce
   Et nato coram dilaceravit eam.
Ille quidem frendens vestem conscindit et atros   55
   Disrumpit crines dilaceratque oculos.
Et sequitur verbis, iterumque iterumque profana
   "Cordoba" voce vocat inlacrimatque diu:
"O Mauri celeres, quo nunc fiducia cessit?
   Promite nunc vires nunc solitas, socii!   60
Unum, per siquid nostri iam cura remansit,
   Deprecor; hoc uno munere laetus ero.
Ipse ego conspexi muro, qua castra remittunt
   Densa, locum, constant raraque linteola:
Me potero insidias inlaesus ferre per illas;   65
   Fors, socii, nota currere ad auxilia.
Vos tantum portas summo servate labore,
   Haud timidi, fratres, huc ego dum redeam;
Nulla quidem fortuna arces vos linquere cogat
   Nec campis, hortor, pergere in arma foras."   70
Multa etiam mandata suis dans cessit ab urbe
   Et latitans furtim praeterit agmen ovans.
Iamque tenebat iter per laeta silentia noctis;
   Infelix nimium protinus hinnit equus.
Quo clamore movent custodes agmina castris   75
   Vocis ad hinnitum moxque sequuntur eum.
Ille pavore viam linquens, vertitque cavallum,
   Sese praecipitem in agmina densa dedit.
Conspicit invisas haud laeta fronte catervas,

52. **haud . . . decet:** i.e., "it would not be fitting to put my horse under your bridle";
CL has *decet* with dative and infinitive. 53. **crudelis:** adjective being used substantively as the subject of this line. **consistit:** i.e., "posted," "established," "set," with *in
arce,* "on the height," "on the wall." 54. **coram:** as a preposition, before or after an
ablative (here *nato*) = "in the presence of. . . ." 55. **ille:** i.e., Zado; in the intervening
lines, this important figure, leader of the Moors at Barcelona, has been introduced
into the narrative. 60. **socii:** vocative. 61. **per siquid:** i.e., "if, by any means. . . ."
nostri: dependent on *cura,* referring to Zado. 63. **muro:** ablative of place without a
preposition. 64. **raraque:** predicate adjective. **linteola:** here used by Ermoldus to
mean "tents." 65. **inlaesus** = CL *illaesus.* 66. **fors:** ellipsis = *fors sit,* "there is the
chance," i.e., "perhaps." **socii:** vocative case. **nota:** perfect passive participle of
noscere = ablative of means, "by a known way." 68. **haud timidi:** with imperative
force = "be not fearful." 77. **pavore:** ablative of cause. **cavallum** = CL *caballum.*
79. **haud laeta fronte:** ablative of specification with adverbial force = "unhappily."

80   Infelix nec habet quo eruat ingenio.
       Mox capitur; merito vincitur, haud mora, loris,
          Ducitur ad regis lintea tecta tremens.
       Fama volans totam turbat terroribus urbem
          Et regem captum nuntiat ore suo.
85   Ingeminant luctum matresque patresque iuvencli;
          Hoc puer exiguus, hocque puella gemit.
       Nec minor in castris passim sonus aethera pulsat
          Laetitiaque fremit unanimi populus.
       Interea nox atra cadens, Aurora reportat
90   Alma diem; Franci regia castra petunt.
       Tum Caroli soboles pacato pectore fatur
          Atque suis famulis dicta benigna dedit:
       "Zadun ad Hispanas cupiens properare catervas,
          Auxilium poscens armaque sive pares,
95   Captus adest nolens vinctusque tenetur inermis
          Ante fores, nostros non fugit ante oculos.
       Fac, Vilhelme, suos possit quo cernere muros
          Et iubeat nobis pandere claustra celer."
       Nec mora. Zado manum sequitur religatus habenis,
100   Et procul expansam sustulit arte manum.
       Nam prius abscedens sociis praedixerat ipse:
       "Seu fortuna nequam, prospera sive cadat,
       Nescio; si casu Francorum incurrero turmis,
          Vos tamen, ut dixi, castra tenete, precor."
105   Tum manus adtendens vocitabat amicos:
       "Pandite iam, socii, claustra vetata diu!"
       Ingeniosus item digitos curvabat et ungues

---

82. **lintea tecta:** i.e., "tents."   85. **iuvencli** = CL *iuvenculi.*   88. **unanimi:** synesis; the correct form is *unanimus.*   89. **nox atra cadens:** nominative absolute; § 3.3.1 (cf. Blaise 67).   91. **Caroli soboles:** i.e., Louis the Pious.   93. **Zadun:** Ermoldus spells this name variously (or it has been copied thusly); here it is nominative masculine. 94. **pares:** *par, paris* as a masculine noun = "companions."   97. **fac:** the construction is *fac possit quo,* lit., "make it so that he is able. . . ."   98. **iubeat:** governed also by *fac quo,* i.e., "and make it so that he orders. . . ."   **celer:** the subject of this line, Zado.   99. **Zado:** this form is nominative masculine.   100. **arte:** from *ars, artis,* but with adverbial force = "skillfully."   102. **nequam:** indeclinable adjective, modifying *fortuna;* as is generally the case where classical quantities are changed in LL/ML, the long "e" of CL *nequam* has become in LL/ML short (Beeson 26).   **cadat:** "occurs," "happens."   103. **casu:** "in the event that. . . ."   **incurrero** + dative = "to run into. . . ."   105. **adtendens** = CL *attendens.*

252

Figebat palmis, haec simulanter agens;
Hoc autem inditio signabat castra tenenda,
Sed tamen invitus "Pandite!" voce vocat.   110
Hoc vero agnoscens Vilhelmus concitus illum
Percussit pugno, non simulanter agens;
Dentibus infrendens versat sub pectore curas,
Miratur Maurum, sed magis ingenium.
—*In hon. Hlud.* 1.140–63, 252–81, 468–527.

108. **simulanter:** this adverb means "pretendedly"; with *haec agens* it really means something like "and he did this in token that the gates were really to be kept closed, in spite of what he said aloud." 109. **inditio** = CL *indicium*, with *hoc* in ablative of means construction. 111. **concitus:** from *conciere*.

PLATE 9. A loose folio from the book of Numbers dating around 825.

PLATE 9

Book of Numbers, c. 825, single folio on parchment
Specimen leaf 132; Koopman Collection
John Hay Library, Brown University

In the Latin Middle Ages, the Bible was the arbiter of all cultural production. When they were not singing from it or reading from it, the students and teachers of the monastic schools of the Carolingian period were thinking about its words or writing about their meaning. Exegetical commentaries formed a great part of the intellectual apparatus of the Carolingian period. But even when they were writing poetry and engaging the best traditions of Latin antiquity, the Carolingian poets were never far from their Scriptural sources, for their own best verses are often written in a prosody owed to both classical and Scriptural dictates.

Many versions of the Bible had been in circulation before the fifth century, and the so-called Latin Bible consisted of widely divergent versions of the same canonical texts. The translation of a new version of the Bible into Latin by Saint Jerome, late in the fourth century, put biblical studies on an entirely new—and much more secure—footing. Jerome's version, called the Vulgate, became normative in the West for all of the Latin Middle Ages. But the Vulgate did not circulate as a single text. Copies of individual books were usually made; sometimes the gospels were circulated together. But in general, to own a "copy" of the Bible meant usually to own many volumes that together comprised its books.

The folio shown here depicts a page from the Book of Numbers. The folio is intact to its original dimensions and is in good shape. It measures 30.5 cm. × 19.5 cm. overall. The verso, shown here, has a left margin of 3 cm.; a right margin of 1 cm.; a top margin of 2.5 cm., and a bottom margin of 4 cm.; the margins are ruled with a dry point, as are the 31 lines of the folio. There are no decorations, penwork, or initials of any colors. The Carolingian minuscule hand, neat and clear, writes in brown ink.

HRABANUS MAURUS

Poems
(*Carmina* 10, 12, 25; c. 820)

Hrabanus Maurus was born around 780 and was educated at Fulda and later at Tours, where he became a prized pupil of Alcuin. It was Alcuin who gave him the second name Maurus, a mark of intellectual distinction and personal devotion, since it was also the name of Saint Benedict's dearest disciple. Hrabanus left Tours for some time but eventually returned, early in the ninth century, and settled on an illustrious teaching career there, training scores of students who went on to hold important posts across the Carolingian empire. Hrabanus's already substantial influence was enlarged in 822, when he was appointed to the abbacy of Fulda, a task to which he devoted the next two decades of his life, resigning in 842 in order to give full time to study. After his resignation, Hrabanus pursued various intellectual projects, including the writing of the *De universo*, an attempt to meld historical and theological knowledge. Of his writings, in addition to the *De universo*, we also possess letters and a body of poetry, three examples of which are reprinted here. In 847, in the full blush of retirement and already quite old, Hrabanus was persuaded by Louis the German, son of Louis the Pious, to become archbishop of Mainz. He served in this important position in a time of increasing turmoil in the Carolingian empire and died in office in 856.

In the poetry of Hrabanus Maurus, one witnesses the slow movement of Medieval Latinity into the cloister. In terms of vision and voice, Hrabanus concentrates on simple and time-honored topics—devotion to God and to friends, purity of heart and mind, wholeness of spirit—but presents them as aspects of private feeling and experience. His style remains classical, but the meter, diction, and word-choice that embody this classicism are less important than the personal expression of immediate feeling. The older traditions of courtly poetry, exhibited in all the poets who wrote between 770 and 840, evanesce in Hrabanus's hands, to be replaced by a less tangible mode of discourse, something more personal in its origins, sentiments, sensibilities.

The selections express Hrabanus's personalizing tendency. While each poem treats straightforwardly an accessible topic—God, a friend—the external measures of sentiment and expression, most notably meter and vocabulary, are less important than a newfound emphasis on the vision itself of Hrabanus's prayer, or on the intimacy of his friendship with Samuel. This tendency will develop for several centuries in the Medieval Latin tradition, especially in the writing of poetry, as poetry becomes, for the first time in the Latin West, something approximating the handmaiden of theology.

The poetry of Hrabanus has been edited by E. Duemmler (*Monumenta Germaniae Historica, Poetae Latini Aevi Carolini*, vol. 2, Berlin, 1884, pp. 154–258). Raby 1, 179ff., analyzes the poetry thoroughly. Godman 246–49 offers translations of some of the poetry (though none of our selections). Duemmler's text is reprinted without change.

A PRAYER

O deus aeterne, mundi sanctissime rector,
Te mea mens ambit, animaeque ac vivida virtus,
Laus, amor atque decus, cordis tu lumen honestum,
Membrorum gestum, tu oculorum reddis et usum,
Auribus auditum, manibus opus indis amatum.   5
Quicquid tellus habet, pontus atque aethera claudunt,
Et quicquid sentit, sapit, est, et vivit ubique,
Omnia nempe tua sapientia condita fulcit,
Vivificat, servat, valido et regit omnia nutu.
Fac me, summe pius, toto te corde fateri,   10
Te sermone loqui, te discere dogmate recto,
Quaerere te manibus, pura te et mente precari.
Tu via, tu virtus, tu vita et ianua vitae,
Tu merces operis, tu factor, tu quoque doctor.
Da mihi nunc veniam misero, et mea crimina laxa: 15
Fac me velle bonum, scire actu, et rite probare,
Sicque tuum laetum tribuas tunc cernere vultum,
Perpetuo, et vera me gaudia carpere fructu.
                                                    —*Carm.* 12.

This poem is written in dactylic hexameters. 8. **condita:** "hidden." 10. **fateri:** this infinitive, like *loqui, discere, quaerere,* and *precari,* in the next verses, is governed by *fac me;* this is an example of the causative *facere* construction, common in LL/ML (Browne xxvii). 13. **tu ... tu ... tu:** in apposition with *via, virtus, vita.* 15. **misero:** in apposition with *mihi.* 17. **tribuas:** jussive subjunctive, with *me* as object and *cernere* and *carpere* dependent on it. 18. **perpetuo:** adverb.

TO A FRIEND

Salve, fidus amor, felix dilectio, salve,
Sospes in orbe mane, sospes in ore mone.
Carmina nempe tua dico meliora Maronis
Carminibus, celsi cantibus Ovidii:
5   Odis, quas cecinit Flaccus, verbosus Homerus,
Corduba quem genuit, Affrica quem tenuit,
Hi quia protulerant pomposis falsa Camenis,
Rite tabescentes morsibus invidiae.
Tu devota piis connectis vincula verbis,
10   Decantans placide pectora amica notans.
Hoc, rogo, noster amor faciat, rogo versibus, oro,
Quod nostris scriptis sedulus ardor eat.
Sermo decorus ovet, servetur regula dictis,
Nexibus et certis versus in arte meet.
15   Sic tua tunc sobrio decoratur fistula cantu,
Laudaturque modo iure poeta bono.
Det tibi summa patris sermonem lingua loquella,
Christus in arce deus, rector in orbe pius.
Spiritus atque suus faciat tibi corda benigna,
20   Mentibus ac verbis ut domino placeas.
Haec tibi nunc breviter festinus calle viator,
Scribere compulerat, tu sine fine vale.

—Carm. 10.

TO SAMUEL

Vive meae vires lassarumque anchora rerum,
Naufragio et litus tutaque terra meo.
Solus honor nobis, urbs tu fidissima semper,

This poem is written in elegiac couplets. 3. **Maronis:** (Publius Vergilius) Maro, i.e., Virgil, the Augustan epicist (d. 19 B.C.E.). 4. **Ovidii:** (Publius) Ovidius (Naso), i.e., Ovid, the author of the *Metamorphoses,* among many other works (d. 17 C.E.). 5. **Flaccus:** (Quintus Horatius) Flaccus, i.e., Horace, the famous Augustan lyric poet (d. 8 B.C.E.). **Homerus:** apparently a pseudonym, the addressee of the poem. 6. **Corduba:** from *Corduba, ae* = Cordova (Sleumer 244). **Affrica** = CL *Africa.* 14. **meet:** from *meare.* 17. **det:** from *dare.*

Later bishop of Worms (841–859), but only a *presbyter* when Hrabanus wrote this poem to him. This poem is written in elegiac couplets. 1. **vive:** imperative = lit., "live well," but with the sense, as in Virg. *Ecl.* 8.58, of "farewell" (cf. LS 2001, s. v. *vivo* C). **lassarumque:** from *lassus, a, um,* modifying *rerum.* 3. **urbs:** used regularly by Hrabanus as an epithet of ecclesiastical figures (Henshaw 75, s. v. *urbs* b).

Curisque afflicto tuta quies animo.
Sintque licet montes inter cum fluctibus arva,   5
    Mens tecum est, nulla quae cohibetur humo.
Te mea mens sequitur, sequitur quoque carmen amoris,
    Exoptans animo prospera cuncta tibi.
Qui mihi te notum dedit et concessit amicum,
    Conservet sanum Christus ubique mihi.   10
Ante solum terrae caelique volubile ciclum
    Praetereant, noster quam quoque cesset amor.
Hocque, pater, monui, moneo te iterumque monebo,
    Sis memor utque mei, sicut et ipse tui.
Ut deus in terris quos hic coniunxit amicos,   15
    Gaudentes pariter iungat in arce poli.

—*Carm. 25.*

11. **ciclum** = CL *cyclum,* with the genitives of this line dependent on it.   **ante . . . quam** + subjunctive: the idiom is "sooner . . . than . . ."   **ipse:** i.e., *ego.*

WALAHFRID STRABO

On Horticulture
(De cultura hortorum 3 & 15; c. 845)

alahfrid Strabo was born around 810. Of his earliest days we know nothing, but he must have displayed an original talent, especially for the composition of poetry, for his first poem, a rendition of a prose account of
a vision experienced by Wetti, of Charlemagne in Hell, was completed
when Walahfrid was just eighteen. Although we lack the details of these
early years, Walahfrid clearly received a solid education at the monastery
at Reichenau, where Wetti was his teacher and where his studies proceeded apace. Walahfrid showed enough promise to be transferred,
around 827, to Fulda, where he became a prized pupil of Hrabanus
Maurus and where, among many other students, Gottschalk, another important Carolingian intellectual, was studying.

Walahfrid seems to have flourished at Fulda, and his reward, in 829,
came in the form of a transfer to the court of Louis the Pious to serve as
a tutor to the future Charles the Bald. There, Charles's mother, Judith,
herself a woman of some learning, became close to Walahfrid and for a
while patronized him. He remained at court as an imperial tutor for a
number of seemingly happy and productive years. Louis the Pious eventually rewarded Walahfrid with the abbacy of Reichenau, whither he returned to devote himself to scholarly, exegetical, and theological pursuits
and to his garden, on which he wrote a lengthy poem, excerpted here.
Walahfrid was briefly caught up in the political turmoils that surrounded
the death of Louis the Pious in 840, and he was banished from Reichenau
in the ensuing dynastic struggles of 840–842. He was eventually re-
instated, however, and spent the remainder of his life at work within
Reichenau's walls, dying there in 849.

Walahfrid's poetry evinces a carefully wrought Latin style, based on
a strong knowledge of the Latin classics and a deft manipulation of imagery, theme, and diction, to create original visions of human experience.
His poem on the cultivation of the garden stands as a bold revision of the
classical *locus amoenus,* where the brutal forces of nature are set against
the beneficence of their bounty and their seemingly innocuous charms.
At once, the terms of Medieval Latin nature poetry are recast, along with
the best traditions informing such poetry. The poem is collected into 27

subsections dealing with specific topics, including treatments of individual plants and specific tasks to be undertaken by the careful gardener. Walahfrid wrote prodigiously, and his works are variously collected. The poetry has been edited by E. Duemmler (*Monumenta Germaniae Historica, Poetae Latini Aevi Carolini*, vol. 2, Berlin, 1884, pp. 259–473). Raby 1, 183ff., discusses the poetry. Godman 222–25 translates parts of the *De cultura hortorum*, though none of our selections; cf. his introduction at 34–40. Duemmler's text is reprinted without change.

THE PERSISTENCE OF THE GARDENER

Denique vernali interdum conspergitur imbre
Parva seges, tenuesque fovet praeblanda vicissim
Luna comas; rursus si quando sicca negabant
Tempora roris opem, culturae impulsus amore,
Quippe siti metuens graciles torpescere fibras,   5
Flumina pura cadis inferre capacibus acri
Curavi studio, et propriis infundere palmis
Guttatim, ne forte ferocior impetus undas
Ingereret nimias, et semina iacta moveret.
Nec mora, germinibus vestitur tota tenellis   10
Areola et quamquam illius pars ista sub alto
Arescat tecto, pluviarum et muneris expers
Squaleat aerii, pars illa perennibus umbris
Diffugiat solem, paries cui celsior ignei
Sideris accessum lateris negat obice duri,   15
Non tamen ulla sibi fuerant quae credita pridem
Spe sine crementi pigro sub cespite clausit.

This poem is written in dactylic hexameters. 2. **praeblanda:** LL/ML neologism = "flattering." 3. **quando:** after *si* = indefinite adverb = "if ever," "if at any time." 4. **impulsus:** the subject is unstated until the appearance of the verb *curavi*. 5. **siti:** ablative of specification. 6. **capacibus:** from *capax, capacis,* modifying *cadis.* 7. **infundere** + dative = "to pour out...." 8. **impetus:** fourth declension. 9. **iacta:** perfect passive participle of *iacere.* 11. **illius:** i.e., *areola.* 12. **expers** + genitive. 13. **aerii:** from *aerius, a, um,* modifying *muneris,* both of which govern *pluviarum.* 14. **cui:** i.e., *pars.* 15. **obice:** *obex, obicis,* ablative of means, governing *lateris duri;* a rough translation of these lines is "to which a higher wall denies access to the sun by the hindrance of its sturdy side." 16. **ulla:** i.e., *semina.* **sibi:** i.e., *illa pars.* **non ... pridem:** a rough translation of this difficult line is "but as there had not been any seeds entrusted to this spot before...." 17. **crementi:** from *crementum, i,* = "increase," a neologism that first appears in Tertullian (Blaise/Chirat 230). **cespite** = CL *caespite.* **clausit:** the subject is *illa pars;* a rough translation of this line is "and so this part is shut off, without hope of increase under the cold earth."

Quin potius quae sicca fere et translata subactis
Suscepit scrobibus, redivivo plena virore
20   Restituit, reparans numeroso semina fructu.
Nunc opus ingeniis, docili nunc pectore et ore,
Nomina quo possim viresque attingere tantae
Messis, ut ingenti res parvae ornentur honore.

LILIES

Lilia quo versu candentia, carmine quove
Ieiunae macies satis efferat arida Musae?
Quorum candor habet nivei simulacra nitoris,
Dulcis odor silvas imitatur flore Sabeas.
5   Non Parius candore lapis, non nardus odore
Lilia nostra premit, necnon si perfidus anguis
Ingenitis collecta dolis serit ore venena
Pestifero, caecum per vulnus ad intima mortem
Corda feram mittens, pistillo lilia praestat
10   Commacerare gravi sucosque haurire Falerno.
Si quod contusum est summo liventis in ore

18. **quin potius:** "in fact rather. . . ."   **fere:** with *sicca* = "nearly dry," but not dry enough to be dead.   21. **opus** = *opus est* + dative, expressing the thing in need = "Now my talents require me to. . . ."   22. **nomina:** the next 23 sections are devoted to considerations of various kind of plants, one of which, on the lily, is the next excerpt.   **quo** = *ut*.   23. **messis:** genitive singular.

    This poem is written in dactylic hexameters.   4. **flore:** i.e., *lilio*.   **silvas Sabeas:** i.e., "Sabean forests"; the land of Saba, in Arabia, was famous for its incomparable incense; the adjective *Sabeus, a, um* is formed on this name (LS 1609).   5. **Parius . . . lapis:** "Parian stone"; Paros was famous for its white marble, hence *lapis* refers here specifically to marble.   **nardus:** "nard," a fragrant ointment.   **odore:** ablative of specification which can be translated as an adjective modifying *nardus* (so, too, with *candore* and *Parius lapis*).   6. **necnon:** this adverb marks a shift from the qualities of beauty exhibited by the lily to the more practical ends to which it can be put.   7. **ingenitis collecta dolis:** *collecta* modifies *venena:* "having gathered together the poisons specific to its inborn deceits."   8. **caecum:** i.e., "random"; governed by *per* (*vulnus*).   9. **corda:** governed by *ad* (*intima*) in the previous line.   **praestat:** impersonal use + infinitive = "it is good to. . . ."   10. **gravi . . . Falerno:** by metonymy for *vino;* Falernus is an area in Campania noted for its wines; *gravi* may suggest taste or mean "undiluted." The remedy for snakebite is to pound the sap from lilies and drink it with Falernian wine.   11. **quod contusum est:** i.e., "that which is beaten," referring to the pulp remaining after the lilies have been pounded.   **summo . . . in ore:** lit., "on the highest face," i.e., "on the surface."   **liventis . . . puncti:** "of the black-and-blue puncture wound."

Ponatur puncti, tum iam dinoscere vires
Magnificas huiusce datur medicaminis ultro.
Haec etiam laxis prodest contusio membris.

—*De cul. hort.* 53–75, 248–61.

12. **dinoscere . . . datur:** *dinoscere* = *dignoscere*; impersonal *datur* + *dinoscere* = "it is possible to know." 14. **contusio:** i.e., *quod contusum est.* **laxis . . . membris:** the object of *prodest*; the sense is "for relaxing the limbs" that have been made tense, presumably by the bite.

John Scottus Eriugena

On the Division of Nature
(*De divisione naturae* I; c. 855)

O f all the work produced by Carolingian intellectuals in the years between Charlemagne's accession and the splintering of his empire, none is conceived in broader terms than the oeuvre of John Scottus Eriugena, whose output includes original works of philosophy, theology, and poetry, and whose intellectual traditions touch on not only the Latin classics but much of the Greek achievement also. Nothing beyond conjecture is known of John's early years, apart from the fact that he was, as his name suggests, born in Ireland (Eriugena, a name coined by John himself, means "born of Ireland"). It is conjectured that he was born around 810. Owing to his career, it can also be conjectured that John was well educated and that his education included a mastery of Greek—a language which, except in Ireland, had fallen from general use in the Carolingian West.

John's Greek learning was put to good use in the philosophical pursuits which dominated his intellectual life. In particular, he read widely in the Neoplatonic tradition, eventually bringing out a Latin translation of the works of the pseudo-Dionysius which was dedicated to his patron, Charles the Bald, in the late 850s. In time, John moved on to more original philosophical work, speculating in a systematic way on issues of theology, cosmology, and nature, in his most famous work, the *De divisione naturae*, excerpted here.

John had arrived at the court of Charles the Bald in the early 840s to assume charge of the school carried on under the patronage of that king. John's supervision of the school seems to have ensured its continued success and, indeed, its enhancement. John was particularly attractive to Charles and his court circle because this King looked eastward for his royal and cultural models. Greek culture and language became a fundament of Charles' outlook, and in the work of John the Scot that outlook is confirmed.

John is not remembered as a teacher so much as a bold, speculative philosopher. The *De divisione naturae*, or *Periphyseon*, which articulates a fourfold division of nature, conceives of a God who is both immanent and transcendent. The tangibility of that God and the close connection of him to his creation is expressed in John's treatise through dialogue, where the give and take of teacher and student—and the inculcation of a direct Latin style—achieve the work's accessibility. Apart from the difficulties presented by the implicit positions John assumes relative to authority, in subsequent centuries much of the work was condemned as heretical by the Church owing to John's presentation of God's immanence, for in subscribing to the Neoplatonic notion of divine participation in all of creation, John sometimes sounds like a pantheist, spying in the smallest creature vestiges of divine knowledge with its bursts of vital creativity. But even when he does not sound the alarm of pantheism (to which he did not adhere), John still allows the divide between divinity and humanity to be crossed too easily—at least for the tastes of the Church. Heresy aside, there is much in the *De divisione naturae* that is owed to earlier Neoplatonic traditions, especially those articulated by the pseudo-Dionysius, but the work was influential especially to a new generation of Platonic thinkers that arose in the Latin West in the twelfth century (see part 5).

John was also an important poet at the court of Charles, though he did not write much by way of quantity. The quality of his poetry, on the other hand, must be measured by the level of experimentation evinced in it. One finds standard pieces in praise of Charles, for example (*Carmen* 9, e.g.), and some smaller pieces on a variety of topics. But there exists in John's output a small collection of Greek poems (3.1–13) which are experimental in tone, style, and content, but which speak most of all to John's willingness to forge ahead in new ways—something he does in his Latin writings consistently. Legend holds that John traveled to Britain near the end of his life to assist in the revival of learning at the court of King Alfred. It is generally assumed that he died no later than 880.

The *De divisione naturae* has been edited by I. P. Sheldon-Williams (*Iohannis Scotti Eriugenae Periphyseon (De Divisione Naturae)*, Dublin, 1968). The poetry is edited by L. Traube (*Monumenta Germaniae Historica, Poetae Latini Aevi Carolini*, vol. 3, Berlin, 1896, pp. 518–53); and by M. Herren (*Iohannes Scottus Eriugena, Carmina*, Dublin, 1993). The poetry is analyzed by Raby 1, 193ff.; it has been partially translated by Godman 300–6 with a useful introduction also at 58–60. M. L. Uhlfelder and J. A. Potter have translated the *De divisione* (*John the Scot, Periphyseon, On the Division of Nature*, Indianapolis, 1973). D. Moran has written on John's philosophical work in general (*The Philosophy of John Scottus Eriugena: A Study of Idealism in the Middle Ages*, Cambridge, 1989). M. Brennan has prepared a bibliography up to 1987 (*A Guide to*

Eriugenian Studies: A Survey of Publications, 1930–1987, Paris, 1989).
Sheldon-Williams's text is given, with the Greek words printed in minus-
cules and "u" and "v" distinguished.

On the Division of Nature

NUTRITOR. Saepe mihi cogitanti diligentiusque quantum vires suppet-
unt inquirenti rerum omnium quae vel animo percipi possunt vel intentio-
nem eius superant primam summamque divisionem esse in ea quae sunt
et in ea quae non sunt horum omnium generale vocabulum occurrit quod
5 graece φύσις, latine vero natura vocitatur. An tibi aliter videtur?
    ALUMNUS. Immo consentio. Nam et ego dum ratiocinandi viam in-
gredior haec ita fieri reperio.
    N. Est igitur natura generale nomen, ut diximus, omnium quae sunt
et quae non sunt?
10   A. Est quidem. Nihil enim in universo cogitationibus nostris potest
occurrere quod tali vocabulo valeat carere.
    N. Quoniam igitur inter nos convenit de hoc vocabulo generale esse,
velim dicas divisionis eius per differentias in species rationem; aut, si tibi
libet, prius conabor dividere, tuum vero erit recte iudicare.
15   A. Ingredere quaesso. Impatiens enim sum de hac re veram rationem
a te audire volens.
    N. Videtur mihi divisio naturae per quattuor differentias quattuor spe-
cies recipere, quarum prima est in eam quae creat et non creatur, secunda
in eam quae et creatur et creat, tertia in eam quae creatur et non creat,
20 quarta quae nec creat nec creatur. Harum vero quattuor binae sibi invicem opponuntur. Nam tertia opponitur primae, quarta vero secundae;
sed quarta inter impossibilia ponitur cuius esse est non posse esse. Rec-
tane tibi talis divisio videtur an non?
    A. Recta quidem. Sed velim repetas, ut praedictarum formarum op-
25 positio clarius elucescat.
    N. Vides, ni fallor, tertiae speciei primae oppositionem (prima nanque
creat et non creatur, cui e contrario opponitur illa quae creatur et non
creat), secundae vero quartae, siquidem secunda et creatur et creat, cui
universaliter quarta contradicit quae nec creat neque creatur.

3. **eius:** i.e., *animi.*   6. **ratiocinandi:** from *ratiocinari.*   7. **haec . . . reperio:** "I find
this to be so."   13. **velim dicas . . . rationem:** *velim* + subjunctive = optative subjunctive; the phrase *dicas . . . rationem* functions as a substantive clause used as the object
of *velim* (AG 442b; cf. 447.1.n, 565.n).   14. **tuum . . . erit:** the idiom is *tuum est* +
infinitive; here, in the future, *iudicare* = "it will fall to you to judge the things that
have been distinguished."

A. Clare video. Sed multum me movet quarta species quae a te addita est. Nam de aliis tribus nullo modo haesitare ausim, cum prima ut arbitror in causa omnium quae sunt et quae non sunt intelligatur; secunda vero in primordialibus causis; tertia in his quae in generatione temporibusque et locis cognoscuntur. Atque ideo de singulis disputari subtilius 5 necessarium est, ut video.

N. Recte aestimas. Sed quo ordine ratiocinationis via tenenda sit, hoc est de qua specie naturae primo discutiendum, tuo arbitrio committo.

A. Ratum mihi videtur ante alias de prima quicquid lux mentium largita fuerit dicere. 10

—*De Divis. Nat.* 1.1.

N. Clare quid velis perspicio ac per hoc ad habitudinis kategoriam transeundum esse video, quae omnium kategoriarum propter nimiam sui amplitudinem obscurissima esse videtur. Non enim est ulla kategoria fere in qua habitus quidam inveniri non possit. Nam et essentiae seu substantiae habitu quodam ad se invicem respiciunt. Dicimus enim rationabilis 5 essentia irrationabilisque qua proportione, id est quo habitu, ad se invicem respiciunt (non enim irrationabilis diceretur nisi ab habitu absentiae rationis, quomodo non aliunde rationabilis vocatur nisi habitu praesentiae rationis). Omnis enim proportio habitus est, quamvis non omnis habitus proportio. Proprie nanque proportio non minus quam in duobus 10 potest inveniri, habitus vero etiam in singulis rebus inspicitur. Verbi gratia: habitus rationabilis animae virtus est. Est igitur proportio species quaedam habitudinis. Si autem exemplo vis declarari quomodo habitus proportionalis in essentia invenitur, ex numeris elige exemplar. Numeri enim, ut aestimo, essentialiter in omnibus intelliguntur. In numeris 15 nanque omnium rerum subsistit essentia. Vides igitur qualis proportio est in duobus et tribus?

A. Video plane. Sesqualteram esse arbitror; et hoc uno exemplo aliorum omnium substantialium numerorum inter se invicem collatorum varias proportionis species possum cognoscere. 20

---

2. **haesitare:** the infinitive in the idiom *ausim* + infinitive = "I would dare to hesitate . . .", in the sense of "pondering." **ausim:** archaic perfect subjunctive of *audere*. 9. **largita:** from *largiri;* predicate adjective.
    1. **habitudinis:** i.e., "state" or "relation." 11. **verbi gratia:** "for instance." 13. **vis declarari quomodo:** indirect question with the indicative: "if you wish it to be demonstrated how . . .."; § 7.11 (cf. Blaise 270). 18. **sesqualteram** = CL *sesquialteram.* 19. **collatorum:** from *conferre.*

N. Intende itaque ad reliqua et cognosce nullas quantitatis species esse
seu qualitatis seu ipsius quae dicitur ad aliquid seu situs locive temporisve
agendi vel patiendi in quibus quaedam species habitudinis non reperiatur.
A. Saepe talia quaesivi et ita repperi. Nam, ut paucis exemplis utar, in
5 quantitatibus magna et parva et media inter se comparata multa pollent
habitudine. Item in quantitatibus numerorum linearum temporum alior-
umque similium habitudines proportionum perspicue reperies. Similiter
in qualitate. Verbi gratia, in coloribus album et nigrum mediusque qualis-
cunque sit color habitu sibimet iunguntur. Album siquidem et nigrum
10 quia extremos colorum locos obtinent, habitu contrarietatis ad se invicem
respiciunt. Color autem ad extrema sui, album dico nigrumque, habitu
medietatis respicit. In ea quoque kategoria quae dicitur πρός τι, id est ad
aliquid, clare apparet, qualis habitus patris ad filium seu filii ad patrem,
amici amico dupli ad simplum caeteraque huius modi. De situ quoque
15 facile patet quomodo stare et iacere habitudinem quandam inter se invicem possideant. Haec enim ex diametro sibi invicem respondent: nequaquam enim intellectum standi absolutum ab intellectu iacendi cogitabis
sed semper simul tibi occurrunt, quamvis in re aliqua non simul appareant. Quid dicendum est de loco quando superiora inferiora et media con-
20 siderantur? Nunquid habitudine carent?
N. Nullo modo. Non enim haec nomina ex natura rerum proveniunt
sed ex respectu quodam intuentis eas per partes. Sursum siquidem et
deorsum in universo non est atque ideo neque superiora neque inferiora
neque media in universo sunt, nam universitatis consideratio haec respuit,
25 partium vero introducit intentio. Eadem ratio est de maiori et minori.
Nullum enim in suo genere parvum aut magnum esse potest, ex cogitati-
one tamen comparantium diversas quantitates talia inventa sunt, ideoque
locorum seu partium contemplatio habitum in talibus gignit. Nulla enim

---

2. **quae . . . aliquid:** i.e., "or of that which is posited of something." 8. **qualis-
cunque** = CL *qualiscumque.* 9. **iunguntur:** by synesis; since *color* is collective, the
verb is plural. 11. **dico:** "namely"; the present active indicative of *dicere* has this
idiomatic meaning in CL also (LS 571, s. v. 2 *dico* II). 14. **de situ:** the topic has
shifted to "position" now. 15. **stare et iacere:** present active infinitives standing as
the nominative forms of the gerund. 16. **ex diametro:** adverb = "diametrically"
(Blaise/Chirat 268). **Haec . . . respondent:** this difficult line means something like
"For each of these [i.e., *stare et iacere*] answers from the part pertaining to itself, which
are in opposition to each other." 20. **nunquid** = CL *numquid;* this adverb always
introduces questions, both direct and indirect, and many times translates in English
idiom as "do?" = "do they lack a state?" 22. **ex respectu . . . intuentis:** i.e., "but
from the point of view of contemplating. . . ." **Sursum . . . deorsum:** the idiom is
sursum deorsum, "up and down."

natura maior aut minor alia natura sit, sicut neque superior neque inferior, cum una omnium subsistat natura ex uno deo condita.

A. Quid de tempore? Nonne in ipsis dum inter se invicem conferuntur luculenter habitus arridet? Verbi gratia: dies ad horas, horae ad punctos, puncti ad momentum, momenti ad atoma. Similiter in superioribus commensurationibus si quis ascenderit reperiet. In his enim omnibus habitus totius ad partes partiumque ad totum perspicitur. 5

N. Profecto non aliter.

A. Quid in diversis agendi et patiendi motibus? Nonne habitus ubique relucet? Nam amare et amari habitudines sunt amantis et amati; siquidem 10 inter se invicem respiciunt sive in una persona sint, quod a Graecis dicitur αὐτοπάθια, id est cum actio et passio in una eademque inspicitur persona, ut me ipsum amo, sive inter duas personas, quod a Graecis dicitur ἑτεροπάθια, id est cum alia persona amantis et alia amati sit, ut "amo te."

N. Et haec vera esse decerno. 15

A. Quaero igitur a te quare ista kategoria habitudinis, cum caeteris kategoriis naturaliter inesse videatur, per se specialiter veluti suis propriis rationibus subnixa suum in denaria kategoriarum quantitate locum obtineat.

N. An forte quia in omnibus invenitur propterea in se ipsa subsistit? 20 Nam quod omnium est nullius proprie est, sed ita est in omnibus ut in se ipsa subsistat. Eadem enim ratio etiam in kategoria essentiae inspicienda est. Quid enim? nunquid, cum decem kategoriae sint, una earum essentia seu substantia dicitur, novem vero accidentia sunt et in substantia subsistunt? Per se enim subsistere non possunt. Essentia in omnibus esse vide- 25 tur, sine qua esse non possunt, et tamen per se locum suum obtinet. Quod enim omnium est nullius proprie est sed omnium commune, et dum in omnibus subsistat per se ipsum propria sua ratione esse non desinit. De quantitate similiter dicendum est. Dicimus enim quanta essentia quanta qualitas quanta relatio quantus situs quantus habitus quam mag- 30 nus locus quam parvum vel spatiosum tempus quanta actio quanta passio. Videsne quam late patet per caeteras kategorias quantitas? Non tamen suum proprium deserit statum. Quid de qualitate? Nonne et ipsa de omnibus aliis kategoriis frequenter praedicari solet? Dicimus enim qualis οὐσία qualis magnitudo qualis relatio situs habitus locus tempus agere 35 pati. Haec enim omnia qualia sunt interrogamus. Non tamen qualitas sui proprii generis rationem deserit. Quid ergo mirum si kategoria habitu-

---

18. **subnixa** + dative = "relying on." **in denaria . . . quantitate:** i.e., "in the ten categories." 35. **agere, pati:** present infinitives = nominative forms of the gerund.

269

dinis dum in omnibus inspicitur propriam suam rationem possidere dicatur?

A. Nullo modo mirandum; nam vera ratio suadet non aliter esse posse.

5 N. Nonne igitur vides divinam essentiam nullius habitudinis participem esse, de ea tamen non incongrue, quoniam ipsius est causa, praedicari posse? Si enim proprie de ipsa habitus praedicaretur nequaquam suimet sed alterius esset; omnis quippe habitus in aliquo subiecto intelligitur et alicuius accidens est, quod de deo, cui nullum accidit et accidit nulli in nulloque intelligitur et nullum in ipso, impium est credere.

10 A. Satis de hac kategoria disputatum est, ut arbitror.

—*De Divis. Nat. 1. 17–20.*

DHUODA

Manual for My Son
(*Liber Manualis;* 843)

Dhuoda is the only woman whose writing survives from the Carolingian period. We know important details about her life. She was the wife of Bernhard, Duke of Septimania, and the mother of two sons, William, born in 826, and the younger Bernhard, born in 841. Both she and her husband were of illustrious families; but her husband, whom she married in 824 in Aachen, achieved particular eminence under Louis the Pious, who appointed him chamberlain in 831. This appointment capped a quick rise to power for Bernhard but also left him little room for maneuvering in the dynastic disputes that plagued the later years of Louis's reign. What were for Bernhard political realities translated for Dhuoda into severe personal losses. She was rarely with her husband, who was constantly traveling, either at the bidding of Louis or in support of his own large holdings of land in Septimania. And, in fact, after their marriage, Bernhard was away from Dhuoda for about fifteen years. She passed the time away raising her son William while ensconced in isolation at a stronghold in Uzès.

At the death of Louis the Pious, Bernhard found that he had few friends, especially in the sons of the dead emperor, who each vied for control of their father's holdings. Bernhard was forced to accept the authority of the youngest of Louis's sons, Charles the Bald, and to pledge as security for that support the life (and custody) of his own son William, then aged 14. Dhuoda's *Liber manualis* was written in response to the removal of her son to the court of Charles the Bald, where he was held, essentially a hostage, as an earnest of his father's goodwill (Dhuoda's infant son was also sent to the court of Charles the Bald at this time). Dhuoda began the *Liber* immediately upon William's captivity, in 841, and she completed it and sent it along to him in 843.

It is doubtful that Dhuoda's *Liber* was read by William. If it was, its wisdom was never put to practical use. The boy was killed around 850 during his vain attempt to avenge his father's execution at the hands of Charles the Bald. Dhuoda's second son may have survived, and it has been conjectured that he was Bernhard Plantevelue, who went on to found the medieval duchy of Aquitaine and to sire a son, William the Pious, who endowed the great abbey at Cluny. Of Dhuoda herself it is presumed that she may well have died before her sons or husband, since she regularly complains of poor health in the *Liber*. No death date is recorded.

The *Liber manualis* is a striking mixture of paradoxes. Gender forms the basis of one such paradox, for the voice of the *Liber* is strongly feminine, although much of the prose exalts the glory and power of men. But the basis for authentic knowledge in the *Liber* is a hidden, subtle species of knowing, one might say a feminine way of knowing, exemplified in obscure phrasing, a love of symbol, and the use of acrostics. Dhuoda's Latin can be evocative, playing on the emotions resident in a mother's love for her son; but appeals of this sort are often balanced by a more detached moralizing tone. It is not CL, to be sure, and it is often difficult to know exactly what she means—reflecting perhaps her own stated sense of writing about a special sort of knowledge that is itself difficult, inaccessible. But Dhuoda's Latin reflects the spoken vernacular of her day, too, so that the *Liber* represents a strain of Medieval Latinity at some remove from other prose writers of the Carolingian period such as Einhard or Alcuin, who followed a classicizing style in their writing. The excerpts that follow give a sense of the range of Dhuoda's prose style and its difficulty. The opening acrostic highlights in its vertical and horizontal lines of narrative the competing kinds of knowledge Dhuoda sets into place in the *Liber,* one masculine and straightforward, the other feminine and harder to distill. The Prologue and Preface, by distinction, speak of Dhuoda's personal situation and of the need for a sweet determination to know and to love God. Yet in making an appeal to love, that is to say, to emotion, Dhuoda stresses again that the best sources of insight and knowing are affective, not rational, and attend not to power politics or to hierarchies of class and status, but to what is uniquely and purely felt. In this way, she teaches her son to love himself and his creator—a knowledge one hopes he put to good use in the tragic end of his life.

The *Liber manualis* has been edited by P. Riché (*Sources chrétiennes,* vol. 225, Paris, 1991, a corrected version of his 1975 edition in the same series). A translation has been prepared by C. Neel (*Handbook for William: A Carolingian Woman's Counsel for Her Son by Dhuoda*, Lincoln, Neb., 1991), which includes an introduction and bibliographical guide. J. Marchand has translated portions of the *Liber* also ("The Frankish Mother Dhuoda," in K. M. Wilson, ed., *Medieval Women Writers*, Athens, Ga., 1984, pp. 1–29), as has M. Thiébaux (*The Writings of Medieval Women*, New York, 1987, pp. 153–69). Godman 274–77 has translated the opening of the *Liber* and discusses the work's themes and Latinity, pp. 52–53. P. Dronke has written a full discussion of Dhuoda also (*Women Writers of the Middle Ages,* Cambridge, 1984, pp. 36–54). Riché's text is reprinted with a punctuation change at v. 31 of the acrostic and with "u" and "v" distinguished.

An Opening Acrostic
In nomine Sanctae Trinitatis

Incipit liber Dhuodane Manualis quem ad filium suum transmisit Wilhelmum.

Cernens plurimas cum suis in saeculo gaudere proles, et me Dhuodanam, o fili Wilhelme, a te elongatam conspiciens procul, ob id quasi anxia et utilitatis desiderio plena, hoc opusculum ex nomine meo scriptum in   5
tuam specietenus formam legendi dirigo, gaudens quod, si absens sum corpore, iste praesens libellus tibi ad mentem reducat quid erga me, cum legeris, debeas agere.

Epigrama operis subsequentis

*D*eus, summe lucis conditor, poli
  Siderumque auctor, rex aeterne, agius,
*H*oc a me coeptum tu perfice clemens.
  Quanquam ignara, ad te perquiro sensum,
*U*t tua capax placita perquiram,   5
  Praesens et futurum tempus curram aptum.

1. **Dhuodane** = *Dhuodanae,* feminine singular genitive. **manualis:** modifies *liber;* the phrase means something like "handbook." 3. **plurimas:** i.e., *feminas.* **cum suis** + *gaudere* = "to enjoy for themselves. . . ." **in saeculo:** ablative of time = "in this age." 5. **scriptum** = *scriptum esse;* Dhuoda means that a scribe wrote down what she dictated (hence *ex nomine meo*). 6. **specietenus** = CL *specie tenus;* the preposition *tenus* (which governs the ablative case) is postpostive. *Specie* has the sense here of "image" or "reflection." **in tuam . . . formam:** lit., "for your form," i.e., "for the shaping of your character." **legendi:** depends on *specietenus;* meaning something like "by means of the reflection of reading" (Riché 73–74, n. 1). 7. **quid:** object of *agere,* which is the complement of *debeas.*

1. Notice the vertical axis of discourse signified by the highlighted initial letters of each couplet, which spell out: *Dhuoda dilecto filio Wilhelmo salutem lege.* 2. **agius** = *hagios, a, on* (see Sleumer 372), from the Greek ἅγιος, "holy," here standing as a substantive. This must be vocative (as are *Deus, conditor, auctor,* and *rex*), though the better form is *hagie* (cf. Blaise/Chirat 69). 3. **hoc:** i.e., *opus.* 4. **quanquam** = CL *quamquam.* **ad** = CL *a.* 5. **capax:** the subject of this line, modifying the subject implicit in the verb. **placita:** from *placitus, a, um,* in the neuter = "beliefs," "tenets," with modifying *tua.* 6. **curram:** more properly *percurram;* the substitution of simple for compound forms is common in ML.

Omnia per cuncta trinus et unus,
 Tuis per saecula prospera largiris.
Digna dignis semper meritis ad singula
10 Tribuis celsam tibi famulantes.
Ad te, ut valeo, poplito flexu,
 Gratias refero conditori largas.
De tua mihi, obsecro, largiri
 Opem, ad dextram sublevans axem.
15 Illic namque credo tuis sine fine
 Manere posse quiesci in regno.
Licet sim indigna, fragilis et exul,
 Limo revoluta, trahens ad imma,
Est tamen michi consors amica
20 Fidaque, de tuis relaxandi crimina.
Centrum qui poli continens girum,
 Pontum et arva concludis palmo,
Tibi commendo filium Wilhelmum:
 Prosperum largiri iubeas in cunctis.
25 Oris atque semper currat momentis;
 Te super omnem diligat factorem.
Filiis cum tuis mereatur felici
 Concito gradu scandere culmen.
In te suus semper vigilet sensus
30 Pandens; per saecula vivat feliciter;

8. **tuis:** lit., "to yours"; i.e., "to those who believe in you." **largiris:** from *largiri*, with *prospera* as object. 9. **dignis . . . meritis:** "by means of apt rewards. . . ." **digna . . . ad singula:** "for every worthy thing. . . ." 10. **celsam:** functions as the substantive object of *tribuis* = "a high prize." **tibi:** *famulantes* + dative = "servants of yours"; although technically *famulantes* is accusative, it stands here with *tibi* as indirect object of *tribuis*, i.e., "you grant to your servants. . . ." 13. **de tua:** with *obsecro*, has the sense of "In supplication before you, I beseech. . . ." **largiri:** infinitive of purpose with *obsecro* = "I beseech you to grant. . . ." 14. **opem:** object of *largiri*. 15. **credo** + dative = "to have faith that . . ."; with *tuis* = "I have faith that your people. . . ." 16. **posse:** infinitive in indirect discourse, with *credo tuis:* "I have faith that your people are able. . . ." **manere . . . quiesci:** complementary infinitives with *posse:* "are able to stay . . . to be made restful . . ."; *quiesci* is the present passive infinitive of *quiescere*. 17. **licet:** conjunction. 19. **michi** = CL *mihi*. 20. **fidaque relaxandi:** *fidaque* modifies *consors amica; relaxandi*, gerund of *relaxare*, depends on it in a phrase meaning something like "confident of the relaxing. . . ." **crimina:** the object of *relaxandi*, it is best translated in English as "of the crimes." 21. **Centrum qui:** i.e., "God the center, who. . . ." **girum** = CL *gyrum*. 25. **oris** = CL *horis*. 27. **felici:** modifies *gradu*. 28. **concito:** from *conciere*, modifying *gradu*.

*L*esus nunquam ille incidat in iram
  Neque separatus oberret a tuis.
*I*ubilet iocundus cursu felici,
  Pergat cum virtute fulgens ad supra;
*O*mnia semper a te abta petat.   35
  Qui das sine fastu, dona illi sensum,
*U*t te intelligat credere, amare,
  Laudare grati<i>s duplicatis agium.
*V*eniat in eum larga tua gratia,
  Pax et securitas corporis et mente,   40
*I*n quo in saeculo vigeat cum prole,
  Ita tenens ista careat ne illa.
*L*egensque revolvat volumen ad tempus,
  Dicta sanctorum obtemperet sensu.
*H*abeat acceptum a te intellectum,   45
  Quid, quando, cui, sublevet opem.
*E*t tibi iugiter quaternas percurrat
  Virtutes, multorum teneat capax.
*L*argus et prudens, pius et fortis,
  Temperantiam necne deserat unquam.   50
*M*is michi similem non habebit unquam,
  Quanquam indigna genitrixque sua,
*O*mnibus semper momentis et oris,
  Rogans te obnixe: miserere illi.
*S*unt michi multae anxiarum turmae,   55
  Flagitans pro illum fragili labore.
*A*d te, largitorem omnium bonorum,
  Eum in cunctis commendo gratantem.
*L*icet sit discors regnum et patria,
  Tu tamen manes solus immutabilis.   60

---

31. **Iesus:** from *laedere,* modifying *ille.*   35. **abta** = CL *apta.*   36. **dona:** imperative.
40. **Pax et securitas:** in apposition with *larga tua gratia.*   **corporis et mente:** genitive and
ablative of specification, respectively, the line means something like "peace and freedom
from the needs of body and of mind."   42. **ita tenens ista:** i.e., "so holding those things
. . ." [i.e., things of the world].   **careat ne illa:** "that he does not lose these things . . ." [i.e.,
things of the next world].   43. **ad tempus:** "at the proper time."   48. **teneat:** intransitive
here.   49. **largus . . . fortis:** the four cardinal virtues are Temperance, Prudence, Fortitude,
and Justice; Dhuoda mentions three of these directly, but lists five in total.   51. **mis** = *mei;*
the form is archaic and is used for emphasis, replicating the sentiment of *mihi,* i.e., "similar
to me, to me" (cf. Riché 79).   54. **miserere:** imperative, with *illi* the dative object.
57. **largitorem:** modifies *te.*   58. **gratantem:** from *gratari,* modifying *eum.*

Utrum digni abta placita perquirant,
In tuo nutu continentur cuncta.
Tuum est regnum tuaque potestas
Plenitudo terrae diffusa per orbem,
65 Et tibi soli famulantur cuncta.
Qui regnas semper, miserere prolis.
Mis duo nati ostensi in saeculo
Vivant, obsecro, teque semper diligant.
Lector qui cupis formulam nosse,
70 Capita perquire abta versorum.
Exin valebis concito gradu
Sensu cognosci quae sim conscripta.
Genitrix duorum masculini sexus,
Rogo, ut ores conditori almo:
75 Erigat ad summum genitorem prolis
Meque cum illis iungat in regnum.

—*Lib. Man.*, Incip.

THE PROLOGUE TO THE MANUAL

Multis plura patent, mihi tamen latent, meae quoque similes, obscurato sensu, carent intellectu, si minus dicam, plus ego. Adest semper ille qui ora aperit mutorum et infantium linguas facit disertas. Dhuoda quanquam in fragili sensu, inter dignas vivens indigne, tamen genitrix tua, fili 5 Wilhelme, ad te nunc meus sermo dirigitur manualis, ut, veluti tabularum lusus maxime iuvenibus inter ceteras artium partes mundanas congruus et abtus constat ad tempus, vel certe inter aliquas ex parte in speculis

---

61. **digni:** "worthy ones," the subject of *perquirant*. **placita:** from *placitus, a, um*, in the neuter = "beliefs," "tenets," with modifying *abta*. 66. **miserere:** imperative with genitive object *prolis* (as common in CL; sometimes a dative object is found). 67. **mis:** *mei*; the form is archaic, here dependent on *nati* in genitive of possession. **duo:** (*duo, ae, o*), masculine plural nominative, modifying *nati*. **ostensi:** perfect passive participle of *ostendere*, modifying *nati*. 69. **nosse** = *novisse*, contracted perfect active infinitive of *noscere*. 72. **cognosci:** present passive infinitive, complement of *valebis* = "you will be able to understand. . . ." **quae sim conscripta:** indirect question which functions as the object of *cognosci*. 74. **ut ores:** i.e., *lector*; Dhuoda is speaking directly to her reader, seeking prayers for her two sons. 75. **ad summum:** "to heaven."
   2. **si minus dicam, plus ego:** the thought is elliptical = " wherein if I say less, I say [or am] more." **ille:** i.e., God; the sentiment is owed to Wisd. of Sol. 10.21. 5. **tabularum lusus:** i.e., "board game." 7. **ad tempus:** prepositional idiom with adverbial force = "at times." **ex parte:** prepositional idiom with adverbial force = "partly."

mulierum demonstratio apparere soleat vultu, ut sordida extergant, exhibentesque nitida, suis in saeculo satagunt placere maritis, ita te obto ut, inter mundanas et saeculares actionum turmas oppressus, hunc libellum a me tibi directum frequenter legere, et, ob memoriam mei, velut in speculis atque tabulis ioco, ita non negligas.   5

Licet sint tibi multa adcrescentium librorum volumina, hoc opusculum meum tibi placeat frequenter legere, et cum adiutorio omnipotentis Dei utiliter valeas intelligere. Invenies in eo quidquid in brevi cognoscere malis; invenies etiam et speculum in quo salutem animae tuae indubitanter possis conspicere, ut non solum saeculo, sed ei per omnia possis placere qui te formavit ex limo: quod tibi per omnia necesse est, fili Wilhelme, ut in utroque negotio talis te exibeas, qualiter possis utilis esse saeculo, et Deo per omnia placere valeas semper.   10

Sunt mihi curae multae, ad te, o fili Wilhelme, verba dirigere salutis, inter quas ardens et vigil meus aestuat animus, ut tibi de tua, auxiliante Deo, nativitate, in hunc codicem libelli ex meo desiderio habeas conscriptum, sicut in sequentibus est utiliter praeordinatum.   15

—*Lib. Man.*, Prol.

THE PREFACE TO THE MANUAL

Anno feliciter, Christo propitio, XI, domno nostro Ludovico condam fulgente in imperio, concurrente V, III Kalendarum iulii diem, in Aquisgrani palatio, ad meum dominum tuumque genitorem Bernardum legalis in coniugio accessi uxor. Et iterum in tertio decimo anno regni eius, III Kalendarum decembrium, auxiliante, ut credo, Deo, tua ex me, desideratissime fili primogenite, in saeculo processit nativitas.   5

Voluente et crescente calamitate huius saeculi miseria, inter multas fluctuationes et discordias regni, imperator praedictus viam omnium isse

2. **obto** = CL *opto.*   6. **adcrescentium** = CL *accrescentium.*   9. **malis:** present active subjunctive of *malle.*   15. **vigil:** from *vigil, vigilis,* "wakeful."

1. **XI:** i.e., the eleventh year of the reign of Louis the Pious = 824.   **domno** = CL *domino.*   **Ludovico:** from *Ludovicus, i* = Louis the Pious (Sleumer 483), the son and successor of Charlemagne, who reigned from 814 to 840.   **condam** = CL *quondam;* (cf. LS 1519, s. v. *quondam*).   2. **Aquisgrani:** from *Aquisgranus, i* = Aachen (Sleumer 121), Louis's capital (built by Charlemagne in the 790s).   4. **accessi:** from *accedere,* with *ad* or *in* + accusative = "to enter into. . . ."   **in tertio . . . eius:** "in the thirteenth year of Louis' reign."   **III Kalendarum decembrium:** i.e., 29 November 826.   6. **in saeculo:** "in the world"; *saeculum* often designates in ML the world of corporal and temporal activity, with a pejorative sense (Blaise/Chirat 732, s. v. *saeculum* 5).   7. **Voluente . . . miseria:** ablative absolute.   **isse:** syncopated perfect active infinitive of *ire.*   8. **imperator . . . viam . . . isse non dubium est:** the thought, elliptically ex-

non dubium est. Nam infra XXVIII anno regni eius, non perveniens ad summum, vitam saeculi debitam finivit. Post mortem quoque eius, in anno sequente, nativitas fratris tui XI Kalendas aprilis: ex meo secundus post te, in Uzecia urbe, Deo miserante, egressus est utero. Etenim parvu-
5 lum illum, antequam baptismatis accepisset gratiam, dominus et genitor Bernardus utrique vestrum, una cum Elefanto, praedictae civitatis epis-copo, et cum ceteris fidelibus suis, in Aquitaniae partibus ad suam fecit adduci praesentiam.

Sed cum diu, ob absentiam praesentiae vestrae, sub iussione senioris
10 mei, in praedicta, cum agone illius iam gaudens, residerem urbe, ex desid-erio utrorumque vestrum hunc codicillum secundum parvitatis meae in-telligentiam tibi transcribi et dirigere curavi.

Item eiusdem. Licet ex multis sim occupata angustiis, ut tuo ali-quando conspicerem aspectu, tamen haec una secundum Deum in arbi-
15 trio Domini constat prior[i]. Volueram quidem, si, daretur mihi virtus de Deo; sed quia longe est a me peccatrice salus, volo, et in hac voluntate meus valde marcessit animus.

Audivi enim quod genitor tuus Bernardus in manus domni te com-mendavit Karoli regis; admoneo te ut huius negotii dignitatem usque ad
20 perfectum voluntati operam des. Tamen, ut ait Scriptura, primum in om-nibus regnum Dei quaere et cetera tunc adicientur, ea quae necessaria sunt animae et corpori tuo fruenda.

—Lib. Man., Praef.

ON LOVING GOD

Diligendus est Deus atque laudandus, non solum a supernis virtuti-bus, sed etiam ab omni humana creatura quae gradiuntur per terram et ad superos tendunt. Inter quos adortor te, fili, ut, in quantum vales, illa semper perquiras ubi cum dignis et abtis Deumque diligentibus, ad cer-

---

pressed, is that "it is indubitable that Louis traveled the road of every obstacle." Dhu-oda refers to the many dynastic challenges put up by the sons of Louis during his reign. 1. **non perveniens ad summum:** lit., "not arriving at the summit," i.e., "prematurely," "not having reached the age for death." 3. **XI Kalendas aprilis:** 22 March 841. 4. **Uzecia:** i.e., Uzès (Riché 84). 6. **una:** adverb. 7. **fecit adduci:** lit., "made [caused] to be moved"; an example of the use in ML of *facere* and the infinitive (Browne xxvii). 10. **cum agone illius . . . gaudens:** i.e., "taking pleasure in the con-tests of Bernhard. . . ."

3. **adortor:** from *adoriri.* **in quantum vales:** i.e., "to whatever extent you are well. . . ."

tum possis scandere culmen, atque una cum illis ad regnum valeas pertingere sine fine mansurum.

Item. Rogo et humiliter suggero tuam iuventutis nobilitatem, quasi praesens, necnon etiam et illos ad quos hunc libellum ad relegendum ostenderis, ne me da<m>pnent vel reprehendant pro eo quod sim temera in   5
tali subintrari agonizatrio acumine laboris, ut tibi aliquid de Deo dirigi audeam sermonem. Certe et ego ipsa, considerans casum humanae fragilitatis meae, me reprehendi indesinenter non cesso, cum sim misera, cinisque et pulvis. Et quid dicam? Si patriarchae et prophetae, et ceteri sancti, a protoplasto usque nunc, eius non valuere plenius intelligere sacramentis   10
documenta, qua<n>to magis ego, exigua et infimi generis orta! Et, si, ut ait Scriptura, coelum et coeli coelorum eum prae magnitudine capere non possunt, quid ego imperitissima valeam dicere?

Legimus in Geneseo quod cum beatus Moyses, ex consortio familiaritatis sermonum Dei, eius voluisset intueri vultum, ita alloquens ait: Si   15
inveni gratiam in conspectu tuo, ostende mihi teipsum ut videam te. Responsum est illi: Non poteris videre faciem meam, nec enim videbit me homo et vivere potest. Et si in sanctis ita, quid putas in terris mihi similes? In hac denegatione conspicuitatis valde meus marcescit animus: aestuat enim sensus.

—Lib. Man. 1.1.1–32.

2. **mansurum:** future active participle of *manere*, modifying *regnum;* the idea is that the kingdom "awaits" William in the future, hence the tense. 4. **necnon . . . ostenderis:** i.e., "and, moreover, even those to whom you show this little book for review. . . ."
5. **da<m>pnent** = CL *damnent*. **pro eo quod sim temera:** lit., "for the thing which I am [considered to be] without cause," i.e., "for being something I am not." **temera** = CL *temere*. 6. **agonizatrio:** from *agonizatrius*, a neologism formed on the Greek ἀγονίζω, meaning "difficulty" (Riché 97). **in tali subintrari . . . laboris:** the thought is redundant and difficult to render into sensible English; lit., "to be involved in such a difficulty, the acme of work," but really meaning something like "to be involved in such a keen and difficult task." 10. **protoplasto:** from *protoplastus, i*, derived from the Greek πρωτοπλαστός, "first-formed," i.e., Adam (Niermeyer 866).
12. **coelum . . . coelorum** = forms of *caelum* in CL. Cf. 1 Kings 8.27 for the sentiment. 14. **in Geneseo:** from *Geneseus, i* = Genesis. **Moyses:** from *Moyses, is* = Moses (Sleumer 531). 15. **alloquens:** from *alloquor*. 17. Cf. Exod. 33.20.
19. **denegatione:** from *denegatio, onis*, "denial" (Blaise/Chirat 254).

Sedulius Scottus

On Christian Leadership; To Bishop Hartgar;
To Bishop Franco
(*De rectoribus christianis* 6; *Carmina* 2.8 & 18; c. 854–859)

The important place Sedulius Scottus holds in the history of Latin literature is at odds with the relative obscurity of his reputation. In the large
body of his work, one finds poetry of every stripe: panegyrics to bishops
and kings, occasional pieces written on a variety of topics, riddles, mock
pastorals evoking the milieu of life at the court of Bishop Hartgar. Much
of this writing is crafted in a classical guise, but adorned with the identifying features of an emerging Medieval Latinity.

Some of those features are owed to the rich traditions of Hiberno-
Latin, for, as his name implies, Sedulius was born and raised in Ireland.
We know nothing, therefore, of his early life and career. He first appears
at Liège in the late 840s, where, along with a group of compatriots, he
was given refuge by Bishop Hartgar. The fact that Hartgar was also the
military and political leader of Liège makes feasible the idea that Sedulius
and his associates accompanied some sort of mission to the continent,
perhaps an overture from Ireland to Charles the Bald. This seems more
likely than that they simply arrived on the continent on a lark, looking
for support for their scholarly and poetic pursuits. Sedulius and his group
found easy company and much support in Bishop Hartgar, who died in
854, whose patronage was continued by his successor, Bishop Franco
(854–901). The dates of Sedulius's birth and death are unknown, but a
floruit of 855 is acceptable, since many of his poems can be dated on
internal evidence to the 850s. It is generally agreed that he died after the
mid 870s.

Much of the importance of Sedulius's work inheres in the variety of
its themes, meters, and tones. Many of his poems were written for formal
occasions, as, for example, *Carmen* 2.18, reprinted here, which celebrates the arrival of Bishop Franco to the see of Liège. Other pieces commemorate important events with praises of individual power and glory,
as the panegyric to Hartgar, *Carmen* 2.8, reprinted here, suggests. In it,
the poet manages to weave Scriptural, classical, and contemporary contexts into an overarching pattern that leaves no doubt of the importance
of Hartgar at every level of society. The use of the Sapphic meter in this
poem proffers the intimacy resident in this meter's long use—it is, after

all, an erotic and intensely personal meter—but demonstrates its new purpose in affirming the social, political, and ecclesiastical familiarity shared by the people of Liège, their leader, and his poet.

Some poems, like the lengthy *De rectoribus christianis,* are more practical, as the excerpt from this poem reprinted here demonstrates. Other poems are more lighthearted and whimsical. Whatever the topic, there is much autobiography and self-effacement throughout, a self-reflective and even a confessional mood that ratifies the balance of intellect and feeling the poet regularly seems to strike in his work. Sedulius is perhaps best known for the debate poem he wrote, in which the rose and the lily vie for supremacy. This poem, which is much like Alcuin's poem on the debate of winter and spring (see pp. 223–25), reminds readers that Sedulius was raised in the Irish literary tradition, which stressed composition in the debate genre. A strong tradition in Irish literary culture, too, insisted on training in Greek, a language Sedulius clearly knew. One finds, not surprisingly, a more pronounced use of Greek neologisms (see *Carmen* 2.18, e.g.) in Sedulius's verse and also a phraseology (see *Carmen* 2.8, e.g.) which tends to be, like much Hiberno-Latin verse, elliptical.

The poetry of Sedulius has been edited by L. Traube (*Monumenta Germaniae Historica, Poetae Latini Aevi Carolini,* vol. 3, Berlin, 1896, pp. 151–240). Raby 1, 193ff., discusses Sedulius in some detail. Several of the poems (though none of the ones reprinted here) have been translated by Godman 282–301, whose introductory comments at 53–57 are also useful. Traube's text is reprinted here without change.

How to Be a Just Judge

Qui cupit rector probus esse iudex,
Lance qui iusti trutinaque gaudet
Inhians pulchri terebrare falsa
    Cuspide veri,
Luminum patrem rutili creantem   5
Solis ac lunae nitidique cosmi
Poscat, ut sensis niteat coruscis
    Luce sophiae;
Vota cognoscat Salemonis aequi,
Quae volaverunt subito per aetram   10

This poem is written in the Sapphic meter.   2. **lance:** from *lanx, lancis,* with adverbial force = "impartially."   **iusti:** from *iustum, i,* dependent on *trutinaque.*   **gaudet** + ablative = "to take delight in. . . ."   9. **Salemonis:** Sedulius always spells Solomon's name this way; more common is *Salomon, onis* (Sleumer 690).   10. **aetram** = CL *aethram.*

Ac penetrarunt domini sabaoth
  Aurea tecta.
Ipse percepit docilemne sensum
Mente lustratus? sapiensne factus
15 Insuper regni columen gubernat
  Gentis Hebraeae?
Quid valet flavi nitor omnis auri?
Ostra quid prosunt rosei decoris?
Gloriae quid sunt Scithicaeque gemmae?
20   Quid diadema?
Orba si mentis acies hebescat,
Lumen ut verum nequeat tueri,
Unde discernat bona prava iusta
  Fasque nefasque—
25 Ergo rectori decus est amare
Te patris verbum sapiensque lumen,
Christe, qui sceptris dominaris orbem
  Celsaque regna;
Cuius in dextra requies beata
30 Constat, in leva locuplesque gaza:
Gloriae princeps humiles coronas,
  Tollis opimos.

—*De Rect. Chris. 6.*

TO BISHOP HARTGAR

Sicut optatus genitor piisque
Advenit gnatis patriaeque magnae,
Sic refers cunctis, pater alme, tecum
  Gaudia laeta.
5 Postque praeclarum rediens tropheum
Hoste prostrato pietatis armis

11. **sabaoth:** indeclinable noun = "heavenly host" (Sleumer 685). 13. **ipse:** i.e., Solomon. 14. **lustratus:** from *lustrari*. 19. **Scithicaeque** = CL *Scythicae,* a general name given by the Romans to the various tribes who lived beyond the Black Sea. 30. **leva** = CL *laeva,* parallel with *dextra.*

1. **genitor:** i.e., Moses; this poem is written in the Sapphic meter. 2. **gnatis** = CL *natis;* in the plural, this means "children." **patriaeque:** i.e., the Promised Land. 3. **pater alme:** i.e., Hartgar, Bishop of Liège, 840–854; the bishops of this relatively new town were also its military and civil leaders, owing to the nearly constant stream of Viking invasions it faced in the ninth century.

Victor exultans manibus decoris
    Prendito palmam.
Te decet talem meruisse florem,
O decus belli meritis coruscum,   10
Arma qui vibras super astra nota,
    Inclite praesul.
Protegis scuto fidei tuosque
Macte lorica galeaque Christi,
Aureo fulgens gladio salutis   15
    Proteris hostes.
Vester insignis niveusque coetus
Corde robusto volitat per hostes,
Conterit turmas agitans per arva
    Herculis armis.   20
Sume florentem meritis coronam,
Quae necas hostes, iuvenum caterva:
Namque Normannus cecidit rebellis
    Praeda cruenta.
Tuncque Golias obiit superbus,   25
Magna qui belli fuerat columna;
Caeteri cedros simulabant altas
    More Ciclopum.
Testis est Rehnus fluvius bicornis,
Testis et campus madidus cruore,   30
Indicat litus rutilum tropaeum
    Ossibus albens.
Unde congaudet populusque totus:
Vosque prae cunctis benedicit ipse,
Laudat hunc vestrum celebratque coetum,   35

---

8. **Prendito:** future active imperative.   13. **tuosque:** i.e., "your own."   14. **macte:** interjection = "well done."   20. **Herculis:** from *Hercules, is.*   23. **cecidit:** intransitive, with only the final "i" long.   **rebellis:** modifies *Normannus*, which means Norsemen or Vikings (Sleumer 551, s. v. *Normanni;* Latham 315); the *Normanni* hailed from Scandinavia and ravaged the northern and western coasts of Europe beginning in roughly the mid 9th century. Liège was from its founding in the eighth century and for several centuries thereafter under virtually continual siege.   24. **praeda cruenta:** in apposition with *Normannus rebellis.*   25. **tuncque:** i.e., when the Normans were defeated, it was like the time when David slew Goliath.   **Golias:** *Golias, ae,* the declinable form of Goliath's name, which is more usually found in its indeclinable form, *Goliath* (Sleumer 363).   27. **caeteri** = CL *ceteri.*   28. **Ciclopum** = CL *Cyclopum* (*Cyclops, opis*).   29. **Rehnus,** more properly *Rhenus,* the Rhine.

Optime pastor.
Sic tibi semper cumulatur astris
Palma pro tali viridans agone,
Te coronando, bone praesul, alma
40   Gratia Christi.

                       —*Carm.* 2.8.

ON THE COMING OF BISHOP FRANCO

Fistola nostra sonet, melicis et concinat odis,
    Musis organizans fistola nostra sonet.
Dulce sonate melos, sollempnica ducite festa:
    Dulcis adest pastor; dulce sonate melos.
5 Christus adest domini sacrato chrismate vernans:
    Plaudite Christicolae, christus adest domini.
Filia pulchra Sion, hymnizans voce sonora
    Gnosce tuum sponsum, filia pulcra Sion.
Hic vir, hic est domini, Lantberti nobilis haeres:
10   Eximius praesul hic vir, hic est domini.
Cunctus ovans populus nunc alleluia cantat,
    Promit osanna novum cunctus ovans populus.
Stella venusta micat Drogonis maxima cura,

40. **gratia:** in apposition with *bone praesul.*
1. **fistola** = CL *fistula;* this poem, written at the arrival of Franco (854–901), Hartgar's successor as Bishop of Liège, is composed in epanaleptic distichs, or *versus serpentini* (like Paul the Deacon's poem to Como, above, pp. 211–12), consisting of elegiac couplets in which the first words of the hexameters are repeated as the last words of the pentameter. 2. **organizans:** from *organizare,* "to compose," "to arrange" (from the Greek ὄργανιζω). 3. **sollempnica** = CL *sollemnia;* the addition of a parasitic consonant is common in ML orthography. 5. **chrismate:** from *chrisma, atis* (Greek Χρίσμα), "unguent," "balm" (Niermeyer 177). 6. **Christicolae:** from *Christicola, ae,* a masculine neologism of the fourth century meaning "worshiper of Christ," here dative with *Plaudite* (Blaise/Chirat 149). 7. **Sion:** from *Sion, onis,* this word has several meanings in ML (Jerusalem, the temple of Jerusalem, the Jewish people, the Church; see Sleumer 729, s. v. 2 *Sion*); here it stands by metonymy for the community of believers at Liège. **hymnizans:** from *hymnizare,* "to chant/sing hymns," a LL neologism found in Prudentius and Irenaeus (Blaise/Chirat 397). 8. **sponsum:** i.e., Franco himself, conceived of here as the groom of the community, his bride. 9. **Lantberti:** i.e., Lambert of Liège. **haeres** = CL *heres.* 11. **alleluia:** indeclinable, here in the accusative case. 12. **osanna** = *hosanna* or *hosiannah;* the addition or deletion of aspirates is common in ML; this form, here in the accusative singular, is indeclinable (Sleumer 391). 13. **Drogonis:** i.e., Drago, Bishop of Metz (d. 855), the son of Charlemagne by his concubine Regina, who, it is suggested in these lines, was involved in the upbringing or training (or both) of Franco.

Ecclesiae specimen stella venusta micat.
Cinnama ferte viro, redolentes spargite flores,   15
    In fialis niveo cinnama ferte viro.
Pistica nardus ei liquidos respiret ordores,
    Profluat ubertim pistica nardus ei.
Splendide pastor, ave, Franco, lux aurea cosmi;
    Florida spes populi, splendide pastor, ave.   20

—*Carm.* 2.18.

16. **fialis** = CL *phialis;* the Romans meant by it "a broad shallow-drinking vessel," "a saucer" (LS 1369), but in EL through the Vulgate it means "censer," as here. (Cf. 1 Chron. 28.17; Apoc. 5.8). **niveo:** referring to Franco's episcopal garments. 17. **pistica:** (Greek πιστικόω), a LL neologism meaning "pure," "genuine" (LS 1380 and cf. John 12.3). **nardus:** this noun is feminine, here modified by *pistica;* in the neuter the nominative form is *nardum.* 19. **Franco:** vocative (from *Franco, onis*).

et eius angelorum quia salus eterna   humano generi ap
paruit.   Gloria in excelsis deo   o et interra pax hom
inibus bo ne uolunta   tis. Quia sal?   Regnans cum
patre natus exmatre xpc nos bndicat. Amen.

ugum enim onerís eius et uirgam humerí eius et
sceptrum exactoris eius supasti sicut indie m
ban· quia omis uiolenta pdatio cū tumultu et
uestimentū mixtū sanguine erit incobustionē·

atore quia ipe est regnum dei amen dico uobis
quia non tardabit·   Laudate pueri dnm
Leuate capita uestra ecce appropinquabit re
demptio uestra   Laudate dnm oms gent
Dum ortus fuerit sol decelo uidebitis regem regum proceden
em apatre tamquam sponsus dethalamo suo·   Laudate nom
Orietur sicut sol·   Laudate dnm quo b·   Iudea
et ierusalem nolite time re cras egrediemini et do minue
rit uobiscum·   Constantes estote uide
bitis auxilium domini sup uos.   Cras egred
um esset desponsata mater iesu maria ioseph ante qua
conuenirent inuenta est inutero habens quod enim inea

PLATE 10. Loose folios (much cut down) from a hymnary, with neumes, or musical notations, written above several of the lines.

PLATE 10

Hymnary (with neumes)
Loose folios on parchment, after 1100
(*top*) AMB ms. 4.2 (2) (b); (*bottom*) AMB ms. 4.2 (1) (a)
Annmary Brown Memorial Collection
John Hay Library, Brown University

Hymns are sung praises to God, and in the Western church of the fourth century they were written both as literary documents—as Christian counterparts to the lyrics of Latin antiquity—and as pieces to be sung. The hymns of Prudentius, for example (see above, pp. 106–10) were literary in nature, while Ambrose's shorter, more direct hymns, written about the same time, were more obviously meant for a wider (and not necessarily well-educated, or even literate) audience. As monasticism grew as an institution and expanded its authority and importance during the Carolingian period, hymns became central, too, to the basic order of the monastic establishment, forming the foundation of the divine office. Hymnaries were common collections, therefore, in the Latin output of the Middle Ages.

Both folios shown here include the rudimentary musical notations, or neumes, which are the forerunner of staffed musical notation. These folios were once part of a larger hymnary that was disassembled, cut down, and used as binding for newer codices, a common practice in the Latin Middle Ages, especially with works such as hymnals. Folio 4.2 (1) (a) is ruled in black ink with red rubrics; as it has been severely cut down, it has no margins. Its dimensions are 11 cm. × 14 cm. Folio 4.2 (2) (b) is of the same dimension, but has a bottom margin of 2 cm. The first five lines are written in a smaller script than the remaining four. All are written in black ink in a late Carolingian hand.

PART FOUR: 900–1100
THE RISE OF MEDIEVAL LATIN

Notker (c. 840–912)
Gerald (fl. c. 850)
Liutprand of Cremona (c. 920–970)
Widukind of Corvey (fl. c. 970)
Richer of St. Remy (fl. c. 975)
Hrotsvita of Gandersheim (c. 925–973)
Medieval Latin Religious Drama
Ekkehard IV of St. Gall (c. 980–1060)
Adam of Bremen (fl. 1075)
The Cambridge Songs (c. 1050)
Peter Damian (1007–1072)

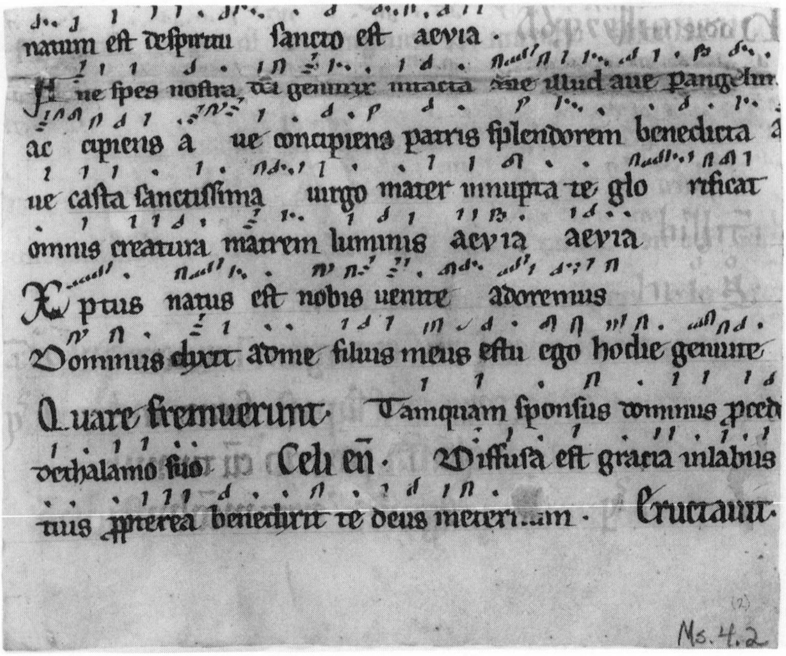

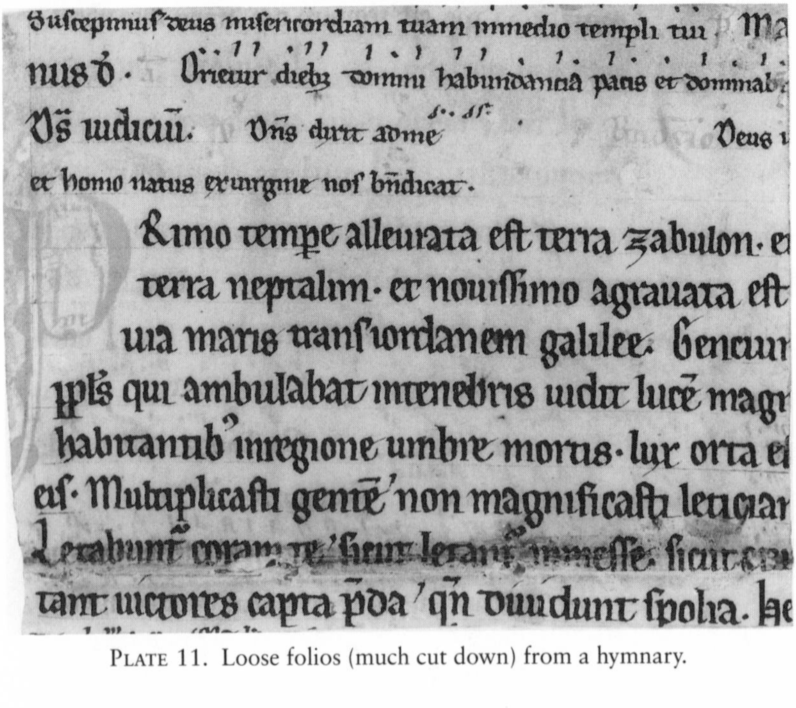

PLATE 11. Loose folios (much cut down) from a hymnary.

PLATE 11

The folios depicted here show the reverse sides of those in plate 10. Folio 4.2 (2) (a) is ruled in black ink. Though the folio has been severely cut down to make it usable as binding material, there is a margin apparent at the left, and the bottom margin, measuring 2 cm., is intact. There are 10 lines. Its dimensions are 11 cm. × 14 cm. The folio is written on parchment in a clear hand. 4.2 (1) (b) preserves 12 lines, but four of those lines are written in a smaller script. The folio is written on parchment in black ink with red initialing.

INTRODUCTION

Antique Latin models had remained a constant in the West for a millennium, and they were to remain important in literary activity to the end of the Latin Middle Ages—indeed, beyond. But increasingly they were forced to compete with newer modes of expression as the international aspirations with which they were best associated gave way to the ethnic, geographic, and political pressures of localism. In fact, the center of literary gravity shifted after the breakup of the Carolingian empire, exacerbating local pressures and portending fundamental changes. Charlemagne's empire had been a phenomenon located generally in what we call northern France and western Germany; its sentiments, as we have seen, tended to be cast in classical guises, hence they remained imprinted with the stamp of the old Mediterranean culture. But after the ninth century, there was a marked shift to the east, to the court of the Ottos of Germany, where a profusion of literary modes were attempted.

Germany under the Ottos was the first "medieval" kingdom to rise from the splintering of Charlemagne's empire. That splintering was rendered final in 877, when Charles the Bald died, a mere three decades after the treaty of Verdun in 843 had divided Charlemagne's empire among his three grandsons. Roughly speaking, the three broad areas of the empire willed to Charlemagne's heirs (i.e., what we call France, Germany, and Italy) became political entities unto themselves. There were already undeniable linguistic and cultural reasons arguing for the separation of these parts of the former empire—reasons which had, in fact, hastened the process along. But in what became France, the forces of localism reigned supreme for much of the ninth and tenth centuries, an outcome also true in Italy. By following the old Carolingian model of ecclesiastical alliances, however, Otto the Great (936–973), the first of three successful German kings so named, managed to build a strong central state in the German portion of the old empire—and to foster much important literary activity as a result.

It was natural that Otto would fashion a continuation of the Carolingian rapprochement with the Church. It was politically wise, to be sure, but it was also judicious from a cultural standpoint, for the church in Germany was a strong, rich institution, comprising important bishoprics, powerful bishops, and prestigious monasteries, including, most famously, the monastery at St. Gall. The vibrant literary culture created at St. Gall was well in place decades before Otto's reign began, as the selections from Notker Balbulus show. St. Gall had always been an active establishment, to be sure, but by the year 900, just a few decades before Otto the Great took power, the monastery experienced some of its most important growth. Among the literary accomplishments owed to its sustaining graces was the development of the sequence, a special musical form sung during the *Jubilus* of the Mass. Under Otto and, indeed, throughout the tenth century, Germany would see numerous continuators of the sequence genre.

Germany in the tenth century also possessed a vibrant sense of history, expectedly, given the strong monarchs of this age. Both Liutprand of Cremona and Widukind of Corvey were associated with Otto I and wrote much about him. They did so by striking off in new directions. Both historians emphasize biography and personal narration in their respective works, as they tend also to focus on secular, rather than sacred, events. Nor does either historian look much to earlier Christian historians as models, much less the antique Latin writers of history. For these reasons, as in so many other respects, the work of Widukind and Liutprand—and the other historians of this age—tends to suggest a new development in historiography, a strain of inquiry and reporting that is truly medieval in theme, tone, presentation, and topic. More medieval, too, is the further development of the epic genre in the ninth century in Germany. It seems logical to think that the interest in German history influenced the writing of the mid ninth century epic the *Waltharius*, whose topic, the German opposition to Attila the Hun, was rendered in classical hexameters suitable for the heroic exploits of the German heroes of the poem. But it is also important to recognize the ways in which this most classical of forms, the hexametric epic, has been taken over by medieval themes, topics, and vocabulary in the *Waltharius*, one of the finest examples of the epicizing strain in the Medieval Latin tradition.

Original in an entirely different way is the work of another tenth-century German writer, Hrotsvita of Gandersheim, who more or less single-handedly reintroduced drama into the literary firmament of the West. Hrotsvita, like Liutprand and Widukind, was presumably an acquaintance of Otto I, for she probably studied at his court. She had news of the court, in the event, from the abbess of Gandersheim, Gerberga, who was the niece of the king. As our selection of religious dramas suggests, Hrotsvita did not work in a vacuum, for there were plenty of dramatic compositions circulating in western Europe (and presumably even more being performed), both before and during her lifetime. In particular, mystery and miracle plays abounded, focusing on sacred events or the important exploits of the most popular saints of the day (Saint Nicholas was consistently popular, for example, in the Latin Middle Ages). But Hrotsvita gave finest and best shape to drama as a genre, mostly by ignoring the traditions of miracle and mystery plays, and paying attention instead to the details of gesture, performance, plot, and structure, inculcating vestiges of antique Latin comedy, and insisting on the use of a wholly original rhythmical prose for her plays.

Germanic monastic institutions such as Gandersheim, where Hrotsvita lived and worked, or St. Gall, where Notker produced his sequences, began in the ninth and tenth centuries to attend to the writing of their own histories, especially as the identity of establishments grew in prestige and pedigree became important to document and sustain. As one of the most important establishments in the West, St. Gall was chronicled early on by its own monks, but in the tenth century, this task was taken over by Ekkehard IV, one of several Ekkehards to be associated with St. Gall and to produce important work in the Latin Middle Ages. In Ekkehard's history of St. Gall, as in other historical works of its kind, much local lore was recorded for posterity, but so too is a nascent prose style retrievable in these histories, which were generally written apart from larger models and by writers who reflect local trends in orthography and syntax.

While monastic establishments were held in special esteem, so too did importance attach to specific bishoprics in the tenth and eleventh centuries. Adam of Bremen's history of the bishops of Hamburg-Bremen demonstrates the importance that could attend to a particular see and also the sorts of power that could accrue to such a see. In the works of Adam and of Ekkehard, in any case, astute historical observers marshaled their talents to tell detailed stories of the growing importance and power of ecclesiastical institutions. In the case of Richer, attention shifts from Germany to France, but the focus remains the same, to communicate the details of a particular past from the purview of the present. Like his near contemporaries Liutprand and Widukind, Richer relies in his history on his own personality to frame his narrative and uses a Latin style that is equally personal and typically medieval.

Medieval in another way is the collection of lyrics known today as the *Cambridge Songs*. This collection, whose modern name associates it with England, is actually German in origin and reflects in its contents lyrics written during the ninth, tenth, and early eleventh centuries. The majority of the lyrics are secular and give vent to a variety of feeling. But feeling remains important in sacred composition too, which prevails in the centuries leading up to the twelfth, as Peter Damian's hymn shows. Damian's more important work was not poetic but political, for he was an intimate of the principles involved in the so-called investiture contest. The origins of this conflict, which climaxed in a lengthy struggle for hegemony between the German king Henry IV and Pope Gregory VII, were rooted in the monastic reform movement associated as early as the tenth century with Cluny, which eventually came to infiltrate the Church as a blanket call for reform. Reform, in the view of ecclesiastical leaders such as Gregory VII or Humbert of Silva Candida, meant removing the Church from the influence of secular power—

precisely the instrument of Germany's relative abundance in the centuries following the demise of the Carolingian achievement.

The investiture contest, as the next part will suggest, brought to the fore the final set of influences that marked the development of Latin in the Middle Ages. But that development was assisted in no small part by the fresh innovations of the writers who worked in the centuries between Charlemagne and Chartres. They were by and large clerical figures, associated with the Church or with powerful leaders. Their learning was owed to monastic schools. They were aware of the ancient pedigree of the literary language in which they wrote, and sometimes spoke, though as a second language, and yet they struck out for novelty and innovation. They worked from close quarters, but what they saw was of a larger scope: nature, emotion, beauty, and power, speaking both to individual longing and to wider assumptions about Christian culture:

> What is all this juice and all this joy?
> A strain of the earth's sweet being in the beginning
> In Eden garden.—Have, get, before it cloy,
>   Before it cloud, Christ, lord, and sour with sinning,
>   Innocent mind and Mayday in girl and boy,
>   Most, O maid's child, thy choice and worthy the winning.

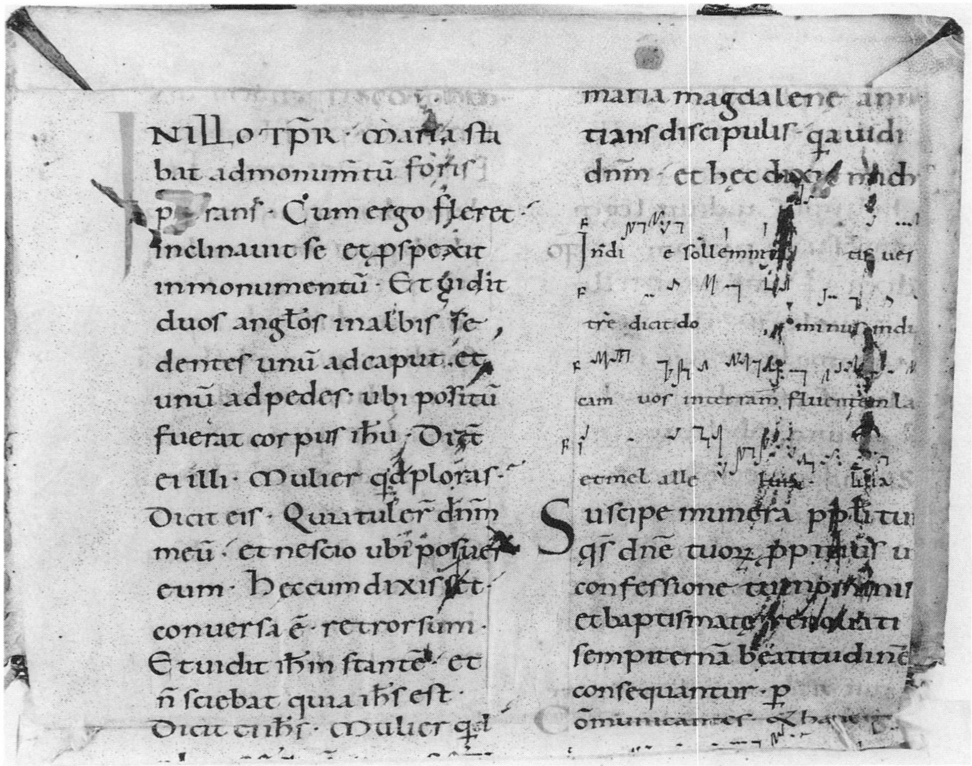

PLATE 12. A loose folio from a hymnary, with neumes.

PLATE 12

Hymnary (with neumes)
Single folio on parchment, after 1000; from the binding of
Quadragesimale doctoris illuminati Francisci Nayronis, Italy, 1491
John Hay Library, Brown University

This loose folio, discovered in the binding of an incunable published in 1491, at one point was part of a much larger page that seems to have been nearly quartered by the Renaissance book-maker who reduced it to scrap. The folio preserves only a 4 cm. left margin and a 1 cm. middle margin separating two columns, the left column preserved entirely, the right cut off abruptly. Musical notations, or neumes, are clearly visible. The folio is written on parchment in brown ink with red initials in a clear, neat Carolingian minuscule.

Notker Balbulus

Sequence for Saint Laurence; Martyrology of Saint Laurence
(*Liber Ymnorum Notkeri; Martyrologium;* c. 900)

I n Notker's lifetime, in the late ninth century, St. Gall must have been an
extraordinary place to live and work. It had always been somewhat iso-
lated geographically, but it was at a remove from those areas (in the east
and north of Europe, especially) that saw a steady stream of invasions,
especially in the late ninth century. By late in the century, it was able to
reap the benefits of its relative stability and experienced both the good
effects of new construction and the intellectual rewards accruing from an
enlarged library—both the result of the earlier work of Abbot Gozbert,
who died in 837, right around the time of Notker's birth, around 840.

Notker lived for all of his adult life at St. Gall, where he was, in
succession, monk and librarian before becoming master. He was influenced intellectually by Hrabanus Maurus, having been instructed by two
of Hrabanus's better pupils, Hartmut and Grimald, both of whom were
at times abbots of St. Gall. Like Hrabanus, Notker seems to have taken
well to teaching, despite the stammer which afflicted him (for which he
was given the added name *Balbulus*). There are contemporary references
to Notker as a warm, witty, and genuinely talented master.

As well as a great teacher, Notker was a litterateur of especial bril-
liance, and he brought his wide-ranging literary instincts to bear on a
number of genres, in each instance reformulating them for future generations, making his position in the development of Medieval Latin all the
more important. Of his prose works, the most famous is the *Gesta Karoli,*
a biography of Charlemagne and a history of his reign, written in the
early 880s. This work, unlike its earlier and equally famous counterpart,
the *Vita Karoli Magni* of Einhard (see pp. 238–46), is anecdotal and personal in its treatment of Charlemagne, relying on the storehouse of lore
and legend that had sprung up around the illustrious king after his death.
In refusing to engage the traditions of ancient historical or biographical
writing, however, and in presenting his material in a direct, even self-
effacing style, Notker achieved for historical prose a new identity owed
more to the simple narratives of saints' lives or monastic histories. Notker
also produced a history of St. Gall, written in prose and verse (now only

fragmentary), and a treatment of Christian martyrs, the *Martyrologium,* from which Laurence's history is excerpted here.

Important in an entirely different way is his *Liber Ymnorum,* which is (seemingly) a complete collection of forty sequences organized liturgically for the ecclesiastical calendar. While the production—not to say the preservation—of such a collection is in itself remarkable, Notker's *Liber* also preserves for the first time in a substantive way the sequence form, a generic invention owed to the Latin Middle Ages. The history of the sequence remains in part obscure, especially in the centuries before Notker wrote. Clearly he did not invent the sequence ex nihilo, but clearly, too, he reformulated the genre and brought it to a new level of sophistication and function, making possible its fullest development in the twelfth century in the hands of Adam of St. Victor (see pp. 521–25).

The sequence developed in the Roman liturgy in the performance of two chants—the Gradual and the Alleluia—that occurred between the reading of the Epistle and the reading of the Gospel. In the chanting of the Alleluia, the tendency developed to prolong the singing of the final *a* sound, which was called by a special name, *Jubilus.* By the late ninth century, the *Jubilus* had been further expanded, from complicated musical patternings, to include prose narratives, set to the *Jubilus*'s musical variations. These prose narratives are called sequences. In the *proemium* to his *Liber,* Notker reports that he wrote his first sequences as a way of remembering the complicated melodies of the *Jubilus.* Whatever his reasons, there can be no doubting his deft balancing of beautiful music and superb narratives. The sequences of Notker are nonmetrical, composed of paired verses of equal syllables, sung to the same tune but with the length of paired verses variable from line to line. In these intense and vivid narratives that often commemorate the passions of Christian belief, one finds the full range of emotion and symbol, compression and drama.

The careful exploitation of imagery in the sequence for the festival of the holy women, for example, based in part on the *Passio Perpetua,* underscores the distinction of gender roles so important to the sequence's larger theme, which celebrates the salvific qualities of Mary against the background of Eve's ancient error. The presentation of earthly and heavenly worlds, and the views they imply, is often the backdrop of Notker's sequences, as in the one written for Laurence reprinted here. While highlighting Laurence's temporal and eternal roles, Notker also plays on the ways in which the former foreshadow the latter. The earthly downfall of Laurence, articulated against the symbols of Roman power and hierarchy, and recalled also in the context of social standing, reaches its most intense depiction precisely at the sequence's midpoint, where one finds Laurence spurning the fasces of Caesar (*Caesaris tu fasces contemnis*) for the surer, soldierly power of David's heaven.

Like the style of his *Gesta Karoli*, the prose of the martyrology is disarmingly simple, exploiting the historical qualities of Notker's vision but relying on a consistently straightforward narrative and a smooth progression from topic to topic. As the excerpt which treats Laurence's martyrdom attests, Notker uses reported dialogue frequently and prefers chronological presentation. There is little time for dramatic effect here or for the potential of emotional appeal. The aim is to set Laurence in a wider context of ecclesiastical history, to demonstrate his special attractiveness as a human, before commending him to God's hands and a better place. Both the treatments given here speak to Notker's penchant for experimenting with form, for the bold tasks he puts to the mixed form in his history of St. Gall are replicated in his versions of the many saints' lives detailed in his *Liber* and his *Martyrologium*.

The sequences of Notker have been edited by W. von den Steinen (*Notker der Dichter und seine geistige Welt*, 2 vols., Bern, 1948). The *Martyrologium* may be found in *PL*, vol. 131. Two of the sequences have been translated by Godman 318–23; his introduction, pp. 64–69, is useful also. Raby 1, 210–19, treats the history of the sequence in some detail, as does P. Dronke ("The Beginnings of the Sequence," in *The Medieval Poet and His World*, Rome, 1984, pp. 115–44). Von den Steinen's text of the sequence and Migne's of the martyrology are reprinted here, both without change.

A SEQUENCE FOR SAINT LAURENCE

A. Laurenti, David magni
martyr milesque fortis:

1. Tu imperatoris tribunal,   2. Tu manus tortorum cruentas

3. Sprevisti, secutus   4. Qui solus potuit
   desiderabilem   regna superare
   atque manu fortem,   tyranni crudelis,

A. **Laurenti:** from *Laurentius, i,* in vocative case.   **David:** indeclinable noun, here in the genitive singular, with modifying *magni*.   2. **cruentas:** modifies *manus*, which governs *tortorum*.   3. **sprevisti:** from *spernere*.   **desiderabilem:** adjective standing as the substantive object of *secutus* (from *sequi*).   **fortem:** adjective standing as the substantive object of *secutus*, with modifying *manu* in ablative of specification.   4. **Qui:** i.e., God.   **tyranni:** i.e., the Emperor Decius, who reportedly witnessed the martyrdom

5. Cuiusque sanctus
sanguinis prodigos
facit amor milites eius,

6. Dummodo illum
liceat cernere
dispendio vitae praesentis.

7. Caesaris tu fasces contemnis
et iudicis minas derides.

8. Carnifex ungulas et ustor
craticulam vane consumunt.

9. Dolet impius
urbis praefectus
victus a pisce assato,
Christi cibo:

10. Gaudet domini
conviva favo
conresurgendi cum ipso
saturatus.

11. O Laurenti,
militum David in-
victissime regis aeterni:

12. Apud illum
servulis ipsius
deprecare veniam semper,

13. Martyr, milesque fortis!

—*De Sancto Laur.*

---

of Laurence in 258. Laurence was scourged and then, as the story goes, he was roasted alive. The lore that surrounds Laurence's death on the gridiron reports also (as the story which is excerpted below from Notker's *Martyrologium* recalls) that the martyr said to the Emperor: "*assasti unam partem, gira et aliam et manduca*" ("you have roasted one side; turn me so the other side can be roasted and then eat me."). Some believe that the scribes copying out this story for circulation misread *passus est* ("he was martyred") as *assus est* ("he was roasted") leading to the details of this unusual method of death. **5. prodigos** + genitive *sanguinis* = lit., "lavish with blood," but as a modifying phrase with *milites* it has predicative force, i.e., "whose holy love made his soldiers flow with blood. . . ." **6. Dummodo . . . dispendio:** *dummodo* + subjunctive *liceat* = a clause of proviso; *licet* + dative *dispendio* and infinitive *cernere* = "it is permissible to/for (something) to . . .," i.e., "if only it is permissible at the cost of the present life to see God [in the next]." **7. fasces:** one of the more important symbols of the authority of the Roman state, the *fasces* traditionally were carried in procession by the lictors. **8. carnifex . . . craticulam:** the *carnifex* and the *ustor* both tortured Saint Laurence, the former by clawing his flesh (hence *ungulas*) and the latter by roasting him (hence *craticulam*, "gridiron"). **9. Urbis praefectus:** i.e., Valerianus, the prefect of the city. **assato:** perfect passive participle of *assare*, "roasted." **Christi cibo:** in apposition with *pisce*. **10. conresurgendi:** from *corresurgere*, "to revive" (Blaise/Chirat 226, s. v. *corresurgure*). **11. David:** genitive case. **12. servulis:** ablative of accompaniment. **deprecare:** present imperative of *deprecor*.

The Story of the Martyrdom of Saint Laurence

IV. ID. AUG. — Romae, via Tiburtina, nativitas sancti Laurentii archidiaconi et martyris sub Decio imperatore. Cui beatus Sixtus omnes facultates et thesauros Ecclesiae, pergens ad coronam martyrii, reliquit. Quos ille munifica liberalitate debilibus et aliis pauperibus, viduisque et
5   indigentibus erogare curavit. Quo audito Decius Caesar fecit eum sibi praesentari; et auditum tradidit eum Valeriano Urbis praefecto, qui et ipse dedit eum in custodiam cuidam Hippolyto, at Hippolytus reclusit eum cum multis. Ibidem beatus Laurentius post sanationem Cyriacae viduae, et illuminationem Crescentionis, Lucillum caecum in nomine Iesu Christi
10   videntem reddidit. Hoc factum audientes, multi caeci veniebant ad beatum Laurentium, et illuminabantur. Quod videns Hippolytus credidit, et catechizatus atque baptizatus est.

    Completis autem tribus diebus, in quibus ex permissu Hippolyti, iam Christiani, omnes facultates Ecclesiae beatus Laurentius pauperibus ex-
15   pendit, praesentavit se ipse in palatio Sallustiano. Decius, iratus, iussit eum exspoliari et caedi scorpionibus; postea vinctus catenis ductus est beatus Laurentius in palatium Tiberii ut ibi audiretur: et iracundia plenus Decius iussit eum nudum caedi. Qui cum caederetur clamabat ad Caesarem: "Ecce, miser, vel modo cognosce quia non sentio tormenta tua."
20   Tunc Decius fustes augeri darique ad latera eius laminas ferreas ardentes iussit. Beatus vero Laurentius dixit: "Domine Iesu Christe, Deus de Deo, miserere mihi servo tuo, quia accusatus non negavi; interrogatus, te Dominum Iesum Christum confessus sum." Et cum diutissime plumbatis caederetur, dixit: "Domine Iesu Christe, qui pro salute nostra dignatus es for-
25   mam servi accipere ut nos a servitio daemonum liberares, accipe spiritum meum." Et audita est vox: "Adhuc multa certamina tibi debentur." Tunc extensus in catasta, et scorpionibus gravissime caesus, subridens et gratias

---

1. **IV. ID. AUG.** = August 10.   **nativitas:** lit., "birth," but referring here to the "birth" of Laurence as a saint; hence this is actually the day of his death. Note the use of an abstract noun for a concrete event.   2. **Sixtus:** Pope Sixtus II (reigned 257–258), martyred three days before Laurence.   5. **fecit . . . praesentari:** *facere* + infinitive (Browne xxvii) is common in ML; with *eum sibi* the phrase literally means "made him [Laurence] to be presented to him [Decius]."   9. **illuminationem:** "giving sight." **Cyriacae . . . Crescentionis, Lucillum:** names of fellow prisoners; Cyriaca was martyred, buried near Laurence, and beatified also.   10. **videntem:** double accusative (with *Lucillum caecum*) meaning "vision."   12. **catechizatus:** from *catechizare* (from the Greek κατηχίζω), "to be instructed [in the faith]" (Blaise/Chirat 138). 22. **mihi** = CL *me; servo tuo* is in apposition with *mihi*.   23. **plumbatis:** from *plumbatae, arum*, "scourges [fitted with leaden balls]" (LS 1388, s. v. *plumbo* B 2). 27. **subridens** = CL *surridens*.

agens, dicebat: "Benedictus es, Domine Deus Pater Domini nostri Iesu Christi, qui nobis donasti misericordiam, quam meriti non sumus; sed tu, Domine, propter tuam pietatem, da nobis gratiam, ut cognoscant omnes circumstantes quia tu consolaris servos tuos." Tunc unus de militibus, nomine Romanus, credidit Domino Iesu Christo, et dixit beato Laurentio: 5 "Video ante te hominem pulcherrimum, stantem cum linteo, et extergentem tua vulnera. Adiuro te per Christum, qui tibi misit angelum suum, ne me derelinquas."

Levatus igitur beatus martyr de catasta et solutus, redditus est Hippolyto, tantum in palatio. Veniens autem Romanus cum urceo, misit se ad 10 pedes beati Laurentii ut baptizaretur; et mox baptizatus, ac se Christianum publica voce professus, eductus foras muros portae Salariae, decollatus est. Decius autem Caesar pergit noctu ad thermas iuxta palatium Sallustii; et exhibito ei sancto Laurentio, allata sunt omnia genera tormentorum: plumbatae, fustes, laminae, ungues, lecti, baculi. Et dixit De- 15 cius beato martyri: "Iam depone perfidiam artis magicae, et dic nobis generositatem tuam." Cui beatus Laurentius dixit: "Quantum ad genus, Hispanus sum eruditus vel nutritus Romanus, et a cunabulis Christianus, eruditus omni lege sancta et divina." Et Decius: "Sacrifica," inquit, "diis, nam nisi sacrificaveris, nox ista in te expendetur cum suppliciis." "Mea," 20 inquit, "illa nox obscurum non habet, sed omnis in luce clarescit." Et cum caederetur lapidibus os eius, ridebat, et confortabatur ac dicebat: "Gratias tibi ago, Domine, quia tu es Dominus omnium rerum."

Allatus est autem lectus cum tribus costis, et exspoliatus beatus Laurentius vestimentis suis extentus est in cratem ferream, et cum furcis 25 ferreis coriatus desuper dixit Decio: "Ego me obtuli sacrificium Deo in odorem suavitatis, quia sacrificium est Deo spiritus contribulatus." Carnifices tamen urgenter ministrabant carbones, mittentes sub cratem, et desuper eum comprimentes furcis ferreis. Sanctus Laurentius dixit: "Disce, miser, quanta est virtus Domini Iesu Christi Dei mei, nam car- 30 bones tui mihi refrigerium praestant, tibi autem supplicium sempiternum.

2. **donasti:** syncopated perfect active indicative, second person singular of *donare* = *donavisti*. 12. **foras:** in CL = adverb; in ML an adverb but also a preposition with the accusative, as here = "outside." 14. **allata sunt:** from *afferre*. 17. **generositatem:** the idea is that Laurence is of high birth or descent, hence *generositas* means something like "position." 24. **lectus cum tribus costis:** lit., "a bed with three ribs," this is another way of describing the gridiron on which Laurence was roasted. 25. **cratem:** from *cratis, is*, "ribs," another way of describing the gridiron. 26. **coriatus:** perfect passive participle of *coriare*, "covered" (Niermeyer 273). 27. **contribulatus:** perfect passive participle of *contribulare*, "afflicted." 31. **refrigerium:** i.e., "coolness."

Quia ipse Dominus novit quia accusatus non negavi, interrogatus
Christum confessus sum, assatus gratias ago." Et vultu pulcherrimo dicebat: "Gratias tibi ago, Domine Iesu Christe, quia me confortare dignatus es." Et elevans oculos suos in Decium, ait: "Ecce, miser, assasti unam
5   partem, regyra aliam, et manduca eam." Gratias igitur agens et glorificans
Deum, dixit: "Gratias tibi ago, Domine Iesu Christe, quia merui ianuas
tuas ingredi," et emisit spiritum.

Mane autem primo, adhuc crepusculo, rapuit corpus eius Hippolytus,
et condivit cum linteis et aromatibus, et hoc factum mandavit Iustino
10 presbytero. Tunc beatus Iustinus et Hippolytus, plorantes et multum
tristes, tulerunt corpus beati Laurentii martyris, et venerunt in via Tiburtina in praedium matronae viduae, nomine Cyriacae, in agro Verano, ad
quam ipse beatus martyr fuerat noctu, cui et linteum dedit, unde sanctorum pedes exterserat, et ibi iam hora vespertina sepeliverunt quarto Idus
15 Augusti. Et ieiunaverunt, agentes vigilias noctis triduo cum multitudine
Christianorum; beatus vero Iustinus presbyter obtulit sacrificium laudis,
et participati sunt omnes. Tunc passi sunt Claudius, Severus, Crescentius
et Romanus, ipso die quo beatus Laurentius, post tertium diem sancti
Sixti martyris. Eodem die Romae militum centum et quadraginta
20 quinque.

—*Mart.* (excerpts).

1. **quia . . . quia:** while the initial *quia* retains its CL sense of "because," the second
quia replaces an infinitive clause (Blaise 262). 4. **assasti:** syncopated perfect active
indicative, second person singular of *assare = assavisti.* 5. **regyra:** from *regyrare,*
"to turn around," here in the imperative mood (Blaise/Chirat 708). **manduca:** from
manducare, lit., "to chew," but here, in the imperative mood = "eat." 10. **multum:**
adverb. 14. **exterserat:** from *extergere.* 19. **centum . . . quinque:** i.e., *passi sunt.*

SEXTI RVFI ILV
RI CENSVLARIS RE
RVM A ROMANIS
gestaru Libro
R E V E
F I E R I
C L E M E

tia tua libellum praecepit · parebo libet
praeceptis · Quippe quom desit facul_
tas Latius eloquendi ac morem secut⁹
calculatorum qui ingentes summas
aere breuiori exprimunt · Res gestaf
signabo non eloquar · Accipe ergo · q̃
breuiter dicta breuiuf computentur ·
ut annosam uetustatem Rei pу Lege
do detineamus · ac praeterita facta tem ·

PLATE 13. A folio from a Latin manuscript of the anonymous *De viris
illustribus urbis Romae*, showing a detailed illumination of an initial B, typical
of much medieval manuscript decoration after the Carolingian period.

PLATE 13

Anonymous, *De viris illustribus urbis Romae*
Latin manuscript on parchment, Italy, c. 1400, fol. 41 verso
Koopman Collection
John Hay Library, Brown University

Much manuscript production was of a workaday kind, but often enough manuscripts were illuminated, as this plate shows. Manuscript illumination had a long pedigree in the Latin Middle Ages—with particularly rich traditions reaching back to Ireland and Anglo-Saxon England. The illumination shown here, of a late medieval date and Italian provenance, nonetheless shows qualities typical of continental illumination in the Latin Middle Ages.

The manuscript from which it comes dates to around 1400. The scribe was Iacobus Laurentianus, who may be responsible for the illuminations also. The *De viris illustribus urbis Romae* is itself an anonymous work that was ascribed in other, earlier copies to a wide variety of classical authors, including Pliny the Younger, Suetonius, Cornelius Nepos, and Sextus Aurelius Victor. The manuscript is 23 cm. in height and contains 60 folios. It is written on parchment in a neat humanistic hand. The binding is of blind stamped goatskin, contemporary with the manuscript's copying, and also traceable to Italy.

GERALD

The Poem on Walter
(*Waltharius;* c. 850)

The problems attending to the date, composition, and traditions of the *Waltharius* do not obscure the fundamental place it holds in the development of the Medieval Latin literary tradition. Yet, the poem remains with respect to date and authorship enigmatic. Several kinds of evidence make it possible to argue convincingly for a ninth-century provenance. It has been shown, for example, that no work written after the year 900 is cited by the Waltharius poet, while it has also been demonstrated, based on quotations gleaned from other authors, that the poem is also no earlier than 820. Certain peculiarities of geographical description in the poem (the ways that cities are styled, for example) suggest that the poem cannot be any later than 890, making it a later Carolingian composition.

But of whose hand? External evidence gleaned from Ekkehard IV of St. Gall, writing in the early eleventh century in his *Casus Sancti Galli* (see pp. 377–90), ascribes the *Waltharius* to his illustrious namesake, Ekkehard I of St. Gall, the monk noted for his learning and teaching. This evidence has been routinely used by scholars to ascribe the poem to his hand. But Ekkehard lived and wrote in the tenth century. The internal evidence that allows us to date the poem, therefore, seems at odds with what we know about Ekkehard's life. Then there is the added problem of the 22-line preface found in several manuscripts of the poem, in which an otherwise unknown Gerald takes credit for the poem and dedicates it to an otherwise unidentified Erkambald. Gerald seems the stronger candidate for authorship, based on the evidence currently to hand.

The issue of authorship is of secondary importance to the qualities of the poem that commend it to modern readers. Like much of the literary materials of the later Carolingian period, the poem is a combination of Classical, Christian, and Germanic traditions, each melded carefully into a larger, cohesive form. The poem's 1,456 hexameters ratify the Homeric emphasis on single combat and the triumph of the hero but also show a reliance on Virgilian vocabulary and tone. Indeed, in one of the excerpts here, the use of Virgilian and Christian material is so prominent that many readers have characterized the lines in question (vv. 725–53) as a cento (on which see pp. 111–16). The epic figures of this poem, of course, are unlike their classical counterparts in their faith, which is present in the texture of the poem as a subtle moral force, suggesting the ways in which heroism from a Christian perspective ought to be pursued. And the figures themselves are unlike anything classical given the Germanic provenance of their story, owed to the body of legends that produced the *Nibelungenlied* and focusing in particular on the exploits of the Aquitanian noble Walter, taken hostage by Attila during his western campaign. Yet the consistencies of tone, vocabulary, and handling of materials suggest the unity of the poet's vision, especially in making a strong place for the epic genre in the Medieval Latin tradition.

The story of the *Waltharius* centers on the exploits of three hostages, captured and taken east by Attila after his western expedition. These hostages—Hagen, Walter, and the princess Hildegund—eventually settle on a plan to escape, an outcome especially welcome for Walter and Hildegund, as they had been as children betrothed to each other. Hagen escapes first; then Walter and Hildegund, as the excerpts detail, plan and execute their flight, loaded down with much treasure that had been stolen by Attila. Walter is eventually challenged by Gunther, a greedy Frankish prince who covets this treasure, at the Vosges mountains. Walter defeats Gunther but is finally wounded by Hagen, who had been persuaded to join in the battle against Walter. The disputants then patch up their quarrel, and Walter and Hildegund are allowed to proceed westward to their homeland.

There are several editions of the *Waltharius,* including those by J. Grimm and A. Schmeller (Berlin, 1838, repr. Amsterdam, 1967), H. Althof (Leipzig, 1905), K. Strecker (Berlin, 1947; and also a subsequent edition by him in *Monumenta Germaniae Historica, Poetae Latini Aevi Carolini,* vol. 6, pt. 1, Weimar, 1951), and D. M. Kratz (*Waltharius and Ruodlieb,* Garland Library of Medieval Literature, vol. 13, New York, 1984), which also contains a translation, a bibliography, and a historical introduction to the poem. English translations have been published by H. M. Smyser and F. P. Magoun, Jr. (*Walter of Aquitaine: Materials for the Study of His Legend,* New London, Conn., 1950) and by C. W. Jones (*Medieval Literature in Translation,* New York, 1950, pp. 192–208). Kratz's text is reprinted here with some minor punctuation changes and consonantal and vocalic "u" distinguished.

Walter and Hildegund Come to an Understanding

Ecce palatini decurrunt arce ministri
illius aspectu hilares equitemque tenebant,
donec vir sella descenderet inclitus alta.
Si bene res vergant, tum demum forte requirunt.
5   Ille aliquid modicum narrans intraverat aulam,
(lassus enim fuerat) regisque cubile petebat.
Illic Hiltgundem solam offendit residentem.
Cui post amplexus atque oscula dulcia dixit
"Ocius huc potum ferto, quia fessus anhelo."
10   Illa mero tallum complevit mox pretiosum
porrexitque viro, qui signans accipiebat
virgineamque manum propria constrinxit; at illa
astitit et vultum reticens intendit herilem,
Walthariusque bibens vacuum vas porrigit olli
15   —Ambo etenim norant de se sponsalia facta—
provocat et tali caram sermone puellam
"Exilium pariter patimur iam tempore tanto,
non ignorantes quid nostri forte parentes
inter se nostra de re fecere futura.
20   Quamne diu tacito premimus haec ipsa palato?"
Virgo per hyroniam meditans hoc dicere sponsum
paulum conticuit, sed postea talia reddit
"Quid lingua simulas quod ab imo pectore damnas,
oreque persuades, toto quod corde refutas,
25   sit veluti talem pudor ingens ducere nuptam?"
Vir sapiens contra respondit et intulit ista
"Absit quod memoras! Dextrorsum porrige sensum!
Noris me nihilum simulata mente locutum
nec quicquam nebulae vel falsi interfore crede.

2. **illius:** i.e., Walter, who has just returned from battle. 6. **regisque cubile:** i.e., "the royal chamber." 9. **ferto:** future active imperative of *ferre*. 10. **tallum:** i.e., "drinking vessel." 11. **signans:** lit., "signing," i.e., "making the sign of the cross." 12. **propria:** modifies an understood *manu*. 13. **herilem** = CL *erilem*, from *erilis, e*. 14. **olli** = *illi*, archaic dative of *ille*. 15. **norant:** contracted form of *noverant*, from *noscere (gnoscere)*. 19. **fecere:** alternate perfect active indicative, third person plural of *facere* = *fecerunt*. 20. **quamne:** *quam* + *ne*, enclitic conjunction introducing a question. **haec ipsa:** i.e., "these very thoughts." 21. **hyroniam** = CL *ironiam*. 27. **quod memoras:** the subject of *absit*; *memorare* has the sense of *dicere* here. 28. **noris** = *noveris*, in jussive subjunctive construction. 29. **interfore** = CL *interesse*; the substitution of *fore* for *esse* is common to ML.

Nullus adest nobis exceptis namque duobus.　　　　　　30
Si nossem temet mihi promptam impendere mentem
atque fidem votis servare per omnia cautis,
pandere cuncta tibi cordis mysteria vellem."
Tandem virgo viri genibus curvata profatur
"Ad quaecumque vocas, mi domne, sequar studiose　　35
nec quicquam placitis malim praeponere iussis."
Ille dehinc: "Piget exilii me denique nostri,
et patriae fines reminiscor saepe relictos
idcircoque fugam cupio celerare latentem.
Quod iam praemultis potuissem forte diebus,　　　　　40
Si non Hiltgundem solam remanere dolerem."
Addidit has imo virguncula corde loquelas
"Vestrum velle meum, solis his aestuo rebus.
Praecipiat dominus, seu prospera sive sinistra
eius amore pati toto sum pectore praesto."　　　　　　45
Waltharius tandem sic virginis inquit in aurem
"Publica custodem rebus te nempe potestas
fecerat, idcirco memor haec mea verba notato
Inprimis galeam regis tunicamque, trilicem
assero loricam fabrorum insigne ferentem,　　　　　　50
diripe, bina dehinc mediocria scrinia tolle.
His armillarum tantum da Pannoniarum,
donec vix unum releves ad pectoris imum.
Inde quater binum mihi fac de more coturnum,

31. **nossem:** imperfect active subjunctive, first person singular of *noscere.* 36. **malim:** present active subjunctive, first person singular of *malle.* **praeponere:** complement of *malim;* with the dative = "to put (something) before"; i.e., "I would not prefer to put anything before the agreeable things you have ordered." 37. **piget** + genitive of the cause of feeling: "Our exile pains me now." 41. **Hiltgundem:** Walter speaks as if he were not addressing Hildegund. **dolorem:** imperfect active subjunctive, first person singular of *dolere.* 42. **loquelas** = CL *loquellas.* 43. **velle:** present infinitive of *volo,* standing as the nominative of the gerund = "wish," modified by *vestrum.* **meum:** supply *est.* 44. **prospera sive sinistra:** "right or wrong." 45. **praesto:** adverb. 47. **publica . . . potestas:** i.e., the Queen. 48. **notato:** future active imperative. 49. **inprimis:** adverb. 51. **mediocria:** "a little larger." **scrinia:** "chest (for carrying goods)." 52. **tantum:** here the neuter singular accusative object of *da* + genitive = "a great quantity of. . . ." **his . . . da:** lit., "give to these (i.e., *scrinia*), i.e., "fill these." **Pannoniarum:** from *Pannonia, ae,* here meaning "people of Pannonia," i.e., Huns (LS 1298). 54. **quater binum:** *binum* modifies *coturnum* and exists in the singular only in ML; *quater,* an adverb, technically modifies *da,* "make four times." The idea, however, is "make me four pairs of shoes." **coturnum** = CL

55 tantundemque tibi patrans imponito vasis.
   Sic fors ad summum complentur scrinia labrum.
   Insuper a fabris hamos clam posce retortos.
   Nostra viatica sint pisces simul atque volucres,
   ipse ego piscator, sed et auceps esse coartor.
60 Haec intra ebdomadam caute per singula comple.
   Audisti, quid habere vianti forte necesse est.
   Nunc quo more fugam valeamus inire, recludo.
   Postquam septenos Phoebus remeaverit orbes,
   regi ac reginae satrapis, ducibus famulisque
65 sumptu permagno convivia laeta parabo
   atque omni ingenio potu sepelire studebo,
   donec nullus erit, qui sentiat hoc, quod agendum est.
   Tu tamen interea mediocriter utere vino
   atque sitim vix ad mensam restinguere cura.
70 Cum reliqui surgant, ad opuscula nota recurre.
   Ast ubi iam cunctos superat violentia potus,
   tum simul occiduas properemus quaerere partes."
   Virgo memor praecepta viri complevit et ecce
   praefinita dies epularum venit, et ipse
75 Waltharius magnis instruxit sumptibus escas.
   Luxuria in media residebat denique mensa,
   ingrediturque aulam velis rex undique saeptam,
   Heros magnanimus solito quem more salutans
   duxerat ad solium, quod bissus compsit et ostrum.
80 Consedit laterique duces hinc indeque binos
   assedisse iubet; reliquos locat ipse minister.

---

cothurnum, the object of *da.* 56. **ad summum . . . labrum:** i.e., "up to the top."
57. **retortos:** from *retorquere,* "twisted," modifying *hamos* = "fish hooks."
59. **coartor** = *cogor,* "I am compelled . . .," with complementary *esse.* 60. **ebdoma-**
dam = CL *hebdomada, ae,* = "week" (LS 848, Sleumer 377). **per singula:** i.e., "one
by one." 61. **habere:** complement of *necesse est.* 62. **quo more:** lit., "by what
way," but = *quomodo,* "how." **quo . . . inire:** this clause is the object of *recludo.*
64. **satrapis:** from *satrapa, ae,* "satraps," "lords" (Sleumer 699). 68. **utere:** alternate
second person singular, present indicative of *uti,* with ablative object. 69. **rest-**
inguere: alternate second person singular, present passive indicative of *restinguere* =
restingueris. 77. **velis:** from *velum, i,* here meaning "tapestries." **saeptam:** perfect
passive participle of *saepire* (sometimes *sepire*), modifying *aulam.* 78. **heros:** nominative singular masculine = Walter. 79. **bissus** = CL *byssus, i,* "linen cloth." **com-**
psit: perfect active indicative, third person singular of *comere.* 81. **assedisse:** contracted perfect active infinitive of *assidere* = *assedivisse,* complement of *iubet.*

Centenos simul accubitus iniere sodales,
diversasque dapes libans conviva resudat.
His et sublatis aliae referuntur edendae,
atque exquisitum fervebat migma per aurum.   85
Aurea bissina tantum stant gausape vasa
et pigmentatus crateres Bachus adornat.
Illicit ad haustum species dulcedoque potus.
Waltharius cunctos ad vinum hortatur et escam.

—Walth. 215–303.

ATTILA DISCOVERS THE FLIGHT OF THE HOSTAGES

Ast urbis populus somno vinoque solutus
ad medium lucis siluit recubando sequentis.
Sed postquam surgunt, ductorem quique requirunt,
ut grates faciant ac festa laude salutent.
Attila nempe manu caput amplexatus utraque   5
egreditur thalamo rex Walthariumque dolendo
Advocat, ut proprium quereretur forte dolorem.
Respondent ipsi se non potuisse ministri
invenisse virum, sed princeps sperat eundem
hactenus in somno tentum recubare quietum   10
occultumque locum sibi delegisse sopori.
Ospirin Hiltgundem postquam cognovit abesse

---

82. **centenos . . . accubitus:** lit., "one hundred places at the table"; *centenos* modifies *accubitus*, a fourth declension masculine noun, meaning "a place at a table." The phrase technically is the object of *iniere*, with *sodales* the subject. It is best rendered in English as "one hundred guests take their place at the table." The grammar of this line is more difficult than one expects in Gerald's poem because he has taken it directly from Prudentius, *Apotheosis* 713.   **iniere:** alternate perfect active indicative, third person plural of *inire = inierunt*.   85. **migma:** from *migma, migmatis*, neuter noun from the Greek μῖγμα, "a mixture," modified by *exquisitum* and referring to wine mixed in the *aurum*, the golden driking vessel.   86. **bissina** = *byssinus, a, um*, adjective from *byssus* = "linen-like"; in the neuter, this form stands as a substantive meaning "vestment" (Blaise/Chirat 120).   **gausape:** modifed by *bissina* in the ablative case, the ablative form should be *gausapa* (*gausapa, ae*; the masculine form is *gausapes, is* and the neuter forms are *gausape, is* (sing. only) and *gausapa, orum* (pl. only); on these forms see LS 803). The ablative phrase here is locative in nature, "on linen coverings."   87. **pigmentatus:** this ML adjective, which can mean "colored," takes its secondary meaning here, "perfumed" (Blaise/Chirat 625).

    5. **caput:** object of *amplexatus*, perfect passive participle of *amplexare*.   **utraque:** modifies *manu*.   12. **Ospirin:** nominative singular feminine, Attila's queen.

nec iuxta morem vestes deferre suetum,
tristior immensis satrapae clamoribus inquit

15   "O destestandas, quas heri sumpsimus, escas!
O vinum, quod Pannonias destruxerat omnes!
Quod domino regi iam dudum praescia dixi,
approbat iste dies, quem nos superare nequimus.
En hodie imperii vestri cecidisse columna

20   noscitur, en robur procul ivit et inclita virtus:
Waltharius lux Pannoniae discesserat inde,
Hiltgundem quoque mi caram deduxit alumnam."

—vv. 358–79.

WALTER DEFEATS HIS OPPONENTS

Tertius en Werinhardus abit bellumque lacessit,
quamlibet ex longa generatus stirpe nepotum,
o vir clare, tuus cognatus et artis amator,
Pandare, qui quondam iussus confundere foedus

5   in medios telum torsisti primus Achivos.
Hic spernens hastam pharetram gestavit et arcum,
eminus emissis haud aequo Marte sagittis
Waltharium turbans. Contra tamen ille virilis
constitit opponens clipei septemplicis orbem,

10   saepius eludens venientes providus ictus.
Nam modo dissiluit, parmam modo vergit in austrum
telaque discussit, nullum tamen attigit illum.
Postquam Pandarides se consumpsisse sagittas

13. **iuxta:** preposition with accusative = "according to." 14. **satrapae:** from *satrapa, ae,* dative singular masculine, referring to Attila 15. **heri:** adverb. **sumpsimus:** from *sumere.* 17. **quod . . . dixi:** *quod* is the object of *dixi; praescia* modifies O*spirin,* the understood subject of *dixi.*

2. **nepotum:** from *nepos, otis,* "descendants." 3. **O vir clare:** vocative case. 4. **Pandare:** vocative case; Pandarus, who was murdered by Turnus, was a famous archer in the Trojan army and the close companion of Aeneas. **iussus:** perfect passive participle of *iubere,* modifying *qui* [Pandarus], with *foedus* the object of the complement *confundere.* 5. **torsisti:** from *torquere.* **Achivos:** i.e., Achaean Greeks. 6. **hic:** i.e., Werinhard. 7. **emissis:** from *emittere,* modifying *sagittis.* **haud aequo Marte:** lit., "with scarcely equal Mars [*Mars, Martis*]," i.e., "with unequal war," "with both sides not equally matched." 9. **septemplicis:** from *semptemplex, icis,* "seven-plated"; modifies *clipei;* shields often were covered with seven thicknesses of bull's hide. **orbem:** here used in its secondary sense of "circle." 11. **in austrum:** from *auster, tri* = lit., "south wind," i.e., "in the air," referring to the motions of Walter's shield. 13. **Pandarides:** *Pandarus + ides* = the patronymic of Pandarus = Werinhard.

incassum videt, iratus mox exerit ensem
et demum advolitans has iactitat ore loquelas   15
"O si ventosos lusisti callide iactus,
forsan vibrantis dextrae iam percipis ictum."
Olli Waltharius ridenti pectore adorsus
"Iamque diu satis expecto certamina iusto
pondere agi. Festina, in me mora non erit ulla."   20
Dixerat et toto conixus corpore ferrum
conicit. Hasta volans pectus reseravit equinum;
tollit se arrectum quadrupes et calcibus auras
verberat effundensque equitem cecidit super illum.
Accurrit iuvenis et ei vi diripit ensem.   25
Casside discussa crines complectitur albos
multiplicesque preces nectenti dixerat heros,
"Talia non dudum iactabas dicta per auras."
Haec ait et truncum secta cervice reliquit.

—vv. 725–53.

THE BATTLE CONTINUES

Nec mora nec requies, bellum instauratur amarum.
Incurrunt hominem nunc ambo nuncque vicissim;
et dum progresso se impenderet acrius uni,
en de parte alia subit alter et impedit ictum.
Haud aliter Numidus quam dum venabitur ursus   5
et canibus circumdatus astat et artubus horret
et caput occultans submurmurat ac propiantes
amplexans Umbros miserum mutire coartat,
tum rabidi circumlatrant hinc inde Molossi

14. **exerit** = CL *exserit*.   15. **loquelas** = CL *loquellas*.   18. **adorsus:** perfect participle of *adoriri*.   19. **expecto** = CL *exspecto*.   21. **conixus:** perfect participle of *coniti*.   23. **arrectum:** perfect passive participle of *arrigere*, modifying *se*.   27. **nectenti:** present active participle of *nectere*, dative singular masculine, modifying an understood Werinhard, with the sense of "making." Its object is *multiplicesque preces*. **heros:** nominative singular masculine.   29. **secta:** perfect passive participle of *secare*.
    2. **ambo:** i.e., Hagen and Gunther; this excerpt picks up in the middle of the action.   3. **progresso:** perfect participle of *progredi*, modifying *se*.   5. **Numidus:** from *Numidus, a, um,* "Numidian."   **haud aliter ... quam dum:** lit., "It is no different from when. . . ."   7. **submurmurat** = CL *summurmurat*.   8. **Umbros:** from *Umber, bri,* an especially good hunting dog (LS 1927, s. v. *Umbri* A 1).   **miserum:** a substantive in the neuter with adverbial force.   9. **Molossi:** from *Molossi, orum,* a people who lived in the eastern part of Epirus, but here = "Molossian dogs," modified by *rabidi*.

10   comminus ac dirae metuunt accedere beluae.
       taliter in nonam conflictus fluxerat horam,
       et triplex cunctis inerat maceratio: leti
       terror et ipse labor bellandi solis et ardor.

—vv. 1333–45.

10. **beluae:** here read as a disyllable.   12. **maceratio:** from *maceratio, onis,* "distress" (Sleumer 488).

LIUTPRAND OF CREMONA

Antapodosis; Mission to Constantinople
(*Antapodosis*, c. 955; *Relatio de legatione Constantinopolitana*, c. 970)

The historical prose of the Latin Middle Ages is characterized by several features. Much of this vast body of writing is controlled by an interest in biography. This in itself is not new, for CL historical writing took as a main focus the lives of important figures. But historical biography in the Latin Middle Ages conceives of the lives it considers in broader terms. The events remembered by Gregory of Tours or Bede are not only records of mundane activity but also guides to the sacred and secular choices that lead to the best kinds of lives to be lived (or to be avoided). Even when the force of Christian epistemology—which surely forms the backdrop of Bede's and Gregory's work—lessens in the centuries following the breakup of the Carolingian empire, there remains in place this longer ethical and, one might say, teleological view.

This body of writing also relies closely on the logic of authorial narration, as against the equally powerful tradition of chronological organization. Many times, as in Bede's *Historia,* chronology and narration coalesce, so that the historian can make powerful statements about the past simply by choosing an alternate chronology, moving, ignoring, or altering the understood order of the past. At other times, the vision of the author demands a certain order that does not necessarily correspond to historical fact or temporal reality. Many times, as in Einhard's *Vita,* these two are in competing balance, with the force of events sometimes controlling organization, only to be superseded at strategic points by the needs of the author's larger vision or purpose (this, in a moderated form, is also at work in Einhard's model text, Suetonius's *De Vita Caesarum*).

Finally, especially after the Carolingian period, there is increasingly a tendency in Medieval Latin historical prose to refract historical phenomena through the prism of secular events. This does not mean that the long dialectic between sacred and secular is abandoned in the tenth century— quite the contrary. It does mean, however, that there is less reliance on overtly Christian models, so that the exemplarism of Bede and the patterns of scriptural continuation in Gregory give way to a more confident acceptance and analysis of events on their own terms. A secondary effect of this tendency is that historical prose becomes more focused ethnically and geographically. Bede and Gregory claimed to be writing about British and Frankish history respectively, but both appended their national histories to the larger contexts of Roman imperial and sacred history. We find Einhard and later writers putting this contextualization to the side.

Whatever the merits of these generalizations with respect to the body of Medieval Latin historical prose, these qualities—an emphasis on biography, on authorial narration, and on secularism—dominate Liutprand of Cremona's historical output, which includes three substantive works based on his own experiences in Italy, Germany, and the Byzantine East. Liutprand was born in Italy around 920. He was associated in Pavia with the Lombard courts of King Hugo and, later, of Berengar and his wife Willa, and he made several trips to Constantinople for Berengar. Unfortunately, he fell out of favor with Berengar in the mid 950s—unfairly, according to his account of these events in the *Antapodosis*. He was forced to leave Italy at this point and eventually made his way to the court of Otto I, king of Germany, who was busy at the time Liutprand reached him in securing for himself and his heirs those parts of the former Carolingian empire that had fallen away during the dynastic disputes of the later ninth century.

Liutprand was especially useful to Otto because of his connections to the East and his Greek learning, both of which were seen as definite boons to the king's international aspirations. Liutprand's eastern connection had been long cultivated. Liutprand's father had been an ambassador to Constantinople from the court of Arles in the 920s; Liutprand himself studied in and made the grand tour of Constantinople in the early 950s, when he was still an intimate of the Lombard royalty. When he found himself the newest member of Otto I's entourage, then, his talent for Greek and his knowledge of the East were put to immediate political use. Otto I's plan was to marry his son, the future Otto II, to Theophano, the daughter of the emperor Nicephorus Phocas. Liutprand was sent on a mission, as the excerpts from the *Legatio* recount, to make these marriage plans a reality. Politics intervened, of course—and the sour relations between Greek East and German West only deteriorated. The marriage never occurred. Liutprand did not suffer for the failure of his mission. He had already been made bishop of Cremona by Otto in 961, and as he was not in the best of health anyway, he did not long survive the ardors he had endured in the East when he finally returned to Otto's court late in the 960s. He died soon after, in the early 970s.

Liutprand's works are, for the most part, records of events in which he took part, and they take on an increasingly narrow focus. His earliest work, the *Antapodosis*, is a history of events in the West between 887 and 949, with the special aim of discrediting his former Lombardic patrons, Berengar and Willa. His subsequent work, *Liber de rebus gestis Ottonis*, treats the affairs of state under Otto I for a period of four years, 960–964. The work offers the praises of Otto and its focus is narrow and detailed. His final work, *Relatio de legatione Constantinopolitana*, deals with his personal mission to Constantinople and is controlled by an intensely personal frame of vision. The discords of ethnicity, belief, habits, customs, and outlook filter Liutprand's every thought and reflection. And here at least, readers enter a new literary space, for despite the affinities, Liutprand's final work is not written in the traditions of prior historical prose. Here, instead, personal experience and the biases it implies control the perspective, and those experiences take best shape against the backdrop of private volition and public assertion, in the sphere of political intrigue, where the desires of the powerful clash against the day-to-day management of human affairs. The Latinity of the works throughout is uniquely medieval: neologisms, Grecisms, simplified phraseology, wide deployment of the principles of Medieval Latin grammar—as the notes indicate.

The works of Liutprand have been edited by E. Duemmler (*Liudprandi Episcopi Cremonensis Opera Omnia*, Hanover, 1877, a revision of Pertz's earlier edition) and J. Becker (*Die Werke Liudprans von Cremona*, Hanover and Leipzig, 1915), whose edition has been reprinted by A. Bauer and R. Rau (*Quellen zur Geschichte der Sächsischen Kaiserzeit*, vol. 8, Darmstadt, 1971) with facing German translation. F. A. Wright has translated Liutprand's entire output (*The Works of Liudprand of Cremona*, London, 1930), and L. H. Nelson and M. V. Shirk have translated the *Relatio de legatione Constantinopolitana* (*Liudprand of Cremona: Mission to Constantinople (968 A.D.)*, Lawrence, Kans., 1972), as has B. Scott (*Relatio de Legatione Constantinopolitana; Liutprand of Cremona*, London, 1993). Becker's text as given in Bauer and Rau is reprinted here (with several punctuation changes and spelling corrections), supplying at Leg. 1.19 *scilicet domorum* and reading at *Leg.* 3.13 *hyopum* for *hyopam* and at *Leg.* 11.14 *quis* for *qui,* as ms. C reports.

A JOKING EMPEROR AND A SHREWD SOLDIER

Alium, quem ipse egit, ludum silentio tegi absurdum esse diiudico. Constantinopolitanum palatium ob imperatoris salutem multorum prae-

---

1. **ipse:** i.e., Leo, who was Byzantine Emperor from 886 to 911.   **diiudico:** "to discern" (LS 579).

sidiis militum custoditur. Custodientibus vero victus censusque cottida-
nus non parvus inpenditur. Contigit itaque XII post corporis refectionem
in ipso diei fervore una in domo quiescere. Mos denique imperatoris erat
cunctis quiescentibus totum perreptare palatium. Qui cum eodem die
5 quadam, quo XII memorati loethoeo sese dederant, pervenisset, ligno
modico, ut non incallidus, ostii pessulo proiecto ingrediendi sibi aditum
praebuit. Undecim vero dormientibus, ut ars artem falleret, duodecimus
pervigil stertere ceu dormiens coeperat contractisque in fatiem brachiis
totum, quod imperator faceret, diligentissime considerabat. Ingressus igi-
10 tur imperator, dum obdormire cunctos perspiceret, aureorum numismatorum libram pectori uniuscuiusque apposuit; moxque clam regressus, ostium, ut prius fuerat, clausit. Eo autem hoc egit, quatinus exitati et de
lucro gratularentur ac, qualiter hoc accideret, non mediocriter mirarentur.
Denique discedente imperatore, qui vigil solus extiterat, surrexit dormi-
15 entiumque nummos aureos sibi adsumpsit atque reposuit; postea vero
quieti sese dedit. Imperator igitur pro hoc ludo sollicitus post nonam
horam XII hos, quos nominavimus, ad se venire praecepit eosque ita convenit: "Si forte vestrum quempiam somnii visio deterruit aut hilarem
reddidit, ut in medium proferat, mea iubet auctoritas; nec minus etiam,
20 si quid novitatis expergefactus quisquam vidit, ut detegat, imperat." Hi
itaque, quemadmodum nihil viderant, nil se vidisse responderant. Magis

1. **victus censusque:** these fourth declension nouns mean, respectively, "livelihood"
and "gifts," but the sense here is something more apropos to military life, i.e., "salary"
and "rations." 2. **inpenditur** = CL *impenditur*. **contigit:** governs here an infinitive
clause (*quiescere*). **XII:** *milites*. 3. **in . . . fervore:** i.e., siesta. **una:** adverb.
4. **cunctis quiescentibus:** ablative of time. 5. **loethoeo** = CL *Lethaeus, a, um* = "Le-
thean," but here used substantively to mean "sleep," by metonymy since Lethe was
the river of forgetfulness. 6. **ostii . . . ingrediendi:** ablative absolute with dependent
genitives. 8. **fatiem** = CL *faciem.* 9. **quod . . . faceret:** indirect question, the clause
is the object of *considerabat.* 10. **numismatorum** = CL *nomismatum*, "coins"; Liutprand seems to use the participial *numismatus* here in place of *nomisma, nomismatis*,
a neuter of the third declension, though other LL/ML writers make the distinction
between these forms (Blaise/Chirat 557, s. v. *nomisma;* 561, s. v. *numismatus*).
11. **libram:** from *libra*, a unit of weight = "pound." **pectori . . . apposuit:** *apponere*
+ dative = "to place on." 12. **eo:** adverb. **quatinus** = CL *quatenus*, used here, as
often in ML, for *ut* in a purpose clause; § 6.1 (cf. Blaise 285). **exitati** = CL *excitati*,
from *excitare.* 15. **adsumpsit** = CL *assumpsit.* 16. **quieti:** from *quies.* **post
nonam horam:** lit., "after the ninth hour" = "in the afternoon." 17. **XII:** i.e., *milites*,
with modifying *hos*, the subject accusative with *venire*, governed by *praecepit.*
18. **quempiam:** from *quispiam*, with *vestrum* = "any of you." 19. **in medium:** idiom
with adverbial force = "publicly"; the *ut* clause stands as the object of *iubet.* 20. **imperat:** the subject remains *mea auctoritas*, with *ut detegat* as object.

autem super hoc admirati, conticuere intentique ora tenebant. Sperans igitur imperator hos non rei inscitia, sed calliditate aliqua reticere, succensus est ut qui magis coepitque nonnulla terribilia reticentibus comminari. Quod qui omnium conscius erat ut audivit, huiusmodi humillima et supplici voce imperatorem convenit: "Φιλάνϑρωπε Βασιλεῦ, filanthrope vasileu," id est, "humanissime imperator, hi quid viderint, nescio; ego tamen delectabile, atque utinam quod persaepe mihi contingeret, somnium vidi. Undecim his conservis meis hodie vere, sed non oportune dormientibus visus sum, quasi non dormiens, vigilare. Ecce autem magnitudo imperii tui quasi occulte ostium reserans clanculumque ingressa libram auri adposuit supra pectus omnium nostrum. Cumque imperium tuum quasi repedare sotiosque hac in visione cernerem dormitare, continuo ceu laetus exurgens undecim dormientium aureorum numismatorum libras tuli meoque in marsupio, in quo una erat, apposui, quatinus ob trangressionem decalogi ne solum essent XI, verum ob memoriam apostolorum mea una adhibita essent et ipsae XII. Visio haec, imperator auguste, bonum sit, usque modo me non deterruit, sed hilarem reddidit. O utinam interpretatio alia imperio tuo non placeat. Nam et me μαντῆν καὶ ὀνιρόπολον, mantin ke oniropolon," id est "divinum et somnii venditorem, esse liquido patet." His auditis magno est imperator cachinno inflatus; verum prudentiam huius atque sollicitudinem plus admiratus protinus infit: "Antehac σὲ ὄυτε μαντῆν ὄυτε ὀνιροπόλον, se ute mantin ute oniropolon,

5

10

15

20

---

1. **conticuere:** alternate perfect active indicative, third person plural of *conticescere* = *conticuerunt*. This tag is owed to Virgil, *Aen*. 2.1. **sperans:** the sense in this context is "thinking." 2. **inscitia . . . calliditate:** ablatives of specification with *reticere; calliditas* = "shrewdness" (Sleumer 181; sometimes spelled *calidias*). 3. **qui** = *imperator*, the subject of *succensus est;* the thought, somewhat difficult to glean from the word order = *qui magis succensus est ut coepit comminari.* . . . 7. **delectabile:** modifies *somnium* in the same line. 9. **vigilare:** the thought is *hodie . . . visus sum . . . vigilare.* **magnitudo imperii tui:** a term of honor = "your imperial highness." 10. **adposuit** = CL *apposuit.* 12. **sotiosque** = CL *sociosque;* palatalization is common in ML. **cumque . . . cernerem:** *cum* + subjunctive; the infinitive clauses governed by *repedare* and *dormitare* are dependent on *cernerem.* 13. **exurgens** = CL *exsurgens.* 14. **marsupio** = CL *marsuppio*, "purse." **quatinus** = CL *quatenus.* 15. **decalogi:** *decalogus, i,* from the Greek δεκαλόγος = Ten Commandments (cf. Sleumer 260, s. v. *decalogus*). **quatinus . . . XI:** this difficult clause means something like, "lest there were only 11 [bags of gold], seeing that [*quatinus*] this goes against [*ob transgressionem*] the number of commandments [*decalogi*]. . . ." **verum . . . XII:** this difficult clause means something like, "with mine having been joined together [*mea una adhibita*], there were 12 bags [*essent et ipsae XII*], recalling thus the memory of the apostles [*verum ob memoriam apostolorum*]." 19. **liquido:** adverb. 22. **se . . . oniropolon:** this tag comes from Lucian, *Gallus* 1.

te neque divinum neque somnii venditorem esse audivi. Hanc vero rem
nunc ita aperte dixti, ut nihil circuitionis usus esses. Sed quia vigilandi
facultatem sive auspicandi scientiam habere non posses, nisi divino tibi
esset munere datum, seu verum sit, ut speramus, immo credimus, seu fal-
5 sum, καθὼς ὃ Λουκιάνος, cathos o Lukianos, id est sicut Lucianus de
quodam dicit, quod dormiens multa reppererit atque a gallo exitatus nihil
invenerit, tu tamen quicquid videris, quicquid senseris, quicquid etiam
inveneris, tuum sit." His auditis, quanta ceteri sint confusione repleti,
quantoque hic sit gaudio plenus, eorum quisque in se personas suscipiens
10 animadvertere poterit.

—*Antap.* 1.12.

THE DEATH OF CONRAD I

Septimo denique regni sui anno vocationis suae ad Deum tempus agnovit. Cumque memoratos principes se adire fecisset, Heinrico solummodo non praesente, ita convenit: "Ex corruptione ad incorruptionem,
ex mortalitate ad inmortalitatem vocationis meae tempus, ut cernitis,
5 praesto est; proin pacem vos concordiamque sectari etiam atque etiam
rogo. Me hominem exeunte nulla vos regnandi cupiditas, nulla praesiden-
di ambitio inflammet. Heinricum, Saxonum et Turingiorum ducem pru-
dentissimum, regem eligite, dominum constituite. Is enim est et scientia
pollens et iustae severitatis censurae habundans." His ita prolatis pro-
10 priam coronam non auro, quo poene cuiuscumque ordinis principes pollent, verum gemmis preciosissimis, non solum inquam ornatam, sed gra-

---

2. **dixti:** syncopated perfect active indicative, second person singular of *dicere* = *dixisti.* **ut . . . esses:** the phrase is idiomatic; lit. it means "so that you were not using the
circuit," which in English idiom is something like "so that you were not beating around
the bush" (as Wright 44 renders it).
1. **agnovit:** the subject is Conrad, Duke of Franconia and King of Germany (d.
918). 2. **memoratos:** "mentioned before" (in a prior chapter of the *Antapodosis*);
memoratos principes is the subject accusative of *adire.* **Heinrico:** Henry I Fowler,
about to be designated by Conrad as his succesor, is the only *princeps* absent. 4. **inmortalitatem** = CL *immortalitatem.* 5. **sectari:** present infinitive of *sector,* governed
by *rogo,* with *vos* its subject and *pacem . . . concordiamque* its objects. 6. **me hominem exeunte:** lit., "with me leaving behind men," i.e., "now that I am dying." 7. **Saxonum et Turingiorum:** *Saxonum* is from *Saxones, um* = Saxons (Sleumer 700); *Turingiorum* is from *Thuringi, orum* = Thuringians; both stand by synecdoche for
Saxony and Thuringia. 9. **habundans** = CL *abundans;* the wider use of aspirates is
common in ML; with the genitive = "abounding in . . ."; § 1.5. **prolatis:** from *proferre.* 10. **poene** = CL *paene.* 11. **inquam:** emphatic parenthetical verb = "I say."
gravatam: perfect passive participle of *gravare* = "weighed down."

vatam, sceptrum etiam cunctaque regalia indumenta in medium venire praecepit ac, prout valuit, huiusmodi verba effudit: "Heredem regiaeque dignitatis vicarium regalibus his ornamentis Heinricum constituo; cui ut oboediatis, non solum consulo, sed exoro. Quam iussionem interitus et interitum mox est oboedientia prosecuta. Ipso namque mortem obeunte 5 memorati principes coronam cunctaque regalia indumenta Heinrico duci contulerunt; atque ut rex Chuonradus dixerat, cuncta per ordinem enarrarunt. Qui regiae dignitatis culmen et prius humiliter delcinavit ac paulo post non ambitiose suscepit. Verum nisi "pallida mors, quae pauperum tabernas regumque turres aequo pulsat pede," Chuonradum regem tam 10 citissime raperet, is esset, cuius nomen multis mundi nationibus imperaret.

—Antap. 2.20.

THE ASSASSINATION OF KING BERENGARIUS I

Igitur post Rodulfi regis abscessum malo Veronenses accepto consilio vitae insidiari Berengarii moliuntur, quod Berengarium non latuit. Tam saevi autem auctor ac repertor facinoris Flambertus quidam erat, quem sibi, quoniam ex sacrosancto fonte filium eius susceperat, compatrem rex effecerat. Pridie vero, quam pateretur, eundem ad se Flambertum venire 5 praecepit. Cui et ait:

"Si mihi tecum hactenus non et multae et iustae causae amoris essent, quoquo modo, quae de te dicuntur, credi possent. Insidiari te vitae meae aiunt; sed non ego credulus illis. Meminisse autem te volo, quantaecumque tibi accessiones et fortunae et dignitatis fuerint, eas te non potu- 10 isse nisi meis beneficiis consequi. Unde et hoc animo in nos esse debes, ut dignitas mea in amore atque in fidelitate tua conquiescat. Neque vero

1. **in medium:** "publicly." 4. **cui ut oboediatis:** *oboedire* takes the dative object *cui;* with *ut* it expresses purpose, with the force of an imperative when read with *consulo* and *exoro:* "I not only advise but entreat you to obey him." **quam . . . interitus:** the phrase is elliptical; *sequitur* is understood, with adverbial *quam* = "quickly," i.e., "death followed this order quickly." 5. **prosecuta:** from *prosequi.* 9. **pallida . . . pede:** the tag is taken from Horace, *Odes* 1.4.13. **nisi . . . is esset:** "except that he was [snatched by death].

1. **abscessum** = CL *assessum,* "company." The idea is that Rodulf left. **Veronenses:** i.e., *cives,* the subject of *moliuntur.* 2. **insidiari:** present infinitive of *insidior* + dative = "to plot against"; this is the complement of *moliuntur.* 4. **compatrem:** "godfather." 5. **quam pateretur:** "as he was to suffer [death]"; *pati* is often used in EL/LL/ML of the death of martyrs. 8. **quoquo modo** = CL *quoquomodo.* **possent:** the subject is the *quae* clause. 11. **consequi:** present infinitive of *consequor,* the complement of *potuisse,* with *eas* its object.

cuiquam salutem ac fortunas suas tantae curae fuisse umquam puto, quanti mihi fuit honos tuus. In quo mea omnia studia, omnem operam, curam, industriam, cogitationem huius civitatis omnem fixi. Unum hoc sic habeto: si a te mihi servatam fidem intellexero, non mihi tam mea
5 salus cara, quam pietas erit in referenda gratia iucunda."

His expletis aureum non parvi ponderis poculum rex ei porrexit atque subiunxit: "Amoris salutisque mei causa, quod continetur, bibito, quod continet, habeto." Vere quippe et absque ambiguitate post potum introivit in illum Sathanas, quemadmodum et de Iuda proditore domini nostri Iesu
10 Christi scriptum est: quia "post bucellam" tunc "introivit in illum Sa- thanas."

Beneficii quippe praeteriti et praesentis immemor insomnem illam re- gis in necem populos instigando pertulit noctem. Rex nocte illa, quemad- modum et solitus erat, iuxta ecclesiam non in domo, quae defendi posset,
15 sed in tuguriolo quodam manebat amoenissimo. Sed et custodes nocte eadem non posuerat nichil suspicans etiam mali.

      Se primum quatiens strepit
      Gallus, cum vigiles facit
      Mortales, solito sonat
20   Et pulsata Deo canit
      Iam tunc aenea machina
      Invitatque docens bene
      Loetheum grave spernere,
      Laudes huic modo reddere,
25   Qui vitam tribuit, dedit
      Et nobis superam bene
      Sanctam quaerere patriam;
      Hic rex ecclesiam petit
      Ac laudes Domino canit.
30   Flambertus properans volat,

2. **quanti:** genitive of value = "so great" (AG 417), functioning with adverbial force: "your honor was of so great value to me. . . ." **honos** = *honor,* masculine singular nominative. 4. **habeto:** future active imperative; the sense of this phrase is "Know this. . . ." 5. **salus:** i.e., "well-being." **cara:** with predicative force here. 6. **non parvi ponderis:** litotes. 7. **causa** + genitive = "for the sake of. . . ." 8. **absque am- biguitate:** i.e., "without a doubt." 9. **illum:** Flambert. **Sathanas:** Satan; normally in ML written *Satan* (indeclinable), but there is a form *Satanas, ae* (Sleumer 699, s. v. *satan, satanas*). 10. **bucellam** = CL *buccellam,* "morsel," but here standing for "din- ner." 13. **pertulit:** i.e., Flambert. 14. **iuxta:** preposition with accusative. 15. **tu- guriolo:** diminuitive of *tugurium* = "little cottage." 17. Luitprand continues the story of Berengarius' murder in a poem written in glyconics. 21. **aenea machina:** periphrasis for "bell."

Quocum multa simul manus,
Ut regem perhimat bonum.
Rex horum vigil inscius
Audit dum strepitum, nichil
Formidans properat citus,   5
Hoc quid visere sit; videt
Armatas militum manus.
Flambertum vocat eminus.
"Quid turbae est," ait, "en bone
Vir? quid nunc populus cupit   10
Armatas referens manus?"
Respondit: "Vereare nil.
Te non ut perhimat ruit,
Sed pugnare libens cupit
Hac cum parte, tuum petit   15
Mox qui tollere spiritum."
Deceptus properat fide
Rex hac in medios simul,
Tum captus male ducitur;
A tergo hunc ferit impius   20
Romphaea; cadit heu pius
Felicemque suum Deo
Commendat pie spiritum!

Denique quam innocentem sanguinem fuderint quantumque perversi
perverse egerint, nobis reticentibus lapis ante cuiusdam ecclesiae ianuam   25
positus, sanguinem eius transeuntibus cunctis ostendens insinuat. Nullo
quippe delibutus aspersusque liquore discedit.

—*Antap.* 2.68–72.

EMPEROR ROMANUS I AND THE PALACE AT CONSTANTINOPLE

Constantinopolitanum palatium non pulcritudine solum, verum
etiam fortitudine omnibus, quas umquam perspexerim, munitionibus
praestat, quod etiam iugi militum stipatione non minima observatur.

2. **perhimat** = CL *perimat;* the wider use of aspirates is common in ML; § 1.5.
4. **nichil** = CL *nihil.*   6. **visere:** complement of *properat;* its object is the indirect
question, *hoc quid sit.*   12. **vereare** = *verearis,* alternate form of the present subjunctive, second person singular of *vereri,* in jussive construction, lit., "be afraid of nothing," i.e., "fear not."   16. **tollere:** with *tuum spiritum* as object, the sense is "to kill
you."   21. **Romphaea** = CL *rhomphaea,* "a [barbarian] spear."   23. **pie:** adverb.
1. **pulcritudine** = CL *pulchritudine.*   2. **omnibus . . . munitionibus . . . praestat:**
"surpasses all other fortresses."   3. **iugi** = CL *iuge.* **stipatione non minima:** litotes.

Moris itaque est hoc post matutinum crepusculum omnibus mox patere, post tertiam vero diei horam emissis omnibus dato signo, quod est mis, usque in horam nonam cunctis aditum prohibere. In hoc igitur Romanos is to chrysotriclinon, id est aureum triclinium, quae praestantior pars est,
5 potentissime degens ceteras palatii partes genero Constantino filiisque suis Stephano et Constantino distribuerat. Hi duo denique, ut praediximus, non ferentes patris iustam severitatem in eorum cubiculis multis copiis congregatis diem constituerunt, quando patrem deicere solique ipsi possent regnare. Cumque dies adveniret optata, cunctis de palatio iuxta
10 morem egressis Stephanus et Constantinus facta congressione super patrem irruunt eumque de palatio civibus ignorantibus deponunt et ad vicinam insulam, in qua caenobitarum multitudo phylosophabatur, tonso ei, ut moris est, capite, phylosophandum transmittunt.

—*Antap.* 5.21 (excerpts).

Liutprand Is Received in Constantinople as an Envoy of Berengar II

Est Constantinopolim domus palatio contigua mirae magnitudinis seu pulchritudinis, quae a Grecis per V loco digammae positam Magnaura, quasi magna aura dicitur. Hanc itaque Constantinus cum ob Hispanorum nuntios, qui tunc eo noviter venerant, tum ob me et Liute-
5 fredum hoc modo praeparari iussit. Aerea, sed deaurata quaedam arbor ante imperatoris sedile stabat, cuius ramos itidem aereae diversi generis

2. **mis:** untranslatable word which represents the sound made to signal for the closing of the gates. 3. **hoc:** i.e., *palatium.* **Romanos:** Emperor until 944, he was deposed by his sons and died in 948. The form of his name is nominative singular masculine, as *is* makes clear. 4. **is:** demonstrative pronoun modifying *Romanos.* 5. **genero:** from *gener, generi.* 12. **caenobitarum:** more properly in ML *coenobitarum,* from *coenobita, ae,* a masculine noun of the first declension, meaning "monk" (Blaise/Chirat 163). **phylosophabatur** = CL *philosophabatur.* **ei:** the object of *transmittunt;* it is common for verbs of motion to take the dative case in ML. 13. **phylosophandum** = CL *philosophandum,* "for the purpose of doing much thinking"; the gerundive is used here in a purpose construction (AG 506).
1. **Constantinopolim:** accusative of place where, without a preposition, common in ML instead of ablative of place where with *in.* The form is *Constantinopolis, eos,* or *is;* the accusative is in *im* (Sleumer 237). **contigua** + dative = "next to. . . ." 2. **Grecis** = CL *Graecis.* **per V:** i.e., *litteram.* **positam:** modifies an understood *litteram* in the prepositional phrase *per V;* the idea is that in the spelling of the name of the palace, "Magnaura," the Greek letter digamma has been replaced by the Roman letter "v" (as often in ancient transliterations from Greek to Latin). 3. **hanc:** i.e., *domum,* object of *iussit praeparari.* **cum . . . tum:** coordinating conjunctions = "not only . . . but also." 5. **deaurata:** perfect passive participle of *deaurare,* "gilded."

deaurataeque aves replebant, quae secundum species suas diversarum avium voces emittebant. Imperatoris vero solium huismodi erat arte compositum, ut in momento humile, exelsius modo, quam mox videretur sublime, quod inmensae magnitudinis, incertum utrum aerei an lignei, verum auro tecti leones quasi custodiebant, qui cauda terram percutientes aperto ore linguisque mobilibus rugitum emittebant. In hac igitur duorum eunuchorum humeris incumbens ante imperatoris praesentiam sum deductus. Cumque in adventu meo rugitum leones emitterent, aves secundum speties suas perstreperent, nullo sum terrore, nulla admiratione commotus, quoniam quidem ex his omnibus eos qui bene noverant fueram percontatus. Tertio itaque pronus imperatorem adorans caput sustuli et, quem prius moderata mensura a terra elevatum sedere vidi, mox aliis indutum vestibus poenes domus laquear sedere prospexi; quod qualiter fieret, cogitare non potui, nisi forte eo sit subvectus ergalio, quo torcularium arbores subvehuntur. Per se autem tunc nihil locutus, quoniam, etsi vellet, intercapedo maxima indecorum faceret, de vita Berengarii et sospitate per logothetam est percontatus. Cui cum consequenter respondissem, interprete sum innuente egressus et in datum mihi hospitium mox receptus.

—Antap. 6.5.

Liutprand's Reception in Constantinople

Ottones Romanorum invictissimos imperatores augustos gloriosissimamque Adelheidem imperatricem augustam Liudprandus sanctae

---

3. **exelsius** = CL *excelsius.* **quam mox:** "how soon. . . ." 4. **inmensae** = CL *immensae.* 6. **rugitum:** *rugitus, us,* "roaring." **in hac:** i.e., *domu.* 7. **humeris** = CL *umeris,* the dative object of *incumbens;* the wider use of aspirates is common in ML; § 1.5. 9. **speties** = CL *species.* 10. **ex his omnibus** = CL *de his omnibus;* an expansion of function and meaning for prepositions is common in ML. **eos:** the object of *percontatus,* and the antecedent of *qui.* 11. **percontatus:** from *percontari.* 12. **moderata mensura:** ablative of place with *quem elevatum.* 13. **poenes** = CL *penes* + accusative. **domus laquear:** *laquear, aris,* neuter noun governed by *poenes,* with modifying *domus.* 14. **ergalio:** *ergalium,* a neologism from the Greek root meaning "work," this word means something like "contraption," "mechanism," etc. **torcularium:** from *torcular, aris* = genitive plural, dependent on *arbores.* 15. **arbores:** lit., "trees," but here meaning something like "beams (as of a winepress)." 16. **intercapedo:** lit., "break," "interruption," but with the more specific sense here of "distance." 17. **sospitate:** from *sospitas, atis,* "health," "welfare," "safety." **logothetam:** a Greek neologism = "secretary." 18. **interprete innuente:** ablative absolute.

1. **Ottones:** Otto I (b. 912; king of Germany 936–973). 2. **Adelheidem:** Queen (later Saint) Adelaide, wife of Otto I.

Cremonensis ecclesiae episcopus semper valere, prosperari, triumphare anhelat, desiderat, optat.

Quid causae fuerit, quod prius literas sive nuntium meum non suscepentis, ratio subsequens declarabit. Pridie Nonas Iunii Constantinopolim
5 venimus et ad contumeliam vestram turpiter suscepti graviter turpiterque sumus tractati. Palatio quidem satis magno et aperto, quod nec frigus arceret, sicut nec calorem repelleret, inclusi sumus; armati milites appositi sunt custodes, qui meis omnibus exitum, ceteris prohiberent ingressum. Domus ipsa solis nobis inclusis pervia, a palatio adeo sequestrata, ut eo
10 nobis non equitantibus, sed ambulantibus anhelitus truncaretur. Accessit ad calamitatem nostram, quod Grecorum vinum ob picis, taedae, gypsi commixtionem nobis impotabile fuit. Domus ipsa erat inaquosa, nec sitim saltem aqua extinguere quivimus, quam data pecunia emeremus. Huic magno vae, vae aliud appositum est, homo scili[cet dom]orum cus-
15 tos, qui cotidianos sumptus praeberet, cui similem si requiras, non terra, sed infernus forsan dabit; is enim, quicquid calamitatis, quicquid rapinae, quicquid dispendii, quicquid luctus, quicquid miseriae excogitare potuit, quasi torrens inundans in nos effudit. Nec in centum viginti diebus una saltem praeteriit, quae non gemitus nobis praeberet et luctus.
20 Pridie Nonas Iunii, ut superius scripsimus, Constantinopolim ante portam Caream venimus, et usque ad undecimam horam cum equis, non modica pluvia, expectavimus. Undecima vero hora non ratus Nicephorus nos dignos esse tam ornatos vestra misericordia equitare venire iussit, et usque in praefatam domum marmoream, invisam, inaquosam, patulam
25 sumus deducti; octavo autem Idus sabbatho primo dierum pentecostes,

---

4. **Pridie Nonas Iunii:** 3 June 968. 9. **pervia:** modifies *Domus ipsa* and governs datives *solis nobis inclusis.* 10. **accessit . . . quod:** "it added to our calamity that. . . ." 11. **Grecorum** = CL *Graecorum.* **picis:** from *pix, picis,* "pitch." **taedae:** from *taeda, ae,* "resin." **gypsi:** from *gypsum, i* = "gypsum." This catalogue refers to the materials used to seal the jars of wine which, over time, coming loose from the seal, had contaminated the wine—which was deemed fit enough still to serve to these unwelcome guests (but cf. Nelson and Shirk for a different view). 13. **sitim** = CL *sitem,* from *sitis.* **extinguere** = CL *exstinguere,* complement of *quivimus,* from *quire.* 14. **vae:** in CL an interjection but in ML a neuter indeclinable substantive also, here in the dative singular, modified by *hiuc magno.* **vae:** nominative singular, modified by *aliud.* 16. **quicquid . . . potuit:** this catalogue is the collective object of *effudit.* 21. **portam Caream:** the Carean gate, allowing entry into Constantinople. 22. **ratus:** from *reri* + accusative and infinitive = "to deem someone worthy to . . ." **Nicephorus:** Byzantine emperor, 963–969. 24. **praefatam:** from *praefari.* 25. **octavo . . . Idus:** i.e., "on the eighth day before the Ides" = 6 June. **sabbatho:** more properly *Sabbato,* from *Sabbatum, i* (cf. Sleumer 685), ablative of time with modifying *primo* = "on the Saturday before. . . ." **pentecostes:** from *Pentecoste, es* = Pentecost, in the

ante fratris eius Leonis coropalati et logothetae praesentiam sum deductus, ubi de imperiali vestro nomine magna sumus contentione fatigati.
Ipse enim vos non imperatorem, id est Βασιλέα sua lingua, sed ob indignationem ῥῆγα, id est regem nostra, vocabat. Cui cum dicerem, quod
significatur, idem esse, quamvis, quod significat, diversum, me ait non   5
pacis, sed contentionis causa venisse; sicque iratus surgens vestras litteras,
vere indignans, non per se, sed per interpretem suscepit, homo ipse ad
personam satis procerus, falso humilis, cui si innisus homo fuerit, manum
eius perforabit.

Septimo autem Idus, ipso videlicet sancto die pentecostes, in domo,   10
quae dicitur Στεφάνα, id est Coronaria, ante Nicephorum sum deductus,
hominem satis monstruosum, pygmaeum, capite pinguem atque oculorum parvitate talpinum, barba curta, lata, spissa et semicana foedatum,
cervice digitali turpatum, prolixitate et densitate comarum satis hyopum,
colore Aethiopem, "cui per mediam nolis occurrere noctem," ventre ex-   15
tensum, natibus siccum, coxis ad mensuram ipsam brevem longissimum,
cruribus parvum, calcaneis pedibusque aequalem, villino, sed nimis veternoso vel diuturnitate ipsa foetido et pallido ornamento indutum, Sicioniis
calceamentis calceatum, lingua procacem, ingenio vulpem, periurio seu
mendacio Ulyxem. Semper mihi domini mei imperatores augusti formosi,   20
quanto hinc formosiores visi estis! Semper ornati, quanto hinc ornatiores!

---

genitive with dependent *dierum* = "of the days of Pentecost." 1. **coropalati:** there
are several forms of this ML neologism compounded of *cura* and *palatium*, though
the more common is *curopalates, ae* (Blaise/Chirat 235); the form used by Liutprand
is *coropalatus, i* = "master of the household," here in the genitive singular modifying
Leonis. **ante . . . praesentiam:** "before" or "into the presence of. . . ." 4. **nostra:**
i.e., *in lingua nostra*. **quod . . . significatur . . . quod significat:** the idea is that "the
thing that is signified is the same [i.e., the notion of ruling a people], though the thing
that signifies it is different [i.e., the words used]." 9. **eius:** here one notes the importance of recognizing that though Liutprand uses ML *eius*, it has the force of CL *suam*,
for it is the hand of the *innisus homo*, not of the king, that gets cut; § 5.3.1. 10. **Septimo . . . Idus:** 7 June. 12. **pygmaeum:** from *pygmaeus a, um*, "pygmy-like."
13. **talpinum:** from *talpinus, a, um*, "mole-like" (LS 1835). **semicana:** from *semica-
nus, a, um*, "half-gray" (LS 1665). **foedatum:** perfect passive participle of *foedare*.
14. **digitali:** *digitalis, e*, with *cervice*, "a neck no bigger than your finger." **hyopum:**
a Greek neologism on ὕωψ, meaning "swine-like" (Becker 238, s. v. *hyops*). 15. The
tag comes from Juvenal 5.53–54. 16. **ad . . . brevem:** "for the shortness of his stature. . . ." 17. **calcaneis:** *calcaneum, i*, "heel"; with *pedibus* the idea is that the Emperor is flat-footed. **villino** = *byssino*, a cotton fabric; the orthography suggests regional pronunciation common in the variances of ML orthography (Becker 246, s. v.
villinus). **veternoso** = CL *vetusto*. 18. **Sicioniis** = CL *Sicyonius, a, um*, "Sicyo-
nian," referring to the territory of Sicyonia in the Peloponnesus.

Semper potentes, quanto hinc potentiores! Semper mites, quanto hinc
mitiores! Semper virtutibus pleni, quanto hinc pleniores! Sedebant ad sinistram, non in eadem linea, sed longe deorsum duo parvuli imperatores,
eius quondam domini, nunc subiecti. Cuius narrationis initium hoc fuit:

5   "Debueramus, immo volueramus te benigne magnificeque suscipere;
sed domini tui impietas non permittit, qui tam inimica invasione Romam
sibi vindicavit, Berengario et Adelberto contra ius fasque vi terram abstulit, Romanorum alios gladio, alios suspendio interemit, oculis alios
privavit, exilio alios relegavit, et imperii nostri insuper civitates homicidio
10   aut incendio sibi subdere temptavit; et quia affectus eius pravus effectum
habere non potuit, nunc te malitiae huius suggestorem atque impulsorem
simulata pace quasi κατάσκοπον, id est exploratorem, ad nos direxit."
        Cui inquam ego: "Romanam civitatem dominus meus non vi aut tyra-
nnice invasit, sed a tyranni, immo tyrannorum iugo liberavit. Nonne ef-
15   feminati dominabantur eius? et quod gravius sive turpius, nonne meretri-
ces? Dormiebat, ut puto, tunc potestas tua, immo decessorum tuorum,
qui nomine solo, non autem re ipsa imperatores Romanorum vocantur.
Si potentes, si imperatores Romanorum erant, cur Romam in meretricum
potestate sinebant? Nonne sanctissimorum paparum alii sunt relegati, alii
20   adeo aflicti, ut neque cotidianos sumptus nec elemosinam habere quirent?
Nonne Adelbertus contumeliosas literas Romano et Constantino, deces-
soribus tuis, imperatoribus misit? Nonne sanctissimorum apostolorum
ecclesias rapinas expoliavit? Quis ex vobis imperatoribus zelo Dei ductus
tam indignum facinus vindicare et sanctam ecclesiasm in statum pro-
25   prium reformare curavit? Neglexistis vos, non neglexit dominus meus, qui
a finibus terrae surgens Romamque veniens impios abstulit et sanctorum
apostolorum vicariis potestatem et honorem omnem contradidit. Postmodum vero insurgentes contra se et domnum apostolicum, quasi iurisiura-

---

7. **Berengario et Adelberto:** ablative of separation with *abstulit.* **abstulit:** from *afferre.* 14. **effeminati:** perfect passive participle of *effiminare,* meaning "those smit-
ten by women." 15. **eius:** i.e., Rome; *dominari* often takes a genitive object (Sleumer
284). 20. **elemosinam:** more properly *eleemosyna, ae,* "alms" (Blaise/Chirat 303).
quirent: from *quire,* with complementary *habere.* 23. **expoliavit** = CL *exspoliavit.*
zelo: *zelus, i,* from the Greek ζῆλος, "zeal." 27. **vicariis:** i.e., the popes, one of whose
titles is Vicar (*vicarius*) of Christ. **contradidit:** perfect active indicative, third person
singular, from *contradere,* "to deliver over wholly." 28. **insurgentes:** the object of
the verbs *cecidit, iugulavit, suspendit,* and *relegavit,* several lines subsequent, with the
catalogue of abusive titles in apposition. **domnum** = *dominum;* syncope (§ 1.1) is
common in ML orthography; the phrase *domnum apostolicum* = "the pope." **iurisi-
urandi:** *iurisiurandum, i,* "oath."

ndi violatores, sacrilegos, dominorum suorum apostolicorum tortores, raptores, secundum decreta imperatorum Romanorum, Iustiniani, Valentiniani, Theodosii et ceterorum, cecidit, iugulavit, suspendit et exilio relegavit; quae si non faceret, impius, iniustus, crudelis, tyrannus esset. Palam est, quod Berengarius et Adelbertus sui milites effecti regnum Italicum sceptro aureo ex eius manu susceperant et praesentibus servis tuis, qui nunc usque supersunt et hac in civitate degunt, iureiurando fidem promiserunt. Et quia suggerente diabolo hanc perfide violarunt, iuste illos quasi desertores sibique rebelles regno privavit; quod ita subditis tibi et postmodum rebellibus faceres."

—*Leg.* 1–5.

SHODDY IMPERIALISM

"Secunda," inquit Nicephorus, "hora iam transiit; προέλευσις, id est processio, nobis est celebranda. Quod nunc instat, agamus. Contra haec, cum opportunum fuerit, respondebimus."

Non pigeat me προέλευσιν ipsam describere et dominos meos audire. Negotiatorum multitudo copiosa ignobiliumque personarum ea sollempnitate collecta ad susceptionem et laudem Nicephori a palatio usque ad Sanctam Sophiam, quasi pro muris, viae margines tenuit, clypeolis tenuibus satis et spiculis vilibus dedecorata. Accessit et ad dedecoris huius augmentum, quod vulgi ipsius potior pars ad laudem ipsius nudis processerat pedibus. Credo sic eos putasse sanctam ipsam potius exornare προέλευσιν. Sed et optimates sui, qui cum ipso per plebeiam et discalceatam multitudinem ipsam transierant, magnis et nimia vetustate rimatis tunicis erant induti. Satis decentius cotidiana veste induti procederent. Nullus est, cuius atavus hanc novam haberet. Nemo ibi auro, nemo gemmis ornatus erat, nisi ipse solus Nicephorus, quem imperialia ornamenta ad maiorum personas sumpta et composita foediorem reddiderant. Per salutem vestram, quae mihi mea carior extat, una vestrorum pretiosa vestis procerum centum horum et eo amplius pretiosior est! Ductus ego ad προέ-

---

5. **palam est:** "it is widely known"; Liutprand uses the adverb *palam* instead of a predicate adjective. 6. **praesentibus servis tuis:** "in the presence of your servants." 9. **quod . . . faceres:** the idea is that "you would do the same thing to those conquered by you who afterward were rebellious toward you."

5. **sollempnitate** = CL *sollemnitate;* the addition of a parasitic consonant is common in ML orthography. 7. **clypeolis:** the better spelling is *clipeolis,* from *clipeolum,* "little shield." 9. **ipsius:** Nicephorus. 11. **discalceatam:** "unshod." 17. **extat** = CL *exstat.*

λευσιν ipsam in eminentiori loco iuxta psaltas, id est cantores, sum constitutus.

Cumque quasi reptans monstrum illud procederet, clamabant adulatores psaltae: "Ecce venit stella matutina, surgit Eous, reverberat obtutu
5 solis radios, pallida Saracenorum mors, Nicephorus μέδων, id est princeps!" Unde et cantabatur: "μέδοντι, id est principi, Nicephoro, πολλὰ ἔτη, id est plures anni sint! Gentes, hunc adorate, hunc colite, huic tanto colla subdite!" Quanto tunc verius canerent: Carbo exstincte veni, μέλε, anus incessu, Sylvanus vultu, rustice, lustrivage, capripes, cornute,
10 bimembris, setiger, indocilis, agrestis, barbare, dure, villose, rebellis, Cappadox! Igitur falsidicis illis inflatus naeniis Sanctam Sophiam ingreditur, dominis suis imperatoribus se a longe sequentibus et in pacis osculo ad terram usque adorantibus. Armiger huius sagitta calamo immissa aeram in ecclesia ponit, quae prosequitur, quo nimirum tempore imperare coep-
15 erit, et sic aeram, qui id non viderunt, intellegunt.

Hac eadem die convivam me sibi esse iussit. Non ratus autem me dignum esse cuipiam suorum praeponi procerum, quintus decimus ab eo absque gausape sedi; meorum nemo comitum, non dico solum mensae non assedit, sed neque domum, in qua conviva eram, vidit. Qua in coena turpi
20 satis et obscena, ebriorum more oleo delibuta alioque quodam deterrimo piscium liquore aspersa multa super potentia vestra, multa super regnis et militibus me rogavit. Cui cum consequenter et vere responderem, "Mentiris!" ait, "domini tui milites equitandi ignari, pedestris pugnae sunt inscii, scutorum magnitudo, loricarum gravitudo, ensium longitudo

1. **eminentiori:** comparative of *eminens,* with *loco.* **psaltas:** from *psaltes, ae,* masculine noun of the first declension, from the Greek ψάλτης (Sleumer 644), which Liutprand translates in the next clause. 4. **Eous:** the morning star. 5. **Saracenorum:** from *Saraceni, orum,* the Saracens (Sleumer 696). 8. **carbo exstincte:** vocative case, "burnt-out piece of coal." **veni:** present active imperative of *venire.* 9. **lustrivage:** *lustrivagus, i,* "wanderer," "hobo" (Niermeyer 623). **capripes:** from *caper + pedes.* 10. **Cappadox:** from *Cappadox, ocis,* "Cappadocian." 11. **naeniis** = CL *neniis,* "songs." 13. **huius:** i.e., Nicephorus. **sagitta calamo immissa:** ablative absolute phrase meaning something like "an arrow being substituted for a pen. . . ." **aeram:** *aera, ae,* "date" or "age"; the ablative absolute phrase suggests that the date is being recorded. 14. **quo nimirum tempore** = CL *ex quo tempore.* 16. **ratus:** from *reri,* "to deem," "to consider." 18. **gausape:** from *gausape* (or *gausapes), is,* it means "tablecloth" or, possibly, "napkin." **dico:** emphatic and parenthetical, to add to the emotion of what is being said. 19. **assedit:** from *assidere* + dative object = "to sit at. . . ." **non . . . solum . . . sed neque:** "not only . . . but not. . . ." **coena** = CL *cena.* 21. **super** = CL *de;* the wider compass accorded to prepositions is a common feature of ML. 22. **rogavit:** with object *me* and predicate accusative *multa.*

galearumque pondus neutra parte eos pugnare sinit," ac subridens: "Impedit," inquit, "eos et gastrimargia, hoc est ventris ingluvies; "quorum Deus venter est," quorum audacia crapula, fortitudo ebrietas, ieiunium dissolutio, pavor sobrietas. Nec est in mari domino tuo classium numerus. Navigantium fortitudo mihi soli inest, qui eum classibus aggrediar, bello maritimas eius civitates demoliar et, quae fluminibus sunt vicina, redigam in favillam. Qui, cedo mihi, etiam in terra copiarum paucitate resistere poterit? Filius non abfuit, uxor non defuit; Saxones, Suevi, Bagoarii, Italici omnes cum eo adfuerunt, et cum civitatulam unam sibi resistentem capere nescirent, immo nequirent, quomodo mihi resistent venienti? quem tot copiae prosequenter,

> Gargara quot segetes, quot habet Methymna racemos,
> Quot caelum stellas, quot mare in flatibus undas!"

—*Leg.* 8–11.

SOME PROPHECIES AND THEIR INTERPRETATIONS

Sed cur exercitum nunc in Assyrios duxerit, quaeso advertite. Habent Greci et Saraceni libros, quos ὁράσεις sive visiones Danielis vocant, ego autem Sibyllanos, in quibus scriptum reperitur, quot annis imperator quisque vivat; quae sint futura eo imperitante tempora, pax an simultas, secundae Saracenorum res an adversae. Legitur itaque huius Nicephori temporibus Assyrios Grecis non posse resistere huncque septennio tan-

---

1. **subridens** = CL *surridens*. 2. **gastrimargia:** explained in the next clause. 5. **inest** + dative = "belongs to. . . ." 7. **cedo:** archaic imperative, "all right," "let's hear it," "out with it," etc. **mihi:** dative object of *resistere,* the complement of *poterit.* 8. **abfuit:** the better spelling is *afuit,* from *absum.* **Bagoarii:** *Bajoarii,* Bavarians (Sleumer 146, s. v. *Bajoaria* and the other forms attending to this region). The orthographical variants of words designating Bavaria and its regions are many. 9. **Italici:** the other names of this catalogue are easier to identify: "Saxons, Swabians, and Italians"; Sleumer gives a full accounting of forms and meanings for these geographical regions and peoples. **adfuerunt** = CL *affuerunt.* **civitatulam:** diminutive of *civitas* = "little city." 12. **Gargara:** city at the base of Mount Ida; also the upper part of Mount Ida itself. **Methymna:** a city on Lesbos, but here by metonymy = Lesbos. These lines come from Ovid, *Ars Am.* 1.57, 59.

1. **duxerit:** the subject is Nicephorus. 2. **Greci** = CL *Graeci.* 3. **Sibyllanos:** i.e., *libros;* the Sibylline books recorded the sayings of the Sibyl at Cumae, a prophetess. 5. **secundae:** modifies *res* = "favorable." 6. **non posse:** verb in the infinitive clause with *Assyrios* as subject and *resistere* as complement; the clause is governed by *legitur.* **huncque:** i.e., Nicephorus. **septennio** = CL *septuennium,* although *septennium* is a collateral form (LS 1676); it means here that Nicephorus will live for only seven years.

tum vivere post cuius obitum imperatorem isto deteriorem—sed timeo, quod inveniri non possit—et magis imbellem debere surgere, cuius temporibus praevalere debent adeo Assyrii, ut in Chalcedoniam usque, quae distat Constantinopoli haud longe, potestative cuncta debeant obtinere.

5 Considerant enim utrique tempora; una eademque re Greci animati insequuntur, Saraceni desperati non resistunt tempus expectantes, cum et ipsi insequantur, Greci interim non resistant.

Sed Hippolytus quidam Siciliensis episcopus eadem scripsit et de imperio vestro et gente nostra—nostram nunc dico omnem, quae sub vestro

10 imperio est, gentem—; atque utinam verum sit, quod de praesentibus scripsit iste temporibus. Cetera, ut scripsit, sunt usque huc completa, quemadmodum per ipsos, qui horum librorum scientiam habent, audivi. Et ex multis eius dictis unum id proferamus in medium. Ait enim nunc completum iri scripturam, quae dicit: λέων καὶ σκίμνος ὁμοδιώξουσιν

15 ὄναγρον. Grece ita. Latinum autem sic: "Leo et catulus simul exterminabunt onagrum." Cuius interpretatio secundum Grecos: Leo, id est Romanorum sive Grecorum imperator, et catulus, Francorum scilicet rex, simul his praesentibus temporibus exterminabant onagrum, id est Saracenorum regem Africanum. Quae interpretatio eo mihi vera non videtur,

20 quoniam leo et catulus, quamvis disparis magnitudinis, unius tamen sunt naturae et speciei seu moris; atque ut mihi mea scientia suggerit, si leo Grecorum imperator, inconveniens est, ut catulus sit Francorum rex. Quamvis enim utrique homines sint, sicut leo et catulus uterque animalia, distant tamen moribus tantum, non dico solum quantum species spe-

25 ciebus, sed quantum sensibilia insensibilibus. Catulus a leone nil nisi tempore distat, forma eadem, rabies una, rugitus idem. Grecorum rex crinitus, tunicatus, manicatus, teristratus, mendax, dolosus, immisericors, vulpinus, superbus, falso humilis, parcus, cupidus, allio, cepe et porris vescens, balnea bibens; Francorum rex contra pulchre tonsus, a muliebri

---

1. **isto**: ablative of comparison, referring to Nicephorus. 4. **potestative**: ablative of means; the *-ve* at the end of *potestati* is an enclitic conjunction = *et*. 5. **utrique**: i.e., "each people." **una eademque re**: ablative of means. 8. **Siciliensis**: *Siciliensis, e* = Sicilian. 9. **nostram**: i.e., *gentem*, which follows at the end of the sentence. 13. **in medium**: "publicly." 14. **completum iri**: future passive infinitive of *complere* = "will be brought to fulfillment." 16. **onagrum**: from *onager* or *onagrus, i*. 24. **dico**: emphatic and parenthetical; Liutprand often uses *dico* in the coordinating construction *non [dico] solum . . . sed. . . .* 25. **tempore**: i.e., "age." 27. **teristratus** = *theristratus*, "wearing a woman's gown" (from *theristrum;* cf. Becker 245, s. v. *teristrum*). 28. **vulpinus**: "fox-like." **cepe** = CL *caepa*, although *cepa* is a CL form also (Liutprand uses the same form below also). 29. **balnea**: "bath-water." **contra**: adverb.

vestitu veste diversus, pileatus, verax, nil doli habens, satis, ubi competit, misericors, severus, ubi oportet, semper vere humilis, nunquam parcus, non allio, cepis, porris vescens, ut possit animalibus eo parcere, quantinus non manducatis, sed venundatis pecuniam congreget. Audistis differentiam; nolite hanc interpretationem suscipere; aut enim futura est, aut 5 haec vera non est. Impossibile est enim, ut Nicephorus, sicut ipsi mentiuntur, sit leo et Otto sit catulus, qui simul exterminent aliquem. "Ante" enim "pererratis amborum finibus exul aut Ararim Parthus bibet aut Germania Tygrim," quam Nicephorus et Otto amicitia coeant et foedera iungant. 10

Audistis Grecorum, audite nunc Liudprandi Cremonensis episcopi interpretationem. Dico autem et non solum dico, sed affirmo, si scriptura haec praesentibus est implenda temporibus, leo et catulus, pater et filius, Otto et Otto, in nullo dispares, tempore distantes tantum, simul hoc praesenti tempore exterminabunt onagrum, id est silvestrem asinum Niceph- 15 orum, qui non incongrue silvestri asino comparatur ob vanam et inanem gloriam incestumque dominae et commatris suae coniugium.

—*Leg.* 39–41 (excerpts).

Liutprand's Farewell to Constantinople

Hanc cum accepissem, vale mihi dicentes dimiserunt oscula praebentes satis iucunda, satis amabilia. Sed dum recederem, legationem mihi non me, sed illis satis dirigunt dignam, scilicet quod mihi soli meisque equos darent, sarcinis nullum; sicque nimis, ut res poscebat, turbatus, διασώστη, id est ductori meo, quinquaginta aureorum res pretio dedi. Et 5 cum non haberem, quod pro malefactis Nicephoro tunc redderem, hos in pariete invisae domus meae et in mensa lignea versiculos scripsi:

Argolicum non tuta fides; procul esto, Latine,
Credere, nec mentem verbis adhibere memento!
Vincere dum possit, quam sancte peierat Argos! 10
Marmore quae vario magnis patet alta fenestris,
Haec inaquosa domus, concluso pervia soli,
Frigora suscipiens, aestum nec saeva repellens;
Praesul ab Ausonia Liudprandus in urbe Cremona,

---

1. **pileatus** = CL *pilleatus*. **satis:** modifies *misericors*. 9. The tag recalls Virgil, *Ecl.* 1.62–63. 17. **commatris:** "godmother."
1. **hanc:** i.e., *litteram*, a formal epistle from Nicephorus to Otto I. 3. **meisque:** i.e., "my companions." 8. **Argolicum:** from *Argolicus, a, um,* this form is genitive, "of the Greeks." 14. **praesul:** in ML a term for bishop (cf. Niermeyer 842–43).

Constantinopolim pacis profectus amore,
Quattuor aestivis concludor mensibus isthic.
Induperator enim Bareas conscenderat Otto,
Caede simul flammisque sibi loca subdere temptans,
5   Sed precibus remeat Romanas victor ad urbes
Inde meis. Nurum promisit Grecia mendax
Quae nisi nata foret, nec me venisse dolerem,
Nec rabiem, Nicephore, tuam perpendere quirem,
Privignam prohibes qui nato iungere herili.
10   Imminet ecce dies, Furiis cum pulsus acerbis,
Ni Deus avertat, toto Mars saeviet orbe
Crimine paxque tuo cunctis optanda silebit!

—Leg. 57.

3. **induperator** = *imperator.* **Bareas:** from *Bareae, arum* = the Italian province of Bari (Becker 215). 7. **foret** = CL *esset.* 9. **nato . . . herili:** i.e., Otto II.

WIDUKIND OF CORVEY

The History of the Saxons
(*Res gestae Saxonicae;* c. 970)

Widukind of Corvey's obscurity is perhaps owed to the very qualities that make his *History* so appealing. It is a work of moderate length, but its scope is rather broad, so compression and imprecision naturally inform its presentation. It is written in a prose style that can be both appreciably simple and ferociously opaque, so that the difficulties of one line become the accessible sentiments of the next. Its narrative moves quickly from topic to topic, taking up tangents of biography, geography, and every manner of detail. Nor does Widukind seem much involved with the work of his predecessors: if he appears not to be a student of the Roman historians, neither is he a follower of the Christian Latin historical tradition. As a monk at the monastery of Corvey, we can assume, he received a basic education, but his writing betrays little of the style of the classicizing schoolbooks he presumably mastered. As with his contemporary, Liutprand of Cremona, Widukind's themes, patterns of organization, and modes of expression are very much of his own confection.

Of Widukind's life we know only that he flourished during the latter part of the tenth century, and that he died around 1004. He was a Benedictine monk associated, so far as is known, for all of his career, with Corvey. The details found in his *Res gestae Saxonicae* suggest that, like Liutprand, Widukind may have had a place at the court of Otto the Great, the first of several kings who ushered a new era of stability into Germanic affairs after the disintegration of the Carolingian empire. The central place accorded to Otto in Widukind's *Res gestae* certainly would suggest as much, especially since the work was composed while Otto was still alive. Widukind should not be considered a mere compiler, nor less a propagandist, however. He has praises to ply, to be sure, but his *History* is too various to allow for a single characterization of its themes or its Latinity. But the insistent development of this thematic and linguistic variety speaks perhaps most clearly to the transformation of LL from its classicizing roots to its various medieval versions, a process that did not reach maturity until the twelfth century.

The *Res gestae Saxonicae* has been edited by G. Pertz (*Widukundi Res Gestae Saxonicae,* Hanover, 1839); by G. Waitz (*Widukundi Rerum*

Gestarum Saxonicarum Libri Tres, Hanover, 1882), and by P. Hirsch and
H. E. Lohmann, reprinted by A. Bauer and R. Rau (*Quellen zur Gesch-
ichte der Sächsischen Kaiserzeit,* vol. 8, Darmstadt, 1971). Bauer and
Rau's reprint is followed here without change.

A Brave Saxon Leads His Countrymen to Victory

Erat autem tunc in castris quidam de veteranis militibus iam senior,
sed viridi senectute adhuc vigens, qui merito bonarum virtutum pater patrum dicebatur, nomine Hathagat. Hic arripiens signum, quod apud eos
habebatur sacrum, leonis atque draconis et desuper aquilae volantis insig-
5   nitum effigie, quo ostentaret fortitudinis atque prudentiae et earum rerum
efficatiam, et motu corporis animi constantiam declarans ait: "Hucusque
inter optimos Saxones vixi, et ad hanc fere ultimam senectutem aetas me
perduxit, et numquam Saxones meos fugere vidi; et quomodo nunc cogor
agere quod numquam didici? Certare scio, fugere ignoro nec valeo. Si fata
10   non sinunt ultra vivere, liceat saltem, quod michi dulcissimum est, cum
amicis occumbere. Exempli michi paternae virtutis sunt amicorum corpora circa nos prostrata, qui maluerunt mori quam vinci, inpigras animas
amittere quam coram inimicis loco cedere. Sed quid necesse habeo exhor-
tationem protrahere tantisper de contemptu mortis? Ecce ad securos ibi-
15   mus, ad caedem tantum, non ad pugnam. Nam de promissa pace ac nostro gravi vulnere nichil suspicantur adversi, hodierno quoque prelio
fatigati quemadmodum sunt, sine metu, sine vigiliis et solita custodia manent. Irruamus igitur super improvisos et somno sepultos, parum laboris
est; sequimini me ducem, et hoc canum caput meum vobis trado, si non
20   evenerit quod dico."
Illius igitur optimis verbis erecti quod supererat diei in reficiendis suis

3. Hathagat: an otherwise obscure Saxon leader (see Pertz 14, n. 1). **4. insignitum:**
perfect passive participle of *insignire;* construed with *effigie,* from *effigies, ei.*
5. earum rerum: i.e., *talium virtutum.* **6. efficatiam** = CL *efficaciam,* "efficiency";
palatalization (§ 1.4) is a common feature of ML phonology. **hucusque** = *huc usque.*
7. fere: adverb. **9. didici:** from *discere;* the *quod* clause is the object of *agere,* itself
the complement of *cogor.* **10. liceat** + dative object *michi* and infinitive *occumbere* = "let it be permitted me to die . . ."; *liceat* is in jussive subjunctive construction.
michi = CL *mihi.* **quod . . . dulcissimum est:** relative clause modifying *occumbere.*
11. exempli = CL *exempla.* **12. maluerunt:** from *malle.* **13. quid necesse habeo:**
the idiom *necesse habere* = "to bother with . . ."; + *quid* = "why do I have to
bother. . . ." **14. protrahere:** complement of *quid . . . habeo;* "why do I have to
bother dragging out an exhortation. . . ." **16. nichil** = CL *nihil.* **prelio** = CL *proelio.* **18. parum laboris est:** "it is hardly any effort at all." **20. quod dico:** this relative clause is the subject of *non evenerit.* **21. quod supererat diei:** the object of *expendebant,* whose subject is *erecti (erigere),* modifying an understood *Saxones.*

corporibus expendebant; deinde prima vigilia noctis dato signo, qua solet
sopor gravior occupare mortales, sumptis armis, precedente duce irruunt
super muros, invenientesque sine vigiliis ac custodiis, ingressi sunt urbem
cum clamore valido. Quo excitati adversarii, alii fuga salutem quaesier-
unt, alii per plateas et muros urbis ut ebrii erraverunt, alii in Saxones,   5
cives suos putantes, inciderunt. Illi vero omnes perfectae aetatis morti
tradiderunt, inpuberes predae servaverunt. Eratque nox illa plena clamoribus, caede atque rapina, nullusque locus in omni urbe quietus, donec
aurora rutilans surgit et incruentam declarat victoriam. Cumque penes
regem, videlicet Irminfridum, summa victoria esset, requisitus cum uxore   10
ac filiis ac raro comitatu evasisse repertus est.

—Res Ges. Sax. 1.11.

Shrewd Methods of Petty Warfare

Sciens autem comitem Isilberhti versutum et callidum nimis nomine
Immonem, artibus illius melius arbitratus est pugnare quam armis. Ille
vero, ut erat astutissimus, meliori ac maiori se subdens, arma sumit contra
ducem; quod ipse dux omnium laborum gravissime tulit, quia eum sibi
adversum sustinere debuisset, cuius consilio ac fidei hactenus se maxime   5
credebat. Augebat quoque indignationem ducis grex porcorum ab Immone callide captus. Nam subulci ducis cum contra portas urbis transirent, Immo porcellum pro porta agitari fecit et omnem gregem porcorum
apertis portis intra urbem recepit. Quam iniuriam dux ferre non valens
coacto exercitu obsedit Immonem. Ille autem plurima apum examina ha-   10
buisse fertur, quae frangens proiecit contra equites. Apes autem aculeis
equos stimulantes in insaniam vertebant, ita ut equites periclitari coepissent. Quo viso Immo prospiciens de muro eruptionem cum sociis mini-
tavit. Huiuscemodi igitur artibus saepius dux ab Immone delusus solvit

9. **incruentam . . . victoriam:** i.e., for the Saxons.   10. **Irminfridum:** King of the
Thuringians, whom the Saxons were fighting.
    1. **sciens:** the subject is King Otto I (reigned 936–972; b. 912).   **Isilberhti:** Giselb-
ert, Duke of Lothringen (Lotharingia) (Pertz 30, n. 1).   2. **Immonem:** Immo, Count
of Lothringen. **illius:** i.e., Immo. **ille:** i.e., Immo.   4. **ducem:** i.e., Giselbert.
quod: the object of *tulit*, with *omnium laborum* dependent on it, the antecedent of
which technically is the subsequent *quia . . . debuisset* clause.   **dux:** i.e., Giselbert.
quia + subjunctive function on the model of CL *cum* + subjunctive, "since. . . ."   **eum
. . . adversum:** prepositional *adversum* takes the accusative *eum.*   5. **sustinere** +
sibi = "to set himself up. . . ."   **debuisset:** *debere* + infinitive = "to be bound/obliged
to . . ."; the subject is Immo.   **se . . . credebat:** "he entrusted himself."   6. **ab Immone
callide:** "by skillful Immo."   10. **ille:** Immo, though under siege, has more tricks up
his sleeve.   12. **periclitari:** present infinitive of *periclitor*, dependent on *coepissent.*
14. **delusus:** perfect passive participle of *deludere*, modifying *dux.*

obsidionem. Discedens vero fertur dixisse: "Immone mecum sentiente omnes Lotharios facile captos tenui, modo ipsum solum cum omnibus Lothariis capere nequeo."

—*Res Ges. Sax.* 2.23.

A FIRE TEST CONVINCES THE DANES

Dani antiquitus erant Christiani, sed nichilominus idolis ritu gentili servientes. Contigit autem altercationem super cultura deorum fieri in quodam convivio rege presente, Danis affirmantibus Christum quidem esse deum, sed alios eo fore maiores deos, quippe qui potiora mortalibus
5   signa et prodigia per se ostenderent. Contra haec clericus quidam, nunc vero religiosam vitam ducens episcopus nomine Poppa, unum verum deum patrem cum filio unigenito domino nostro Iesu Christo et spiritu sancto, simulacra vero daemonia esse et non deos testatus est. Haraldus autem rex, utpote qui velox traditur fore ad audiendum, tardus ad lo-
10   quendum, interrogat, si hanc fidem per semet ipsum declarare velit. Ille incunctanter velle respondit. Rex vero custodire clericum usque in crasti-num iubet. Mane facto ingentis ponderis ferrum igne succendi iubet, cler-icumque ob fidem catholicam candens ferrum portare iussit. Confessor Christi indubitanter ferrum rapit tamdiuque deportat, quo ipse rex decer-
15   nit. Manum incolumem cunctis ostendit, fidem catholicam omnibus pro-babilem reddit. Ad haec rex conversus Christum deum solum colendum decrevit, idola respuenda subiectis gentibus imperat, Dei sacerdotibus et ministris honorem debitum deinde prestitit. Sed et haec virtutibus merito patris tui adscribuntur, cuius industria in illis regionibus ecclesiae sacer-
20   dotumque ordines in tantum fulsere.

—*Res Ges. Sax.* 3.65.

1. **Dani:** from *Dani, orum,* the Danes (Sleumer 257). **antiquitus:** adverb. **nichilom-inus** = CL *nihilominus.* 2. **servientes** + dative = "were followers of/to. . . ." **con-tigit:** impersonal verb with infinitive clause *altercationem . . . fieri.* 4. **eo:** i.e., *Deus,* in ablative of comparison construction. **fore** = CL *esse,* as often in ML. 6. **Poppa:** an otherwise unknown figure. 8. **Haraldus:** King Harold of the Danes. 9. **utpote** . . . **audiendum:** this ellipitcal line means something like "inasmuch as he was the one who [*utpote qui*] had it ordered [*traditur*] to be quick [*velox . . . fore*] for the presenta-tion [*ad audiendum*]." 11. **incunctanter:** "without delay." **velle:** lit., "he responded without delay that he wished to do so," = "yes." 15. **probabilem:** predicate adjective with *omnibus.* 17. **respuenda:** from *respuere.* 18. **prestitit** = CL *praestitit.* 19. **tui:** i.e., Matilda, the daughter of Otto I, to whom Widukind dedicated his history. **adscribuntur** = CL *asscribuntur.* 20. **in tantum:** "to such a degree." **fulsere:** alter-nate perfect active indicative, third person plural of *fulgere* = *fulserunt.*

RICHER OF ST. REMY

The History of France
(*Historiarum libri quatuor;* c. 998)

R icher exemplifies most readily the wide compass granted in Medieval
Latin historical prose to personal recollection—a tendency, as we have
seen, that informs much of the historical output of Liutprand and Widukind also. This has the effect of dramatizing the narrative, of making it
appear to be more a collection of anecdotes than a longer narrative devoted to an enormously important theme—the coming of the Capetians
to the throne of France. At the same time, much like Widukind and Liutprand, Richer expresses his vision of the past in a Latin style reflective
less of the formal models of classical or Christian historical prose, and
more beholden to local influences. These influences are apparent in the
elliptical syntax that Richer regularly employs, and in his word-choice,
which favors Greek neologisms or words of a Greek provenance. By the
same token, his syntax is accessible, though the conversational quality of
his prose tends sometimes to obscure, rather than illuminate, the point
he is making.

Richer's background, such as we have it, makes the topic of his work
an outgrowth of his upbringing, for we know on evidence that he himself
supplies in his *History* that he hailed from a family that had close connections to the Capetian royal house—his main topic in the *History.* Richer's
father, Raoul, was a soldier who had served Louis IV closely, who took a
keen interest in the world of politics, and who had experience of the royal
circle at first hand. Other details of Richer's background are lacking. We
do not know when he was born, nor do we know much about his education, except that it seems to have included the study of medicine and
other sciences, a facet of his training that is evident in many of the autobiographical passages of the *History.* We do know, too, that Richer was
a monk connected to the abbey of St. Remy at Reims. It is conjectured
that he entered the monastery around 965 (though hardly on conclusive
evidence). We know that he lived to at least the year 998, as that is the
last year mentioned in the *History.* And it is logical to surmise that Richer
died soon after 998, as the *History* remains unfinished, stopping abruptly
in this year.

The *Historiarum libri quatuor* has been edited by, among others,

G. Pertz (*Richeri Historiarum Libri IIII,* Hanover, 1839), G. Waitz (*Richeri Historiarum Libri IIII,* Hanover, 1877), and R. Latouche (*Richer, Histoire de France (888–995),* Paris, 1930). Latouche's text is reprinted with some minor spelling changes.

VERDUN IN THE TENTH CENTURY

VIRDUNI EXPUGNATIO. Quae civitas eo situ posita est ut a fronte planitie pervia meantibus accessum praebeat, a tergo inacessibilis sit; ibi enim a summo in posteriora, profundo hiatu circumquaque distenditur. Ab inferioribus vero ad summum rupibus praeruptis artatur. Quae non
5 solum scatens fontibus puteisque, incolis accommoda, sed et fluvio Mosa eam a praerupta parte abluente nemorosa. Ubi ergo a fronte planitiem praefert, pugnaturi machinas bellicas generis diversi aptavere. Nec minus qui in urbe erant, ad resistendum sese expediebant. Pugnatum est tandem VIII ferme continuis diebus. At cives cum viderent nulla a suis extrinsecus
10 suffragia mitti, nec iugis praelii pondus se tolerare posse, consilio inito, indempnes et intacti hostibus cessere; urbem aperuerunt et sese Lothario victi obtulerunt.

Quibus peractis, rex ad urbem tuendam reginam Emmam in ea reliquit. Ipse cum exercitu Laudunum rediit, suos etiam ad sua redire per-
15 misit; tantae benivolentiae favore apud eos usus ut repetito itinere se ulterius ituros, si iuberet, pollicerentur et, neglectis pro tempore domibus et natis, cum hoste comminus dimicaturos. Lotharius interea apud suos deliberabat utrum potius foret sese ulterius ire, armisque et viribus totam Belgicam sibi subiugare, an residendo Virduni, per legatos habitis sua-
20 sionibus, mores hostium ad suum animum informare. Si enim eos ferro vinceret, cum id sine multo sanguine fieri non posset, cogitabat in posterum minus eis credendum, eo quod amicorum labem eis intulerit. Si vero per benivolentiam reversuros expectaret, cavendum putabat ne in tanta otio hostes insolentiores redderentur.

1. **VIRDUNI:** from *Virdunum, i* = Verdun (Sleumer 824). 4. **praeruptis:** from *praerumpere,* "broken." **non solum . . . sed:** coordinating conjunctions. 5. **Mosa:** from *Mosa, ae,* masculine noun = the river Meuse (Sleumer 530). 7. **pugnaturi:** the subject of *aptavere.* **aptavere:** alternate perfect active indicative, third person plural of *aptare* = *aptaverunt.* 9. **ferme:** sometimes spelled *fere* = adverb. 10. **suffragia:** i.e., *auxilium.* **praelii:** alternate spelling for *proelii.* **inito:** perfect passive participle of *inire,* in ablative absolute construction. 11. **indempnes** = CL *indemnes.* **Lothario:** Lothar, King of France (954–986), son of Louis IV. 14. **Laudunum:** the better spelling is *Laudanum, i* = Laon (Sleumer 465). 18. **foret** = *esset;* the substitution of *fore* for *esse* is common in ML. 21. **in posterum:** "in the future." 22. **eo quod:** "because." 23. **reversuros:** future active participle of *revertere.* **cavendum:** gerund of *cavere* = "caution."

VIRDUNI INVASIO A BELGIS. Dum haec multa consultatione venti-
laret, Belgicae dux Teodericus, necnon et vir nobilis ac strenuus Godefridus, Sigefridus quoque vir illustris, Bardo etiam et Gozilo fratres claris-
simi et nominatissimi, aliique principes nonnulli latenter pertemptant
Virdunum irrumpere, eamque ab Gallis evacuare; factisque insidiis, nego-   5
tiatorum claustrum, muro instar oppidi extructum, ab urbe quidem Mosa
interfluente seiunctum, sed pontibus duobus interstratis ei annexum, cum
electis militum copiis ingressi sunt.

Annonam omnem circumquaque milites palantes advectare fecerunt.
Negotiatorum quoque victus in usum bellicum acceperunt. Lignorum   10
trabes ex Argonna aggregari iusserunt, ut, si ab hostibus extra machinae
muris applicarentur, ipsi quoque interius obnitentibus machinis obstare
molirentur. Crates quoque viminibus et arborum frondibus validas intex-
uerunt, machinis erectis, si res exposceret, supersternendos, sudes ferro
acuminatos et igne subustos ad hostes transfodiendos quamplures aptav-   15
erunt; missilia varii generis per fabros expedire; funium millena volumina ad usus diversos convexerunt; clipeos quoque habendae testudini ordinandos instituerunt. Preterea centena mortis tormenta non defuere.

— *Hist.* 3.101–3.

1. **BELGIS:** from *Belgae, arum,* Belgium (Sleumer 152).   2. **Belgicae:** from *Belgicus,
a, um* = Belgians (Sleumer 153).   **Teodericus:** Thierry I, Duke of Haute-Lorraine.
Godefridus: Godfrey, Count of Verdun.   3. **Sigefridus:** Sigfried, Count of Luxem-
bourg.   **Bardo . . . Gozilo:** both were counts and nephews of Godfrey, Count of Verdun.   6. **extructum** = CL *exstructum,* from *exstruere.*   9. **advectare fecerunt:** lit.
"made to carry," i.e., "conveyed," an example of the use of *facere* as a helping verb,
common in ML.   10. **negotiatorum:** "sellers."   **victus:** i.e., "provisions."   11. **ex
Argonna:** *Argonna, ae,* "from the Argonne forest."   **machinae:** Richer means something like "devices" to be used to scale the walls of the city.   12. **applicarentur** +
dative object = "to apply something to. . . ."   **obnitentibus machinis:** lit., "opposing
devices," i.e., devices that will do the same sort of thing from *interius,* inside the city
walls, in order to repel the invaders.   **obstare:** complement of *molirentur,* with a dative
object = "oppose with. . . ."   14. **supersternendos:** from *supersternere,* modifying
crates validas, "that could be covered over," *si res exposceret.*   15. **quamplures** = CL
quam plurimos, adverbial phrase modifying *hostes.*   16. **expedire:** alternate perfect
active indicative, third person plural = *expedierunt.*   **millena:** *milleni, ae, a,* "thousand."   17. **clipeos . . . ordinandos:** the thought here is difficult but means something
like: "shields [*clipeos*] that had to be arranged [*ordinandos*] for the besiegers [*testudini*] who needed to have them [*habendae*]." *Testudo* has as a military meaning the
covering besiegers use to advance while remaining protected (LS 1864, s. v. *testudo* II
3 a & b).   18. **preterea** = CL *praeterea.*   **defuere:** alternate perfect active indicative,
third person plural = *defuerunt.*

A HARD JOURNEY IN PURSUIT OF LEARNING

DE DIFFICULTATE SUI ITINERIS AB URBE REMORUM CARNO-
TUM. Ante horum captionem, diebus ferme XIIII, cum aviditate discendi
logicam Yppocratis Choi de studiis liberalibus saepe et multum cogi-
tarem, quadam die equitem Carnotinum in urbe Remorum positus of-
5 fendi. Qui a me interrogatus, quis et cuius esset, cur et unde venisset,
Heribrandi clerici Carnotensis legatum sese et Richero sancti Remigii mo-
nacho se velle loqui respondit. Ego mox, amici nomen et legationis causam advertens, me quem querebat indicavi, datoque osculo semotim sec-
essimus. Ille mox epistolam protulit hortatoriam ad *Aphorismorum*
10 lectionem. Unde et ergo admodum laetatus, assumpto quodam puero
cum Carnotino equite, iter Carnotum arripere disposui.

Digressus autem ab a[bbate] m[eo] unius tantum parvaredi solatium
accepi. Nummis etiam, mutatoriis, ceterisque necessariis vacuus, Orbatium perveni, locum multa caritate inclitum, ibique domni abbatis D. col-
15 loquio recreatus, simulque et munificentia sustentatus, in crastino iter usque Meldim peragendum arripui. Ingressus vero cum duobus comitibus
lucorum anfractus, non defuere infortunii casus. Nam fallentibus biviis,
sex leugarum superfluitate exorbitavimus. Transmisso vero Teodorici
castello, parvaredus ante visus bucephalus fieri coepit asello tardiusculus.

1. **REMORUM:** *Remi, orum,* Reims; as this line suggests, this chapter of the *History* relates a journey made by Richer himself (*sui itineris*) from Reims to Chartres.   **CAR-NOTUM:** (also *Carnuntum* or *Carnutum, i*), Chartres (the orthography is various; cf. Sleumer 190 for the diversity of forms).   2. **ante . . . XIIII:** "approximately 14 days before their capture . . ."; *horum captionem* refers to the capture of Charles of Lorraine and Archbishop Arnulf of Reims by Adalberon.   3. **Yppocratis Choi:** i.e., Hippocrates of Cos; in the genitive case.   4. **equitem Carnotinum:** (*Carnotinus, a, um*) "a Chartrian horseman."   6. **legatum:** supply *esse.*   8. **querebat** = CL *quaerebat.* **semotim:** "to the side" (Blaise/Chirat 751; Latham 432).   9. **hortatoriam:** *hortatorius, a, um,* "encouraging" (cf. Blaise/Chirat 394, s. v. *hortatorius*). *Aphorismorum:* i.e., *Aphorismi,* the sayings of Hippocrates, his most celebrated work.   12. **parvaredi** = CL *paraveredi,* "saddle horse." **solatium** = CL *solacium,* modified by *tantum.* 13. **mutatoriis:** *mutatorius, a, um* in the neuter = "change of clothes." **vacuus** + ablative = "lacking. . . ." **Orbatium:** i.e., Orbais.   14. **domni:** by syncope for CL *domini.* **abbatis:** *abbas, atis,* "abbot" (Sleumer 64).   **D.:** standing for the name of an abbot, otherwise unknown (cf. Latouche 227, n. 2).   16. **Meldim:** accusative form for the city of Meaux; the orthography attending to this city is various (see Sleumer 513, for the diversity of forms).   18. **leugarum** = CL *leuca, ae,* "league," a unit of measurement.   **exorbitavimus:** from *exorbitare,* "we wandered off the beaten track." **Teodorici castello:** i.e., Château-Thierry.   19. **bucephalus:** by metonymy for *equus;* Bucephalus was the name of the famous horse belonging to Alexander the Great.

Iam sol a mesembrino discesserat, totoque aere in pluvias dissoluto, in occasum vergebat, cum fortis ille bucefalus supremo labore victus inter femora insidentis pueri deficiens corruit et, velut fulgure traiectus, VI^to miliario ab urbe exspiravit. Quanta tunc fuit perturbatio, quanta anxietas, illi perpendere valent qui casus similes aliquando perpessi sunt et ex 5 similibus similia colligant. Puer inexpertus tanti itineris difficultatem fessus toto corpore equo amisso iacebat. Impedimenta sine vectore aderant. Imbres nimia infusione ruebant; caelum nubila praetendebat; sol iam in occasu minabatur tenebras.

Inter haec omnia dubitanti consilium a Deo non defuit. Puerum 10 namque cum impedimentis ibi reliqui; dictatoque ei quid interrogatus a transeuntibus responderet, et ut somno imminenti resisteret, solo equite Carnotino comitatus, Meldim perveni. Pontem quoque vix de luce videns ingredior; et dum diligentius contemplarer, novis iterum infortuniis angebar. Tantis enim et tot hiatibus patebat ut vix civium necessarii die 15 eadem per eum transierint. Carnotinus inpiger et in peragendo itinere satis providus, naviculam circumquaque inquirens et nullam inveniens, ad pontis pericula rediit et ut equi incolumes transmitterentur e caelo emeruit. Nam in locis hiantibus equorum pedibus aliquando clipeum subdens, aliquando tabulas abiectas adiungens, modo incurvatus, modo erectus, 20 modo accedens, modo recurrens, efficaciter cum equis me comitante pertransiit.

Nox inhorruerat mundumque tetra caligine obduxerat, cum basilicam sancti Pharonis introii, fratribus adhuc parantibus potum caritatis. Qua die sollempniter pranserant, recitato cap[itulo] de cellarario mon- 25 asterii, quod fuit causa tam serae potationis. A quibus ut frater exceptus, dulcibus alloquiis, cibisque sufficientibus recreatus sum. Carnotinum

---

1. **mesembrino:** from *mesembrinos, i,* from the Greek μεσημβρίνος, "midday" (Blaise/ Chirat 528; Latham 297).   3. **fulgure** = CL *fulgore.*   **VI^to:** i.e., *sexto;* read with *miliario.*   4. **miliario:** from *miliarium,* lit., the milestone marking the distances from ancient cities, i.e., "miles."   6. **inexpertus:** has the force of a participle in predicate adjective construction, with *difficultatem* its object: "the boy, who had not experienced the difficulty of so trying a journey. . . ."   11. **quid:** object of *responderet.*   **interrogatus:** modifies *puer,* the understood subject of *responderet,* and governs the prepositional phrase *a transeuntibus.*   13. **comitatus:** perfect passive participle with *solo . . . Carnotino* in ablative of accompaniment.   **vix de luce:** lit., "scarcely from the light," i.e., "for the poor light."   16. **inpiger** = CL *impiger.*   23. **tetra** = CL *taetra.* 24. **sancti Pharonis:** Saint Faron. (Latouche 229).   25. **sollempniter** = CL *sollemniter;* the addition of a parasitic consonant is common in ML.   **pranserant** = CL *pranderant,* perfect active indicative, third person plural of *prandere,* "to eat breakfast."   **capitulo:** i.e., the rules of the monastery.   **cellarario:** *cellararium, i,* "steward."

equitem cum equis vitata pontis pericula iterum attemptaturum puero
relicto remisi. Arte praemissa pertransiit et ad puerum secunda noctis vigilia errabundus pervenit; vixque eum saepius inclamatum repperit. Quo
assumpto cum ad urbem devenisset, suspectus pontis pericula, quae per-
5 nitiosa experimento didicerat, cum puero et equis in cuiusdam tugurium
declinavit; ibique per totam diem incibati, nocte illa ad quiescendum, non
ad cenandum collecti sunt.

    Quam noctem ut insomnem duxerim, et quanto in ea cruciatu tortus
sim, perpendere possunt qui cura carorum aliquando vigilasse coacti
10 sunt. Post vero optata luce reddita, nimia esurie confecti, maturius affuerunt. Eis etiam cibi illati; annona quoque cum paleis equis anteposita est.
Dimittensque abbati Aug[ustino] puerum peditem, solo Carnotino comitatus Carnotum raptim deveni. Unde mox equis remissis, ab urbe Melde-
nsi puerum revocavi.

15   Quo reducto et omni sollicitudine amota, in *Aphorismis* Yppocratis
vigilanter studui apud domnum Herbrandum, magnae liberalitatis atque
scientiae virum. In quibus cum tantum prognostica morborum accepissem, et simplex egritudinum cognitio cupienti non sufficeret, petii etiam
ab eo lectionem eius libri, qui inscribitur *De Concordia Yppocratis, Ga-*
20 *lieni et Surani.* Quod et obtinui, cum eum in arte peritissimum, dinamidia
farmaceutica, butanica atque cirurgica non laterent.

— Hist. 4.50.

2. **arte praemissa:** "by the way previously described"; Richer has sent the Chartrian
horseman back to the boy they left behind, and he refers here to the unique way in
which he and the horseman had been able to cross the bridge in order to get to St.
Faron in the first place. 4. **pernitiosa** = CL *pernicioso.* 6. **incibati:** *incibatus, a,*
um, "without food." 9. **vigilasse:** syncopated perfect active infinitive of *vigilare* =
vigilavisse. 10. **esurie:** *esuries, ei,* "hunger." 11. **illati:** perfect passive participle of
inferre. 15. **amota:** perfect passive participle of *amovere.* 16. **domnum:** by syncope for *dominum.* **Herbrandum:** Heribrand, otherwise unknown. 18. **egritudi-**
num = CL *aegritudinum.* 20. **dinamidia:** *dynamidia, orum,* lit., "efficacy" (Blaise/
Chirat 296), i.e., "cures." 21. **farmaceutica** = CL *pharmaceuticus, a, um,* from the
Greek φαρμακευτικός, "pharmeceutical." **butanica** = CL *botanicum, a, um,* from
the Greek βοτανικόν, "botanical." **cirurgica** = CL *chirurgica,* from the Greek χειρο-
υργικός, "of surgery."

PLATE 14. A folio from a late medieval breviary, showing the liturgical calendar.

PLATE 14

Breviary, Latin manuscript on parchment, sixteenth century, fol. 7 verso
John Hay Library, Brown University

The breviary (from the Latin *breviarium*) is rooted in the Old Testament, with its fixed hours of prayer and ritual, but in its medieval context it arises with the rule of Saint Benedict in the sixth century. Benedict, whose simple ordering of monastic life was to prove so influential to the Latin Middle Ages, called for communal prayer and devotion at set times during the day and night (see plate 6 for a full discussion). In time, a canon of prayer arose—including psalms, canticles, quotations and hymns from the fathers, lives of the saints, and prayers and devotionals of other kinds—which was anthologized into the Latin breviary. Eventually, the breviary itself was more formally organized around the seasons of the liturgical year, with set groupings of prayers for liturgical observances, veneration of the Virgin, daily devotion, and other specialized occurrences. Since they were collections specific to the liturgical calendar, therefore, breviaries often included formal calendars, as the plate here shows.

The breviary from which this folio comes is from the late Middle Ages and is in excellent shape. It is bound in wood boards covered with stamped calfskin and retains its brass clasps. The pages have been marked with knots to allow easy reference to specific parts of the collection. It is written in Gothic script in black ink, with red used to highlight certain days and observances, and is of German origin.

351

HROTSVITA OF GANDERSHEIM

Dulcitius

(*Passio Sanctarum Virginum Agapis Chioniae et Hirenae; c. 960*)

A s Western Europe reconfigured itself in fundamental ways after the
breakup of the Carolingian empire—no less in artistic than in political,
economic, or social terms—vibrant literary cultures appeared at the
courts of Charlemagne's successors, especially Otto I and his sons. In the
rush of literary activity attending to the patronage of this powerful and
learned king (whose influence touched Liutprand and Widukind also),
Hrotsvita is perhaps the most significant figure. Not much can be told of
Hrotsvita's life apart from what she tells us in her writings. We know
with certainty that she was born between 912 and 940 (this from evidence internal to her collection) and that she died some time after 973.
She was associated with the abbey of Gandersheim for all her productive
life, and that association tells us that she was of noble birth (as all the
inhabitants of this abbey were). She may have studied at the court of Otto
I, although it is certain that she was educated at Gandersheim under the
watchful (and influential) eye of Gerberga, its abbess, who also happened
to be a niece of Otto I. Hrotsvita, in any case, was clearly an intimate of
the goings-on at the court, whose patronage in a variety of ways both
direct and indirect influenced her own substantial output.

Hrotsvita is best remembered for her dramatic work. Easy to forget
is the relative isolation in which she produced these dramas, for she had
no models ready to hand to which she could turn for guidance or inspiration. To be sure, there were the remote Senecan tragedies, written nearly
a millennium earlier, but not even Seneca's contemporaries had known
quite what to do with these bleak and exotic pieces (if they were available
to Hrotsvita at all). Less remote in terms of tone and topic were Terence's
comedies, to which Hrotsvita did turn for precedent, but these masterpieces of Latin comedy can hardly have offered much assistance. They
preceded Seneca, after all, by some two centuries and told the stories—
written in a fast-paced VL—of lowlifes, slaves, and compromising situations. More ominously, no substantial tradition of Christian drama existed (see pp. 366–76 on Medieval Latin drama). That she revivified an
abandoned genre and placed it on surer footing would be enough to en-

sure her reputation and secure her place in the development of the Medieval Latin literary tradition.

She did not confine herself exclusively to drama, however, choosing to work in hagiography and epic also. Her hagiographic output, collectively called *The Legends,* consists of eight poems devoted to the lives of Christian martyrs, all written in hexameters save the concluding elegiac piece. Her epics, also written in hexameters, are more worldly. The *Poem on the Deeds of the Emperor Otto* is an account of the reign of Otto I, while the *Beginnings of the Abbey of Gandersheim* is a history of Hrotsvita's own abbey down to the year 919.

But it is to the dramas, one of which is excerpted here, that students of Medieval Latin return consistently. They do so because Hrotsvita's dramas offer such rich variety: quick-paced dialogue, gesture, and performance; the tensions of comedy and the affect of tragedy; simple, direct plots. Well versed in the metrical traditions of Roman comedy, Hrotsvita nonetheless put to the side the poetic qualities of ancient drama, choosing rhythmic prose instead. So, too, is there a consistency of presentation in Hrotsvita's dramas: the crisp, efficient Latin of her dialogues, beholden to classical rhetorical norms best learned in Terence, animates a system of core beliefs that flow naturally from Christianity but also, and perhaps more importantly, from the discrete situations Hrotsvita recreates for her readers and listeners.

The works of Hrotsvita have been edited by P. von Winterfeld (*Hrotsvithae Opera,* Berlin, 1902), K. Strecker (*Hrotsvithae Opera,* Leipzig, 1930), H. Homeyer (*Hrotsvithae Opera,* Munich, 1970), and F. Bertini and P. Dronke (*Rosvita Dialoghi Drammatici,* Milan, 1986; with facing Latin and Italian translation and some grammatical notes). P. Pascal has written a commentary and Latin edition of the *Dulcitius* alone (*Hrotsvitha: Dulcitius and Paphnutius,* Bryn Mawr, 1985). Many translations exist, most recently by L. Bonfante (*The Plays of Hrotsvitha of Gandersheim,* New York, 1979) and K. Wilson (*The Plays of Hrotsvit of Gandersheim,* New York, 1989), whose introduction is especially excellent on matters of Hrotsvita's Latinity. P. Dronke has written a useful introduction to Hrotsvita (*Women Writers of the Middle Ages: A Study of Texts from Perpetua (203) to Marguerite Porete (1310),* Cambridge, 1984, pp. 55–83, 293–97). Raby 1, 208ff., discusses Hrotsvita in some detail.

Perhaps the most famous of her plays, the *Dulcitius,* as it is commonly known, excerpted here, is a dramatization of the martyrdom of three sisters who lived during the persecution of Diocletian (the last to be waged against the Christians, late in the third century and early in the fourth, and probably the most vicious) and who were murdered in Thessalonica in 290. It is a serious drama, though not a tragedy in the classical sense, but there are moments of comedy, too. The text of Bertini and Dronke is reprinted without change.

Dulcitius

Passio Sanctarum Virginum
Agapis Chioniae et Hirenae

quas sub nocturno silentio Dulcitius praeses clam adiit, cupiens earum amplexibus saturari; sed mox ut itravit, mente captus ollas et sartagines pro virginibus amplectendo osculabatur, donec facies et vestes horribili nigredine inficiebantur. Deinde Sisinnio comiti ius super puniendas vir-
5 gines cessit; qui, etiam miris modis illusus, tandem AG. et CHION. concremari et HIR. iussit perfodi.

Diocletianus, Agapes, Chionia, Hirena, Dulcitius, Milites

I

DIOCLETIANUS. Parentelae claritas ingenuitatis vestrumque serenitas pulchritudinis exigit, vos nuptiali lege primis in palatio copulari, quod nostri iussio annuerit fieri si Christum negare nostrisque diis sacrificia
10 velitis ferre.

AGAPES. Esto securus curarum, nec te gravet nostrum praeparatio nuptiarum, quia nec ad negationem confitendi nominis, nec ad corruptionem integritatis ullis rebus compelli poterimus.

DIOCLETIANUS. Quid sibi vult ista, quae vos agitat, fatuitas?
15 AGAPES. Quod signum fatuitatis nobis inesse deprehendis?

DIOCLETIANUS. Evidens magnumque.

AGAPES. In quo?

DIOCLETIANUS. In hoc praecipue, quod, relicta vetustae observantia religionis, inutilem christianae novitatem sequimini superstitionis.
20 AGAPES. Temere calumpniaris statum dei omnipotentis. Periculum.

---

4. **nigredine:** from *nigredo, inis* = "blackness." 7. **parentelae:** *parentela, ae,* lit., "relationship," with the sense that the reference is specifically to "parents." 8. **primis:** i.e., "to one of the nobles." 9. **iussio:** from *iussio, onis,* "order," "command." 14. **fatuitas:** in CL = "folly," "silliness," but here with the sense of "madness." 20. **temere:** adverb. **calumpniaris** = CL *calumniaris,* from *calumniari;* the insertion of "p" between "m" and "n" is a scribal expedient used to make it easier to read

DIOCLETIANUS. Cuius?

AGAPES. Tui reique publicae, quam gubernas.

DIOCLETIANUS. Ista insanit; amoveatur!

CHIONIA. Mea germana non insanit, sed tui stultitiam iuste reprehendit.

DIOCLETIANUS. Ista inclementius bachatur; unde nostris conspectibus ae- 5
que subtrahatur, et tertia discutiatur.

HIRENA. Tertiam rebellem tibique penitus probabis renitentem.

DIOCLETIANUS. Hirena, cum sis minor aetate, fito maior dignitate.

HIRENA. Ostende, quaeso, quo pacto!

DIOCLETIANUS. Flecte cervicem diis et esto sororibus exemplum correc- 10
tionis et causa liberationis.

HIRENA. Conquiniscant idolis, qui velint incurrere iram celsitonantis! Ego
quidem caput regali unguento delibutum non dehonestabo pedibus
simulachrorum submittendo.

DIOCLETIANUS. Cultura deorum non adducit inhonestatem, sed praeci- 15
puum honorem.

HIRENA. Et quae inhonestas turpior, quae turpitudo maior, quam ut servus veneretur ut dominus?

DIOCLETIANUS. Non suadeo tibi venerari servos, sed dominos princi-
pumque deos. 20

HIRENA. Nonne is est cuiusvis servus, qui ab artifice pretio comparatur
ut empticius?

DIOCLETIANUS. Huius praesumptio verbositatis tollenda est suppliciis.

HIRENA. Hoc optamus, hoc amplectimur, ut pro Christi amore suppliciis
laceremur. 25

DIOCLETIANUS. Istae contumaces nostrisque decretis contraluctantes catenis inretiantur et ad examen Dulcitii praesidis sub carcerali squalore serventur.

"mn"; it is pronounced like "nn." (Bertini/Dronke 86, n. I 3). **Periculum:** aposiopesis,
a common feature of Hrotsvita's Latin; supply *est*. 6. **discutiatur:** from *discutere;* the
sense in ML is "to discuss," "to question," "to examine" (LS 590). 8. **fito:** future
active imperative singular of *fieri*. 9. **quo pacto:** idiomatic = "how," modifying *ostende*. 10. **esto:** future active imperative singular of *sum*. 12. **conquiniscant:** from
conquiniscere, "to cower," to "bow down." **celsitonantis:** *celsitonans, antis* = *Deus*.
19. **suadeo** + dative object = "to urge." 21. **cuiusvis:** from *quivis*. 22. **empticius:**
empticius, a, um = "bought," "purchased." 26. **contraluctantes** = *contra* + *luctans,
luctantis*, i.e., "resisting with much force." The word is not found in CL. 27. **inretiantur** = CL *irretiantur*, "let them be ensnared. . . ." **praesidis:** *praeses, idis*, with *Dulcitii*, "Governor Dulcitius." **carcerali:** from *carceralis*, modifying *squalore*.

I I

DULCITIUS. Producite, milites, producite, quas tenetis in carcere!

MILITES. Ecce, quas vocasti.

DULCITIUS. Papae! quam pulchrae, quam venustae, quam egregiae puellulae!

5 MILITES. Perfectae decore.

DULCITIUS. Captus sum illarum specie.

MILITES. Credibile.

DULCITIUS. Exaestuo illas ad mei amorem trahere.

MILITES. Diffidimus te praevalere.

10 DULCITIUS. Quare?

MILITES. Quia stabiles fide.

DULCITIUS. Quid, si suadeam blandimentis?

MILITES. Contempnunt.

DULCITIUS. Quid, si terream suppliciis?

15 MILITES. Parvi pendunt.

DULCITIUS. Et quid fiet?

MILITES. Praecogita.

DULCITIUS. Ponite illas in custodiam in interiorem officinae aedem, in cuius proaulio ministrorum servantur vasa.

20 MILITES. Ut quid eo loci?

DULCITIUS. Quo a me saepiuscule possint visitari.

MILITES. Ut iubes.

I I I

DULCITIUS. Quid agant captivae sub hoc noctis tempore?

MILITES. Vacant hymnis.

25 DULCITIUS. Accedamus propius.

MILITES. Tinnulae sonitum vocis a longe audiemus.

DULCITIUS. Observate pro foribus cum lucernis, ego autem intrabo et vel optatis amplexibus me saturabo.

MILITES. Intra, praestolabimur.

---

2. **vocasti:** contracted perfect active indicative, second person singular of *vocare* = *vocavisti.* 3. **puellulae:** diminutive of *puella.* 13. **contempnunt** = CL *contemnunt.* 15. **parvi pendunt:** "they don't care." 19. **proaulio:** from *proaulium, i* (neuter neologism from the Greek προαυλή) = "vestibule" (Niermeyer 853). 20. **ut quid:** "why?" 21. **saepiuscule** = CL *saepicule,* "very often." 26. **a longe:** the use of the preposition with an adverb is a feature common to VL and ML. 27. **foribus:** *foris, is,* "doors."

IV

AGAPES. Quid strepat pro foribus?

HIRENA. Infelix Dulcitius. Ingreditur.

CHIONIA. Deus nos tueatur!

AGAPES. Amen.

CHIONIA. Quid sibi vult collisio ollarum, caccaborum et sartaginum? 5

HIRENA. Lustrabo. Accedite, quaeso, per rimulas perspicite!

AGAPES. Quid est?

HIRENA. Ecce, iste stultus, mente alienatus, aestimat se nostris uti amplexibus.

AGAPES. Quid facit? 10

HIRENA. Nunc ollas molli fovet gremio, nunc sartagines et caccabos amplectitur, mitia libans oscula.

CHIONIA. Ridiculum.

HIRENA. Nam facies, manus ac vestimenta adeo sordidata, adeo coinquinata, ut nigredo, quae inhaesit, similitudinem Aethiopis exprimit. 15

AGAPES. Decet, ut talis appareat corpore, qualis a diabolo possidetur in mente.

HIRENA. En, parat egredi. Intendamus, quid illo egrediente agant milites pro foribus expectantes.

V

MILITES. Quis hic egreditur? Daemoniacus. Vel magis ipse diabolus. Fugiamus! 20

DULCITIUS. Milites, quo fugitis? state, expectate; ducite me cum lucernis ad cubile.

MILITES. Vox senioris nostri, sed imago diaboli. Non subsistamus, sed fugam maturemus: fantasma vult nos pessumdare. 25

DULCITIUS. Ad palatium ibo et, quam abiectionem patiar, principibus vulgabo.

VI

DULCITIUS. Hostiarii, introducite me in palatium, quia ad imperatorem habeo secretum.

---

5. **caccaborum** = CL *cacaborum,* "cooking pots." 6. **rimulas:** the diminutive of *rima, ae,* "cracks." 14. **coinquinata:** from *coinquinare,* "infected." 20. **daemoniacus:** this word, as a masculine substantive, means "one who is possessed by the devil" (LS 510); it comes to ML from the Greek, δαιμονιακός, through EL. 25. **fantasma** = CL *phantasma,* "apparition." **pessumdare** = CL *pessum dare*: "to bring to ruin," "to kill."

OSTIARII. Quid hoc vile ac detestabile monstrum, scissis et nigellis pan-
niculis obsitum? Pugnis tundamus, de gradu praecipitemus, nec ultra
huc detur liber accessus.

DULCITIUS. Vae, vae! quid contigit? Nonne splendidissimis vestibus indu-
5   tus totoque corpore videor nitidus? et quicumque me aspicit, velut
horribile monstrum fastidit! Ad coniugem revertar, quo ab illa, quid
erga me actum sit, experiar. En, solutis crinibus egreditur, omnisque
domus lacrimis prosequitur!

VII

CONIUX. Heu, heu! mi senior Dulciti, quid pateris? Non es sanae mentis.
10   Factus es in derisum christicolis.

DULCITIUS. Nunc tandem sentio, me illusum illarum maleficiis.

CONIUX. Hoc me vehementer confudit, hoc praecipue contristavit, quod,
quid patiebaris, ignorasti.

DULCITIUS. Mando, ut lascivae praesententur puellae et abstractis vesti-
15   bus publice denudentur, quo versa vice, quid nostra possint ludibria,
experiantur.

VIII

MILITES. Frustra sudamus, in vanum laboramus: ecce, vestimenta vir-
gineis corporibus inhaerent velut coria; sed et ipse, qui nos ad expoli-
andum urgebat, praeses stertit sedendo nec ullatenus excitari potest a
20   somno. Ad imperatorem adeamus ipsique res, quae geruntur, propalemus.

IX

DIOCLETIANUS. Dolet nimium, quod praesidem Dulcitium audio adeo illusum, adeo exprobratum, adeo calumniatum. Sed, ne viles mulierculae iactent se impune nostris diis deorumque cultoribus illudere, Sisin-
25   nium comitem dirigam ad ultionem exercendam.

---

1. **Ostiarii:** *Hostiarii.*   2. **obsitum:** from *obserere*, modifying *monstrum*.   7. **egreditur:** the subject is *coniunx*.   10. **christicolis:** from *christicola, ae,* masculine noun of
the first declension = "Christians," here in ablative of means (Blaise/Chirat 149).
13. **ignorasti** = contracted perfect active indicative, second person singular of *ignorare* = *ignoravisti*, with *quid patiebaris* its object.   15. **versa vice:** lit., "with fortune
reversed."   20. **propalemus:** from *propalare*, "to disclose," "to report" (Sleumer
639).   22. **quod . . . audio:** *quod* = CL *cum* in temporal construction, dependent on
dolet: "it grieves me very much when I hear that. . . ."

X

SISINNIUS. O milites, ubi sunt lascivae, quae torqueri debent, puellae?

MILITES. Affliguntur in carcere.

SISINNIUS. Hirenam reservate et reliquas producite.

MILITES. Cur unam excipis?

SISINNIUS. Parcens infantiae. Forte facilius convertetur, si sororum prae-   5
sentia non terrebitur.

MILITES. Ita.

XI

MILITES.   Praesto sunt, quas iussisti.

SISINNIUS. Praebete assensum, Agapes et Chionia, meis consiliis.

AGAPES. Si praebebimus.   10

SISINNIUS. Ferte libamina diis.

CHIONIA. Vero et aeterno patri eiusque coaeterno filio sanctoque amborum paraclyto sacrificium laudis sine intermissione libamus.

SISINNIUS. Hoc vobis non suadeo, sed poenis prohibeo.

AGAPES. Non prohibebis, nec umquam sacrificabimus daemoniis.   15

SISINNIUS. Deponite duritiam cordis et sacrificate. Sin autem: faciam vos
interfectum iri iuxta praeceptum imperatoris Diocletiani.

CHIONIA. Decet, ut in nostri necem obtemperes iussis tui imperatoris, cuius nos decreta contempnere noscis; si autem parcendo moram feceris,
aequum est, ut tu interficiaris.   20

SISINNIUS. Non tardetis, milites, non tardetis; capite blasphemas has et in
ignem proicite vivas!

MILITES. Instemus construendis rogis et tradamus illas bachantibus
flammis, quo finem demus conviciis.

AGAPES. Non tibi, domine, non tibi haec potentia insolita, ut ignis vim   25
virtutis suae obliviscatur, tibi obtemperando. Sed taedet nos mora-
rum; ideo rogamus solvi retinacula animarum, quo extinctis corporibus tecum plaudant in aethere nostri spiritus.

MILITES. O novum, o stupendum miraculum! Ecce, animae egressae sunt

---

11. **libamina:** from *libamen, libaminis.*   13. **paraclyto:** *paraclytus, i,* from the Greek
παράκλητός = "the Holy Spirit" (Bertini/Dronke 98, n. XI 1).   17. **interfectum iri:**
future passive infinitive of *interficere,* read with *faciam vos.*   18. **iussis:** dative plural
object of *obtemperes.*   21. **blasphemas:** from *blasphemus, a, um,* on the Greek word
βλασφημός, standing as a substantive for "blasphemers."   26. **taedet** + accusative of
person and genitive of cause = "we are tired of delay."   28. **aethre** = CL *aethere,*
from *aether, eris,* "heaven."   29. **egressae sunt:** from *egredi.*

corpora, et nulla laesionis repperiuntur vestigia, sed nec capilli, nec
vestimenta ab igne sunt ambusta, quo minus corpora.

SISINNIUS. Proferte Hirenam.

XII

MILITES. Eccam.

5 SISINNIUS. Pertimesce, Hirena, necem sororum et cave perire exemplo illarum.

HIRENA. Opto exemplum earum moriendo sequi, quo merear cum eis ae-
ternaliter laetari.

SISINNIUS. Cede, cede meae suasioni.

10 HIRENA. Haut cedam facinus suadenti.

SISINNIUS. Si non cesseris, non citum tibi praestabo exitum, sed differam
et nova in dies supplicia multiplicabo.

HIRENA. Quanto acrius torqueor, tanto gloriosius exaltabor.

SISINNIUS. Supplicia non metuis? Admovebo, quod horrescis.

15 HIRENA. Quicquid irrogabis adversi, evadam iuvamine Christi.

SISINNIUS. Faciam te ad lupanar duci corpusque tuum turpiter coin-
quinari.

HIRENA. Melius est, ut corpus quibuscumque iniuriis maculetur, quam
anima idolis polluatur.

20 SISINNIUS. Si socia eris meretricum, non poteris polluta ultra intra contu-
bernium computari virginum.

HIRENA. Voluptas parit poenam, necessitas autem coronam; nec dicitur
reatus, nisi quod consentit animus.

SISINNIUS. Frustra parcebam, frustra miserebar huius infantiae.

25 MILITES. Praescivimus; nullatenus ad deorum culturam potest flecti, nec
terrore umquam potest frangi.

SISINNIUS. Non ultra parcam.

MILITES. Rectum.

SISINNIUS. Capite illam sine miseratione et, trahentes cum crudelitate,
30 ducite ad lupanar sine honore.

HIRENA. Non perducent.

SISINNIUS. Quis prohibere poterit?

---

4. **eccam** = *ecce* + *eam*, lit., "behold her," i.e., "here she is"; the usage is probably
owed to Hrotsvita's reading of Terence (Bertini/Dronke 102 XII 1).   13. **quanto** . . .
tanto: coordinating conjunctions = "the . . . the. . . ."   15. **iuvamine**: from *iuvamen,*
inis, "aid."   23. **reatus**: *reatus, us,* fourth declension masculine noun = "offense."
24. **miserebar**: *miserere* takes the genitive of the object of pity.

HIRENA. Qui mundum sui providentia regit.

SISINNIUS. Probabo.

HIRENA. Ac citius libito.

SISINNIUS. Ne terreamini, milites, fallacibus huius blasphemae praesagiis.

MILITES. Non terremur, sed tuis praeceptis parere nitimur.   5

XIII

SISINNIUS. Qui sunt hi, qui nos invadunt? Quam similes sunt militibus, quibus Hirenam tradidimus! Ipsi sunt.—Cur tam cito revertimini? Quo tenditis tam anheli?

MILITES. Te ipsum quaerimus.

SISINNIUS. Ubi est, quam traxistis?   10

MILITES. In supercilio montis.

SISINNIUS. Cuius?

MILITES. Proximi.

SISINNIUS. O insensati et hebetes totiusque rationis incapaces.

MILITES. Cur causaris? cur voce et vultu nobis minaris?   15

SISINNIUS. Dii vos perdant!

MILITES. Quid in te commisimus? Quam tibi iniuriam fecimus? Quae tua iussa transgressi sumus?

SISINNIUS. Nonne praecepi, ut rebellem deorum ad turpitudinis locum traheretis?   20

MILITES. Praecepisti, nosque tuis praeceptis operam dedimus implendis, sed supervenere duo ignoti iuvenes, asserentes se ad hoc ex te missos, ut Hirenam ad cacumen montis perducerent.

SISINNIUS. Ignorabam.

MILITES. Agnoscimus.   25

SISINNIUS. Quales fuerunt?

MILITES. Amictu splendidi, vultu admodum reverendi.

SISINNIUS. Num sequebamini illos?

MILITES. Sequebamur.

---

3. **libito** = CL *libeto;* the change of "e" to "i" is common in ML orthography. 5. **parere:** from *pareo* + dative object; this infinitive is the complement of *nitimur.* **nitimur:** from *niti* + infinitive = "to try to. . . ." 11. **supercilio:** with the secondary meaning of "summit." 14. **incapaces:** from *incapax, acis,* "incapable," this usage is common to EL and LL also (Bertini/Dronke 104, n. XIII 2). 15. **minaris:** from *minari* + dative object = "to threaten. . . ." 21. **operam dedimus** + dative: the idiom is *operam dare:* "to pay attention to. . . ." 22. **supervenere:** alternate perfect active indicative, third person plural = *supervenerunt.*

SISINNIUS. Quid fecerunt?

MILITES. A dextra laevaque Hirenae se locaverunt et nos huc direxerunt, quo te exitus rei non lateret.

SISINNIUS. Restat, ut ascenso equo pergam et, qui fuerint, qui nos tam
5   libere illuserunt, perquiram.

MILITES. Properemus pariter.

XIV

SISINNIUS. Hem! Ignoro, quid agam; pessumdatus sum maleficiis christicolarum: en, montem circueo, et, semitam aliquoties repperiens, nec ascensum comprehendere nec reditum queo repetere.

10 MILITES. Miris modis omnes illudimur nimiaque lassitudine fatigamur; et si insanum caput diutius vivere sustines, te ipsum et nos perdes.

SISINNIUS. Quisquis es meorum, strenue extende arcum, iace sagittam, perfode hanc maleficam.

MILITES. Decet.

15 HIRENA. Infelix, erubesce, Sisinni, erubesce, teque turpiter victum ingemisce, quia tenellae infantiam virgunculae absque armorum apparatu nequivisti superare.

SISINNIUS. Quicquid dedecoris accedit, levius tolero, quia te morituram haut dubito.

20 HIRENA. Hinc mihi quam maxime gaudendum, tibi vero dolendum, quia pro tui severitate malignitatis in tartara dampnaberis; ego autem, martiri palmam virginitatisque receptura coronam, intrabo aethereum aeterni regis thalamum; cui est honor et gloria in saecula.

                                                               —*Dulc.*

2. **a dextra laevaque:** i.e., "on the right and left side. . . ."   4. **qui fuerint:** relative clause serving as the object of *perquiram*.   8. **aliquoties** = CL *aliquotiens*.   11. **insanum caput:** i.e., Hirena.   18. **morituram:** future active participle of *mori* 21. **dampnaberis** = CL *damnaberis*.   22. **martiri:** better *martyrii*, from *martyrium, i,* "martyrdom" (Sleumer 50), dependent on *palmam*.   **receptura:** future active participle of *recipere*.

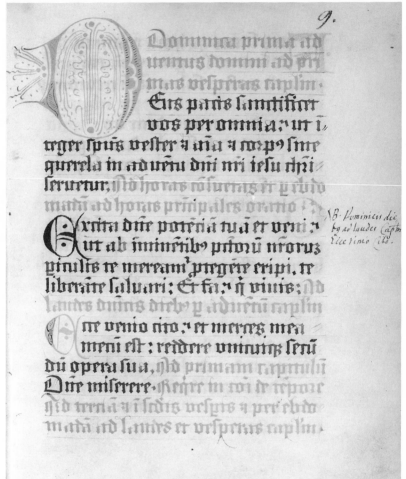

PLATE 15. A folio from a late medieval breviary of German provenance.

PLATE 15

Breviary, Latin manuscript on parchment, sixteenth century, fol. 9 recto
John Hay Library, Brown University

The religious observances that would have marked a normal day at the monastery at Gandersheim would have involved Hrotsvita in communal prayer and devotion. Latin breviaries, which were normalized in the eleventh century, would have been used by her and her sisters to help organize their public devotion and to ensure that the daily observances would correspond with the larger liturgical seasons. Saint Benedict had prescribed the daily office of prayer in the sixth century, but the complexities of ecclesiastical organization and liturgical observance made breviaries, such as the one shown here, an absolute necessity by Hrotsvita's day.

The folio displayed here is written in a Gothic script in red and black ink, with the illumination of the initial "D," predominantly in black, gold, and red, showing some penwork flourishes. The folio's margins and 20 lines are ruled in ink. (See plate 14 for discussion of the manuscript itself.)

MEDIEVAL LATIN RELIGIOUS DRAMA

A Mystery Play on the Resurrection; A Miracle Play on Saint Nicholas

(Mysterium resurrectionis D. N. Ihesu Christi; Miraculum Sancti Nicholai; c. 1050)

When Tertullian railed against the theater in his treatise *On Spectacles* ("You, O Christian, will hate the theater, whose authors you are not able but to hate," sec. 10), he did more than speak to a contemporary audience about the moral implications of *ludi,* or "plays." His comments (and others like them from later writers—among others, Augustine [cf. *Conf.* 1]) had the effect of expunging the very genre from Christian literary culture, which turned its back on drama for over five hundred years. It is not until the ninth century that we have solid evidence for the drama again, but in versions different in conception and purpose from those against which Tertullian wrote.

Like its classical counterpart, Medieval Latin drama can be divided into serious and comedic categories, though it is not proper to speak of Medieval Latin tragedies per se. Comedy, however, is a discrete form of drama in the Medieval Latin tradition, and it seems almost certain that it never entirely died out in the West—in spite of the vigilance with which the Church strove to control or root out drama altogether. The Roman theaters were closed in the West during the fifth and sixth centuries, making private theater the only option for dramatic performance. But comedy in various guises seems especially to have been preserved in performances of mime, a tradition that continued throughout the Middle Ages. At the same time, by the eleventh century there is a host of evidence demonstrating that, quite apart from mime, comedic performances were staged. Church injunctions in particular regularly condemn such performances, while contemporary accounts speak of time wasted watching such performances and of the money to be made in staging them. There can be no denying, in any case, the huge popularity of literary comedy also.

Surely most of the comedies written and performed are lost to us—and many of these were probably not highly accomplished. But the comedies that have come down to us exhibit a bawdiness and directness that appeals to the reader and belies the garb of moral purity with which students still associate the Middle Ages. Their appeal is also owed to literary accomplishment, for many of the better Medieval Latin comedies were written by those well versed in the ancient comedies of Terence (Plautus was less readily available, though manuscripts of his works were in circulation in southern and central France from the ninth century onward and in Italy for all of the Middle Ages). These were works, therefore, that, in addition to being performed, were read by a learned audience of religious and lay people alike. In fact, the most famous Medieval Latin comedy, the *Pamphilus,* an anonymous work of around 1100, was so popular that it was copied out literally hundreds of times in little manuscript copies— whence our term, "pamphlets." In addition to the anonymous *Pamphilus* and a host of other anonymous works, we possess comedies written by Vitalis of Blois, William of Blois, and Arnulf of Orléans. These extant comedies represent a higher, literary strain and are often indebted to Terence in structural, verbal, and thematic ways, as well as to the specific features of Latin that lend it to comedic diction and performance.

Serious drama existed variously for several centuries before its form was perfected by Hrotsvita (see previous section), but it is impossible to state with certainty its origins or even to chart its development before her time. A host of influences—the maturation of the Medieval Latin sequences, hymnology, developments in music, liturgical performance, and dramatic traditions already in place—all clearly figure in this development. Three kinds of drama predominate: mystery plays, usually based on gospel narratives; morality plays, more loosely constructed in terms of sources than mystery plays, but with perhaps a heavier pedagogical aim, extolling general ethical principles; and miracle plays, drawing on ecclesiastical materials, especially the lives of saints and other exemplary figures, for inspiration. These plays, with their often severe plots and compressed dialogues, were invariably sung, unlike their lighter comedic counterparts, and some of their music survives in the manuscripts.

The anonymous works presented here exemplify collections of dramas produced throughout the Latin Middle Ages on set themes or individuals. The miracle play on Saint Nicholas draws on an enormous tradition of writing about Nicholas that dates from the ninth century in the West and even earlier in the East. In addition to various Nicholas plays, there are many hymns, sequences, and lives of Nicholas that survive from the tenth century onward. The manuscript that records it, the Fleury play-book, dates to the thirteenth century, though the composition itself is no later than the twelfth century and almost certainly older. The musical notation survives in the manuscript. The mystery play is from the Fleury play-book also, featuring the three Marys at the tomb of the already risen Jesus—a motif common in medieval drama. Both dramas feature a sparse, quickly paced, sung dialogue comprising accentual verses, with the rule of an equal number of syllables rigidly adhered to, and generally with two-syllable end rhyme.

Medieval Latin comedy and drama are accessible in large collections (F. Bertini, ed., *Commedie latine del XII e XIII secolo*, 4 vols., Sassari, 1976–83, with Latin texts and facing Italian translations of 16 comedies; K. Young, *The Drama of the Medieval Church*, 2 vols., Oxford, 1933) and variously in individual studies on single plays. A. G. Elliott's translation of seven comedies (*Seven Medieval Latin Comedies*, New York, 1984) contains a full bibliography of primary and secondary sources for the comedies she treats. P. Dronke's bilingual edition of nine plays in the Cambridge Medieval Classics series (*Nine Medieval Latin Plays*, Cambridge, 1994), in addition to bringing the plays he treats up to date in textual matters, also includes a useful introduction to Medieval Latin drama in general and full bibliography. The Nicholas plays of the Fleury play-book have been separately edited and studied by O. E. Albrecht (*Four Latin Plays of St. Nicholas from the 12th Century Fleury Playbook: Text, Commentary, with a Study of the Music of the Plays, and of the Sources and Iconography of the Legends*, Philadelphia, 1935). Much work remains to be done in this genre of Medieval Latin literature. Young's texts, vol. 1, pp. 393–97, 666, and vol. 2, pp. 330–32, are followed with "u" and "v" distinguished and some minor changes in spelling and formatting. Bracketed material indicates stage directions and explanatory material found in the manuscripts.

A MYSTERY PLAY ON THE RESURRECTION

[Ad faciendam similitudinem Dominici Sepulchri primum procedant tres fratres preparati et vestiti in similitudinem trium Mariarum, pedetemtim et quasi tristes alternantes hos versus cantantes:]

PRIMA [earum dicat]

5 Heu! pius pastor occidit,
 quem culpa nulla infecit.
 O res plangenda!

SECUNDA
 Heu! verus pastor obiit,
10 qui vitam functis contulit.
 O mors lugenda!

2. **trium**: from *tres, tria, trium*. **Mariarum**: i.e., the "three Marys": Mary Magdalene, Mary Jacobi, Mary Salome, common in mystery plays of this sort (cf. Dronke 1, 83 ff.).

TERTIA
Heu! nequam gens Iudaica,
quam dira frendet vesania.
Plebs execranda!

PRIMA   5
Cur nece pium impia
dampnasti seva, invida?
O ira nefanda!

SECUNDA
Quid iustus hic promeruit   10
quod crucifigi debuit?
O gens dampnanda!

TERTIA
Heu! quid agemus misere,
dulci magistro orbate?   15
Heu, sors lacrimanda!

PRIMA
Eamus ergo propere,
quod solum quimus facere
mente devota.   20

SECUNDA
Condimentis aromatum
ungamus corpus sanctissimum,
quo preciosa.

TERTIA   25
Nardi vetet commixcio
ne putrescat in tumulo
caro beata.

[Cum autem venerint in chorum, eant ad Monumentum et quasi queren-
tes, et cantantes omnes simul hunc versum:]   30
Sed nequimus hoc patrare sine adiutorio;
Quisnam saxum hoc revolvet ab monumenti hostio?
[Quibus respondeat ANGELUS sedens foris ad caput Sepulcri, vestitus

---

7. **dampnasti:** contracted perfect active indicative, second person singular of *damn-
are* = *damnavisti.*   11. **crucifigi:** present passive infinitive of *crucifigere,* "to be fixed
to a cross."   15. **orbate:** perfect passive participle of *orbare,* with its object in the
ablative expressing separation.   22. **aromatum:** from *aroma, atis,* from the Greek ἀρ-
ύμα, "spices."   24. **preciosa** = CL *pretiosa.*   26. **commixcio** = CL *commixtio, onis,*
"a mixing."   27. **putrescat** = CL *putescat.*

alba deaurata, mitra tectus caput etsi deinfulatus, palmam in sinistra, ra-
mum candelarum plenum tenens in manu dextra, et dicat moderata et
admodum gravi voce:]

    Quem queritis in sepulcro,

5   O Christicole!

MULIERES

    Ihesum Nazarenum crucifixum,

    O celicola!

[Quibus repondeat] ANGELUS:

10   Quid, Christicole, viventem queritis cum mortuis?

    Non est hic, sed surrexit, predixit ut discipulis.

    Mementote quid iam vobis locutus est in Galilea,

    Quia Christum opportebat pati atque die tercia

        Resurgere cum gloria.

15 [MULIERES converse ad populum cantet:]

    Ad monumentum Domini venimus gementes, angelum Dei sedentem

        vidimus et dicentem quia surrexit a morte.

[Post hec MARIA MAGDALENE, relictis duabus aliis, accedat ad Sepulcrum, in quod sepe aspiciens, dicat:]

20   Heu dolor! heu quam dira doloris angustia,

    Quod dilecti sum orbata magistri praesencia!

    Heu! quis corpus tam dilectum sustulit e tumulo?

[Deinde pergat velo<citer> ad illos qui in similitu<di>ne Petri et Iohannis pr<e>stare debent ere<cti>, stansque ante eos quasi trist<is>,

25 dicat:]

    Tulerunt Dominum meum,

    et nescio ubi posuerunt eum,

    Et monumentum vacuum est inventum,

    Et sudarium cum sindone intus est repositum.

30 [Illi autem hec audientes, vel<ociter> pergant ad Sepulcrum acsi cur-
re<ntes> sed iunior, scilicet Iohannes, preveniens st<et> extra Sepulcrum; senior vero, scilicet Pe<trus>, sequens eum, statim intret; postquam et Ioh<annes in>tret. Cum inde exierint, IOHANNES quasi
<ad>mirans dicat:]

35   Miranda sunt que vidimus!

    An furtim sublatus est Dominus?

---

1. **mitra:** *mitra, ae,* "mitre" (Sleumer 524). **deinfulatus:** from *de* + *infulatus* =
"wearing fillets." 5. **Christicole:** from *Christicola, ae,* masculine noun of the first
declension = "Christians." 8. **celicola** = CL *caelicola.* 12. **Mementote:** future imperative plural. 29. **sindone:** *sindon, onis,* "cloth."

[Cui] PETRUS
Imo, ut predixit vivus,
surrexit, credo, Dominus.

IOHANNES
Sed cur liquit in sepulcro 5
sudarium cum lintheo?

PETRUS
Ista, quia resurgenti
non era\<n\>t necessaria,
Imo Resurrectionis 10
restant hec indicia.

[Illis autem abeuntibus, acced\<at\> MARIA ad Sepulcrum, et prius dicat:]
Heu dolor, heu quam dira doloris angustia,
Quod dilecti sum orbata magistri praesencia!
Heu! quis corpus tam dilectum sustulit e tumulo? 15

[Quam alloquantur DUO ANGELI sedentes infra Sepulcrum, dicentes:]
Mulier, quid ploras?

MARIA
Quia tulerunt Dominum meum,
et nescio ubi posuerunt eum. 20

ANGELUS
Noli flere, Maria, resurrexit Dominus,
alleluia!

MARIA
Ardens est cor meum desiderio 25
videre Dominum meum;
quero et non invenio
ubi posuerunt eum,
alleluia!

[Interim veniat quidam preparatus in similitudinem Hortolani, stansque 30
ad caput Sepulcri et dicat:]
Mulier, quid ploras? Quem queris?

MARIA
Domine, si tu sustulisti eum, dicito mihi ubi posuisti eum, et ego
eum tollam. 35

Et ILLE:
Maria!

---

2. **imo** = CL *immo*.   30. **Hortolani:** *hortulanus, i,* "gardener" (Sleumer 390).

371

[Que procidens ad pedes eius MARIA dicat:]
    Raboni!
[At ille subtrahat se, et, quasi tactum eius devitans, dicat:]
    Noli me tangere, nondum enim ascendi ad Patrem meum, et Patrem
5   vestrum, Deum meum, et Deum vestrum.
[Sic discedat Hortolanus. MARIA vero conversa ad populum dicat:]
    Congratulamini mihi omnes qui diligitis Dominum, quia quem quer-
      ebam apparuit mihi, et dum flerem ad monumentum, vidi Domi-
      num meum, alleluia!
10 [Tunc DUO ANGELI exeant ad hostium Sepulcri, ita ut appareant foris,
    et dicant:]
    Venite et videte locum ubi positus erat Dominus,
      alleluia!
    Nolite timere vos.
15   Vultum tristem iam mutate;
    Ihesum vivum nunciate;
    Galileam iam adite.
    Si placet videre, festinate.
    Cito euntes dicite discipulis quia surrexit Dominus,
20   alleluia!
[Tunc MULIERES discedentes a Sepulcro dicant ad plebem:]
    Surrexit Dominus de sepulcro,
    qui pro nobis pependit in ligno,
    alleluia!
25 [Hoc facto, expandant sindonem, dicentes ad plebem:]
    Cernite, vos socii, sunt corporis ista beati
    Linthea, que vacuo iacuere relicta sepulcro.
[Postea ponant sindonem super altare, cum qua revertentes alternent
hos versus:]
30 PRIMA [dicat:]
    Resurrexit hodie Deus deorum.
SECUNDA
    Frustra signas lapidem, plebs Iudeorum.
TERTIA
35   Iungere iam populo Christianorum.

2. **Raboni:** indeclinable masculine noun (an Aramaic word transcribed in the Greek New Testament and repeated in the Vulgate, John 20.16) = "lord," "master" (Sleumer 654, s. v. *Rabboni*). 27. **iacuere:** alternate perfect active indicative, third person plural = *iacuerunt*.

[Item PRIMA dicat:]
Resurrexit <h>odie rex angelorum.
SECUNDA
Ducitur de tenebris turba piorum.
TERTIA   5
Reseratur aditus regni celorum.
[Interea is qui ante fuit Hortolanus in similitudinem DOMINI veniat,
dalmaticatus candida dalmatica, candida infula infulatus, filacteria preci-
osa in capite, crucem cum labaro in dextra, textum auro paratum in sin-
istra habens, et dicat mulieribus:]   10
Nolite timere vos; ite, nunciate fratribus meis ut eant in Galileam;
ibi me videbunt, sicut predixi eis.
CHORUS
Alleluia,
resurrexit hodie Dominus!   15
[Quo finito, dicant OMNES insimul:]
Leo fortis, Christus, filius Dei.
[Et CHORUS dicat:]
Te Deum laudamus
[Explicit.]   20

                                   —*Myst. Res. Ih. Chr.*

A Miracle Play on Saint Nicholas
Miraculum Sancti Nicholai

PRIMUS CLERICUS
Nos quos causa discendi literas
apud gentes transmisit exteras,
dum sol aduc extendit radium,
perquiramus nobis hospicium.   5
SECUNDUS CLERICUS
Iam sol equos tenet in litore,
quos ad presens merget sub equore.

---

8. **dalmaticatus:** *dalmaticatus, a, um,* "adorned in priestly garments." **dalmatica:**
dalmatica, ae, "undergarment" worn by a priest during Mass. **infula infulatus:** lit.,
"filleted with a fillet," i.e., "wearing a fillet." **filacteria** = CL *phylacterium, i,* neuter
noun from the Greek φυλακτήριον = "phylacteries" (LS 1373). 9. **labaro:** *labarum,
i,* neuter noun from the Greek λαβαρόν = "labarum," a richly decorated staff or standard terminating in a crown, cross, and the initial letters of Christ's name. 16. **insimul:** adverb = "at the same time."

Nec est nota nobis hec patria;
ergo queri debent hospicia.

TERTIUS CLERICUS

Senem quemdam maturum moribus
5   hic habemus coram luminibus;
forsan, nostris compulsus precibus,
erit hospes nobis hospitibus.

[Insimul CLERICI ad Senem dicant:]

Hospes care, querendo studia
10   huc relicta venimus patria;
nobis ergo prestes hospicium,
dum durabit hoc noctis spacium.

SENEX

Hospitetur vos factor omnium,
15   nam non dabo vobis hospicium;
nam nec mea in hoc utilitas,
nec est ad hoc nunc op<p>ortunitas.

[CLERICI ad Vetulam:]

Per te, cara, sit impetrabile
20   quod rogamus, etsi non utile.
Forsan propter hoc beneficium
vobis Deus donabit puerum.

MULIER [ad Senem:]

Nos his dare, coniux, hospicium,
25   qui sic vagant querendo studium,
sola saltem compellat karitas;
nec est dampnum, nec est utilitas.

SENEX a[d Uxorem:]

Acquiescam tuo consilio,
30   et dignabor istos hospicio.

[Ad Clericos:]

Accedatis, scolares, igitur;
quod rogastis vobis conceditur.

24. **coniux:** this explains the relationship of the *vetula* to the *senex*. **nos his dare** . . . **hospicium:** "let us give shelter to these men . . .."; the use of the infinitive for an imperative is common in ML and modeled on the Greek, mediated through the influence of EL. It is common, as here, for the subject of the infinitive to be in the accusative case (Blaise 337). 32. **scolares:** *scholaris, is* = "scholars" (Sleumer 702, s. v. *schola* 2).

SENEX [ad Uxorem, Clericis dormientibus:]
  Nonne vides quanta marsupia?
  Est in illis argenti copia;
  haec a nobis absque infamia
  possideri posset pecunia.   5
VETULA
  Paupertatis onus sustulimus,
  mi marite, quamdiu viximus;
  hos si morti donare volumus,
  paupertatem vitare possumus.   10
  Evagines ergo iam gladium,
  namque potes morte iacencium
  esse dives quamdiu vixeris;
  atque sciet nemo quod feceris.
NICHOLAUS   15
  Peregrinus, fessus itinere,
  ultra modo non possum tendere;
  huius ergo per noctis spacium
  michi prestes, precor, hospicium.
SENEX [ad mulierem:]   20
  An dignabor istum <h>ospicio,
  cara coniux, tuo consilio?
VETULA
  Hunc persona commendat nimium,
  et est dignum ut des hospicium.   25
SENEX
  Peregrine, accede propius.
  Vir videris nimis egregius;
  si vis, dabo tibi comedere;
  quidquam voles temptabo querere.   30
NICHOLAUS [ad mensam:]
  Nichil ex his possum comedere;
  carnem vellem recentem edere.
SENEX
  Dabo tibi carnem quam habeo,   35
  namque carne recente careo.

---

2. **marsupia** = CL *marsuppia*. 11. **evagines:** from *evaginare*, "to unsheath."
36. **careo:** takes an ablative object.

NICHOLAUS

Nunc dixisti plane mendacium;
carnem habes recentem nimium;
et hanc habes magna nequicia,
5   quam mactari fecit pecunia.

SENEX [et] MULIER [simul:]

Miserere nostri, te petimus,
nam te sanctum Dei cognovimus.
Nostrum scelus abhominabile,
10   non est tamen incondonabile.

NICHOLAUS

Mortuorum afferte corpora,
et contrita sint vestra pectora.
Hi resurgent per Dei graciam;
15   et vos flendo queratis veniam.

[Oratio] SANCTI NICHOLAI

Pie Deus, cuius sunt omnia,
celum, tellus, aer et maria,
ut resurgant isti praecipias,
20   et hos ad te clamantes audias.

[Et post] OMNIS CHORUS [dicat:]

Te Deum laudamus.

—*Mir. S. Nich.*

10. **incondonabile:** "unpardonable." 17. **pie Deus:** vocative case. 18. **celum** = CL *caelum.*

EKKEHARD IV OF ST. GALL

The History of St. Gall
(*Casus Sancti Galli;* c. 1035)

On the authority of a comment made by his namesake, Ekkehard IV, the first Ekkehard of St. Gall is thought to have written the important Medieval Latin epic, *Waltharius* (though that ascription is hardly certain [see pp. 310–18]). That comment is recorded in the fourth Ekkehard's richly detailed and philologically unique history, the *Casus Sancti Galli,* a work Ekkehard continued after its originator, Ratpert, died around 890. In addition to its unique Latinity and importance generically, Ekkehard's *History* also reveals important details about one of the more illustrious monastic establishments of the Latin Middle Ages.

St. Gall had been founded on the burial site of Gallus, a disciple of Columban, who had been left behind when Columban had abandoned Alemannia for the less rugged countryside of Italy (where he founded Bobbio). The abbey's school, for which it became justly famous, had been initiated by its first abbot, Othmar. Later, it was split into "inner" and "outer" establishments. The "outer" school, for general instruction to laymen, soon became a center of learning without peer—especially under the leadership of a series of strong abbots after the middle of the ninth century.

Perhaps the most important intellectual to hail from St. Gall was Notker (see pp. 300–306), who is well remembered by Ekkehard in our first excerpt, as a supreme example of erudition, piety, and devotion to duty. But Ekkehard, too, appears through the words of his *History* as a man of enormous energy and literary skill, an organizer of anecdote and detail into a larger narrative that wavers between hagiography and gossip, subtle criticism and blind acceptance of legend. Of Ekkehard personally we know very little beyond the fact that he was born, probably near St. Gall, around 980 and that he died around 1060. He seems to have been trained at St. Gall, and he clearly spent most of his life there, paying lavish attention to his monastery's past, though he was also for a time in charge of a school in Mainz.

That Ekkehard was a teacher there can be little doubt, for his *History* is much concerned with moral instruction and institutional memory, with preserving the past for his brethren while insisting on the exemplarism that the past ennobles. At the same time, Ekkehard's *History* speaks also to fresh currents in Medieval Latin literary culture. With respect to genre, for example, the *History* embodies a new set of tasks put to historical prose—the collation and celebration of an institutional past. The necessity, and the impetus, to write such histories, of course, had to wait for the fuller development of monasticism as an institution within western Christianity—a development hastened along by the rapprochement of the Church to the Carolingian and, later, the Ottonian state.

Hardly a function of institutional necessity, however, are the linguistic changes in evidence in Ekkehard's work, for the Latin of his *History* marks an important point in the development of ML. In the first place, Ekkehard Latinizes everything that comes before him, so that his writing bristles with the variety of German regional place-names, not to mention the institutional figures of German stock who peopled St. Gall (*Ungros, Ratpert, Tuotilo,* e.g.). In part, too, his Latinity reflects a more technical vocabulary attending to the architecture, organization, and governance of St. Gall, with words such as *cursus, capitulum, refectorarius, praelatus, prior, laus, scriptorio* opening up the private spaces of St. Gall to readers. At the same time, Ekkehard's syntax points to the influences of the vernacular German which St. Gall's monks by the early eleventh century clearly spoke. One can spy vestiges of Old High German especially in idioms (*super se, se caveret, cedere habuisset*). ML idioms abound also, of course (*secundum quod,* the infinitive of purpose, the infinitive with *facere,* etc.). This linguistic variety adds to the dazzling spectacle of Ekkehard's version of ML, a variety displayed in the passages excerpted here, which include also snippets of Old High German and Greek that add to the richness of this most important work.

G. Meyer von Knonau comments fully on the Latinity of Ekkehard in his old edition (*Mittheilungen zur Vaterländischen Geschichte,* St. Gall, 1877, pp. 1–450). Most recently, H. Haefele has brought out a bilingual edition with facing German and Latin text (*Ekkehard IV, St. Galler Klostergeschichten,* in *Ausgewählte Quellen zur Deutschen Geschichte des Mittelalters,* vol. 10, Darmstadt, 1980), which includes a brief introduction and list of names. Haefele's text is followed here, with his subscripts normalized. The following changes have been made: at section 35, *Notkerus* for *Nothkerus, Ratpertus* for *Rapertus, inquit* for *inquid* (these based on the consistent use of the alternatives elsewhere in the text); and at section 41, *'awe'* for *awe.* At section 53, *ubi* replaces the misprinted *ub* and *frustrati* for *frustati.*

THREE FRIENDS AND A TELLTALE

De Notkero, Ratperto, Tuotilone, discipulis eius et Marcelli, quoniam quidem cor et anima una erant, mixtim, qualia tres unus fecerint, quantum a patribus audivimus, narrare incipimus. Hi quidem ab Hisone cum in divinis non mediocriter essent praelibati, Marcello, ut iam diximus, sunt coniuncti. Qui in divinis eque potens et humanis, septem liberales 5 eos duxit ad artes, maxime autem ad musicam. Quae cum ceteris naturalior et, quamvis difficilius apprehensa, usu quidem sit iocundior, tantum in ea tandem valuerant, quantum in operibus singulorum, quae iam ante quiddam tetigimus, apparet. Enimvero hi tres quamvis votis essent unicordes, natura tamen, ut fit, erant dissimiles. 10

Notker corpore non animo gratilis, voce non spiritu balbulus, in divinis erectus, in adversis patiens, ad omnia mitis, in nostratium acer erat exactor disciplinis; ad repentina timidulus et inopinata praeter demones infestantes erat, quibus quidem se audenter opponere solebat. In orando, legendo, dictando creberrimus. Et ut omnes sanctitatis eius in brevi con- 15 plectar dotes: sancti spiritus erat vasculum, quo suo tempore habundantius nullum.

At Tuotilo longe aliter bonus erat et utilis, homo lacertis et omnibus menbris, sicut Favius athletas eligere docet. Erat eloquens, voce clarus, celaturae elegans et picturae artifex. Musicus sicut et sotii eius, sed in 20 omnium genere fidium et fistularum prae omnibus; nam et filios nobilium in loco ab abbate destinato fidibus edocuit. Nuntius procul et prope sollers, in structuris et ceteris artibus suis efficax, concinnandi in utraque lingua potens et promtus natura, serio et ioco festivus: adeo, ut Karolus noster aliquando ei maledixerit, qui talis naturae hominem monachum 25 fecerit. Sed inter haec omnia, quod prae aliis est, in choro strenuus, in

1. **Notkero:** *Notkerus, i* = Notker Balbulus, a monk of St. Gall and a famous literary artist in his own right (cf. above, pp. 300–306). **Ratperto, Tuotilone . . . Marcelli:** *Ratpertus, i* = Ratpert, *Tuotilo, onis* = Tuotilo, *Marcellus, i* = Marcellus; all three are monks of St. Gall. 2. **mixtim:** in ML = "together as a group" (Blaise/Chirat 537). 3. **Hisone:** *Hiso* (or *Iso*), *onis* = Iso, a monk of St. Gall and teacher. 4. **praelibati:** perfect passive participle of *praelibare*, lit., "to taste beforehand," but with the sense here of "tested." 5. **eque** = CL *aeque*. 11. **gratilis** = CL *gracilis*. 12. **nostratium:** *nostrates, ium* = "country folk" (Sleumer 551). 15. **conplectar** = CL *complectar*. 16. **habundantius** = CL *abundantius*. 19. **menbris** = CL *membris*. **Favius:** i.e., M. Fabius Quintilianus, the first century C.E. rhetorician, author of the *Institutiones Oratoriae* (cf. *Inst. Orat.* 10.1.33). 20. **celaturae:** the better spelling is *caelaturae*, from *caelatura, ae* = "(carved) ceiling" (Niermeyer 162). **sotii** = CL *socii;* palatalization in ML phonology is common. 24. **promtus** = CL *promptus,* perfect passive participle of *promere*. **Karolus noster:** i.e., Charles III (the Fat).

latebris erat lacrimosus; versus et melodias facere praepotens, castus ut
Marcelli discipulus, qui feminis oculos clausit.

Ratpertus autem inter ambos, quos diximus, medius incedebat, scolarum ab adolescentia magister, doctor planus et benivolus, disciplinis
5   asperior, raro praeter fratres pedem claustro promovens, duos calceos annum habens; excursus mortem nominans, sepe Tuotilonem itinerarium,
ut se caveret, amplexibus monens. In scolis sedulus plerumque cursus et
missas negligebat: "Bonas," inquiens, "missas audimus, cum eas agi do-
cemus." Qui cum labem maximam claustri impunitatem nominasset, ad
10   capitulum tamen nonnisi vocatus venit, cum sibi officium capitulandi et
puniendi gravissimum, ut ait, sit traditum.

Tales cum essent tres isti nostrae reipublicae senatores, quod semper
doctorum est et utilium, ab otio vacantibus et in levitate ambulantibus
detractiones et dorsiloquia patiuntur assidua, sed maxime, quia minus
15   refellere solebat, sanctus, ut vere asseram, domnus Notkerus. Tuotilo
quidem et Ratpertus, acriores talibus minusque ad contumelias habiles,
rarius ab eis ledebantur. Notkerus autem, hominum mitissimus, quid iniurie essent, in semet ipso didicit.

De quibus pluribus unum aliquem, ut quantum satanas in talibus
20   praesumat, ab uno discas omnes, introducere volumus. Erat hic quidem
refectorarius nomine Sindolfus, postremo autem, fictis obsequelis, cum

3. **scolarum:** the better spelling is *scholarum,* from *scholar, aris,* "scholars" (Sleumer
702, s. v. *schola* 2).   4. **benivolus** = CL *benevolus* (the form used here by Ekkehard
is common from antiquity in inscriptions and attested to in many manuscripts; cf. LS
232).   5. **claustro:** *claustrum, i,* has the common meaning of "cloister" (Sleumer
214).   6. **sepe** = CL *saepe.*   7. **cursus:** *cursus, us* = a technical term referring to the
daily ordering of prayers, psalms, hymns, etc., prescribed for the monks of St. Gall
(Sleumer 254).   8. **missas:** *Missa, ae* = Mass (Sleumer 522–24).   9. **nominasset:**
syncopated pluperfect active subjunctive, third person singular, of *nominare* = *nomi-
navisset.*   10. **capitulum:** this word has a variety of meanings in ML; here it designates a meeting of all the monks of St. Gall for general instruction, counsel, etc. (Niermeyer 136–37, s. v. *capitulum* 12, 13).   **nonnisi** = *non* + *nisi.*   **capitulandi:** gerund
of *capitulare.* Ekkehard uses this verb to mean "reproving," "reprehending," although
it is not primarily used to mean this (cf. Niermeyer 136, s. v. *capitulare* 5, but cf. 1-4).
14. **dorsiloquia:** *dorsiloquim, i,* probably a neologism of Ekkehard = "backbiting"
(Niermeyer 357).   15. **domnus** = CL *dominus;* syncopation is common in ML orthography.   17. **ledebantur** = CL *laedebantur.*   **iniurie** = CL *iniuriae.*   19. **satanas:**
sometimes spelled *satan,* this masculine noun is indeclinable (Sleumer 699).   21. **refectorarius:** from *refectorarius, i,* masculine noun = "steward," "refector"; there is in
ML also an adjectival form, *refectorarius, a, um* (cf. Niermeyer 898, s. v., *refectorarius*).   **Sindolfus:** Sindolf, the monk of the refectory, who figures in several other stories told by Ekkehard.   **obsequelis:** from *obsequela, ae* = obsequiousness (LS 1241,
s. v. *obsequela*).

alias in nullo esset utilis, accusans fratres criminibus coniectis, a Salomone operariorum positus est decanus. Enimvero cum esset refectorarius, pro commodis incommoda, quibus ausus erat, exhibebat, prae ceteris autem Notkero. Salomone autem in plurimis occupato nec adtendere ad singula sufficienti, alimonia interdum fratribus cum aut detraheretur aut   5
depravaretur, clamabant plures pro iniusticia; inter quos aliquando aetiam tres, quos dicimus, isti aliqua locuti parebant. At Sindolfus, discordiae semper fomes, sciens antiquam condiscipulorum odii facem et causam, accommodat se auribus Salomonis, quasi pro suo honore rem sibi sit dicturus. Ille vero etsi nihil nocivius scisset praelatis a subditis   10
quam susurros audire, quid novi afferret, quesivit. Ille vero tres illos semper super se verba iacere solitos hesterno, quae Deo importabilia sint, mentitur locutos. Credidit ille sermoni et nihil mali opinantibus rancorem portavit, tandem et ostendit. At illi cum nihil ab eo reatus sui exsculpere possent, Sindolfi se tegnis ariolantur fuisse circumventos. Re tandem co-   15
ram fratribus discussa, cum ipsi, testantibus cunctis nihil omnino se contra episcopum dixisse, cum ceteris eum vincerent, vindictam super falsidicum quisque sibi rogant. Quod ille cum dissimulasset, taciti quieverant.

   Erat tribus illis inseperabilibus consuetudo, permisso quidem prioris, in intervallo laudum nocturno convenire in scriptorio collationesque tali   20
horae aptissimas de scripturis facere. At Sindolfus sciens horam et colloquia quadam nocte fenestrae vitreae, cui Tuotilo assederat, clandestinus

---

1. **Salomone:** *Salomon, onis,* = Salomon, Bishop of Constance and abbot of St. Gall from after 890 to 920.   2. **operariorum:** from *operarius, i* = "workers" (Niermeyer 739).   **decanus:** *decanus, i* = "chief" (LS 516).   4. **adtendere** = CL *attendere.* **Salomone … sufficienti:** ablative absolute.   6. **aetiam** = CL *etiam.*   10. **nocivius:** comparative of the adjective *nocivus,* modifying *nihil.*   **scisset:** contracted pluperfect active subjunctive, third person singular of *scire* = *scivisset.*   **praelatis:** from *praelatus, i* = "prelates" (this word has various meanings in ML, see Niermeyer 834).   11. **quesivit** = CL *quaesivit.*   12. **importabilia:** from *importabilis,* modiyfing *verba* = "intolerable" (LS 908).   14. **reatus:** a fourth declension masculine noun in ML = "guilt" (Niermeyer 885).   15. **tegnis** = CL *technis,* from *techna, ae.*   **ariolantur** = CL *hariolantur.*   18. **dissimulasset:** contracted pluperfect active subjunctive, third person singular of *dissimulare* = *dissimulavisset.*   19. **inseperabilibus** = CL *inseparabilibus.*   **prioris:** *prior, oris,* this word has various technical meanings in ML, one of which is to designate the abbot of a monastery, as here (cf. on the other meanings Niermeyer 851–52).   20. **laudum:** from *laus, laudis,* a word with literally dozens of meanings in ML; here it is used to designate "lauds," a period of prayer for the monastic community. On the various meanings of this word, see Niermeyer 587–89; on the specific meaning used by Ekkehard here, see sec. 19. **scriptorio:** *scriptorium, i,* the "writing room" of the monastery where manuscripts were copied.

foris appropiat aureque vitro affixa, si quid rapere posset, quod deprava-
tum episcopo traderet, auscultabat. Senserat illum Tuotilo, homo pervi-
cax lacertisque confisus, Latialiterque, quo illum, qui nihil intellegeret,
lateret, compares alloquitur: "Adest ille," inquit, "et aurem fenestrae
5 affixit. Sed tu, Notker, quia timidulus es, cede in aecclesiam! Ratperte
autem mi, rapto flagello fratrum, quod pendet in pyrali, deforis accurre!
Ego enim illum, cum appropinquare te sensero, vitreo citissime redaperto
captum capillis ad meque pertractum violenter tenebo. Tu autem, anime
mi, confortare et esto robustus, flagelloque illum totis viribus increpita et
10 Deum in illo ulciscere!" Ille vero, sicut semper erat ad disciplinas acutissi-
mus, modeste exiens, rapto flagello cucurrit celerrimus hominemque intro
capite tractum totis viribus a dorso ingrandinat. Et ecce ille manibus pedibusque renisus, flagellum incussum capiens tenuit. At ille virgam propius
aspectam rapiens ictus ei validissimos infregit. Cum autem parci sibi male
15 mulctatus incassum petisset: "Voce," inquit, "opus est," et exclamans
vociferavit. At fratrum pars, voce audita tali tempore insolita, stupens
accurrit luminibus et, quidnam esset, quesivit. Tuotilo autem diabolum
se coepisse creber ingeminans, lumen adhiberi rogat, ut, in cuius illum
imagine teneret, certius inspiceret. Capite autem inviti hac et illac ad in-
20 spicientes versato, si Sindolf esset, quasi nescius interrogat. Omnibus
autem vere ipsum esse clamitantibus et, ut illum dimitteret, rogantibus,
relicto eo: "Me miserum," ait, "in auricularem et intimum episcopi manus misisse!" Ratpertus vero fratribus acurrentibus in partem cedens clam
se subduxit. Neque enim ipse, qui passus est, a quo cederetur, scire pot-
25 erat. Querentibus autem aliquibus, ubinam domnus Notkerus Ratper-
tusque abissent: "Ambo," inquit, "ad opus Dei diabolum sentientes abier-
unt meque cum illo in negotio perambulante in tenebris dimiserunt. Vere
autem omnes scitote angelum Domini ictus ei manu sua incussisse!"
    Discedentibus tandem fratribus a partium sectatoribus surgunt, ut fit,

1. **appropiat** = CL *appropriat*; in ML *appropriare* means "to approach," "to draw
near" (cf. Niermeyer 53, s. v. *appropriare;* cf. LS 144, s. v. *approprio*). 3. **Latialiterque:** i.e., "in Latin" (Niermeyer 583); the form is found in CL also (LS 1039, s. v.
Latium II D). 5. **timidulus:** diminutive of *timidus.* **aecclesiasm** = CL *ecclesiam.*
6. **pyrali:** from *pyrale, pyralis* = "hearth" (Niermeyer 797, s. v. *pyrale* 2), but referring here to a room in which there was a large hearth. 9. **confortare:** i.e., "to
strengthen" (LS 416). 12. **ingrandinat** = CL *grandinare* + *in* = "to hail down
upon." This appears to be a neologism owed to Ekkehard. 22. **auricularem:** from
auricularius, aris, third declension noun = "intimate counselor," "confidant" (Niermeyer 73). 24. **cederetur** = CL *caederetur.* 28. **scitote:** future active imperative
plural of *scire.* **incussisse:** perfect active infinitive of *incutire* + dative object.

multiloquia. Alii Dei iudicio, ut auscultatores clandestini publicarentur, factum dicebant; alii autem tali viro, nisi quod angelum Dei praetendit, tale opus non decuisse. Occultabat autem se confractus ille corporis pariter et mentis dolore. Interrogatque tandem episcopus post aliquos dies, ubinam tandiu moraretur suus famidicus—sic enim hominem nominare   5
erat solitus nova semper aliqua sibi clam adportantem. Re, ut erat, veraciter comperta, quoniam tantae auctoritati pro tam turpiter reo nihil imputare volebat, consolatur accitum: "Quoniam," inquit, "illi a pueritia mei semper invidi male tibi fecerant, ego quidem, si vixero, melius tibi facere habebo." Data est post non multum temporis occasio, et plerisque   10
omnibus, ne rem loci tam praeclaram in tali homine deiceret, contradicentibus, ut supra praelibavimus, operariorum factus est ab ipso decanus.

—Cas. Sanc. Gal. 33–36.

NOTKER'S ENCOUNTER WITH THE DEVIL

Notkerus autem spiritualiter, ut diximus, fortis, quantum Tuotilo in homines, tantum ipse valuit in demones; alias autem corpore, ut ieiunans et vigilans, tener, ut diximus, et macer. Accidit autem, ut quadam nocte in aecclesia praeveniens in maturitate altariaque circuiens, ut solebat, clamaret. In criptam vero veniens XII apostolorum sanctique Columbani,   5
acriores de post aram oculi eius cum deducerent lacrimas, quasi canem audierat mussitantem. Cumque interea suis vocem grunnientis mixtam sentiret, intellexit temptatorem: "Esne tu," inquit, "iterum ibi? Quam

1. **multiloquia:** from *multiloquium, ii* = "to say many things" (Niermeyer 543). 5. **famidicus:** formed on *fama* and *dicere* = "rumor teller" (Du Cange 318, who alone reports it; Haefele 85 translates it *Gerüchteerzähler*). 6. **adportantem** = CL *apportantem.* 12. **ut . . . praelibavimus:** "as we have mentioned before above . . ."; in CL, *praelibare* means "to taste beforehand," but in ML comes to mean, as Ekkehard uses it here, "to mention before" (Niermeyer 834).

2. **demones:** the better spelling is *daemones,* from *daemon, onis* = "demons." 4. **in maturitate:** in ML the phrase more commonly means "early in the morning" (Sleumer 508, s. v. *maturitas*), but here, given *quadam nocte,* the less common meaning of "midnight" seems better (see Niermeyer 664, s. v. *maturitas*). **clamaret:** *clamare* commonly means "to pray" in ML (Niermeyer 184–85). 5. **criptam** = CL *cryptam.* **Columbani:** When Columban left Alemannia for Italy to found the monastery of Bobbio, he left behind a companion, Gallus, who in due course became a holy man of some legend and whose place of death marked the location of the abbey of St. Gall, named after him. 6. **de post:** lit., "from behind," i.e., "behind"; the combination of two prepositions, or prepositions with adjectives or adverbs, is common in ML (Latham 131, s. v. *de*). 7. **grunnientis:** present active participle of *grunire,* "to grunt."

bene tibi, miser, contigit nunc mussitanti et grunnienti post gloriosas voces illas, quas in caelis habueras!" Accensoque lumine, quo angulo lateret, quaesivit. Ille vero sinistro angulo appropiantem tanquam canis rabidus vestes lacerat. "Eia," inquit ille, "servitium tuum foris criptam sa-
5   tagere habeo; neque enim penae ille valent, quas, ut aiunt, iam pateris: acrius tibi aliquid paraturus sum. Praecipio tibi autem in nomine istorum sanctorum et Domini mei, ut me in eodem, quo nunc indutus es, canino corpore exspectes." Et ille: "Faciam," inquit, "si volo." Et Notkerus velocius abiens: "Confido," ait, "in Domino, quia, velis nolis, me exspec-
10   tabis." Festinato autem aram sancti Galli adiens, cambotam suam et magistri eius, multarum virtutum operatricem, cum spera illa sanctae crucis notissima rapuit et, in introitu criptae dextero spera posita, cum baculo sinistrorsum caninum illum aggressus est diabolum. Cum autem illum baculo sancto cedere coepisset, voces suas anteriores altius gannitu edidit et
15   grunnitu. Tandem vero cum ad speram sanctissimam cedendo cedentem fugiens venisset, ultra iam progredi non valens constitit, et tot iam ictus et incussiones ferre non sustinens, barbarice clamans: "Auwe mir we!" vociferavit. At interea edituus cum basilicam intrasset vocesque horridas audisset, lumen velox in manibus sumpsit et ad criptam acceleravit. At
20   ille cum ei ictum ultimum fecisset, baculum sanctum in locis confregit. Et nisi edituus speram videns allevasset canemque sic abire permisisset, adhuc eum cedere habuisset. Edituus vero baculo inspecto attonitus: "Baculumne sanctum, domine mi, in cane fedasti?" Illo conticente addidit:

3. **appropiantem** = CL *appropriantem*, but in ML *appropriare* means "to approach," "to draw near" (Niermeyer 53, s. v. *appropriare*); a comparable CL word is *appropinquantem*. 4. **eia**: interjection, meaning something like "ah." 5. **penae** = CL *poenae*; the substitution of "e" for "oe" is common in ML; § 1.3.1. 10. **cambotam**: there are various spellings for this first declension noun, which means "walking stick" (see Niermeyer 118, s. v. *cambuta*; Blaise/Chirat 125, s. v. *cambocta, cambucia, cambuta*); the comparable CL noun is *baculus*, which Ekkehard uses subsequently. 11. **virtutum**: in ML *virtus* has over a dozen meanings, but most commonly, as here, means "miracle" (Niermeyer 1111, s. v. *virtus* 2). **spera** = CL *sphaera*. 13. **baculo**: specifically, the sense here is the "staff" of the spiritual shepherd. 14. **cedere** = CL *caedere*. 17. **auwe mir we**: cries of pain (in old High German). 18. **edituus**: the better spelling is *aedituus* or *aeditumus*, both second declension nouns = "sexton," "sacristan" (Sleumer 83, s. v. *aedituus* and *aeditumus* and Niermeyer 366, s. v. *aedituus*). **intrasset**: contracted pluperfect active subjunctive, third person singular of *intrare* = *intravisset*. 21. **allevasset**: contracted pluperfect active subjunctive, third person singular of *allevare* = *allevavisset*. **adhuc** = "still," as often in ML. 23. **fedasti** = CL *foedasti*, the contracted perfect active indicative, second person singular of *foedare* = *foedavisti*. **conticente**: present active participle of *conticere*, a strengthened LL verb on *tacere* = "to be silent," here with *illo* in ablative absolute construction.

"Quisnam ille erat," inquit, "qui 'awe' vociferavit?" Putansque illum pro
pietate furem aliquem caelare, ivit in pedes per totam aecclesiam, furem
comprehendere cupiens. Sed cum neque furem inveniret, neque canem,
graditur secum mirans, quia aecclesiam post se introiens clauserat, quidnam esse posset, quod contigerat. Virum denique regularem iam semel 5
sibi tacitum amplius alloqui non ausus est praesumere. Et ille, secundum
quod humilis erat et prudens, edituo foras ire significans, in partem eum
sumpsit, benedictioneque praelata: "Quoniam baculum," inquit, "fili mi,
confregi, nisi tu iuveris, secreta mea habent efferri. Sed quoniam meum
non est ambulare in magnis et in mirabilibus super me, silentio fidei tuae, 10
quod factum est, committo." Sicque ei rem, ut facta est, enucleavit. At ille
baculo per fabrum latenter reparato, quod factum est, ad tempus occulta-
vit. In temporis autem processu res, ut erat, in medium venit.

—*Cas. Sanc. Gal.* 41.

HERIBALD AND THE HUNGARIAN INVASION

Ibant exploratores per nota sibi loca nocte dieque, adventum hostium
fratribus, sanctum Gallum unquam a barbaris invadi nimis incredulis, ut
ad castellum fugerent, praedicturi. Engilbertus enim et ipse talibus as-
sentiens pene sero carissimas sancti Galli res castello intulit. Unde et ciborium Otmari relictum est hostibus. Nam hostes non simul ibant; sed tur- 5
matim, quia nemo restiterat, urbes villasque invaserant et spoliatas
cremaverant, ideoque inprovisi, qua vellent, imparatos insiliebant. Silvis
quoque centeni vel minus interdum latentes eruperant. Fumus tamen et
caelum ignibus rubens, ubi essent turmae quaeque, innotuit.

Erat autem tunc inter nostrates frater quidam simplicissimus et fat- 10
uus, cuius dicta et facta sepe ridebantur, nomine Heribaldus. Huic, cum

1. 'awe': a repetition of part of an old High German expression of pain.   5. regularis: *regularis, is,* masculine third declension noun = "monk" or "nun" (Niermeyer
904; the adjective *regularis, e,* refers to anyone or anything associated with the keeping
of normal orders, vows, rules, etc.).   6. secundum quod: ML idiom = "seeing that,"
"according as," "given the fact that . . ." (Blaise/Chirat 747, s. v. *secundum* 4).
7. edituo = *aedituo.*   in partem eum sumpsit: lit., "raised him in part," i.e., "took
him into his confidence."   9. habent efferri = CL *effrenda sunt*; it is more common
in ML to have the infinitive of purpose with a verb than to use the CL constructions,
such as *effrenda sunt,* to express the same idea; cf. §§ 7.2.2, 7.9.

2. barbaris: i.e., the Hungarians, who invaded the region of St. Gall in 915.
3. Engilbertus: i.e., Engilbert or Engilpert (Haefele 289, s. v. *Engilpertus*), an important figure at St. Gall at the time of the invasion, later abbot (925–933).
4. pene = CL *paene.*   ciborium Otmari: the canopy or altar cloth of Othmar, the
first abbot of St. Gall (720–760).   7. inprovisi = CL *improvisi.*

ad castellum fratres primo pergerent, ut et ipse fugeret, cum terrore quidam dicerent: "Enimvero," ait ille, "fugiat, qui velit; ego quidem, quia
corium meum ad calceos camerarius hoc anno non dedit, nusquam fugiam." Cum autem illum fratres, ut secum pergeret, in novissimo articulo
5 vi cogere vellent, multa reluctatus, nisi annotinum corium sibi ad manus
daretur, nusquam se iuravit iturum. Sicque Ungros ingruentes imperterritus exspectabat. Fugiunt tandem pene sero fratres cum aliis incredulis,
horridis vocibus hostes instanter irruere perculsi; sed ipse intrepidus in
sententia permanens otiose deambulabat.
10   Ingruunt tandem pharetrati illi, pilis minantibus et spiculis asperi. Locum omnem perscrutantur solliciti; nulli sexui vel aetati certum est miser-
eri. Inveniunt solum illum in medio stantem intrepidum. Quid velit
curque non fugerit, mirati, ferro interim parcere necatoribus iussis, primipilares per interpretes interrogantes, fatuitatis monstrum ubi sentiunt,
15 omnes illi risibiles parcunt. Aram lapideam sancti Galli, quod prius crebro talibus frustrati nihil intus nisi ossa vel cineres cum invenissent, nec
tangere curant. Requirunt tandem a fatuo suo, ubi thesaurus loci sit conditus. Quos cum ille alacer ad gazophilatii duceret occultum ostiolum,
effracto illo nihil ibi nisi candelabra et coronas deauratas reperientes,
20 quas in fugam festinantes reliquerant, deceptori suo alapas dare palmis
intentant. Duo ex illis ascendunt campanarium, cuius cacuminis gallum
aureum putantes deumque loci sic vocatum non esse nisi carioris metalli
materia fusum, lancea dum unus, ut eum revellat, se validus protendit, in
atrium de alto cecidit et periit. . . .
25   Erant autem in cellario fratrum communi duo vasa vinaria usque ad
sigillos adhuc plena. Quae, quia in articulo illo nemo boves iungere aut
minare est ausus, ita sunt relicta. Haec vero, nescio quo loci fortunio,
nisi quod talibus in vehiculis praedarum habundaverant, hostium nullus

---

3. **calceos:** from *calceus, i* = "shoe." **camerarius:** from *camerarius, i*, this term designates a monastic office involving the oversight of finances and the appropriation of
goods to the brothers, as the description here clearly suggests (Niermeyer 120).
6. **Ungros:** from *Hungari, orum* = Hungarians (on the various forms see Sleumer
393, s. v. *Hungari*). 13. **necatoribus:** from *necator, oris* = "murderers. **primipilares:** from *primipilaris, is* = "captain." 15. **risibiles:** from *risibilis, e* = "laughing."
18. **gazophilatii:** the better spelling is *gazophylacii*, from the Greek γαζοφυλάκιον =
"storehouse of treasures" (Sleumer 353, s. v. *gazophylacium*). 21. **campanarium:**
from *campanarium, i* = "bell tower" (Niermeyer 122). 23. **fusum:** perfect passive
participle of *fundere* = "alloyed." 25. **cellario:** from *cellarium, i* = "pantry" (Niermeyer 163, s. v. *cellarium* 1). 27. **nescio quo:** the idiom is *nescio quid* = "something
or other," with *quo* modifying *fortunio*. **fortunio:** from *fortunium, i* = "fortune"
(Niermeyer 448). 28. **habundaverant** = CL *abundaverant*.

aperuit. Nam cum quidam illorum ascia vibrata unum retinaculorum suc-
cideret, Heribaldus inter eos iam domestice versatus: "Sine," inquit, "vir
bone! Quid vis vero, ut nos, postquam abieritis, bibamus?" Quod ille per
interpretem audiens et cachinnans socios, ne fatui sui vascula tangerent,
rogavit. Sicque usque ad abbatis conspectum Ungris locum deserentibus   5
sunt servata.

   Exploratores autem, qui silvas et quaeque latentia sollicitissime scru-
tarentur, certatim illi mittunt; eos, si quid novi referant, operiuntur. Spar-
guntur tandem, Wiborada iam passa, per atrium et prata ad prandia copiosa. Cyborium quoque Sancti Otmari argento vestitum nudant, quod   10
repente invasi fugientes asportare non poterant. Primipilares quidem
claustri planitiem tenentes omni copia convivantur. Heribaldus aetiam
coram illis plus quam unquam, ut ipse postea dicebat, saturatus est.
Cumque more suo super viride foenum singuli ad prandendum absque
sedilibus recumberent, ipse sibi et clerico cuidam praeda capto sellulas   15
posuit. Ipsi vero cum armos et caeteras victimarum portiones semicrudas
absque cultellis dentibus laniando vorassent, ossa obaesa inter se unus
quidem in alterum ludicro iecerant. Vinum quoque plenis cubbis in medio
positum sine discretione, quantum quemque libuerat, hausit.

   Postquam vero mero incaluerant, horridissime diis suis omnes vocifer-   20
abant. Clericum vero et fatuum suum id ipsum facere coegerant. Clericus
autem linguae bene eorum sciolus, propter quod aetiam eum vitae servav-
erant, cum eis valenter clamabat. Cumque iam satis lingua illorum insanis-
set, antiphonam de sancta cruce, cuius postera die inventio erat, "Sanc-
tifica nos" lacrimans incoeperat. Quam Heribaldus cum eo, quamvis voce   25
raucosus, et ipse decantabat. Conveniunt omnes, qui aderant, ad insoli-
tum captivorum cantum, et effusa laeticia saltant coram principibus et

1. **ascia**: from *ascia, ae* = "trowel," "axe." 9. **Wiborada**: a virgin martyr who had
prophesied the invasion of the Hungarians, and who lost her life at their hands on 1st
May 915. 10. **cyborium**: the better spelling, as above, is *ciborium*. 14. **foenum** =
CL *faenum* (or *fenum*), modified by *viride*; the tag comes from Mark 6.39. 17. **laniando**: from *laniare*. **vorassent**: contracted pluperfect active subjunctive, third person
plural of *vorare* = *voravissent*. **obaesa** = CL *obesa*; the substitution of "ae" for "e"
is common in ML orthography; § 1.3.1. 18. **cubbis** = CL *cupa* = "cup"; the better
spelling in ML is *cuppa* (but many forms exist (*coppa, cupa, coupa*); see Niermeyer
287, s. v. *cuppa*). 19. **discretione**: *discretio, onis* = "discretion," "discrimination";
the word has a variety of meanings in ML (see Niermeyer 338). 22. **sciolus**: *sciolus,
a, um* + genitive = "knowledgeable in . . ." (Niermeyer 946, s. v. *sciolus* 1). 23. **in-
sanisset**: contracted pluperfect active subjunctive, third person singular of *insanire* =
insanivisset. 24. **antiphonam**: *antiphona, ae* = "hymn" (Niermeyer 47). **inventio**:
i.e., the anniversary of its discovery. 25. **incoeperat** = CL *inceperat*. 27. **laeticia** =
CL *laetitia*.

luctantur. Quidam aetiam armis concurrentes, quantum disciplinae belli-
cae nossent, ostenderant. Interea clericus ille pro relaxatione sua rogandi
tempus oportunum in tali alacritate arbitratus, sanctae crucis implorans
adiutorium, provolvitur miser principum cum lacrimis pedibus. At illi
5 nimis effero spiritu sibilis et quasi grunnitu horrido satellitibus, quid velint, insinuant. Illique rabidi advolant, hominem dicto cicius corripiunt,
cultellos, ut ludicrum, quod Teutones "picchin" vocant, in coronam eius
facerent, antequam capite illum plecterent, exigunt.

Interim dum talia parant, exploratores in silva, quae castellum vergit,
10 subitanea tubarum et vocum significatione accelerant. Castellum cum
armatis legionibus obfirmatum improximo sibimet esse asserunt; clerico
ibi et Heribaldo relictis solis in claustro, celeres pro se quisque viri foras
festinant et, ut assueti erant, priusquam quisquam credat, parati in acie
stabant. Audita autem castelli natura, quod obsideri non possit, locum
15 autem longo collo et artissimo impugnantibus maximo damno certoque
periculo adibilem, tutores eius suae multitudini, dum victualia habeant,
modo viri sint, nunquam cessuros, monasterio, eo quod Gallus deus eius
ignipotens sit, tandem omisso, villae domos, ut videre possint—nam nox
proxima erat—aliquas incendunt et silentio tubis et vocibus indicto via,
20 quae Constanciam ducit, abeunt. Castellani autem cum monasterium
ardere putassent, abitu eorum comperto per compendia eos insecuti, exploratores de longe multitudinem prosecutos in faciem aggressi, quosdam
occidunt, unum autem vulneratum captum aveunt; ceteri vix fuga lapsi
multitudini tubis, ut caveant, significant. At illi campos et planitiem,
25 quam citissime poterant, optinentes aciemque, prout copia esset, alacriter
instruentes vehiculis et caeteris impedimentis circumpositis noctem vigiliis partiuntur fusique per herbas vino et somno taciti indulgent. Mane
autem prima villas proximas incurrentes, si quid fugientes reliquerint, investigant et rapiunt cunctaque; quae praetereunt, aedificia exurunt.

2. **nossent:** contracted pluperfect active subjunctive, third person plural of *noscere*
(*gnoscere*) = *novissent*.   6. **cicius** = CL *citius*.   7. **Teutones:** *Teutoni, orum* = "Germans" (Sleumer 775).   **picchin:** old High German equivalent of "to stab."   **coronam:**
i.e., the tonsure characteristic of monastic communities.   11. **improximo** = *inprox-
imo*.   16. **adibilem:** from *adibilis, e* = "approachable" (Blaise/Chirat 51).   20. **Constanciam:** better spelled *Constantia* = Constance; there are, in addition to the German
Constance, three other medieval cities with this name, see Sleumer 237, s. v. *Constantia 2–5*.   **castellani:** i.e., the occupants, for the time being, of the castle.   21. **putassent:** contracted pluperfect active subjunctive, third person plural of *putare* = *pu-
tavissent*.   23. **aveunt** = CL *avehunt;* the lack of aspirates is common in ML
orthography; § 1.5.   26. **caeteris** = CL *ceteris*.

At Engilbertus, hostium invasionis primicerius, castellum repetere caeteris dimissis, cum paucis eque audacibus monasterium vitabundus inambulat; si aliqui ad insidias relicti sint, explorat. Heribaldi fratris fatuitatem, bene quidem nati, miserans, si vel corpus eius ad sepeliendum inveniant, sollicite investigant. Illo quidem nusquam reperto—nam cacu- 5 men proximi montis, vix a clerico persuasus, cum ipso occupans inter arbusta et frutecta latuit—miserebatur adhuc, si tantae simplicitatis mancipium hostes quidem secum abegerint. Miratus aetiam vini vasa ab hostibus nimium bibulis vitata, gratias Deo egit.

—Cas. Sanc. Gal. 52–55.

THE DUCHESS HADWIG AT HER MORNING LESSON WITH EKKEHARD

Altera dein die cum diluculo, ut ibi solebant, silentium regulae, cuius et ipsa exactrix erat sollicita, de more persolvisset—nam iam monasterium in monte statuere coeperat—magistrum lectura adiit. Et cum sedisset, ad quid puer ille venerit, ipso astante inter caetera quesivit. "Propter Grecismum," ille ait, "domina mi, ut ab ore vestro aliquid raperet, alias 5 sciolum vobis illum attuli." Puer autem ipse pulcher aspectu, metro cum esset paratissimus, sic intulit:

"Esse velim Grecus, cum sim vix, domna, Latinus."

In quo illa, sicut novarum rerum cupida, adeo est delectata, ut ad se tractum osculata scabello pedum proximius locaret. A quo, ut repentinos 10 sibi adhuc versus faceret, curiosa exegerat. Puer vero magistros intuitus, quasi talis osculi insuetus, haec intulit:

"Non possum prorsus dignos componere versus.
Nam nimis expavi duce me libante suavi."

1. **primicerius:** from *primicerius, i,* the word has a variety of technical meanings, but here = "abbot" (cf. Niermeyer 848, s. v. *primicerius* 1–9). 2. **eque** = CL *aeque.* 6. **ipso** = CL *illo;* in ML *ipse* often does the work of CL *ille;* § 5.2.1 (cf. Blaise 158). 7. **frutecta:** from *frutectum, i,* = "shrubs." 8. **abegerint:** from *abigere.* 1. **regulae:** i.e., the monastic rule. 2. **exactrix:** *exactrix, exactricis* = "demander" (LS 671), modified by *ipsa;* the phrase refers to Hadwig, Duchess of Swabia, whom Ekkehard II instructed at the castle of Hohentweil, to which *monasterium* refers here. 3. **magistrum:** i.e., Ekkehard II, nephew of Ekkehard I, a distinguished scholar. 4. **caetera** = CL *cetera.* 5. **Grecismum** = *Graecum, i* = "Greek language" (Haefele 195). 6. **puer:** i.e., Purchard II, abbot of St. Gall, 1001–1022. 8. **Grecus** = CL *Graecus.* **domna:** by syncope for *domina.* 10. **scabello** = CL *scabillo.*

Illa vero extra solitam severitatem in chachinnos versa, tandem puerum coram se statuit et eum antiphonam, "Maria et flumina," quam ipsa in Grecum transtulit, canere docuit ita: "Thalassi ke potami, eulogiton kiryon; ymnite pigonton kyrion alleluia." Crebroque illum postea, cum va-
5 casset, ad se vocatum, repentinis ab eo versibus exactis, grecissare docuit et unice dilexit. Tandem quoque abeuntem Oratio et quibusdam aliis, quos hodie armarium nostrum habet, donavit libris.

—*Cas. Sanc. Gal.* 94.

1. **chachinnos** = CL *cachinnos;* the addition of aspirates is common in ML.   2. **ipsa:** Hadwig was learned in Greek because she had been betrothed to a Greek.   3. **Thalassi . . . alleluia:** a rough translation of this Greek passage, which comes from Dan. 3.77ff., is "Your seas and rivers, praise the Lord, praise Him, your font, the Lord, alleluia."   4. **vacasset:** contracted pluperfect active subjunctive, third person singular of *vacare* = *vacavisset.*   5. **grecissare:** the better spelling is *graecizare* (or *graecissare*) = "to speak/sing Greek" (Niermeyer 475).   7. **armarium:** in ML = "archive," hence "library" (Niermeyer 60).

ADAM OF BREMEN

A Description of the Islands of the North
(*Descriptio insularum aquilonis*; c. 1075)

When Helmold, the twelfth-century chronicler, set about justifying his discussion of the bishops of Oldenburg in his *Chronicle of the Slavs,* he inadvertently gave to posterity the name of the author of the *Gesta Hammaburgensis ecclesiae pontificum,* one of his best sources. But for Helmold's casual mention of "master Adam," we would know Adam of Bremen only by his initial, "A," and he would be simply an anonymous hand writing in obscure devotion of the illustrious bishops of Hamburg-Bremen.

Not that his work would lack any of its importance absent our knowledge of his name, for Adam's sense of the aims of historical inquiry are implicit in the design and execution of his work. The scope of that design is belied by the title of his work, for though Adam does in fact recall in his *History* the bishops of Hamburg-Bremen, he also works out by stages from their individual exploits to the larger history of the church in Hamburg-Bremen, to a review of diocesan affairs especially under Adalbert, and then to the details of Baltic and Scandinavian history, including a treatment of the exploits of Leif Ericsson and his cohorts in "Vinland." The four books of the *History* reflect successively these shifts of focus, and the fourth book, from which our excerpts come, has, owing to its focus, its own title, *Descriptio insularum aquilonis.*

Adam tells us that he came to Bremen as his patron, Bishop Adalbert, was celebrating twenty-four years in his episcopal chair—around 1067. He had apparently come to the attention of Adalbert for his scholarly skills: a good command of Latin, a fluent writing style, an obvious control of the Latin classics—and had been invited to Bremen to teach and write. He was quickly appointed a canon of the cathedral chapter at Bremen by Adalbert, and almost immediately started on his work. Adam's birthplace can only be conjectured, though he clearly hailed from some part of Germany. Bamberg and Würzburg have been put forward on various kinds of (inconclusive) evidence. Whatever his city of origin, Adam seems to have conceived of his *History* at least in part as a work of thanks to Adalbert for having made him a canon. But Adam's original concept, to write a history of Adalbert and his predecessors, soon became something much larger as he made his way through the records of those earlier bishops, who had always looked with interest to the North, and especially when he came to treat Adalbert's more expansive plans for a northern patriarchate administered from Bremen. This aspect of Bremen's episcopal past resulted in those sections of Adam's *History* that consider the peoples, geography, and practices of northern Europe. Adam worked on his history for a number of years—probably for most of the decade of the 1070s. He died sometime in the first half of the 1080s—possibly as early as 1081, certainly no later than 1085.

In a sense, Adam's project reverses the norms that had informed Medieval Latin historical prose for a century or more. In Liutprand and Widukind, for example, the tendency had been to focus on local history by emphasizing individual biography and secular power, while taking for granted the larger Christian context that underlay such a view. Adam works out from the details of individual biography and power to a perspective much more in line with the earlier historians of the Latin Middle Ages, such as Gregory of Tours, Bede, or Paul the Deacon, where the larger contexts of local history dominate the presentation of historical detail. Adam's reliance on a broad array of documents, sources, and reports also reminds one more of Bede than, say, Liutprand, as does his consistent use of tags from CL authors. He collated, read, and reconfigured information from at least several dozen earlier works. He read widely in and consulted with contemporary experts on matters of cartography and geography. His interest in accuracy, as well as his concern for dating, ethnography, and the association of power and personality, lend to his work a sophistication revelatory of high talents.

The *Gesta Hammaburgensis ecclesiae pontificum* has been edited by, among others, J. M. Lappenberg (*Monumenta Germaniae Historica, Scriptores Rerum Germanicarum*, Hanover, 1846, pp. 267–89; rev. 1876 under the editorship of K. Weiland and J. W. Waitz) and by B. Schmeidler (*Adam von Bremen, Hamburgische Kirchengeschichte*, Hanover, 1917), which includes extensive word and name lists helpful on difficult usages. F. J. Tschan has published an English translation (*Adam of Bremen: History of the Archbishops of Hamburg-Bremen*, New York, 1959), which includes an extensive introduction, excellent explanatory notes, and a full bibliography. Schmeidler's text is reprinted without change.

THE NORSEMEN DISCOVER AMERICA

Praeterea unam adhuc insulam recitavit a multis in eo repertam oceano, quae dicitur Winland, eo quod ibi vites sponte nascantur, vinum optimum ferentes. Nam et fruges ibi non seminatas habundare non fabulosa opinione, sed certa comperimus relatione Danorum.

Item nobis retulit beatae memoriae pontifex Adalbertus in diebus 5 antedecessoris sui quosdam nobiles de Fresia viros causa pervagandi maris in boream vela tetendisse, eo quod ab incolis eius populi dicitur ab ostio Wirrahae fluminis directo cursu in aquilonem nullam terram occurrere preter infinitum occeanum. Cuius rei novitate pervestiganda coniurati sodales a littore Fresonum laeto celeumate progressi sunt. Deinde 10 relinquentes hinc Daniam, inde Britanniam pervenerunt ad Orchadas. Quibus a laeva dimissis, cum Nortmanniam in dextris haberent, longo traiectu glacialem Island collegerunt. A quo loco maria sulcantes in ultimam septentrionis axem, postquam retro se omnes, de quibus supra dic-

---

1. **recitavit:** the speaker is the King of the Danes. 2. **Winland:** Vineland, the term used by the Norsemen to designate that part of North America which they discovered early in the eleventh century. Adam uses an adjectival form, *Winlandensis*, also (Schmeidler 322, s. v. *Winland; Winlandensis*). **eo quod:** CL and ML idiom = "because." 3. **habundare** = CL *abundare*, with *fruges*, governed by *comperimus*. The wider use of aspirates is common in ML orthography. 5. **pontifex:** *pontifex, pontificis* = "archbishop"; the word designates several ecclesiastical ranks, including pope and bishop (cf. Sleumer 617). **Adalbertus:** archbishop of Hamburg–Bremen and Adam's teacher at the cathedral school there, he is a prominent figure in Adam's *History*. 6. **antedecessoris:** *antedecessor, oris* = "predecessor" (Niermeyer 47), modified by *sui*. **Fresia:** more commonly in ML = *Frisia, ae* = Frisia (Sleumer 344). 7. **tetendisse:** perfect active infinitive of *tendere*, read with *retulit* and *quosdam nobiles . . . viros*. 8. **Wirrahae:** *Wirraha, ae*, the Weser River, modified by *fluminis* (Schmeidler 322, s. v. *Wirraha*). 9. **preter** = CL *praeter*. **occeanum** = CL *oceanum;* the doubling of a single CL consonant (and vice versa) is common in ML orthography. 10. **Fresonum:** more commonly in ML = *Frisones, um* = Frisia (Sleumer 344, s. v. *Frisones*). **celeumate** = CL *celeusma, atis*, neuter noun from the Greek κέλευσμα, modified by *laeto*, the call of the chief oarsman which gave the time to the rowers. The feminine form *celeusma, ae* also exists (cf. LS 309, s. v. *celeusma*). 11. **Daniam:** *Dania, ae* = Denmark, object of *relinquentes* (Sleumer 257, s. v. *Dania*). **inde:** with *hinc,* coordinating conjunctions, "here, . . . there. . . ." **Orchadas:** spelled variously in Adam, but most commonly as a first declension noun, *Orchada, ae* = the Orkney Islands (Schmeidler 311, s. v. *Orcades insulae*). 12. **Nortmanniam:** *Nortmannia, ae* = Norway (Schmeidler 310, s. v. *Nortmannia*). 13. **Island:** spelled variously in Adam = Iceland, modified by *glacialem* (Schmeidler 306, s. v. *Island*). **collegerunt** = CL *legerunt*, "sailed." 14. **septentrionis:** *septentrio, trionis* = "north"; the form is classical (cf. LS 1675, s. v. *septentriones;* cf. Sleumer 710, s. v. *septentrio*). **omnes:** i.e., *insulae*.

tum est, insulas viderunt, omnipotenti Deo et sancto confessori Willehado suam commendantes viam et audatiam subito collapsi sunt in illam
tenebrosam rigentis oceani caliginem, quae vix oculis penetrari valeret.
Et ecce instabilis oceani euripus ad initia quaedam fontis sui archana re-
5 currens infelices nautas iam desperatos, immo de morte sola cogitantes
vehementissimo impetu traxit ad chaos [—hanc dicunt esse voraginem
abyssi—] illud profundum, in quo fama est omnes recursus maris, qui
decrescere videntur, absorberi et denuo revomi, quod fluctuatio crescens
dici solet. Tunc illis solam Dei misericordiam implorantibus, ut animas
10 eorum susciperet, impetus ille recurrens pelagi quasdam sociorum naves
abripuit, ceteras autem revomens excursio longe ab alteris post terga repulit. Ita illi ab instanti periculo quod oculis viderant, oportuno Dei auxilio liberati toto nisu remorum fluctus adiuvarunt.

Et iam periculum caliginis et provintiam frigoris evadentes, insperate
15 appulerunt ad quandam insulam altissimis in circuitu scopulis ritu oppidi
munitam. Huc visendorum gratia locorum egressi reppererunt homines
in antris subterraneis meridiano tempore latitantes. Pro quorum foribus
infinita iacebat copia vasorum aureorum et eiusmodi metallorum, quae
rara mortalibus et preciosa putantur. Itaque sumpta parte gazarum, quam
20 sublevare poterant, laeti remiges festine remeant ad naves. Cum subito
retro se venientes contemplati sunt homines mirae altitudinis, quos nostri
appellant Cyclopes. Eos antecedebant canes magnitudinem solitam ex-
cedentes eorum quadrupedum, quorum incursu raptus est unus de sociis,
et in momento laniatus est coram eis. Reliqui vero suscepti ad naves evas-
25 erunt periculum, gygantibus, ut referebant, pene in altum vociferando sequentibus. Tali fortuna comitati Fresones Bremam perveniunt, ubi Alebrando pontifici ex ordine cuncta narrantes pio Christo et confessori eius
Willehado reversionis et salutis suae hostias immolarunt.

—*Descrip. Ins. Aquil.* 39–41.

1. **Willehado:** *Willehadus, i* = Willehad, Bishop of Bremen (Schmeidler 322). 2. **audatiam** = CL *audaciam.* 4. **euripus:** *euripus, i,* from the Greek εὔριπος (LS 664),
"channel." 8. **descrescere . . . absorberi . . . revomi:** these infinitives are governed by
videntur. 11. **repulit** = CL *reppulit,* from *repellere.* 14. **provintiam** = CL *provinciam;* palatalization is a common feature of ML phonology. 16. **munitam:** perfect
passive participle of *munire,* modifying *insulam,* with *ritu oppidi* dependent on it.
25. **gygantibus** = CL *gigantibus,* "giants." 26. **Alebrando pontifici:** Bishop Ale-
brand, also known as Bescelinus (Schmeidler 291, s. v. *Alebrandus*).

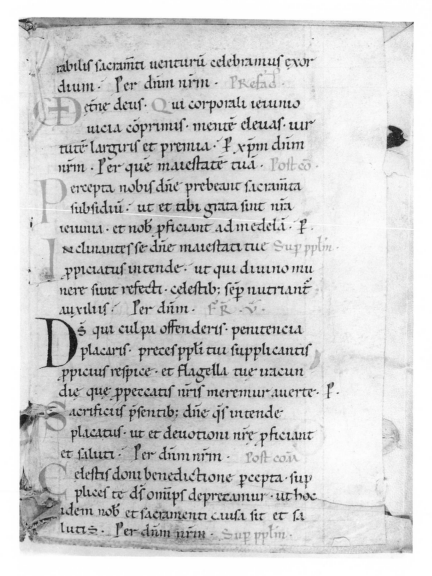

PLATE 16. A loose folio from a hymnary, found in the backing of Petrus Haedus, *De amoris generibus*, published in 1492.

PLATE 16

Hymnary, single folio on parchment, eleventh century
Annmary Brown Memorial Collection
John Hay Library, Brown University

This well-preserved folio from a Latin hymnary, shown here still attached to the backing of Petrus Haedus's *De amoris generibus* (published in 1492), is 21 cm. in height and written in Carolingian minuscule. The folio is cut only at the bottom, otherwise showing its original left, right, and top margins. It is ruled and shows 24 lines, though it clearly was longer than this originally. It has red and blue initials. It dates from the eleventh century and is probably from Italy. See plate 7 for a fuller discussion of the recycling of earlier manuscripts in the production of later codices and in the printing of incunables.

THE CAMBRIDGE SONGS

(*Carmina Cantabrigiensia;* c. 1050)

The place-names with which the authors of the previous selections have been associated—St. Gall, Corvey, Gandersheim, Bremen—affirm the fundamental place Germany holds in the study of Medieval Latin literature. The *Cambridge Songs* help to ratify this place, for, though the modern title of the collection signals an English provenance for the lone manuscript preserving it, many of the poems of the collection are German in origin. To the important developments in Germany in Medieval Latin prose, historiography, and drama, therefore, to which the works of Liutprand, Widukind, Ekkehard, and Hrotsvita speak, can be added unique inroads in thematics, prosody, and musical composition represented by the *Cambridge Songs*.

It is important, however, apart from its obvious Germanicism, to understand also the collection's internationalism, for aside from the songs contained within it of French and Italian origin is the fact that it was sent to—and copied in—(Anglo-Saxon) England. We call the poems the *Cambridge Songs* because the (lone) manuscript recording them is housed in the Cambridge University Library. The manuscript itself was produced at the monastery of Saint Augustine in Canterbury, probably just before the Norman invasion of England, and remained there until the dissolution of the Catholic Church in the sixteenth century, after which it arrived in Cambridge. The songs themselves stand at the end of an enormous compilation of Latin poetry of late antique, Carolingian, and Anglo-Latin authors. They would seem, then, to form the end point of an anthology of Medieval Latin verse. The latest date retrievable from the *Cambridge Songs* themselves is 1039, and it seems clear that the manuscript as a whole was prepared in the following decade.

Until the 1980s, the *Cambridge Songs* were thought to consist of poems 1–49, conventionally numbered, as they were found in the manuscript and associated with each other based on an obvious incipit in the manuscript at folio 432 r. 1, and on the fact that they were copied out from the exemplar by a single hand. It had always been thought, however, that several leaves were missing from the manuscript; miraculously, one of them was located in Germany in 1982 and returned to the codex—

where the scribal hand as well as the pagination added in the fifteenth century accorded perfectly with what remained. This leaf was incontrovertibly part of the *Cambridge Songs* collection, and its contents—a cohort of twenty-seven *carmina* composed of initial passages of the *metra* of Boethius's *Consolation of Philosophy* (see pp. 138–42)—have now become poems 50–76 of the collection. The most recent work on the *Songs* would also add seven more songs located subsequent to the collection in the manuscript, but written in a different hand and treating different thematic concerns. There are good grounds to include these poems also in the collection, and to see it now as a total collection of 83 songs.

The poems of the collection display a diversity of form, content, and function. Classical quantities are used, as well as rhythmic meters. The meters do not, however, correspond in set ways to topics, so that the genres of the *Cambridge Songs*—as is the case with much Medieval Latin poetry—are unique. We can extricate praise poetry for kings and bishops, erotic verses (some of which have been erased or inked out), nature poems, and other sorts of writing less easily classified. As a collection, this variety is perhaps to be expected. Less accessible is the overall function intended for the collection—a schoolbook? a handbook for wandering singers? a formal anthology for pleasure and edification?—and the musical foundation of many of the poems.

Collateral German manuscripts help to strengthen the musical basis of several of the *Cambridge Songs,* including the second song excerpted here, the *Modus Ottinc,* whose title (though it is not found in the Cambridge manuscript per se), not to mention contents, affirms the sung quality of its lines (*modus* means "melody" in ML). This poem in particular also points to Germanic traditions, for it recounts the story of the singing of a melody by the minstrels of the castle in order to awaken Otto I after it was discovered that his palace was on fire. The poem, written in uneven intervals of iambic and trochaic verses, is also a panegyric on Otto II and Otto III. After celebrating the rout of the Hungarians at the Battle at the River Lech by Otto I, Otto II is mentioned (5b) before a fuller panegyric on Otto III (6a,b) is offered. Poem 17, reprinted here, on the death of Henry II, the great-grandson of Otto I, is a rhythmic sequence with a refrain written in dactylic hexameters. Poem 15, about famous liars, represents an old Germanic tradition of writing about this topic, much as the poem on Heriger probably represents an older vernacular German original. Poems 24 and 35 are written in ancient meters, while Poem 23, on summer, is in the accentual Sapphic stanza popular in the Latin Middle Ages. The first selection, on the nightingale, most likely has a

French provenance. It is not clear how, if at all, the collection was originally arranged, and arguments for and against thematic design have been made. Similarly to the debates over Catullus's collection, however, arrangement would seem to remain in the eye of the beholder.

The *Cambridge Songs* have been edited by K. Breul (*The Cambridge Songs: A Goliard's Song Book of the XIth Century,* Cambridge, 1915, which contains photographic copies of excellent quality of poems 1–49, transcriptions (though with some rearrangement and minor alterations of the Latin text), thorough notes, and discussions of the text and its antecedents); K. Strecker (*Carmina Cantabrigiensia: Die Cambridger Lieder,* Hanover, 1926), with copious notes (in German); W. Bulst (*Carmina Cantabrigiensia,* Heidelberg, 1950); and J. Ziolkowski (*The Cambridge Songs (Carmina Cantabrigiensia),* New York, 1994), which accords with the ordering of the poems as recorded in the manuscript, includes the new songs recently rediscovered and/or now considered part of the collection, and contains introduction, notes, an English translation, and bibliography. M. T. Gibson, M. Lapidge, and C. Page have analyzed the discovery of the missing leaf, which added a cohort of poems to the collection ("Neumed Boethian *metra* from Canterbury: A Newly Recovered Leaf of Cambridge, University Library, Gg. 5.35 (the 'Cambridge Songs' manuscript)," *Anglo-Saxon England* 12 (1983): 141–52). Raby 2, 291ff., 328ff., offers a full discussion of the collection also. Ziolkowski's text is reprinted with consonantal and vocalic "u" distinguished.

CARMEN 10: THE NIGHTINGALE

1. Aurea personet lira   clara modulamina,
   Simplex corda sit extensa   voce quindenaria,
   Primum sonum mese reddat   lege ypodorica.
2. Philomele demus laudes   in voce organica,
5   Dulce melos decantantes   sicut docet musica,
   Sine cuius arte vera   nulla valent cantica.

---

1. **lira** = CL *lyra*. **modulamina**: from *modulamen, inis* = "melody" (Blaise/Chirat 537). 2. **quindenaria**: the poet refers to this poem itself, composed in mono-rhymed fifteen-syllable trochaic verses (except for 6.2 which does not end in "a"). 3. **mese**: from *mese, es* = "middle note" (LS 1138; TLL 8.854.37–50). **ypodorica**: the better spelling is *hypodorica*, from *hypodoricus, a, um* = "hypodorian" (Blaise/Chirat 398; Latham 232). 4. **Philomele** = CL *Philomelae*. **organica**: from *organicus, a, um* = "melodious" (Ziolkowski 195).

3. Cum telluris vere nova   producuntur germina
    Nemorosa circumcirca   frondescunt et brachia,
    Flagrat odor quam suavis   florida per gramina.

4. Hilarescit philomela   dulcis vocis conscia   10
    Et extendens modulando   gutturis spiramina
    Reddit voces ad estivi   temporis indicia.

5. Instat nocti et diei   voce sub dulcisona
    Soporatis dans quietem   cantus per discrimina
    Nec non pulchra viatori   laboris solatia.   15

6. Vocis eius pulchritudo   clarior quam cithara
    Vincit omnes cantitando   volucrum catervulas
    Implens silvas atque cuncta   modulis arbuscula.

7. Volitando scandit alta   arborum cacumina
    Gloriosa valde facta   veris pro letitia   20
    Ac festiva satis gliscit   sibilare carmina.

8. Felix tempus cui resultat   talis consonantia.
    Utinam per duodena   mensium curricula
    Dulcis philomela daret   sue vocis organa.

9. Sonos tuos vox non valet   imitari lirica,   25
    Quibus nescit consentire   fistula clarisona,
    Mira quia modularis   melorum tripudia.

10. O tu parva, numquam cessa   canere, avicula.
    Tuam decet symphoniam   monocordi musica
    Que tuas <laude>s <frequenta>t   voce diatonica.   30

11. Nolo, nolo ut quiescas   temporis ad otia,
    Sed ut letos des concentus   tua volo ligula,
    Cuius laude memoreris   in regum palatia.

12. Cedit auceps ad frondosa   resonans umbracula,
    Cedit cignus et suavis   ipsius melodia,   35
    Cedit tibi timpanista   et sonora tibia.

---

8. **circumcirca**: ML adverb = "entirely around" (Niermeyer 182). 11. **spiramina**: from *spiramen, inis* = "little breaths" (LS 1742). 12. **estivi** = CL *aestivi*. 15. **solatia** = CL *solacia*. 17. **catervulas**: diminutive of *caterva* = "small crowd" (Latham 76); if the MS is correct, this is the only line that does not end in "a." 20. **letitia** = CL *laetitia*. 24. **sue** = CL *suae*, modifying *vocis*. 25. **lirica** = CL *lyrica*. 29. **symphoniam** = "harmonious accord," "symphony," "consonance" (Blaise/Chirat 805). **monocordi**: the better spelling is *monochordum, i* = single-chord instrument, here in the genitive (Blaise/Chirat 539). 30. **que** = CL *quae*. **diatonica**: from *diatonicus, a, um* = "diatonic" (LS 569), modifying *voce*. 32. **letos** = CL *laetos*. **ligula**: from *lingua* (sometimes *lingula*), *ae* = "little tongue" (Blaise/Chirat 496). 36. **timpanista** = CL *tympanista, ae* = "a drummer," "a tympanum player" (LS 1921).

13. Quamvis enim videaris   corpore premodica,
    Tamen te cuncti auscultant.   nemo dat iuvamina,
    Nisi solus rex celestis,   qui gubernat omnia.

40 14. Iam preclara tibi satis   dedimus obsequia,
    Que in voce sunt iocunda   et in verbis rithmica,
    Ad scolares et ad ludos   digne congruentia.

15. Tempus adest, ut solvatur   nostra vox armonica,
    Ne fatigent plectrum lingue   cantionum tedia,
45 Ne pigrescat auris prompta   fidium ad crusmata.

16. Trinus deus in personis,   unus in essentia,
    Nos gubernet et conservet   sua sub clementia
    Et regnare nos concedat   cum ipso in gloria.

CARMEN II: THE OTTO MELODY

1a. Magnus cesar Otto,   1b. Stant ministri regis,
    quem hic modus refert   timent dormientem
    in nomine,   attingere
    Otdinc dictus,   et cordarum
    quadam nocte   pulsu facto
    somno membra   excitatum
    dum collocat,   salvificant,
    palatium   et domini
    casu subito   nomen carmini
    inflammatur.   inponebant.

2a. Excitatus   2b. Iuxta litus
    spes suis surrexit,   sedebant armati,
    timor magnus   urbes, agros,
    adversis mox venturus   villas vastant late,
    nam tum fama volitat   matres plorant filios
    Ungarios   et filii
    signa in eum   matres undique
    extulisse.   exulari.

38. **iuvamina:** from *iuvamen, inis* = "help," "aid," "assistance" (LS 1020).   41. **rith-mica** = CL *rythmica.*   43. **armonica** = CL *harmonica;* the loss of aspirates in ML orthography is common.   45. **crusmata:** from *crusma, atis* = "string music" (LS 485) but more specifically the single note of of stringed music (TLL 4.1252.55–59; Ziolkowski 196).

    Carm. 11. The poem comprises six pairs of strophes without rhyme (see Ziolkowski 202).   1a. **cesar** = Caesar, i.e., Otto I.   **dictus:** i.e., "called," with *Otdinc*, in the genitive = "called of Otto."   2a. **Ungarios:** from *Hungari, orum* = Hungarians (on the various forms see Sleumer 393).   2b. **armati:** from *armatus, a, um,* but standing as a substantive here = "troops."   **exulari** = CL *exsulari.*

3a. "Hei quis ego" dixerat
Otto "videor Partis?
diu, <diu> milites
tardos moneo frustra.
dum ego demoror,
crescit clades semper.
ergo moras rumpite
et Parthicis
mecum <hostibus>
obviate."

4a. His incensi
bella fremunt,
arma poscunt,
hostes vocant,
signa sequuntur;
tantus tubis;
clamor passim oritur
et milibus
centum Teutones
inmiscentur.

5a. Parva manu
cesis Parthis,
ante et post
sepe victor,
communem cunctis
movens luctum,
nomen, regnum, optimos
hereditans
mores filio
obdormivit.

3b. Dux Cuonrad intrepidus,
quo non fortior alter,
"miles" inquit "pereat,
quem hoc terreat bellum.
arma induite;
armis instant hostes.
ipse ego signifer
effudero
primus sanguinem
inimicum."

4b. Pauci cedunt,
plures cadunt;
Francus instat,
Parthus fugit.
vulgus exangue
undis obstat;
Licus rubens sanguine
Danubio
cladem Parthicam
ostendebat.

5b. Adolescens
post hunc Otto
imperavit
multis annis
cesar iustus,
clemens, fortis.
unum modo defuit,
nam inclitis
raro preliis
triumphabat.

3a. **Partis:** from *Parthi, orum,* here used to mean *Hungari.*   3b. **Cuonrad:** *Cuonrad, atis* = Conrad, Duke of Franconia, the hero of the battle of the River Lech, in which the Hungarians were defeated, and to which these lines refer.   **quo:** ablative of comparison. 4a. **incensi:** perfect passive participle of *incendere,* the subject of *fremunt,* with ablative of means *his (verbis)* dependent on it.   **milibus:** ablative of *mille* = "with thousands."   **centum Teutones:** *Teutoni, orum* = "Germans" (Sleumer 775).   **inmiscentur** = CL *immiscentur.*   4b. **exangue** = CL *exsangue,* modifying *vulgus.*   **Licus** = CL *Lycus,* here designating the River Lech (LS 1090, s. v. *Lycus* VII A–F).   **Danubio** = CL *Danuvio* = the Danube.   **Parthicam:** *Parthicus, a, um* = "Parthian," modifies *cladem.*   5a. **cesis** = CL *caesis,* the perfect passive participle of *caedere.*   **sepe** = CL *saepe.*   **hereditans:** present active participle of *hereditare* = "bequeathing."   5b. **adolescens . . . Otto:** i.e., Otto II.

6a. Eius autem
    clara proles
    Otto, decus
    iuventutis,
    ut fortis, <ita>
    felix erat.
    arma quos numquam
      militum
    domuerant,
    fama nominis
    satis vicit.

6b. Bello fortis,
    pace potens,
    in utroque
    tamen mitis,
    inter triumphos,
    bella, pacem
    semper suos pauperes
    respexerat,
    inde pauperum
    pater fertur.

7. Finem demus modo,
    ne forte notemur
    ingenii culpa
    tantorum virtutes
    ultra quicquam
    deterere,
    quas denique
    Maro inclitus
    vix equaret.

CARMEN 15: A CLEVER LIAR

1. Mendosam quam cantilenam ago,
    puerulis commendatam dabo,
    quo modulos per mendaces risum
    auditoribus ingentem fera<nt>.

5 2a. Liberalis et decora
    cuidam regi erat nata,
    quam sub lege huius modi
    procis obponit querendam:

2b. Si quis mentiendi gnarus
10   usque adeo instet fallendo
    dum cesaris ore fallax
    predicitur, is ducat filiam.

6a. **Otto:** i.e., Otto III. **ut . . . erat:** this line is owed to Cicero, *Pro Mur.* 38.   7a. **Maro:** i.e., Virgil.
    Carm. 15. The poem is written in no recognizable meter (for a fuller discussion see Ziolkowski 220–21).   8. **obponit** = CL *opponit.*   **querendam** = CL *quaerendam.*

3a. Quo audito Suevus
    nil moratus inquit
    "raptis armis ego   15
    cum venatu\<m\> solus irem,
    lepusculus inter feras
    telo tactus occumbebat.
    mox effusis intestinis
    caput avulsum cum cute cedo.   20
3b. Cumque cesum manu
    levaretur caput,
    lesa aure effunduntur
    mellis modii centeni
    sotiaque auris tacta   25
    totidem pisarum fudit.
    quibus intra pellem strictis
    lepus ipse dum secatur,
    crepidine summa caude
    kartam regiam latentem cepi,   30
  4. Que servum te firmat esse meum."
    "mentitur" clamat rex "karta et tu!"
    Sic rege deluso Suevus falsa
    gener regius est arte factus.

CARMEN 17: LAMENT FOR THE DEATH OF HENRY II
(1024 C.E.)

1. Lamentemur nostra,   socii, peccata;
   lamentemur \<et ploremus\>.   quare tacemus?
   pro iniquitate   corruimus late;
   scimus celi hinc offensum   regem inmensum.

    Heinrico requiem, rex Christe, dona perhennem.   5

2. Non fuimus digni   munere insigni
   munus \<dico\> sive donum,   Heinricum bonum

---

13. **Suevus:** the better spelling is *Suebus, i* = "Swabian" (Sleumer 752, s. v. *Suebia: Suebi*). 17. **lepusculus:** i.e., "a little hare" (LS 1052). 20. **avulsum:** perfect passive participle of *avellere*. **cedo** = CL *caedo*. 30. **kartam** = CL *chartam*.

    Carm. 17. This poem has been written in alternating twelve-syllable and thirteen-syllable lines, with internal end-rhyme, four of which total one strophe. The refrain is a hexameter. 4. **inmensum** = CL *immensum*. 5. **Heinrico:** from *Heinricus, i* = Henry II. **perhennem** = CL *perennem;* the use of aspirates is common in ML orthography.

qui ex iuventute	magne fuit vite
procreatus regum stirpe	rexit et ipse.

10   Heinrico requiem, rex Christe, dona perhennem.

3. Orbis erat pignus,   regno fuit dignus.
imperator Romanorum,   rector Francorum
imperabat Suevis,   Saxonibus cunctis,
Bauvaro truces Sclavos   fecit pacatos.

15   Heinrico requiem, rex Christe, dona perhennem.

4. Possumus mirari   de domino tali:
res tractando laicatus   fit litteratus,
prudens in sermone,   providus opere,
viduarum tutor bonus,   orphanis pius.

20   Heinrico requiem, rex Christe, dona perhennem.

5. Heinricus secundus,   plangat illum mundus,
fines servans Christianos   pellit paganos,
stravit adversantes   pacem persequentes,
voluptati contradixit,   sobrie vixit.

25   Heinrico requiem, rex Christe, dona perhennem.

6. Quis cesar tam largus   fuit pauperibus?
quis tam loca sublimavit   atque ditavit
atria sanctorum   ubere bonorum?
ex propriis fecit magnum   episcopatum.

30   Heinrico requiem, rex Christe, dona perhennem.

7. Ploret hunc Europa   iam decapitata;
advocatum Roma ploret,   Christum exoret,

---

8. **magne . . . vite** = CL *magnae . . . vitae;* the substitution of "e" for "ae" is common in ML orthography.   12. **Francorum:** *Franci, orum* = "the Germans" (Sleumer 341)   13. **Suevis:** the better spelling is *Suebi, orum* = "Swabians," a people who lived east of the Rhine and north of the Danube (Sleumer 752, s. v. *Suebia: Suebi*). **Saxonibus:** *Saxones, um* = "Saxons" (Sleumer 700).   14. **Bauvaro:** the better spelling is *Bavaro* = "Bavarian" (Sleumer 151).   **Sclavos:** the better spelling is *Slavos* = "the Slavs" (Sleumer 731, s. v. *Slavi*).   17. **laicatus:** a fourth declension noun, *laicatus, us* = "laity" (Niermeyer 579).   23. **stravit:** from *sternere.*   27. **sublimavit:** from *sublimare* = "to exalt."   29. **magnum episcopatum:** i.e., Bamberg, founded and endowed by Henry, and where he was buried also.   32. **advocatum:** i.e., in his role as the Holy Roman Emperor.

| ut sibi fidelem | prestet seniorem, |
| recognoscat grave dampnum | ecclesiarum. |

Heinrico requiem, rex Christe, dona perhennem.   35

8. Dicamus Heinrico   domini amico,
   ut quiescat post obitum   semper in evum,
   dicat omnis clerus   anime illius
   'pace Christi <re>quiescat,   gaudia noscat.'

Heinrico requiem, rex Christe, dona perhennem.   40

CARMEN 23: A SONG FOR SUMMER

1. Vestiunt silve tenera ramorum
   virgulta, suis onerata pomis;
   canunt de celsis sedibus palumbes
   carmina cunctis.

2. Hic turtur gemit, resonat hic turdus,   5
   pangit hic priscus me<ru>lorum sonus
   passer nec tacens, arripit garritu
   alta sub ulmis.

3. Hic leta canit philomela frondis,
   longum effundit sibilum per aura<s>   10
   sollempne; milvus tremulaque voce
   aethera pulsat.

4. Ad astra volans aquila, in auris
   alauda canit, modulis resolvit,
   desursum vergit, dissimili modo   15
   dum terram tangit.

5. Velox plipiat iugiter hirundo,
   pangit coturnix, gracula resultat:
   aves sic cunctis celebrant estivum
   undique carmen.   20

33. **prestet** = CL *praestet*.   **seniorem:** this is a technical term in ML that has many meanings; here it is used in a quasi-feudal sense to mean "lord," or "seigneur" (cf. Niermeyer 957, s. v. *senior* 1).   34. **dampnum** = CL *damnum;* the addition of a parasitic consonant is common in ML orthography.   37. **evum** = CL *aevum.*   38. **anime** = CL *animae.*

    Carm. 23. The poem is written in Sapphics.   1. **silve** = CL *silvae.*   9. **leta** = CL *laeta;* with *frondis* dependent on it.   11. **sollempne** = CL *sollemne*, modifies *sibilum.* 19. **estivum** = CL *aestivum.*

6. Nulla inter aves similis est api,
que talem gerit tipum castitatis,
nisi que Christum portavit <in> alvo
inviolata.

Carmen 24: The Bishop and the Braggart

1. Heriger, urbis Maguntiacensis
antistes, quendam vidit prophetam,
qui ad infernum se dixit raptum.
2. Inde cum multas referret causas,
subiunxit totum esse infernum
accinctum densis undique silvis.
3. Heriger illi ridens respondit
"meum subulcum illuc ad pastum
nolo cum macris mittere porcis!"
4. Vir ait falsus "fui translatus
in templum celi Christumque vidi
letum sedentem et comedentem.
5. Iohannes baptista erat pincerna
atque preclari pocula vini
porrexit cunctis vocatis sanctis."
6. Heriger ait "prudenter egit
Christus Iohannem ponens pincernam,
quoniam vinum non bibit umquam.
<7. . . . . >
8. Mendax probaris, cum Petrum dicis
illic magistrum esse cocorum,
est quia summi ianitor celi.

21. **api:** from *apis, is.* 22. **tipum** = CL *typum.* **castitatis:** the idea of chastity with respect to bees is old and consistently applied, both in ancient and medieval literature (cf. Virgil, *Geo.* 4.197–202, e.g.). 23. **alvo:** this feminine noun means both "beehive" and "womb."

Carm. 24. This poem is written in paired end-rhyming adonics (i.e., the fourth line of the Sapphic stanza). 1. **Heriger:** Bishop of Mainz (913–927); the poem is later than his episcopate and is probably based on a German version contemporary with his reign. **Maguntiacensis:** *Maguntiacensis, is* = "Mainz" (cf. Sleumer 491, s. v. *Magontiacum*). 3. **infernum:** "the after world." 6. **accinctum:** perfect passive participle from *accingere.* 9. **macris:** from *macer, era, erum.* **comedentem:** present active participle of *comedere.* 13. **pincerna:** "cup-bearer" (LS 1377). 19. Although no lacuna appears in the MS, it seems likely that something is missing here, considering what is said of Peter in the following stanza. 22. **celi** = CL *caeli,* and elsewhere in this poem.

9. Honore quali
   habuit ibi?
   volo ut narres
10. Respondit homo
    partem pulmonis
    hoc manducavi
11. Heriger illum
    loris ligari
    sermone duro
12. "Si te ad suum
    Christus, ut secum
    cave ne furtum

te deus celi
ubi sedisti?
quid manducasses."   25
"angulo uno
furabar cocis.
atque recessi."
iussit ad palum
scopisque cedi,   30
hunc arguendo
invitet pastum
capias cibum,
facias."

CARMEN 35: THE PRIEST AND THE WOLF

1. Quibus ludus est animo
   hoc advertant ridiculum.
2. Sacerdos iam ruricola
   vivebat amans pecudis;
3. Ad cuius tale studium
   nisi foret tam proxima
4. Hi minuentes numerum
   dant impares ex paribus.
5. Qui dolens sui fieri
   quia diffidit viribus,
6. Fossam cavat non modicam
   Et ne pateret hostibus,
7. Humano datum commodo
   lupus, dum nocte circuit,
8. Accurrit mane presbiter,
   intus protento baculo

et iocularis cantio,
est verum, non fictit<i>um.
aetate sub decrepita
hic enim mos est rusticis.
Omne patebat commodum,   5
luporum altrix silvula.
perdentes summam generum
et pares ex imparibus.
detrimentum peculii,
vindictam querit artibus.   10
intus ponens agniculam,
Superne tegit frondibus.
nil maius est ingenio.
spe prede captus incidit.
gaudet vicisse taliter.   15
lupi minatur oculo.

25. **manducasses:** syncopated pluperfect active subjunctive, second person singular of *manducare* = *manducavisses*.   30. **scopisque:** from *scopa, ae* = "rod," "birch" (LS 1646, s. v. 1 *scopa*).   31. **arguendo:** the gerund of *arguere*, in the ablative, with the force of a present participle, a common construction in ML.   34. **facias:** the MS ends with *facias*, but metrically this will not do; several conjectures have been suggested (see Ziolkowski 244, who chooses not to emend).
    Carm. 35. This poem is written in dactylic hexameters.   8. **impares . . . imparibus:** i.e., by taking one at a time the wolf makes the number alternately odd and even. 11. **agniculam:** diminutive of *agnus* = "little lamb" (LS 72).   14. **prede** = CL *praedae*, dependent on *spe*.   15. **presbiter:** the better spelling is *presbyter, eri* = "priest" (Sleumer 632). **vicisse:** perfect active infinitive of *vincere*.

9. "Iam," inquit "fera pessima,   tibi rependam debita.
   aut hic frangetur baculus   Aut hic crepabit oculus."
10. Hoc dicto simul impulit,   Verbo sed fatum defuit
    Nam lupus servans oculum   morsu retentat baculum.
11. At ille miser vetulus,   dum sese trahit firmius,
    Ripa cedente corruit   Et lupo comes incidit.
12. Hinc stat lupus, hinc   timent, sed dispariliter,
    presbiter;
    Nam ut fidenter arbitror,   lupus stabat securior.
13. Sacerdos secum musitat   septemque psalmos ruminat,
    sed revolvit frequentius   "miserere mei, deus."
14. "Hoc" inquit, "infortunii   Dant mihi vota populi,
    Quorum neglexi animas,   Quorum comedi victimas."
15. Pro defunctorum merito   cantat "placebo domino"
    et pro votis viventium   totum cantat psalterium.
16. Post completum psalterium   commune prestat commodum
    Sacerdotis timiditas   atque lupi calliditas.
17. Nam cum acclinis presbiter   perfiniret "pater noster"
    Atque clamaret domino   "Sed libera nos a malo,"
18. Hic dorsum eius insilit   Et saltu liber effugit
    et cuius arte captus est,   illo pro scala usus est.
19. Ast ille letus nimium   Cantat "laudate dominum"
    Et promisit pro populo   se oraturum amodo.
20. Hinc a vicinis queritur   Et inventus extrahitur
    sed numquam <post> devotius Oravit nec fidelius.

CARMEN 42: THE LAZY ABBOT

1. In gestis patrum veterum   quoddam legi ridiculum,
   exemplo tamen habile,   quod vobis dico rithmice.
2. Iohannes abba parvulus   statura, non virtutibus,
   ita maiori socio,   quicum erat in heremo,

30. **psalterium:** from *psalterium, i* = "the psalter" (Sleumer 644).   33. **perfiniret:** from *perfinire* = "to finish" (Blaise/Chirat 611).   38. **amodo:** i.e., "henceforth" (Blaise/Chirat 77); the combination of CL particles into new forms, as here, is common to ML.

Carm. 42. This poem is written in paired verses of eight syllables with internal rhyme, four of which comprise a strophe.   2. **rithmice** = CL *rythmice*, from *rhythmice, is* = "rhythmical poem."   4. **heremo:** the better spelling is *eremo*, from *eremus, i* = "desert" (on the various forms and meanings of this word see Niermeyer 380, Blaise/Chirat 313).

3. "Volo" dicebat, "vivere   secure sicut angelus,   5
    nec veste nec cibo frui,   qui laboretur manibus."
4. Maior dicebat "moneo,   ne sis incepti properus,
    frater, quod tibi postmodum   sit non cepisse sacius."
5. At minor "qui non dimicat,   non cadit neque superat"
    ait et nudus heremum   interiorem penetrat.   10
6. Septem dies gramineo   vix ibi durat pabulo
    octava fames imperat,   ut ad sodalem redeat.
7. Qui sero clausa ianua   tutus sedet in cellula,
    cum minor voce debili   "frater," apellat "aperi!
8. Iohannes opis indigus   notis assistit foribus   15
    nec spernat tua pietas,   quem redigit necessitas."
9. Respondit ille deintus   "Iohannes factus angelus
    miratur celi cardines.   ultra non curat homines."
10. Iohannes foris excubat   malamque noctem tolerat
    et preter voluntariam   hanc agit penitentiam.   20
11. Facto mane recipitur   satisque verbis uritur
    sed intentus ad crustula   fert patienter omnia.
12. Refocilatus domino   grates agit et socio.
    dehinc rastellum brachiis   temptat movere languidis.
13. Castigatus angustia   de levitate nimia,   25
    cum angelus non potuit,   vir bonus esse didicit.

8. **cepisse** = CL *coepisse.*   20. **preter** = CL *praeter.*   23. **refocilatus:** from *refocilare* (sometimes *refocillare*) = "revived" (Blaise/Chirat 705).   24. **rastellum:** diminutive of *rastrum* = "little rake," "little hoe" (LS 1525).

PLATE 17. A folio from a fifteenth-century collection of sermons, written in French.

PLATE 17

Book of Sermons
French manuscript on paper, fifteenth century, fol. 290 verso
John Hay Library, Brown University

In the twelfth, thirteenth, and fourteenth centuries, there occurred a substantial increase in the writing and collection of sermons, a process stimulated in large part by the formulation of the various *artes praedicandi*—manuals for the instruction of preachers. Collections of sermons were usually organized under the rubrics of homilies aimed at a wider audience not necessarily versed in Latin, and university sermons intended for an educated audience whose intellectual exchanges would have been exclusively conducted in Latin. Both Latin and the vernacular languages, therefore, were used in the composition, collection, and dissemination of sermons.

The folio reproduced here comes from a lengthy collection of sermons written in French in a lively cursive script. The copyist used black ink with some red initials. The manuscript contains 382 leaves, with some blank pages, all of which have lines and margins ruled with a dry point. The manuscript is 22 cm. in height and bound with wood boards, with vellum covering the spine.

PETER DAMIAN

Poem on the Joy of Paradise
(*Rhytmus de gaudio paradisi;* c. 1050)

When Charlemagne was crowned Holy Roman Emperor on Christmas day in 800, he ushered in a long era of rapprochement with the western Church that was not threatened until the late eleventh century and that remained operative for another century. But in the last quarter of the eleventh century, after a generation of militant goading from within and without, the Church took the full measure of its spiritual powers—powers it had gained with the assistance of Charlemagne and his heirs, to be sure—and asserted its rights of self-government. Lay investiture, usury, simony, among other abuses, were to be abandoned; monastic reforms, already under way for several generations, were encouraged and expanded. The power of the papacy was reconfigured and more fully articulated in the face of the old habits of secular encroachment. The Church's spiritual authority was clearly waxing—and much of the activity attending to this burst of ecclesiastical and political reconfiguration was manifested in a fresh outburst of literary activity, marking the commencement of a century of EL poetry and prose that is one of the chief hallmarks of the Latin Middle Ages.

One of the most prolific of the reformists, Peter Damian has left us a large body of work by which to gauge the influence of political and ecclesiological affairs on Latin literary culture. Much of Damian's writings was work-a-day: letters dashed off quickly, treatises hurriedly compiled to meet the most recent pedagogical or ecclesiastical query, dry and humorless tracts on church governance. But much of the remainder of Damian's work is of another order. There are, in addition to formal treatises on theology, monastic life, and communal and spiritual living, a collection of hymns, prayers, sermons, and lives of the saints. This great body of work was not compiled quickly but, on the contrary, was polished slowly in the seclusion of the Italian abbey at Fonte Avellana in which Damian lived and over which he eventually ruled as abbot.

Damian was born in Ravenna in 1007, an orphan of a poor family. He was able to secure an education only through the good offices of the priest who adopted him and whose name, Damiani, the young Peter subsequently took to honor him. Through this initial training, Damian was

able to leave behind a life of abject poverty (he had worked for a time as
a swineherd). He studied by turns at Ravenna, Faenza, and Parma and
took up teaching for a short while at Parma before joining the hermits of
the Holy Cross of Fonte Avellana and embracing the monastic life. He
became head of the monastery there in 1043, a role that afforded Damian
a prominence that his talents exploited. He quickly came to the notice of
Pope Leo IX, who appointed him bishop and cardinal of Ostia. After this
appointment, Damian quickly became a leading figure at the highest levels of the church.

Damian rose to prominence in the Church at a time of swift change
and controversy. The reforming tendencies of the eleventh century were
in full vogue, and Damian was in the forefront of efforts to assert the
superior spiritual powers of the Church against a long-entrenched secular
authority. In this regard, he counted as his close associates not only Hildebrand, who was to become Pope Gregory VII (see pp. 437–43); but also
Pope Nicholas II, another reformer, whose elevation to the papacy was
in part engineered by Damian, and Bishop Anselm of Lucca, who accompanied Damian to Milan to settle disputes there, and who came later
to the papacy as Alexander II. Damian was active as a papal emissary
throughout western Europe especially during the pontificate of Alexander, settling monastic disputes between bishops and the abbot of Cluny
in France and managing in Germany to dissuade Emperor Henry IV from
divorcing his queen, Bertha. He died in 1072.

Of particular interest in Damian's large output is his poetry, comprising hexameters, elegiacs, and lyrical meters, in addition to accentual meters used especially in the hymns, one of which, selected here, is written
in accentual trochaic septenarii. This hymn, part of a larger series that
reaches back thematically to celebrate key figures of the Old and New
Testaments, also reaches back in terms of meter, word-choice, and syntax
to the traditions of LL spiritual poetry. This is not surprising, since the
outlook of the reformists was decidedly backward-looking. But when one
compares the traditions resident in, say, the *Cambridge Songs*, which
were copied out in England probably in the same decade when Damian
wrote our selection, the differences are striking, even when one takes into
account the disparity of intended function of the poems. The movement
of religious poetry to the cloister and away from the classicizing habitat
of Carolingian poets, a tendency best exemplified, as we have seen, in the
poetry of Hrabanus Maurus (see pp. 256–59), is now reversed. Damian
takes his readers to an older place, where emotion and spiritual reflection
are refracted through the controlling prism of ancient genre and meter

and a vocabulary almost as old. It was one more way that Damian, now in a literary venue, could return yet again to the foundational sources of his life's work, where he and others like him were certain paradise could be more securely culled.

The poetry of Peter Damian has been edited by M. Lokrantz (*L'opera poetica di S. Pier Damiani*, Stockholm, 1964). The hymns have been edited separately and appear in various volumes of *Analecta Hymnica Medii Aevi*, 55 vols. (Leipzig, 1886–1922; for specific volume references for each hymn, see Lokrantz's edition, pp. 44–48). Raby 1, 250ff., offers a full discussion of Damian.

Lokrantz's text is reprinted with consonantal and vocalic "u" distinguished.

The Joy of Paradise

1. Ad perennis vitae fontem mens sitivit arida.
   Claustra carnis praesto frangi clausa quaerit anima,
   Gliscit, ambit, eluctatur exsul frui patria.

2. Dum pressuris ac aerumnis se gemit obnoxiam,
   Quam amisit, cum deliquit, contemplatur gloriam,
   Praesens malum auget boni perditi memoria.

3. Nam quis promat, summae pacis quanta sit laetitia,
   Ubi vivis margaritis surgunt aedificia,
   Auro celsa micant tecta, radiant triclinia?

4. Solis gemmis pretiosis haec structura nectitur;
   Auro mundo tamquam vitro urbis via sternitur;
   Abest limus, deest fimus, lues nulla teritur.

5. Hiems horrens, aestas torrens illic numquam saeviunt;
   Flos purpureus rosarum ver agit perpetuum;
   Candent lilia, rubescit crocus, sudat balsamum.

6. Virent prata, vernant sata, rivi mellis influunt;
   Pigmentorum spirat odor liquor et aromatum;
   Pendent poma floscidorum non lapsura nemorum.

5

10

15

---

2. **praesto:** adverb.   12. **lues:** from *lues, is*, feminine noun of the third declension = "plague" (LS 1084).   17. **aromatum:** from *aroma, atis* = "aroma" (Blaise/Chirat 97).   18. **floscidorum:** from *floscidus, a, um* = "flower bearing" (Lokrantz 225).

7. Non alternat luna vices, sol vel cursus siderum;
   Agnus est felicis urbis lumen inocciduum;   20
   Nox et tempus desunt, aevum diem fert continuum.

8. Nam et sancti quique velut sol praeclarus rutilant,
   Post triumphum coronati mutuo coniubilant
   Et prostrati pugnas hostis iam securi numerant.

9. Omni labe defaecati carnis bella nesciunt;   25
   Caro facta spiritalis et mens unum sentiunt;
   Pace multa perfruentes scandala non perferunt.

10. Mutabilibus exuti repetunt originem
    Et praesentem veritatis contemplantur speciem;
    Hinc vitalem vivi fontis hauriunt dulcedinem.   30

11. Inde statum semper idem exsistendi capiunt:
    Clari, vividi, iucundi nullis patent casibus;
    Absunt morbi semper sanis, senectus iuvenibus.

12. Hinc perenne tenent esse, nam transire transiit;
    Inde virent, vigent, florent; corruptela corruit;   35
    Immortalitatis vigor mortis ius absorbuit.

13. Qui scientem cuncta sciunt, quid nescire nequeunt
    Nam et pectoris arcana penetrant alterutrum;
    Unum volunt, unum norunt, unitas est mentium.

14. Licet cuique sit diversum pro labore meritum,   40
    Caritas hoc suum facit, quod amat in altero;
    Proprium sic singulorum commune fit omnium.

---

20. **inocciduum:** from *inocciduus, a, um* = "that does not set" (Blaise/Chirat 450).
23. **mutuo:** adverb. 25. **defaecati:** perfect passive participle of *defaecare.*
27. **scandala:** from *scandalum, i* = "dispute," "quarrel," "strife" (Niermeyer 942).
28. **exuti:** perfect passive participle of *exuere,* the subject of this line, with dependent *mutabilibus* (i.e., *rebus*). 34. **tenent:** the subject remains *exuti* from stanza 10. **esse:** in effect, the present active infinitive acts as a nominative gerund = "being," modified by *perenne*; the thought is *exuti perenne tenent esse.* **transire:** the present active infinitive acts as the nominative of the gerund = "dying." 37. **qui . . . sciunt:** this clause means something like "these are the ones who have a knowledge of all things. . . ." 38. **alterutrum:** in ML an adverb = "mutually" (Blaise/Chirat 74, s. v. *alteruter* 1 c).

15. Ubi corpus, illic iure congregantur aquilae;
    Quo cum angelis et sanctae recreantur animae;
45 Uno pane vivunt cives utriusque patriae.

16. Avidi semper et pleni, quod habent, desiderant.
    Non satietas fastidat, neque fames cruciat;
    Inhiantes semper edunt et edentes inhiant.

17. Novas semper harmonias vox meloda concrepat,
50 Et in iubilum prolata mulcent aures organa;
    Digna, per quem sunt victores, regi dant praeconia.

18. Felix, caeli quae praesentem regem cernit, anima
    Et sub sede spectat altam orbis volvi machinam,
    Solem, lunam et globosa bini cursus sidera.

55 19. Christe, palma bellatorum, hoc in municipium
    Introduc me post solutum militare cingulum;
    Fac consortem donativi beatorum civium.

20. Praebe vires inexhausto laboranti proelio,
    Ut quietem post procinctum debeas emerito,
60 Teque merear potiri sine fine praemio.

                                    Amen.
                          —*Rhyt. de Gau. Par.*

50. **iubilum:** from *iubilum, i* = "shouts." **prolata:** perfect passive participle of *pro-ferre*, modifying *organa*. 58. **praebe:** present active imperative of *praebere;* parallel with *introduc* and *fac* in stanza 19. 59. **procinctum:** from *procinctus, us* = "battle" (LS 1452). 60. **potiri:** present infinitive, complement of *merear* + ablative object = "to gain," "to acquire."

PLATE 18. Two folios from a decretal issued by Pope Sixtus IV to the Augustinians, confirming prior papal decretals dating back to the pontificate of Boniface VIII.

PLATE 18

Augustinian Decretals
Latin manuscript on parchment, fifteenth century, fols. 3 verso and 4 recto
Koopman Collection
John Hay Library, Brown University

One of the chief means by which papal authority was propagated was through the assertion of authoritative positions, articulated as responses to specific questions. A decretal was in the Latin Middle Ages strictly speaking a papal letter offered in response to a specific question, harboring the force of law within the pope's jurisdiction. Decretals are almost coeval with the institution of the Church itself; the first one in existence dates from the late fourth century. Collections of decretals were made thereafter, including the famous "False Decretals," a series of forgeries of letters drawn up to bolster the cause of papal supremacy. The folios shown here come from a collection of the decretals of various popes concerning the Augustinian order, collected by Pope Sixtus IV (1471–1484) in 1474 to confirm previous papal decretals to the order. The text of the decretal from Sixtus concerns the rights, privileges, and rules of the order. The folios have initials in red and blue and the manuscript is bound in limp parchment with an external tie. There is in the left margins of both folios some penwork floreation. The margins and lines are ruled with a dry point and are still visible. This copy of Sixtus' original decretal of 1474 was written in 1486 by Pontenuovo for presentation by Cardinal Raphael Galeotto Sansone-Riario (1451–1521) to his University.

PART FIVE: 1100–1350
VARIETIES OF MEDIEVAL LATIN

SAINT ANSELM (1033–1109)
GREGORY VII (1021–1085)
THE ALEXANDER ROMANCES (c. 1100)
RAYMOND OF AGUILERS (fl. c. 1100)
WILLIAM OF MALMESBURY (c. 1095–1143)
FULCHER OF CHARTRES (c. 1060–1127)
PETER ABELARD (1079–1142)
HELOISE (c. 1100–1164)
GEOFFREY OF MONMOUTH (c. 1090–1155)
ADAM OF SAINT VICTOR (fl. c. 1145)
NIVARDUS (fl. c. 1148)
BERNARDUS SILVESTRIS (c. 1100–1165)
BERNARD OF MORLAS (fl. c. 1150)
BERNARD OF CLAIRVAUX (1090–1153)
THE ARCHPOET (fl. c. 1160)
HILDEGARD OF BINGEN (1098–1179)
THE SONGS OF BEUERN (c. 1150–1200)
ALAN OF LILLE (c. 1116–1203)
NIGEL WHITEACRE (c. 1130–1210)
JOHN OF HAUVILLE (fl. c. 1185)
WALTER OF CHATILLON (c. 1135–1204)
WALTER MAP (c. 1135–1210)
MATTHEW PARIS (c. 1220–1259)
SAINT BONAVENTURE (1221–1274)
ROGER BACON (c. 1215–1292)

Nuq̃o fron dicet homo et hō natus ē
do nartauit in ſcriptūs ꝑꝓloꝛ et ꝑ
Sic letātiū oīum hitatio ī te ~
    Omie ꝫ ſalutis mee ī die d
    ſntret in coſpectu tuo oꝛo mea
Qma repleta ē malis aīa mea et
Extimatus ſū cū deſcēdctibȝ ī lacū
Sic uulnerati doꝛmietes ī ſepulcꝛo
poſueriit meī lacu iſerioꝛi in ten
Sup me ꝓfirmat' eſt furoꝛ tuis et õꝫ
Longe fecıſti notos meȝ a me poſuıe
Tradıtus ſum et nō egꝛediebar dc
Clamaui ad te dīe tota die exꝑ
Nuq̃o nartabit alıq̃s ī ſepulcꝛo m
Nuq̃o moꝛtuis facıes mırabılıa aut
Numq̃o cogſcētur ī tenebrıs mıra
Et ego ad te dō clamaui et mane
Vt quıd dīe repellıs oꝛonē meam
paup ſum ego et ı laboꝛıbȝ a ıuue
ın me trāſıeriit ıre tue et oꝛoꝛes
Cırcūdederē me ſıc aqua tota die
Elōgaſtı a me amıcū et ꝓxımum
    ſbicoꝛdıaꝫ dō ī etnıȝ cātabo

PLATE 19

Psalter, Latin manuscript on parchment, late fourteenth century, fol. 33 verso
Koopman Collection
John Hay Library, Brown University

Collections of psalms were made in earliest times in the Church, and parts of the Old Latin Psalter are preserved in the Verona Psalter, which dates from the sixth–seventh century, but which records a collection of psalms in use as early as the mid fourth century. Saint Jerome translated groupings of psalms from the Septuagint in the late fourth century that became the basis of the so-called Gallican and Hebrew psalters. The Gallican psalter, made in 392 by Jerome, became popular in Gaul especially in succeeding centuries (hence its name), and by the ninth century, under the influence of Alcuin, it had replaced the Hebrew psalter, which Jerome had made in around 400, in most manuscripts of the Vulgate. In some copies of the Vulgate, however, even though the Gallican is preferred, all three versions of the psalter—Hebrew, Gallican, and Roman (Old Latin)—are presented in parallel columns.

The folio shown here, from a late medieval psalter undoubtedly used for private devotional purposes, gives a sense of how small (11 cm. in height) and compact (90 leaves) the manuscript is. It has a red initial "O" and a more elaborately decorated "M." Its lines are ruled with a dry point. The manuscript is bound in blind stamped wooden boards covered with calfskin. The knotwork on the binding suggests an Italian provenance, and the front endpaper is signed "Latanzia Pambara" (in a later hand than the manuscript itself). The script is a neat, bold, Roman minuscule.

INTRODUCTION

It is difficult to summarize the diversity of literary activity produced in the Latin West between the late eleventh and the mid thirteenth centuries. This era is fraught with social changes advanced by economic expansion, ecclesiastical accomplishment, political shifts, and linguistic development. The epoch began with a substantial increase in papal prestige, grounded in the challenges to imperial authority fronted by the reformist agenda of Pope Gregory VII. That agenda, which helped to fuel a new-found sense of purpose within the larger Church, was modified in the twelfth century, leading to the accumulation of further power and prestige and influencing a fresh output of literary activity. This newfound prestige and power was reflected, for example, in writings from the papal chancery—including letters produced by (and for) popes (of which the letter from Gregory VII presented here is an example). Ecclesiastical writing of a different sort was produced by exemplary churchmen also, such as Bernard of Clairvaux, who wrote in a host of genres long associated with the Church, but whose prose style was quite unlike anything produced in those genres in earlier centuries.

Along with developments in these areas, writing that more directly engaged spirituality, both in prose and poetry, arose in profusion in this period. Private devotion became a mainstay of high medieval culture, and the prayers and meditations of Anselm evince a renewed tendency toward mystical, introspective reflection spurred on by the patronage of a devout, wealthy nobility (cf. also the various discussions of the books of hours in plates 18ff.). A similar interest in spiritual exploration, but from the foundation of a simple piety intended for the widest possible audience, supports much of the output of Saint Bonaventure, who writes a century and a half after Anselm. The further development of the sequence in the twelfth century is another aspect of spiritual writing in this period, and the refinements of this form at the monastery of St. Victor were especially important. Sequences were also written by Hildegard of Bingen, whose work in liturgical poetry, painting, mystical and visionary writing, and music perhaps best demonstrates the medieval emphasis on the integration of artistic forms.

An emphasis on spiritual expression in a variety of media is balanced in the Latin Middle Ages by novelty and innovation of literary forms. New genres take mature shape, such as the beast fable best represented by the work of Nivardus or Nigel Whiteacre, and irony, parody, and sarcasm are more fully developed especially in the work of these two poets, whose allegories also speak to the strains of the expansions of medieval culture at all levels—expansions which allowed their work to flourish.

Historical writing, too, flourished in this age, spurred on by the international exploits of the Crusaders, by the nationalistic feelings of the rising "states" of medieval Europe, and by an interest in linking the glorious past of Rome or of some such similar ideal to the more tangible present of contemporary times. Crusader narratives fill the pages of Raymond of Aguilers's work and of the account by Fulcher of Chartres. More local in their historical concerns, William of Malmesbury and Geoffrey of Monmouth both key into the earlier historical traditions of Bede, but Geoffrey especially expands the realm of historical inquiry to include myth, lore, and legend, inculcating a palpable sense of poetry to his composition that is otherwise lacking in the straightforward narratives of William. Historical in a different sense is the Alexander tradition, which reached its maturest form in the eleventh century in the various recensions of the Alexander romances, a tradition owed principally to the translations from the Greek of Leo of Naples and which would take its most classical form in the epic of Walter of Châtillon, the *Alexandreis,* in the twelfth century.

New directions in learning took shape in the twelfth century, too, and as economic and social expansion allowed for greater civic opportunities, there arose a wider lay class, with secular literary aspirations. In the work of the so-called Goliardic tradition, those aims were merged with the effects of the new learning, for many of the so-called Goliards were wandering students, whose work, reflected in the Archpoet's verses and in many of the *Carmina Burana,* spoke to a new sense of the role and function of affect in Christian culture and in personal endeavor. The work of Abelard and Heloise reflects the easy joining of new models of learning with an interest in affect also, as both of these important figures attempted to make better sense of the devastation of their emotional lives within the larger context of Christian culture—now exposed to them in wider relief by the aims and methods of scholastic philosophy, though perhaps not to any sort of (personally) agreeable conclusion.

Later developments in Christian theological and philosophical exposition occurred—in the thirteenth century in the work of Aquinas—but there was also an explosion of scientific work produced contemporaneous to Aquinas's bold project. In part influenced by the rise of Islamic and Byzantine scientific texts, in part the result of the reintroduction of Greek philosophy full scale into the Western tradition again, and owing also to natural curiosity, the work of thirteenth-century thinkers such as Roger Bacon in physics, optics, and the organization of knowledge was foundational. At the same time, a revolution in cosmological speculation took root, in part a result of Islamic influences and the rediscovery of

Aristotle. Bold speculative cosmologies, worked out by thinkers such as Bernardus Silvestris or Alan of Lille were balanced by more cynical views of the world and of humanity's place in it.

Yet perhaps the most important trend in this complex and diverse period was the emphasis on humanity in the literary works of the eleventh, twelfth, and thirteenth centuries. Bernard of Morlas's cynical digs at a world of corruption and vice or Walter Map's collection of stories, which gives vent to a multiplicity of worldly perspectives, offer up a harshly cynical view of humanity. But John of Hauville's optimistic portrayal of the so-called Arch-Weeper, in search of moral perfection, contrasts with the more traditional view of heroic action set against the backdrop of Alexander's life in Walter of Châtillon's *Alexandreis*. In pursuing this king's paths to glory, however, Walter does more than participate in the classical, Virgilian epic tradition, for the model of Alexander, much like the model of Merlin, Arthur, or any medieval type, holds out the hope of perfection, the chance of recovery, renewal, integration—and innovation on personal and cultural levels. And, ultimately, it is innovation, matched by renewal and integration, that is most accurately the marker of the diverse literary activity reflected in this part, the fullest literary bounty of the Latin Middle Ages.

> The fine delight that fathers thought; the strong
> Spur, live and lancing like the blowpipe flame,
> Breathes once and, quenched faster than it came,
> Leaves yet the mind a mother of immortal song. . . .
>
> The roll, the rise, the carol, the creation,
> My winter world, that scarcely breathes that bliss
> Now, yields you, with some sighs, our explanation.

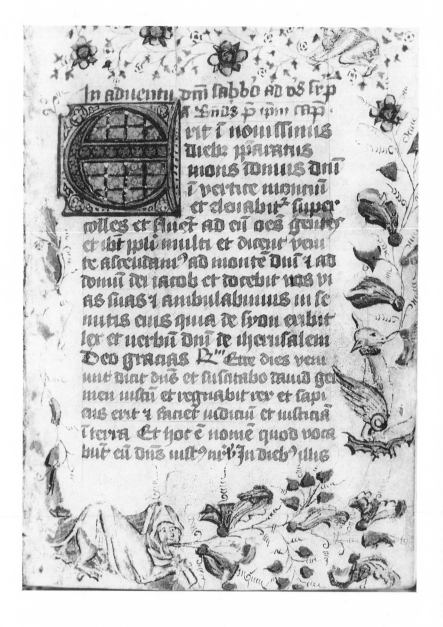

PLATE 20. The opening folio from a Latin Book of Hours of the late thirteenth–century, showing an intial "E."

PLATE 20

Book of Hours
Latin manuscript on parchment, late thirteenth century, fol. 1 recto
John Hay Library, Brown University

The Latin breviary arose in the eleventh century as a formal collection of prayers, hymns, lessons, and readings for the divine office. The rise of popular private devotion, however, occasioned the production of Books of Hours, which normally included psalms, biblical passages, hymns, and prayers. These devotionals were often commissioned by wealthy individuals, who saw to it that they were colorfully decorated. Many of the Books of Hours paid special attention in their collections of material to the observation of the hours of devotion owed the Virgin Mary, and eventually a series of events in the life of the Virgin came to be associated with the set hours of her observance. The social context of Anselm's prayers and meditations is not unlike that attending to the production of the later tradition of Books of Hours. He was asked to write his prayers by a wealthy patron, Matilda of Tuscany, and both she and several of Anselm's colleagues apparently had the right to send Anselm's works back to him for revision or complete overhaul.

The patronized production of devotionals, leading to the flowering of the Book of Hours form, arises from the earlier trend represented by the prayers of Anselm. The production of these later books was much more complicated than the simple process of writing and revising practiced by Anselm. The books had first to be physically produced on animal skin, which was prepared by being soaked in lime, shaved down to a relatively consistent thickness, and rubbed smooth with a pumice stone. Then the skins were stretched and dried before being cut down for collation. Three visual components are common: the text itself, written first, ornamental border decoration, as shown here, followed by illumination with full-scale pictures of whatever scenes were required. The visual aspect of these books was important not only in an artistic sense but also owing to the fact that many of their owners could not read the language and used the scenes depicted in the book to find their place (they presumably knew the prayers associated with the pictures by heart).

This Book of Hours from the late thirteenth century includes some illuminated initials and decorations, and an elaborate initial with much marginal floreation in vivid primary colors. Most subsequent folios are undecorated. At some point after its production, a red or purple velvet cover was added (now faded), which suggests its continual usage. Its wide margins and 20 lines are ruled in pencil. It is 10.5 cm. in height and has 55 folios.

431

St. Anselm

The Prayer to the Virgin Mary
(*Oratio ad Sanctam Mariam*; c. 1072)

A nselm is most famous as a scholastic philosopher and theologian, yet his importance in the development of two strains of Medieval Latinity, rhythmic prose and devotional writing, is of the first moment. By the late eleventh century, a long tradition of Latin prose *cursus* was already in place. But the ancient experiments of Cicero and the Christian innovations of Augustine and his Carolingian successors did not have the final word. Medieval Latin prose *cursus* remained to be perfected in the twelfth century in the hands of such masters as John of Salisbury.

Anselm was surely aware of prose stylistics, but when he turned to prose writing early in his career, he settled on a new path by circumventing traditional prose *cursus,* with its elaborate symmetries, its balanced cola, its calculus of style and sense, relying instead on the same feature of Latin that Notker had exploited in his prose sequences—the rhythms innate to the Latin language. That Anselm's work marks a true development in prose writing is confirmed by his many subsequent imitators. But no one has ever matched the simplicity of his prose style or the ways in which he managed to balance purity of sound with sparseness of word, while simultaneously exploiting internal and end rhymes in such a way as to ballast the sense of what he was saying.

It is on the merits of what Anselm did, in fact, say that we chiefly return to his prayers and meditations, and herein another fundamental aspect of Anselm's collection becomes apparent. In that he is writing prayers in his *Orationes sive meditationes,* Anselm is much more directly engaging the tradition of meditative prayer that had been in place for centuries in the West. But many of his prayers, though they were used in a monastic context, were initially written for the private devotion of lay people, especially women of station and means. Many of these women, having at their disposal the ability to patronize the production of personal devotionals, also had it within their sights to participate fully in the reform movements sweeping the Church and cloister in the late eleventh century (most famously, Countess Matilda of Tuscany). Anselm wrote most of his prayers, it is important to remember, during the 1070s and

1080s, when the full rigor of the Gregorian reform was resonant (see pp. 437–43).

The materials of his prayers are unique also. Before him, prayers invariably relied on excerpts drawn from the Psalms, which formed the bulwark of the monastic offices and hence figured prominently in private devotionals as well. In contrast, Anselm's prayers were not excerpts from the Psalms at all but original creations, expressing all the emotional and spiritual zeal their author could muster. The circulation of Anselm's prayers created in short order a new genre of private devotion based on the personal affect and spiritual longings of an individual—and contemporary—believer. Much like the stir accompanying the publication of Augustine's *Confessions,* the circulation of Anselm's prayers ensured that private devotional writing would never be the same again.

Anselm was born in 1033 in Aosta and studied at the monastery of Notre Dame at Bec in Normandy as a young man. There he met Lanfranc, prior of Bec, who was important in Anselm's life as a mentor and intellectual colleague and whom he replaced as prior when Lanfranc was assigned to other duties. In 1078, Anselm became abbot of Bec, and in 1093 he was appointed archbishop of Canterbury by William II (succeeding Lanfranc), a position he held until his death in 1109. Anselm's tenure as archbishop was an unhappy period for Church–state relations, culminating in the forfeiture of his see, in 1097, when he made a trip to Rome without receiving the permission of the king. The two men had clashed over the right of the king to invest bishops—a sore point throughout western Christendom in the late eleventh century. After William II's death in 1100, however, Anselm was able to return to Canterbury, though he soon fell into conflicts with the new king, Henry I, which remained persistent almost up until Anselm's death in 1109. Amid a life of administrative duties at Bec and in Canterbury, Anselm managed to produce a large amount of important philosophical and theological writing.

The wealth of his accomplishment as a prose stylist and writer of devotionals is evinced in the prayer to Mary excerpted here, one of three such works written to the Virgin. We know that Anselm sent them from Bec, where they were written, some time around 1072, to his colleague, Gundolf. Anselm's letter to Gundolf indicates that he, Anselm, had been asked to write a prayer to Mary—the first prayer—which when it was sent to its patron was deemed unacceptable. Thus the second prayer was written and sent, with the same response. Finally, the third prayer satisfied the (otherwise unnamed) patron (perhaps fictitiously constructed by Anselm), giving rise to the collection of Marian poems, of which the second is reprinted here.

For many centuries the collections of prayers and meditations of Anselm included literally dozens of works which were not from Anselm's hand. The authentic works were established only with the publication of Dom Wilmart's book (*Auteurs spirituels et textes dévots du moyen âge latin,* Paris, 1932, pp. 162–201). The authentic works have been edited in the larger collection of all of Anselm's writings by F. S. Schmitt (*S. Anselmi Cantuariensis Archiepiscopi Opera Omnia,* 6 vols., Edinburgh, 1938–61; the *Prayers and Meditations* are in vol. 3, 1946). An English translation has been prepared by B. Ward for the Penguin Classics (*The Prayers and Meditations of St. Anselm with the Proslogion,* Harmondsworth, 1973).

Schmitt's text is reprinted without change.

To Mary, When the Mind Is Troubled by Fear

Virgo mundo venerabilis, mater humano generi amabilis, femina angelis mirabilis, Maria sanctissima, cuius beata virginitate omnis sacratur integritas, cuius glorioso partu omnis salvatur foecunditas; domina magna, cui gratias agit contio laeta iustorum, ad quam territa fugit turba
5 reorum: ad te, praepotens et misericors domina, ego peccator et utique nimis peccator anxius confugio.

Videns enim me, domina, ante districti iudicis omnipotentem iustitiam, et considerans irae eius intolerabilem vehementiam, perpendo peccatorum meorum enormitatem et condignam tormentorum immanitatem.
10 Tanto igitur, domina clementissima, horrore turbatus, tanto pavore perterritus: cuius enixius implorabo interventionem, quam cuius uterus mundi fovit reconciliationem? Unde securius velocem in necessitate subventionem sperabo, quam unde mundo processisse propitiationem scio? Aut cuius intercessio facilius reo veniam impetrabit, quam quae illum
15 generalem et singularem iustum ultorem et misericordem indultorem lactavit? Sicut namque, beatissima, impossibile est ut haec merita tibi tam singularia, nobis tam necessaria obliviscaris: sic, mitissima, incredibile est ut supplicantibus miseris non miserearis. Bene quippe novit mundus, nec nos mundi peccatores ullatenus dissimulari patimur; satis, inquam, o do-
20 mina, satis novimus, quis "filius hominis" vel cuius hominis filius "venit"

---

3. **foecunditas** = CL *fecunditas.* 13. **propitiationem:** from *propitiatio, ionis* = "mercy," "pardon" (Niermeyer 862).

"salvum facere quod perierat." Numquid ergo tu, domina mea, mater spei meae, numquid oblivisceris tu odio mei quod mundo tam misericorditer est intimatum, tam feliciter divulgatum, tam amanter amplexatum? Ille bonus filius hominis venit perditum sponte salvare, et mater dei poterit perditum clamantem non curare? Bonus ille filius hominis venit "vo- 5 care" peccantem "ad paenitentiam," et mater dei contemnet precantem in paenitentia? Ille, inquam, bonus deus, mitis homo, misericors filius dei, pius filius hominis venit quaerere peccatorem errantem, et tu, bona mater eius, potens mater dei, repelles miserum orantem?

Ecce enim, o virgo homo, de qua natus est deus homo, ut salvaretur 10 peccator homo: ecce coram bono filio tuo et coram bona matre eius paenitet et confitetur, gemit et orat peccator homo. Obsecro ergo vos, bone domine et bona domina, obsecro vos, pie fili et pia mater, obsecro vos per hanc ipsam veritatem, per hanc singularem spem peccatorum, ut sicut vere tu es filius eius et tu mater eius ut salvetur peccator: sic, sic absolvatur 15 et curetur, sanetur et salvetur hic peccator. Probet in se, probet hic vester peccator quia vere estis, sentiat in se quia propter salutem peccatorum estis tu filius et tu mater. Vester certe amborum peccator.

Cum enim peccavi in filium, irritavi matrem, nec offendi matrem sine iniuria filii. Quid ergo facies, peccator? Quo igitur fugies, peccator? Quis 20 enim me reconciliabit filio inimica matre? Quis mihi placabit matrem irato filio? Sed etsi pariter ambo offensi estis: nonne et ambo clementes estis? Fugiat ergo reus iusti dei ad piam matrem misericordis dei. Refugiat reus offensae matris ad pium filium benignae matris. Ingerat se reus utriusque inter utrumque. Iniciat se inter pium filium et piam matrem. 25

Pie domine, parce servo matris tuae. Pia domina, parce servo filii tui. Bone fili, placa matrem tuam servo tuo. Bona mater, reconcilia servum tuum filio tuo. Qui me inicio inter duas tam immensas pietates, non incidam in duas tam potentes severitates. Bone fili, bona mater, non sit mihi frustra quod confiteor de vobis hanc veritatem, nec erubescam quod spero 30 in vobis hanc pietatem. Amo enim veritatem quam confiteor de vobis, et deprecor pietatem quam spero in vobis.

Dic, mundi iudex, cui parces, dic, mundi reconciliatrix, quem reconciliabis, si tu, domine, damnas et tu, domina, averteris homunculum bona vestra cum amore, mala sua cum maerore confitentem. Salvator singu- 35 laris, dic quem salvabis, salutis mater, dic pro quo orabis, si te, domine,

---

1. Cf. Luke 19.10. 2. **misericorditer:** adverb = "with compassion," "with mercy" (Niermeyer 693). 6. Cf. Luke 5.32. 34. **homunculum:** from *homunculus, i,* the diminutive of *homo, inis,* Anselm uses this term to designate himself in his wretched, fallen state.

praecipiente et te, domina, consentiente tormenta vexant peccatorem se execrantem, vos obsecrantem. Si infernus absorbet reum se accusantem, vos deprecantem. Si tartara devorant pauperem in se desperantem, in vobis sperantem.

5   Deus, qui factus es filius feminae propter misericordiam, femina, quae facta es mater dei propter misericordiam: aut miseremini miseri, tu parcendo, tu interveniendo, aut ostendite ad quos tutius fugiam misericordiores, et monstrate in quibus certius confidam potentiores. Si enim est, immo quia est tam magna mea iniquitas et tam modica fides mea, tam tepida caritas mea, tam fatua mea oratio, tam imperfecta mea satisfactio, ut nec merear delictorum veniam nec salutis gratiam: hoc est, hoc est ipsum quod supplico, ut in quo merita mea mihi videtis non sufficere, in eo misericordiae vestrae non dignentur deficere. Precor itaque, precor exaudite me, sed propter vos, non propter me, per pietatem qua exundatis, per potestatem qua abundatis, ut evadam meritos dolores damnatorum et intrem in gaudia beatorum, te deum laudaturus, qui es benedictus et superlaudabilis in saecula saeculorum. Amen.

—*Or. ad Sanct. Mar.*

3. **tartara:** CL *Tartarus* often in ML = Hell. 15. **abundatis:** from *abundare* = "to overflow," "to be full" (LS 13). 16. **intrem:** present active subjunctive, first person singular of *intrare*. 17. **superlaudabilis:** from *superlaudabilis, is* = "beyond all praise" (Latham 467).

GREGORY VII

A Letter to Emperor Henry IV
(*Registrum* 3.10; 8 January 1076)

The first pope to take the name Gregory called on the full resources of the
Latin at his command in order to perform the duties of the papacy in the
sixth century. Nearly 500 years later, Gregory I's namesake, Gregory VII,
did much the same, marshaling in his voluminous output the full measure
of Latin's unique features—limited vocabulary, fluid word order, econ-
omy of syntax and diction—in order to make his case to the world. That
case had changed considerably in the years since the first Gregory had
written to the Empress Constantina Augusta, politely refusing her request
for the holy relics of Saint Peter (see pp. 169–73). As the letter reprinted
here demonstrates, the papacy had widened its spheres of influence appreciably since the sixth century. Gregory VII was only too willing, in the
full blush of the reform movements of the eleventh century, to make demands of the Holy Roman Emperor that both demeaned the king politically in his German homeland and notably lessened his power base there.

The path by which the papacy arrived at this pinnacle of power—
short-lived and precarious though it was—is part and parcel a function
of the full development of ML as a language of Church and state; and in
the letters of Gregory VII one glimpses more specifically the mature form
of EL prose, one of the hallmarks of ML. Perhaps only the writings of
Innocent III a century later rank higher in importance in this regard. The
Latin style of Gregory VII is, as need be, direct or elliptical, obtuse or
simple. In this letter, one of the more important in the correspondence
between the Pope and Emperor Henry IV over the latter's practice of investing bishops, one witnesses Gregory's ability to fall into and out of
bureaucratic diction; to exploit the relationship of sound and sense; and,
when scolding the emperor, to rely on EL directness and simplicity. Especially near the letter's end, when the stakes are raised and the confronta-
tion is explicit, the prose replicates a father scolding a child—terse, a bit
condescending, but fully communicating the firm voice of a powerful
leader of an important institution.

Gregory VII, known before his pontificate as Hildebrand, came from
a poor family whose low station was hardly predictive of the kinds of
success the future pope would attain. Gregory was born in Tuscany in

1021 and was educated at the monastery of Santa Maria in Rome but soon left the monastic life, taking up a more active role in the service of the church hierarchy. He rose quickly in it. He first served Pope Gregory VI, but it was Leo IX who lifted Gregory the highest, making him a papal emissary to France and Germany and raising his profile throughout western Europe substantially. He had become famous within the Church for the rigor of his reformist positions and his somewhat unbending adherence to them. In particular, Gregory called for a Church divorced from worldly influences, for which reason he worked especially hard to root out simony, i.e., the buying and selling of church offices, and lay investiture, the practice in place since the days of the Carolingians in which the king held the prerogative of choosing and investing bishops of the church (see also above, pp. 193–96).

Gregory's unbending line on these key issues often put him at odds with his colleague in the College of Cardinals, Peter Damian (see pp. 414–18). A comparison of their respective bodies of work reveals the extent to which Damian was more a mystic and idealist, less a politician set on pursuing a discrete agenda, and more a Latin writer of an earlier, and passing, moment. Like many reformers, however, Gregory VII was a man of various contradictions—a reformer who stood for a less worldly church but was himself immersed in the politics of his age; a man of peace and spiritual depth who fought fiercely and with a bitterness against his enemies perceived or real. Gregory died in exile, defeated by Henry IV over the investiture contest and replaced by a pope of the emperor's choosing, in 1085. Later popes would have to finish his work.

The letters of Gregory VII were considered by the Church a precious commodity and, almost immediately after his death, they were collected in the *Registrum,* a nearly complete compilation, and the first such collection made by the Church since the letters of Gregory I had been gathered subsequent to his pontificate. The *Registrum* consists of nine books, one for each of the first seven years of Gregory's reign, and two final books, of a more disorganized and unwieldy nature, presumably reflecting the contemporary recording of papal correspondence.

The letters have been edited for modern readers by P. Jaffé (*Registrum Gregorii VII, in Monumenta Gregoriana, Bibliotheca rerum Germanicarum,* vol. 2, Berlin, 1865), E. Caspar (*Gregorii VII Registrum, Das Register Gregors VII, in Monumenta Gregoriana, Epistolae selectae,* vol. 2, 1920–23), and F.-J. Schmale (*Quellen zum Investiturstreit: Ausgewählte Briefe Papst Gregors VII, in Ausgewählte Quellen zur deutschen Geschichte des Mittelalters,* vol. 12a, Darmstadt, 1978). E. Emerton has translated selected letters from the *Registrum* (*The Correspondence of Pope Gregory VII: Selected Letters from the* Registrum, in Columbia Records of Western Civilization, New York, 1932), with a complete historical and literary introduction. Schmale's text is reprinted without change, but I have normalized his orthography with respect to the use of subscripts for vowels, and I have, for ease of reading, placed scriptural tags in quotation marks, rather than retain the editor's italics.

A LETTER TO EMPEROR HENRY IV: 8 JANUARY 1076

Gregorius episcopus servus servorum Dei Henrico regi salutem et apostolicam benedictionem, si tamen apostolicae sedi, ut christianum decet regem, oboedierit.

Considerantes ac sollicite pensantes, quam districto iudici de dispensatione crediti nobis per beatum Petrum apostolorum principem ministerii rationem reddituri sumus, cum dubitatione apostolicam tibi benedictionem mandavimus, quoniam iudicio sedis apostolicae ac synodali censura excommunicatis communionem tuam scienter exhibere diceris. Quod si verum est, tu ipse cognoscis, quod nec divinae nec apostolicae benedictionis / gratiam percipere possis, nisi his qui excommunicati sunt a te separatis et compulsis ad paenitentiam de transgressione tua condigna penitudine et satisfactione prius absolutionem consequaris et indulgentiam. Unde excellentiae tuae consulimus, ut, si in hac re te culpabilem sentis, celeri confessione ad consilium alicuius religiosi episcopi venias, qui cum nostra licentia congruam tibi pro hac culpa iniungens paeniten-

5

10

15

---

3. **oboedierit** + dative object.   4. **quam:** adverb.   **districto:** perfect passive participle of *distringere* = "strict," "severe" (Blaise/Chirat 286, s. v. *districtus* 2).   **dispensatione:** a word with various meanings in ML, here = "governance" (Niermeyer 341, s. v. *dispensatio* 6).   5. **crediti:** perfect passive participle of *credere*, modifying *ministerii*, with dependent *nobis*.   **ministerii:** a word of fundamental importance in the ML lexicon, with dozens of meanings; here, Gregory indicates his ministry as the *servus servorum Dei*, a political as well as sacramental charge (cf. Blaise/Chirat 532, Niermeyer 687–90).   6. **rationem reddituri:** the future active participle of *reddere*, it picks up the sense of *ratio* here as an "accounting" = "rendering the account of the ministry. . . ."   7. **synodali:** from *synodalis, e* = "synodal" (Sleumer 764).   8. **excommunicatis:** perfect passive participle of *excommunicare* = "those who have been excommunicated."   10. **gratiam . . . possis:** the negation of the previous line is implicit here also.   12. **penitudine:** *paenitudo* and *poenitudo* are better spellings, with the former having the sense of "penance" (the meaning here), the latter, "pain," "weariness" (Blaise/Chirat 589, s. v. *paenitudo;* Niermeyer 783, s. v. 1 *paenitudo,* 2 *poenitudo*).   13. **consulimus** + dative object.   14. **religiosi:** *religiosus, a, um* = "pious," "religious" (Blaise/Chirat 709).

tiam te absolvat et nobis tuo consensu modum paenitentiae tuae per epistolam suam veraciter intimare audeat.

De caetero mirum nobis valde videtur, quod totiens nobis tam devotas
epistolas et tantam humilitatem tuae celsitudinis per legatorum tuorum
5 verba transmittis, filium te sanctae matris ecclesiae et nostrum vocas in
fide subiectum in dilectione unicum in devotione precipuum, postremo
cum omni affatu dulcedinis et reverentiae te commendas, re tamen et
factis asperrimum canonicis atque apostolicis decretis in his, quae ecclesiastica religio maxime poscit, te contrarium ostendis. Nam, ut de reliquis
10 taceamus, quod de causa Mediolanensi per matrem tuam, per confratres
nostros episcopos, quos ad te misimus, nobis promiseras, qualiter attend-
eris aut quo animo promiseris, ipsa res indicat. Et nunc quidem, ut vulnus
vulneri infligeres, contra statuta apostolicae sedis tradidisti Firmanam et
Spoletanam ecclesiam, si tamen ab homine tradi ecclesia aut donari
15 potest, quibusdam personis nobis etiam ignotis, quibus non licet nisi pro-
batis et ante bene cognitis regulariter manum imponere.

Decuerat regiam dignitatem tuam, cum te filium ecclesiae confiteris,
honorabilius magistrum ecclesiae, hoc est beatum Petrum apostolorum
principem, intueri. Cui, si de dominicis ovibus es, dominica voce et potes-
20 tate ad pascendum traditus / es dicente sibi Christo: "Petre, pasce oves
meas," et iterum: "Tibi tradite sunt claves regni caelorum; et quodcunque
ligaveris super terram, erit ligatum et in caelis; et quodcunque solveris
super terram, erit solutum et in caelis." In cuius sede et apostolica amministratione dum nos qualescunque peccatores et indigni divina dispositione
25 vicem suae potestatis gerimus, profecto, quicquid ad nos vel per scripta

3. caetero = CL cetero. 4. tuae celsitudinis: "of your highness"; celsitudo, inis is
an honorific reserved in ML for the emperor (and sometimes for high dignitaries; Niermeyer 164). 5. te: in apposition to filium. 6. precipuum: precipuus, a, um = "superior," "eminent" (Habel/Gröbel 302). 7. re tamen: "and yet in fact. . . ."
8. asperrimum: the object of ostendis, modifying te. ecclesiastica religio: a technical
term = the constitutions of the Church (Niermeyer 906, s. v. religio 7). 10. Mediolanensi: Mediolanensis, e = Milanese (Sleumer 511, s. v. Mediolanum). 13. Firmanam: Firmanus, a, um, adjective formed on Firmum, i = Fermo (Sleumer 335, s. v.
Firmum), hence, this word = "Fermean" and modifies ecclesiam. 14. Spoletanam:
Spoletanus, a, um, adjective formed on Spoletum, i = Spoleto (Sleumer 739, s. v.
Spoleto), hence this word = "Spoletan" and modifies ecclesiam. 15. quibusdam personis: indirect object of tradidisti. 16. manum imponere: a technical term, lit., "to
place the hand," i.e., "to consecrate" (on the shades of this meaning see Blaise/Chirat
414, s. v. impono). 17. decuerat: pluperfect active indicative of decet. 19. intueri:
complementary infinitive with decuerat, with magistrum and principem as objects.
20. This famous quotation comes from Matt. 16.19. 23. amministratione = CL
administratione (also the better spelling in ML). 25. profecto: adverb.

aut nudis verbis miseris, ipse recipit et, dum nos aut elementa percurrimus aut loquentium voces auscultamus, ipse, ex quo corde mandata prodierint, subtili inspectione discernit. Quapropter providendum esset tuae celsitudini, ne erga sedem apostolicam in verbis et legationibus tuis aliqua inveniretur discrepantia voluntatis, et in his, per quae christiana fides et 5
status ecclesiae ad aeternam salutem maxime proficit, non nobis sed Deo omnipotenti debitam non denegares reverentiam, quamquam apostolis eorumque successoribus Dominus dicere dignatus sit: "Qui vos audit, me audit, et qui vos spernit, me spernit." Scimus enim, quoniam, qui fidelem Deo oboedientiam exhibere non rennuit, in his, quae sanctorum patrum 10
statuta sequentes diximus, veluti si ab ore ipsius apostoli accepisset, nostra monita servare non spernit. Nam si propter reverentiam cathedre Moysi Dominus precepit apostolis, ut, quaecunque scribe et farisei super eam sedentes dicerent, observarent, non dubium est, quin apostolica et evangelica doctrina, cuius sedes et fundamentum Christus est, cum omni 15
veneratione a fidelibus per eos, qui in ministerium predicationis electi sunt, suscipienda et tenenda sit.

Congregata nanque hoc in anno apud sedem apostolicam synodo, cui nos superna dispensatio presidere voluit, cui etiam nonnulli tuorum interfuere fidelium, videntes ordinem christianae religionis multis iam labe- 20
factatum temporibus et principales ac proprias lucrandarum animarum causas diu prolapsas et suadente diabolo conculcatas concussi periculo et manifesta perditione Dominici gregis ad sanctorum patrum decreta doctrinamque recurrimus nichil novi, nichil adinventione nostra statuentes, sed primam et unicam ecclesiasticae disciplinae regulam et tritam sancto- 25
rum viam relicto errore repetendam et sectandam esse censuimus. Neque

1. **ipse:** i.e., Peter himself. **elementa:** i.e., written documents; *elementum* can mean "letters of the alphabet," hence the sense here. 3. **tuae celsitudini:** dative of agency with *providendum.* 7. **denegares:** from *denegare.* 8. This quotation comes from Luke 10.16. 12. **cathedre** = CL *cathedrae,* a term designating royal throne, bishop's chair, scholar's seat, among other meanings. Here it refers to the "seat of Moses" (Niermeyer 158). 13. **Moysi:** *Moyses, is* = Moses (Sleumer 531). **scribe** = *scribae;* the form is first declension masculine = "scribes" (Niermeyer 947). **farisei:** the better spelling is *Pharisaei* = Pharisees (Blaise/Chirat 623). 14. **non dubium est, quin:** the CL idiom is *non dubito quin,* "I do not doubt that"; here the comparable ML phrase is "there is no doubt that. . . ." 18. **nanque** = CL *namque* (and the better spelling in ML also). **synodo:** from *synodus, i,* feminine noun of the second declension = "synod" (Sleumer 764), modified by *congregata* in ablative absolute construction. 19. **presidere** = CL *praesidere.* **interfuere:** alternate perfect active indicative, third person plural = *interfuerunt.* 21. **lucrandarum:** from *lucrari* = "gaining," "acquisition." 24. **nichil** = CL *nihil.* **adinventione:** from *adinventio, onis* = "invention" (LS 36).

enim alium nostrae salutis et aeternae vitae introitum Christi ovibus eorumque pastoribus patere cognoscimus, nisi quem ab ipso monstratum qui
dixit: "Ego sum ostium; per me si quis introierit, salvabitur et pascua
inveniet," et ab apostolis predicatum et a sanctis patribus observatum in
5 evangelica et in omni divinarum scripturarum pagina didicimus. Huius
autem decreti, quod quidam dicunt humanos divinis honoribus preponentes importabile pondus et inmensam gravitudinem, nos autem magis
proprio vocabulo recuperandae salutis necessariam veritatem vocamus et
lucem, non solum a te vel ab his, qui in regno tuo sunt, sed ab omnibus
10 terrarum principibus et populis, qui Christum confitentur et colunt, devote suscipiendam et observandam adiudicavimus, quamquam hoc multum desideremus et te permaxime deceret, ut, sicut caeteris gloria honore
virtuteque potentior, ita esses et in Christi devotione sublimior.
Attamen, ne haec supra modum tibi gravia aut iniqua viderentur, per
15 tuos fideles tibi mandavimus, ne pravae consuetudinis mutatio te com-
moveret, mitteres ad nos, quos sapientes et religiosos in regno tuo invenire
posses, qui si aliqua ratione demonstrare vel astruere possent, in quo
salvo aeterni regis honore et sine periculo animarum nostrarum promul-
gatam sanctorum patrum possemus temperare sententiam, eorum consi-
20 liis condescenderemus. Quod quidem etsi a nobis tam amicabiliter moni-
tus non fuisses, aequum tamen fuerat, ut prius, in quo te gravaremus aut
tuis honoribus obstaremus, rationabiliter a nobis exigeres, quam apostolica decreta violares. Verum, quanti aut nostra monita aut observantiam
iustitiae feceris, in his, quae postmodum a te gesta et disposita sunt, de-
25 claratur.
Sed quia, dum adhuc longa Dei patientia ad emendationem te invitat,

3. The quotation comes from John 10.9. 5. huius decreti: Gregory refers here to
his specific decree against lay investiture. On *decretum* see Niermeyer 309. 6. humanos: the accusative object of *preponentes*, modifying an understood *honores*. preponentes = CL *praeponentes* + accusative and dative objects = "to place something
before something else. . . ." 7. importabile: *importabilis, e* = "intolerable," "unman-
ageable." 8. necessariam: *necessarius, a, um*: predicative. 10. devote: adverb =
"faithfully." 11. suscipiendam et observandam: these gerundives modify collectively
veritatem and *lucem*. 12. permaxime: adverb = "particularly." caeteris = CL *ceteris*, in ablative of comparison. 14. supra modum: in ML an adverbial phrase =
"very" (Niermeyer 1009). 15. fideles: a word of many technical meanings in ML,
here it refers to men who have sworn fealty to Henry IV (see Niermeyer 422–23, s. v.
fidelis 3). 17. astruere: "to furnish," "to supply"; parallel with *demonstrare*, both of
which are complements of *possent*. 22. rationabiliter: adverb = "reasonably,"
"rightfully." 23. verum: adverb. quanti: in genitive of price, with *feceris*, it has adverbial force in indirect question = "what you made of our warnings and of the observance of justice. . . ."

crescente intellegentia tua ad oboedientiam mandatorum Dei cor et animum tuum flecti posse speramus, paterna te caritate monemus, ut Christi supra te imperium recognoscens honorem tuum eius honori preponere quam sit periculosum, cogites et libertatem ecclesiae, quam sponsam sibi caelesti consortio iungere dignatus est, non iam tua occupatione imped- 5
ias, sed, quo maxime crescat, Deo omnipotenti et beato Petro, a quibus et tua mereatur amplificari gloria, auxilium tuae virtutis fideli devotione exhibere incipias. Quod nimirum pro collata tibi ex hostibus tuis victoria nunc te permaxime illis debitum fore cognoscere debes, ut, dum te memorabili prosperitate laetificant, ex concessis beneficiis devotiorem videant. 10
Atque hoc ut timor Dei, in cuius manu et potestate omne regnum est et imperium, precordiis tuis altius quam nostra ammonitio infigat, in mente habeas, quid Sauli post adeptam victoriam, qua propheta iubente usus est, de suo triumpho glorianti et eiusdem prophetae monita non exequenti acciderit et qualiter a Domino reprobatus sit, quanta vero gratia 15
David regem ex merito humilitatis inter virtutum insignia subsecuta fuerit.

Denique super his, quae in epistolis tuis visa hac cognita reticemus, non antea tibi certa responsa dabimus, donec legati tui Rabbodi Adelpreth et Uodescalki, quem his adiunximus, ad nos reversi super his, quae 20
illis tecum agenda commisimus, tuam nobis plenius aperiant voluntatem. Data Rome VI. Idus Ianuarii, Indictione XIIII.

—*Reg.* 3.10.

2. **flecti:** present passive infinitive of *flectere,* complement of *posse,* itself the verb of the infinitive clause governed by *speramus.* 3. **preponere** = CL *praeponere.* 12. **in mente habeas:** lit., "have in mind" (jussive subjunctive) = "remember," with the *quid* clause as object. 13. **Sauli:** *Saulus, i;* there are several forms of this name in ML = Saul (cf. Sleumer 700, s. v. *Saul, Sauli, Saulitae, Saulus*). **adeptam:** perfect participle of *adipisci.* **usus est:** from *uti,* the meaning here is "enjoyed" in the sense of "achieved." 16. **David:** indeclinable noun modified by *regem* here. 19. **legati . . . Uodescalki:** the royal legates Radbod, Adalbert, and Odescalcus. 22. **Indictione:** from *indictio, onis* = a period of fifteen years.

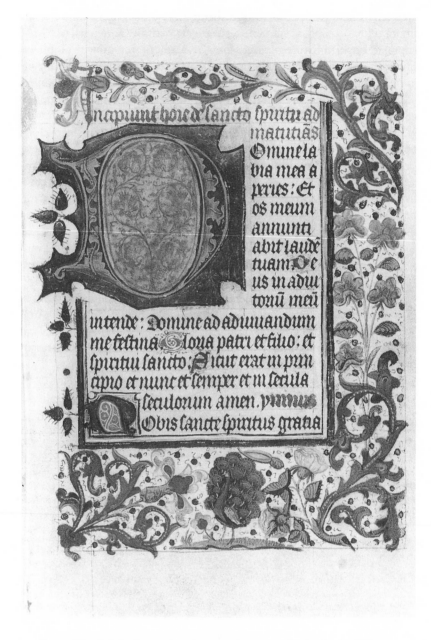

PLATE 21. A folio from a late fourteenth–century Latin Book of Hours, showing an initial "D."

PLATE 21

Book of Hours
Latin manuscript on parchment, late fourteenth century, fol. 14 recto
John Hay Library, Brown University

This folio, with a large, decorated initial "D," properly 14 recto, actually begins the work itself, being preceded by prefatory material common in Books of Hours—lists of saints and matters pertaining to the organization and use of individual prayers. The folio is vigorously adorned with marginal floreation of bright colors—red, green, blue—and the initial D is decorated along its edges by gilding. Its lines and margins are ruled in pencil and still visible. The book opens with the lines *Incipiunt hor[a]e de sancto spiritu ad matutinas; Domine labia mea aperies et os meum annuntiabit laudem tuam; Deus in adiutorium meum intende*—these commonly found in Books of Hours. The manuscript is plainly bound in wooden boards showing much wear (on the Book of Hours tradition, see plate 20). It is 17 cm. in height and has 60 folios.

The Alexander Romances

(*Historia de preliis* (J1 Recension); c. 1100)

O ne of the boldest literary innovations of the Latin Middle Ages was the development of romance—and a comparison to our modern romance novels is not far-fetched. The romance tradition itself in Latin was long-standing, and its most famous (though by no means its only) exemplar was Apuleius's *Metamorphoses*. The tradition was carried on in a variety of ways after him but reached perhaps its most popular (if not polished) form in the various late antique versions of the life of Alexander the Great. Nor was an interest in Alexander new. The specific tradition at-tending to the details of Alexander's life derived from several ancient works, both Greek and Roman. From the Latin side, of particular influ-ence were the history of Quintus Curtius, written in the middle of the first century C.E., which offered much biographical detail; and a history of the world commissioned by Augustine and executed by Orosius in the fourth century, which added further specifics to the portrait. On the Greek side, a third century C.E. accounting of Alexander's life and ex-ploits, the so-called *Alexander Romance,* gave impetus to the growth of the myths surrounding the life of the king in its combination of fact and fiction.

But though all of these works, especially the Greek *Alexander Ro-mance,* combined to make possible the medieval versions of Alexander's life, it fell to the Latin Middle Ages to perfect the genre as such. The most important link in this process was the tenth-century Latin translation of the *Alexander Romance,* produced by Leo of Naples. Leo's work was not a highly polished literary product, to be sure. His Latin was simple and sometimes awkward, and he seems to have been copying from an abbrevi-ated Greek exemplar, a process that magnified the already numerous de-ficiencies of syntax and grammar that characterize his version. But these deficiencies did not suppress the popularity of Leo's translation, which was deemed important enough to warrant revision and polishing. Those tasks were undertaken by the redactor called J1, who made Leo's transla-tion into a longer and more accomplished work of literary art, called the J1 recension, brought out some time around 1100.

In addition to polishing Leo's language, the J1 redactor expanded the scope of Leo's treatment of Alexander's life by including material that Leo had not included (or had not known about): most importantly, the legends surrounding Alexander's travels in India, parts of which are excerpted here. And quite apart from its direct importance for the Medieval Latin tradition, the J1 recension was influential also in the development of the romantic tradition in medieval vernacular literature. In particular, it was fundamental in the writing of the (now fragmentary) twelfth-century poem on Alexander by Alberic of Pisancon, and in the creation of the late twelfth century *Roman d'Alexandre,* in which Alexander was made to play the part of an Arthurian prince. The importance of the J1 recension is felt also in the production of two later recensions, J2 and J3, from which one can trace the writing of Middle English Alexander narratives, the Italian *I nobili fatti d'Alessandro Magno,* several Middle High German and French versions, and perhaps most famously, Walter of Châtillon's *Alexandreis* (see pp. 632–36).

The Latin of the J1 redactor is simple. His task was to make Leo of Naples's original—and somewhat messy—translation passable. This he does by rearranging words, modifying syntax, expanding vocabulary, and framing his narratives in fresh ways. Because this is a translation of a translation written in the second century, there are many CL words and phrases, though the syntax remains medieval throughout, as, for example, in this passage: *Videns autem hoc Philippus rex turbatus est valde et vocavit ad se ariolum et narravit ei quod viderat.* Here infinitive clauses are abandoned for the simplified syntax of the indicative mood, even in something as uncomplicated as an indirect question. But CL constructions, though used sparingly, are not abandoned (e.g., *sperans deum esse Apollinem descendentem de celis,* or *tunc precepit Alexander accendi focos plurimos*). The mingling of CL and ML results in a style reflecting certain limits of expression imposed by translation, rather than any definitive version of eleventh-century Latin in general.

The Latin Alexander romances have been edited separately. Leo of Naples' *Historia de preliis* has been edited by F. Pfister (*Der Alexanderroman des Archpresbyters Leo,* Heidelberg, 1913), the J1 recension by A. Hilka and K. Steffens (*Historia Alexandri Magni (Historia de preliis), Rezension J1,* Meisenheim am Glan, 1979), the J2 recension by A. Hilka (*Historia Alexandri Magni (Historia de preliis), Rezension J2 (Orosius Rezension),* 2 vols., Meisenheim am Glan, 1976–77), and the J3 recension by K. Steffens (*Die Historia de Preliis Alexandri Magni, Rezension J3,* Meisenheim am Glan, 1975). Translations have been made of the Greek *Alexander Romance* by E. Haight (*The Life of Alexander of*

Maecedon, New York, 1928) and most recently by B. P. Reardon (*Collected Ancient Greek Novels,* Berkeley, 1989). A complete overview of the romance tradition with excellent notes, bibliography and translations of much of the primary material has been written by D. Katz (*The Romances of Alexander,* in Garland Library of Medieval Literature, vol. 64, Series B, New York, 1991). The text of Hilka and Steffens is reprinted here without change.

SELECTIONS FROM THE LIFE OF ALEXANDER THE GREAT

Post paucos vero dies sedens Philippus rex solus in palatio suo, et apparuit ei parva atque mitis avis, volans et sedens in gremio eius et generavit ovum, et cecidit ipsum ovum de gremio eius in terram atque divisum est, et statimque exiit ex eo parvissimus serpens congiratusque ovum
5   voluit introire in eum; et antequam ibi caput inmitteret, mortuus est. Videns autem hoc Philippus rex turbatus est valde et vocavit ad se ariolum et narravit ei quod viderat. Cui ariolus ait: "Rex Philippe, nascetur tibi filius qui debet regnare post obitum tuum et circuire totum mundum subiugando sibi omnes; et antequam revertatur in terram nativitatis sue, in
10   parvis annis morietur."
                                                              —*Hist. Prel.* 1.11.
Et inde amoto exercitu perrexit in Mediam et Armeniam magnam et subiugavit eas. Deinde ambulavit dies multos et ingressus est in locum aridum et cavernosum in quo non inveniebatur aqua. Et transiens per locum qui dictur Andriaci venit ad flumen Eufraten et castra metatus est
15   ibi. Statimque iussit afferri ligna et preparari pontem super fluvium et iussit ligari eum clavis et catenis ferreis et precepit militibus suis ut transirent. Illi autem videntes magnitudinem fluminis et cursum validissimum timuerunt intrare in ipsum pontem ut non frangerentur ipse catene. Videns autem eos Alexander dubitare precepit custodibus suis qui animalia
20   custodiebant ut transirent primum, deinde omnis apparatus de ipso exercitu. Post hec iussit militibus suis ut transirent. Illi vero dubitabant. Alex-

---

1. **Philippus:** King Philip, son of Amyntas and father of Alexander the Great. 4. **congiratusque** = CL *congyratus.* 5. **inmitteret** = CL *immitteret.* 6. **ariolum** = CL *hariolum.* 8. **circuire:** sometimes spelled *circumire,* complement of *debet.* 9. **sue** = CL *suae.* 11. **amoto:** perfect passive participle of *amovere.* **perrexit:** from *pergere.* **Mediam:** i.e., *Media, ae,* modern Azerbaijan. **Armeniam magnam:** i.e., *Armenia, ae,* the term used by the Romans to designate the eastern portion of the larger country of Armenia. 14. **Andriaci:** "Andriaci," otherwise unknown. **Eufraten** = CL *Euphrates, is,* the Euphrates River. 16. **eum:** i.e., *pontem.* **precepit** = CL *praecepit.* 18. **ipse catene** = CL *ipsae catenae.* 21. **hec** = CL *haec.*

ander autem videns eos iterum dubitare iratus est valde et convocatis principibus suis cepit transire primum ipse, deinde principes et omnis exercitus. Fluvius itaque Tigris et Eufrates pergunt per Mediam et Mesopotamiam et Babiloniam et intrant in fluvium Nilum. Referunt enim alii quia, quando fluvius Nilus irrigat Egyptum, ista flumina evacuantur; et 5 quando iterum regreditur in alveo suo, ista flumina intumescunt. Cum autem transisset Alexander et omnis exercitus eius fluvium Eufraten, castra metatus est ibi et fecit incidere ipsum pontem. Videntes autem hoc milites eius tristati sunt valde et murmurantes inter se ceperunt vociferare et dicere: "Si acciderit nobis ut fugiamus e prelio, non erit transitus no- 10 bis." Quibus Alexander dixit: "Quid est hoc quod inter vos confertis dicentes quia, si acciderit nobis ut fugiamus e prelio, non est transitus nobis? Nam pro certo scitote quia inde feci ego incidere ipsum pontem, ut aut pugnetis viriliter et vincatis aut, si vultis e prelio fugere, pereatis, quia pugna et victoria non erit de his qui fugiunt, sed de illis qui insequuntur. 15 Pro quo confertetur mens vestra et fortitudo pugne estimetur vobis ludus, quia certissime scitote, nullomodo videbitis Macedoniam, quousque subiugabo cunctos barbaros, et tunc cum victoria revertamur illuc.

—*Hist. Prel.* 2.9.

Cum autem audisset mater Darii imperatoris quod preparasset se Darius filius eius cum exercitu, ut aliam pugnam cum Alexandro committeret, tristis effecta est valde, sed tamen scripsit ei epistolam continentem ita: "Regi Dario dulcissimoque filio mater eius dirigat illi gaudium. Audivimus itaque quia congregasti populum tuum et alias gentes plurimas et vis alia vice pugnare cum Alexandro. Quin immo si totum mun- 20

---

3. **Tigris:** *Tigris, idis* = Tigris River. **Mesopotamiam:** *Mesopotamia, ae*, the country between the Tigris and Euphrates. 4. **Babiloniam** = CL *Babylonia, ae* (the preferred ML spelling also; cf. Sleumer 145), i.e., a Roman province in Syria which comprises Mesopotamia and other parts of the Middle East situated between the Tigris and Euphrates rivers. **Nilum:** *Nilus, i* = Nile River. **referunt** = *dicunt.* 5. **quia:** with *evacuantur, quia* forms the object clause of *referunt* in the indicative that stands for CL infinitive clause; § 7.10 (cf. Blaise 262). 7. **Alexander et omnis exercitus:** collective object considered singular in number—hence *transisset.* 8. **fecit incidere:** *facere* + infinitive is common in ML, here = "destroyed." 9. **ceperunt** = CL *coeperunt.* 12. **quia . . . non est:** object clause in the indicative of *dicentes* = CL infinitive clause. 16. **pugne** = CL *pugnae.* **estimetur** = CL *aestimetur.* 17. **Macedoniam:** i.e., Macedonia, ae, the homeland of Alexander and his troops. **quousque:** in ML = "until" (Niermeyer 880). **subiugabo:** from *subiugare,* "to bring under the yoke," "to subdue" (LS 1777). 20. **eius:** i.e., *mater.* 23. **quia:** with *audivimus* + indicative *congregasti* = CL infinitive clause, "we have heard that you have gathered your people. . . ." 24. **alia vice:** idiomatic = "again." **quin immo:** idiomatic phrase emphasizing what follows = something like "but indeed. . . ."

dum adunare potueris, non potes ei resistere, quia prospera et victoria concessa sunt ei a diis. Pro quo dimitte sensum altitudinis tue et reclina paululum a gloria tua, quia, si in ipsa perseverare volueris, perdes vitam et induces malum super nos et facies nos perdere honorem quem apud
5 eum habemus. Certus namque esto, fili mi, quia in maximo honore nos habet. Et noli matri tue amplius preparare angustiam, quia fiducia mihi est quod poteris venire in bonum ordinem cum Alexandro, si volueris." Relecta itaque Darius epistola flevit et turbatus est valde, veniendo illi in memoriam parentes sui.

—*Hist. Prel.* 2.12.

10 Interea Alexander amoto exercitu cepit appropinquare ad civitatem in qua erat Darius. Et ita appropinquavit ei, ut milites sui conspicerent sublimissima loca montium que erant super civitatem Darii. Videns autem hec Alexander statim precepit militibus suis ut inciderent ramos arborum atque evellerent herbas et ligarent eas in pedibus equorum et
15 camelorum et mulorum qui erant in ipso exercitu; hoc enim ingenium proinde fecit Alexander, ut maiorem pulverem facerent et ut videntes eam Perses ab excelsis montibus obstupescerent de plenitudine hostium.

Et veniens iuxta civitatem Susis in qua erat Darius itinere dierum quinque et castra metatus est ibi et convocatis principibus suis dixit: "In-
20 veniamus hominem quem mandemus Dario dicendo: ut subiuget se sub potestate nostra aut pugnet nobiscum." Eadem igitur nocte apparuit Alexandro deus Ammon in figura Mercurii, portans regalem clamidem atque Macedonicam vestem et dicens illi: "Fili Alexander, quando necesse est tibi adiutorium, paratus sum nuntiare tibi. Sed missum quem dixisti
25 dirigere Dario vide ne feceris. Volo itaque ut induaris figuram meam et

1. **adunare:** "to unite" (LS 47).   2. **tue** = CL *tuae*.   **reclina:** present active imperative from *reclinare*.   5. **eum:** i.e., Alexander.   6. **habet:** the subject is Alexander.   8. **relecta:** perfect passive participle from *relegere*.   10. **cepit** = CL *coepit*.   12. **que** = CL *quae*.   16. **eam:** i.e., *pulverem;* one expects *eum*, standing for masculine *pulveris*.   18. **Susis:** from *Susis, idis,* adjective formed on *Susa, orum,* the ancient capital of Persia; here the author seems to construe *Susis* as a genitive, though one would more properly expect *Susorum;* if the adjective is meant, then *Susidem* is better (on the forms see LS 1818, s. v. *Susa*).   20. **dicendo:** the gerund in *do* often functions as an infinitive in ML and here, on the model of an infinitive of purpose = "whom we might send to Darius to say that he might subject himself to our power or . . ." (cf. Blaise 341).   22. **Ammon:** a name of Jupiter (sometimes *Hammon;* cf. LS 107).   23. **Macedonicam:** *Macedonicus, a, um* = "Macedonian."   **fili:** vocative case.   24. **missum quem dixisti:** object clause of *dirigere* = "the messenger which you spoke of . . ."; *missus, i* = "messenger," "envoy," "legate" (Niermeyer 695–97).   25. **dirigere . . . vide ne feceris:** a negative purpose clause with imperative = "see to it that you do not . . ."; *feceris* = *facere* + infinitive *dirigire* = "to order," "to send."

pergas tu ibi, quamvis periculosa res sit ire regem pro legato. Sed tamen noli expavescere, quia deus est in adiutorium tibi nullamque angustiam sustineberis." Exurgens autem Alexander a somno repletus est gaudio magno et convocatis amicis suis narravit somnium quod viderat. At illi dederunt ei consilium ut ita faceret quemadmodum dictum est ei per   5 somnium.

—Hist. Prel. 2.13.

Statimque Alexander vocavit unum ex principibus militie sue cui nomen erat Eumilio; erat autem ipse vir audax et fidelissimus Alexandro, et iussit ei ut unum equum ascenderet et alium vacuum traheret et sequeretur eum. Factumque est. Et cum perrexissent ambo ad fluvium qui dicitur   10 Granicus qui Persica lingua Stragana appellatur, invenerunt eum coagulatum. Statimque Alexander mutato habitu induit se vestimentum quod in somno viderat et principem militie sue dimisit ibi cum duobus equis et ille cum equo in quo sedebat transiens ipsum fluvium et cepit ire contra civitatem Darii. Princeps vero rogabat eum dicens: "Maxime imperator,   15 permitte me transire tecum fluvium et venire, ne forte eveniat tibi aliqua angustia." Cui Alexander dixit: "Expecta me hic, quia in meo adiutorio veniet ille qui in somno mihi apparuit." Iste enim fluvius de quo superius diximus hiemali et vernali tempore tota nocte permanet coagulatus; mane vero cum incaluerit sol, dissolvitur et efficit se nimium rapidissimum, et   20 quicumque ibi ingressus fuerit, rapit et absorbet eum. Est enim latitudo ipsius fluvii stadium unum. Cum autem venisset Alexander ad portam civitatis, videntes eum Perses mirabantur in figura eius, estimantes illum deum esse, statimque interrogaverunt eum dicentes: "Quis es tu?" Et ille respondit: "Apocrisarius sum regis Alecandri." Darius itaque imperator   25 tunc erat per montana terre sue vociferando et congregando multitudinem hostium, ut aliam pugnam cum Alexandro committeret. Qui cum venisset ad portam civitatis et invenisset Alexandrum loqui cum Persis, miratus est valde in figura eius, sperans deum esse Apollinem descendentem de celis, statimque adoravit eum et dixit illi: "Quis est tu?" Cui ille   30

---

7. **militie sue** = CL *militiae suae.*   8. **Eumilio:** i.e., Eumelus.   10. **perrexissent:** pluperfect active subjunctive, third person plural, from *pergere.*   11. **Granicus:** *Granicus, i* = the River Granicus, in Mysia.   **Stragana:** a Latin transliteration of the otherwise untranslatable Persian name for Granicus.   **coagulatum:** perfect passive participle from *coagulare* = "frozen" (LS 356).   19. **hiemali:** from *hiemalis, e* = "wintry" (LS 854). **vernali:** from *vernalis, e* = "spring-like" (LS 1974).   20. **incaluerit:** from *incalescere.* 22. **stadium:** *stadium, ii* = a unit of measure equivalent to about 607 feet (cf. LS 1750). 23. **Perses** = *Persae, arum,* masculine first declension noun = "Persians" (Sleumer 596, s. v. *Persae*).   25. **apocrisarius** = CL *apocrisiarius, ii* = "envoy," "delegate," "legate" (LS 138).   26. **terre sue** = CL *terrae suae.*   30. **celis** = CL *caelis.*

respondit: "Misit me rex Alexander ad te dicens: ut quid moram facis ut timidus homo exire preliando cum inimicis tuis? Aut subiuga te sub potestate nostra aut constitue diem pugnandi." Audiens autem hec Darius dixit ei: "Forsitan enim tu es Alexander qui cum tanta audacia loqueris?
5 Ut video, non loqueris tu sicut nuntius, sed sicut idem ipse Alexander. Pro certo scias quia nullomodo me turbant dicta tua. Sed tamen comede hodie mecum ad cenam meam sicut missus, quia et Alexander invitavit missos meos ad cenam suam." Et hec dicens tetendit manum suam et apprehendit eum per dexteram manum suam, introducens illum in palatium
10 suum. Alexander enim cepit cogitare et intra se dicere: "Bonum signum in me fecit barbarus iste, introducens me per dexteram in hoc palatio; certissime etenim adiuvantibus diis in proximo meum erit istud palatium." Et ingressus Darius una cum Alexandro in triclinium suum in quo erat ipsa cena preparata, sedit Darius imperator, sedit et Alexander sede-
15 runtque et principes militie Darii cum Alexandro facie ad faciem. Erat enim ipsum triclinium totum ornatum ex auro.

—*Hist. Prel.* 2.14.

Perses itaque sedentes in convivio despexerunt staturam Alexandri eo quod esset parva, ignorantes qualis sapientia et qualis virtus et audacia erat in tali corpusculo. Parapsides autem et mense et scamna omnia erant
20 ornata ex auro. Pincerne vero ferebant sepius pocula in vasis aureis ornatis ex pulchrioribus gemmis. Mediante vero convivio cum porrectum fuisset Alexandro poculum aureum, bibit et misit eum in sinum suum. Allatum est illi et vas aliud, et fecit similiter, deinde usque ad tertium. Allatores vero vasculorum cum hoc vidissent, retulerunt Dario impera-
25 tori. Audiens autem hec Darius erexit se et dixit Alexandro: "Amice, quid est hoc quod facis? Quare abscondis vasa aurea in sinu tuo?" Cui Alexander respondit: " In convivio nostri senioris talis est consuetudo ut convive, si volunt, tollant sibi vascula cum quibus bibunt. Sed quia talis non est consuetudo apud vos qualis apud nostrum seniorem, reddo a vobis." Et

---

1. **quid:** adverb. **ut:** "as if." 2. **timidus:** predicative here, with *exire*. 5. **ut video:** idiomatic = "the way I see it. . . ." 7. **missus:** an important word in ML = "legate," "envoy," "messenger" (Niermeyer 695–97). 17. **despexerunt:** perfect active indicative, third person plural of *despicere*. **eo quod** = "because." 19. **Parapsides** = CL *paropsides*, from *paropsis, idis* = "large dish"; from EL usage (cf. Matt. 23.25; 26.23; cf. Blaise 595 and LS 1305). **mense** = CL *mensae*. **scamna:** from *scamnum, i* = "benches" (cf. LS 1638). 20. **pincerne** = CL *pincernae*, from *pincerna, ae*, masculine noun of the first declension = "servant," "butler" (cf. LS 1377). 21. **porrectum:** perfect passive participle of *porrigere*. 23. **allatum:** perfect passive participle of *afferre*. 24. **allatores:** from *adlator, oris* = "servants" (Blaise/Chirat 52). 27. **convive** = CL *convivae*.

hec dicens reddidit ea pincernis. Perses vero dicebant inter se mutuo: "Ista consuetudo valde bona est." Quidam vero ex principibus militie Darii cui nomen erat Anepolis, sedens in convivio et intuens faciem Alexandri— viderat enim illum tunc quando direxerat eum Darius cum aliis Macedoniam Philippo tollere censum—et intelligens vocem et figuram eius cepit 5 cogitare intra se: "Nonne iste est Alexander filius Philippi?" Et statim erigens se et accessit propius Dario imperatori et dixit ei: "Maxime imperator, iste missus quem vides ipse est Alexander Philippi filius." Alexander autem videns eos inter se mutuo loqui, intelligens quia de agnitione eius dicerent, statim exiliens de sedio suo, exiens foras triclinium et invenit 10 quendam ex Persis tenentem in manu faculam, ascendit equum suum et cum magna celeritate cepit ire. Perses vero videntes hoc omnes armati ascenderunt equos suos et cum magna velocitate secuti sunt eum. Erat enim obscura nox. Alexander itaque portans in manu faculam tenebat iter rectum; insequentes autem illum alii oberrabant deviantes, alii percu- 15 tiebant facies suas per ramos arborum, alii cadebant in foveas. Sedente autem Dario in throno suo et cogitante de hoc quod fecit Alexander, aspexit contra statuam auream Xersen regis que sedebat sub tribunal triclinii, et statim cecidit ipsa statua. Videns enim hoc Darius dolore ductus cepit flere amarissime et dicere: "Hoc prodigium desolationis est 20 domus mee et detrimentum regni Persarum." Alexander autem venit ad fluvium Granicum invenitque eum coagulatum et transiit; et antequam de fluvio exiret, mortuus est equus eius et dissolutus est fluvius et tulit eum. Ille vero iunctus est cum Eumilo principe militie sue et reversus est ad suos. 25

—*Hist. Prel.* 2.15.

Alio itaque die congregato exercitu suo pervenit ad numerum centum viginti milia hominum, et ascendens in ementiori loco confortabat exercitum dicens: "Non equabitur multitudo Persarum ad multitudinem hominum nostrorum, quia multi plures sumus nos quam illi. Sed tamen si illi

1. **ea:** adverb. 3. **Anepolis:** the nominative singular form of the name of someone who is otherwise unknown. 4. **direxerat:** from *dirigere*. **Macedoniam:** accusative of place to which without a preposition (common in ML; cf. Blaise 75). 5. **Philippo:** ablative of source without a preposition. **tollere:** complement of *direxerat*, with *censum* its object. 13. **secuti sunt:** from *sequi*. 18. **Xersen** = CL *Xerxen*, from *Xerxes, is*; the form is accusative by attraction to the prepositional phrase, although it clearly goes with *regis* = "of King Xerxes." **tribunal:** from *tribunal, tribunalis;* with *sub* one expects *tribunale*. 21. **mee** = CL *meae*, modifying *domus*, which is also genitive singular here. 27. **ementiori** = CL *eminentiori*, comparative form of the present active participle of *eminere* = "higher," "loftier." 28. **equabitur** = CL *aequabitur*.

multi plures nobis fuissent, etiam centupliciter, non nos deberent turbare, quia multitudo muscarum nullam lesionem prevalet facere parvitati vespium." Audiens autem hoc omnis exercitus elevata voce magna ceperunt laudare eum.

5   Darius itaque imperator amoto exercitu suo venit ad fluvium Granicum transiensque ipsum fluvium castra metatus est ibi. Erat enim exercitus Darii magnus valde et fortis habebatque falcatos currus decem milia. Alio namque die convenerunt in campo utreque hostes, Alexander cum suis et Darius imperator cum suis. Alexander enim ascendens equum qui

10   dicebatur Bukefalas et amoto eo cursu velocissimo stetit in medio ante omnes suos. Videntes enim Perses ex adverso obstupefacti sunt; timebant enim eum pro eo quod terribilis videbatur ab omnibus. Sonuerunt itaque tubas bellicas et facto impetu contra eos statim mixta est utraque hostis et ceperunt pugnare inter se acriter et ex ambabus partibus sonabant tube.

15   Fortior enim erat sonitus armorum pugnantium quam sonitus tubarum, et cadebant ex utraque parte multitudo militum. Erat enim sagittariorum plenitudo maxima per partes qui cooperiebant ipsum aerem de sagittis sicut nubes; alii autem manu ad manum pugnabant cum ensibus, alii vero cum sagittis et contis. Et erat planctus in eis et tribulatio magna eratque

20   campus plenus ex mortuis et semivivis et vulneratis, et inchoatum est prelium ab ortu solis et pugnatum est usque ad occasum eius. Inter hec autem multi ceperunt cadere a parte Persarum. Videns enim Darius suos in bello deficere terga versus est et iniit fugam ceperuntque et Perses fugere cum eo. Erat enim iam obscura nox. Multitudo falcatorum curruum fugientes

25   occidebant suos et cadebant pedestres homines ante eos sicut messis cadit in campo ante plenitudinem equitum. Veniens autem Darius ad fluvium invenit eum coagulatum et transiit. Plenitudo vero Persarum post eum fugientes ingressi sunt in ipsum fluvium et impleverunt illum ab una ripa in alteram, et statim rupta est glacies eius et absorbuit eos. Alii vero ven-

30   ientes ad ipsum fluvium, et cum transire non possent, insequentes eos Macedones interficiebant illos. In hoc itaque bello interfecti sunt ex Persis trecenta milia homines absque eis quos tulit ipse fluvius.
                                                              —*Hist. Prel.* 2.16 (excerpts).

1. **centupliciter:** "even a hundredfold more . . ."   2. **prevalet** = CL *praevalet.*   **parvitati:** *parvitas, atis* = "small horde."   **vespium:** in CL the form is *vespa, ae,* but in ML this noun becomes third declension = *vespa, is* (Latham 509).   8. **utreque** = CL *utraeque.*   10. **Bukefalas** = CL *Bucephalas,* from *Bucephalas, ae* (LS 254), the famous horse of Alexander.   14. **tube** = CL *tubae.*   17. **aerem:** from *aer, aeris.*   20. **prelium** = CL *proelium.*   21. **eius:** i.e., *solis.*   24. **curruum:** from *currus, us.*   32. **absque eis:** i.e., "not counting those. . . ."

ALEXANDER IN INDIA

Altera autem die expugnavit ipsam civitatem Pori apprehendensque
eam ingressus est palatium eius et invenit ibi que incredibilia humanis
mentibus videbantur, id est quadringente columne auree cum capitellis
aureis, et vinea pendebat inter ipsas columnas que habebat folia aurea, et
racemi illius erant alii de cristallo, alii de margaritis et unionibus, alii de   5
smaragdis et onichitis. Et erant parietes illius palatii investiti de laminis
aureis quas incidebant Macedones, et inveniebantur grosse ad instar digiti
hominis de manu, erantque ipsi parietes ornati ex margaritis et unionibus
et carnbunculis et smaragdis et ametistis. Porte vero predicti palatii erant
eburnee et lacunaria ebena et camere eius de lignis cipressinis. Et in aula   10
ipsius palatii erant posite statue auree, et inter ipsas stabant platani aurei
in quorum ramis erant multa genera avium, et invenit unamquamque
avem tinctam secundum suum colorem habebantque ungulas et rostra in-
aurata, et in auribus earum pendebant margarite et uniones, et quando
volebat Porus rex, per musicam omnes melodificabant secundum suam   15
naturam. Et invenit in ipso palatio multa vasa aurea et gemmea, seu et
cristallina, ex omni genere facta, ad obsequium hominum pertinentia, erantque ex ipsis pauca argentea.

—Hist. Prel. 3.3 (excerpts).

Girantes autem ipsum fluvium ex alia parte circa horam undecimam
venerunt ad stagnum mellifluum ac dulce et castra metatus est ibi in lati-   20
tudine et longitudine ad tria miliaria. Deinde iussit incidere ipsam silvam
que erat in circuitu de ipso stagno, eratque ipsa silva ex predictis calamis.
Et erat spatiosus ipse stagnus ad unum miliarium. Tunc precepit Alexander accendi focos plurimos. Cumque luna lucere inciperet, subito ceperunt venire scorpiones ad bibendum in ipso stagno. Deinde ceperunt venire   25
serpentes et dracones mire magnitudinis ex diversis coloribus, et tota ipsa
terra resonabat ex sibilis eorum. Exierant enim ex ipsis montibus et venie-

1. **Pori:** *Porus, i* = Porus, the King of India, where Alexander now has made his way in
this part of the story.   3. **quadringente columne auree** = CL *quadringentae columnae
aurea.*   5. **cristallo** = CL *crystallo.*   6. **onichitis:** in CL there are two forms for
"onyx": *onyx, onychis* and *onychitis, onychitides;* this form, *onichitus, i,* in the ablative, is technically neither of these.   7. **grosse** = CL *grossae.*   9. **ametistis** = CL *am-
ethystis.*   **predicti** = CL *praedicti.*   10. **eburnee** = CL *eburneae.*   **camere** = CL
camerae.   **cipressinis** = CL *cupressinus* (or *cypressinus*), adjective formed on *cupres-
sus* = "cypress-like" (LS 499).   11. **posite statue auree** = CL *positae statuae aureae.*
14. **margarite** = CL *margaritae.*   17. **cristallina** = CL *crystallina,* from *crystallinus,
a, um.*   19. **Girantes:** from CL *gyrantes,* the subject of *venerunt* with the sense of
"crossing back" (Blaise/Chirat 383, s. v. *gyro*).   22. **predictis** = CL *praedictis*
26. **mire** = CL *mirae.*

bant ad bibendum ex ipsa aqua. Ipsi namque dracones habebant cristas in capite et adducebant pectora erecta, ora aperta; flatus eorum erat mortalis et de oculis eorum scintillabat venenum. Videntes enim eos ipse exercitus timore perterriti existimabant se omnes mori. Tunc Alexander cepit
5 confortare eos dicens: "O commilitones fortissimi, non turbetur animus vester, sed sicut me videritis facere, ita facite." Et hec dicens statim apprehendit venabulum et scutum et cepit pugnare cum draconibus et serpentibus qui super illos veniebant. Videntes autem hoc milites eius confortati sunt valde apprehendentesque armas ceperunt et illi similiter pugnare
10 cum eis. Alios occidebant cum armis, alios vero ad ignem, et interfecti sunt viginti milites a draconibus et triginta servi eius. Deinde exierunt cancri ex ipso arundineto mire magnitudinis, habentes dorsa duriora sicut cocodrilli. Iactantes super eos lanceas suas, et nullomodo intrabant in dorsa eorum; sed tamen multos ex eis occiderunt ad ignem, alii intraver-
15 unt in ipsum stagnum. Iam venerat quinta vigilia noctis, et subito venerunt super eos leones albi maiores sicut tauri et cum magna murmuratione concutiebant cervices suas, et facto impetu contra eos recipiebant eos milites in venabulis suis et sic interficiebant eos. Post hec ceperunt venire sues mire magnitudinis, habentes dentes per longum cubitum unum et
20 erant mixti inter eos homines agrestes, mares et femine, habentes per singulos sex manus et occurrebant super eos una cum sues. Milites autem recipiebant eos in venabulis suis et interficiebant eos. Angustiabatur plurimum Alexander et omnis eius exercitus statimque precepit accendi focos plurimos extra ipsum exercitum.

—Hist. Prel. 3.17.3.

25 Deinde venit super eos bestia mire magnitudinis, fortior elephanto, et erat similis equo, caput habebat nigrum et in fronte eius tria cornua erant armata; nominabatur autem ipsa bestia secundum Indicam linguam Odontetiranno. Et antequam de ipsa aqua biberet, dedit impetum super eos. Alexander autem discurrens huc atque illuc confortando milites suos.
30 Ex alia parte irruit super eos ipsa bestia et occidit ex ipsis viginti sex, et quinquaginta et duos ex eis conculcavit; sed tamen occiderunt illam.

—Hist. Prel. 3.17.4.

---

12. **cancri:** from *cancer, cancri.* **arundineto** = CL *harundineto*, from *harundinetum, i* = "thicket of reeds" (LS 841). 13. **cocodrilli** = CL *crocodilus, i* = "crocodile" in genitive of specification with *durioria sicut* = "harder than those of crocodiles"; cf. AG 349d. 19. **sues:** from *sus, suis.* 20. **femine** = CL *feminae.* 28. **Odontetiranno** = CL *odontotyranno*, from *odontotyrannus, i* = "a beast" (LS 1256).

Deinde exierunt ex ipso arundineto mures maiores sicut vulpes et comedebant corpora mortuorum; et quanta de animalibus mordebant, statim moriebantur; homines vero nullomodo nocebat morsus eorum, ut exinde morerentur. Volabant et ibi vespertiliones maiores sicut columbe, dentes eorum ut dentes hominum, feriebantque in facies eorum et plaga- 5 bant eos, ad alios tollebant nares et ad alios aures. Appropinquante luce venerunt aves magne ut vultures; colorem habebant rubicundum, pedes et rostra habebant nigros; et non nocuerunt eos, sed impleverunt totam ripam de ipso stagno et ceperunt exinde trahere pisces et anguillas et com- edebant eos. 10

Deinde amoto exercitu dimiserunt loca periculosa et venerunt in loca Bactrianorum que erant plena de auro et aliis divitiis, et benigne receper- unt eum homines ipsius terre, steteruntque ibi dies viginti. Et invenerunt ibi gentes que nominantur Seres. Erantque ibi arbores que mittebant ipsa folia velut lana, que ipsa gens colligebant et vestimenta exinde sibi facie- 15 bant. Milites enim Alexandri ceperunt habere fortem animum propter victorias et prospera que habuerunt ex ipsis feris.

—*Hist. Prel.* 3.17.5.

4. **columbe** = CL *columbae*.   6. **nares:** from *naris, is.*   7. **magne** = CL *magnae.*
12. **Bactrianorum:** from *Bactriani, orum* = the Bactrians (LS 219, s. v. *Bactra* C2).

PLATE 22. A folio from a late fourteenth–century Latin Book of Hours, showing the Crucifixion.

PLATE 22

Book of Hours
Latin manuscript on parchment, late fourteenth century, fol. 52 verso
John Hay Library, Brown University

This folio, which comes from the same manuscript as that in plate 21, depicts the Crucifixion of Christ, and is placed near the end of the work. Like its counterpart discussed above, this folio is vigorously decorated with marginal floreation of bright colors—red, green, blue—and much intricate detailing, including animals, insects, and human figures. The crucifixion scene is framed by a drawn border, suggestive of a window view or of a portrait hung on the wall. Within its frames there is some gilding and much continued attention to color and vivid detail. Mary is shown on the left, and John, "the disciple whom Jesus loved most," is on the right. Jerusalem, the site of so much of the Crusader literature and the focus of Raymond of Aguilers's narrative, is plainly visible in the distance. The manuscript is bound in wooden boards showing much wear (on the Book of Hours tradition, see plate 20). It is 17 cm. in height and has 60 folios.

RAYMOND OF AGUILERS

The History of the Franks Who Captured Jerusalem
(*Historia Francorum qui ceperunt Iherusalem*; c. 1100)

I n 1070, the Seljuk Turks seized Jerusalem from the control of the Fatamids, who had ruled Egypt and the Holy Land and had allowed substantial
liberties of movement, worship, and commerce for Christians there. In
short order, atrocities and desecrations were reported to the West. About
the same time, the Turks began a concerted assault on Byzantium from
the east: a horrible defeat was suffered at Manzikert in 1071; Edessa,
Antioch, Tarsus, and Nicaea were taken by 1085; the West itself seemed
vulnerable when, in 1095, the Byzantine Emperor, Alexius I, appealed to
the West for assistance. In March of that year, at Piacenza, Urban II presided over a council set to determine whether a holy war should be waged
against the Turks. For the better part of the next seven months, Urban
traveled from Piacenza through northern Italy and into southern France,
gauging the mood—both public and princely—for such a war. In November, at Clermont, he presided over another council, and on the 27th
of that month to the gathered crowds preached the First Crusade. William of Malmesbury (see pp. 473–75) reported that many nobles knelt at
the feet of the pope and vowed to take up arms against the Turks, pledg-
ing their property for the effort. A similar response swept much of
Europe.

When the Crusaders reached the Holy Land—after pillaging much
of eastern Europe, the suburbs of Constantinople, and Nicaea along the
way—mostly French contingents remained, thus making the First Crusade largely a French affair, a fact that accords well with the sentiments
and perspective of Raymond of Aguilers, an eyewitness to much of the
action, as recorded in his *Historia Francorum qui ceperunt Iherusalem*,
excerpted here. Raymond was attached to the army of Count Raymond
of Toulouse, who had already fought against Islam in Spain, where inroads had been made against Muslim control earlier in the eleventh century. Here now, in 1097, Raymond's army joined up with the troops of
Godfrey of Bouillon, Bohemund of Taranto, and Tancred of Hauteville,
and this collective host made its way into the Holy Land. The decisive
prize was to be Antioch.

The excerpts recount an important event in the days following the capture of Antioch. The capture itself had taken place on 3 June 1098. But a fierce Moslem army, led by Kerbogha of Mosul, was only days away at the time. Many Christians fled their newly won city, fearful that they would be slaughtered by Kerbogha; Emperor Alexius, on his way to help, heard in error that the Christians had been defeated, and turned back; morale was low. At this point, Peter Bartholomew, a priest from Marseille, claimed to have found the Holy Spear, the lance that had pierced the side of Christ as he hung on the Cross. He used the lance to good effect to lift morale and inspire the troops. The first excerpt details the discovery of the spear; the second, which describes a later occasion, explains its powers and Peter Bartholomew's insistence on its true identity. In the event, the Crusaders defeated Kerbogha and arrived, eventually, at Jerusalem in 1099—a full year after the Fatamids of Egypt had retaken the city from the Seljuks. Godfrey of Bouillon was chosen to rule Jerusalem, which was easily taken from the Egyptians in the summer of 1099 (and about which Raymond of Aguilers has much to tell also), and from this cohort of armies, battles, and victories arose the Latin Kingdom of Jerusalem.

Raymond of Aguilers tells us that he was a chaplain in the retinue of Count Raymond IV of Toulouse, that he accompanied the Count on the First Crusade, and that he was made a priest while on the journey to the Holy Land. We do not know when he was born or died. He was clearly not a historian by calling or a literary scholar by training, like Richer or Liutprand of Cremona. He reports that he wrote his history as a collaborative venture with Pons of Balazun. But Pons died from wounds suffered at the battle of 'Arqah, leaving Raymond to complete the work on his own. Both men were presumably commissioned to their historical task, especially since their stated aim in producing their work was to suppress criticism of the First Crusade in the West (if nothing else, this demonstrates that Raymond undertook his history after the Latin Kingdom of Jerusalem had been established, for the cynicism surrounding its foundation is more than likely the "criticism" Raymond has in mind).

Given his training, background, and aims, there are no obvious threads of the Medieval Latin historiographic tradition informing Raymond's narrative. Nor is he much of a participant in the high literary culture of his day. He writes in a roughly chronological fashion, and he controls his story through first person narration and impersonal chronicling of events, but he has no larger purposes other than to extol the virtues of Christianity as against the heathen tendencies of Islam, or, when he is not doing this, to sing the praises of his patron, Count Raymond IV of Toulouse. The tone of the *Historia Francorum*, therefore, is didactic, while the Latin is simple, reflecting not a high literary prose but a more common style that arose as the Church itself developed a literate class of clerics to do its work in the late eleventh and throughout the twelfth century. Indeed, this prose style, which is firmly indicative of EL standards, is evocative of Scripture itself, and many scriptural quotations are used by Raymond in his descriptions of historical figures. Other characteristics of what might be called Raymond's "middle" prose style include many features of ML prose in general: a tendency to use prepositions with adverbs (e.g., *a longe*); the deployment of *dum* with the subjunctive; the use of the ablative of the gerund as a present participle, expressing the circumstances under which the action of the gerund occurs; the use of *de* to replace the inflection of a noun into the genitive; the deployment of *quia* (also *quod* or *quoniam*) to introduce indirect discourse, with the indicative; or result clauses construed with the indicative mood. The *Historia* was written almost contemporaneously with the events it describes. The ways in which it was mined for information by Fulcher of Chartres (see pp. 478–88) allows us to say with some certainty that it was finished no later than 1101.

Raymond's *Historia* has been edited by Philippe Le Bas (*Raimundus de Aguilers, Historia Francorum qui ceperunt Iherusalem,* in *Recueil des historiens des croisades, Historiens occidentaux,* Académie des Inscriptions et Belles-Lettres, 5 vols., Paris, 1866, vol. 3, pp. 231–309) and by J. H. Hill and L. L. Hill (*Le Liber de Raymond d'Aguilers,* in "Documents relatifs à l'histoire des croisades," Académie des Inscriptions et Belles-Lettres, Paris, 1969); they have also translated the work into English (*Raymond D'Aguilers: Historia Francorum qui ceperunt Iherusalem,* Philadelphia, 1968), with excellent notes, introduction, and bibliography. The text of Hill and Hill is reprinted with subscripts normalized.

THE DISCOVERY OF THE HOLY SPEAR

Itaque ut diximus dum nostri conturbarentur, et cum in desperationem ruerent, divina clementia eis affuit, et quae lascivientes filios correxerat, nimium tristes tali modo consolata est. Igitur cum capta esset civitas Antiochiae, usus sua potentia et benignitate dominus, pauperem

---

4. **Antiochiae:** from *Antoiochia, ae* = Antioch, feminine noun of the first declension (Sleumer 114).

quendam rusticum elegit, provincialem genere, per quem omnes nos confortavit, et comiti et Podiensi episcopo, haec verba mandavit. Andreas Dei et Domini nostri Ihesu Christi apostolus, me quater olim monuit et iussit ut ad vos venirem, et lanceam quae Salvatoris latus aperuit, capta civitate vobis redderem. Hodie autem cum ad pugnam profectus essem extra civitatem cum reliquis, atque comprehensus a duobus equitibus pene suffocatus in regressu fuissem, quasi exanimis illic super lapidem quendam tristis resedissem. Cumque pre dolore et timore sicut tristis titubarem, venit ante me beatus Andreas cum socio quodam multum michi interminatus, nisi cito vobis landeam redderem. Cumque ab eo comes et episcopus revelationis et iussionis apostolicae ordinem requirerent, respondit: in primo terraemotu qui apud Antiochiam factus est, cum exercitus Francorum obsideret eam, tantus timor me invasit, ut nichil preter Deus adiuva me dicere possem. Erat enim nox et ego iacebam, nec in tugurio meo erat aliquis cuius consorcio refoverer. Cum autem ut dixi concussio terrae diutius duraret, et timor meus semper excresceret, coram me duo viri astiterunt in veste clarissima. Alter erat senio rufo conoque capillo. Oculi nigri, et convenientes faciei. Barba vero cana et lata et prolixa et statura eius media. Alter vero et iunior et procerior erat. Speciosus forma pre filiis hominum. Et ait michi senior: quid agis? et ego maxime timui quia nullum adesse sciebam, et respondi: quis es tu? et ait: surge, et noli timere; et audi quae ego loquor ad te: Ego sum Andreas apostolus. Congrega episcopum Podiensem, et comitem Sancti Egidii, et Petrum Raimundum de Altopullo, et hoc dices ad illos: cur negligit episcopus predicare et commonere et cum cruce quam prefert cotidie signare populum? Etenim multum prodesset illis et addidit: veni et ostendam tibi lanceam patris nostri Ihesu

1. **provincialem:** from *provincialis, is* = Provençal (Sleumer 643, s. v. 2 *provincialis*). The Provençal peasant meant here is Peter Bartholomew, who is mentioned below by name.   2. **comiti:** i.e., Count Raymond IV of Toulouse, one of the leaders of the First Crusade, and the patron of the author of this work, Raymond of Aguilers. **Podiensi:** from *Podiensis, is* = Le Puy, a bishopric in France (Hill and Hill 51); Adhémar, bishop of Le Puy, is meant by the phrase *Podiensi episcopo*.   **mandavit:** i.e., *rusticus.*   **Andreas:** from *Andreas, ae,* masculine noun of the first declension = Saint Andrew (Sleumer 108).   4. **Salvatoris:** from *Salvator, oris* = Christ.   6. **pene** = CL *paene*.   11. **respondit:** i.e., Peter Bartholomew.   12. **terraemotu:** i.e., an earthquake.   16. **astiterunt:** from *assistere*.   23. **Egidii:** from *Aegidius, i,* = St.-Gilles (Sleumer 83); with *comitem* = Count of St.-Gilles.   **Raimundum:** with *Petrum* = Peter Raymond, a vassal of Raymond IV of Toulouse and fellow Crusader.   **Altopullo:** i.e., Hautpoul (Hill and Hill 52).   24. **episcopus:** i.e., Adhémar, bishop of Le Puy.

Christi, quam comiti donabis, etenim Deus eam concessit illi ex quo genitus est. Surrexi itaque et secutus sum eum in civitatem nullo circumdatus
amictu preter camisiam et induxit me in aecclesiam beati Petri apostoli
per septentrionalem portam quam antea Sarraceni maumariam fecerant.
5 In aecclesia vero duae lampades erant, quae tantum lumen ibi reddebant
ac si meridies illuxisset. Et dixit michi: expecta hic. Et iussit me assistere
columnae quae [proxima] erat gradibus quibus ascenditur ad altare a
meridie et socius eius a longe stetit ante gradus altaris. Ingressusque sub
terram sanctus Andreas produxit lanceam atque in manibus michi tradi-
10 dit. Et dixit michi: ecce lancea quae latus eius aperuit, unde tocius mundi
salus emanavit. Dumque eam in manibus meis tenerem, lacrimando pre
gaudio dixi ei: domine si vis portabo eam et reddam comiti. Et dixit
michi: sine modo. Futurum est enim ut civitas capiatur. Et tunc venies,
cum .xii. viris et queres eam hic unde ego abtraxi, et ubi eam recondam.
15 Et recondidit eam. His ita peractis super murum civitatis reduxit me in
domum meam, et sic a me recesserunt. Tunc ego mecum recogitans, et
paupertatis meae abitum et vestram magnitudinem, veritus sum ad vos
accedere. Post illud tempus cum profectus essem ad quoddam castrum
quod est iuxta Roiam propter alimoniam, prima die quadragesime in galli
20 cantu affuit beatus Andreas in eodem abitu et cum eodem sotio quo prius
venerat, et magna claritas domum replevit. Et ait beatus Andreas: vig-
ilasne? Sic expergefactus respondi: non domine. Domine mi non dormio.
Et ait michi: dixisti ea quae dudum tibi dicenda mandavi? Et respondi:
domine nonne ego precatus sum vos ut alium eis mitteretis, etenim met-
25 uens paupertati meae accedere ante illos dubitavi. Et dixit michi: nescisne
cur Deus huc vos adduxit? et quantum vos diligit, et quomodo vos pre-

---

1. **comiti:** i.e., Raymond IV of Toulouse.　3. **camisiam:** from *camisia, ae* = "under-
shirt," in ML also *camisa, camisum, camisium;* cf. Niermeyer 121.　4. **Sarraceni:** the
better spelling is *Saraceni, orum* = the Saracens (Sleumer 696).　**maumariam:** from
mafumaria, ae = "mosque" (Hill and Hill 52; Latham 286); the phrase means, "in
front of which the Saracens had built a mosque."　6. **assistere** + dative object.
7. **altare:** from *altare, is* = "altar" (Niermeyer 38).　8. **a longe** = CL *longe;* the use
of prepositions with adverbs is common in ML.　11. **dumque . . . tenerem:** it is common in ML for *dum* + imperfect subjunctive = *cum;* "and while I
was holding the sword in my hands . . ." (cf. Blaise 310).　**lacrimando:** it is common in ML for the ablative of the gerund to function as a present participle, expressing the circumstances under which the action of the gerund occurs = "crying for
joy . . ." (Blaise 343).　14. **abtraxi:** from *abstrahere.*　17. **veritus sum:** from *vereri.*
19. **Roiam:** from *Roia, ae* = Edessa (Hill and Hill 53).　**quadragesime** = *quadragesimae,* from *quadragesima, ae* = Lent (Sleumer 648).

cipue elegit? Pro contemptu sui et suorum vindicta vos huc venire fecit. Diligit vos adeo ut sancti iam in requie positi divine dispositionis gratiam prenoscentes in carne esse et concertare nobiscum vellent. Elegit vos Deus ex omnibus gentibus sicut triticeae spicae de avenaria colliguntur, etenim meritis et gratia preceditis omnes qui ante et post vos venient, sicut aurum 5 precio precedit argentum. Post haec discesserunt, et me tanta egritudo oppressit ut lumen oculorum perderem et dispositionem tenuissime paupertatis meae facerem. Tunc ego cepi mecum cogitare, quod ob neglegentiam apostolicae iussionis tuae iuste michi contingerent. Confortatus itaque ad obsidionem reversus sum. Rursus paupertatis mee debilitatem 10 recogitans, timere cepi si ad vos venirem, famelicum me esse et pro victu talia ea referre me proclamaretis, itaque ea vice conticui. Defluente itaque tempore cum apud portum Sancti Symeonis sabbato in palmis essem, atque cum domino meo Willelmo Petri, infra tentorium una recubarem, affuit beatus Andreas, cum socio et habitu eodem quo prius venerat, 15 atque michi sic locutus est: cur non dixisti comiti et episcopo et aliis quae ego preceperam tibi? Et respondi: domine nonne ego precatus sum te ut alium pro me mitteres? Qui et sapientor esset, et quem audire vellent? Preterea Turci sunt in itinere qui venientes et abeuntes interficiunt. Et ait sanctus Andreas: noli timere, quia nichil tibi nocebunt. Haec quoque 20 dices comiti cum venerit ad Iordanem fluvium non intinguatur ibi sed navigio transeat. Cum autem transierit, camisia et bragis lineis indutus de flumine aspergatur, et postquam siccata fuerint eius vestimenta reponat ea et conservet cum lancea Domini. Et haec dominus meus Willelmus Petrus audivit, licet non videret apostolum. Confortatus igitur, ad exerci- 25 tum reversus sum. Cumque hoc vobis haec pariter dicere vellem, coadunare vos non potui. Itaque profectus sum ad portum de Mamistra, ibi vero

1. **venire fecit**: the infinitive with *facere* is common in ML (cf. Browne xxv); lit. "he made you to come here," i.e., "he ordered you here." 4. **avenaria**: from *avenaria, ae* = "field of oats" (Niermeyer 74). 12. **conticui**: from *conticescere*. 13. **Symeonis**: from *Simeon, onis* = Saint Simeon (Sleumer 726), bishop of Jersualem and martyr to the faith c. 105; with *portum* = port of St. Simeon. 14. **Willelmo Petri**: *Willelmus Petrus*, i.e., William Peter, a pilgrim on the crusade, otherwise unknown (Hill and Hill 54, n. 4). 16. **comiti et episcopo**: i.e., Raymond IV of Toulouse and Adhémar. 20. **nocebunt**: the subject is *Turcae*. 21. **Iordanem**: from *Iordanis, is* = River Jordan (with *fluvium*) (Sleumer 445). 22. **bragis** = CL *bracae, arum*. 26. **coadunare** = "to bring together" (Niermeyer 193); the phrase means "I was not able to bring you together." 27. **de**: the use of *de* to replace the inflection of a noun in the genitive is, among other such usages, common in ML. **Mamistra**: with *portum de* = the port of Mamistra (Hill and Hill 54).

cum navigare in Cyprum insulam pro victualibus vellem, comminatus est michi multum sanctus Andreas, nisi cito reverterem et vobis iniuncta michi referrem. Cumque cogitare mecum quomodo reverterem ad castra, aberat enim portus ille ab exercitu quasi per tres dies, amarissime flere
5 cepi. Cum redeundi facultatem reperire non possem, tandem a sociis et domino meo conmonitus navigium ingressus, in Cyprum remigare cepimus. Et cum per totam diem remis et prosperis ventis ageremur, usque ad solis occasum orta subito tempestate, in spatio unius hore vel duarum ad relictum portum reversi sumus. Sicque secundo et tercio a transitu proibiti
10 in insulam, ad portum Sancti Symeonis reversi sumus, ibi langorem gravissimum incurri. Capta autem civitate ad vos veni, et nunc si vobis placet experimini quae dico: episcopus autem nichil esse preter verba putavit. Comes vero ilico credidit, et illum qui hoc dixerat capellano suo Raimundo custodiendum tradidit.

15 (A)pparuit in ipsa nocte quae secuta est Dominus noster Ihesus Christus cuidam sacerdoti nomine Stephano lacrimanti pro interitu suo et sociorum quem futurum ilico sperabat, etenim terruerant eum quidam qui de castello descenderant, dicentes Turcos iam descendere de monte in civitatem, atque nostros fugere et victos esse, propterea sacerdos volens
20 habere Deum mortis suae testem, ingressus aecclesiam beatae Mariae abita confessione, et sumpta venia cum quibusdam sociis psalmos cantare coepit. Dormientibusque aliis cum solus vigilaret, atque cum dixisset, Domine quis habitabit in tabernaculo tuo aut quis requiescet in monte sancto tuo, stetit coram eo vir quidam ultra omnem speciem pulcher, et
25 dixit ei: homo, quaenam est haec gens quae civitatem ingressa est? Et ait presbiter: christiani. Et dixit ille: cuiusmodi christiani? Et sacerdos: qui credunt Christum de virgine natum, et in cruce passum, mortuum, et sepultum, et resurrexisse tercia die, atque in caelum ascendisse. Et dixit vir ille: et si christiani sunt cur paganorum multitudinem verentur? Et ad-
30 didit: agnoscisne me? et respondit presbiter: non agnosco te, nisi quod

1. **Cyprum:** from *Cyprus, i* = Cyprus (Sleumer 255). 2. **iniuncta:** from *iniunctum, i* = "injunction," "order," "instruction" (Niermeyer 538). 13. **capellano:** from *capellanus, i* = "chaplain" (but with a host of other meanings also; see Niermeyer 131–32). **Raimundo:** i.e., the author of this work. 16. **Stephano:** from *Stephanus, i* = Stephen, otherwise unknown, he is sometimes called Stephen Valentine (cf. Hill and Hill 55, and n. 7). 18. **Turcos:** from *Turcae, arum;* the better spelling is *Turcas* (Sleumer 796) = Turks. 21. **psalmos:** from *psalmus, i* = "psalms" (Sleumer 644). 25. **quaenam:** from *quisnam.* **civitatem:** i.e., Antioch. 26. **presbiter:** from *presbyter, eris* = "priest" (Sleumer 632), i.e., Stephen. **sacerdos:** from *sacerdos, otis* = "priest" (Sleumer 686). 28. **resurrexisse:** from *resurgere.*

pulcherrimum omnium te video. Et ait vir: diligentissime intuere me.
Cumque in eum perspicaciter sacerdos intenderet, de capite eius speciem,
crucis sole multum clariorem procedere vidit. Et ait viro interroganti de
se: domine imagines Ihesu Christi esse dicimus, quae similem tibi speciem
preferant. Et dixit illi dominus: bene dixisti quia ego sum. Nonne   5
scriptum est de me quia sum dominus fortis et potens in prelio? Et quis
est dominus in exercitu? Et respondit presbiter: Domine non fuit ibi unus
solus dominus umquam, sed magis episcopo credunt. Et dixit Dominus:
haec dices episcopo. Populus iste male agendo me elongavit a se, et ideo
dicat eis: convertimini ad me et ego revertar ad vos. Et cum pugnam inier-   10
int, haec dicant: congregati sunt inimici nostri et gloriantur in virtute sua
contere fortitudinem illorum domine et disperge illos ut cognoscant quia
non est alius qui pugnet pro nobis nisi tu Deus noster. Et haec quoque
dices ad illos: si feceritis quae ego precipio vobis, usque ad quinque dies,
vestri miserebor. Haec autem eo dicente mulier Maria mater Ihesu Christi   15
quedam supra modum inflammati vultus accessit. Et intuita Dominum,
dixit ei: Domine et quid huic viro dicitis? et Dominus ad illam: Quero ab
eo de hac gente quae civitatem ingressa est quae sit. Et ait domina: O
Domine mi, hi sunt pro quibus ego tantum te rogo. Cumque sacerdos
socium suum qui prope se dormiebat pulsaret, ut tante visionis testem   20
habere potuisset, ab oculis eius sublati sunt. Mane autem facto in montem
sacerdos ascendit, ubi principes nostri morabantur, contra Turcorum
castellum preter ducem. Ille enim castellum quod erat in septentrionali
colle servabat. Convocata itaque contione, habuit haec verba ad nostros
principes, atque ut verum esse monstraret, super crucem iuravit. In-   25
credulis autem satisfacere volens vel transire per ignem vel precipitari de
altitudine turris voluit. Tunc iuraverunt principes, quod de Antiochia non
fugerent neque egrederentur nisi de communi consilio omnium. Etenim
populus ea tempestate existimabat quod principes vellent fugere ad portum. Confortati sunt itaque multi, etenim in nocte preterita pauci steter-   30
unt in fide qui fugere non voluissent. Quod nisi episcopus et Boiamundus

2. **perspicaciter:** adverb = "with wisdom" (Blaise/Chirat 618). 6. **quia:** it is common in ML for *quia* (also *quod* or *quoniam*) to introduce indirect discourse, with the
indicative. 8. **episcopo:** i.e., Adhémar. 9. **elongavit:** from *elongare* = "to alien-
ate," "to remove," "to take away," on the model of the *Vulgate,* Psalm 54.7, e.g. (cf.
Blaise/Chirat 305). 10. This quotation comes from Zach. 1.3. 23. **ducem:** i.e.,
Godfrey of Bouillon. 31. **episcopus:** i.e., Adhémar. **Boiamundus:** *Boimundus, i* =
Bohemund, son of Robert Guiscard, a rival of Count Raymond IV of Toulouse, who
helped to capture Antioch in 1098.

portas civitatis reclusissent, admodum pauci remansissent. Fugit tamen Guillelmus de Grandismainil et frater eius, et multi alii laici et clerici. Multis autem contigit ut cum de civitate cum maximo periculo evasissent in manus Turcorum maius periculum mortis incurrebant. Eo tempore
5 contigerunt nobis plurime revelationes per fratres nostros, et signum in caelo mirabile vidimus. Nam stella quedam maxima per noctem super civitatem stetit, quae post paulum in tres partes divisa est, atque in Turcorum castris cecidit. Confortati igitur aliquantulum nostri diem quintum quem predixerat sacerdos expectabant. Die autem illa preparatis nec-
10 essariis duodecim viri cum homine illo qui de lancea dixerat eiectis de aecclesia Beati Petri omnibus aliis, fodere coepimus. Fuit autem in illis .xii. viris, episcopus Aurasicensis, et Raimundi comitis capellanus, qui haec scripsit, et ipse comes, et Pontius de Baladuno, et Faraldus de Tornaiz. Cumque a mane usque ad vesperum fodissemus, in vespere desper-
15 are quidam de inventione lanceae ceperunt. Discesserat enim comes propter castelli custodiam. Sed loco illius et aliorum qui fodiendo fatigabantur, alios recentes inducebamus qui viriliter operi insisterent. Videns autem iuvenis qui de lancea dixerat nos defatigari, discinctus et discalciatis pedibus in camisia in foveam descendit, atque obtestatus est nos ut Deum
20 deprecaremur, quatinus nobis lanceam suam redderet, in confortationem et victoriam suae plebis. Tandem per gratiam pietatis suae commonitus est Dominus, ut lanceam suam nobis ostendat. Et ego qui scripsi haec

2. **Guillelmus de Grandismainil:** i.e., William of Grand-Mesnil, brother-in-law of Bohemund; the better spelling is *Wilhelmus* (Hill and Hill 57 and n. 12). **laici:** from *laicus, i* = "laity" (Blaise/Chirat 484). **clerici:** from *clericus, i* = "clergy" (Blaise/Chirat 159). 4. **Turcorum:** specifically, the Turkish leader Kerbogha is meant here. **ut . . . incurrebant:** a result clause construed with the indicative mood, as often in ML (Blaise 291). 7. **Turcorum:** from *Turcae, arum;* the better spelling is *Turcarum* (Sleumer 796); with *partes* = "the Turkish camp." 8. **diem quintum:** i.e., the "fifth day" proclaimed by Peter Bartholomew as the day in which the lance would be reclaimed. 11. **Petri:** from *Petrus, i* = Peter, with *de aecclesia Beati* = Church of Blessed Peter. 12. **episcopus Aurasicensis:** i.e., the bishop of Orange (Hill and Hill 57). **Raimundi . . . capellanus:** i.e., Raymond of Aguilers, the author of this work, as the *qui* clause subsequently makes clear. 13. **ipse comes:** i.e., Raymond of St.-Gilles. **Pontius de Baladuno:** i.e., Pons of Balazun (Hill and Hill 57), the coauthor of the *History* with Raymond, who was killed before he could complete much of his task at the Battle of 'Arqah. **Faraldus de Tornaiz:** i.e., Farald of Thouars (Hill and Hill 57), another French crusader. 18. **iuvenis:** i.e., Peter Bartholomew. **discinctus:** from *discingere.* **discalciatis:** perfect passive participle from *discalceare,* with *pedibus* = "with bare feet" (cf. Blaise/Chirat 276). 20. **quatinus** = CL *ut* + subjunctive *redderet* in a purpose clause, as often in ML (Blaise 290). **confortationem:** from *confortatio, onis* = "consolation" (Blaise/Chirat 197).

cum solus mucro adhuc appareret super terram, osculatus sum eam. Quantum gaudium et exultatio tunc civitatem replevit, non possum dicere. Inventa est, autem lancea octavo decimo, kalendas iulii.

—*Hist. Franc.* 10 (excerpts)

THE VIRTUE OF THE HOLY SPEAR

Accessit autem et episcopus Attensis dicens: Insomnis ego an non viderim ista certum nescio Deus scit. Vir quidam venit indutus albis et stetit ante me, at tenebat dominicam lanceam, lanceam dico istam in manibus suis, et dixit michi: Credis hanc lanceam esse Domini? et respondi: credo domine. Dubitaveram ego aliquando de ea. Cumque secundo id et tercio 5 graviter exigisset a me, dixi ad eum: Credo domine hanc esse lanceam Domini mei Ihesu Christi, et post haec dimisit me. Et ego qui haec scripsi, coram fratribus et episcopis haec ibi dixi: Interfui ego dum effoderetur, et antequam tota super terram apparuisset, mucronem obsculatus sum, et sunt in exercitu plures qui mecum ista viderunt. Et addidi: Et alius qui- 10 dam sacerdos Bertrannus nomine Podiensis, qui familiaris episcopo Podiensi erat, in vita ipsius. Hic autem sacerdos infirmatus est, usque ad mortem apud Antiochiam. Cumque iam de vita sua desperaret, venit ante eum episcopus Podiensis cum Eraclio vexillifero suo qui in bello maximo facto apud Antiochiam in facie percussus sagitta, cum intrepidus agmina 15 Turcorum prosterneret, et inde vitam finierat. Et dixit ei episcopus: Bertrande quid agis? Et dixit Heraclius: Domine infirmus est. Et respondit episcopus: Propter incredulitatem infirmatur. Et sacerdos ad haec: Domine nonne ego de lancea Domini credo, sicut et de passione Domini? Et dixit ei episcopus: Et adhuc alia multa te oportet credere. Et licet ad hoc 20 negocium non pertineat, tamen quia egregium est, gratia bonorum hominum aliquid adiungam. Cum resedisset sacerdos ad presentiam episcopi et Heraclii domini sui, infirmus enim erat nec stare poterat, vidit in facie

---

3. **octavo decimo, kalendas iulii:** lit., "on the 18th day before the Kalends (*Kalendae*) of July (*Iulii,* from *Iulius, i*) = 14 June.

1. **episcopus Attensis:** i.e., the bishop of Apt, a Provençal bishopric (Hill and Hill 98 and n. 15). 3. **dominicam:** from *dominicus, a, um* = "royal," "lordly" etc. (on the variety of meanings see Niermeyer 352–53). 11. **Bertrannus . . . Podiensis:** *Bertrannus, i* = Bertrand of Le Puy; *Podiensis, is* = Le Puy (Hill and Hill 99 and n. 16). **episcopo Podiensi:** i.e., Adhémar. 14. **Eraclio:** from *Heraclium, i* = Heraclius, otherwise unknown, whose function is explained by *vexillifero.* **vexillifero:** from *vexillifer, eri* = "standard-bearer" (Niermeyer 1084). **qui:** i.e., Heraclius. 16. **episcopus:** i.e., Adhémar. 17. **Heraclius:** Heraclius answers for Bertrand, who, as Heraclius explains, is sick. 22. **adiungam:** Raymond is announcing here that what follows is not exactly pertinent, but useful because of its beneficial content.

domini sui vulnus unde ipse vitae mortalis labores finierat. Et dixit ei presbiter: Domine nos iam credebamus quod vulnus hoc vestrum sanatum
esset. Quid est hoc? Et respondit Heraclius: Bene hoc quesisti. Cum ego
veni ante dominum meum deprecatus sum eum quatenus numquam haec
5   plaga clauderetur, quoniam propter eam vitam finieram: Et hoc michi
concessit dominus. Haec et multa alia episcopus et Heraclius sacerdoti
dixerunt, quae modo non sunt necessaria. His atque pluribus aliis auditis,
credidit Arnulfus, et confessus est. Promisitque episcopo Albariensi quod
coram omni populo pro incredulitate sua veniam faceret. Die autem con-
10 stituta cum venisset vocatus ad consilium Arnulfus, cepit dicere quod
bene crederet, sed cum domino suo volebat loqui antequam veniam faceret. Cum vero haec audisset Petrus Bartholomeus iratus nimium sicut
homo simplex, et qui veritatem obtime noverat dixit: Volo ac deprecor ut
fiat ignis maximus, et cum lancea Domini transibo per medium. Et si est
15 lancea Domini incolumis transeam, sin autem conburar in igne. Video
enim quia nec signis nec testibus creditur. Placuerunt haec omnia nobis.
Et indicto ei ieiunio, diximus quod eo die fieret ignis, quo Dominus pro
nostra salute plagatus cum ea in cruce fuit, et post .iiii. diem erat paras-
cevem. Itaque illuscescente die constituta ignis preparatus est post meri-
20 diem. Convenerunt eo principes et populus usque ad .lx. milia virorum.
Fuerunt ibi sacerdotes, nudis pedibus et induti sacerdotalibus indumentis.
Factus est de oleis siccis, et habuit in longitudine .xiii. pedes et erant duo
aggeres et inter utrosque spacium quasi unius pedis. Et in altitudine ag-
gerum erant quatuor pedes. Cum vero ignis vehementer accensus esset,
25 dixi ego Raimundus coram omni multitudine: Si Deus omnipotens huic
homini locutus est facie ad faciem, et beatus Andreas lanceam dominicam
ostendit ei cum iste vigilaret, transeat iste illesus per ignem. Sin autem est
mendatium conburatur iste cum lancea quam portabit in manu sua. Et
omnes flexis genibus responderunt amen. Exestuabat ita incendium, ut
30 usque ad .xxx. cubitos aera occuparet. Accedere vero prope nullus poterat. Tunc Petrus Bartholomeus indutus solummodo tunica, et flexis genibus ante episcopum Albariensem, Deum testem invocavit, quod facie ad
faciem ipsum in cruce viderit, et haec quae suprascripta sunt ab eo audivit. Et a beato Petro et Andrea neque quicquam eorum quae sub nomine
35 sancti Petri vel sancti Andreae, vel ipsius Domini dixit se conposuisse. Et

8. **Arnulfus:** from *Arnulfus, i* = Arnulf of Chocques (Hill and Hill 99). **episcopo
Albariensi:** from *Albariensis, is* = the Bishop of Albara (Hill and Hill 100).   18. **para-
scevem:** from *Parasceve, es* = Good Friday (Sleumer 581).   21. **sacerdotalibus:** from
sacerdotalis, is = "priestly" (Niermeyer 926).   34. **Petro et Andrea:** *Petrus, i* = Peter;
Andrea, ae = Andrew.

si quicquam mentitus erat, presens incendium numquam transisset. Caetera quae ipse commisisset et in Deum et in proximum dimitteret ei Deus, et pro his oraret episcopus, atque omnes alii sacerdotes et populus qui ad hoc spectandum convenerat. Post haec cum episcopus posuisset ei lanceam in manu, flexis genibus et facto signo crucis sibi cum lancea viri-   5
liter et inperterritus incendium ingressus est. Atque per spacium quoddam in medio ignis demoratus est, et sic per Dei gratiam transivit. Sunt autem nonnulli adhuc qui hoc signum ibi viderunt, quod antequam egrederetur rogum, quedam avis desuper volans lustrato igne se intus inmisit. Hoc vidit Ebrardus sacerdos ille cuius mencionem superius fecimus,   10
qui Ierosolimis pro Deo postea remansit. Et Guillelmus Bonofilius obtimus miles, et boni testimonii patria Arelatensi. Hoc ipsum se vidisse testatur alius quidam miles honestus genere Biterensis, nomine Guillelmus Maluspuer. Quod antequam Petrus ingrederetur in flamma, quendam hominem indutum veste sacerdotali, nisi quod casulam habebat replicatam   15
super capud ingredi in ignem vidit. Et cum videret quod non egrederetur, existimans Petrum Bartholomeum esse, lacrimari cepit, credens eum esse extinctum in igne. Erat ibi multitudo hominum, nec poterant omnes videre omnia. Et alia multa nobis revelata sunt et facta, quae nos metuentes legentibus fastidium scribere noluimus. Cum ad omnem causam tres ido-   20
nei testes sufficiunt, hoc unum non pretermittamus. Postquam Petrus Bartholomeus per ignem transivit, licet multum estuaret incendium, tamen populus ita avide ticiones collegit et carbones cum cinere, ut in brevi spatio nichil inde appareret. In fide etenim illorum multas per hec virtutes operatus est postea Dominus. Ut vero Petrus de igne egressus est, ita ut   25
nec tunica eius conbusta fuerit, nec etiam pannus ille subtilissimus de quo lancea Domini involuta erat, signum alicuius lesionis habuisset accepit eum omnis populus cum signasset eos tenens manu lanceam et clamasset

1. **caetera** = CL *cetera*.   6. **inperterritus** = CL *imperterritus*.   8. **nonnulli**: litotes. 10. **Ebrardus**: from *Ebrardus, i*, Ebrard, otherwise unknown (Hill and Hill 101). 11. **Ierosolimis**: from *Hierosolyma, orum* = Jerusalem, here in the locative case (see AG 427).   **Guillelmus Bonofilius**: i.e., William Bonofilius, a knight of Arles (Hill and Hill 101, n. 18).   12. **Arelatensi**: from *Arelatensis, e* = Arles (Sleumer 124, s. v. *Arelate*).   13. **Biterensis**: i.e., Béziers (Hill and Hill 101, n. 18).   **Guillelmus Maluspuer**: William Malopuer, a knight, as Raymond suggests, from Béziers (Hill and Hill 101). 15. **casulam**: from *casula, ae* = "hood" (cf. Niermeyer, s. v. *casula* 4; the word has other meanings).   23. **ticiones**: from *titio, onis* = "firebrand" (LS 1874).   24. **nihil . . . appareret**: i.e., nothing was left of the bed of fire except the blackened ground. **per hec**: i.e., "through these [relics]."   28. **signasset** = contracted pluperfect active subjunctive, third person singular of *signare* = *signavisset*.   **clamasset** = contracted pluperfect active subjunctive, third person singular of *clamare* = *clamavisset*.

alta voce Deus adiuva, accepit eum et traxit eum per terram et conculcavit eum omnis pene illa multitudo populi. Dum quisɩ ᴜe volebat eum tangere, vel accipere de vestimento eius aliquid, et dum credebat eum esse quisquam apud alium. Itaque tria vel .iiii. vulnera fecerunt in eius cruribus
5 abscidentes de carne eius, et spinam dorsi eius confringentes, crepuerunt eum. Expirasset ibi animam Petrus sicut nos credimus, nisi Raimundus Pelet miles nobilissimus et fortis, fultus agmine sociorum, irrupisset in agmine turbae turbatae, et usque ad mortem pugnando liberasset eum. Sed nos in sollicitudine et in angustia modo positi, amplius de his scribere
10 non possumus. Cum vero detulisset Raimundus Pelet, Petrum ad domum nostram colligatis eius vulneribus cepimus querere ab eo quare moram fecisset in ignem. Ad haec ipse respondit: Dominus michi occurrit in medio igne, et apprehendens me per manum, dixit michi: Quid dubitasti de inventione lanceae, cum beatus Andreas ostendisset tibi eam, non sic
15 transibis illesus, sed infernum non videbis. Et hoc dicto me dimisit. Videte itaque si vultis adustionem meam, et erat aliquantula adustio in cruribus, verum non multa. Sed plage erant magnae. Post haec convocavimus omnes qui de lancea Domini dubitaverant, ut venirent et viderent faciem eius et capud atque capillos et reliqua menbra, et intelligerent quod verum
20 est, quicquid ipse de lancea dixerat, et de aliis cum pro testimonio eorum, non extimuisset intrare tale incendium. Venerunt itaque multi, et videntes faciem eius atque totum corpus glorificabant Dominum dicentes: Bene potest nos Dominus custodire inter gladios inimicorum nostrorum qui hominem istum liberavit, de tanto incendio flammarum. Certe non crede-
25 bamus, quod sagitta aliqua sic transire possit illesa per ignem quomodo iste transivit.

—Hist. Franc. 18 (excerpts).

6. **expirasset** = contracted pluperfect active subjunctive, third person singular of *expirare* = *expiravisset*(= CL *exspirare*); the subject is still Peter Bartholomew, who has just been attacked by the crowd frenzied over his miraculous walk on the fire. **Raimundus Pelet:** i.e., Raymond of Pilet, a Limousin knight of the Provençal army (Hill and Hill 102 and n. 19). 8. **liberasset** = contracted pluperfect active subjunctive, third person singular of *liberare* = *liberavisset*. 13. **dubitasti:** contracted perfect active indicative, second person singular of *dubitare* = *dubitavisti*.

WILLIAM OF MALMESBURY

The Deeds of the Kings of England
(*Gesta regum Anglorum;* c. 1125)

B etween the writing of Bede's *Historia ecclesiastica gentis Anglorum* (see pp. 179–84) and the completion of William of Malmesbury's *Gesta regum Anglorum* lies nearly four hundred years, yet the model of Bede seems never to be far from William of Malmesbury's mind. The virtues of Bede's historical output—accuracy, honesty, simplicity of style, control of material—served as examples for William as he completed his project. Less obvious an influence are Bede's general aims for his *History,* for William's treatment of the deeds of the kings of England is more beholden to the goals envisioned by the historians of Germany and France, his closer contemporaries (see pp. 319–48). Those aims, recall, settled on the importance of biography and the logic of authorial narration as against the equally powerful tradition of chronological organization and the use of secular events as the backdrop against which historical phenomena were cast. All three tendencies inform William's *History.*

Born around 1095, William of Malmesbury spent all of his productive career at the Benedictine abbey at Malmesbury, serving as librarian there and producing a variety of historical works, the most important of which, excerpted here, is his *Deeds of the Kings of England.* That work, as these passages suggest, is synthetic, topical, and personal. Its Latin is clear and never strays too far from the prose standards established by Bede, as one would expect of a work written so carefully in Bede's shadow. The time span covered in William's *Gesta* is large (449–1120), and his treatment is therefore anecdotal. William is one of the more prolific of medieval writers: he also produced a history of the bishoprics of England, the *Gesta pontificum* (with a heavy emphasis on pre-Norman materials), and the *Historia novella,* "new" in the sense that it treated contemporary events of the reigns of Henry I and Stephen. William also dabbled in saints' lives, the histories of monastic institutions (Glastonbury, for example), and biblical commentaries. He died around 1143.

The *Gesta regum Anglorum* has been edited by W. Stubbs (*Willelmus Malmesbiriensis Monachus, De Gestis Regum Anglorum Libri Quinque,* Rolls Series 90, 2 vols., London, 1887–89). An English translation was produced by J. A. Giles (*William of Malmesbury: Chronicles of the Kings of England,* London, 1847). A general treatment of William has been written by R. M. Thompson (*William of Malmesbury,* London, 1987). A. Gransden has a full account of William (*Historical Writing in England, c. 550–1307,* Ithaca, N. Y., 1974). Stubbs's text is reprinted without change.

THE MAGNANIMITY OF WILLIAM RUFUS

Egressus rex tabernaculo, vidensque eminus hostes superbum inequitantes, solus in multos irruit, alacritate virtutis impatiens, simulque confidens nullum sibi ausurum obsistere; moxque occiso sub feminibus deturbatus equo, quem eo die quindecim marcis argenti emerat, etiam per
5   pedem diu tractus est; sed fides loricae obstitit ne laederetur. Iamque miles, qui deiecerat, manum ad capulum aptabat ut feriret, cum ille, periculo extremo territus, exclamat, "Tolle, nebulo! rex Angliae sum!" Tremuit, nota voce iacentis, vulgus militum; statimque reverenter de terra levato equum alterum adducunt. Ille, non expectato ascensorio, sonipedem
10   insiliens, omnesque circumstantes vivido perstringens oculo, "Quis," inquit, "me deiecit?" Mussitantibus cunctis, miles audacis facti conscius non defuit patrocinio suo, dicens: "Ego, qui te non putarem esse regem, sed militem." Tum vero rex placidus, vultuque serenus, "Per vultum," ait, "de Luca," sic enim iurabat, "meus a modo eris, et meo albo insertus
15   laudabilis militiae praemia reportabis." Macte animi amplissime rex, quod tibi praeconium super hoc dicto rependam? A magni quondam Alexandri non degener gloria, qui Persam militem se a tergo ferire conatum, sed pro perfidia ensis spe sua frustratum, incolumem pro admiratione fortitudinis conservavit.

— *Gesta Reg. Ang.* 4. 309.

OTHER EXAMPLES OF THE KING'S MAGNANIMITY

Veruntamen sunt quaedam de rege praeclarae magnanimitatis exempla, quae posteris non invidebo. Venationi in quadam silva intentum nun-

---

1. **egressus:** perfect participle of *egredi.* **superbum:** adverb (cf. LS 1805, s. v. *superbus—Superbus* B3). **inequitantes:** present active participle of *inequitare* = "to ride up" (LS 940). 3. **deturbatus:** from *deturbare* = "to cut off," "to cast down" (LS 564). 4. **marcis:** from *marca, ae,* formulaic with *argenti* = "silver piece" (cf. Niermeyer 653, 2 *marca*). 9. **ascensorio:** from *ascensorium* = "stirrup" (Blaise/ Chirat 100). 14. **a modo:** "from now on. . . ." **albo:** "album" or list of worthy soliders. 15. **macte:** vocative case.

   1. **veruntamen** = CL *verumtamen.* 2. **intentum:** i.e., King William.

tius detinuit ex transmarinis partibus, obsessam esse civitatem Cenomannis, quam nuper fratre profecto suae potestati adiecerat. Statim ergo
ut expeditus erat retorsit equum, iter ad mare convertens. Admonentibus
ducibus exercitum advocandum, paratos componendos, "Videbo," ait,
"quis me sequetur; putatis me non habiturum homines? si cognovi iuven-   5
tutem meam, etiam naufragio ad me venisse volet." Hoc igitur modo pene
solus ad mare pervenit. Erat tunc nubilus aer et ventus contrarius; flatus
violentia terga maris verrebat. Illum statim transfretare volentem nautae
exorant ut pacem pelagi et ventorum clementiam operiatur. "Atqui," inquit rex, "nunquam audivi regem naufragio interiisse. Quin potius solvite   10
retinacula navium, videbitis elementa iam conspirata in meum obsequium."

   Ponto transito obsessores, eius audita fama, dissiliunt. Auctor tur-
barum, Helias quidam, capitur; cui ante se adducto rex ludibundus, "Habeo te, magister!" dixit. At vero illius alta nobilitas, quae nesciret in tanto   15
etiam periculo humilia sapere, humilia loqui: "Fortuitu," inquit, "me cep-
isti; sed si possem evadere, novi quid facerem." Tum Willelmus, prae furore fere extra se positus, et obuncans Heliam, "Tu," inquit, "nebulo! tu,
quid faceres? Discede, abi, fuge! concedo tibi ut facias quicquid poteris;
et, per vultum de Luca! nihil, si me viceris, pro hac venia tecum paciscar."   20
Nec inferius factum verbo fuit, sed continuo dimisit evadere, miratus potius quam insectatus fugientem. Quis talia de illitterato homine crederet?
Et fortassis erit aliquis qui, Lucanum legens, falso opinetur Willelmum
haec exampla de Iulio Caesare mutuatum esse; sed non erat ei tantum
studii vel otii ut litteras unquam audiret; immo calor mentis ingenitus et   25
conscia virtus eum talia exprimere cogebant. Et profecto, si Christianitas
nostra pateretur, sicut olim anima Euforbii transisse dicta est in Pythagoram Samium, ita possit dici quod anima Iulii Caesaris transierit in regem Willelmum.

—Gest. Reg. Ang. 4.320.

1. **obsessam:** perfect passive participle of *obsidere*. **Cenomannis:** i.e., Le Mans
(Sleumer 200).   6. **pene** = CL *paene*.   8. **transfretare:** "to pass over the seas" (LS
1890).   14. **Helias:** *Helias, ae,* an otherwise unknown figure.   18. **obuncans:** present active participle from *obuncare* = "gesturing at" (Latham 319).   27. **Euforbii** =
CL *Euphorbi*, from *Euphorbus, i,* the son of Panthus, whose soul Pythagoras claimed
to possess through the process of "transmigration," as William suggests here (cf. LS
664).   **Pythagoram Samium:** i.e., Pythagoras of Samnos, the famous ancient Greek
philosopher.

PLATE 23. Facing folios from a Latin Book of Hours from the fifteenth century.

PLATE 23

Book of Hours
Latin manuscript on parchment, fifteenth century, fols. 13 verso and 14 recto
John Hay Library, Brown University

These folios, from the opening of a fifteenth-century Book of Hours, depict the Virgin on the verso and a large, decorated "A" on the recto. The book's functionality is suggested by the quality of its binding and the care with which it was produced, as the brass clasps attached by leather to the back of the manuscript, and visible at the right, show. The verso picture is of the annunciation, with Mary turning to see Gabriel. The picture is framed and catches much vivid detail; the margins, ruled in pencil (still visible) are floreated by simple patterns of bright color. The recto folio is dominated by the "A" of "alleluia," with its rich details and clear colors. The margins, like the lines of the folio, are ruled in pencil and are filled with much detail, including some intricate penwork. The binding of this lengthy Book of Hours is of sturdy leather. It is 11 cm. in height and contains 232 folios.

FULCHER OF CHARTRES

A History of the Expedition to Jerusalem
(*Historia Hierosolymitana;* c. 1130)

R aymond of Aguilers's account of the First Crusade is direct and simple, composed still in the bright glare of the events of which he writes (see pp. 460–72). Fulcher of Chartres's account is much more a formally historical enterprise, written over the course of a long span of time and taking the story of the Crusaders down to 1127. His *Historia Hierosolymitana* stands, along with Raymond's work and the anonymous *Gesta Francorum,* in an important group of eyewitness accounts of the First Crusade, but of these three works, Fulcher's is the most accomplished in a literary sense.

That accomplishment is owed no doubt to Fulcher's training; it can be surmised that he was well educated in the Latin Classics and Scripture and that he was no ordinary cleric. In his *History,* in addition to his own eyewitness accounts of events, he marshals evidence from letters and other shorter works, in addition to the longer treatments of Raymond and the anonymous chronicler of the First Crusade. He also uses older sources—Rufinus's Latin translation of two works pertaining to the Holy Land, originally written in Greek by Flavius Josephus; and Solinus's epitome of Pliny's *Historia naturalis.* As he was in Jerusalem, he seems clearly to have used documentary material available to him there in libraries also. His talents as a historian, in any case, led him to some renown, for Fulcher is mentioned, on the fame of the circulation of his *History,* by three important twelfth-century historians—William of Malmesbury, Guibert of Nogent, and Ordericus Vitalis.

Fulcher's prose style is quintessentially medieval and includes the use of neologisms, the deployment of the gerund as a present participle, the use of pronouns and adjectives (*is, ea, id; unus, a, um*) as modifiers that act as articles, the deployment of the ablative absolute in the main clause of a sentence, and the subordination of the oblique cases to prepositional phrases, especially the use of ablative prepositional phrases for the genitive. Fulcher uses classical allusion and quotation frequently, and even (as in the excerpts here) is fond of lifting passages directly from classical authors. Scriptural quotations, needless to say, are used to frame characterization and events in both obvious and subtle ways.

Of Fulcher's early life we know next to nothing. He tells us that he was 66 years old in 1125. Presumably he was born in Chartres around 1060. His French background is obvious from his name and also from other evidence, including the fact that he longs to be "home" in Chartres at several points in his descriptions of battles in his *History.* Fulcher made his way to the Holy Land in the retinue of Robert of Normandy and Stephen of Blois, leaving not long after Urban II's famous sermon at Clermont (on which Fulcher reports at length—he may even have been an eyewitness to it). Along the way, however, he became the chaplain of Baldwin I, lord of Edessa (though he does not say why he chose to take up this post). In the event, he remained in the Holy Land for the rest of his life, living in Jerusalem from 1100 until he disappears from the evidence in 1127.

The excerpt recounts the approach to and the capture of Jerusalem by the Crusaders in 1099. Fulcher presumably was not an eyewitness to these events, since we know he left the main army of the Crusaders to join the retinue of Baldwin I of Edessa. He relies, therefore, on the accounts of Raymond of Aguilers and the anonymous *Gesta Francorum* for most of what is reprinted here, though he adds his own stylistic touches, including the direct quotation of poetry from Ovid and one set of verses of his own confection. Fulcher began writing his *Historia* around 1100, almost certainly after he came to live in Jerusalem. His text had a complicated life, owing to the fact that it was composed over a number of years and revised considerably by its author. Of its three books, most chapters of the first two were in circulation by 1106, when they were taken up by two anonymous writers who added their own knowledge to Fulcher's accounts and in many cases changed his Latin. One edition, known as the version of "Bartolf of Nangis," ends at 2.35. The other version, known as Codex L, is more a direct copy of Fulcher until book 2, where substantial changes in story line and style occur; Codex L veers away from Fulcher's text entirely at chapter 33. In any case, Fulcher eventually returned to his work to take the story of the Crusaders down to the late 1120s, finishing his second book and adding a third. The third book does not seem to be complete, however, suggesting that Fulcher continued to write until his death—which is surmised to have occurred in 1127, where his narrative leaves off. One senses, too, that he died a happy man, for, though early on in his work he had bemoaned the loss of his homeland for the faraway haunts of the east, his later ruminations on the topic are entirely as a lover of his adopted home, as someone who recognized how easily one's former life and language could be replaced by the exotic attractiveness of the Holy Land.

The *Historia* has been edited by H. Wallon (*Fulcher of Chartres, Historia Iherosolymitana: Gesta Francorum Iherusalem peregrinantium (MXCV–MCXXVII) auctore Domno Fulcherio Carnotensi*, in *Recueil des historiens des croisades, Historiens occidentaux*, Académie des Inscriptions et Belles-Lettres, 5 vols., Paris, 1866, vol. 3, pp. 311–485) and by H. Hagenmeyer (*Fulcheri Carnotensis Historia Hierosolymitana (1095–1127)*, Heidelberg, 1913). M. E. McGinty has translated Fulcher (*Fulcher of Chartres, Chronicle of the First Crusade*, in "Translations and Reprints from the Original Sources of History," ser. 3, vol. 1, Philadelphia, 1941), as has F. R. Ryan (*Fulcher of Chartres, A History of the Expedition to Jerusalem, 1095–1127*, Knoxville, Tenn., 1969) with an excellent introduction (by H. S. Fink), running notes, and bibliography. Hagenmeyer's text is reprinted here, with the initial letters of sentences capitalized and some minor changes in formatting.

THE CRUSADERS CAPTURE JERUSALEM

Mora quippe ibi per IV dies facta, cum basilicae S. Georgii episcopum praefecissent et in arcibus urbis homines ad custodiendum locassent, Hierosolymam iter suum protenderunt. Ipso die usque castellum, quod Emaus dicitur, ambulaverunt, quod iuxta se habet Modin, civitatem Ma-
5 chabaeorum. Nocte vero sequenti C milites de probioribus conscenderunt equos, qui aurora clarescente prope Iherusalem transeuntes usque Bethleem properaverunt: de quibus erat Tancredus unus, alter vero Balduinus.

1. **S. Georgii:** from *Georgius, i,* Christian martyr, c. 303 (cf. Sleumer 356); the bishop chosen was Robert of Rouen; both William of Tyre and Raymond of Aguilers (see pp. 460–72) report information about these events also. **cum . . . praefecissent:** *cum* temporal construction with the subjunctive, as in CL; *praefecissent* is from *praeficere.* 2. **locassent** = contracted pluperfect active subjunctive, third person plural of *locare* = *locavissent.* 3. **Hierosolymam:** accusative of place to which without *ad* or *in* (cf. AG 426). 4. **Emaus:** i.e., Emmaus, modern 'Amwas (Hagenmeyer 277). **quod . . . Modin:** the idiom *se habere,* lit., "to be," "to feel," etc. seems to be meant here as a periphrasis for *est* = "which is near to Modin." *Modin* is seven miles north of Emmaus (Hagenmeyer 278). **civitatem Machabaeorum:** "a city of the Maccabees" (cf. 1 Mac. 2.1–15), from *Machabaei, orum* (cf. Sleumer 488 and Hagenmeyer 277). 5. **C** = 100. **milites de probioribus:** from *probus* = "soliders of better qualities"; CL would call for a noun for *probioribus* to modify in the genitive of quality, but ML uses *de* + ablative in place of the genitive of quality. 6. **Iherusalem:** from *Hierosolyma, orum* = Jerusalem (cf. Sleumer 385 for various forms and spellings). **Bethleem:** the better spelling is *Bethlehem,* usually indeclinable = Bethlehem (cf. Sleumer 163 for various forms and spellings). 7. **Tancredus:** from *Tancredus, i* = Tancred of Hauteville, one of the leaders of the First Crusade, a nephew of Bohemund of Taranto. **Balduinus:** i.e., Baldwin of Le Bourg, eventually count of Edessa and king of Jerusalem (cf. Ryan 115, n. 13).

Quod cum Christiani, qui inibi conversabantur, comperirent, Graeci videlicet et Syri, Francos illuc advenisse, gravisi sunt gaudio magno valde. Ig-
norabant tamen primitus quae gens essent, putantes eos vel Turcos vel
Arabes esse. Sed cum aperte propius eos intuerentur et eos non dubitarent
esse Francos, statim gaudenter crucibus adsumptis et textis, obviam   5
flendo et pie cantando processerunt eis: flendo, quoniam metuebant ne
tantillum gentis a multitudine tanta paganorum, quos in patria esse scie-
bant, facillime quandoque occiderentur; cantando, quoniam congratula-
bantur eis quos diu desideraverant esse venturos, quos Christianismum, a
nefandis tamdiu pessumdatum, in honorem debitum et pristinum relev-   10
are sentiebant.

Facta autem ilico in basilica beatae Mariae supplicatione ad Deum
devota, cum locum in quo Christus natus fuit visitassent, dato Syris osculo pacifico, ad urbem sanctam Iherusalem celeriter regressi sunt. Ecce
subsequens exercitus, relicta in sinistra parte Gabaon, quae ab Ihero-   15
solymis L distat stadiis, ubi Josue soli imperavit et lunae, civitati tunc ad-
propinquavit. Et cum praecursores signiferi vexilla elevata civibus monstrassent, protinus contra eos interni hostes exierunt. Sed qui festini sic
exierant, festinatius in urbem mox repulsi sunt.

---

1. **Graeci:** from *Graecus, i* = Greeks (cf. Sleumer 364, s. v. *Graeci—Graecis*); stands
in apposition to *Christiani,* along with *Syri.* 2. **Syri:** from *Syrus, a, um* = Syrians (cf.
Sleumer 764, s. v. *Syra—Syrus*); stands in apposition to *Christiani,* along with *Graeci.*
Francos illuc advenisse: object of *comperirent,* with *Christiani* the subject. **gravisi:**
with *gaudio magno* the sense is "rejoiced." 3. **Turcos:** from *Turcae, arum;* the better
spelling is *Turcas* (Sleumer 796) = Turks. 4. **Arabes:** from *Arabs, abis* = Arabs
(Sleumer 121). 5. **adsumptis** = CL *assumptis.* 6. **pie:** adverb. **flendo . . . cantando:** it is common in ML for the ablative of the gerund to function as a present
participle, expressing the circumstances under which the action of the gerund occurs =
"crying . . . singing"; § 3.4 (cf. Blaise 343). Thus in the clauses that follow, too, *flendo*
and *cantando* are akin to present active participles in the nominative, modifying *Christiani.* 9. **Christianismum:** from *Christianismus, i* = "Christianity" (Niermeyer 178).
10. **pessumdatum:** the idiom is *pessum dare* = "to send to the bottom," to sink to
ruin"; here it functions as an adjective modifying *Christianismum,* and, with the
phrase *a nefandis tamdiu,* meaning something like "having been ruined by wickedness
for a long while. . . ." 12. **Mariae:** from *Maria, ae* = Mary. 13. **visitassent:** contracted pluperfect active subjunctive, third person plural = *visitavissent;* this is *cum*
temporal construction + subjunctive, as in CL. 15. **Gabaon:** i.e., Gibeon; Fulcher
situates this city geographically and in terms of Scripture. 16. **L** = 50. **stadiis:** from
stadium, a measure of length (Latham 450), here construed with *L.* **Josue:** from
Josue, indeclinable noun = Joshua (Sleumer 447); the orders of which Fulcher speaks
are recounted at Josh. 10.12–13. 17. **monstrassent:** contracted pluperfect active subjunctive, third person plural = *monstravissent.*

Lucis septenae iam Iunius igne calebat,
Iherusalem Franci cum vallant obsidione.

Est equidem civitas Iherusalem in montano loco posita, rivis, silvis
fontibusque carens, excepto fonte Siloe, distante ab urbe quantum iactus
5 est arcus, ubi sufficienter aqua interdum habetur, interdum vero raro
haustu attenuatus invenitur: qui fonticulus in vallis est fundo sub monte
Sion in decursione torrentis Cedron, qui tempore hiemali per vallem mediam Iosaphat defluere solet. Cisternae autem multae et aquis satis abundae in urbe habentur, quae imbribus hibernis reservantur. Extra urbem
10 quoque plures inveniuntur, quibus homines et pecora refocillantur. Constat civitas haec condecenti magnitudine facta per circuitum, ita ut nec
parvitate nec magnitudine cuiquam videatur fastidiosa, quae interius a
muro usque ad murum quantum iacit arcus quater sagittam est lata. Habet siquidem ab occasu turrim Davidicam, utroque latere supplentem civi-
15 tatis murum; montem Sion a meridie paulo minus quam iaciat arcus sagittam; ad orientem Oliveti montem mille passibus ab urbe distantem.
Praedicta quidem Davidis turris usque ad medietatem sui ab imo solide
massata est et de lapidibus caementata quadris et magnis et plumbo fusili
sigillatis: quae si bene munita cibario fuerit, XV homines vel XX ab omni
20 adsultu hostium defendere poterunt. Et est in eadem urbe Templum dominicum, opere rotundo conpositum, ubi Salomon alterum prius instituit

4. **fonte Siloe:** i.e., the font of Siloam (Ryan 116). 6. **fundo:** from *fundus, i* =
"bottom," "base," but here with adverbial force = "at the base . . ." **monte Sion:** i.e.,
Mount Zion (Sleumer 729). 7. **torrentis Cedron:** i.e., "of the brook Kedron . . .";
Cedron is indeclinable, but functions here in the genitive (Sleumer 198). 8. **Iosaphat:**
from *Iosaphat,* indeclinable = Jehoshaphat (cf. Sleumer 446 for the various forms).
abundae: from *abundus, a, um* = "abundant" (LS 14). 10. **constat:** used impersonally = "it is established that. . . ." 11. **condecenti:** present active participle from *con-
decet* = "becoming," "pleasing." 12. **interius:** adverb. 13. **quantum iacit arcus
quater sagittam:** lit., "how much the bow throws four arrows," i.e., "the distance of
four bowshots"; the basic sentence is "*quae* [*civitas*] *est lata;* the *quantum* clause is
adverbial to *est lata* = "the city is as wide as the distance of four bowshots." 14. **turrim:** from *turris, is.* **Davidicam:** from *Davidicus, a, um,* patronymic of David = "of
David," here modifying *turrim.* 16. **Oliveti montem:** from *Mons Oliveti,* i.e., the
Mount of Olives (Sleumer 565, s. v. *olivetum—Mons Oliveti*). **mille passibus:** i.e.,
one thousand paces; on this form of measurement see AG 135c. 18. **massata:** from
massatus, a, um = "massed" (Latham 293) referring to the masonry of the tower, as
Fulcher goes on to explain. **caementata:** from *caementatus, a, um* = "solidly built"
(Blaise/Chirat 122). 20. **adsultu** = CL *assultu.* **dominicum:** from *dominicus, a,
um* = "lordly" (Niermeyer 352) but here functioning as a substantive in the genitive =
domini. 21. **conpositum** = CL *compositum.*

mirificum, quod quamvis illi priori schemati nullatenus sit comparandum, istud tamen opere mirabili et forma speciosissima factum est. Sepulcri dominici ecclesia forma rotunda similiter, quae nunquam fuit tecta, sed semper foramine patulo architecti sapientis magisterio artificiose machinato, hiatu perpetuo aperta claret in summo. Nec valeo nec audeo   5
nec sapio multa, quae inibi habentur, quaedam quidem adhuc praesentia, quaedam vero iam praeterita recitare, ne in aliquo vel haec legentes vel haec audientes fallam. Cum in templi medio, quando prius intravimus et postea per XV fere annos, rupes quaedam ibi nativa habetur, in qua divinabant esse arcam foederis Domini cum urna et tabulis Moysi sigil-   10
latim conclusam, eo quod Iosias, rex Iuda, poni eam iussit dicens: "nequaquam portabitis eam de loco isto." Praevidebat enim captivitatem futuram; sed istud obest, quod is descriptionibus Ieremiae legimus in libro Machabaeorum secundo, quod ipse Ieremias eam in Arabia occultaverit, dicens nequaquam illam esse inveniendam, donec gentes multae congre-   15
garentur. Ipse quidem contemporaneus huius regis Iosiae fuit; tamen vivendi finem fecit rex, antequam Ieremias defungeretur occisus. Super rupem etiam praedictam dicebant angelum Domini stetisse et populum peremisse, propter dinumerationem insipienter a David factam et Domino displicentem. Rupes autem illa, quia Templum Domini deturpabat,   20
postea cooperta est et marmore pavimentata, ubi nunc est altare suppositum et clerus ibi adaptavit chorum. Hoc Templum dominicum in veneratione magna cuncti Saraceni habuerant, ubi precationes suas lege sua libentius quam alibi faciebant, quamvis idolo in nomine Mahumet facto eas

1. **mirificum:** from *mirificus, a, um* = "wonderul," "awe-inspiring" (Habel/Gröbel 242), modifying *alterum*, which itself modifies an understood *templum*. This is the Qubbat as-Sakhrah mosque (cf. Ryan, p. 117, n. 2). **schemati:** from *schema, atis,* neuter noun = "plan" (Blaise/Chirat 742). **nullatenus:** adverb = "in no way" (Niermeyer 724). 3. **nunquam** = CL *numquam.* 7. **recitare:** complement of *valeo, audeo,* and *sapio.* 10. **divinabant:** i.e., *dicebant.* **Moysi:** from *Moyses, is* = Moses, an alternate genitive form is *Moysi*, used here (cf. Sleumer 531). **sigillatim** = CL *singulatim.* 11. **Iosias:** from *Iosias,* indeclinable noun = Josiah (Sleumer 447). **Iuda:** the better form is *Iudaeorum,* from *Iudaei, orum* = Jews (Sleumer 451). 12. Cf. 2 Chron. 35.3. 13. **Ieremiae:** from *Ieremias, ae* = Jeremiah (Sleumer 403). 14. **Machabaeorum:** *Machabaei, orum* = Maccabees, here, with modifiers = "the second book of Maccabees" (Sleumer 488). 17. Cf. 2 Mac. 2.4–9. 20. Cf. 2 Chron. 3.1; 2 Sam. 24.1–2, 15–25; 1 Chron. 21.15. 21. **altare:** from *altare, is* = "altar" (Sleumer 99). 23. **Saraceni:** from *Saraceni, orum* = Saracens (Sleumer 696). 24. **Mahumet:** here in the genitive with *in nomine . . . facto* = "made in the name of Muhammad." On the forms of *Mahumet,* see Sleumer 491, s. v. *Mahumetus; Mahumites.*

vastarent, in quod etiam nullum ingredi Christianum permittebant. Alterum Templum, quod dicitur Salomonis, magnum est et mirabile. Non est autem illud idem, quod ipse Salomon fabricari fecit, quod quidem non potuit propter inopiam nostram in statu quo illud invenimus sustenari;
5 quapropter magna iam ex parte destruitur. Non desunt etiam civitati per vicos aquaeductus, per quos imbrium tempore omnes spurcitiae diluuntur. Hanc urbem etiam Aelius Hadrianus imperator mirifice decoravit et vicos et plateas decenter pavimentis exornavit. De cuius nomine Iherusalem Aelia vocata est. Ex his et ceteris huiusmodi venerabilis est et gloriosa civitas.
10 osa civitas.

Quam cum aspicerent Franci et viderent eam ad capiendum gravem, iussum est a principibus nostris scalas ligneas fieri, quibus muro admotis deinde et erectis, cum impetu feroci per eas in summum muri scandentes, urbem Deo iuvante ingrederentur. Quod cum fecissent, die septimo se-
15 quenti, monitu procerum, sonantibus bucinis mane claro, impetu miro civitatem undique adsilierunt. Et cum usque ad horam diei sextam adsiluissent et per scalas quas aptaverant, eo quod paucae erant, introire nequirent, adsultum tristes dimiserunt. Tunc adunato consilio, iussum est ab artificibus machinas fieri, quibus muro admotis, spei effectum, auxiliante
20 Deo, adipiscerentur. Quod ita factum est. Interim quidem nec panis nec carnis inopiam passi sunt; sed quia locus ille aridus et inaquosus et sine fluminibus exsistat, tam viri quam iumenta eorum egebant aqua nimis ad potandum. Quapropter, quia monebat hoc necessitas, longe aquam quaeritabant et a IV miliariis vel V laboriose ad obsidionem in utribus
25 suis cotidie apportabant. Machinis autem paratis, arietibus scilicet et scrophis, ad adsiliendum urbem item paraverunt. Inter artificia vero illa turrim unam ex lignis exiguis, quia magna materies in locis illis non habetur, compegerunt, quam noctu, edicto proinde facto, ad unum civitatis

2. **Templum . . . Salomonis:** i.e., the Temple of Solomon, from *Salomon, onis* (Sleumer 690). 5. **destruitur:** Fulcher is referring here to the al-Aqsa mosque, which had been stripped of its lead roof by King Baldwin for the purpose of raising money (cf. Ryan 118, n. 6). 7. **Aelius Hadrianus:** i.e., Hadrian, who was Roman emperor from 117 to 138. 11. **eam:** i.e., *civitatem.* 12. **iussum est:** impersonal, with ablative of agency, *a principibus nostris,* i.e., "it was ordered by our leaders. . . ." 16. **adsilierunt** = CL *assilierunt.* **adsiluissent** = CL *assiluissent.* 17. **eo quod:** idiomatic = "because." 18. **adsultum** = CL *assultum.* 20. **quod ita factum est:** idiomatic = "and thus it was done." 24. **miliariis:** from *milliarium* = "mile." 26. **scrophis:** from *scropha, ae,* there is no single English term with which to translate this word; it means "a device for the destruction of walls" (Habel/Gröbel 357), parallel with *arietibus,* both of which are in apposition to *machinis paratis.* **adsiliendum** = CL *assiliendum.*

cornu frustatim detulerunt. Et sic mane ipso cum petrarias et cetera ad-
minicula paravissent, citissime haud longe a muro compactam erexerunt.
Quam erectam et de coriis deforis bene munitam, paulatim promovendo
muro propius impegerunt. Tum vero rari milites, tamen audaces, monente
cornu, ascenderunt super eam, contra quos Saraceni nihilominus se de-   5
fendendo faciebant, et ignem cum oleo et adipe vividum cum faculis ap-
tatis praedictae turri et militibus, qui erant in ea, fundibulis suis iacu-
labantur. Multis igitur utrorumque sic invicem certantium mors erat praesens et festina. Ea quidem in parte, qua Raimundus comes et homines eius
adsistebant, scilicet in monte Sion, cum machinis suis adsultum magnum   10
dabant. Ex alia vero parte, qua dux erat Godefridus et Robertus Normanniae comes, Robertus quoque Flandrensis, maior erat muro adsultus. Illo
die sic agitur. Sequenti quoque die laborem eundem, facto bucinarum
concrepitu, virilius inierunt, ita ut in uno loco cum arietibus pulsando
murum perforarent. Pendebant nempe ante muri propugnacula duo as-   15
seres, funibus illic adligati, quos Saraceni sibi praeparaverant, ut inruenti-
bus et lapides in eos iacientibus obstaculum eis utile fierent. Sed quod pro
incremento sibi fecerant, idem ad detrimentum suum, Domino provide-
nte, postea exceperunt. Nam turri praefata muro admota rudentibusque,
quibus ligna praedicta pendebant, falcibus sectis, de eisdem tignis unum   20
pontem sibi Franci coaptaverunt, quem de turri super murum callide extensum iactaverunt. Iamiamque ardebat arx una in muro lapidea, supra
quam machinatores nostri torres flammeos iniecerant, unde, foco paulatim inter lignorum materiam nutrito, fumus flammaque sic prodire coepit, ut nec unus quidem custodum civium ibi ulterius morari posset. Mox   25
igitur Francis hora meridiana urbem magnifice intrantibus, die quae Veneris habebatur, qua Christus etiam in cruce totum mundum redemit, cornibus insonantibus, cunctis tumultuantibus, viriliter impetentibus, "Adiuva

1. **frustatim:** adverb = "bit by bit." **petrarias:** from *petraria, ae* = "catapult" (Habel/
Gröbel 287); the CL word is *ballistas*. 3. **deforis** = ML adverb (*de* + *foris*), "from
without" (Latham 136). 6. **adipe:** from *adeps, adipis*. 7. **fundibulis:** from *fun-
dibulum, i* = "slingshot" (Habel/Gröbel 162). 9. **Raimundus comes:** from *Raimundus, i* = Count Raymond. 10. **adsistebant** = CL *assistebant*. 11. **Godefridus:**
from *Godefridus, i* = Godfrey, Duke of Bouillon. **Robertus Normanniae comes:** i.e.,
Count Robert of Normandy (*Normannia, ae;* cf. Sleumer 551). 12. **Robertus quoque Flandrensis:** i.e., Robert of Flanders (Ryan 120; cf. Sleumer 336 for collateral
forms). 16. **adligati** = CL *alligati*. 20. **unum pontem:** in CL *unum* is unnecessary;
this usage is common in ML as the harbinger of the Romance indefinite article.
21. **coaptaverunt:** from *coaptare* = "to fit together" (Latham 92). 26. **Francis:** from
Francus, i = Frank (Sleumer 343). **Veneris:** from *Venus, eris* = Venus; with *die* =
Friday.

Deus" exclamantibus, vexillum in muri fastigio statim elevantibus, pagani omnino exterriti, per vicorum angiportus audaciam suam in fugam celerem commutaverunt omnes. Qui cum velociter fugerent, velocius fugati sunt. Hoc nondum comes Raimundus advertebat, qui ex altera urbis
5 parte cum gente sua fortiter adsiliebat, donec per muri apicem Saracenos exsilire conspexerunt. Quo viso, ad urbem laetissimi quantocius cucurrerunt et cum aliis hostes nefarios persequi et occidere non cessaverunt. Tum quidem alii, tam Arabes quam Aethiopes, in arcem Daviticam fugientes se intromiserunt, alii vero in Templum Domini atque Salomonis se incluserunt, in quorum atriis impetus in eos agebatur nimius: nusquam erat
10 etiam locus, quo Saraceni gladiatores evadere possent. Supra Salomonis templum, quod fugiendo ascenderant, multi eorum ad mortem sagittati sunt et deorsum de tecto praecipitati, in quo etiam templo X milia fere decollati sunt. Quod si inibi essetis, pedes vestri sanguine peremptorum
15 usque ad bases tingerentur. Quid narrabo? Nullus ex eis vitae est reservatus. Sed neque feminis neque parvulis eorum pepercerunt.

Mirabile autem quid videretis, cum scutigeri nostri atque pedites pauperiores, calliditate Saracenorum comperta, ventres eorum iam mortuorum findebant, ut de intestinis eorum bisantios excerperent, quos vivi
20 faucibus diris transglutiverant. Quapropter post dies aliquot, acervo magno de cadaveribus facto et cinere tenus combusto, aurum memoratum in eodem cinere facilius reppererunt. Tancredus autem Templum dominicum festino cursu ingressus, multum auri et argenti lapidesque pretiosos adripuit. Sed hoc restaurans, eadem cuncta vel eis appretiata loco
25 sacrosancto remisit, licet in eo nihil tunc deicum ageretur, cum Saraceni legem suam idolatriae superstitioso ritu exercerent, qui etiam Christianum nullum in id ingredi sinebant.

---

5. **apicem:** from *apex, apicis.* 6. **quantocius:** adverb = "as quickly as possible" (LS 1506). **Aethiopes:** from *Aethiopes, Aethiopum* = Ethiopians (Sleumer 86). **Daviticam:** the better spelling is *Davidicam,* from *Davidicus, a, um,* patronymic of *David* = "of David," here modifying *arcem.* 9. **Salomonis:** dependent on *Templum,* as is *Domini.* 14. **quod si . . . tingerentur:** anacoluthon; the complete construction is something like *"si fuissetis, vidissetis pedes tinctos."* 16. This is a description of the massacre at the al-Aqsa Mosque; cf. Ryan 122, n. 10. 17. **scutigeri:** from *scutiger, eri* = "shield-bearer," "squire" (Latham 427) 19. **bisantios:** from *bisantius, i* = "bezants," "gold coins" of the Eastern Roman Empire (see Latham 61, s. v. *byzantius—bazantius,* for the various forms of this word). 20. **transglutiverant:** from *transglutiare* = "to swallow" (Latham 490). 24. **adripuit** = CL *arripuit.* **appretiata:** perfect passive participle from *appretiare* = "valued," here with *eis* = "things equal in value to those things he took . . ." (cf. Niermeyer 52). 25. **deicum:** from *deicus, a, um* = "divine" (Latham 136), here modifying *nihil.*

Ensibus exemptis currit gens nostra per urbem;
Nec cuiquam parcunt etiam miserere precanti.
Vulgus erat stratum, veluti cum putrida motis
Poma cadunt ramis, agitataque ilice glandes.

Et post stragem tantam ingressi sunt domos civium, rapientes quae- 5
cumque in eis reppererunt: ita sane, ut quicumque primus domum introisset, sive dives sive pauper esset, nullatenus ab aliquo alio fieret iniuria,
quin domum ipsam aut palatium et quodcumque in ea repperisset, ac si
omnino propria sibi adsumeret, haberet et possideret. Hoc itaque ius invicem tenendum stabilierant. Unde multi inopes effecti sunt locupletes. 10
Tunc autem ad Sepulcrum Domini et Templum eius gloriosum euntes,
clerici simul et laici, exsultationis voce altisona canticum novum Domino
decantando, loca sacrosancta tamdiu desiderata, cum oblationibus faciendis supplicationibusque humillimis, laetabundi omnes visitaverunt. O
tempus tam desideratum! o tempus inter cetera tempora memorandum! 15
o factum factis omnibus anteferendum! Vere desideratum, quoniam ab
omnibus fidei catholicae cultoribus interno mentis desiderio semper desideratum fuerat, ut locus, in quo cunctarum creaturarum creator munus
salutiferae recreationis, Deus homo factus, humano generi pietate sua
multiplici, nascendo, moriendo resurgendoque contulit, a paganorum 20
contagione inhabitantium quandoque mundatus, tamdiu superstitione
eorum contaminatus, ab in se credentibus et confidentibus in modum
pristinae dignitatis reformaretur. Et vere memoriale et iure memorandum,
quia quaeque Dominus Deus noster Iesus Christus, in terra homo cum
hominibus conversans, egit et docuit, ad memoriam celeberrimam reno- 25
vata et reducta sunt orthodoxis. Et quod idem Dominus per hunc populum suum tam, ut opinor, dilectum et alumnum familiaremque, ad hoc
negotium praeelectum, expleri voluit, usque in finem saeculi memoriale
linguis tribuum universarum personabit et permanebit.

Anno milleno centeno quominus uno 30
Virginis a partu Domini qui claruit ortu,
Quindecies Iulio iam Phoebi lumine tacto

---

1. These verses come from Ovid, *Met.* 7.585–86.   7. **nullatenus:** adverb = "in no
way" (Niermeyer 724).   9. **adsumeret** = CL *assumeret.*   10. **tenendum:** better read
as *tenendi.*   12. **clerici:** from *clericus, i* = "clerics," a word of several meanings in
ML (cf. Niermeyer 190–91). **laici:** from *laicus, i* = "laity" (Niermeyer 579).
13. **decantando:** the ablative gerund functions as a present active participle in ML; §
3.4 (cf. Blaise 343).   14. **laetabundi:** from *laetabundus, a, um* = "joyful" (LS 1029;
Sleumer 460).   26. **orthodoxis:** from *orthodoxus, a, um* = "orthodox" (Sleumer
572).   32. **Iulio:** i.e., the month.

Iherusalem Franci capiunt virtute potenti
Quippe Godefrido patriae mox principe facto.

Quem ob nobilitatis excellentiam et militiae probitatem atque patientiae
modestiam, necnon et morum elegantiam in urbe sancta regni principem
5   omnis populus dominici exercitus ad illud conservandum atque regen-
dum elegit. Tunc etiam locati sunt in ecclesia dominici Sepulcri canonici,
atque in Templo eiusdem ipsi servituri. Patriarcham autem tunc decrever-
unt nondum ibi fieri, donec a Romano papa quaesissent, quem ipse laud-
aret praefici. Interea Turci et Arabes, nigri quoque Aethiopes, quingenti
10   fere, qui in arcem Daviticam se intromiserant, petierunt Raimundo comite, qui prope turrim illam hospitatus erat, ut pecunia eorum in arce ipsa
retenta, vivos tantum eos abire permitteret. Hoc concessit, et hinc Ascalonem adierunt. Placuit tunc Deo, quod inventa est particula una crucis
dominicae in loco secreto, iam ab antiquo tempore a viris religiosis oc-
15   cultata, nunc autem a quodam homine Syro, Deo volente, revelata, quam
cum patre suo inde conscio diligenter ibi et absconderat et conservarat.
Quam quidem particulam in modum crucis reformatam, aurea partim et
argentea fabrica contectam, ad dominicum Sepulcrum, dehinc etiam ad
Templum congratulanter psallendo et gratias Deo agendo, qui per tot dies
20   hunc thesaurum suum et nostrum sibi et nobis servaverat, omnes una in
sublime propalatam detulerunt.

                                            —Hist. Hier. 1.25.13–1.30.

3. **quem:** i.e., Godfrey of Bouillon; note how the antecedent, in the poem, is in ablative
absolute construction.   6. **canonici:** from *canonicus, i* = "canons" (on the various
meanings see Niermeyer 128, s. v. *canonicus* 1.).   7. **Patriarcham:** from *Patriarcha,
ae* = "Patriarch" (Niermeyer 773–74); Arnulf of Chocques was chosen for this important post (see Ryan 124, n. 3).   8. **quaesissent:** contracted pluperfect active subjunctive, third person plural = *quaesivissent,* from *quaerere.*   12. **Ascalonem:** from
Ascalon, onis, though more often indeclinable (on which cf. Sleumer 130) = Ascalon
(cf. Ryan 124 and n. 4).   15. **homine Syro:** from *Syrus, i* = Syrian, with *homine* =
"Syrian man" (Sleumer 764).   19. **psallendo et gratias Deo agendo:** notice the continued use of the gerund in ablative as a present active participle.   21. **propalatam:**
perfect passive participle of *propalare* = "to make known to all" (Hagenmeyer 311,
n. 14).

PETER ABELARD

The History of My Misfortunes; Hymn for Vespers; Lament of Dinah

(*Historia calamitatum* = *Epistula* I, c. 1132; *Sabbato ad Vesperas; Planctus Dinae, filiae Jacob;* c. 1135)

B ecause we tend often to think of him in caricature—as a figure consumed by romantic love, or, conversely, as an intellectual zealot brought down by his own hubris—Peter Abelard's literary influence tends to be downplayed. Yet, the effect he had on the development of ML into a language fully competent to the tasks of philosophy, theology, and lyric cannot be underestimated. Abelard's work falls into three broad categories—philosophical-theological, lyrical, and personal—and in each of these a separately evolved Latinity was developed and deployed by Abelard.

The philosophical-theological works, the most substantial in terms of sheer volume, include the treatises by which Abelard made his reputation and for which he is normally remembered, i.e., *Yes and No, Know Thyself, Christian Theology,* and *On the Unity and Trinity of God.* In these works, the qualities of Latin best required for the scholastic enterprise were exploited. One finds a vocabulary consistently and systematically deployed, a clear syntax, a simple presentation. The personal works would include sermons on various topics and the letters Abelard wrote in response to Heloise's requests for guidance after she had assumed the abbacy of the convent of the Paraclete. These works, though they often treat topics similar to those in the philosophical and theological vein, evince nonetheless a more complex Latin, fronted by a fresh vocabulary of affect and ascent. The style reflects a pedagogical aim, much as in the philosophical and theological treatises, but always with the more restricted audience of the Paraclete in view. The learning of Abelard (and of Heloise) comes across in the many quotations from Scripture and allusions to the classical canon that are dispersed through these collections. Included in this group, too, would be the so-called *Historia calamitatum,* properly the first of the *Letters,* excerpted here—in essence an autobiography of Abelard down to about a decade before his death.

The third group, perhaps least well known, includes the *Planctus,* a series of sequences written on various Old Testament themes, and the *Hymnarius Paraclitensis,* a series of 133 hymns written for the Paraclete at Heloise's request and sent to the convent in three collections with dedicatory letters. These poetic works are of a kind in the ML tradition, both as to their formal qualities of diction and meter and as to their thematic concerns, symbolism, and theology. The hymn for Saturday vespers, reprinted here, for example, is written in twelve-syllable end-rhyming couplets, but it also features prominent internal rhyming, alliteration, and parallel construction. The lament of Dinah, in contrast, exhibits a complicated sequential structure reflecting the antiphonal nature of the earliest sequences, in which the melody of the *Jubilus* was broken up into parts and sung alternately by choirs of men and boys (cf. pp. 300–306 and 521–25). Whether or not such choirs performed these roles in the singing of Abelard's *Planctus*, there is little doubt that they were meant to be sung, as the music for them has come down to us.

Broken down into its constituent parts, the opening verses of the lament of Dinah look like this, with (1a) and the Refrain sung collectively, and (1b) and (1c) performed antiphonally:

[1a]	Abrahe proles,	Israel nata,	
	patriarcharum	sanguine clara,	
[1b] Incircumcisi	viri rapina	[1c] Generis sancti	macula summa,
hominis spurci	facta sum preda,	plebis adverse	ludis illusa.
	[Refrain:] Ve mihi misere	per memet prodite!	

Abelard was born of a minor noble family at Le Pallet, near Nantes in Brittany, in 1079. He was the eldest of several sons but nonetheless renounced his rights in favor of his younger brothers to take up the life of a scholar. He was a prodigious student who, as he tells us in the *Historia calamitatum,* was fond of showing up his teachers' inadequacies, much to their chagrin and to the delight of his fellow students. He studied at Loches under Roscelin of Compiègne, and then, around 1100, attached himself to the Cloister School of Notre Dame. There, not long after his arrival, he experienced the first of a series of confrontations with his teacher, William of Champeaux, which ended only when William's reputation suffered for his inability to counter Abelard's challenges to his views on universals.

Abelard then took up the gauntlet against another teacher, Anselm of Laon, whom he describes in the *Historia calamitatum* as a rotten oak ready to fall at the next bolt of lightning. William of Champeaux had been a dialectician. Anselm was a theologian, and it was to the methods of theology that Abelard now turned his criticism. Rather than use the collection of commentaries as aids in the understanding of Scripture (the method extolled for centuries on the model of Saint Benedict and championed by Anselm), Abelard preferred a simpler method, in which students read Scripture unaided by a commentary, relying on their own innate abilities to make sure sense of what they were reading.

Abelard's challenges to authority made him a popular teacher, and students flocked to him. He eventually taught in schools at Corbeil, Melun, and Paris. Then around 1115, as these excerpts from the *Historia* recount, he made the acquaintance of Heloise, the niece of Fulbert of Chartres, who had arrived in Paris to stay with her uncle. As Abelard remembers, the two quickly fell in love and proceeded to have a lengthy affair, which resulted eventually in marriage and the birth of a son, Astrolabe. Once the affair was found out, however, the rage of Fulbert was channeled into a plot—successfully accomplished—to castrate Abelard. Thereafter, Heloise became a nun at Argenteuil and Abelard, who recovered from his wounds, became a monk at St. Denis. Abelard went on to pursue teaching yet again and was condemned at Soissons in 1121, not for the last time, as a heretic. In 1122, Abelard took up teaching in Champagne, and by the end of the decade he was abbot of St. Gildas-de-Rhuys in Brittany. By 1135 or so, we find him back in Paris, teaching yet again, only to be vilified by his persecutor, Bernard of Clairvaux, who accused him of heresy (this time with assistance from William of St. Thierry) at a council in Sens. Abelard died, unexonerated, in 1142.

The first letter was not called the *Historia calamitatum* by Abelard (although by Petrarch's time the title *Historia suarum calamitatum* was in wide use); more probably a working title for the *Historia* in the century after Abelard's death was *Ad amicum suum consolatoria* (though this title would not seem to be owed to Abelard, either). There are nine MSS of the letters, none of which is earlier than the late thirteenth century. There is no independent MS, so far as is known, of the *Historia calamitatum,* although Heloise speaks of possessing one in *Ep.* 2 (see pp. 504–511). The letters were brought out in the thirteenth century, presumably based on a collection of documents pertaining to the Paraclete that came directly from Heloise.

The works of Abelard have been variously edited but remain difficult to obtain in good editions. The complete works have been edited by V. Cousin (*Petri Abaelardi Opera*, Paris, 1849). No modern edition of the complete correspondence exists, although an edition and translation of Abelard's letters is under way in the Cambridge Medieval Classics Series. The *Historia Calamitatum* (and, separately, the other letters) has been edited by J. T. Muckle ("Abelard's Letter of Consolation to a Friend (*Historia Calamitatum*)," *Mediaeval Studies* 12 (1950): 163–213), and by J. Monfrin (*Historia Calamitatum: Texte critique avec introduction*, Paris,

1962, with letters 1 and 3 of Heloise (2 and 4 if one counts the *HC* as letter 1) included in an appendix). There are several translations into English of the *Historia Calamitatum,* including those by J. T. Muckle (*The Story of Abelard's Adversities,* Toronto, 1964) and by B. Radice, prepared for the Penguin Classics and including the other letters (*The Letters of Abelard and Heloise,* Harmondsworth, 1974).

The hymns have been edited by G. Drèves (*Petri Abaelardi Peripatetici Palatini Hymnaris Paraclitensis,* Paris, 1891); in the *Analecta Hymnica* (vol. 48, pp. 144–223); and by J. Szövérffy (*Peter Abelard's Hymnarius Paraclitensis,* 2 vols., Leiden, 1975). The *Planctus* have been edited by W. Meyer ("Petri Abaelardi Planctus i, ii, iv, v, vi," *Romanische Forschungen* 5 (1890): 419–45, and also in *Gesammelte Abhandlungen zur mittellateinischen Rhythmik,* vol. 1, Berlin, 1905, pp. 340–74); in the *Analecta Hymnica* (vol. 48, pp. 223–32), by G. Vecchi (*Pietro Abelardo, I Planctus,* Rome, 1951); and in part by P. Dronke (*Poetic Individuality in the Middle Ages: New Departures in Poetry, 1100–1150,* Oxford, 1970, pp. 121–23 and 146). See also Raby 1, 319ff., for a general discussion.

Muckle's text of the *Historia calamitatum, Mediaeval Studies* 12, pp. 182–84, 185–89, is reprinted here, with some minor punctuation and formatting changes. I have also corrected one misprint, involving the quotation of Seneca, *Ep.* 72, *Resistendum est occupationibus, nec explicandae sunt sed submovendae,* which is part of Seneca's text, not, as reprinted in Muckle, part of the *HC.* The text of the hymn for Sabbath vespers is taken from the *Analecta Hymnica,* p. 163, without change; and the text of the lament of Dinah is taken from Dronke, *Poetic Individuality,* p. 146, without change.

THE HISTORY OF MY MISFORTUNES

Erat quippe in ipsa civitate Parisiensi adolescentula quaedam nomine Heloisa, neptis canonici cuiusdam qui Fulbertus vocabatur, qui eam, quanto amplius diligebat, tanto diligentius in omnem qua poterat scientiam litterarum promoveri studuerat. Quae, cum per faciem non esset

1. **Parisiensi:** *Parisiensis, e,* adjective = "Parisian" (Sleumer 582, s. v. *Parisii*) but more easily translated "in the city of Paris." 2. **canonici:** *canonicus, i* = "canon," a technical term in ML designating two bodies of religious, a "regular" group of monks who lived in a monastery and followed a rule (*regula,* hence their title); and a "secular" group, who did not live a monastic life or follow a set rule. Fulbert, the uncle of Heloise, was a secular canon. On the various meanings of the term see Niermeyer 127-28. 3. **quanto ... tanto:** "the ... the. ..." **qua:** adverb. 4. **studuerat:** intransitive.

infima, per abundantiam litterarum erat suprema. Nam, quo bonum hoc, litteratoriae scilicet scientiae, in mulieribus est rarius, eo amplius puellam commendabat et in toto regno nominatissimam fecerat. Hanc igitur, omnibus circumspectis quae amantes allicere solent, commodiorem censui in amorem mihi copulare et me id facillime credidi posse. Tanti quippe tunc   5
nominis eram et iuventutis et formae gratia praeminebam ut quamcumque feminarum nostro dignarer amore nullam vererer repulsam. Tanto autem facilius hanc mihi puellam consensuram credidi, quanto amplius eam litterarum scientiam et habere et diligere noveram, nosque etiam absentes scriptis internuntiis invicem liceret praesentare, et pleraque   10
audacius scribere quam colloqui, et sic semper iocundis interesse colloquiis.

In huius itaque adolescentulae amorem totus inflammatus occasionem quaesivi qua eam mihi domestica et quotidiana conversatione familiarem efficerem et facilius ad consensum traherem. Quod quidem ut fieret,   15
egi cum praedicto puellae avunculo, quibusdam ipsius amicis intervenientibus, quatenus me in domum suam quae scholis nostris proxima erat sub quocumque procurationis pretio susciperet, hanc videlicet occasionem praetendens quod studium nostrum domestica nostrae familiae cura plurimum praepediret et impensa nimium me gravaret. Erat autem cu-   20
pidus ille valde, atque erga neptim suam ut amplius semper in doctrinam proficeret litteratoriam plurimum studiosus. Quibus quidem duobus facile eius assensum assecutus sum, et quod optabam obtinui, cum ille videlicet et ad pecuniam totus inhiaret et neptim suam ex doctrina nostra aliquid percepturam crederet. Super quo vehementer me deprecatus, supra   25
quam sperare praesumerem, votis meis accessit et amori consuluit, eam videlicet totam nostro magisterio committens ut, quotiens mihi a scholis reverso vacaret, tam in die quam in nocte ei docendae operam darem, et eam, si negligentem sentirem, vehementer constringerem. In qua re quidem quanta eius simplicitas esset vehementer admiratus, non minus   30

2. quo . . . eo: "the . . . the . . ."; with *bonum hoc, quo* is redundant. **litteratoriae:** *litteratorius, a, um* = "literary," or, more specifically, "grammatical" (Niermeyer 616, s. v. *litteratorius* 2) modifying *scientiae*, with the phrase dependent on *bonum hoc*. 8. **tanto . . . quanto:** "the . . . the. . . ." 15. **ut fieret:** "so that it might come about." 17. **quatenus:** the postclassical sense of "that," "whereby," "so that" is standard in ML. 20. **plurimum:** adverb. 21. **neptim:** accusative singular of *neptis, is;* in CL = "granddaughter"; in ML = "niece" (Niermeyer 717). 22. **litteratoriam:** modifies *doctrinam.* 22. **quibus . . . duobus:** "by these two means," i.e., Fulbert's greed and his desire for Heloise to be well educated. 25. **super quo:** "concerning which." **deprecatus:** perfect participle of *deprecari,* "beseeched," modifying an understood "Fulbert." **supra quam** = "more than."

apud me obstupui quam si agnam teneram famelico lupo committeret. Qui cum eam mihi non solum docendam, verum etiam vehementer constringendam traderet, quid aliud agebat quam ut votis meis licentiam penitus daret, et occasionem, etiam si nollemus offerret ut quam videlicet
5   blanditiis non possem, minis et verberibus facilius flecterem? Sed duo erant quae eum maxime a turpi suspicione revocabant, amor videlicet neptis et continentiae meae fama praeterita. Quid plura? Primum domo una coniungimur, postmodum animo. Sub occasione itaque disciplinae amori penitus vacabamus et secretos recessus quos amor optabat studium lec-
10   tionis offerebat. Apertis itaque libris, plura de amore quam de lectione verba se ingerebant; plura erant oscula quam sententiae . . . .

Et quo me amplius haec voluptas occupaverat, minus philosophiae vacare poteram et scholis operam dare. Taediosum mihi vehementer erat ad scholas procedere, vel in eis morari pariter et laboriosum, cum noctur-
15   nas amori vigilias et diurnas studio conservarem. Quem etiam ita negligentem et tepidum lectio tunc habebat ut iam nihil ex ingenio sed ex usu cuncta proferrem, nec iam nisi recitator pristinorum essem inventorum, et, si qua invenire liceret carmina, essent amatoria, non philosophiae secreta. Quorum etiam carminum pleraque adhuc in multis, sicut et ipse
20   nosti, frequentantur et decantantur regionibus ab his maxime quos vita similis oblectat. Quantam autem maestitiam, quos gemitus, quae lamenta nostri super hoc scholares assumerent, ubi videlicet hanc animi mei occupationem, immo perturbationem, praesenserunt, non est facile vel cogitare. Paucos enim iam res tam manifesta decipere poterat ac neminem,
25   credo, praeter eum ad cuius ignominiam maxime id spectabat, ipsum videlicet puellae avunculum. Cui quidem hoc, cum a nonnullis nonnunquam suggestum fuisset, credere non poterat tum, ut supra memini, propter immoderatam suae neptis amicitiam, tum etiam propter anteactae vitae meae continentiam cognitam. Non enim facile de his quos pluri-
30   mum diligimus turpitudinem suspicamur, nec in vehementi dilectione turpis suspicionis labes potest inesse. Unde et illud est Beati Hieronymi in Epistola ad Sabinianum:

---

1. **obstupui** = CL *obstipui*, from *obstipescere*. 3. **quid aliud agebat quam:** "what else was he doing than. . . ." 9. **secretos recessus:** object of *offerebat*. 13. **taediosum:** *taediosus, a, um* = "irksome" (LS 1834). 28. **anteactae:** perfect passive participle of *anteagere* = "actions formerly done" (Blaise 84). 31. **Hieronymi:** *Hieronymus, i* = Saint Jerome, translator of the Vulgate and an important figure in the Western church in the late fourth and early fifth centuries; he died in 419. 32. **ad Sabinianum** = the title Abelard gives to Jerome's letter to Castrician, *Ep.* 147; the passage that Abelard quotes comes from line 10.

Solemus mala domus nostrae scire novissimi, ac liberorum ac coniugum vitia vicinis canentibus ignorare.

Sed quod novissime scitur utique sciri quandoque contingit, et quod omnes deprehendunt, non est facile unum latere.

Sic itaque pluribus evolutis mensibus, et de nobis accidit. O quantus 5
in hoc cognoscendo dolor avunculi! quantus in separatione amantium dolor ipsorum! quanta sum erubescentia confusus! quanta contritione super afflictione puellae sum afflictus! quantos maeroris ipsa de verecundia mea sustinuit aestus! Neuter quod sibi, sed quod alteri, contigerat querebatur; neuter sua sed alterius plangebat incommoda. Separatio autem haec corp- 10
orum maxima erat copulatio animorum, et negata sui copia amplius amorem accendebat. . . .

Illico ego ad patriam meam reversus amicam reduxi ut uxorem facerem, illa tamen hoc minime approbante, immo penitus duabus de causis dissuadente, tam scilicet pro periculo quam pro dedecore meo. Iurabat 15
illum nulla unquam satisfactione super hoc placari posse, sicut postmodum cognitum est. Quaerebat etiam quam de me gloriam habitura esset cum me ingloriosum efficeret et se et me pariter humiliaret; quantas ab ea mundus poenas exigere deberet, si tantam ei lucernam auferret; quantae maledictiones, quanta damna ecclesiae, quantae philosophorum lacry- 20
mae hoc matrimonium essent secuturae; quam indecens, quam lamentabile esset ut quem omnibus natura creaverat uni me feminae dicarem et turpitudini tantae subicerem. Detestabatur vehementer hoc matrimonium quod mihi per omnia probrosum esset atque onerosum. Praetendebat infamiam mei pariter et difficultates matrimonii ad quas quidem vitandas 25
nos exhortans Apostolus ait: "Solutus es ab uxore? Noli quaerere uxorem. Si autem acceperis uxorem, non peccasti, et si nupserit virgo, non peccabit. Tribulationem tamen carnis habebunt huiusmodi. Ego autem vobis parco." Item: "Volo autem vos sine sollicitudine esse."

Quod si nec Apostoli consilium, nec sanctorum exhortationes de 30
tanto matrimonii iugo susciperem, saltem, inquit, philosophos consulerem et quae super hoc ab eis vel de eis scripta sunt attenderem. Quod

---

3. **sed . . . contingit**: this somewhat obscure line means something like, "But what is known of late, turns out at any rate to be known sometime." 5. **accidit**: impersonal = "it happened . . .," i.e., what Abelard describes as inevitable in the previous line; Fulbert found out about the liaison between Abelard and Heloise. 16. **illum**: i.e., Fulbert. **super hoc**: "concerning this matter." 19. **ei**: i.e., *mundus;* with *tantam lucernam* = "a light so great to it." 20. **lacrymae** = CL *lacrimae.* 26. **apostolus**: i.e., Paul; the quotations that follow come from 1 Cor. 7.27, 28, 32.

plerumque etiam sancti ad increpationem nostram diligenter faciunt. Quale illud est beati Hieronymi in primo *Contra Iovinianum* ubi scilicet commemorat Theophrastum intolerabilibus nuptiarum molestiis assiduisque inquietudinibus ex magna parte diligenter expositis, uxorem sapi-
5   enti non esse ducendam evidentissimis rationibus astruxisse ubi et ipse illas exhortationis philosophicae rationes tali fine concludens:

> "Hoc," inquit, "et huiusmodi Theophrastus disserens quem non suffundat Christianorum?"

Idem in eodem:

10   "Cicero," inquit, "rogatus ab Hirtio ut post repudium Terentiae sororem eius duceret, omnino facere supersedit, dicens non posse se et uxori et philosophiae operam pariter dare.

Non ait: "operam dare," sed adiunxit: "pariter," nolens quicquam agere quod studio aequaretur philosophiae. Ut autem hoc philosophici studii
15   nunc omittam impedimentum, ipsum consule honestae conversationis statum. Quae enim conventio scholarium ad pedissequas, scriptoriorum ad cunabula, librorum sive tabularum ad colos, stilorum sive calamorum ad fusos? Quis denique sacris vel philosophicis meditationibus intentus pueriles vagitus, nutricum quae hos mitigant nenias, tumultuosam famil-
20   iae tam in viris quam in feminis turbam sustinere poterit? Quae etiam inhonestas illas parvulorum sordes assiduas tolerare valebit? Id, inquies, divites possunt quorum palatia vel domus amplae deversoria habent, quorum opulentia non sentit expensas nec quotidianis sollicitudinibus cruciatur. Sed non est, inquam, haec condicio philosophorum quae divitum, nec
25   qui opibus student vel saecularibus implicantur curis divinis seu philosophicis vacabunt officiis.

Unde et insignes olim [philosophi] mundum maxime contemnentes, nec tam relinquentes saeculum quam fugientes, omnes sibi voluptates in-

---

1. **increpationem:** *increpatio, onis* = "rebuke" (Niermeyer 524). 2. **in primo** . . . *Iovinianum* : i.e., the first book of Jerome's *Against Jovinian;* Abelard is discussing here 1.47. 5. **astruxisse:** perfect active infinitive of *astruere* = "to have affirmed." 10. **Hirtio:** i.e., *Hirtius,* who asked Cicero to marry his sister after he, Cicero, had divorced Terentia. **Terentiae:** Cicero's former wife, divorced by him. 15. **consule:** present active imperative singular of *consulere;* with Heloise the implied speaker here. 16. **scriptoriorum:** *scriptorium, i* = "the writing room" (Niermeyer 948). 20. **tam** . . . **quam:** coordinating conjunctions = "the . . . the. . . ." 21. **inquies:** i.e., "you [Abelard] will say"; in response to the implied discourse that Abelard reports here from the point of view of Heloise. 28. **nec tam** . . . **quam:** the sense here is "not so much . . .as. . . ."

terdixerunt ut in unius philosophiae requiescerent amplexibus. Quorum unus et maximus Seneca Lucilium instruens ait:

> Non cum vacaveris philosophandum est; omnia negligenda sunt ut huic assideamus cui nullum tempus satis magnum est. . . . Non multum refert utrum omittas philosophiam an intermittas; non enim, ubi interrupta est, manet. Resistendum est occupationibus, nec explicandae sunt sed sub-movendae.

5

Quod nunc igitur apud nos amore Dei sustinent qui vere monachi di-cuntur, hoc, desiderio philosophiae, qui nobiles in gentibus exstiterunt philosophi. In omni namque populo, tam gentili scilicet quam Iudaico sive Christiano, aliqui semper exstiterunt fide seu morum honestate ceteris praeeminentes, et se a populo aliqua continentiae vel abstinentiae singularitate segregantes. Apud Iudaeos quidem antiquitus Nazaraei qui se Domino secundum legem consecrabant, sive filii prophetarum, Heliae vel Helisaei sectatores, quos, beato attestante Hieronymo, monachos legimus in veteri Testamento. Novissime autem tres illae philosophiae sectae quas Iosephus in libro Antiquitatum distinguens, alios Pharisaeos, alios Sadducaeos, alios nominat Essaeos. Apud nos vero monachi qui videlicet aut communem Apostolorum vitam aut priorem illam et solitariam Ioannis imitantur; apud gentiles autem, ut dictum est, philosophi. Non enim sapientiae vel philosophiae nomen tam ad scientiae perceptionem quam ad vitae religionem referebant, sicut ab ipso etiam huius nominis ortu didicimus, ipsorum quoque testimonio sanctorum. Unde et illud est beati Augustini octavo de Civitate Dei libro genera quidem philosophorum distinguentis:

10

15

20

25

2. **Lucilium:** the quotation that follows comes from Seneca, *Ep.* 72.3; Lucilius, as often, is the intended recipient. 8. **monachi:** *monachus, i* = "monk." 10. **gentili:** *gentilis, is* = "heathen" (Niermeyer 466). **Iudaico:** from *Iudaicus, a, um* = Jewish (Sleumer 451). 13. **Iudaeos:** from *Iudaei, orum* = Jews (LS 1015, s. v. *Iudaea* II A). **antiquitus:** adverb. **Nazaraei:** from *Nazaraei, orum* = Nazirites (Sleumer 540); cf. Num. 6.21 and Judges 16.17. 14. **Heliae** = *Elias, ae* or *Elia, ae* = the prophet Elijah; the form is as early as the third century (cf. LS 637, s. v. 2 *Elias*). 15. **Helisaei:** *Helises, ei* = Elisha. **Hieronymo:** Jerome, *Ep.* 125.7. 16. **veteri Testamento:** i.e., the Old Testament; Abelard (in the voice of Heloise) refers here specifically to 2 Kings 6.1. 17. **Iosephus:** Jewish historian (37 C.E.–c. 100 C.E.). **Antiquitatum:** i.e., *The Antiquities of the Jews,* 18.1.11. **Pharisaeos:** *Pharisaeus, i* = Pharisees, a Jewish sect (Sleumer 604). **Sadducaeos:** *Sadducaei, orum* = Sadducees, a Jewish sect (Sleumer 687). 18. **Essaeos:** *Essaei, orum* = Essenes, a Jewish sect. 20. **non . . . tam . . . quam:** "not so much . . . as. . . ." 23. **beati Augustini:** *Augustinus, i* = Saint Augustine (d. 430). 24. **de Civitate Dei:** i.e., Augustine's *City of God;* Abelard quotes from 8.2 here.

Italicum genus auctorem habuit Pythagoram Samium a quo et fertur ipsum philosophiae nomen exortum. Nam cum antea sapientes appellarentur qui modo quodam laudabilis vitae aliis praestare videbantur, iste interrogatus quid profiteretur philosophum se esse respondit, id est studi-
5   osum vel amatorem sapientiae, quoniam sapientem profiteri arrogantissimum videbatur.

Hoc itaque loco cum dicitur:

Qui modo quodam laudabilis vitae aliis praestare videbantur, . . .

aperte monstratur sapientes gentium, id est, philosophos ex laude vitae
10   potius quam scientiae sic esse nominatos. Quam sobrie autem atque continenter ipsi vixerint non est nostrum modo ex exemplis colligere ne Minervam ipsam videar docere. Si autem sic laici gentilesque vixerunt, nulla scilicet professione religionis astricti, quid te clericum atque canonicum facere oportet ne divinis officiis turpes praeferas voluptates, ne te praecip-
15   item haec Charybdis absorbeat, ne obscoenitatibus istis te impudenter atque irrevocabiliter immergas? Qui si clerici praerogativam non curas, philosophi saltem defende dignitatem. Si reverentia Dei contemnitur, amor saltem honestatis impudentiam temperet. Memento Socratem uxoratum fuisse, et quam foedo casu hanc philosophiae labem ipse primo
20   luerit ut deinceps ceteri exemplo eius cautiores efficerentur; quod nec ipse praeterit Hieronymus ita in primo *Contra Iovinianum* de ipso scribens Socrate:

1. **Pythagoram Samium:** i.e., Pythagoras of Samos, the famous ancient Greek philosopher. 9. **monstratur:** i.e., based on the quotation from Augustine just repeated, "it is demonstrable that. . . ." 11. **Minervam** = Minerva, the goddess of wisdom, arts, and science (= Pallas Athena). 12. **laici:** *laicus, i* or *laica, ae* = "layman" or "laywoman" (Niermeyer 579, s. v. 1 *laicus*). 13. **astricti:** perfect passive participle of *astringere,* modifying *laici gentilesque.* **clericum:** *clericus, i* = "clerk," generally (though not always) referring to one who has lower orders only, i.e., is not ordained a priest, but who can say Mass and teach (cf. Niermeyer 190–91 and Muckle 188, n. 81). **canonicum:** Abelard was a secular canon (as was Fulbert, the uncle of Heloise). The term has various meanings, see Niermeyer 127–28; for the complications of Abelard's status as canon, see Muckle 188, n. 81. 15. **Charybdis:** from *Charybdis, is* = the dangerous whirlpool between Italy and Sicily (opposite Scylla), often characterized as a female monster. **obscoenitatibus** = CL *obscenitatibus.* 16. **praerogativam:** ML a feminine noun of the first declension = "privilege" (Blaise/Chirat 652). 18. **Socratem:** *Socrates, is* = Socrates, the famous ancient Greek philosopher and teacher of Plato. 19. **uxoratum:** perfect participle of *uxorari* = "married" (Niermeyer 1056). 21. **Contra Iovinianum:** Jerome's *Against Jovinian,* 1.48.

Quodam autem tempore, cum infinita convicia ex superiori loco ingerenti Xanthippae restitisset, aqua profusus immunda nihil respondit amplius quam, capite deterso: "Sciebam," inquit, "futurum ut ista tonitrua imber sequeretur."

Addebat denique ipsa et quam periculosum mihi esset eam reducere, et 5
quam sibi carius existeret mihique honestius amicam dici quam uxorem ut me ei sola gratia conservaret, non vis aliqua vinculi nuptialis constringeret, tantoque nos ipsos ad tempus separatos gratiora de conventu nostro percipere gaudia, quanto rariora. Haec et similia persuadens seu dissuadens, cum meam deflectere non posset stultitiam, nec me sustineret 10
offendere, suspirans vehementer et lacrymans perorationem suam tali fine terminavit: "Unum," inquit, "ad ultimum restat ut in perditione duorum minor non succedat dolor quam praecessit amor." Nec in hoc ei, sicut universus agnovit mundus, prophetiae defuit spiritus.

—*Ep.* 1 (excerpts).

HYMN FOR VESPERS ON THE SABBATH

O quanta qualia sunt illa Sabbata,
quae semper celebrat superna curia!
quae fessis requies, quae merces fortibus,
cum erit omnia deus in omnibus!

Vera Ierusalem est illa civitas   5
cuius pax iugis est, summa iucunditas,
ubi non praevenit rem desiderium,
nec desiderio minus est praemium.

Quis Rex, quae curia, quale palatium,
quae pax, quae requies, quod illud gaudium!   10
huius participes exponant gloriae,
si, quantum sentiunt, possint exprimere.

2. **Xanthippae:** *Xanthippa, ae* = Xanthippe, Socrates' wife. 5. **addebat ... ipsa:** Abelard concludes the fiction of Heloise's reported dialogue, but notes here that "she added. . . ." 6. **amicam:** lit., "friend," but the sense is "lover." **dici:** present passive infinitive of *dicere* = "to be called," with *amicam ... quam uxorem* as objects. 11. **lacrymans** = CL *lacrimans*.

1. **sabbata:** *sabbata, orum,* from *sabbatum, i* = Sabbath, i.e., Saturday evening (Sleumer 685, s. v. *sabbata;* cf. *sabbatum*). 5. **Ierusalem:** from *Ierusalem,* indeclinable feminine noun (Sleumer 404). 6. **iugis:** adjective. 8. **desiderio:** ablative of comparison with *minus.* 11. **huius ... gloriae:** dependent on *participes,* referring to the preceding catalogue of qualities; *participes* is the subject of *exponant.*

Nostrum est interim mentem erigere,
et totis patriam votis appetere,
15   et ad Iersualem a Babylonia,
post longa regredi tandem exsilia.

Illic, molestiis finitis omnibus,
securi cantica Sion cantabimus,
et iuges gratias de donis gratiae
20   beata referet plebs tibi, Domine.

Illic ex Sabbato succedet Sabbatum,
perpes laetitia sabbatizantium,
nec ineffabiles cessabunt iubili,
quos decantabimus et nos et angeli.

25   Perenni Domino perpes sit gloria,
ex quo sunt, per quem sunt, in quo sunt omnia:
ex quo sunt, Pater est, per quem sunt, Filius,
in quo sunt, Patris et Filii Spiritus.

—Sabb. ad vesp.

LAMENT OF DINAH

Abrahe proles,   Israel nata,
patriarcharum   sanguine clara,

Incircumcisi   viri rapina
hominis spurci   facta sum preda,

5   Generis sancti   macula summa,
plebis adverse   ludis illusa.
    Ve mihi misere   per memet prodite!

15. **Babylonia:** from *Babylonia, ae* = Babylon (Sleumer 145), the reference is to the Babylonian captivity of the Jews. 16. **regredi:** parallel with *appetere* and *erigere*, all of which complement *nostrum est.* 18. **securi:** adjective acting as substantive subject of *cantabimus.* **Sion:** sometimes declined as a third declension feminine noun, but here, as often, indeclinable, but in the genitive singular, dependent on *cantica* = "songs of Zion" (Sleumer 729). 22. **sabbatizantium:** present active participle, genitive plural, of *sabbatizare* = "to make or celebrate Sabbaths" (Sleumer 685). 1. **Abrahe:** better *Abrahae,* the genitive of *Abraham,* otherwise indeclinable (Sleumer 67). **Israel:** genitive singular of indeclinable *Israel* (Sleumer 450); *nata* refers to Dinah. 4. **preda** = CL *praeda.* 6. **adverse** = CL *adversae.* **illusa:** perfect passive participle of *illudere.* 7. **ve** = CL *vae.* **misere** = CL *miserae.* **memet:** "met" added to pronouns (here, *me*) is emphatic. **prodite** = CL *proditae* = "betrayer of myself."

Quid alienigenas iuvabat me cernere?
Quam male sum cognita volens has cognoscere!
 Ve mihi misere per memet prodite!   10

Sichem, in exicium nate tui generis,
nostris in obprobrium perpes facte posteris!
 Ve tibi misero per temet perdito!

Frustra circumcisio fecit te proselitum,
non valens infamie tollere prepucium.   15
 Ve tibi misero per temet perdito!

Coactus me rapere, mea raptus spetie,
quovis expers venie non fuisses iudice!
Non sic, fratres, censuistis, Symeon et Levi,
in eodem facto nimis crudeles et pii!   20
Innocentes coequastis in pena nocenti,
Quin et patrem perturbastis: ob hoc execrandi!

Amoris impulsio, culpe satisfactio,
quovis sunt iudicio culpe diminutio!
Levis etas iuvenilis minusque discreta   25
ferre minus a discretis debuit in pena.
Ira fratrum ex honore fuit lenienda,
quem his fecit princeps terre ducta peregrina.
 Ve mihi, ve tibi, miserande iuvenis:
 in stragem communem gentis tante concidis! 30

         —Planc. Din.

8. **quid . . . iuvabat . . . cernere:** *iuvare* with infinitive + *quid* = "what good/help was it for me to. . . ." 11. **Sichem:** i.e., Sichem, son of Hemor (cf. Gen. 34); indeclinable (Sleumer 722–23). **exicium** = CL *exitium.* **nate:** vocative with *Sichem.* 12. **obprobrium** = CL *opprobrium.* 14. **frustra:** adverb. **circumcisio:** from *circumcisio, onis* = "circumcision" (Niermeyer 182). **proselitum:** from *proselytus, i* = "stranger" (Niermeyer 865). 15. **infamie** = CL *infamiae.* **prepucium** = CL *praeputium.* 17. **spetie** = CL *specie.* 18. **venie** = CL *veniae.* 19. **Symeon:** indeclinable noun = Simeon, brother of Dinah, son of Jacob (Sleumer 726). **Levi:** indeclinable noun = Levi, brother of Dinah and son of Jacob (Sleumer 47). 23. **culpe** = CL *culpae.* 25. **etas** = CL *aetas.* 26. **pena** = CL *poena.* 28. **terre** = CL *terrae.* 30. **tante** = CL *tantae.*

Septem psalmos
Domine ne in furore
tuo arguas me neqz
in ira tua compias me

PLATE 24. A folio from a fifteenth-century Book of Hours, showing Bathsheba.

PLATE 24

Book of Hours
Latin and French manuscript on parchment, fifteenth century, fol. 61 recto
John Hay Library, Brown University

Originally, Books of Hours were commissioned by the wealthy laity for their private devotion, and the prayers and hymns attending to the veneration of the Virgin were always central to these collections. The day was normally divided into eight equal parts. Each portion equaled an "hour" of devotion. The office for each hour consisted of whatever service was set to be performed for any given time—this model follows closely the divine office established by Saint Benedict and followed by the Church for centuries (see pp. 186–87). The Book of Hours from which this folio comes was produced in the fifteenth century—the greatest century for the production of such manuscripts—and it is written in both French and Latin. The opening folios 1 recto to 12 verso give a calendar of liturgical observances (in French), followed (in Latin) by prayers, the epistles, the gospels, hymns to the Virgin, and psalms, thus making this a rather complete liturgical book. Books such as this one were in increasing demand as the number of private Masses commonly heard among the nobility increased in the Middle Ages.

The folio shown here, depicting Bathsheba, is richly colored in red and green, with floreated margins filled with geometric shapes. The folio is ruled in pencil, as are the four lines of text shown below the picture. The manuscript is bound in wooden boards, covered by stamped leather. It is 18 cm. in height and has 117 folios.

Heloise

Letter to Abelard
(*Epistula 2;* c. 1135)

Because we tend to dragoon Heloise into the constellation of events re-counted so vividly in Peter Abelard's *Historia calamitatum,* we often fail to recognize her own accomplishments. It is important to remember that Heloise was a gifted woman in her own right who eventually became a respected abbess, and, in the two decades following Abelard's death, went on to pursue important work at the Paraclete, the monastic establishment given to her by Abelard.

We know nothing of Heloise's early life. The accepted conjecture for her birth is around 1100. Some have suggested that she may have been illegitimate. She was raised at the convent of St. Marie of Argenteuil dur-ing her formative years and seems to have received an education that, if it did not accommodate her extraordinary talents, was nonetheless out of the ordinary for a woman in the early twelfth century. Her talents are confirmed, too, by the fact that she came to Paris around 1115 to live with her uncle, Fulbert of Chartres, to further her study. In later life, Abelard reported in his letters that Heloise knew Greek and Hebrew, in addition to Latin and the vernacular French of their day.

Still a teen when she arrived at Paris, Heloise came almost at once to the attention of Abelard, who was then in his mid thirties and who al-ready had an international reputation as a teacher of the first order. Their fateful meeting, representing the final phase in Abelard's stormy life, sym-bolizes in Heloise's only the first juncture in a series of intellectual and spiritual pursuits. Those pursuits, as is well known, were inspired by Abe-lard, who, as he relates in the *Historia calamitatum* (see pp. 489–501) conspired to insinuate himself into Fulbert's household in order to be closer to the exotic and alluring woman. To his surprise and delight, Fulbert gave Abelard complete charge of Heloise's education and train-ing, and their affair quickly developed. Part and parcel of that affair was an attention, at least initially, to the rounding off of Heloise's education. But that aim quickly was pushed aside as the affair commenced in earnest.

The details of their life together after this initial stage are well known: Fulbert became aware of the scandal; the couple left for Brittany; they were married and a son, Astrolabe, was born; Abelard was castrated by the henchmen of a furious Fulbert; and, in the complications arising from competing desires on the parts of both Abelard and Heloise as to what should be done next, the couple separated, each taking religious vows.

At this point, in the early 1120s, Heloise returned to Argenteuil and eventually became prioress there. She did not have contact with Abelard for the better part of a decade. Abelard entered the monastery of St. Denis, was accused of heresy and condemned at the Council of Soissons in 1121, and then fled to Champagne, building near Troyes the oratory he called the Paraclete. In 1126 he left the Paraclete to become abbot of St. Gildas de Rhuys, in Brittany. The abandonment of the Paraclete coincided with the confiscation of Argenteuil by Suger of St. Denis, who claimed that the monastery belonged to St. Denis. Heloise and her nuns found themselves homeless in 1127—at which point Abelard interceded and offered them the Paraclete, which had been more or less abandoned for several years. The nuns were there by 1129, with Heloise as prioress. Her literary output derives from the tasks she assumed in this important position.

In addition to the *Historia calamitatum*, which is properly epistle 1 of the collected letters, there are four "personal" epistles, consisting of two letters sent to Abelard from Heloise and Abelard's responses to each, which center on the emotional and spiritual desolations and potentials of life after their separation. To this are added three other letters, the so-called letters of "direction," one from Heloise to Abelard, and two from Abelard to her, in which the details of the management of the Paraclete are taken up. Several other letters exist as well which are not normally included in the collection, viz., Abelard's so-called "confession of faith" to Heloise, and his various letters written to accompany works requested of him by Heloise (i.e., his sermons, the *Hexaemeron*, and the hymns and sequences); and, from Heloise's hand, a letter introducing the so-called "problems" of Heloise.

Because there is a gap of over a century between the composition of the letters, in the 1130s, and the earliest manuscript preserving them, which dates from the late thirteenth century, scholars have always had grounds, if not good reason, to doubt the collection's authenticity. No manuscript ascribes the letters to any other figures, but many have wondered specifically over the contents of the collection, especially the personal revelations they gather. This scholarly puzzlement reached its apex in the early 1970s, when it was argued that political needs internal to the Paraclete in the late thirteenth century led to the forging of the correspondence in order to introduce a male-centered rule to the monastery and to allow for the eating of meat. But there remains no substantive evidence arguing for forgery, and much literary evidence supports their authenticity.

In returning to the personal letters, the first of which is excerpted here, one discovers a unique Latinity that gives some sense of Heloise as an intellect: a consistent vocabulary, a tendency to write complex periods with parallel coordination, and, in terms of content, a fierce and persistent self-reflection, aided by the ebb and flow of a now simple, now complex syntax. In these excerpts, Heloise gives a full sense of her spiritual and emotional state; her need of Abelard, her devotion to him, her feelings as to their separation and his particular lack of attention toward her. This letter is exemplary both in terms of its Latinity, evincing all the characteristics of the best ML prose style, and in terms of its vision and voice, for there are few comparable works in prose or verse that are as self-reflective.

The collection of letters as we have them is presumably based on a like collection of documents pertaining to the Paraclete that derives from Heloise herself. V. Cousin has edited the letters (*Petri Abaelardi Opera*, Paris, 1849), as has J. T. Muckle ("The Personal Letters Between Abelard and Heloise," *Mediaeval Studies* 15 (1953): 47–94 (for letters 1–4) and 17 (1955): 240–81 (for letters 5–6); T. P. McLaughlin, *Mediaeval Studies* 18 (1956): 241–92 has edited letter 7). B. Radice has translated the letters most recently for the Penguin Classics, and her introduction and bibliography are excellent (*The Letters of Abelard and Heloise*, Harmondsworth, 1974). R. W. Southern has written on the authenticity issue ("The Letters of Heloise and Abelard," in *Medieval Humanism and Other Studies*, Oxford, 1970), as have P. Dronke (*Abelard and Heloise in Medieval Testimonies*, Glasgow, 1976) and B. Newman ("Authority, Authenticity, and the Repression of Heloise," *Journal of Medieval and Renaissance Studies* 22 (1992): 121–57).

Muckle's text, *Mediaeval Studies* 15: 68–71, is reprinted here, with quotation marks substituted for the italics used by him to designate scriptural passages.

LETTER TO ABELARD

Domino suo immo patri, coniugi suo immo fratri, ancilla sua immo filia, ipsius uxor immo soror, Abaelardo Heloisa.

Missam ad amicum pro consolatione epistolam, dilectissime, vestram

ad me forte quidam nuper attulit. Quam ex ipsa statim tituli fronte
vestram esse considerans, tanto ardentius eam coepi legere, quanto
scriptorem ipsum carius amplector ut, cuius rem perdidi, verbis saltem
tamquam eius quadam imagine recreer. Erant memini huius epistolae fere
omnia felle et absinthio plena quae scilicet nostrae conversionis miserabi-   5
lem historiam et tuas, unice, cruces assiduas referebant. Complesti revera
in epistola illa quod in exordio eius amico promisisti ut videlicet in com-
paratione tuarum suas molestias nullas vel parvas reputaret. Ubi quidem
expositis prius magistrorum tuorum in te persecutionibus deinde in corpus tuum summae proditionis iniuria ad condiscipulorum quoque   10
tuorum Alberici videlicet Remensis et Lotulfi Lombardi execrabilem invidiam et infestationem nimiam stilum contulisti. Quorum quidem sug-
gestionibus quid de glorioso illo theologiae tuae opere quid de te ipso
quasi in carcere damnato actum sit non praetermisisti.

Inde ad abbatis tui fratrumque falsorum machinationem accessisti et   15
detractiones illas tibi gravissimas duorum illorum pseudo-apostolorum a
praedictis aemulis in te commotas atque ad scandalum plerisque subortum de nomine Paracliti oratorio praeter consuetudinem imposito.
Denique ad intolerabiles illas et adhuc continuas in te persecutiones crude-
lissimi scilicet illius exactoris et pessimorum quos filios nominas mona-   20
chorum profectus miserabilem historiam consummasti.

Quae cum siccis oculis neminem vel legere vel audire posse aestimem.
Tanto dolores meos amplius renovarunt, quanto diligentius singula ex-
presserunt et eo magis auxerunt, quo in te adhuc pericula crescere retulisti

1. **attulit:** from *afferre.* **ex ipsa . . . tituli fronte:** i.e., Heloise sees at once from the
superscription that the letter was from Abelard. 2. **tanto . . . quanto:** "the . . . the
. . .," coordinating the comparatives *ardentius* and *carius.* 4. **recreer:** from *recreare,*
read with *ut.* **memini:** parenthetical. 5. **conversionis:** i.e., the entry into orders of
Heloise, who became a nun after Abelard's disgrace. 6. **unice:** vocative case. **revera:** adverb. 8. **suas:** i.e., *amicus,* who is the subject of the *ut* clause. 10. **iniuria:**
ablative case, parallel with *expositis persecutionibus,* with an understood *exposita*
modifying it. **ad:** governs *execrabilem . . . nimiam* and forms the prepositional phrase
which serves as the object of *stilum contulisti,* i.e., "you turned your pen to. . . ."
11. **Alberici . . . Remensis . . . Lotulfi Lombardi:** i.e., Alberic of Rheims and Lotulf of
Lombardy, both heads of the cathedral school at Rheims, and enemies of Abelard from
his student days, as Abelard recounts in the *Hist. Cal.* 511ff. (Muckle 192). 13. **quid
. . . quid . . . actum sit:** indirect questions serving as the objects of *non praetermisisti.*
17. **aemulis:** i.e., Alberic and Lotulf. **scandalum:** from *scandalum, i* = "hatred,"
"discord," "displeasure," rather than "scandal" (cf. Niermeyer 942). **subortum:** perfect participle of *suboriri.* 18. **oratorio:** from *oratorium, i* = "oratory," "chapel" (cf.
Niermeyer 743).

ut omnes pariter de vita tua desperare cogamur et quotidie ultimos illos de nece tua rumores trepidantia nostra corda et palpitantia pectora expectent.

Per ipsum itaque qui te sibi adhuc quoquo modo protegit Christum
5 obsecramus quatinus ancillulas ipsius et tuas crebris litteris de his in quibus adhuc fluctuas naufragiis certificare digneris ut nos saltem quae tibi solae remansimus doloris vel gaudii participes habeas. Solent etenim dolenti nonnullam afferre consolationem qui condolent et quodlibet onus pluribus impositum levius sustinetur sive defertur. Quod si paululum haec
10 tempestas quieverit, tanto amplius maturandae sunt litterae, quanto sunt iucundiores futurae. De quibuscumque autem nobis scribas, non parvum nobis remedium conferes hoc saltem uno quod te nostri memorem esse monstrabis. Quam iucundae vero sint absentium litterae amicorum ipse nos exemplo proprio Seneca docet ad amicum Lucilium loco sic scribens:

15 Quod frequenter mihi scribis gratias ago. Nam quo uno modo potes te mihi ostendis. Numquam epistolam tuam accipio quin protinus una simus. Si imagines nobis amicorum absentium iocundae sunt quae memoriam renovant et desiderium absentiae falso atque inani solatio levant quanto iocundiores sunt litterae quae amici absentis veras notas afferunt?

20 Deo autem gratias quod hoc saltem modo praesentiam tuam nobis reddere nulla invidia prohiberis, nulla difficultate praepediris, nulla, obsecro, negligentia retarderis.

Scripsisti ad amicum prolixae consolationem epistolae et pro adversitatibus quidem suis sed de tuis. Quas videlicet tuas diligenter commem-
25 orans cum eius intenderes consolationi nostrae plurimum addidisti desolationi et, dum eius mederi vulneribus cuperes, nova quaedam nobis vulnera doloris inflixisti et priora auxisti. Sana, obsecro, ipsa quae fecisti qui quae alii fecerunt curare satagis. Morem quidem amico et socio gessisti et tam amicitiae quam societatis debitum persolvisti. Sed maiori te

---

4. **quoquo modo** = CL *quoquomodo*. 5. **quatinus** = CL *quatenus,* here, as often in ML = *ut* + subjunctive *digneris* introducing a result clause (cf. Blaise 290). **ancillulas:** in CL *ancillula* = "young slave girl" but in ML = "virgin," thus, "nun" (Sleumer 107). 6. **certificare:** complement of *digneris* = "to declare" (Niermeyer 172). 7. **participes:** appositional to *nos* = "you have us, a participant of [your] joy and grief." 13. **quam . . . amicorum:** this indirect question is, along with *nos,* the object of *docet.* 14. **Lucilium:** Seneca wrote a series of letters to Lucilius; this is from *Ep.* 40.1. 24. **tuas:** i.e., *adversationes.* 27. **auxisti:** from *augere.* **sana:** imperative mood. **quae . . . quae:** the antecedent in both clauses is *vulnera.* 29. **te:** with *astrinxisti* = "you have joined yourself. . . ."

debito nobis astrinxisti quas non tam amicas quam amicissimas non tam socias quam fillias convenit nominari vel si quod dulcius et sanctius vocabulem potest excogitari.

Quanto autem debito te erga obligaveris non argumentis non testimoniis indiget ut quasi dubium comprobetur et si omnes taceant, res ipsa 5 clamat. Huius quippe loci tu post Deum solus es fundator, solus huius oratorii constructor, solus huius congregationis aedificator. Nihil hic super alienum aedificasti fundamentum. Totum quod hic est tua creatio est. Solitudo haec feris tantum sive latronibus vacans nullam hominum habitationem noverat, nullam domum habuerat. In ipsis cubilibus ferarum, 10 in ipsis latibulis latronum ubi nec nominari Deus solet, divinum erexisti tabernaculum et Spiritus Sancti proprium dedicasti templum. Nihil ad hoc aedificandum ex regum vel principum opibus intulisti cum plurima posses et maxima ut quicquid fieret tibi soli posset ascribi. Clerici sive scholares huc certatim ad disciplinam tuam confluentes omnia ministra- 15 bant necessaria. Et qui de beneficiis vivebant ecclesiasticis nec oblationes facere noverant sed suscipere et qui manus ad suscipiendum non ad dandum habuerant hic in oblationibus faciendis prodigi atque importuni fiebant.

Tua itaque vere tua haec est proprie in sancto proposito novella plan- 20 tatio cuius adhuc teneris maxime plantis frequens ut proficiant necessaria est irrigatio. Satis ex ipsa feminei sexus natura debilis est haec plantatio et infirma etiam si non esset nova. Unde diligentiorem culturam exigit et frequentiorem iuxta illud apostoli: "Ego plantavi, Apollo rigavit, Deus autem incrementum dedit." Plantaverat apostolus atque fundaverat in fide 25 per praedicationis suae doctrinam Corinthios quibus scribebat. Rigaverat postmodum eos ipsius apostoli discipulus Apollo sacris exhortationibus et sic eis incrementum virtutum divina largita est gratia. Vitis alienae vineam quam non plantasti in amaritudinem tibi conversam admonitionibus saepe cassis et sacris frustra sermonibus excolis. Quid tuae debeas 30 attende qui sic curam impendis alienae.

Doces et admones rebelles nec proficis. Frustra ante porcos divini eloquii margaritas spargis. Qui obstinatis tanta impendis quid obedientibus debeas considera. Qui tanta hostibus largiris quid filiabus debeas medi-

---

1. **quas:** the antecedent is *nobis;* Heloise, like Cicero, uses the "royal" we throughout this letter. 4. **erga:** *nos* is understood here. 24. **"Ego ... dedit":** the quotation comes from 1 Cor. 3.6. 27. **eos:** i.e., the Corinthians. **Apollo:** i.e., Apollos, the disciple of Saint Paul. 32. **frustra:** adverb. 34. **considera:** imperative mood, with the *quid* clause its object. **filiabus:** dative plural, as in CL.

tare. Atque ut ceteras omittam, quanto erga me te obligaveris debito pensa ut quod devotis communiter debes feminis unicae tuae devotius solvas.

Quot autem et quantos tractatus in doctrina vel exhortatione seu
5 etiam consolatione sanctarum feminarum sancti patres consummaverint et quanta eos diligentia composuerint, tua melius excellentia quam nostra parvitas novit. Unde non mediocri admiratione nostrae tenera conversationis initia tua iam dudum oblivio movit quod, nec reverentia Dei nec amore nostri nec sanctorum patrum exemplis admonitus, fluctuantem me
10 et iam diutino moerore confectam vel sermone praesentem vel epistola absentem consolari tentaveris. Cui quidem tanto te maiore debito noveris obligatum, quanto te amplius nuptialis foedere sacramenti constat esse astrictum et eo te magis mihi obnoxium, quo te semper ut omnibus patet immoderato amore complexa sum.
15 Nosti carissime, noverunt omnes quanta in te amiserim et quam miserabili casu summa et ubique nota proditio me ipsam quoque mihi tecum abstulerit ut incomparabiliter maior sit dolor ex amissionis modo quam ex damno. Quo vero maior est dolendi causa, maiora sunt consolationis adhibenda remedia non utique ab alio sed a teipso ut qui solus es in causa
20 dolendi solus sis in gratia consolandi. Solus quippe es qui me contristare, qui me laetificare seu consolari valeas. Et solus es qui plurimum id mihi debeas et nunc maxime cum universa quae iusseris in tantum impleverim ut cum te in aliquo offendere non possem me ipsam pro iussu tuo perdere sustinerem. Et quod maius est dictuque mirabile, in tantam versus est
25 amor insaniam ut quod solum appetebat, hoc ipse sibi sine spe recuperationis auferret, cum ad tuam statim iussionem tam habitum ipsa quam animum immutarem ut te tam corporis mei quam animi unicum possessorem ostenderem.

Nihil umquam, Deus scit, in te nisi te requisivi, te pure non tua con-

1. **atque . . . omittam**: lit., "and so that I might pass over all other things," i.e., "putting all else aside. . . ." 7. **non mediocri admiratione**: litotes; *admiratio* is used here in its less positive conotation of "surprise." 8. **oblivio**: in ML the feminine *oblivio, onis* = "forgetfulness" (Sleumer 557); modified here by *tua*. 10. **moerore** = CL *maeror, oris,* modified by *diutino*. 11. **noveris**: from *noscere,* with an infinitive clause here. 13. **astrictum**: from *astringere,* the verb in an infinitive clause dependent on *contsat.* **obnoxium**: the sense here is "bound" or "obliged" rather than something more negative. **eo . . . quo**: coordinating conjunctions, akin to *tanto . . . quanto* = "the . . . the. . . ." 15. **nosti**: syncopated form from *noscere.* 17. **abstulerit** = CL *attulerit,* from *afferre.* 19. **teipso** = *te* + *ipso,* an intensive form of the personal pronoun = "you yourself."

cupiscens. Non matrimonii foedera, non dotes aliquas expectavi, non denique meas voluptates aut voluntates sed tuas, sicut ipse nosti, adimplere studui.

—*Ep.* 2 (excerpts).

2. **adimplere:** "to fill" in the sense of "fulfill" here (cf. LS 36).

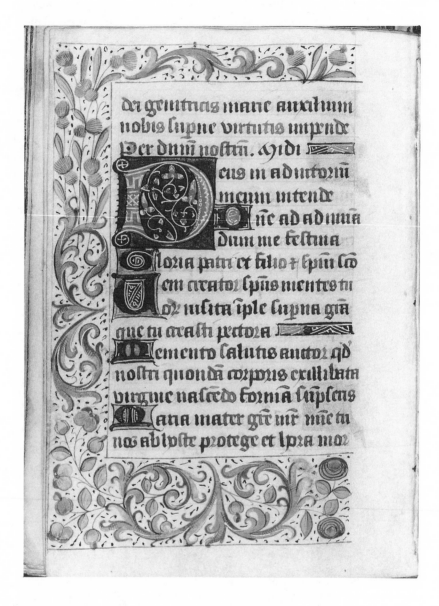

PLATE 25. A folio from a fifteenth-century Book of Hours, showing a decorated initial "D."

PLATE 25

Book of Hours
Latin and French manuscript on parchment, fifteenth century, fol. 45 verso
John Hay Library, Brown University

The Book of Hours from which this folio comes was produced in the fifteenth century and is written in both French and Latin. This folio shows the common lines used in the hours of the Virgin, and the decorated "D" announces the phrase *Deus in adiutorium meum intende.* The initial folios of the book give a calendar of liturgical observances (in French), followed (in Latin) by prayers, the epistles, the gospels, hymns to the Virgin, and psalms.

This folio has much marginal floreation in bright colors and is ruled in pencil. The decoration within the frame of the folio is colorful and dominated by deep hues. The manuscript is bound in wooden boards covered with stamped leather. It is 18 cm. in height and has 117 folios. (On this manuscript and the traditions informing it, see plate 24.)

GEOFFREY OF MONMOUTH

The History of the Kings of Britain
(*Historia regum Britannie;* c. 1138)

Although there are important traditions of historical writing in Germany, France, and (especially earlier) in Italy in the Latin Middle Ages, English historical prose developed in the twelfth century in unique ways. The most influential English historian was Bede (see pp. 179–84), a figure much esteemed, as we have seen, by one of his more important successors, William of Malmesbury. It was William, recall, who brought forward the traditions of historical inquiry and reporting best exemplified in Bede, even as he added certain features to his presentation more in line with contemporary historical writing in France and especially in Germany (see pp. 473–75). All the same, a further, more literary strain of historical prose developed in the twelfth century in England, which took Bede and William as models but made allowance for authorial creativity. This strain of historical prose might be called historical romance or novelistic history. Whatever it is called, however, it was practiced most vigorously by Geoffrey of Monmouth in his *Historia regum Britannie,* and with long-lasting influence.

Geoffrey's *Historia* falls into a larger body of Anglo-Norman writing, produced in the late eleventh century and throughout the twelfth, that aimed to reinvestigate the history of Anglo-Saxon England—still in the mid twelfth century a relatively new land to the Norman invaders. This was one of the main reasons, for example, that William of Malmesbury, not to mention another important Anglo-Latin historian, Henry of Huntingdon, both worked as continuators of Bede, meshing Bede's Anglo-Saxon material with later events and working to suggest the larger flow of English history from antiquity to contemporary times.

Geoffrey focused, however, not on continuing Bede, but rather on fleshing out the origins of the race of people whose island the Normans had taken over. Much of his account in the *Historia* deals precisely with the Roman and Trojan origins of King Arthur and other earlier British leaders, as our excerpts from the *Historia* suggest. Geoffrey relied in this project as much on histories such as Gildas's *De excidio et conquestu Britonum,* which preceded Bede's *Historia,* as on compilations such as

Nennius's *Historia Britonum,* which, while later than Bede, also presumably included material culled from sources or traditions prior to him.

Apart from the aim of increasing the contemporary Anglo-Norman prestige by glorifying its ancient bases, Geoffrey also took up a strain of inquiry he had worked on earlier—magic and prophecy. His first work had focused directly on this topic and the *Prophetie Merlini,* which Geoffrey claimed was a translation from Anglo-Saxon of the prophecies delivered to King Vortigern by the magician Merlin, eventually found its way into the *Historia* itself. When that larger work was completed, some time around 1138, the prophecies and life of Merlin formed the concluding sections, to which was appended the declaration of Geoffrey that his work was a translation of an earlier historical work written in "the British language," a declaration with which the work had begun also (cf. sections 2, 208).

This assertion is a commonplace—and cannot be proven one way or the other at the present time. Less difficult to ascertain are the aims and affinities of Geoffrey's project. In two ways, Geoffrey works within the broad tradition of historical prose writing already in place in Germany and France: viz., in his tendency to focus on powerful individuals and in his willingness to construct his story along the lines of his own powers of vision and voice. This becomes especially apparent as the *Historia* concludes. There, as the life of Merlin winds down, one becomes aware of the symbolic and perhaps even allegorical role of Merlin as the talented individual, able to weave magic, to create, to influence events and people. Just the same, Merlin's life evanesces into those themes it comes to best represent: solidity of purpose and character, erudition, the fundamental attractions of friendship, the potency of power in all its versions—magical, prophetic, or in terms of personality. One senses Geoffrey as much as Merlin in these lines, a sense that ratifies a new level of artistic involvement in the construction of national history.

At the same time, too, that construction involves a simple and clear Latinity, whose stumbling blocks really are ethnographic, not grammatical. There are many exotic place names, figures, and objects designated in the *Historia,* and for these Geoffrey relies on the adaptations already in place in Latin vocabulary, but also on his own ability to stretch the language at points to suit his purposes. The words for North and South Wales, for example—*Vendotia, ae* and *Demetia, ae*—demonstrate this tendency, as does the reporting of Old Norse directly, when Latin simply will not do, in the phrases "*Drincheil*" and "*Waesseil.*" But in general

Geoffrey's Latin reflects in its structure and syntax the feature of ML prose most generally praised: its direct simplicity.

The date of Geoffrey's birth is unknown. He may have been of Breton origin, and he clearly seems to have been associated with Monmouth, since he styles himself of this place at several points in his works. He was born no earlier than the last decade of the eleventh century, perhaps in Monmouth. We know that Geoffrey was in Oxford by the early 1130s, teaching and writing. The *Historia* was completed by the end of this decade. Geoffrey continued on in Oxford for some time, working in a small group of important and influential churchmen and nobles, including Alexander of Lincoln and Walter of Oxford. Near the end of his life, Geoffrey took up the bishopric of St. Asaph, in Wales, although it is considered doubtful that he actually traveled to his bishopric personally. It is reported that Geoffrey died in 1155, though this is not conclusively known.

The standard text of the *Historia regum Britannie,* called the Vulgate, is currently being reedited, a monumental task given the number of manuscripts and their vexed history. The work has been edited by E. Faral (*La légende arthurienne: Études et documents,* 3 vols., Paris, 1929, vol. 3), A. Griscom and R. E. Jones (*The Historia Regum Britanniae of Geoffrey of Monmouth with Contributions to the Study of Its Place in Early British History Together with a Literal Translation of the Welsh Manuscript No. LXI of Jesus College Oxford,* London, 1929), and N. Wright (*The Historia Regum Britannie of Geoffrey of Monmouth I: Bern, Burgerbibliothek, MS. 568,* Cambridge, 1985). In 1951 Jacob Hammer published his variant edition of the *Historia,* based on a family of manuscripts that sometimes give readings substantially different from those of the Vulgate (*Geoffrey of Monmouth: Historia Regum Britanniae: A Variant Version Edited from Manuscripts,* Cambridge, Mass., 1951); this family has recently been reedited by N. Wright (*The Historia Regum Britannie of Geoffrey of Monmouth II: The First Variant Version: A Critical Edition,* Cambridge, 1988). Wright's interim edition of the Vulgate and his new edition of the variant version both have substantive introductions, notes, and bibliographies that treat fully the issues attending to Geoffrey's text. The *Historia* has been translated by L. Thorpe (*Geoffrey of Monmouth, History of the Kings of Britain,* Harmondsworth, 1966). M. J. Curley surveys Geoffrey's life and work, with relevant bibliography (*Geoffrey of Monmouth,* in Twayne's English Authors Series, New York, 1994). Wright's Vulgate text is reprinted here, with a few minor punctuation changes and "u" and "v" distinguished.

The Beginning of "Waesseil" in England

Interea vero reversi sunt nuntii ex Germania conduxerantque .x. et
.viii. naves electis militibus plenas. Conduxerunt etiam filiam Hengisti
vocabulo Renwein cuius pulcritudo nulli secunda videbatur. Postquam
autem venerunt, invitavit Hengistus Vortegirnum regem in domum suam
[u]t novum edificium et novos milites qui applicuerant videret. Venit ilico   5
rex privatim et laudavit tam subitum opus et milites invitatos retinuit. Ut
ergo regiis epulis refectus fuit, egressa est puella de thalamo aureum ciphum plenum vino ferens. Accedens deinde propius regi flexis genibus
dixit: "Lauerd king, Waesseil!" At ille, visa facie puelle, ammiratus est
tantum eius decorem et incaluit. Denique interrogavit interpretem suum   10
quid dixerat puella et quid ei respondere debeat. Cui interpres dixit: "Vocavit te dominum regem et vocabulo salutationis honoravit. Quod autem
respondere debes, est 'Drincheil.'" Respondens deinde Vortegirnus
"Drincheil" iussit puellam potare cepitque ciphum de manu ipsius et osculatus est eam et potavit. Ab illo die usque in hodiernum mansit consue-   15
tudo illa in Britannia quia in conviviis qui potat ad alium dicit "Waesseil."
Qui vero post illum recipit potum, respondet "Drincheil." Vortegirnus
autem diverso genere potus inhebriatus intrante Sathana in corde suo,
[amavit puellam, et postulavit eam a patre suo. Intraverat, inquam, Sathanas in corde suo] quia, cum Christianus esset, cum pagana coire desidera-   20
bat. Hengistus ilico, ut erat prudens, comperta levitate animi regis con-

---

2. **electis militibus:** i.e., the Jutes, who were invited by King Vortigern to come from
Scandinavia to England to help him fight the Picts (from Scotland), sometime in the
fourth century. **Hengisti . . . Renwein:** *Hengistus, i* = Hengist, a prince of the Jutes,
who is also on this voyage, with, as this line suggests, his beautiful daughter, Renwein,
whose name is otherwise indeclinable (neither name is given in Latham). 4. **Vortegirnum:** *Vortegirunus, i* = Vortigern, a legendary British king whose career was generally
seen as disastrous for the native Britons, since he invited in the Jutes as mercenaries,
and they never left (the name is not given in Latham). 5. **edificium** = CL *aedificium.*
7. **ciphum:** the better spelling is *scyphum*, from *scyphus, i* = "bowl," "goblet," "cup"
(Latham 427). 8. **genibus:** from *genus, genus.* 9. **Waesseil:** lit., "be in good
health" (= Old Norse *ves* or *ver heill;* cf. Anglo-Saxon *was hál,* Middle English *waes
haeil* and, for more on these forms, OED, s. v. *wassail*). The numerous MSS of the
Historia record many different spellings for this word. **ammiratus est** = CL *admiratus est.* 10. **incaluit:** from *incalescere,* used here in the sense of becoming passionate
or, literally, "hot with passion." 13. **"Drincheil":** "drink good health," or "good
luck" (= Old Norse *drinc heill;* cf. Middle English *drinc hail* and, on the forms OED,
s. v. *Drinkhail*). 18. **inhebriatus** = CL *inebriatus;* the addition of aspirates in ML
orthography is common. **Sathana:** the better spelling is *Satana,* from *Satanas, ae,*
masculine noun of the first declension = "Satan" (Sleumer 699, s. v. *satan* and *satanas*).

suluit fratrem suum Horsum ceterosque maiores natu qui secum aderant quid de peticione regis facerent. Sed omnibus unum consilium fuit ut puella regi daretur et ut peterent pro ea provinciam Cantie ab illo. Nec mora data fuit puella Vortegirno et provincia Cantie Hengisto nesciente
5 Gorangono comite qui in eadem regnabat. Nupsit itaque rex eadem nocte pagane que ultra modum placuit ei; unde inimicitiam procerum et filiorum suorum citissime incidit. Generaverat nanque filios primitus quibus erant nomina Vortimer, Katigernus, Paschent.

—*Gest. Reg. Brit.* 100.

THE CORONATION OF KING ARTHUR

Omnibus igitur in urbe congregatis sollennitate instante archipresules ad palatium ducuntur ut regem diademate regali coronent. Dubricius ergo, quoniam in sua diocesi curia tenebatur, paratus ad celebrandum obsequium huius rei curam suscepit. Rege tandem insignito, ad templum
5 metropolitane sedis ordinate conducitur. A dextro enim et a levo latere duo archipontifices ipsum tenebant. Quatuor autem reges, Albanie videlicet atque Cornubie, Demetie et Venedotie, quorum ius id fuerat, quatuor aureos gladios ferentes ante illum preibant. Conventus quoque multimodorum coronatorum miris modulationibus precinebat. Ex alia autem

1. **Horsum:** i.e., Horsa, who was the brother of Hengist, from *Horsus, i.* 2. **peticione** = CL *petitione,* i.e., the request for Renwein's hand in marriage to King Vortigern. 3. **Cantie** = *Cantiae,* from *Cantia, ae,* = Kent (Sleumer 186). 5. **Gorangono:** Gorangonus, King of Kent. 6. **pagane** = CL *paganae.* **que** = CL *quae.* 7. **nanque** = CL *namque.*

1. **sollennitate:** from *solemnitas, atis* = "solemn service" (Latham 443, s. v. *solemne—itas*). **archipresules:** from *archipresul, ulis* = "archbishop" (Latham 28). 2. **Dubricius:** *Dubricius, i* = Dubricius, archbishop of the City of the Legions, who crowned Arthur, according to the legend recounted here, at Silchester; Arthur's grandfather had been crowned in the same city in his time (Curley 79). 4. **templum:** i.e., *ecclesia.* 5. **metropolitane** = *metropolitanae,* from *metropolitanus, a, um* = "metropolitan," modifies *sedis* (cf. Niermeyer 676). The phrase *"metropolitane sedis ordinate"* is periphrastic for *archipresul.* **sedis:** i.e., "episcopal see" (cf. the variety of meanings attending to this important EL word in Niermeyer 952–54). **ordinate** = CL *ordinatae.* **conducitur:** in CL the subject of an ablative absolute, here *rex,* would never also be the subject of the main clause, as happens here. This is common in ML, however; § 3.3.4 (cf. Blaise 114). **levo** = CL *laevo.* 6. **archipontifices:** from *archipontifex, archipontifices* = "archbishop" (Latham 28). **Albanie** = *Albaniae,* from *Albania, ae* = Albany (cf. Curley 86). 7. **Cornubie** = *Cornubiae,* from *Cornubia, ae* = Cornwall (Sleumer 245). **Demetie** = *Demetiae,* from *Demetia, ae* = South Wales (also called *Dyfed;* Curley 86). **Venedotie** = *Venedotiae,* from *Vendotia, ae* = North Wales (Curley 86). 8. **preibant** = CL *praeibant,* from *praeire.* 9. **modulationibus:** from *modulatio, onis* = "melodies," "singing" (Niermeyer 700). **precinebat** = CL *praecinebat.*

parte reginam suis insignibus laureatam archypresules atque pontifices
ad templum dedicatarum puellarum conducebant. Quatuor quoque pre-
dictorum regum regine quatuor albas columbas more preferebant. Mulieres omnes que aderant illam cum maximo gaudio sequebantur. Postremo peracta processione tot organa tot cantus in utrisque fiunt templis   5
ita ut pre nimia dulcedine milites qui aderant nescirent quod templorum
prius peterent. Catervatim ergo nunc ad hoc, nunc ad illud ruebant nec si
totus dies celebrationi [adesset], tedium aliquod ipsis generaret. Divinis
tandem obsequiis in utroque celebratis rex et regina diademata sua deponunt assumptisque levioribus ornamentis ipse ad suum palacium cum   10
viris, ipsa ad aliud cum mulieribus epulatum incedunt. Antiquam nanque
consuetudinem Troie servantes Britones consueverant mares cum mari-
bus, mulieres cum mulieribus festivos dies separatim celebrare. Collocatis
postmodum cunctis [ut dignitas] singulorum expetebat [K]aius dapifer
herminio ornatus, mille vero nobilibus comitatus, qui omnes herminio   15
induti fercula cum ipso ministrabant. Ex alia vero parte Bedverum pincernam vario totidem amicti secuntur qui in cyphis diversorum generum
multimoda pocula cum ipso distribuebant. In palatio quoque regine innumerabiles ministri diversis ornamentis induti obsequium suum prestabant morem suum exercentes. Quem si omnino describere pergerem, nim-   20
iam prolixitatem historie generarem. Ad tantum etenim statum dignitatis
Britannia tunc reducta erat quod co[pi]a diviciarum, luxu ornamen-
torum, facecia incolarum cetera regna excellebat. Quicunque vero famo-
sus probitate miles in eadem erat unius coloris vestibus atque armis uteba-
tur. Facete etiam mulieres consimilia indumenta habentes nullius amorem   25
habere dignabantur nisi tertio in milicia probatus esset. Efficiebantur ergo
caste et meliores et milites pro amore illarum probiores.

---

2. **dedicatarum puellarum:** i.e., "girls dedicated to virginity." 3. **regine** = CL *reginae.* 5. **organa:** i.e., musical instruments. 6. **pre** = CL *prae.* **quod** = CL *quid,*
with *templorum.* 8. **tedium** = CL *taedium.* 10. **palacium** = CL *palatium.*
12. **Troie** = CL *Troiae,* from *Troia, ae.* 14. **[K]aius:** *Kaius, i,* = Caius, the court
steward. **dapifer:** from *dapifer, eri* = "steward" (Niermeyer 301). 15. **herminio:** or
erminio, from *erminium, i* = "ermine" (Latham 169). 16. **Bedverum:** *Bedverus, i* =
Bedevere, Arthur's cupbearer (Curley 83). 17. **secuntur** = CL *sequntur.* 21. **prolixitatem:** from *prolixitas, atis* = "long-windedness" (Latham 376, s. v. *prolix/ia—
itas*). **historie** = CL *historiae.* 22. **diviciarum** = CL *divitiarum.* 23. **facecia** =
CL *facetia;* in ML this stands in the singular as well as in the plural; in CL it is in
the plural only. **cetera . . . excellebat:** this is properly a result clause with the indicative, as often in ML (cf. Blaise 291). 26. **milicia** = CL *milita.* 27. **caste** = CL
castae.

THE CORONATION GAMES AND SPORTS

Ut tandem epulis peractis diversi diversos ludos composituri campos
extra civitatem adeunt, mox milites simulachrum prelii sciendo eques-
trem ludum componunt; mulieres in edito murorum aspicientes in furiales
amores flammas ioci more irritant. Alii cum cestibus, alii cum celtibus,
5 alii cum hasta, alii ponderosorum lapidum iactu, alii cum scaccis, alii cum
aleis ceterorumque iocorum diversitate contendentes quod diei restabat
postposita lite pretereunt. Quicunque ergo victoriam ludi sui adeptus erat
ab Arturo largis muneribus ditabatur. Consumptis ergo primis in hunc
modum tribus diebus instante quarta vocantur cuncti qui ei propter hon-
10 ores obsequium prestabant et singuli singulis possessionibus, civitatibus
videlicet atque castellis, archiepiscopatibus, episcopatibus, abbaciis, ceterisque honoribus donantur.

—*Hist. Reg. Brit.* 157.

2. **simulachrum:** the better spelling is *simulacrum*. **prelii** = CL *proelii*. 4. **cestibus** = CL *caestibus*. **celtibus:** from *celtis, is* = "chisel" (Habel/Gröbel 55).
5. **scaccis:** from *scacci, orum,* generally in the plural only = "chessmen," by metonymy = "chess" (Latham 421). 8. **Arturo:** from *Arturus, i* = King Arthur. 11. **archiepiscopatibus:** from *archiepiscopatus, us,* fourth declension noun, which can designate both physical objects, such as metropolitan cathedrals, and also the abstract
power of an archbishop; the latter is probably meant here, in the sense of holding
an office (Niermeyer 56–57). **episcopatibus:** from *episcopatus, us,* fourth declension
noun = "episcopal cathedral" or "power of a bishop," "bishopric," etc. (cf. Niermeyer
375–76). **abbaciis:** better spelled *abbatiis,* from *abbatia, ae* = "power of abbots,"
"abbotships," etc. (cf. Niermeyer 1–3 for the various meanings of this important EL
word).

ADAM OF ST. VICTOR

Sequences on Christ
(*In resurrectione Domini; In ascensione Domini;* c. 1145)

In the Roman liturgy in the Latin Middle Ages, two chants—the Gradual and the Alleluia—occurred between the reading of the Epistle and the reading of the Gospel. In particular, in the chanting of the Alleluia, the prolongation of the final *a* sound developed, to be called by a special name, the *Jubilus*. By the late ninth century, the *Jubilus* had been further expanded from complicated musical patternings to include prose narratives set to the *Jubilus*'s musical variations. These prose narratives are called sequences, one of the more important literary forms of the Latin Middle Ages.

The most important early practitioner of the sequence form was Notker Balbulus of St. Gall (see pp. 300–306), who set many prose narratives to the musical varieties encouraged by the *Jubilus*. After Notker, Ekkehard I of St. Gall and Wipo (associated with the courts of Kings Conrad II and Henry III of Germany), among others, had a hand in ensuring the continued use and slow development of the sequence. It was not until the twelfth century, however, that the mature form of the sequence, the development of the so-called regular sequence, occurred. No one is more important to that development than Adam of St. Victor.

Virtually nothing is known of Adam's life. He was born around 1112, perhaps in England, but probably in Brittany. He became associated with the Augustinian monastery at St. Victor, in Paris, in the early 1130s, though the details of that association are lacking. He was presumably well trained before he arrived, but the intellectual atmosphere at St. Victor must have proven all the more stimulating, for we know that Adam had as associates there two other famous intellectuals of the twelfth century, Hugh and Richard. Both these thinkers are important philosophers in their own right, who articulated mystical and allegorical Christian cosmologies, heralding the rise in the twelfth century of Platonic conceptions of the universe that have come to be grouped under the rubric of Christian Platonism and Chartrian humanism.

Although mysticism is an important ingredient in his work, the sequences of Adam are not projects in mystical cosmology. Adam's concerns are always more temporal and corporal—the ruinous flirtations of

Christians with the flesh, the separation of humanity from the perfections of Christ, the weakness of the soul, the human longing for Christ's love and redemption. The vision of Adam's poetry is always well grounded in a discrete time, place, and situation; one is always looking up toward, seeking, God. The fallenness of humanity is implicit in virtually every sequence he wrote.

Difficulty has always surrounded the attribution to Adam of those sequences associated with him by tradition. There are about fifty such sequences, but several are clearly not his and others are not unproblematically ascribed to him. Clearly Adam wrote sequences, and clearly St. Victor was a locale in which the so-called regular sequence was more fully developed. We can perhaps more easily speak of Victorine sequences, but when we do we are surely talking about Adam more than anyone else.

The most important developmental feature of Adam's work is the linking in his sequences of natural word accent and rhyme to the principles of accentual metrics. This appropriation of rules of meter literally "regularized" these sequences—hence the name regular sequence. The earliest sequences, recall, were simply prose pieces set to preexisting melodies of the *Jubilus*. Adam's sequences were now formally poetic and were written to continue for the whole of the *Jubilus*, not just parts of it.

More specifically, his sequences combed the full resources of Latin, bringing together natural word accent into trochaic lines of a set number of syllables (usually, but not always, seven and eight syllables), with regular caesura at the end of the fourth foot and always occurring at the end of a word. The first sequence reprinted here exploits these basic tenets. In this tour de force of sequential rhythms, Adam presents variations of accentual possibilities from strophe to strophe. The complexity and variety of these possibilities can be gleaned from a brief examination of strophe one:

> Salve, dies, dierum gloria,
> Dies felix
>   Christi victoria
> Dies digna iugi laetitia,
>   Dies prima.

Here, the first and fourth lines have ten syllables each, with caesura after the fourth syllable; while the second and third lines, which together have ten syllables, contain, respectively, four and six syllables; and the last line contains four syllables. Other strophes present other combinations.

Syllabification, which connects the first and fourth lines, is confirmed by rhyme, but the use of an end-rhyming "a" in the third and fifth lines connects them also to their longer counterparts.

These sorts of complications, with modulations of sound and vocabulary, meter and structure, make Adam's work and the traditions of the Victorine sequences of the first moment in the development of ML poetry. More traditional is the second sequence here, all of whose sixteen strophes contain two eight-syllable lines followed by a concluding seven-syllable line—the normal configuration for the regular sequence. The caesura is after the fourth foot in the first two lines of each strophe, corresponding strictly to word-ending, with these two lines connected also by rhyme, which is always different from the concluding line of each strophe:

> Postquam hostem et inferna
> Spoliavit, ad superna
> Christus redit gaudia.

The sequences of Adam have been edited in a number of venues but are best had in vol. 54 of the *Analecta Hymnica* (C. Blume and H. M. Bannister, eds., *Liturgische Prosen des Übergangsstiles und der zweiten Epoche insbesondere die dem Adam von Sanct Victor*, Leipzig, 1915). An overview of Christian Latin hymnody has been written by J. Szövérffy (*A Concise History of Medieval Latin Hymnody: Religious Lyrics between Antiquity and Humanism*, in Medieval Classics: Texts and Studies, vol. 19, Leiden, 1985); his *Latin Hymns* (Turnhout, 1989) is a guide to research. Raby 1, 344–75, is a thorough discussion of Adam and the Victorine school also. The text of Blume and Bannister from the *Analecta Hymnica*, vol. 54, pp. 222, 231–32, is reprinted here. In the second selection, at strophe 6.1, *moriturus* is read for *morituros*.

Sequence on the Resurrection of the Lord

1. Salve, dies, dierum gloria,	2. Lux divina caelis irradiat,
Dies felix	In qua Christus
Christi victoria	infernum spoliat,
Dies digna iugi laetitia,	Mortem vincit et reconciliat
5 Dies prima.	Summis ima. 10

---

6. **caelis:** ablative of source without a preposition (cf. Blaise 107). 8. **infernum:** i.e., Hell.

3. Sempiterni regis sententia
Sub peccato conclusit omnia,
Ut infirmis
   superna gratia
15   Subveniret;
4. Dei virtus et sapientia
Temperavit iram clementia,
Cum iam mundus
   in praecipitia
20   Totus iret.
5. Insultabat
   nostrae miseriae
Vetus hostis,
   auctor malitiae,
25 Quia nulla spes erat veniae
   De peccatis.
6. Desperante
mundo remedium
Dum tenerent
30   cuncta silentium
Deus pater emisit filium
   Desperatis.
7. Praedo vorax,
   monstrum tartareum,
35 Carnem videns,
   non cavens laqueum,
In latentem ruens aculeum
   Aduncatur.

8. Dignitatis
   primae condicio   40
Reformatur
   nobis in filio,
Cuius nova nos resurrectio
   Consolatur.
9. Resurrexit   45
   liber ad inferis
Restaurator
   humani generis
Ovem suam
   reportans umeris   50
   Ad superna.
10. Angelorum
   pax fit et hominum,
Plenitudo
   succrescit ordinum;   55
Triumphantem
   laus decet Dominum,
   Laus aeterna.
11. Harmoniae caelestis patriae
Vox concordet   60
   matris ecclesiae,
Alleluia frequentet hodie
   Plebs fidelis.
12. Triumphato mortis imperio
Triumphali   65
   fruamur gaudio
In terra pax et iubilatio
   Sit in caelis.
                —*Anal. Hym.* 146.

---

20. **iret:** imperfect active subjunctive, third person singular of *ire*, with *cum*. 21. **in-sultabat** + dative object; the subject is *auctor malitiae*, i.e., Satan. 38. **aduncatur:** from *aduncare* = "to bend," "to curve" (Niermeyer 24). 40. **condicio** = CL *conditio*. 47. **Restaurator:** from *restaurator, oris* = Christ (Blaise/Chirat 719). 50. **umeris:** from *umerus, i*.

Sequence on the Ascension of the Lord

1. Postquam hostem et inferna
Spoliavit, ad superna
   Christus redit gaudia.
2. Angelorum ascendenti
Sicut olim descendenti
   Parantur obsequia.
3. Super astra sublimatur,
Non apparet, absentatur
   Corporis praesentia;
4. Cuncta tamen moderatur,
Cuius patri coaequatur
   Honor et potentia.
5. Modo victor, modo tutus
Est in caelis constitutus
   Rector super omnia;
6. Non est rursum moriturus
Nec per mortem mundaturus
   Hominum contagia.
7. Semel enim incarnatus,
Semel passus, semel datus
   Pro peccatis hostia,
8. Nullam feret ultra poenam,
Nam quietem habet plenam
   Cum summa laetitia.

9. Cum recessit, ita dixit,   25
Intimavit et infixit
   Talia discipulis:
10. "Ite, mundum circuite,
Universos erudite
   Verbis et miraculis.   30
11. Iam ad patrem meum ibo
Sed sciatis, quod redibo,
   Veniet paraclitus,
12. Qui disertos et loquaces
Et securos et audaces   35
   Faciet vos penitus.
13. Super aegros et languentes
Manus vestras imponentes
   Sanitatem dabitis.
14. Universas res nocentes,   40
Inimicos et serpentes
   Et morbos fugabitis.
15. Qui fidelis est futurus
Et cum fide suscepturus
   Baptismi remedium,   45
16. A peccatis erit purus
Et cum iustis habiturus
   Sempiternum praemium."
           —*Anal. Hym.* 151.

2. **spoliavit:** the reference is to the harrowing of Hell. 4. **ascendenti:** in ML *ascendens* is a substantive designating consanguinity (Niermeyer 62; cf. CL usage also [LS 171, s. v. *ascendo—ascendens* B]), but here meaning something more like "ascent," it is the dative object of *parantur,* with dependent *angelorum.* 5. **descendenti:** in CL and ML *descendens* has the primary meaning of "descendent" but here means "descent" (cf. LS 554–55, s. v. *descendere—descendens*), parallel with *ascendenti.* 6. **obsequia:** from *obsequium, i* = "service"; on the many meanings of this word in ML, see Niermeyer 729–30. 22. **ultra:** adverb.

PLATE 26. The opening folio from an anonymous life of Christ, written in French.

PLATE 26

Anonymous, *Vie de Jesus Christ*
French manuscript on paper, around 1450, fol. 1 recto
John Hay Library, Brown University

Lives of Christ were common in the Middle Ages and circulated widely both in Latin and in the vernacular languages. This folio comes from a prose life of Christ written in French but translated from a Latin exemplar around 1450. The title given to this manuscript, *Vie de Jesus Christ*, is supplied by a later hand. This folio well represents the others of the manuscript, written clearly in black ink in a distinctive hand with strong downstrokes. The capital is in red, with some pen-work flourishes. Chapter and section headings are rubricated by another hand. The manuscript is numbered in the old Roman style. The margins and lines are not visibly ruled. There are worm holes in the first and last leaves, and the last twenty leaves have a small burn hole in them, about 0.5 cm. in width. The manuscript is 30 cm. in height and has 221 folios.

Nivardus

Ysengrimus
(*Ysengrimus;* c. 1148)

In the middle of the eleventh century, an otherwise unknown poet wrote a mock epic about a calf who escaped from his stall and was captured by a wolf, only to be rescued after spending a terrifying night in the wolf's cave not knowing from one moment to the next if or when he would be eaten. In the end, the wolf was captured and hanged and the calf went on to a happy life. The competition of the calf and the wolf, and the allegory by which the calf was to be seen as a monk, formed the crux of the so-called *Ecbasis captivi*, whose composition marks the beginning of beast poetry in ML, one of the more important genres of poetry in the Latin Middle Ages.

Beast poetry gained wide currency in the century after the *Ecbasis captivi*, all the more as poets were able to bring to maturity strategies of allegory in order to criticize contemporary culture. Indeed, owing to the ways in which culture criticism, wit, linguistic playfulness, and comedy coalesce in beast poetry, it is perhaps fair to say that no other genre of writing is more typical of the Latin Middle Ages. Beast poetry is not, to be sure, a medieval invention, for there are beast poems from antiquity and an attention to personifying animals throughout the Western literary tradition. Yet the Latin Middle Ages perfected the genre as such, and perhaps never more than in the hands of Nivardus, the twelfth-century poet to whose creativity is owed the *Ysengrimus,* the longest beast poem of the Latin Middle Ages.

The length of Nivardus's poem (seven books; 3,287 elegiac couplets) affords its readers plenty of opportunity to perceive the work's virtues. Chief among them—apart from the engaging plot lines that involve the archcompetitors Ysengrimus the wolf and Reynard the fox—is the poem's unique Latinity. One is aware in a profound way of having entered a new literary world upon reading Nivardus's lines. The poem offers a mixture of Latinities. CL standards predominate: there are plenty of CL idioms and the normal constructions one associates with the older version of the language (including the use of archaisms, and rare forms such as *redies*). But Nivardus also relies on VL, especially in the dialogues he reports in direct quotation. Those dialogues can be straightforward or obscure, as need be, but they are framed by constructions that lead to a difficulty of reading and interpretation: heavy use of the subjunctive mood, ellipses, widespread use of deponent verbs and of verbal forms that tend to confuse (imperatives of deponents, alternate forms of verbs, etc.). Nivardus also fully exploits the hypotactic and paratactic potentials of Latin.

Perhaps more subtle is Nivardus's talent for constructing narratives whose style is reflective of sense. There is a careful relationship between the larger moral element which forms much of the poem's didactic aim, and the Latin style used to express it. When Ysengrimus is dissembling, his sentences are obscure, choppy, difficult—and so, too, when Reynard is being disingenuous. But when Ysengrimus is at wit's end, when the stakes are clear and not to be clearer, he can express himself in a Latin as direct, and as funny, as anything ever written in the language. When Reynard is chiding Ysengrimus, for example (see vv. 885ff.), for not getting up quickly enough (knowing full well that Ysengrimus cannot get up because his tail is frozen into the ice), Ysengrimus comes back at him with these words, perfect in terms of tone and fully exploitative of the strengths of the elegiac couplet:

> Captus ad hec captor: "nescis, quid, perfide, dicas,
> Clunibus impendet Scotia tota meis."

> And the prisoner said this to his captor: "You don't know what you're saying, sneak, the whole of Scotland is hanging from my ass."

We know next to nothing about Nivardus as a historical figure, except that he hailed from Ghent and that he completed his poem in 1148 or 1149. Nivardus is clearly engaging a full and varied tradition of beast poetry in *Ysengrimus,* and he adds to that tradition by giving names to his main characters, thus inaugurating with the name Reynardus the long tradition of so-called Reynard epics that eventually were written in the vernacular languages of western Europe, including the French *Roman de Renart,* the Dutch *Van den Vos Reynaerde* and *Reinaerts Historie,* and the Low German *Reynke de Vos.*

Nivardus's text has been edited by E. Voigt (*Ysengrimus,* Halle, 1884, which contains full notes, a glossary, and introduction), and by J. Mann (*Ysengrimus: Text, with Translation, Commentary, and Introduction,* in Mittellateinische Studien und Texte 12, Leiden, 1987, with excellent notes, grammatical and orthographical sections, and introduction). N. F. Blake has surveyed the tradition of Reynard tales (*The History of Reynard the Fox,* Oxford, 1970), as has T. W. Best (*Reynard the Fox,* Boston,

1983, though with very little on the *Ysengrimus* itself); J. Ziolkowski has surveyed beast poetry in general in the Medieval Latin tradition, with a chapter on *Ysengrimus* (*Talking Animals: Medieval Latin Beast Poetry 750–1150*, Philadelphia, 1993). See also Raby 2, vol. 2, 151ff.

The *Ysengrimus* is divided in Voigt's edition into seven books and features twelve stories involving the fox and the wolf (some scholars hold that there are actually fourteen tales, based on a different set of assumptions in reading them). In the excerpts (from Book 1), Reynard has just been cheated by Ysengrimus of a ham and is determined to get even. He meets up with the wolf in the dead of winter and conspires to trick him into ice-fishing with his tail, planning all the while to immobilize his foe, after which time he will lead an angry mob of townsfolk against him. These lines recount the details of Reynard's scheme. The text is Mann's improvement of Voigt, reprinted with "u" and "v" distinguished.

Reynard Takes Ysengrimus Fishing

Venerat ergo dies vindicte lectus, uterque
Hostis agens hosti, non temere actus, obit.
Visa vulpe senex hilaris concinnat inanes
Blanditias, blesa calliditate loquens:
5   "Tempore felici venias, cognate! quid affers?
Nunc, si quid dederis, partior absque dolo."
Cui vulpes: "refer ergo fidem, que, patrue, primam
Divisit, tibi si perna secunda placet.

—*Yseng. 529–36.*

1. **vindicte** = CL *vindictae*. **lectus:** from *legere*, modifying *dies*. **uterque hostis:** i.e., the fox, Reynard, and the wolf, Ysengrimus. 2. **non temere actus:** periphrastic construction with adverbial force, lit., "not having done it carelessly," i.e., "thoughtfully." **agens hosti . . . obit:** ellipsis for *quod ageretur hosti obit*, i.e., each one was considering what he might do to the other. . . ." 3. **vulpe:** Reynard. **senex hilaris:** Ysengrimus, the wolf; he is happy because he got the better of Reynard in a previous encounter, in which a ham, procured mostly through the good efforts of the fox, was devoured by Ysengrimus before Reynard could claim his share. 4. **blesa** = CL *blaesa*. 5. **cognate:** vocative, meaning something like "relative," but perhaps best translated as "nephew," since Reynard often likes to call Ysengrimus "uncle" (*patrue*). **quid affers:** referring, sarcastically, to their previous encounter in which the fox lost his share of a ham. 6. **si quid:** note the CL idiom in which *quid* after *si, nisi, num,* or *ne* becomes indefinite. **absque dolo:** lit., "apart from deceit," i.e., "without trickery"—the trickery by which Reynard had been cheated out of the ham by Ysengrimus. 7. **que** = CL *quae*. **patrue:** vocative, "uncle," the term for Ysengrimus used commonly by Reynard.

Et nunc divideres socialiter? immo videtur,
  Ne pecces iterum, res facienda secus.
Non prohibet pisces tibi regula, tuque fuisti
  Monachus, et non est semper edenda caro;
Fac dapibus licitis insanum assuescere ventrem,
  Cuius ob ingluviem noxia nulla times.

—vv. 553–58.

Omne malum vice nemo mala nisi pessimus equat,
  Ergo, ne pereas, consiliabor item.
Piscibus innumeris vivaria subdita novi;
  Emoritur stricto plurima turba vado.

—vv. 597–600.

"Sit quamvis in ventre tuo tam creber et amplus
  Angulus, es numquam vel satiandus ibi."
Ille reclamat ovans: "furimus, Reinarde? quid istic
  Figimur? accelera! mors, nisi piscer, adest!
Vis vivam, in pisces age me, carnem abdico prorsus.
  Tu prisci sceleris ne meminisse velis.

—vv. 605–10.

Et veterem patruum capiendis piscibus induc."
  Precedit vulpes subsequiturque lupus;

—vv. 615–16.

Moverat algorem Februi violentia, quantus
  Stringere Danubias sufficiebat aquas.
Nacta locum vulpes dixit: "Sta, patrue dulcis,"

10

15

20

25

9. **divideres:** i.e., Ysengrimus will divide up fairly whatever the pair finds this time to eat, something he failed to do in their previous encounter.   11. **regula:** i.e., the monastic rule, since Ysengrimus was once a monk, as Reynard makes clear here.   12. **monachus:** Ysengrimus.   14. **cuius ... noxia nulla times:** lit., "no poisons of which you fear . . .," i.e., "whose poisions you do not fear. . . ."   15. **vice:** ablative of *vicis,* with *omne malum* = "in exchange for every evil."   **equat** = CL *aequat;* the sense here is "proffer," rather than CL "to make even," though this meaning is retained in ML also (cf. Sleumer 84, s. v. *aequo*).   17. **subdita** = *subdita esse,* with *novi;* this is hypallage for *novi innumeros pisces vivariis subditos.*   22. **nisi piscer:** "unless I fish," *piscer* is present subjunctive of *piscari;* it is in winter when the pair meet up again, and both are quite hungry.   23. **vis vivam:** *velle* + subjunctive expressing a command = lit., "you wish that I live," i.e., "let me live"; parallel to *age me.*   24. **meminisse** + genitive = "to be reminded of. . . ."   26. **precedit** = CL *praecedit.*   28. **stringere:** the literal meaning is "to constrict," "to compress," but here it is used figuratively to mean "to freeze."   **quantus ... sufficiebat:** "the extent to which was sufficient"; *stringere* completes the thought.   29. **locum:** object of *nacta (nancisci),* modifying *vulpes.*

30   (Hiscebat glacies rupta recenter ibi)
    "Hic impinge tuam, carissime patrue, caudam,
     Rete aliud nullum, quo potiaris, habes.
    Utere more meo (quotiens ego piscor, eundem
     Piscandi quovis sector in amne modum):
35   Utque experta loquar, si multum linea claudant
     Retia, ter tantum cauda tenere solet.

               —vv. 665–74.

    Anguillas percasque tene piscesque minores,
     Qui tibi sint, quamvis plurima turba, leves. . . .
    Lucratur temere, qui perdit seque lucrumque;
40   Interdum lucris proxima dampna latent.
    Ne capiens capiare, modum captura capescat;
     Virtutum custos est modus atque dator."
    Retifer econtra: "ne quid michi consule, frater,
     Da tibi consilium, consule memet agor!"

          —vv. 679–80, 683–88.

45   "Pauper ovat modico, sum dives, multa capesco;
     Tangit parva super paupere cura deum.
    Divitibus fecit deus omnia, servat et offert;
     Dives qui sapiant scit bona, nescit inops.
    Scit dives scitasque cupit queritque cupitas,
50   Quas sibi querendas premeditatur, opes;
    Quesitas reperit, fruitur parcitque repertis
     Ordine, proventu, tempore, lege, loco,
    Colligit ac spargit, colitur, laudatur, amatur,
     Cominus et longe cognitus atque placens.

31. **caudam:** the wolf's tail will act as a net. 32. **rete aliud nullum:** i.e., "no net of another kind"; the phrase is the object of *habes* and explains Reynard's order in the previous line. **potiaris** = CL *possis;* the meaning is clear enough with *potior,* i.e., "by which you might obtain fish." 34. **piscandi:** the complete thought is *eundem piscandi . . . modum,* "the same mode of fishing." 36. **ter tantum:** "three times as much." 40. **dampna** = CL *damna;* the addition of a parasitic consonant is common in ML. 41. **capiare:** alternate form for the present passive subjunctive, second person singular, of *capere.* **capescat** = *capessat,* "to seize," "capture"; the line means something like, "lest you are captured in the capturing, endeavor to capture in the way I have taught you." 43. **retifer:** Ysengrimus, whose tail is to be used as a net. 46. **super** + ablative = *de.* 48. **qui** = *quo;* this is an archaic form that has adverbial force; here with *sapiant,* the meaning is something like "however they taste." 49. **queritque** = CL *quaeritque.* 50. **querendas premeditatur** = CL *quaerendas praemeditatur.* 51. **quesitas** = CL *quaesitas.* 54. **cominus** = CL *comminus;* with *longe* = "near and far."

Infelix, qui nulla sapit bona, nulla requirit,   55
 Vivat et absque bono, vivat honore carens.
Nullus amet talem, nullus dignetur odire!
 Ergo ego piscabor, qua michi lege placet.
Proximitas quedam est inter cupidumque deumque:
 Cuncta cupit cupidus, prebet habetque deus." 60
"Patrue," dux inquit, "moneo, non quero docere;
 Perfectus sapiens absque docente sapit.
At timeo tibi, debet amans hoc omnis amanti,
 Vincula preterea nos propiora ligant.
Huc me igitur duce ductus ades lucrumque locumque 65
 Indice me nosti—temet agenda doce.
Sic studeas lucris, ne dampnum lucra sequatur;
 Quid valeas, pensa, ne vide, quanta velis.
Perfeci, quecumque michi facienda fuerunt;
 Ire michi restat, cetera mando tibi.   70
Quid vel ubi faceres, dixi, facienda subisti;
 Securus dixi—tu facis, esto pavens."

        —vv. 701–28.

Emergente die Reinardus, ut arte ferocem
 Eliciat turbam, proxima rura subit.
Iamque sacerdotis stantis secus atria gallum 75
 Ecclesiam populo circueunte rapit,
Intenditque fuge; non laudat facta sacerdos,
 Nec laudanda putat nec patienda ioco.
"Salve, festa dies!" cantabat, ut usque solebat
 In primis feriis, et "kyri" vulgus "ole." 80
"Salve, festa dies!" animo defecit et ori,

---

58. **lege:** from *lex, legis* but with adverbial force, "legally." 59. **quedam** = CL *quaedam.* 60. **prebet** = CL *praebet.* 61. **dux:** Reynard now picks up the narrative again. **quero** = CL *quaero.* 62. **absque** = *sine*, governing *docente.* 63. **amans:** the term is one used to denote monastic friendship. 64. **preterea** = CL *praeterea.* 66. **temet:** as in CL, the enclitic "met" is added to pronouns in order to provide emphasis. 69. **quecumque** = CL *quaecumque.* **michi** = CL *mihi.* **quecumque . . . fuerunt:** this clause acts as the object of *perfeci.* 75. **secus:** preposition + accusative = "beside," "near to"; this usage is common in ML but is attested to in every other period of Latin writing except CL (cf. Blaise/Chirat 748, s. v. II *secus,* but cf. LS 1657, s. v. 2 *secus* III for instances that appear in early and later Latin). 76. **ecclesiam:** object of *circueunte*, with *populo* in ablative absolute construction. 77. **fuge** = CL *fugae.* 80. **kyri . . . ole** = transliterated Greek phrase equivalent to "*Salve Domine.*"

Et dolor ingeminat: "ve tibi, mesta dies!
Ve tibi, mesta dies, toto miserabilis evo,
Qua letus spolio raptor ad antra redit!
85   Cum michi festa dies vel maximus hospes adesset,
Abstinui gallo, quem tulit ille Satan";

—vv. 735–48.

Protinus inceptum populo comitante relinquens
Clamitat: "o proceres, accelerate, probi!
Me quicumque volunt pro se meruisse precari,
90   Et qui fida michi corda deoque gerunt."
Arma omnes rapiunt, arma omnia visa putantur;
"Hai! hai!" continuant, "hai!" sine fine fremunt.
Per iuga, per valles, per plana, per hirta sequuntur,
Post hostem profugum milia mille rotant:
95   Clerus vasa, crucum baculos, candelabra, capsas,
Edituus calicem, presbiter ipse librum,
Sacras deinde cruces, saxorum milia vulgus,
Presbiter ante omnes voce manuque furit.
Pertigerat gnarus, quo vellet tendere, raptor,
100   Qua piscaturum liquerat ante senem,
Et procul increpitans, ut vix clamaret ad illum,
Turbat, ut ad furcam tractus, anhela loquens:
"Ibimus? esne paratus adhuc? rue, patrue, cursim!
Si cupis hinc mecum currere, curre celer!
105   Non equidem veni cum libertate morandi,
Si venies, agili strennuitate veni!"
Talia clamanti succlamans ille reclamat:
"Audio! quid clamas? non ego surdus adhuc!
Desine bachari, nos nulla tonitrua terrent,
110   Nec tremor est terre iudiciive dies.
Ad quid precipitur via tam rapienda repente?

82. **ve . . . mesta** = CL *vae . . . maesta* (and in the next line also). 83. **evo** = CL *aevo*. 84. **letus** = CL *laetus*. 87. **inceptum:** i.e., the Mass (that had just begun). 89. **me . . . volunt . . . meruisse precari:** lit., "whoever wishes that I render for them prayer . . .," i.e., "whoever wants me to pray for them." 94. **milia mille:** "a great thousand"; *mille* is modified by *milia*, which has the meaning of "great," "large" in number (cf. Blaise/Chirat 531, s. v., *mille* 1, 2). 95. **clerus:** "clergy," in a collective sense. 99. **pertigerat:** from *pertingere*, with the *quo* clause as object. 100. **liquerat:** from *linquere*. 107. **ille:** Ysengrimus. 110. **terre** = CL *terrae*. **iudiciive:** *iudicium* + enclitic conjunction *ve* = "or." 111. **ad quid:** lit., "to what end," i.e., "why," equivalent to *quare*. **precipitur** = CL *praecipitur*.

Colligo nunc primum, captio cepta fere est;
Dic tamen, an fuerit, si scis, michi pluris abisse
Quam tenuisse moram." turbidus ille refert:
"Nescio, suspendisse viam tibi prosit an obsit,   115
Dicturi veniunt post mea terga tibi.
Non michi dignaris, dignabere forsitan illis
Credere, sed prodest accelerare michi;
Collige constanter, siquidem lucrabere, persta."
Hic pavidus paulum repplicat ipse precans: 120
"Ecce celer tecum venio, subsiste parumper!"
Respondet patruo taliter ille suo:
"Non ego pro septem solidis tria puncta morarer.
Ad tua sedisti lucra, morare satis!
Quod capere optabam, fors obtulit, heret in unco."   125
Serio formidans ille precatur item:
"Fige gradum sodes! et quos fugis, eminus absunt;
Dux meus huc fueras, esto reductor abhinc!
Ne dicare dolo duxisse, merere reducens;
Pondus amicitie tristia sola probant.   130
Pura fides etiam personam pauperis ornat,
At fraus purpuream privat honore togam.
Non rebar captos, quantis fore sentio plures;
Sarcina me prede detinet, affer opem!
Auxiliare seni patruo! scelerate, quid heres?"   135
Clamat ovans vulpes: "ista profecto velim!

112. **captio:** collectively referring to the fish set to be caught. **cepta** = CL *coepta.*
113. **michi pluris abisse:** the idiom is *pluris esse* with *pluris* in the genitive of value = "it is better"; here the perfect active infinitive replaces *esse* and the phrase is the object of *an fuerit:* "whether it will be better for me to depart. . . ." 114. **quam tenuisse moram:** completes the thought of *an fuerit michi pluris abisse:* "rather than to stay put (lit., "to stick to delay"). 115. **prosit an obsit:** present subjunctives, expressing two distinctive options, in indirect question. 117. **dignabere:** alternate form for *dignaberis.* 119. **lucrabere:** alternate form for *lucraberis.* 120. **repplicat** = CL *replicat.* 123. **pro septem solidis:** *solidus* = gold piece, here modified by indeclinable *septem* and governed by *pro.* **tria puncta:** "three moments," "three seconds." 124. **morare:** alternate present passive indicative, second person singular. 125. **heret** = CL *haeret.* 127. **sodes** = *si audes,* CL idiom = "please," "if you will." 129. **ne dicare dolo duxisse:** lit., "lest you are said to have led (me here) by deceit," i.e., "unless you have tricked me into being here. 130. **amicitie** = CL *amicitiae.* 133. **captos:** i.e., *pisces.* 134. **prede** = CL *praedae.* **affer opem:** the idiom is *opem ferre,* "to proffer help"; here it is a command, "help me." 135. **quid heres:** *heres* = CL *haeres;* i.e., "why are you standing there?"

Subvenientis eges, non castigantis egebas—
   Venit ad hoc "vivum linquere velle nichil!"
Dedecus et dampnum piscatus es atque dolorem;
140   Qui queritur de te, perpetiatur idem.
Quid iuvit clamare: "modum servare memento?"
   Incidis erumpnam transitione modi.
Captus es a captis, periit modus, hocque peristi,
   Et nunc operiar subveniamque iube!
145   Scilicet exspectem mundo in mea terga ruente
   Cum canibus, gladiis, fustibus atque tubis!
Fortunam misero non vult coniungere felix;
   Differimus multum stans ego tuque iacens.

                                                        —vv. 753–814.

"Leniter ergo cuba, donec pausaris, ego ibo;
150   Solus habe pisces, sat michi gallus agit."
"Ergo," inquit, "redies patruo, Reinarde, relicto?
   Tam consanguinee nil pietatis habes?
Si pietate cares, saltem cogente pudore
   Ibimus hinc pariter, me michi redde prius.
155   Nulla mei michi cura, tuo fac server honori!"
   Galliger econtra: "patrue, nolo mori."

                                                        —vv. 825–32.

Dixit et absiliens iterum simulabat abire;
   Piscator revocat: "quo, scelerate, ruis?
Quo sine me properas?" subsistens ille reclamat:
160   "Patrue, vis aliquid? precipe, nolo roges.
Sed quia multa soles dominorum more iubere,
   Atque ego proposui singula iussa sequi,
Una dies spatium iussis non equat et actis;

---

137. **eges** + dative or ablative = "to be in need of," "to require the assistance of. . . ."
138. **venit**: impersonal. **nichil** = CL *nihil*. 142. **erumnam** = CL *aerumnam;* the inclusion of a parasitic consonant is common in ML. 144. **operiar** = CL *opperiar*.
iube: often in ML *iubeo* takes the subjunctive, forming a purpose clause that expresses a command (as in CL; see AG 565). The subjunctives *operiar* and *subveniam* can be translated: "you order me to . . . and to. . . ." 149. **cuba:** imperative, from *cubare.*
151. **redies:** one expects *redibis,* but *redies* is attested to in Apuleius (*Met.* 6,9) and Seneca (*De Ben.* 1,2,3). 152. **consanguinee** = CL *consanguineae.* 155. **fac** + subjunctive *server* = imperative: lit., "allow that I might be saved by your honor."
156. **galliger:** a neologism of Nivardus' confection = *gallus* + *gero.* 160. **nolo** + subjunctive *roges* = imperative: lit., "don't ask," spoken in response to the rhetorical question posed at the beginning of the line, "*vis aliquid?*"

536

Tu iubeas hodie, cras ego iussa feram."
"Perfide," respondit, "iubeo nichil, obsecro solvi!"   165
   Galliger obstrepuit: "patrue, nonne furis?
Tu piscaris adhuc—et velle recedere iuras?
   Esse nimis captum dicis—et usque capis?
Absolvique petis? simulas, per sidera celi;
   Mens aliter versat, quam tua lingua sonat."   170
                 —vv. 869–82.

"Quid defixus, iners, heres, velut inter Ianum
   Februus et Martem, si tibi cura fuge est?
Emolire loco piscosaque retia subduc,
   Et, nisi non egeas, auxiliabor ego."
Captus ad hec captor: "nescis, quid, perfide, dicas,   175
   Clunibus impendet Scotia tota meis.
Undecies solvi temptans, immobilis hesi;
   Alligor, immota firmius Alpe sedens."
                 —vv. 885–92.

Galliger iratum cernens incumbere vulgus
   Maioresque moras posse nocere salit. . . .   180
Serio festinat, iam non discedere fingit,
   Tam letus caude quam levitate pedum.
           —vv. 931–32, 937–38.

165. **solvi:** present passive infinitive of *solvere.*   169. **celi** = CL *caeli.*   172. **fuge** =
CL *fugae.*   173. **emolire:** present imperative with *loco,* in ablative of separation: "get
up from this place. . . ."   175. **hec** = CL *haec.* 176. **Scotia:** Scotland.   177. **hesi** =
CL *haesi.*   178. **alligor:** Ysengrimus's tail, which he was using as a fishing net, is
frozen into the water; he cannot move.   **immota . . . Alpe:** ablative of comparison with
firmius.   180. **posse nocere:** "were able to bring harm. . . ."

BERNARDUS SILVESTRIS

The Cosmography
(*Cosmographia*; c. 1148)

The twelfth century was home to a cohort of social and intellectual changes that had a profound impact on literary activity. There were, in the first instance, the accomplishments of scholasticism, which marshaled a rigorous method of analytical inquiry grounded in the dialectic method. At the same time, a fresh interest in the best remains of classical antiquity arose, an inheritance which had been, as we have seen, put to the side as medieval literary forms developed in earnest after the ninth century. New currents of thought, from the Greek East and the Arab fringe, also infiltrated the West. Simultaneous to these currents was a full-blown expansion of economic activity, which had the effect of creating new social possibilities. One of the happy consequences of this, the so-called commercial revolution, was an increased urbanization, an enrichment of urban churches and cathedrals, and a surplus of resources that went into the production of cultural accoutrements.

The intellectual benefits of these important advances in the twelfth century were long-lived and profound. Not the least of these attended to a new sense of the human situation and a tendency to revisit cherished assumptions, a process that was hastened and emboldened by an engagement of the Platonic tradition in the work of the Chartrian humanists (see pp. 602–13). Bernardus Silvestris's *Cosmographia* evidences this ongoing process of intellectual renewal and revival. It revisits the problems of humanity's relationship to God, the broader order of the cosmos, and the negotiations required of nature, humanity, and divinity in their mutual relations; but it does so from a Platonic framework, and with a sense of both the glories and the limits of humanity's place in the order of the universe and of humanity's ability to comprehend that order.

Bernardus's work is also important in a formal sense, not just for the questions it raises, but for the way it frames those questions. Because the *Cosmographia* is a prosimetrum (or Menippean satire), like Boethius's *Consolation* (see pp. 138–42) or Dhuoda's *Manual* (see pp. 271–79), it broaches its best themes from two perspectives, rational and affective. In fact, beyond the gathering of themes in two venues, Bernardus is often

538

able to insinuate his good points through the very manipulation of prose and poetry, implying positions that are not espoused outright. At the same time, Bernardus's Latin serves broader interpretive goals by remaining faithful to classical norms while making a place for medieval innovation. Especially in his use of the *cursus,* or rhythmic prose cadences, Bernardus applies classical symmetry but in a measure unusual for classical prose, in effect poeticizing his prose. His deployment of prose and poetry, in the event, is carefully strategized.

Very little is known of Bernardus's life. He was born around 1100. He taught in Tours for a decade, beginning around 1130. His obvious training in the platonizing traditions of Chartrian humanism was buttressed by a solid knowledge of Arab intellectual currents. He knew Thierry of Chartres and Matthew of Vendôme, two other important twelfth-century intellectual figures, and shared their intellectual milieus. He seems to have been positively influenced, especially in the study and practice of poetry, by Hildebert of Le Mans, whom Bernardus must have known when Hildebert was made Archbishop of Tours. But apart from these scraps of information, little else can be surmised. A rough date of 1165 is conjectured for his death.

The *Cosmographia* has been edited by C. S. Barach and J. Wrobel (*De mundi universitate (Cosmographia),* Innsbruck, 1876). A. Vernet's École Nationale des Chartes dissertation offers a new edition, but has yet to be published, some sixty years after its completion (*Bernardus Silvestris: Recherches sur l'auteur et l'oeuvre suivies d'une édition critique de la "Cosmographia,"* Paris, 1938). P. Dronke has published the L manuscript, a competent witness to the *Cosmographia,* and controls its readings by consulting some seven other MSS (*Bernardus Silvestris, Cosmographia,* Leiden, 1978). Dronke supplies especially good notes, introduction, and comments on Bernardus's Latinity. W. Wetherbee has translated the *Cosmographia* into English in the Columbia Records of Western Civilization series (*The Cosmographia of Bernardus Silvestris,* New York, 1973). Wetherbee 1, 11ff. and 152 ff., offers a fuller sense of Chartrian humanism, Christian Platonism, and the twelfth-century intellectual currents attending to these important facets of the Latin Middle Ages in the work of Bernardus. Dronke's text is reprinted without change.

An Aspect of the Cosmos

"Perspice, mente sagax, que mundi forma, quibusque
Internexa sibi sint elementa modis,
Quo studio Noys alma rudem digessit acervum
Ut stabilem teneant contiguamque fidem;
5   Quid mediis extrema liget, quid federa iungat,
Quid celum moveat, quidve moretur humum;
Astrorum motus et que sit cuique potestas,
Ortus, occasus, puncta gradus, numeri;
Cur Aplanen contra septenos impetus orbes
10   Volvat, et amfractus per sua signa vagos;
Cur Veneris sint blandicie, cur prelia Martis,
Frigora Saturni, temperiesque Iovis;
Que Solis, que Mercurii Luneque potestas,
Et qua discurrant signa gradusque mora,
15   Quod, si pretemptes numeros, si consulis artem,
Quid fati series det ve neget ve probas;
Cur constringat hyemps, ver laxet, torreat estas,
Auptumnique metant tempora, mente vides;
Cur gelidus Boreas, mollisque Favonius, alter
20   Floribus expoliet, vestiat alter humum,
Coniugis in gremium Iove descendente novetur
Mundus, et in partu turgeat omnis humus,
Inveniatque Ceres quesitam cum face prolem,

1. que = CL *quae;* supply an understood *sit.* 2. internexa: from *internectere* = "intertwined." 3. Noys: in Bernardus' work, Noys represents the cause of created life; for a full discussion of Noys see Wetherbee 2, 53–55. 4. fidem: here *fides* should be translated in a more formally philosophical sense as "harmony," rather than in a theological sense as "faith" (cf. Wetherbee 2, 109). 5. federa = CL *foedera.* 6. celum = CL *caelum.* moretur: these and the other verbs of this catalogue are in indirect question. 8. puncta: here used in a spatial sense. gradus: used here in the sense of "motion." numeri: i.e., in the sense of "rules." 9. Aplanen: from *aplanes, is* = "unmoving" (Latham 24); here in the nominative singular, modifying *impetus* = "the force of the firmament" (on *Aplanen* see Dronke 2, 52, 71, 168). 10. amfractus = CL *anfractus.* 11. blandicie = CL *blanditiae.* prelia = CL *proelia.* **Martis:** from *Mars, Martis.* 13. Luneque = CL *Lunaeque.* 14. qua . . . mora: *mora* here = "space of time," in the ablative, modified by *qua.* 15. pretemptes = CL *praetemptes,* here in present active subjunctive. 17. hyemps = CL *hiems.* estas = CL *aestas.* 18. auptumnique = CL *autumnique.* 23. prolem: from *proles, is,* here = Persephone; the reference is to her removal from Hades and the coming of Spring.

Ut proserpendo proferat illa capud,
In silvis volucres, pisces generentur in undis,   25
   Floreat omnis ager, frondeat omne nemus;
Que membris animam numeri proportio iungat,
   Ut res dissimiles uniat unus amor.
Cum terrena caro, mens ignea, cumque repugnent—
   Hec gravis, illa movens, hec hebes, illa sagax—   30
Simplicitas anime sic transit in alteritatem
   Divisumque genus dividit illud idem.
Sed que compedibus, que carcere clausa tenetur,
   En quasi corporea mole sepulta iacet!
Ad natale iubar, ad regna paterna redibit,   35
   Si sapiat; si non—coniuga carnis eat.
Quid morti licitum, que mortis causa, quis auctor,
   Alcius evolvens philo<so>phando vide—
Quo trahit imperio sorbetque voragine quicquid
   Aura levat, tellus sustinet, equor alit.   40
Si tamen inspirat verum mens conscia veri,
   Rem privat forma, non rapit esse rei.
Res eadem subiecta manet, sed forma vagatur
   Atque rei nomen dat nova forma novum.
Forma fluit, manet esse rei, mortisque potestas   45
   Nil perimit, sed res dissociat socias.
Quid placeat per se, que sint aliunde petenda,
   Quid deceat, quid non, philosophando vide.
Iniustum iusto, falso discernere verum
   Sedula pervideas et ratione probes."

                      —*Cos., Mic.* 8.

24. **proserpendo:** the ablative gerund = present active participle, modifying *illa* here; note the pun on Persephone's name (i.e., *Proserpina*). **capud** = CL *caput*. 27. **numeri:** here in the sense of the "rules" that sustain *proportio*. 30. **hec ... hec** = CL *haec ... haec*. 31. **anime** = CL *animae*. **cum ... sic:** *cum* concessive = "although" + *sic* = "nonetheless." **alteritatem:** from *alteritas, atis* = "otherness" (Latham 16; cf. Wetherbee 2, 109, 161). 33. **compedibus:** from *compes, compedis*. 37. **quid morti licitum:** i.e., "what is permitted to death...." 38. **alcius** = CL *altius*. 40. **equor** = CL *aequor.* 42. **esse:** i.e., "the being," "the essence"; the present active infinitive functions here as the nominative gerund, as in CL.

An Aspect of Creation

Primum igitur hominem, quem pagina designabat ab occipitis regione, longa longis hystoriis fatorum series sequebatur. In ea namque fortuna calcata—plebis humilitas, in ea regum venerabilis celsitudo, in ea vel paupertas miserias vel redundancia fecerat voluptates. Sortis plerique
5 medie ab alterutro temperabant. In ea vel sudatum milicie vel literis vigilatum, ceteraque operum functione vita fataliter actitata. Secularis illa continentia, purioribus ex auro iniciata principiis, paulatim degenerante materia, in ferrum via est terminare.

Erat quoque et liber recordationis, non conmunibus literis, verum caractere notisque conscriptus, brevis ad sentenciam, et pagina pauciore contentus. In ea quidem brevitate res providencie fatique congeste subnotari poterant: poterant subintelligi, non poterant pervideri. Liber enim recordationis non aliud quam qui de rebus se ingerit et compellat memoriam intellectus, ratione sepe veridica, sed probabili sepius coniectura.

15 Illic eadem—sed non eodem iuditio—naturarum omnium que precesserant argumenta. Verumtamen eorum que visuntur corporea consummatior inibi et multo plenior disciplina. Illic quatuor mundani corporis materie, ad eternam sententiam de nativo litigio revocate. Suberat ratio unde amor, unde parta sodalitas, ut conponencia conpositum membra
20 corpus efficerent, et divisa se traderet pluralitas unitati. Illic aquei pennatique generis cognata germanitas, divisiva per species, qualitatibus differens et figuris. Suberat ratio unde squamas, unde plumas alterutris Natura comparet tegumentum, unde avibus lingua dulcissona, pisces perpetuo conticescunt. Illic pedestrium alia domestice mansuetudinis, alia moribus
25 ad maliciam efferatis. Suberat ratio cur leonibus et apris excandencior iracundia, cur in cervo vel lepore relanguit vis ignita. Illic de herbarum potenciis familiarior contemplatus. Suberat ratio unde illa seminibus,

2. **hystoriis** = CL *historiis*. 3. **celsitudo**: from *celsitudo, inis* = "elevation" (Latham 78). 4. **redundancia** = CL *redundantia*. 5. **sudatum**: perfect passive participle of *sudare,* here used substantively = "labor," "toil," etc. **milicie** = CL *militiae.* **literis** = CL *litteris.* 7. **iniciata** = CL *initiata.* 9. **non . . . verum** = "not . . . but. . . ." **caractere**: the better spelling is *charactere,* from *character, is* = "character," i.e., a written letter of the alphabet (Latham 82). 10. **sentenciam** = CL *sententiam.* 11. **providencie** = CL *providentiae.* **congeste** = CL *congestae,* modifying *res.* 14. **sepe** = CL *saepe.* **sepius** = CL *saepius.* 15. **iuditio** = CL *iudicio,* i.e., "discernment." 18. **materie** = CL *materiae.* **revocate** = CL *revocatae,* modifying *materiae.* 19. **conponencia**: the better spelling is *componentia,* a substantive here used as an adjective, modifying *membra* (cf. Latham 101, s. v. *compositio—componibilis—entia*). 24. **domestice** = CL *domesticae.* 25. **maliciam** = CL *malitiam.* 27. **potenciis** = CL *potentiis.*

succis altera, hec efficacior in radice. Illic quicquid vel ingressus ad sub-
stantiam generatio provehit, vel egressus a substantia destruit corruptela.
Tanta igitur naturarum multitudine, labore Physis plurimo speciem de-
prehendit humanam, sublustrem, tenuem, et pagine terminantis ex-
tremam.   5

—*Cos., Mic.* 11.9–11.

3. **Physis:** i.e., Physis, the material principle of nature, partnered in Bernardus' work
with Urania, the spiritual principle, and Natura, the coalescent principle (on these see
Wetherbee 2, 45ff. and Dronke 2, 44ff.)

BERNARD OF MORLAS

The Contempt of the World
(*De contemptu mundi;* c. 1150)

One of the strongest seats of ecclesiastical reform in the Western Church throughout the tenth and eleventh centuries was the abbey of Cluny, founded in 910 by William of Aquitaine. The focus of the work of William and his successors was to sanitize Benedictine monasticism—that is, to live closely by Saint Benedict's *Rule,* to concentrate monasticism's efforts on instilling into monks a rigorous ethic of liturgical observance and discipline, and to ensure that other monasteries followed suit. The effect of their work was two-pronged: on the one hand, much of the impetus for ecclesiastical reform in general in the eleventh century (see pp. 437–43) was spearheaded by the Cluniac reform; on the other hand, and more importantly, Cluniac reform helped to reinvigorate Benedictine monasticism in general, especially against the rise of competing monastic movements, such as the Cistercians (see pp. 554–62).

Of the many abbots of Cluny, however, Peter the Venerable is perhaps the most important. He took up his duties in 1122 amidst the difficulties left in the wake of his predecessor's unsuccessful abbacy. Peter's abbacy, in contrast, was anything but unsuccessful. The abbey continued to be influential in monastic reform, to be sure, but under Peter it also became a center for the composition of sacred poetry. Peter himself was a hymnist of some power, and also a prose stylist. In one remarkable instance, too, he seems to have served as an inspiration to an otherwise obscure monk in his charge, Bernard of Morlas, whose work *De contemptu mundi,* dedicated to Peter, is one of the more important poems of the ML tradition.

Of Bernard we know precious little. Even the place of his birth is a matter of some controversy, for he is sometimes styled Bernard of Morlaix (in northwestern France), though it is generally believed that he hailed from Morlas. He clearly was well educated, as the classical reminiscences in his poem suggest, and he was also an astute observer of his own time. It is perhaps not surprising that a biting commentary on the corruptions of the world should come from a Cluniac monk. But what is striking is Bernard's metrical skill, for the *De contemptu mundi* is written in dactylic hexameters in which both leonine and end rhymes are maintained in every verse. The poem is also noteworthy for its length—nearly

3,000 lines. It treats the failings of the world from various perspectives in book 1, while in book 2 the Golden Age is contrasted to more recent times. In book 3, finally, Bernard brings the full force of his attack on contemporary culture, yet his ending verses merge the criticism of the present age with a nostalgia for all that can, with God's help, still yet be:

Aurea tempora, primaque robora redde,—rogamus.
Nos modo dirige, postmodo collige,—ne pereamus.

It is difficult to find in the ML tradition a more straightforward expression of the love of God merged with the desire to express that longing in the best way. In this regard temperamentally, though not in terms of tradition, Bernard stands with the Goliardic poets (see pp. 566–71), and spiritually with Pope Gregory VII (see pp. 437–43), seeking always a higher, clearer vantage point from which to instruct and to purify.

The *De contemptu mundi* has been edited by T. Wright (*The Anglo-Latin Satirical Poets and Epigrammatists of the Twelfth Century*, vol. 2, London, 1872) and by H. C. Hoskier (*De Contemptu Mundi: A Bitter Satirical Poem of 3000 Lines upon the Morals of the XIIth Century by Bernard of Morval, Monk of Cluny (fl. 1150)*, London, 1929), which contains a rambling but useful preface, with critiques of the various translations into English of Bernard's poem.

Hoskier's text is reprinted here with some minor formatting changes.

THIS FLEETING WORLD, THE JUDGMENT, HEAVEN, HELL, WARNINGS, AND EXHORTATIONS

Hora novissima, tempora pessima sunt, vigilemus.
Ecce minaciter imminet arbiter, ille supremus.
Imminet, imminet ut mala terminet, aequa coronet,
Recta remuneret, anxia liberet, aethera donet.
Auferat, aspera duraque pondera mentis onustae,   5
Sobria muniat, improba puniat, utraque iuste.
                                        —*De Cont. Mun.* 1.1–6.
Tunc erit omnibus inspicientibus ora tonantis
Summa potentia, plena scientia, pax rata sanctis;
Pax erit omnibus, illa fidelibus, illa beata,
Inresolubilis, invariabilis, intemerata;   10
Pax sine crimine, pax sine turbine, pax sine rixa,

---

7. **tonantis:** from *tonans, tonantis,* lit., "thunderer," a name in CL for Jupiter and in ML a synonym for *Deus;* here it is akin to *arbiter, ille supremus* in the previous lines.
10. **inresolubilis** = CL *irresolubilis* = "indissoluble" (LS 1001).

Meta laboribus atque tumultibus, anchora fixa.
Pax erit omnibus unica, sed quibus? immaculatis,
Pectore mitibus, ordine stantibus, ore sacratis.
15 Pax ea pax rata, pax superis data, danda modestis,
Plenaque vocibus atque canoribus atria festis.
Hortus odoribus affluet omnibus hic paradisus,
Plenaque gratia, plenaque gaudia, cantica, risus;
Plena redemptio, plena refectio, gloria plena,
20 Vi, lue, luctibus aufugientibus, exule poena.
Nil ibi debile, nil ibi flebile, nil ibi scissum;
Res ibi publica, pax erit unica, pax in idipsum.
Hic furor, hic mala scismata, scandala, pax sine pace;
Pax sine litibus et sine luctibus in Sion arce.
25 O sacra potio, sacra refectio, visio pacis;
Mentis et unctio, non recreatio ventris edacis.
                                    —De Cont. Mun. 1.115–34.
Hic breve vivitur, hic breve plangitur, hic breve fletur.
Non breve vivere, non breve plaudere, retribuetur.
O retributio, stat brevis actio, vita perennis;
30 O retributio, coelica mansio stat lue plenis.
Quid datur? Et quibus? Aether egentibus, et cruce dignis,
Sidera vermibus, optima sontibus, astra malignis.
                                    —De Cont. Mun. 1.167–72.
O bona patria, lumina sobria, te speculantur,
Ad tua nomina, sobria lumina collacrimantur;
35 Est tua mentio pectoris unctio, cura doloris:
Concipientibus aethera mentibus ignis amoris.
Tu locus unicus, illeque coelicus es Paradisus.
Non ibi lacrima, sed placidissima gaudia, risus.
Est ibi consita laurus, et insita cedrus hysopo;

16. **canoribus:** from *canor, canoris.* 20. **vi:** from *vis.* **lue:** from *lues, is.* **exule** = CL *exsule,* from *exsul, exsulis.* 22. **idipsum** = *id* + *ipsum.* 23. **hic:** the contrast of *hic* to the previous catalogue featuring *ibi* is emphatic. **scismata** = CL *schismata,* from *schisma, atis* = "schism" (LS 1641). 24. **Sion:** from *Sion, onis* = Zion (Sleumer 729); Bernard treats it as an indeclinable noun throughout (here it is genitive). 26. **recreatio:** from *recreatio, onis* = "refreshment" (on the various meanings of this term see Latham 395). **edacis:** from *edax, acis.* 30. **retributio:** from *retributio, onis* = "reward" (Niermeyer 918). **coelica** = CL *caelica,* from *caelicus, a, um* = "heavenly" (Blaise/Chirat 122) 32. **sontibus:** from *sons, sontis.* 39. **consita:** perfect passive participle from *conserere.* **insita:** perfect passive participle from *inserere* = "to sow," "to plant." **hysopo:** from *hyssopus, i* (the better spelling) = "holy

Sunt radiantia iaspide moenia, clara pyropo.   40
Hinc tibi Sardius, inde Topazius, hinc Amethystus;
Est tua fabrica concio coelica, gemmaque Christus,
Lux tua mors crucis, atque caro ducis est crucifixi.
Laus, benedictio, coniubilatio personat ipsi.

                                  —*De Cont. Mun.* 1.235–46.

Urbs Sion aurea, patria lactea, cive decora,   45
Omne cor obruis, omnibus obstruis et cor et ora.
Nescio, nescio quae iubilatio, lux tibi qualis,
Quam socialia gaudia, gloria quam specialis.
Laude studens ea tollere mens mea, victa fatiscit.
O bona gloria vincor in omnia laus tua vicit.   50
Sunt Sion atria coniubilantia, martyre plena,
Cive micantia, principe stantia, luce serena.
Sunt ibi pascua mitibus afflua praestita sanctis.
Regis ibi tonus agminis et sonus est epulantis,
Gens duce splendida, concio candida vestibus albis,   55
Sunt sine fletibus in Sion aedibus, aedibus almis;
Sunt sine crimine, sunt sine turbine, sunt sine lite,
In Sion arcibus editioribus Israhelitae.
Pax ibi florida, pascua vivida, viva medulla;
Nulla molestia, nulla tragoedia, lacrima nulla.   60
O sacra potio, sacra refectio, pax animarum;
O pius, o bonus, o placidus sonus, hymnus earum.
Sufficiens cibus est Deus omnibus ipse redemptis,
Plena refectio, propria visio Cunctipotentis.

---

water sprinkler" (Latham 232).   40. **iaspide** = CL *iaspis, idis* = "jasper" (i.e., a green precious stone; cf. LS 874).   **pyropo:** from *pyropus, i* = "ruby," "carbuncle" (Latham 384).   41. **Sardius:** from *sardius, ii* = "carnelian" (a precious stone; cf. LS 1631).   **Topazius:** the better spelling is *topazos, i* = "topaz" (LS 1878).   **Amethystus:** from *amethystus, i* = "amethyst" (LS 105).   42. **concio** = CL *contio.* 44. **benedictio:** from *benedictio, onis* = "blessing" (cf. Niermeyer 89 to get an idea of the variety of meanings that exist for this word).   **coniubilatio:** from *coniubilatio, onis* = "joint celebration."   45. **Sion:** here with *urbs.*   51. **coniubilantia:** from *coniubilare* = "to rejoice together" (Latham 107).   **martyre:** from *martyr, is* = "martyr" (Blaise/Chirat 516).   53. **afflua** = CL *effluus, a, um* = "flowing out" (LS 631), predicative here, modifying *pascua* with *mitibus* the object = "pastures flowing with softness. . . ."   **praestita:** perfect passive participle of *praestare,* predicative here, with *sanctis* as object.   58. **editioribus:** from *editus, a, um.*   **Israhelitae:** the better spelling is *Israelitae,* from *Israelita, ae* = Israelites (Sleumer 450).   64. **Cunctipotentis:** from *cunctus + potens = Deus.*

65 Eius habent satis, his tamen est sitis eius anhela,
Absque doloribus, absque laboribus, absque querela.
—De Cont. Mun. 1.268–90.
Rex tibi praesidet, et tua possidet atria magnus,
Qui patris unicus est leo mysticus, et tamen agnus.
Rex tibi filius unicus illius ille Mariae,
70 Stirps sacra virginis, auctor originis, osque Sophiae.
Hic sapientia, linguaque patria, patria dextra.
Continet arbiter, omnia sub, super, intus et extra,
Astra regit Deus, astra cinis meus audet in illo,
Qui quasi propria continet omnia, facta pugillo.
75 Cum patre filius, atque paraclitus aequus utrique,
Omnia continet, omnibus eminet, omnis ubique.
Hunc bene quaerimus, ergo videbimus, immo videmus.
Hunc speculabimur, hoc satiabimur, hunc sitiemus.
Cernere iugiter atque perenniter ora tonantis
80 Dat lucra iugia, perpetualia, dat lucra sanctis.
O sine luxibus, o sine luctibus, o sine lite,
Splendida curia, florida patria, patria vitae,
Urbs Sion inclyta, patria condita littore tuto,
Te peto, te colo, te flagro, te volo, canto, saluto.
—De Cont. Mun. 1.321–38.
85 Gens pia vocibus, impia gressibus, invida morum,
Cur male vivitis, et bona perditis illa bonorum?
Gens adamantina, saxea gramina, gramina dura,
Quid bona spernitis, atque requiritis interitura?
Gens male provida, turbaque turbida turbine mortis,
90 Gens foris actibus, introque cordibus orba retortis,
Quid retro ceditis, illaque spernitis intima dona?
Manna relinquitis, atque recurritis ad Pharaona.

---

74. **pugillo:** from *pugillum, i* = "fist," or perhaps better here, "hand" (LS 1487).
75. **paraclitus:** from *paraclitus, i* = Holy Spirit (Sleumer 580).   79. **iugiter:** adverb =
"constantly" (Blaise/Chirat 479).   81. **luxibus:** from *luxus, us.*   83. **inclyta** = CL
inclita.   87. **adamantina:** from *adamantinus, a, um* = " extremely hard" (Blaise/
Chirat 47).   88. **interitura:** future active participle of *interire,* the object of *requiritis.*
89. **turbida:** predicative here.   92. **manna:** from *manna, ae* = this word means both
"manna," the nourishment of the Hebrews in the desert and also the fragrance emanating from the tombs of the saints (cf. Blaise/Chirat 514; Niermeyer 638); given the rest
of the line, the former meaning is meant here, though the latter is subtly present also.
Pharaona: the better spelling is *Pharum,* from *Pharum, i* = Pharaoh; (cf. Sleumer
604–5 for the various forms of this word as a noun and adjective).

Cur ea quaeritis, unde peribitis, unde ruetis?
Cur pereuntia fine, ruentia morte tenetis?
Turba theatrica, turba phrenetica, quo properatis?   95
Quo rea pectora, quo rea corpora praecipitatis?
Quid, rogo, spernitis ante requiritis ire retrorsum?
Perdita gens satis, ad scelus os datis, ad bona dorsum.
Fluxa manentibus, obruta stantibus, ultima primis,
Cur homo praeficis, altaque despicis, omnis in imis?   100
                    —*De Cont. Mun.* 1.393–408.
Nox simul omnibus est habitantibus in regione
Mortis. Homo geme, plange, dole, treme, terrea pone.
Ignea vincula denique singula membra catenant,
Corpora lubrica, membraque scenica vincula frenant.
Stat cruce triplice gens rea, vertice mersa deorsum,   105
Ora tenet sua, dorsa simul sua versa retrorsum,
Sunt superhorrida, nam lue sordida, crura, pedesque,
Inferius caput. Haec mala sunt apud infera certe.
                    —*De Cont. Mun.* 1.541–48.
Pars habet aethera, perditur altera strata ruinae.
Corpora lubrica, corda tyrranica percrucientur,   110
Frigore grandinis haec, face fulminis illa cremantur.
Arctat, arat, terit, angit, agit, ferit illa gehenna,
Vi, cruce, pondere, frigore, verbere, perpete poena.
Est ibi, credite, crux sine stipite, mors sine morte,
Vox sine carmine, lux sine lumine, nox sine nocte.   115
Non ibi publicus arbiter Aeacus, aut Rhadamanthus;
Non ibi Cerberus, aut furor inferus, ultio, planctus.
Non ibi navita, cymbaque praedita voce Maronis;

---

95. **theatrica:** from *theatricus, a, um* = "theatrical," "of the theater" (Blaise/Chirat 815). 96. **rea:** from *reus, a, um* = "guilty" (Latham 393). 103. **catenant:** from *catenare* = "to chain" (Latham 76). 104. **scenica** = CL *obscena*, from *obscenus, a, um.* 107. **superhorrida:** from *superhorridus, a, um* = "exceedingly horrible." 109. **strata:** from *stratum, i* = "pavement," "highway" (Sleumer 745). 112. **gehenna:** from *gehenna, ae* = Hell (Niermeyer 464). 113. **perpete:** adverb = "perpetually" (Latham 344, s. v. *perpet/uatio*). 116. **Aeacus:** from *Aeacus, i* = son of Jupiter by Europa, and king of Aegina; owing to his good judgment, he was made arbiter of the lower regions, along with Minos and Rhadamanthus (cf. LS 51). 117. **Cerberus:** from *Cerberus, i,* = Cerberus, the three-headed monster, guardian of the underworld (cf. LS 318). 118. **Maronis:** from *Maro, onis* = Publius Vergilius Maro, or Virgil (d. 19 B.C.E.), the famous Latin poet.

Sed quid? adustio, nox, cruciatio, mors Babylonis.

120 Non tenet Orphea, lex data Typhea fortia lora,

Non lapis hic gravis, aut lacerans avis interiora.

Poena nigerrima, poena gravissima, poena malorum,—

Mens male conscia, cordaque noxia, vermis eorum.

—*De Cont. Mun.* 1.580–94.

Ignea flumina, nigra volumina flamma retorquet,

125 Brumaque torrida, flammaque frigida pectora torquet.

Vermis edax scatet et puteus patet altus abyssi.

Sunt ibi pectore, sunt ibi corpore quique remissi.

Ludite, vivite, foenore divite, gens aliena.

Vos caro decipit hic,—ibi suscipit illa gehenna.

130 Non ibi visio, non ibi mansio luce repleta,

Non locus ordinis, aulaque luminis, arvaque laeta.

O Maro falleris hic ubi conseris arva piorum,

Elysios ibi non reperis tibi scriptor eorum.

Musa poetica, lingua scholastica, vox theatralis,

135 Haec quia disseris et male falleris, et male fallis.

Fulgurat ignibus haud radiantibus illa gehenna,

Plena nigredine, plenaque turbine, plenaque poena.

—*De Cont. Mun.* 1.635–48.

Cur homo nascitur, aut puer editur? Ut moriatur.

Exit in aera, sustinet aspera, migrat, humatur.

140 Glarea labilis, aura volatilis est homo natus.

Mane stat aggere, nec mora vespere fertur humatus.

Qui modo flos fuit, in spacio ruit unius horae.

Mox rapitur, licet ingenio micet, atque decore.

Fit cinis infimus, ille probissimus et preciosus,

145 Irreparabilis, irrevocabilis, officiosus.

Gleba reconditur atque recluditur hospite tumba.

Laus stat imaginis, umbraque nominis, immo nec umbra.

—*De Cont. Mun.* 1.765–74.

---

119. **cruciatio:** from *cruciatio, onis* = "torture" (Niermeyer 283). **Babylonis:** from *Babylon, onis* = Babylon (Sleumer 145). 126. **abyssi:** from *abyssus, i* = "abyss" (Sleumer 70). 133. **Elysios:** from *Elysium, i* = Elysium, in Roman mythology, the place where the blessed spent eternity; Virgil speaks of it in the *Georgics* and the *Aeneid*. 140. **labilis:** from *labilis, is* = "slippery," "unstable" (cf. for the various meanings Niermeyer 575). 142. **spacio** = CL *spatio*. 146. **gleba** = CL *glaeba*. **tumba:** from *tumba, ae* = "tomb" (Niermeyer 1047).

Est ubi gloria nunc Babylonia, nunc ubi dirus
Nabuchodonosor, et Darii vigor, illeque Cyrus?
Qualiter orbita viribus incita praeterierunt.　　　　　　　　150
Fama relinquitur, illaque figitur, hi putruerunt.
Nunc ubi curia, pompaque Julia? Caesar, obisti.
Te truculentior, orbe potentior ipse fuisti.
　　　　　　　　　　　　　　　—*De Cont. Mun.* 1.933–38.
Nunc ubi Marius atque Fabricius, inscius auri?
Mors ubi nobilis et memorabilis actio Pauli?　　　　　　　155
Diva Philippica vox ubi coelica nunc Ciceronis?
Pax ubi civibus atque rebellibus ira Catonis?
Nunc ubi Remulus, aut ubi Romulus, aut ubi Remus?
Stat rosa pristina nomine, nomina nuda tenemus.
　　　　　　　　　　　　　　　—*De Cont. Mun.* 1.947–52.
Gens temeraria, dum licet, impia facta fleamus.　　　　　160
Ille minaciter advenit arbiter, expaveamus.
Nemo capescere ius, mala plangere nemo relinquat;
Gaudia flentibus, irreverentibus ira propinquat.
Iam tuba septima, plaga novissima, lux pia, dira,
Intonat, ingruit, emicat, irruit, et venit ira.　　　　　　165
Gens male conscia, lubrica gaudia flendo tegamus,
Gens male conscia, quae fugientia sunt, fugiamus.
Stare refugimus, ad mala fluximus; ad bona stemus.
Hora novissima, tempora pessima sunt vigilemus!
　　　　　　　　　　　　　　—*De Cont. Mun.* 1.1069–78.

149. **Nabuchodonosor:** indeclinable = Nebuchadnezzar (Sleumer 535), here in the nominative. **Darii:** from *Darius, ii* = Darius, the famous King of Persia (LS 512). **Cyrus:** from *Cyrus, i* = Cyrus, the founder of the Persian monarchy (LS 508). 154. **Marius:** i.e., C. Marius, the conqueror of Jugurtha and consul seven times (cf. LS 1115). **Fabricius:** i.e., C. Fabricius Luscinus, famous Roman leader under the Republic (cf. LS 713). 155. **Pauli:** L. Aemilius Paulus, a famous consul and military leader (cf. LS 1318). 156. **Philippica:** *Philippicus, a, um,* referring to the series of speeches by Cicero against Antony. **Ciceronis:** from *Cicero, onis* = Cicero, the famous orator and politician (d. 43 B.C.E.). 157. **Catonis:** from *Cato, onis* = Cato, the enemy of Caesar who committed suicide after the battle of Pharsalia. 158. **Remulus:** from *Remulus, i* = Remulus, a king of Alba (LS 1564). **Romulus . . . Remus:** i.e., Romulus and Remus, the legendary brothers, the former was the founder and first king of Rome. 161. **expaveamus:** from *expavere* = "to be mightily afraid" (LS 691).

PLATE 27. A folio from a Flemish Book of Hours from the fifteenth century.

Plate 27

Book of Hours, Flemish manuscript on parchment, fifteenth century,
fol. 113 verso
John Hay Library, Brown University

The folio shown here depicts the adoration of the Lamb and comes from a Book of Hours produced in Flanders in the fifteenth century, with richly illustrated and decorated leaves. This folio has floreated margins with much shading and deep coloring. The frame of the picture harnesses royal colors—deep red, blue, and gold. The manuscript itself is in excellent condition, with wood-board binding in leather, stamped, with functional brass clutches. It is 17 cm. in height and has 192 folios.

Bernard of Clairvaux

The Steps of Humility; Advice To Pope Eugenius

(*De gradibus humilitatis et superbiae*, c. 1120; *De consideratione ad Eugenium Papam*, c. 1153)

The life and writings of Bernard of Clairvaux are intimately bound up with the ecclesiastical and political developments of twelfth-century Europe, for at the height of his powers Bernard was perhaps the most famous, not to mention the most powerful, ecclesiastic in the West. He hailed from Fontaine-les-Dijon, in Burgundy, where he was born in 1090. He was one of the younger children of a large and somewhat prosperous family, for whom a career in the Church was natural. Bernard's easy intellectual gifts accorded well with this career path, and he entered the small monastery at Cîteaux in 1112 (so it is said, with many of his friends, his uncle, and his brothers), where he remained for three years. In 1115 he was chosen by the abbot of Cîteaux, Stephen Harding, to found a daughter house, and for his new abbey Bernard eventually settled on a heavily wooded, secluded spot some ninety miles from Cîteaux, called Clairvaux. It flourished quickly. Bernard remained affiliated with Clairvaux for the rest of his life, devoting all his energy, time, and skill to teaching, administration, and reflection. Bernard's accomplishments are attested to by the hundreds of students he trained, including Pope Eugenius III, whose admonitions from Bernard, taken from the *De consideratione*, are excerpted here. They are equally measured by the full flowering of Cistercian monasticism, the development of which is owed as much to Bernard's work at Clairvaux as to the proselytizing maintained from the mother house at Cîteaux. (It is estimated that by mid-century, Clairvaux had founded or made affiliated to it some seventy daughter houses, which, in turn, produced over ninety more such houses; in total, by 1150, there were some 280 daughter houses of Cîteaux, and by 1200, some 530.) The flavor of that proselytizing, the kinds of care lavished on his monastic charges by Bernard, are in evidence in the excerpts from *De gradibus humilitatis*, Bernard's treatment of mystical ascent and contemplation.

It is important to cast Bernard's life in the context of the Gregorian reform movement, spearheaded as we have seen by Peter Damian and Gregory VII (see pp. 414–18, 437–43). Cîteaux was an important locus of monastic reform in the late eleventh century, and when Bernard entered it in the early twelfth century, he surely had on his mind the spirit of reformation that had informed its founding in 1098 by Robert of Molesmes. It was from Stephen Harding, however, that Bernard learned to be a devoted father to his charges (or, to use his terminology, a mother to his sons). As much as he operated from principles of spiritual purity and apart from the corruption of Church, however, he also was attracted to the power that naturally flowed from the papacy and the institutional Church in the twelfth century, for though the Church was much troubled in the decades following Gregory VII's death in 1085, it reached the apogee of its powers and prestige over the course of the next hundred years—and Bernard both assisted and retarded this process.

Bernard first came into contact with the power politics of the Church in the 1130s, when he involved himself in the papal split between Innocent II and Anacletus II. As a result of a series of sermons Bernard preached in France on Innocent's behalf—sermons based on Bernard's belief that Innocent represented the true strain of reform in the Western Church—Innocent II was slowly able to accrue adherents to his cause, including the kings of France and England, and this success brought Bernard into the inner circle of Innocent's advisors. Bernard thereafter became an eloquent spokesman for the pope and was with Innocent as all the major kingdoms of Europe came slowly to his support. When Innocent II arrived in Rome in 1138 to replace the ousted Anacletus II, no one was more powerfully ennobled by the victory than Bernard. And, as the next several popes were all reformists of the mold of Innocent II, Bernard's power remained intact from Innocent's accession down to Bernard's own death in 1153. It was perhaps never greater than after 1145, when Eugenius III, a former student of Bernard's, became pope. It was this pope who took as his spiritual disciple Louis VII and whose influence, combined with Bernard's rhetorical skill, launched the Second Crusade, preached by Bernard in 1146.

One can discern Bernard's rhetorical skills in the excerpts here, which are drawn from two of his more important works. The first, treating the steps required for mystical ascent and union with God, was written c. 1120. It accords with the notions of mystical union developed in Bernard's *De diligendo deo* and in his sermons on the Song of Songs, a huge compilation of commentary on this most mystical of Old Testament texts. The second excerpt, written in stops and starts between 1148 and Bernard's death in 1153, is noteworthy for the way it moves between a high style (with which is starts) and a much simpler, more conversational style (with which it ends). Throughout, however, as in most of his writings, Bernard calls upon an erotics of expression that blurs gender distinctions and the normal roles assumed by man and woman. While both treatises evince a Medieval Latin style burnished in the cloister schools, both treatises are quintessentially medieval; *quod* functions, for example, in Bernard's exquisite prose as an all-purpose conjunction, much akin to the French *que* or the English "that," but also to introduce consecutive and final clauses, with or without the subjunctive. Syntax is simple and the structure of the sentences sometimes reflects the spoken French of Bernard's day.

There are numerous editions of the works of Bernard, but the best is the multivolume series by J. Leclercq and H. Rochais (*Sancti Bernardi Opera*, 8 vols, Rome, 1957–77; the *De consideratione* and the *De gradibus humilitatis* are both in vol. 3). There are also numerous translations into French, German, and English of Bernard's works. The *De consideratione* has been translated by J. D. Anderson and E. T. Kennan (*Five Books on Consideration: Advice to a Pope*, in The Works of Bernard of Clairvaux, vol. 13, = vol. 37 of the Cistercian Fathers Series, Kalamazoo, Mich., 1976). This translation has excellent notes and introduction. G. B. Burch has translated the *De gradibus humilitatis* (*The Steps of Humility, by Bernard, Abbot of Clairvaux*, Cambridge, Mass., 1940), which also contains excellent notes. One should consult the multivolume *Bibliographie Bernardine*, published most recently in *Documentation Cistercienne*, for current work on Bernard. The text of Leclercq and Rochais is reprinted here with quotation marks, rather than capital letters, designating scriptural passages.

THE STEPS OF HUMILITY: THE RAPTURE OF ST. PAUL

Putas hos gradus Paulus non transierat, qui usque ad tertium caelum se raptum fuisse dicebat? Sed quare raptum, et non potius ductum? Ut videlicet si tantus Apostolus raptum se dicit fuisse, quo nec doctus scivit, nec ductus potuit ire, me, qui procul dubio minor sum Paulo, ad tertium caelum nulla mea virtute, nullo meo labore pervenire posse praesumam, ne vel de virtute confidam, vel pro labore diffidam. Qui enim docetur aut ducitur, ex hoc ipso quod docentem vel ducentem sequitur, laborare con-

---

1. **ad tertium caelum:** i.e., Paradise; cf. 2 Cor. 12.2.   3. **quo:** conjunction.   4. **me:** object of *pervenire*.   **procul dubio:** idiom = "without a doubt."   **Paulo:** ablative of comparison with *minor*.   6. **ne . . . confidam vel . . . diffidam:** negative purpose clauses = "lest I am confident of my virtue or shy of the work."   7. **docentem vel ducentem:** present active participles used as substantives, i.e., "teacher or leader."   **laborare convincitur:** the object of *docetur aut ducitur,* i.e., "who is taught or is led is proven to work," with *ex hoc . . . quod sequitur* subordinate to this main thought.

vincitur, et aliquid de se agit, ut ad destinatum vel locum vel sensum per-
trahatur, ita ut dicere possit: "Non autem ego, sed gratia Dei mecum."
Qui vero rapitur, non suis viribus, sed alienis innixus, tamquam nescius,
quocumque portatur, nec de toto in se, nec de parte gloriatur, ubi nec per
se, nec cum alio aliquid operatur. Ad primum itaque sive ad medium cae-   5
lum ductus vel adiutus Apostolus ascendere potuit; ad tertium autem ut
perveniret, rapi oportuit. Nam et Filius ad hoc legitur descendisse, ut
iuvaret ascensuros ad primum, et Spiritus Sanctus missus fuisse, qui per-
duceret ad secundum. Pater vero, licet Filio et Spiritui Sancto semper
cooperetur, numquam tamen aut de caelo descendisse, aut ad terras le-   10
gitur missus fuisse. Lego certe, quod "Misericordia Domini plena est
terra, et pleni sunt caeli et terra gloria tua," et multa huiuscemodi. Lego
et de Filio: "Postquam venit plenitudo temporis, misit Deus Filium
suum"; et ipse Filius loquitur de se: "Spiritus Domini misit me." Et per
eumdem Prophetam: "Et nunc," inquit, "Dominus misit me et Spiritus   15
eius." Lego et de Spiritu Sancto: "Paraclitus autem Spiritus Sanctus, quem
mittet Pater in nomine meo," et: "Cum assumptus fuero, mittam vobis
eum," haud dubium quin Spiritum Sanctum. Patrem autem in sua persona, licet nusquam non sit, nusquam tamen invenio nisi in caelis, ut in
Evangelio: "Et Pater meus qui in caelis est," et in oratione: "Pater noster,   20
qui es in caelis."

Unde nimirum colligo, quod quia Pater non descendit, Apostolus, ut
eum videret, ad tertium caelum ascendere quidem non potuit, quo tamen
se raptum memoravit. Denique: "Nemo ascendit in caelum, nisi qui descendit de caelo." Et ne putes de primo dictum vel secundo, dicit tibi Da-   25
vid: "A summo caelo egressio eius." Ad quod iterum non subito raptus,
non furtim sublatus, sed: "Videntibus," inquit, "Illis," id est Apostolis,
"elevatus est." Non sicut Elias, qui unum, non sicut Paulus, qui nullum,—
vix enim vel seipsum testem aut arbitrum habere potuit, ipso perhibente:

2. Cf. 1 Cor. 15.10.   3. **innixus:** perfect participle of *inniti* = "supported," with ablative of means.   6. **adiutus:** perfect passive participle of *adiuvare.*   7. **rapi:** present
passive infinitive of *rapere*, complement of *oportuit.*   **ad hoc:** i.e., "for this reason";
the subsequent purpose clause spells out this reason.   **legitur:** it is probably easiest to
read this impersonally, i.e., "it is read [in Scripture] that. . . ."   11. **quod:** note how
quod functions as an all-purpose conjunction, much akin to the French *que* or the
English "that"; § 5.4.   Cf. Psalm 32.5.   12. Cf. *Preface* to the Mass.   13. Cf. Gal.
4.4.   14. Cf. Isa. 61.1; Luke 4.18.   15. Cf. Isa. 48.16.   16. Cf. John 14.26.
17. Cf. John 16.7.   18. **haud dubium quin:** i.e., with *Spiritum Sanctum* = "without
a doubt the Holy Spirit [is meant]."   20. Cf. both Matt. 16.17 and Matt 6.9.
24. Cf. John 3.13.   26. Cf. Psalm 18.7.   27. Cf. Acts 1.9.   28. **Elias:** i.e., the
prophet Elijah.

"Nescio, Deus scit—" sed ut omnipotens, qui quando voluit descendit, quando voluit ascendit, pro suo arbitrio arbitros et spectatores, locum et tempus, diem et horam exspectans, "Videntibus illis," quos scilicet tanta visione dignatur, "Elevatus est." Raptus est Paulus, raptus est Elias, 5 translatus est Enoch; Redemptor noster legitur "Elevatus," hoc est ex seipso levatus, non aliunde adiutus. Denique non currus vehiculo, non angeli adminiculo, sed propria virtute subnixum "Suscepit eum nubes ab oculis eorum." Cur hoc? An fessum iuvit? An pigrum impulsit? An cadentem sustinuit? Absit. Sed suscepit eum ab oculis carnalibus discipulorum, 10 qui etsi Christum noverant secundum carnem, sed ultra iam non noscerent. Quos ergo ad primum caelum per humilitatem Filius vocat, hos in secundo per caritatem Spiritus aggregat, ad tertium per contemplationem Pater exaltat. Primo humiliantur in veritate, et dicunt: "In veritate tua humiliasti me." Secundo congaudent veritati, et psallunt: "Ecce quam bo-15 num et quam iucundum, habitare fratres in unum," de caritate quippe scriptum est: "Congaudet autem veritati." Tertio ad arcana veritatis rapiuntur, et aiunt: "Secretum meum mihi, secretum meum mihi."

—De Grad. Hum. 8.

ADVICE TO POPE EUGENIUS

Subit animum dictare aliquid, quod te, Papa beatissime Eugeni, vel aedificet, vel delectet, vel consoletur. Sed nescio quomodo vult et non vult exire laeta quidem, sed lenta oratio, dum certatim illi contraria imperare

1. Cf. 2 Cor. 12.2. **quando voluit:** a common ML construction = "when he wished." 5. **Enoch:** the prophet Enoch. 7. Cf. Acts 1.9. 10. **secundum:** preposition + accusative. 13. Cf. Psalm 118.75. 14. **humiliasti:** syncopated perfect active indicative, second person singular = *humiliavisti*, from *humiliare* = "to humble" (Blaise/Chirat 396). **congaudent:** from *congaudere* = "to rejoice together" (Blaise/Chirat 199). **psallunt:** from *psallere* = "to sing" (Blaise/Chirat 681). Cf. Psalm 132.1. 16. Cf. 1 Cor. 13.6. 17. Cf. Isa. 24.16.

1. **Papa beatissime Eugeni:** i.e., *Papa beatissimus Eugenius* = Eugenius III, who reigned from 15 February 1145 to 8 July 1153; Eugenius was a Cistercian and former student of Bernard; and Bernard, knowing him as a master knows a student, worried from the start over Eugenius's temperament. Bernard called him "a delicate son . . . more accustomed to retirement than to treat of external affairs . . . [I] fear that he will not fulfill his apostolic task with all the authority he ought" (Anderson and Kennan 183). **quod te . . . consoletur:** the construction is quintessentially ML, i.e., *quod* + subjunctive expressing purpose, expanding on the meaning of *aliquid*; § 6.1. 2. **quomodo:** adverb = "how." 3. **laeta . . . sed lenta oratio:** technically the subjects of *vult et non vult*, with *exire* the intransitive complement of these two verbs; *laeta* and *lenta* should be read as opposites, something like "informal and formal" (or, more literally, "happy and tough" (cf. Anderson and Kennan 23).

contendunt maiestas atque amor. Nempe urget ille, inhibet illa. Sed intervenit tua dignatio, qua hoc ipsum non saltem praecipis, sed petis, cum praecipere magis te deceat. Maiestate igitur tam dignanter cedente, quidni cedat pudor? Quod enim si cathedram ascendisti? Nec si ambules super pennas ventorum, subduceris affectui. Amor dominum nescit, agnoscit filium et in infulis. Per se satis subiectus est, obsequitur sponte, gratis obtemperat, libere reveretur. Non sic aliqui, non sic; sed aut timore ad ista impelluntur, aut cupiditate. Hi sunt qui in facie benedicunt, mala autem in cordibus eorum; blandiuntur coram, in necessitate deficiunt. At "Caritas numquam excidit." Ego, ut verum fatear, matris sum liberatus officio, sed non depraedatus affectu. Olim mihi invisceratus es: non mihi e medullis tam facile abstraheris. Ascende in caelos, descende in abyssos: non recedes a me, sequar te quocumque ieris. Amavi pauperem spiritu, amabo pauperum et divitum patrem. Non enim, si bene te novi, quia pater pauperum factus, ideo non pauper spiritu es. In te hanc mutationem factam esse confido, non de te, nec priori statui tuo successisse promotionem, sed accessisse. Monebo te proinde, non ut magister, sed ut mater: plane ut amans. Amens magis videar, sed ei qui non amat, ei qui vim non sentit amoris.

—*De Cons.* Praef.

Unde iam ergo incipiam? Libet ab occupationibus tuis, quia in his maxime condoleo tibi. Condoleo dixerim, si tamen doles et tu. Aliter enim "doleo" magis dixisse debueram, quia non est condolere, ubi nemo qui doleat. Itaque si doles, condoleo; si non, doleo tamen, et maxime, sciens longius a salute absistere membrum quod obstupuit, et aegrum sese non sentientem periculosius laborare. Absit autem ut de te id suspicer. Novi quibus deliciis dulcis quietis tuae non longe antehac fruebare. Non potes his dissuevisse tam cito, non potes ita subito non dolere nuper subtractas. Plaga recens dolore non caret. Neque enim iam occalluit vulnus, nec in tam brevi versum in insensibile est. Quamquam, si non dissimules, non deest tibi iugis materia iusti doloris a quotidianis damnis. Invitus, ni fallor, avelleris a tuae Rachelis amplexibus, et quoties id pati contigerit,

1. **ille:** i.e., *amor.* **illa:** *maiestas.* 5. **affectui:** the dative object of [*n*]*ec subduceris.* 6. **et:** as in CL, in its emphatic usage = "and even." 7. **non sic:** emphatic repetition. 10. **matris:** notice the erotic, parental, and filial vocabulary used here and throughout this preface. 11. **depraedatus:** from *depraedari* = "to be deprived," "to lose," "to be stripped" (LS 551), with *affectu* in ablative of specification construction. 16. **priori statui tuo:** dative object of *successisse.* 26. **fruebare:** alternate second person singular, imperfect indicative of *fruor* = *fruebaris.* 28. **occalluit:** from *occallescere.* 31. **Rachelis:** from *Rachel, elis* = Rachel; cf. Gen. 29.6 ff. **quoties . . . toties:** idiomatic = "however many . . . this many. . . ."

toties dolor tuus renovetur necesse est. At quando non contingit? Quoties vis, et incassum? Quoties moves, nec promoves? Quoties conaris, et non datur ultra; eniteris, et non paris? Tentas, et abriperis, et ubi incipis, ibi deficis, et dum adhuc ordiris, succidunt te? "Venerunt filii usque ad par-
5 tum," ait Propheta, "et vires non habet parturiens." Nosti hoc? Nemo te melius. Attritae frontis es, et instar vitulae Ephraim doctus diligere trituram, si, pace tua, sic se tuae res habent. Absit: haec est pars illius, qui datus est in reprobum sensum. Ab his sane cupio tibi pacem, non cum his. Nihil plus metuo tibi pace ista. Miraris si umquam possit accidere?
10 Etiam, dico tibi, si res, ut assolet, per consuetudinem in incuriam venerit.
—*De Cons.* 1.1.1.

Libri superiores, etsi De consideratione inscribantur, plurimum tamen habent actionis admixtum, dum res aliquas non considerandas tantum, sed agendas docent vel monent. At qui in manibus modo est, sola in consideratione versabitur. Quae enim supra sunt, — id quidem instat—, actu
15 non indigent, sed inspectu. Non est quod in eis actites, quae uno modo semper sunt, et in aeternum; porro aliqua et ab aeterno. Et hoc velim sollerter advertas, vir sagacissime Eugeni, quia toties peregrinatur consideratio tua, quoties ab illis rebus ad ista deflectitur inferiora et visibilia, sive intuenda ad notitiam, sive appetenda ad usum, sive pro officio dispo-
20 nenda vel actitanda. Si tamen ita versatur in his, ut per haec illa requirat, haud procul exsulat. Sic considerare, repatriare est. Sublimior iste praesentium ac dignior usus rerum, cum, iuxta sapientiam Pauli, "invisibilia Dei per ea quae facta sunt, intellecta conspiciuntur." Sane hac scala cives non egent, sed exsules. Quod vidit ipse huius sententiae auctor, qui, cum
25 diceret invisibilia per visibilia conspici, signanter posuit: "A creatura mundi." Et vere quid opus scalae tenenti iam solium? Creatura caeli illa est, praesto habens per quod potius ista intueatur. Videt Verbum, et in

---

1. **necesse est:** lit., "it is necessary," but with adverbial force = "necessarily." 6. **attritae frontis es:** lit., "you are of a worn appearance"; *frons, frontis* is modified by the perfect passive participle *attritae,* from *atterere.* 11. **superiores:** i.e., the previous four books of the *De Consideratione.* This excerpt comes from the beginning of book 5. 13. **qui:** i.e., *liber V.* 14. **quae supra sunt:** the topic is "those things which are above" Eugenius. 15. **non est quod:** i.e., "There is no way that. . . ." **in eis actites:** jussive subjunctive construction, with *non est quod* = "there is no way that you act on those things. . . ." 17. **Eugeni:** vocative case. **toties . . . quoties:** "as many times . . . that many times. . . ." 22. Cf. Rom. 1.20. 26. **quid opus:** idiomatic = "what need/use is there. . . ." **scalae:** the genitive complement of *quid opus* = "what need is there of a ladder . . ." **tenenti iam solium:** dative of the person in need, with *quid opus* = "what need is there of a ladder for the one already holding the throne"; *solium* (from *solium, ii*) is the object of *tenenti.*

Verbo facta per Verbum. Nec opus habet ex his quae facta sunt Factoris notitiam mendicare. Neque enim, ut vel ipsa noverit, ad ipsa descendit, quae ibi illa videt, ubi longe melius sunt quam in seipsis. Unde nec medium requirit ad ea corporis sensum: sensus ipsa sibi, seipsa sentiens. Optimum videndi genus, si nullius egueris, ad omne quod nosse libuerit, te   5
contentus. Alioquin iuvari aliunde, obnoxium fieri est, minusque a perfecto istud, et minus liberum.

Quid quod et inferioribus eges? Nonne praeposterum hoc et indignum? Plane superiorum quaedam iniuria est, inferiorum operam desiderare, a qua iniuria nemo hominum perfecte vindicabitur, nisi cum quisque   10
evaserit in libertatem filiorum Dei. Nempe erunt hi omnes docibiles Dei et, nulla interveniente creatura, solo beati Deo. Repatriasse erit hoc, exisse de patria corporum in regionem spirituum. Ipsa est Deus noster, maximus spiritus, maxima mansio spirituum beatorum, et, ne quid hic sibi usurpet carnis sensus seu imaginatio, veritas est, sapientia est, virtus,   15
aeternitas, summum bonum. Unde interim absumus, et ubi sumus, vallis est, et vallis lacrimarum, in qua sensualitas regnat et consideratio exsulat, in qua libere quidem et potestative se exserit sensus corporeus, sed intricatus caligat oculus spiritualis. Quid igitur mirum, si ope indigenae advena indiget? Et felix secundum tempus viator, qui civium beneficium, sine quo   20
transire non potest, in obsequium convertere potuit, utens, non fruens; urgens, non petens, exactor, non supplex.

—*De Cons.* 5.1.1, 2.

Magnus ille, qui usum sensuum, quasdam veluti civium opes, expendere satagit, dispensando in suam et multorum salutem. Nec ille minor, qui hunc sibi gradum ad illa invisibilia philosophando constituit, nisi   25
quod hoc dulcius, illud utilius, hoc felicius, illud fortius esse constat. At omnium maximus, qui, spreto ipso usu rerum et sensuum, quantum quidem humanae fragilitati fas est, non ascensoriis gradibus, sed inopinatis excessibus, avolare interdum contemplando ad illa sublimia consuevit. Ad hoc ultimum genus illos pertinere reor excessus Pauli: excessus,   30
non ascensus, nam raptum potius fuisse quam ascendisse ipse se perhibet.

5. **egueris**: from *egere*. 8. **quid quod**: "why is it that. . . ." **eges** + dative object.
11. Cf. Rom. 8.21. **docibiles**: from *docibilis, e* = "teachable" (cf. Blaise/Chirat 288) but predicative with *erunt* = "Indeed they will all be taught about God. . . ."
12. **beati**: predicative with *erunt* = "they will all be [made] blessed by God alone"; *solo Deo* is ablative of means. **repatriasse**: syncopated perfect active infinitive = *repatriavisse*, here in a purpose construction with *erit hoc*, i.e., "this will be an instance of having returned home . . ."; *exisse* functions in the same way, i.e., "this will be an instance of having gone from the land of the body into the region of the spirit."
18. **potestative**: adverb = "forcefully" (Niermeyer 821).

Inde est quod dicebat: "Sive mente excedimus, Deo." Porro haec tria ita contingunt, cum consideratio, etsi in loco peregrinationis suae, virtutis studio et adiutorio gratiae facta superior, sensualitatem aut premit ne insolescat, aut cogit ne evagetur, aut fugit ne inquinet. In primo potentior,

5 in secundo liberior, in tertio purior: puritatis siquidem et alacritatis pariter alis fit ille volatus.

Vis tibi has considerationis species propriis distingui nominibus? Dicamus, si placet, primam dispensativam, secundam aestimativam, tertiam speculativam. Horum nominum rationes diffinitiones declarabunt. Dis-

10 pensativa est consideratio sensibus sensibilibusque rebus ordinate et socialiter utens ad promerendum Deum. Aestimativa est consideratio prudenter ac diligenter quaeque scrutans et ponderans ad vestigandum Deum. Speculativa est consideratio se in se colligens et, quantum divinitus adiuvatur, rebus humanis eximens ad contemplandum Deum. Puto vigi-

15 lanter advertis aliarum hanc esse fructum, ceteras, si non referantur ad istam, quod dicuntur videri posse, sed non esse. Et prior quidem absque intuitu huius multa serit et nihil metit, sequens vero, nisi ad istam se dirigat, vadit, sed non evadit. Ergo quod prima optat, secunda odorat, tertia gustat. Ad quem tamen gustum perducunt et ceterae, etsi tardius, nisi

20 quod prima laboriosius, secunda quietius pervenitur.

—*De Cons.* 5.2.3, 4.

1. Cf. 2 Cor. 5.13.   9. diffinitiones = CL *definitiones*.

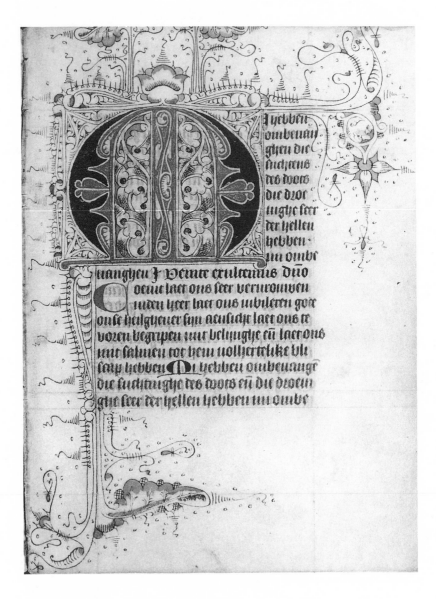

PLATE 28. A folio from a fifteenth-century Book of Hours produced in Flanders.

PLATE 28

Book of Hours, Flemish manuscript on parchment, fifteenth century,
fol. 161 recto
John Hay Library, Brown University

The folio shown here is the recto facing a verso depiction of the raising of Lazarus.
The Book of Hours from which it comes was produced in Flanders in the fifteenth
century, with richly illustrated and decorated leaves. This folio has floreated margins with much detailed penwork, and an initial "M" decorated with rich colors.
This page has margins and lines ruled in pencil, as does the manuscript as a
whole, though some pages are lined but not filled in. They may have been meant
for pictures never realized, since the manuscript seems to be a complete Book of
Hours otherwise. The manuscript itself is in excellent condition, with wood-
board binding in leather, stamped, with functional brass clasps. It is 17 cm. in
height and contains 192 folios.

THE ARCHPOET

Confession
(*Estuans intrinsecus: Carmen* 10; c. 1160)

Just as ML poetry reoriented itself in the ninth century to a closer accom-
modation to the cloister and to the affect of Christian spirituality, so in
the twelfth century was that process irrevocably reversed. By the close of
the century, the enormous gathering of Latin and vernacular songs we
now call the *Carmina Burana* had presumably been collected (see pp.
586–99), with its fresh celebrations of gender difference, its ritualized
singings of the violence and the rigors of love, its bows to the glories
of nature (owed to simultaneous developments in Christian speculative
theology, on which see pp. 602–13). A similar thematic strain of poetic
abandon and celebration occurred, however, by the middle of the century
with the development of so-called "Goliardic" verse, owed mostly to the
best known exemplars of the genre, Hugh Primas of Orléans and the
Archpoet.

The term "Goliardic" verse derives from "Golias," or "Goliath," the
Old Testament Philistine giant who was slain by David (1 Sam. 17). It
was common by the ninth century to associate Goliath with Satan and to
describe particularly evil clerics as belonging to the family of Golias. Bernard of Clairvaux, in condemning Peter Abelard, called him a new Goliath, perhaps setting off the new lease on life that Golias achieved in the
twelfth century. By the middle of the century, indeed, Golias had become
a more affable figure, a poet-beggar who served as a patron saint to poetic
practitioners of the genre named after him. To follow him, as many seem
to have done in the twelfth century, meant adopting an attitude toward
the world, striking a pose, above all, scorning many of the accoutrements
of contemporary culture. In particular, Goliards enjoyed striking a satiric
pose: mocking institutions, celebrating drunkenness, exposing the vanities of human passion, reveling in gambling. *Carmina Burana* 219 famously announces the "formation" of the "order" of vagrants (the *ordo
vagorum*) to which the "Goliards" belonged, and its beginning lines, par-
odying the verses of Mark 16.15, also satirize the flourishing of monastic
reform movements in the twelfth century (Cluny, Cistercians, Carthu-
sians), of which this "order" is but the newest:

1. Cum in orbem universum
   Decantatur, "Ite,"
   Sacerdotes ambulant
   Currunt cenobite,
   Et ab evangelio
   Iam surgunt levite
   Sectam nostram subeunt
   Que salus est vite.

2. In secta nostra scriptum est:
   "Omnia probate,
   Vitam nostram optime
   Vos considerate,
   Contra pravos clericos
   Vos perseverate,
   Qui non large tribuunt
   Vobis in caritate."

This poem, which goes on for over one hundred lines, does much to demolish the pretenses of spirituality, the longings at once to purify and also to leave this world, and the contrary tendencies of a Church devoted to divesting itself of worldly accoutrements at the same time that it was gathering them in perhaps in greatest abundance. The irony was not lost on Hugh Primas of Orléans, to be sure, who is also good at summarizing cultural attitudes and crashing them to the ground in his collection, which consists of 23 poems written in classical and accentual meters. But the Archpoet is perhaps better known than Hugh, owing to the selection reprinted here, the so-called "Confession," sometimes called the "Confession of Golias," in which the aesthetic principles of Goliardic culture are best expressed.

Yet its author, the Archpoet, is an unknown quantity in the literary history of the Latin Middle Ages. We know that he was patronized by Rainald of Dassel, archchancellor to Emperor Frederick Barbarossa, later archbishop of Cologne, as the poem attests. But even the designation "Archpoet" is little more than a literary affectation—*Archipoeta* (like *Primas*) was a title used by (or granted to) various poets who wrote Goliardic (or similarly themed) verse. The Archpoet presumably was not a cleric or religious of any sort. He tells us he studied medicine at one point early in his career, before attaching himself to the court of Frederick Barbarossa. He was of the elite class—a knight by birth—and, as one would expect of his class, well educated. He seems to have had access to an unusually wide variety of classical poetry (in part the reason why it has been speculated that he studied for a spell at Orléans with Hugh, where a school existed that held a collection of such poetry). We know also that the Archpoet lived for a while at the monastery of St. Martin in Cologne. What we lack in identity, however, apart from a possible (but by no means certain) German birthright, we have in output, for we possess from the hand of the Archpoet ten substantive poems of excellent craftsmanship and range.

There are differences between Hugh Primas of Orléans and the Archpoet, though both represent the best of the Goliardic tradition. Less important are the small divergences of meter, word-choice, and tone found in a comparison of the works of the two authors, though clearly the Archpoet took Hugh as his metrical exemplar. His use of leonine hexameters is especially telling in this regard. In the poem reprinted here, there is also a much bolder statement of personal identity on the part of the Archpoet than one finds in Hugh, framed by a careful, balanced use of scriptural and classical allusion, the scriptural references framing the opening strophes, to be replaced by Ovidian material at the poem's bold conclusion. There is also, finally, perhaps the finest development of the most popular meter of the Goliardic tradition, the so-called "Vagantenstrophe," which consists of thirteen-syllabled end-rhymed lines, with a caesura after the seventh syllable, and end rhyme consistent within each strophe.

The poetry of the Archpoet has been edited by M. Manitius (*Die Gedichte des Archipoeta,* Munich, 1916, 2d ed., 1929), K. Langosch (*Hymnen und Vagantenlieder,* Basel, 1954), and H. Watenphul and H. Krefeld (*Die Gedichte des Archipoeta,* Heidelberg, 1958). F. Adcock has published a translation of Hugh Primas and the Archpoet (*Hugh Primas and the Archpoet,* in Cambridge Medieval Classics 2, Cambridge, 1994), which contains notes, bibliography, and a historical introduction (and a second introduction on both poets' identities by P. Dronke). See also Raby 2, vol. 2, 180ff. (on the Archpoet), and vol. 2, 171ff. (on Hugh Primas).

Our selection, poem 10, is normally published with two substantive omissions—as below. The first involves an additional five strophes appended to the poem in a copy of it preserved in the Codex Buranus— the *Carmina Burana*—which are pretty clearly not of the Archpoet's confection. The second omission involves six strophes—what would be 14–19—which repeat strophes 10–15 of poem 4 and do not well fit in with poem 10 thematically or topically. Some editors print them as part of poem 10, as do Watenphul and Krefeld. Their text is reprinted here with strophes 14–19 omitted.

A GOLIARDIC CONFESSION

Estuans intrinsecus ira vehementi
in amaritudine loquar mee menti:
factus de materia levis elementi
folio sum similis de quo ludunt venti.

1. **estuans** = CL *aestuans.*   2. **mee** = CL *meae.*

Cum sit enim proprium viro sapienti   5
supra petram ponere sedem fundamenti,
stultus ego comparor fluvio labenti
sub eodem aere nunquam permanenti.

Feror ego veluti sine nauta navis,
ut per vias aeris vaga fertur avis.   10
non me tenent vincula, non me tenet clavis,
quero mei similes et adiungor pravis.

Mihi cordis gravitas res videtur gravis,
iocus est amabilis dulciorque favis;
quicquid Venus imperat, labor est suavis;   15
que nunquam in cordibus habitat ignavis.

Via lata gradior more iuventutis,
inplico me viciis immemor virtutis,
voluptatis avidus magis quam salutis,
mortuus in anima curam gero cutis.   20

Presul discretissime, veniam te precor:
morte bona morior, dulci nece necor;
meum pectus sauciat puellarum decor,
et quas tactu nequeo, saltem corde mechor.

Res est arduissima vincere naturam,   25
in aspectu virginis mentem esse puram;
iuvenes non possumus legem sequi duram
leviumque corporum non habere curam.

---

5. **cum sit:** concessive. 6. **ponere:** complementary with *cum sit . . . proprium.*
8. **nunquam** = CL *numquam.* 14. **favis:** ablative of comparison with *dulciorque;*
from *favus, i.* 16. **que** = CL *quae,* i.e., Venus. 17. **via lata:** ablatives of specification which essentially function as the object of *gradior:* "I follow the wide path. . . ."
18. **inplico** = CL *implico.* 20. **curam gero cutis:** the CL idiom *cutem curare,* "I look
out for my own skin," may well carry over here. 21. **presul** = CL *praesul;* in ML =
"bishop," "archbishop," "abbot," but here, with *discretissime* in the vocative, refers to
the addressee of the poem, Rainald of Dassel, Archbishop (elect) of Cologne (on the
various meanings of *presul,* better spelled in ML *praesul* see Niermeyer 842–43).
precor: with double objects here. 22. **nece:** from *nex, necis.* 24. **mechor** = CL
moechor. 25. **vincere . . . esse:** both infinitives are complements of *Res est arduis-*
sima. 28. **leviumque corporum:** i.e., *puellarum.* **sequi . . . non habere:** as in the
first two lines of this strophe, here also two infinitives are complements of a verb
phrase, i.e., *non possumus.* The second complement, *non habere,* with *non possumus,*
is an example of litotes.

Quis in igne positus igne non uratur?
30   quis Papie demorans castus habeatur,
ubi Venus digito iuvenes venatur,
oculis illaqueat, facie predatur?

Si ponas Ypolitum hodie Papie,
non erit Ypolitus in sequenti die:
35   Veneris in thalamos ducunt omnes vie;
non est in tot turribus turris Alethie.

Secundo redarguor etiam de ludo,
sed cum ludus corpore me dimittit nudo,
frigidus exterius mentis estu sudo;
40   tunc versus et carmina meliora cudo.

Tercio capitulo memoro tabernam.
illam nullo tempore sprevi neque spernam,
donec sanctos angelos venientes cernam
cantantes pro mortuis "Requiem eternam."

45   Meum est propositum in taberna mori,
ut sint vina proxima morientis ori.
tunc cantabunt letius angelorum chori:
"Sit deus propitius huic potatori."

Poculis accenditur animi lucerna;
50   cor inbutum nectare volat ad superna.
mihi sapit dulcius vinum de taberna
quam quod aqua miscuit presulis pincerna.

---

30. **Papie:** from *Papia, ae* = Pavia (Sleumer 580).   31. **digito:** ablative of means.
32. **predatur** = CL *praedatur.*   33. **Ypolitum** = *Hippolytus, i* (cf. LS 856), son of
Theseus and Hippolyta, his stepmother, Phaedra, fell in love with him, but he was
repulsed by her and she subsequently accused him of misconduct. He is in the Middle
Ages a symbol of chastity and sexual continence. Cf. Virgil, *Aen.* 7.761ff. and Ovid,
Met. 15.487ff.   35. **Veneris:** from *Venus, eris.*   **vie** = CL *viae.*   36. **tot:** indeclinable
adjective, with *turribus.*   **Alethie** = CL *Alethia,* i.e., Truth, or, more specifically here,
Virtue as the embodiment of sexual continence (cf. LS 83).   37. **secundo:** adverb; the
Archpoet here begins a second set of charges.   **ludo:** i.e., gambling.   39. **estu** = CL
aestu.   40. **cudo:** the sense in modern English = "I hammer out" (cf. Adcock 117).
42. **sprevi:** from *spernere.*   44. **eternam** = CL *aeternam;* the phrase comes from the
Introit to the Mass for the Dead.   47. **letius** = CL *laetius.*   48. The Archpoet
changes one strategic word from Luke 18.13—*peccatori* becomes *potatori.*
50. **nectare:** from *nectar, aris.*

Ecce mee proditor pravitatis fui,
de qua me redarguunt servientes tui.
sed eorum nullus est accusator sui,   55
quamvis velint ludere seculoque frui.

Iam nunc in presentia presulis beati
secundum dominici regulam mandati
mittat in me lapidem neque parcat vati,
cuius non est animus conscius peccati.   60

Sum locutus contra me quicquid de me novi
et virus evomui quod tam diu fovi.
vita vetus displicet, mores placent novi;
homo videt faciem, sed cor patet Iovi.

Iam virtutes diligo, viciis irascor,   65
renovatus animo spiritu renascor;
quasi modo genitus novo lacte pascor,
ne sit meum amplius vanitatis vas cor.

Electe Colonie, parce penitenti,
fac misericordiam veniam petenti   70
et da penitenciam culpam confitenti:
feram quicquid iusseris animo libenti.

Parcit enim subditis leo rex ferarum
et est erga subditos immemor irarum,
et vos idem facite, principes terrarum: 75
quod caret dulcedine, nimis est amarum.

—Est. Intrin.

64. **Iovi:** from *Iovis, is,* here dative with *patet; Iovis* stands here, as often in ML, for *Deus.* 69. **electe Colonie:** vocative case, referring to Rainald of Dassel. 71. **penitenciam:** often spelled *paenitentiam,* from *paenitentia* = "penance" (Niermeyer 783). 73. **rex ferarum:** in apposition to *leo.*

HILDEGARD OF BINGEN

Know the Way; The Symphony of Harmony
of Celestial Revelations
(*Scivias;* c. 1151; *Symphonia armonie celestium revelationum,* c. 1175)

Because our own age is unaccustomed to it, it is easy to downplay the close connection of visual, aural, and verbal media in the Latin Middle Ages. In the twelfth century, a particular confluence of trends helped to situate literary production in a cohort of other media. In the first instance, this century witnessed a general increase in literacy and literary production, an increase assisted by the good effects of the monastic reforms of the eleventh and early twelfth centuries, which fostered private devotion and spiritual inspiration on a scale not before seen or possible. At the same time, the new movements of private spirituality and devotion engendered not only verbal but, as in the case of Hildegard of Bingen, visual depictions, a development that coincided with the maturation of the musical forms (many of them monastic, or at least liturgical, in origin or use) attending to the sequence, the trope, and the drama. Finally, a newfound sophistication in producing and disseminating illuminated manuscripts, psalters, hymnbooks, etc., and a fuller accounting of musical notation made possible an increased publication of sung and performed works with musical notations and illustrations. The twelfth century, in short, fostered in every way a multimedia artistic scene—a scene that would continue well into the thirteenth century with the historical and artistic achievements of, among other figures, Matthew Paris (see pp. 644–51).

No one is more exemplary of that scene in the twelfth century than Hildegard of Bingen. Her output is enormous and includes music, poetry (including drama), herbal and medicinal treatises, and painting. Her longest work is the *Scivias,* which means something like "Know the Way," a series of twenty-six visions, reprinted in three books dealing with, respectively, creation, redemption, and salvation (a passage of which is excerpted below). This extraordinary work of mystic penetration and salvific explanation also includes illuminations of the visions very likely produced under Hildegard's supervision (extant now only in copies of the originals). This was the work that inspired hundreds of pilgrims to come to Hildegard's abbey in Germany, especially after Pope Eugenius III, at the insistence of Bernard of Clairvaux, read parts of the *Scivias* in Trier in 1148 and promptly declared his support and protection for Hildegard (on Bernard and Eugenius see pp. 554–62). Later works include the *Book of Life's Merits; On the Activity of God;* her scientific works, the *Physica* and the *Book of Compound Cures;* her drama, the *Ordo virtutum,* written for performance by the nuns of her monastery; a series of autobiographical reminiscences; and a substantial collection of letters.

Her literary masterpiece, however, is the *Symphonia armonie celestium revelationum,* written over a long stretch of time and excerpted here. The songs collected in this lengthy work were all written for the monastic liturgy, that is, for the singing of the Divine Office that ordered the activities of monastic life. Over half the songs in the *Symphonia* are antiphons—simple verses with melody which were sung before and after the psalm set for singing in each of the seven Divine Offices. The *Symphonia* also includes responsories—verses with melody (usually more complex musically than antiphons) set for both individual and choral performance that were sung after the scriptural lessons which followed the antiphons. Also included (in addition to several pieces for the Mass) are hymns and a group of sequences written in the Carolingian tradition of nonmetrical composition (on Notker's model, see pp. 300–306). The music of the *Symphonia* survives complete, and in this aspect of her creativity, Hildegard tends to be a complex composer. She dislikes the simplicity occasioned by the correspondence of single notes to single syllables in her compositions, and she often ventures into complicated musical patternings, where single syllables are sung in several notes or more.

Because she wrote an autobiography, and because several (hagiographic) biographies were written about her, we know important details about the life and career of Hildegard. She was born in 1098 in Bermersheim, near Mainz. In 1106, she was given as an oblate to the monastery of St. Disibod, and she came under the instruction there of Jutta. Her education seems to have been singularly unremarkable, and Hildegard lived in total obscurity until the 1130s. In 1136, however, she was chosen abbess of the nuns associated with St. Disibod, and in taking this post she became at once more visible to her community and to the wider world. It was only after the assumption of her duties as abbess that Hildegard began to write. But with prompting from Saint Bernard (with whom she corresponded in 1147) and affirmation by Pope Eugenius, Hildegard became a famous visionary and mystic—a position which encouraged her to establish her own monastery for her nuns at Rupertsberg, on the site of a monastery founded earlier by the mother of Saint Rupert. Although initially faced with many difficulties, the establishment was founded and eventually prospered, though it continually faced opposition from many quarters.

It is important to recognize, as her contemporaries did, that Hildegard was a mystic, a visionary, for the function of visions is fundamental to her output. We can gain a full sense of her peculiar brand of mysticism only by listening to performances of her songs, viewing her illuminations, and reading her words—hence the songs included here can only suggest, not embody, the range of Hildegard's aesthetic practices. Also included is one of the prose descriptions of a vision of Hildegard, which depicts a peculiar version of Satan in relation to a group of believers. In her description, Hildegard is direct. The liturgical pieces are more complex, mostly because of the compression of diction demanded by the venue. Nonetheless, simplicity remains the norm, and there is nothing here resembling the compression of Abelard's *Planctus* (pp. 489–501) or even of the sequences of Adam of St. Victor (pp. 521–25). Hildegard died in 1179 and was almost immediately recognized as a saint in Germany.

The *Symphonia* has been edited by P. Barth, M.-I. Ritscher, and J. Schmidt-Görg (*Hildegard von Bingen: Lieder*, Salzburg, 1969) and by Barbara Newman (*Saint Hildegard of Bingen: Symphonia: A Critical Edition of the Symphonia armonie celestium revelationum [Symphony of the Harmony of Celestial Revelations]*, Ithaca, N. Y., 1988). Newman's edition offers translations as well as Latin texts and includes a substantive introduction on all aspects of the *Symphonia;* a complete bibliography, including a full list of other English translations; and a section on discography, for Hildegard's musical compositions have of late been performed and recorded in several venues. Sidwell 287 lists discography down to 1995. The *Scivias* has been edited by A. Führkötter and A. Carlevaris (*Hildegardis Scivias*, in Corpus Christianorum, Continuatio Mediaevalis, vols. 43–43a, Turnholt, 1978), which includes superb reproductions of the illuminations of Hildegard's visions. The *Scivias* has been translated by C. Hart and J. Bishop (*Scivias*, New York, 1990). A good discussion of Hildegard's life and work has been written by P. Dronke (*Women Writers of the Middle Ages*, Cambridge, 1984, pp. 144–201). See also K. Wilson, *Medieval Women Writers* (Athens, Ga., 1984, pp. 109–29). Newman's edition of the *Symphonia* is reprinted without change (including her numbering); the edition of the *Scivias* of Führkötter and Carlevaris is reprinted here, with consonantal and vocalic "u" distinguished.

CARMEN 2

O virtus Sapientie
que circuiens circuisti,
comprehendendo omnia
in una via que habet vitam,
tres alas habens,   5
quarum una in altum volat
et altera de terra sudat
et tercia undique volat.
Laus tibi sit, sicut te decet,
o Sapientia.   10

CARMEN 3

O quam mirabilis est
prescientia divini pectoris
que prescivit omnem creaturam.
Nam cum Deus inspexit
faciem hominis quem formavit,   5
omnia opera sua
in eadem forma hominis
integra aspexit.
O quam mirabilis est inspiratio
que hominem sic suscitavit.   10

CARMEN 4

O pastor animarum
et o prima vox
per quam omnes creati sumus,
nunc tibi, tibi placeat
ut digneris   5
nos liberare de miseriis
et languoribus nostris.

Carm. 2. Antiphon. 1. **Sapientie** = CL *Sapientiae*. 2. **que** = CL *quae*. **circuiens circuisti:** both forms are from *circumire* (sometimes spelled *circuire*). 3. **comprehendendo:** the gerund in the ablative often functions as a present active participle, equivalent here to *comprehendens;* § 3.4 (cf. Blaise 341, 343).

Carm. 3. Antiphon. 2. **prescientia:** the better ML spelling is *praescientia* = "foreknowledge" (Niermeyer 838). 3. **prescivit** = CL *praescivit*.

Carm. 4. Antiphon.

CARMEN 5

O cruor sanguinis
qui in alto sonuisti,
cum omnia elementa
se implicuerunt
5   in lamentabilem vocem
cum tremore,
quia sanguis Creatoris sui
illa tetigit,
ungue nos
10   de languoribus nostris.

CARMEN 7

O eterne Deus,
nunc tibi placeat
ut in amore illo ardeas
ut membra illa simus
5   que fecistis in eodem amore,
cum Filium tuum genuisti
in prima aurora
ante omnem creaturam,
et inspice necessitatem hanc
10   que super nos cadit,
et abstrahe eam a nobis
propter Filium tuum,
et perduc nos in leticiam salutis.

CARMEN 10

O splendidissima gemma
et serenum decus solis
qui tibi infusus est,
fons saliens
5   de corde Patris,

Carm. 5. Antiphon. 1. **cruor sanguinis:** both words mean fundamentally the same thing, i.e., "blood"; *cruor* puns on *cruciare,* "to be crucified," the source of the blood recalled here. The repetition is emphatic. 9. **ungue:** present imperative of *ungere.*
    Carm. 7. Psalm antiphon. 13. **leticiam** = CL *laetitiam.* **salutis:** in CL = "health," "safety" but in EL/LL/ML = "salvation" (cf. Blaise/Chirat 734 for variations of meaning).
    Carm. 10. Psalm antiphon (for the Virgin Mary).

quod est unicum Verbum suum,
per quod creavit
mundi primam materiam,
quam Eva turbavit.
Hoc Verbum effabricavit tibi   10
Pater hominem,
et ob hoc es tu illa lucida materia
per quam hoc ipsum Verbum exspiravit
omnes virtutes,
ut eduxit in prima materia   15
omnes creaturas.

CARMEN 11

Hodie aperuit nobis
clausa porta
quod serpens in muliere suffocavit,
unde lucet in aurora
flos de Virgine Maria.   5

CARMEN 12

Quia ergo femina mortem instruxit,
clara virgo illam interemit,
et ideo est summa benedictio
in feminea forma
pre omni creatura,   5
quia Deus factus est homo
in dulcissima et beata virgine.

CARMEN 17

1. Ave generosa,
gloriosa et intacta puella.
Tu pupilla castitatis,
tu materia sanctitatis,
que Deo placuit.   5

9. **Eva:** from *Eva, ae* = Eve, the source of Original Sin (Sleumer 313). 10. **effabri-cavit:** from *effabricare* = "fashion," "make" (Newman 115). **tibi:** i.e., Mary. 11. **hominem:** double object of *effabricavit*, with *Hoc Verbum*; the subject is *Pater*.
    Carm. 11. Psalm antiphon (for the Virgin Mary). 2. **clausa:** perfect passive participle from *claudere*.
    Carm. 12. Psalm antiphon (for the Virgin Mary). 5. **pre** = CL *prae*.
    Carm. 17. Hymn (to the Virgin Mary).

2. Nam hec superna infusio
in te fuit,
quod supernum Verbum
in te carnem induit.

10   3. Tu candidum lilium
quod Deus ante omnem creaturam
inspexit.

4. O pulcherrima et dulcissima,
quam valde Deus in te delectabatur,
15   cum amplexionem caloris sui
in te posuit,
ita quod Filius eius
de te lactatus est.

5. Venter enim tuus gaudium habuit
20   cum omnis celestis symphonia de te sonuit,
quia virgo Filium Dei portasti,
ubi castitas tua in Deo claruit.

6. Viscera tua gaudium habuerunt
sicut gramen super quod ros cadit
25   cum ei viriditatem infundit,
ut et in te factum est,
o mater omnis gaudii.

7. Nunc omnis ecclesia in gaudio rutilet
ac in symphonia sonet
30   propter dulcissimam Virginem
et laudabilem Mariam,
Dei Genitricem.
Amen.

CARMEN 19

1. O viridissima virga, ave,
que in ventoso flabro sciscitationis
sanctorum prodisti.

6. hec = CL *haec*. **infusio:** from *infusio, onis* = "flood," "pouring in" (LS 949).
15. **amplexionem:** from *amplexio, onis* = "embrace" (Latham 18).   20. **celestis** =
CL *caelestis*, here modifying *symphonia* (with *omnis*).
    Carm. 19. Hymn to the Virgin.   2. **flabro:** here in the singular, the form is usually
flabra, orum = "gusts of wind" (Blaise/Chirat 354).   **sciscitationis:** from *sciscitatio,*

2. Cum venit tempus
quod tu floruisti in ramis tuis,   5
ave, ave fuit tibi,
quia calor solis in te sudavit
sicut odor balsami.

3. Nam in te floruit pulcher flos
qui odorem dedit   10
omnibus aromatibus
que arida erant.

4. Et illa apparuerunt omnia
in viriditate plena.

5. Unde celi dederunt rorem super gramen   15
et omnis terra leta facta est,
quoniam viscera ipsius frumentum protulerunt
et quoniam volucres celi
nidos in ipsa habuerunt.

6. Deinde facta est esca hominibus   20
et gaudium magnum epulantium.
Unde, o suavis Virgo,
in te non deficit ullum gaudium.

7. Hec omnia Eva contempsit.

8. Nunc autem laus sit Altissimo.   25

CARMEN 21

O tu suavissima virga
frondens de stirpe Iesse,
o quam magna virtus est
quod divinitas

---

onis = "questioning" (Blaise/Chirat 744). 6. **fuit:** used impersonally here, i.e., "it
was. . . ." 11. **aromatibus:** from *aroma, atis,* neuter noun = "spices" (Blaise/Chirat
97). 14. **viriditate:** from *viriditas, atis* = "greenness" (Habel/Gröbel 427).
15. **celi** = CL *caeli.* 16. **leta** = CL *laeta.* 17. **ipsius:** i.e., "of Mary herself," dependent on *viscera,* which means here "womb" rather than something biologically more
general. 19. **in ipsa:** i.e., in Mary's womb. 21. **epulantium:** present participle of
epulari.

    Carm. 21. Responsory (for the Virgin Mary). 2. **Iesse:** from *Iesse,* indeclinable
noun = Jesse (Sleumer 405).

5 in pulcherrimam filiam aspexit,
sicut aquila in solem
oculum suum ponit:

Cum supernus Pater claritatem Virginis
adtendit
10 ubi Verbum suum
in ipsa incarnari voluit.

Nam in mistico misterio Dei,
illustrata mente Virginis,
mirabiliter clarus flos
15 ex ipsa Virgine
exivit:

Cum supernus Pater claritatem Virginis
adtendit
ubi Verbum suum
20 in ipsa incarnari voluit.
Gloria Patri et Filio
et Spiritui sancto,
sicut erat
in principio.

25 Cum supernus Pater claritatem Virginis
adtendit
ubi Verbum suum
in ipsa incarnari voluit.

CARMEN 23

O tu illustrata
de divina claritate,
clara Virgo Maria,
Verbo Dei infusa,
5 unde venter tuus floruit
de introitu Spiritus Dei,
qui in te sufflavit
et in te exsuxit

---

9. adtendit = CL *attendit*. 12. mistico = CL *mystico*. misterio = CL *mysterio*.
 Carm. 23. Antiphon (for the Virgin Mary). 8. exsuxit: from *exsugere*. 9. abstulit: from *auferre*.

quod Eva abstulit
in abscisione puritatis,   10
per contractam contagionem
de suggestione diaboli.

Tu mirabiliter abscondisti in te
inmaculatam carnem
per divinam racionem,   15
cum Filius Dei
in ventre tuo floruit,
sancta divinitate eum educente
contra carnis iura
que construxit Eva,   20
integritati copulatum
in divinis visceribus.

CARMEN 64

1. O Ecclesia,
oculi tui similes
saphiro sunt,
et aures tue monti Bethel,
et nasus tuus est   5
sicut mons mirre et thuris,
et os tuum quasi sonus
aquarum multarum.

2. In visione vere fidei
Ursula Filium Dei amavit   10
et virum cum hoc seculo reliquit
et in solem aspexit
atque pulcherrimum iuvenem
vocavit, dicens:

10. **abscisione:** from *abscisio, onis* = "breach" (Niermeyer 6; the word also can mean in ML "castration" and "excommunication"). 11. **contractam:** perfect passive participle of *contrahere*. 15. **racionem** = CL *rationem*. 21. **copulatum:** modifies *eum* in the prior line.
      Carm. 64. Sequence (irregular, on the model of Notker). 3. **saphiro:** from *saphirus, i* = "sapphire" (Sleumer 696). 4. **tue** = CL *tuae*. **Bethel:** indeclinable noun, here in the dative with *monti* = Mount Bethel (Sleumer 162). 6. **mirre:** the better spelling is *myrrhae*, from *myrrha, ae* = "myrrh" (Sleumer 534). **thuris:** from *thus, thuris* = "incense" (Sleumer 782). 9. **vere** = CL *verae*. 10. **Ursula:** i.e., Saint Ursula. 11. **virum:** i.e., her betrothed. **seculo** = CL *saeculo*.

15   3. In multo desiderio
desideravi ad te venire
et in celestibus
nuptiis tecum sedere,
per alienam viam ad te currens
20   velut nubes que in purissimo aere
currit similis saphiro.

       4. Et postquam Ursula
sic dixerat,
rumor iste
25   per omnes populos exiit.
Et dixerunt:
Innocentia puellaris ignorantie
nescit quid dicit.

       5. Et ceperunt ludere cum illa
30   in magna symphonia,
usque dum ignea sarcina
super eam cecidit.
Unde omnes cognoscebant
quia contemptus mundi est
35   sicut mons Bethel.

       6. Et cognoverunt etiam
suavissimum odorem
mirre et thuris,
quoniam contemptus mundi
40   super omnia ascendit.

       7. Tunc diabolus
membra sua invasit,
que nobilissimos mores
in corporibis istis
45   occiderunt.

       8. Et hoc in alta voce
omnia elementa audierunt
et ante thronum Dei
dixerunt:

    17. **celestibus** = CL *caelestibus*.   27. **ignorantie** = CL *ignorantiae*.

9. Wach!   50
rubicundus sanguis innocentis agni
in desponsatione sua
effusus est.

10. Hoc audiant omnes celi
et in summa symphonia   55
laudent Agnum Dei,
quia guttur serpentis antiqui
in istis margaritis
materie Verbi Dei
suffocatum est.   60

THE SEVENTH VISION OF THE SECOND PART

Deinde vidi ardentem lucem tantae magnitudinis, ut aliquis mons
magnus et altus est, in summitate sua velut in multas linguas divisam. Et
coram luce ista quaedam multitudo albatorum hominum stabat, ante
quos velut quoddam velum tamquam crystallus perlucidum a pectore usque ad pedes eorum extensum erat. Sed et ante multitudinem istam quasi   5
in quadam via velut quidam vermis mirae magnitudinis et longitudinis
supinus iacebat, qui tanti horroris et insaniae videbatur ultra quam homo
effari potest. Ad cuius sinistram quasi forum erat, ubi divitiae hominum
atque deliciae saeculares et mercatus diversarum rerum apparuerunt, ubi
etiam quidam homines multa celeritate currentes nullum mercatum facie-   10
bant, quidam autem tepide euntes et venditioni et emptioni ibi insiste-
bant. Vermis autem ille niger et hirsutus atque ulceribus et pustulis plenus
erat, quinque varietates a capite per ventrum suum usque ad pedes in
modum zonarum descendentes in se habens, quarum una viridis, alia
alba, alia rubea, quaedam crocea, quaedam nigra apparebat, plenae ven-   15
eno mortifero. Sed caput eius ita contritum fuit, quod et sinistra maxilla

---

50. **wach:** Middle High German exclamation, akin to something like "ach!" (cf. Newman 243, 314). 52. **desponsatione:** from *desponsatio, onis* = "betrothal" (Niermeyer 325). 59. **materie** = CL *materiae.*
The visions of the *Scivias* are divided into three books, representing creation, salvation, and redemption; there is a total of twenty-six visions, each of which includes
much exegetical commentary by Hildegard also. 2. **linguas:** "tongues" is meant here
literally. 4. **crystallus** = CL *crystallum.* 6. **vermis:** a common word in Hildegard's
writings, here = Satan, as often in ML (cf. Latham 508; Blaise/Chirat 843). 12. **pustulis:** from *pustula, ae* = "pustule" (Sleumer 647).

ipsius iam dissolvi videbatur. Oculi vero eius extrinsecus sanguinei et intrinsecus ignei, aures autem rotundae et hispidae, nares vero et os secundum nares et os viperae, sed manus secundum manus hominis, pedes
autem ut pedes viperae, et cauda brevis et horribilis apparebat. Et collo
5   eius catena imposita fuerat, quae et manus et pedes ipsius alligaverat, ita
quod et eadem catena in lapidem abyssi fortissime firmata illum tam val-
ide constrinxerat, quod se nec hac nec illac secundum nequitiam voluntatis suae movere poterat. Ex ore autem eius multae flammae exeuntes in
quattuor partes se diviserunt, quarum pars una usque ad nubes ascende-
10 bat, et alia inter saeculares homines, alia autem inter spiritales se extende-
bat, quaedam vero usque in abyssum descendebat. Sed flamma illa quae
nubes petebat contra homines illos proeliabatur qui ad caelos ire vole-
bant. Quorum tres acies videbam.

Nam acies una prope nubes, et una in medietate illa quae inter nubes
15 et terram est, et una iuxta terram pergebat, omnes repetitis vocibus "per-
gamus ad caelos" vociferantes. Sed a flamma illa hac et illac proiecti, quidam non cadebant, alii autem pedibus suis se vix sustentabant, alii vero
ad terram cadentes, sed iterum surgentes, ad caelos tendebant. Flamma
autem illa quae se inter saeculares homines diffudit, quosdam ex eis com-
20 burens in taeterrimam nigredinem vertit, quosdam autem suo acumine ita
transfixit, quod eos quocumque volebat inflexit. De qua tamen quidam se
eripientes et ad illos qui caelos petebant pergentes "o vos fideles, praestate
nobis adiutorium" iterato clamore vociferabantur; quidam autem ita
transfixi permanserunt. Illa vero flamma quae se inter spiritales extende-
25 bat, eos sua caligine obtexit. Quos etiam in sex modis considerabam.

Nam alios eadem flamma crudeliter incendio laesit; quos autem laedere non potuit, hos aut viridi aut albo aut rubeo aut croceo aut nigro
mortifero veneno illo quod a capite eiusdem vermis usque ad pedes eius
descendebat, ardenter afflavit. Sed flamma quae abyssum petebat, di-
30 versas poenas illorum in se habebat qui per fontem baptismatis non loti
lucem veritatis et fidei ignorantes Satanam pro Deo coluerant.

Et vidi etiam ex ore ipsius acutissimas sagittas perstrepentes, et a pectore eius nigrum fumum volantem ac a lumbis ipsius ardentem umorem
ebullientem, et ab umbilico eius fervidum turbinem flantem atque ab ex-
35 tremitate ventris ipsius velut immunditiam ranarum scaturientem, quae
omnia magnam inquietudinem in hominibus faciebant. Sed et de ipso

6. **abyssi:** from *abyssus, i* = "abyss" (Sleumer 70).   30. **baptismatis:** from *baptisma, atis* = "baptism" (Sleumer 148).   35. **scaturientem** = CL *scaturrientem*.

taeterrima nebula cum pessimo foetore egrediens multos homines sua
perversitate infecit. Et ecce magna multitudo hominum in multa claritate
fulgentium veniebat, quae eundem vermem fortiter ubique conculcans
acriter eum cruciabat, ita tamen quod ipsa nec a flammis nec a veneno
illius laedi poterat. Audivique iterum vocem mihi de caelo dicentem.   5

—*Scivias* 7.2.

The Songs of Beuern

(*Carmina Burana;* c. 1150–1200)

Of the many features that characterize literary activity during the last half of the twelfth century, one of the most important is the rise of vernacular literary cultures. Vernacular languages were already in place by the Carolingian period, fostering in due course their own traditions in popular and folk literature. But it was not until the twelfth century that the clear division between high literature, written in Latin, and more popular literary forms, written in the vernaculars, began to blur. It would be another century before Dante would render for the first time a full-scale literary project in the vernacular, in many ways thereby marking the end of the Latin Middle Ages. But already in the poems of the *Carmina Burana* collection, one sees a lessening of the boundaries between vernacular and Latin.

Nor is this lessening merely a function of linguistic variety. More important perhaps than the fact that Occitan or Middle High German wend their way through many of the poems of the collection (often in combination with Latin) is the infiltration of themes and genres of a vernacular provenance that are given fresh airing in Latin. It is a gathering of fundamental importance also for its size (228 poems), and for the manifold voices of its many poets, most of whom remain anonymous, but several of whom—Peter of Blois, Walther von der Vogelweide (d. 1228), Otloh of St. Emmeram, Marbod of Rennes (d. 1123), Godfrey of Winchester (d. 1107), Godfrey of St. Victor (d. c. 1195), and the Marner (d. c. 1265)— are well-known figures in medieval French and German literary culture.

The Codex Buranus, the lone manuscript that records the collection we call the *Carmina Burana* (though not the lone witness for all of the poems) was found in Bavaria at Benediktbeuern abbey in 1803. Later the manuscript was moved to Munich. It was recorded (by three hands) in the early thirteenth century, though for what purpose remains unclear. It was first published in 1847. The collection is dominated by songs, and several of the works have accompanying musical notation, but it is not entirely composed of performed pieces. There are three broad themes in the collection, corresponding to the general order of the works: poems 1–55 are moralizing and satirical pieces; 56–186 are the so-called love lyrics (though a dozen of these poems, 122–34, are not properly love lyrics at all); and 187–228 are goliardic and celebratory pieces on a variety of themes and topics.

It is difficult to know why the collection was made. It is a polyglot amalgam of mainly Latin pieces, with some Occitan and Middle High German works. The traditions evinced in the collection are equally various: the German songs seem consistently to point to folk origins, as if the German pieces might have been added to please an audience less well acquainted with Latin or Latin traditions. French courtly literary influences are clearly at work in many of the Latin compositions, including examples of the pastourelle, or shepherdess' song, itself a development out of French folk tradition. French is often enough used, as poem 118, included here, exemplifies. It is the Latin, however, that dominates these pieces, and in them one finds vestiges of classical authors, especially Ovid, and classical meters, especially the hexameter and the elegiac couplet, as well as accentual meters with leonine and end-rhyming, which dominate the collection.

Because the poems of the collection are written by many authors, reflect various literary traditions, both high and low, and presumably represent a wide chronological range, it is difficult to generalize about their Latinity, apart from the fact that they are in most respects typical of ML poetry. Poems 17 and 24, for example, are characteristic of ML accentual verse, with two verses composed in rhyming trochaic dimeters, followed by a trochaic tetrameter (catalectic). The topics of both poems, too, the fickleness of fate and the constant threats of fortune's wheel, are common in other poems of the collection and to ML (and especially Goliardic) poetry generally (see pp. 566–571). But even given their thematic similarities, one can see the differences of presentation of material in the two poems, suggestive of differing traditions and poetic priorities. Poem 17, for example, is much more worldly in its consideration of fortune's power and humanity's lot, much more resigned in its concluding call to all humans to share in the situation it imagines for them. Poem 24, in contrast, while bemoaning much the same lot, frames its depiction in the context of Christian faith and scriptural allusion, so that the resignation of 17 is now transformed into something more positive.

More original in theme and form, poem 62 celebrates the connections of sleep, imagination, physiology, and eroticism. It has been the subject of much debate, mostly because the singularity of its themes and its irregular metrical patterns have made it seem to some editors to be corrupt, a conflation of several poems, or hopelessly bungled. Stanzas 1–4 have been considered by many to be the authentic poem (Schumann), with 5–8 treated as a later addition unworthy to be printed as part of the collection.

Others have argued for the authenticity of stanzas 5–8 (Dronke) and have cited among other evidence the parody of poem 62 in the *Carmina Burana* collection itself—poem 197, *Dum domus lapidea,* which is longer than four stanzas. This is hardly conclusive proof, and all attempts to justify exclusion or inclusion must rest ultimately on subjective grounds. The poem moves from its initial verses, in which sleep is celebrated in a complex web of metrical variations that set the rigors of bodily need in the context of cosmology and myth, to a set of lines which relate sleep to lovemaking, before concluding with a rumination on the physiology of the brain in relation to sleep and a general celebration of the pleasures of sexual release and rest. In its collation of physical and cosmological themes, moreover, the poem taps into the contemporary developments in speculative theology, philosophy, and poetry most famously associated with the school of Chartres and Platonic humanism (see pp. 602–13).

Poem 72, ascribed to Peter of Blois, treats a similar topic, but from a completely different perspective. The poem takes up the literary convention of the lover as soldier, marching forward to do the bidding of Venus (a prominent theme in other poems of the collection, e.g., 62), as it affirms the five stages of love well known in the Latin Middle Ages through Ovid and Donatus. It is unique, however, in the violence it depicts—and celebrates—quite apart from twelfth-century theories of love that sanctioned the rape of country girls, and neither the formal polish nor the traditional motifs do much to blunt the boldness of the poet's voice, or the violence to which it gives pronounced shape.

More conventional in theme is poem 186, which takes up the issue of fidelity through the symbolism of the rose, a commonly deployed medieval image. Less conventional is the meter of this piece, which is written, with the exception of the final elegiac couplet, in dactylic hexameters with leonine rhyme. More metrically consonant with the collection as a whole, poem 118 is a mixture of French and Latin written in accentual meters of various patterns. The smaller pieces, poems 51a, 130, and 174, also feature languages other than Latin and tie into popular traditions. 51a is a crusading song that records a somewhat botched version of the Trisagion, a form of the doxology, as it affirms Christian power against the incursions of Islam against the Latin Kingdom of Jerusalem. Poem 130, in contrast, offers the perspective of a swan that has been spiced, cooked, and is on the verge of being eaten—indeed the final verse of the poem records the gnashing teeth that the swan, with some trepidation, sees approaching its body. 174, finally, presumably arises in folk celebrations of spring, where ritualized dancing and singing helped to affirm the advent of nature's bounty. Here, one finds part of that celebration recorded in nonsense—"hyria hyrie / nazaza trillirivos!"—which seems more to embody the motion implicit in the song's wider context than anything internal to the poem's situation of discourse. Here, too, as in the other shorter pieces, the Latin is simpler than one finds in the longer, more rhetorically laden works, such as 62, where compression and vocabulary often render the Latin difficult to translate or to understand easily.

The *Carmina Burana* have been edited by J. A. Schmeller (*Carmina Burana*, Stuttgart, 1847), who prints the songs as they are recorded in the manuscript, an ordering that was later corrected by W. Meyer through careful physical study of the manuscript (which also eventually led to the discovery of several additional poems, now called the *Fragmenta Burana*). The songs were later (partially) edited by R. Peiper (*Gaudeamus! Carmina vagorum selecta in usum laetitiae*, Leipzig, 1877) and by L. Laistner (*Golias: Studentenlieder des Mittelalters: aus dem lateinischen*, Stuttgart, 1879), whose partial edition was later revised by E. Brost and W. Bulst (*Carmina Burana: Lateinisch und Deutsch: Lieder der Vaganten*, Heidelberg, 1961).

Poems 1–186 have been edited by A. Hilka and O. Schumann (*Carmina Burana*, Band 1, Text: (1) *Die Moralisch-satirischen Dichtungen*, Heidelberg, 1930; *Carmina Burana*: Band 1, Text: (2): *Die Liebeslieder*, Heidelberg, 1941); poems 187–228 have been edited by O. Schumann and B. Bischoff (*Carmina Burana*, Band 1, Text: (3): *Die Trink- und Spielerlieder, Die geistlichen Dramen, Nachträge*, Heidelberg, 1970). A commentary on poems 1–55 has been written by A. Hilka and O. Schumann (*Carmina Burana*: Band 2, Kommentar: (1) *Einleitung (Die Handschrift der Carmina Burana); Die moralisch-satirischen Dichtungen*, Heidelberg, 1930). The commentaries on the remaining poems have yet to be published. The work of Hilka, Schumann, and Bischoff is now the standard edition of the *Carmina Burana*.

Most recently, P. G. Walsh has edited a selection of poems 56–186 (*Love Lyrics from the Carmina Burana*, Chapel Hill, 1993), which contains an excellent introduction, commentary, and English translations. Walsh also has published a useful anthology of poems from the collection (*Thirty Poems from the Carmina Burana*, Reading, Eng., 1976), which has text and notes for the poems selected. David Parlett has translated selections from the whole collection for the Penguin Classics (*Selections from the Carmina Burana: A New Verse Translation*, Harmondsworth, 1986), and E. D. Blodgett and R. A. Swanson have translated the love songs (*The Love Songs of the Carmina Burana*, New York, 1987, with notes). Cf. Raby 2, vol. 2, 256ff. Sidwell 337 provides a list of recent discography.

The text of Hilka and Schumann is reprinted here, with stanzas 5–8 of poem 62 printed as part of the poem.

CARMEN 17

1. O Fortuna,
   velut luna
statu variabilis,
   semper crescis
5   aut decrescis;
vita detestabilis
   nunc obdurat
   et tunc curat
ludo mentis aciem,
10   egestatem,
   potestatem
dissolvit ut glaciem.

2. Sors immanis
   et inanis,
rota tu volubilis,   1
   status malus,
   vana salus
semper dissolubilis,
   obumbratam
   et velatam   2
michi quoque niteris;
   nunc per ludum
   dorsum nudum
fero tui sceleris.

3. Sors salutis   2
   et virtutis
michi nunc contraria
   est affectus
   et defectus
semper in angaria.
   hac in hora
   sine mora
corde pulsum tangite;
   quod per sortem
   sternit fortem,   3
mecum omnes plangite!

Carm. 17. This poem is found only in the *Carmina Burana* collection. The lines are accentual, with two rhyming trochaic dimeters followed by a trochaic tetrameter catalectic. 3. **statu:** ablative of respect. 9. **ludo:** "as if a game." 13. **Sors:** i.e., Fate; in the collection this poem appears on a folio with an illumination of Fortune's wheel. 15. **tu:** in apposition with the catalogue of nouns and adjectives that follow. 19. **obumbratam:** from *obumbrare* = "obscurity." 20. **velatam:** from *velare* = "hiddenness." 21. **michi** = CL *mihi*. 30. **angaria:** the word has several meanings in ML, including, more concretely, "conveyance for military purposes," but here the sense is more abstract, centering on "oppressive service" or "unlawful duty," the idea being that Fate has overly and unfairly burdened the speaker of the poem (on *angaria,* see Niermeyer 43–44).

CARMEN 24

Iste mundus	furibundus	falsa prestat gaudia,	
Quia fluunt	et decurrunt	ceu campi lilia.	
Laus mundana,	vita vana	vera tollit premia,	
Nam impellit	et submergit	animas in tartara.	
Lex carnalis	et mortalis	valde transitoria	5
Fugit, transit	velut umbra,	que non est corporea.	
Quod videmus	vel tenemus	in presenti patria,	
Dimittemus	et perdemus	quasi quercus folia.	
Fugiamus,	contemnamus	huius vite dulcia,	
Ne perdamus	in futuro	pretiosa munera!	10
Conteramus,	confringamus	carnis desideria,	
Ut cum iustis	et electis	in celesti gloria	
Gratulari	mereamur	per eterna secula!	

Amen.

CARMEN 51A

1. Imperator rex Grecorum,
minas spernens paganorum,
auro sumpto thesaurorum
parat sumptus armatorum.
   Ayos   5
o theos athanathos
ysma sather yskyros!
miserere kyrios,
salva tuos famulos!

Carm. 24. This poem is found in one other manuscript; it is written in accentual verses, with two rhyming trochaic dimeters followed by a trochaic tetrameter catalectic. Each line ends in rhyming "a." **1. prestat** = CL *praestat.* **3. premia** = CL *praemia.* **4. tartara:** i.e., Hell. **6. que** = CL *quae.* **9. vite** = CL *vitae.* **11. carnis:** from *caro, carnis.* **12. celesti** = CL *caelesti.* **13. eterna secula** = CL *aeterna saecula.*

   Carm. 51a. This poem is printed as the last part of *Carmen* 51, though clearly a separate song. It treats events in the Holy Land between the end of the Second Crusade, whose aim had been to prop up the Latin kingdoms established by the First Crusade (see pp. 460–72; 478–88), and the beginning of the Third Crusade after the capture of Jerusalem by Saladin in 1187. The stanzas are accentual, trochaic, and monorhythmical. **1. Grecorum** = CL *Graecorum;* with *Imperator rex* = the Byzantine Emperor Manuel Comnenus. **2. paganorum:** i.e., the Islamic kingdom of Fatamid Egypt. **5. Ayos . . . famulos:** this formulation, which functions as a refrain in this poem, is a somewhat altered version of the Greek Tersanctus or Trisagion, one of several versions

10 2. Almaricus miles fortis,
    rex communis nostre sortis,
    in Egypto fractis portis
    Turcos stravit dire mortis.
        Ayos
15 o theos athanathos
    ysma sather yskyros!
    miserere kyrios,
    salva tuos famulos!

    3. Omnis ergo Christianus
20 ad Egyptum tendat manus!
    semper ibi degat sanus,
    destruatur rex paganus!
        Ayos
    o theos athanathos
25 ysma sather yskyros!
    miserere kyrios,
    salva tuos famulos!

                CARMEN 62

        1. Dum Diane vitrea
        sero lampas oritur
        et a fratris rosea
        luce dum succenditur,
5   dulcis aura zephyri
        spirans omnes etheri
            nubes tollit;
            sic emollit
        vi chordarum pectora

---

of the Christian doxology, which offers praise to God in the words taken from Isaiah's
seraphic hymn. A rough translation is, "Listen, O eternal God, save your servants and
spare them, lord.   10. **Almaricus:** i.e., Amalric, king of Jerusalem, who, along with
the Byzantine Emperor Manuel Comnenus, attacked Fatamid Egypt in 1168.
11. **nostre** = CL *nostrae*.   13. **Turcos:** from *Turcae, arum* = Turks (Sleumer 796).
stravit: from *sternere*.   **dire** = CL *dirae*.

    Carm. 62. The poem is found only in the *Carmina Burana* collection; it is written in
accentual verses of varying lengths.   1. **Diane** = CL *Dianae* = the moon.   3. **fratris:**
i.e., Diana's brother, Apollo = the sun.   6. **etheri** = CL *aetheri;* this is an ablative.

et immutat   10
cor, quod nutat
ad amoris pignora.
2. Letum iubar Hesperi
gratiorem
dat humorem   15
roris soporiferi
mortalium generi.
3. O quam felix est antidotum soporis
quot curarum tempestates sedat et doloris!
dum surrepit clausis oculorum poris,   20
ipsum gaudio equiperat dulcedini amoris.
4. Morpheus in mentem
trahit impellentem
ventum lenem segetes maturas,
murmura rivorum per harenas puras,   25
circulares ambitus molendinorum,
qui furantur somno lumen oculorum.
5. Post blanda Veneris commercia
lassatur cerebri substantia.
hinc caligant mira novitate   30
oculi nantes in palpebrarum rate.
hei, quam felix transitus amoris ad soporem,
sed suavior regressus ad amorem!
6. Ex alvo leta fumus evaporat,
qui capitis tres cellulas irrorat;   35
hic infumat oculos
ad soporem pendulos
et palpebras sua fumositate
replet, ne visus exspacietur late.
unde ligant oculos virtutes animales,   40
que sunt magis vise ministeriales.

---

13. letum = CL *laetum*.   **20. surrepit:** from *surrepere* + dative object.   **21. equiperat** = CL *aequiperat* + dative object; *gaudio* is ablative of respect; *ipsum*, the subject (= *antidotum*).   **26. molendinorum:** from *molendinum, i* = "mill" (Niermeyer 700). **35. capitis tres cellulas:** i.e., the three cells of the brain; medieval anatomists considered the brain to be a three-chambered organ.   **38. fumositate:** from *fumositas, atis* = "fume," "vapor" (Latham 204).   **39. exspacietur** = CL *exspatietur*.   **41. que** = CL *quae*.   **vise** = CL *visae*, predicative.

7. Fronde sub arboris amena,
dum querens canit philomela,
suave est quiescere,
45   suavius ludere
in gramine
cum virgine
speciosa.
si variarum
50   odor herbarum
spiraverit,
si dederit
torum rosa,
dulciter soporis alimonia
55   post Veneris defessa commercia
captatur,
dum lassis instillatur.
8. O in quantis
animus amantis
60   variatur vacillantis!
ut vaga ratis per equora,
dum caret ancora,
fluctuat inter spem metumque dubia
sic Veneris militia.

CARMEN 72

1a. Grates ago Veneri,
que prosperi
michi risus numine
de virgine
mea gratum
et optatum
contulit tropheum.

1b. Dudum militaveram,
nec poteram
hoc frui stipendio;
nunc sentio
me beari,
serenari
vultum Dioneum.

42. **amena** = CL *amoena*.   43. **querens:** from *queri*.   60. **vacillantis:** present active participle of *vacillare*, used substantively here = "vacillations."   61. **equora** = CL *aequora*.

Carm. 72. This poem is recorded in one other manuscript, London, B. L. Arundel 384 (though it is not complete there, lacking stanzas 5a and b). It is attributed to Peter of Blois (c. 1135–1204). The poem is in the form of a sequence, with five pairs of stanzas each sharing the same accentual, end-rhymed scheme. 1a. **que** = CL *quae*. **michi** = CL *mihi*. **risus:** genitive, with modifying *prosperi*. **numine:** ablative of means.   1b. **Dioneum:** from *Dioneus, a, um* (= CL *Dionaeus, a, um*) = "pertaining to Venus" (LS 583), here

2a. Visu, colloquio,
　　contactu, basio
frui virgo dederat;
　　　　sed aberat
linea posterior
　　et melior
　　　　amori.
quam nisi transiero
　　de cetero
sunt que dantur alia
　　materia
　　　　furori.

2b. Ad metam propero.
　　sed fletu tenero
mea me sollicitat,
　　　　dum dubitat
solvere virguncula
　　repagula
　　　　pudoris.
flentis bibo lacrimas
　　dulcissimas;
sic me plus inebrio,
　　plus haurio
　　　　fervoris.

3a. Delibuta lacrimis
oscula plus sapiunt,
blandimentis intimis
mentem plus alliciunt.
ergo magis capior,
　　et acrior
vis flamme recalescit.
sed dolor Coronidis
　　se tumidis
exerit singultibus
　　nec precibus
　　　　mitescit.

3b. Preces addo precibus
basiaque basiis;
fletus illa fletibus,
iurgia conviciis,
meque cernit oculo
　　nunc emulo,
nunc quasi supplicanti;
nam nunc lite dimicat,
　　nunc supplicat;
dumque prece blandior,
　　fit surdior
　　　　precanti.

---

modifying *vultum*, but better rendered as a substantive, i.e., "Venus' face." 2a. **dederat:** *frui* completes the meaning = "had given to enjoy," with ablative objects. **linea posterior:** i.e., the "last stage" of love; the four earlier stages are recorded in the prior lines with the nouns *visa, colloquio, contactu, basio,* i.e., "looking," "speaking," "touching," and "kissing." These stages are a commonplace in CL and ML poetry; cf. Ovid, *Met.* 10.342 and, in the *Carmina Burana,* poems 88 and 154. 3a. **delibuta:** predicative. **plus sapiunt:** *sapiunt* is intransitive here, with *plus* having the sense of "better." **flamme** = CL *flammae*. **Coronidis:** from *Coronis, onidis* = the mother of Asclepius by Apollo; she is used here as a symbol for feminine grief. Coronis was a Thessalian princess before she was killed by Apollo for infidelity, but not before her unborn son, Asclepius, was snatched from her womb by Apollo. 3b. **emulo** = CL *aemulo,* modifies *oculo.* **supplicanti:** present active participle of *supplicare,* modifying *oculo.*

4a. Vim nimis audax infero.
hec ungue sevit aspero,
    comas vellit,
    vim repellit
    strenua,
    sese plicat
    et intricat
    genua,
    ne ianua
pudoris resolvatur.

4b. Sed tandem ultra milito,
triumphum do proposito.
    per amplexus
    firmo nexus,
    brachia
    eius ligo,
    pressa figo
    basia;
    sic regia
Diones reseratur.

5a. Res utrique placuit,
et me minus arguit
mitior amasia,
    dans basia
    mellita

5b. Et subridens tremulis
semiclausis oculis,
veluti sub anxio
    suspirio
    sopita.

Carmen 118

1. Doleo, quod nimium
patior exilium.
pereat hoc studium,
    si m'en iré,
5 si non reddit gaudium,
    cui tant abé

2. Tua pulchra facies
me fey planser milies;
pectus habet glacies.
    a remender   10
statim vivum facies
    per un baser!

4a. **hec** = CL *haec.* **sevit** = CL *saevit.* 4b. **Diones:** i.e., Venus. 5a. **amasia:** from *amasia, ae* = "lover" (Niermeyer 39; Walsh 46). 5b. **subridens** = CL *surridens.* **sopita:** perfect passive participle of *sopire,* modifying *amasia.*
    Carm. 118. This poem is found only in the *Carmina Burana* collection. The first three verses of each stanza are written in seven-syllable, accentual rhymes, followed by three lines alternating between four and seven syllables, also in accentual rhymes. 4. **si m'en iré:** French = "I will go." 5. **reddit:** i.e., *hoc studium.* 6. **cui tant abé:** French = "for whom I long so much." 8. **me fay planser** = French = "makes me cry." **milies:** the better spelling of this adverb is *millies* = "a thousand times" (Sleumer 520). 10. **a remender:** French = "to cure." 11. **vivum:** the Latin object (*vivus, a, um*) of the French *a remender,* it is difficult to bring into English, but means something like, "to cure me at once and to make me alive...." 12. **per un baser:** French = "with a kiss"; with *facies* and the preceding lines the meaning is something like "kiss my face."

3. Prohdolor, quid faciam?
ut quid novi Franciam?
15 perdam amicitiam
de la gentil?
miser corde fugiam
de cest pays?

4. Cum venray in mon pays,
20 altri drud i avra bris.
podyra, mi lassa dis.
me miserum!
suffero par sue amor
supplicium.

5. Dies, nox et omnia   25
michi sunt contraria.
virginum colloquia
me fay planszer.
oy suvenz suspirer plu
me fay temer.   30

6. O sodales, ludite!
vos qui scitis, dicite;
michi mesto parcite:
grand ey dolur!
attamen consulite   35
per voster honur!

7. Amia, pro vostre amur
doleo, suspir et plur;
par tut semplant ey dolur
grande d'amer.   40
fugio nunc; socii,
lassé m'aler!

1. Olim lacus colueram
olim pulcher exstiteram,
dum cygnus ego fueram.
miser! miser!
5 Modo niger
et ustus fortiter!

2. Eram nive candidior,
quavis ave formosior;
modo sum corvo nigrior.
miser! miser!   10
Modo niger
et ustus fortiter!

13. **prohdolor:** exclamation = *pro + dolor.*   16. **de la gentil:** French = "of the lady."
18. **de cest pays:** French = "from this country."   19. **cum ... dis:** these lines are
written in French and mean something like, "When I come home, / another love she
will have taken. / It is hard to forget old times."   23. **par sue amor:** French = "for
love of her."   28. **me fey planszer:** French = "makes me lament."   29. **oy suvenz
suspirer plu:** French = "I sigh and weep much."   30. **me fay temer:** French = "makes
me fearful."   33. **mesto** = CL *maesto.*   34. **grand ey dolur:** French = "great suffering."   36. **per voster honur:** French = "for your honor."   37. **Amia, pro vostre
amur:** French = "Dear friend, for your love."   38. **suspir et plur:** French = "I sigh
and weep."   39. **par tut semplant ey dolur / grande d'amer:** French = "the great
suffering of the lover is well known by all."   42. **lassé m'aler:** French = "let me go."

Carm. 130. This poem appears only in the *Carmina Burana* collection. The poem
is written in eight-syllable, accentual iambics. 2. **exstiteram:** as often in ML, *ex-
stare = esse* (cf. Blaise/Chirat 337). 7. **nive ... ave ... corvo:** ablatives of comparison with *candidior, formosior,* and *nigrior,* respectively.

3. Me rogus urit fortiter,
   gyrat, regyrat garcifer;
15 propinat me nunc dapifer.
       miser! miser!
       Modo niger
     et ustus fortiter!

4. Mallem in aquis vivere,
   nudo semper sub aere,   20
   quam in hoc mergi pipere.
       miser! miser!
       Modo niger
     et ustus fortiter!

5. Nunc in scutella iaceo   25
   et volitare nequeo;
   dentes frendentes video—
       miser! miser!
       Modo niger
     et ustus fortiter!

CARMEN 174

1. Veni, veni, venias
   ne me mori facias!
   hyria hyrie
   nazaza trillirivos!

2. Pulchra tibi facies, 5
   oculorum acies,
   capillorum series—
   o quam clara species!

3. Rosa rubicundior,
   lilio candidior,   10
   omnibus formosior,
   semper in te glorior!

CARMEN 186

I. Suscipe, flos, florem,   quia flos designat amorem!
   Illo de flore,   nimio sum captus amore;

14. **garcifer:** from *garcifer, eris* = "cook" (Latham 208; Habel/Gröbel 163).
21. **mergi:** present passive infinitive of *mergere*, complement of *mallem*, parallel with
vivere.   27. **dentes frendentes:** this phrase plays on the idiom *dentibus frendere*, "to
gnash the teeth."
   Carm. 174. This poem is found only in the *Carmina Burana* collection; the poem
is (with the exception of 1.3) written in seven-syllable, accentual, end-rhymed lines.
Along with several other poems in the collection, these simple verses probably arose
in the celebration of spring's arrival and included participation of bachelors and un-
married women in ritualized dancing.   3. **hyria . . . trillirivos:** v. 3 of this stanza is
the only one to have six syllables; the lines are nonsense words.   6. **acies:** i.e., "sharp-
ness," or "brightness."
   Carm. 186. This poem is found only in the *Carmina Burana* collection; part 1 is
in dactylic hexameters; part 2 is an elegiac couplet; both parts have leonine rhyme.

Hunc florem, Flora   dulcissima, semper odora!
Nam velut aurora   fiet tua forma decora.
Florem, Flora, vide!   quem dum videas, michi ride!   5
Flori fare bene!   tua vox cantus philomene.
Oscula des flori!   rubeo flos convenit ori.

II. Flos in pictura   non est flos, immo figura;
Qui pingit florem,   non pingit floris odorem.

6. **fare:** imperative of *for, fari* = "speak." 8. The sentiments of these lines are strikingly similar in theme and vocabulary to the final *carmen* of Ausonius' *De Bissula* (see pp. 85–88).

PLATE 29. A folio from a French Book of Hours from the fifteenth century.

PLATE 29

Les heures de notre dame en francois
Manuscript on paper, fifteenth century, fol. 187 recto
Koopman Collection
John Hay Library, Brown University

This Book of Hours, written in French in the fifteenth century, has a strong semi-Gothic hand, as this folio shows. The initials on this folio, and throughout, are in red and blue, with some decoration. The hand shows consistent lines and down-strokes, and almost every page is brightly adorned with red and blue penstrokes, as here, filling out the lines on the page. The Gothic initial shown here is in gold and red. The folios have margins and lines ruled in pencil, 18 to a page, and visible here. The binding of the manuscript, which is contemporary to it, is of blind stamped sheepskin. The manuscript is 16 cm. in height and has 275 folios.

Alan of Lille

The Lament of Nature; Against Claudian
(*De planctu naturae,* c. 1170; *Anticlaudianus,* c. 1182)

The twelfth century witnessed numerous changes at various cultural levels, but perhaps the most significant intellectual shift occurred in the area of cosmology. Before the twelfth century, cosmological speculation had been a much more settled matter. The Augustinian view offered a clear dichotomy between the temporal world of earthly affairs and the timeless retreat of God's heaven. By the early twelfth century, however, this view, with its implicit divide between perfection and imperfection, temporal and eternal, was feeling the pressure of fresh perspectives, formulated under the influence of newly imported Platonic notions of participation and ascent. Alan of Lille is one of the more important poets to make use of the Platonic tradition in the twelfth century.

Platonic notions had been implicit in Christian thinking since the second century C.E., and some of the work of Plato had been available to the West since that time in Latin translations. But Platonic tendencies in the twelfth century were much more widely felt, and the larger sphere of their influence included an important effect on the development of Medieval Latin poetry—for poetry became an important venue to frame the new views of Platonic cosmologies. The leading center of this work in philosophy and poetry was the so-called school of Chartres. There, for much of the century, experiments in cosmology, allegory, and philosophy conspired to create a body of work that was both poetic and philosophical and that had profound influences on later writers of the Latin and vernacular traditions, most notably Dante and Chaucer.

One reason for the Chartrian achievement was the fact that Chartres had the most liberal curriculum devoted to the Classics of any school in the twelfth century. Chartrians, unlike many other scholars of this period, were not plagued by pangs of guilt or conscience when they read the classical authors. They felt that all knowledge was integrative and that all the powers a human could muster ought to be brought to bear in constructing human self-knowledge. The emphasis in the curriculum on Platonic and Neoplatonic teachings had the pedagogical effect of closely linking the classicizing impetus of poetry writing to the larger philosophical and theological concerns of the Platonic revival.

The work of the Chartrian school over the course of the twelfth century developed in several ways (and not only at the cathedral school, for Chartrian humanism represents a way of thought as much as a physical place). Symbol and analogy were important tools in much of the work of the Chartrians, especially in those writers who believed that individual things embodied the divine mystery. The bases for this mode of thought were the tradition of scriptural exegesis, coupled with the writings of Boethius (see pp. 138–42) and John Scottus Eriugena (see pp. 264–70), among others. Hymns and prayers of mystical ascent usually figured prominently in the work of thinkers subscribing to this perspective, and the work of Anselm or Bernard of Clairvaux is exemplary in this regard (see pp. 432–36 and 554–62).

Some Chartrians took a more practical tack in analyzing the problem of cosmology. A group of thinkers, including Alan of Lille, approached the issue from a rational and formally philosophical perspective. These thinkers believed that the mind and cosmos were mutually intelligible. The ideal world, which both mind and cosmos reflect, is analogous to the real world and thus metaphorically accessible. Less rational and analytical in their approach were those Platonists who approached cosmological issues from the standpoint of what is now called psychology. They held that the power of the mind could give symbolic expression to its affections and that it could discover the bases of emotion and affect. The cosmos became, in such a view, the setting for a complex web of human relations and feelings.

For such an important figure in the Medieval Latin tradition, the details of Alan's life are woefully lacking. He was born at Lille around 1116. He studied at St. Peter's in Lille, then proceeded to Paris and Chartres. He eventually took up teaching duties at Paris. He died around 1203. He was a prodigious writer, and has left, in addition to the two major poems excerpted here, numerous works of theology, exegesis, and rhetoric. The *De planctu naturae*, excerpted here, was written some time around 1170, though this date is by no means certain. It seems to be written, in any case, well before the *Anticlaudianus*. It is a Menippean satire—that is, it is written, like Boethius's *Consolation* (see pp. 138–42), in verse and prose. The work takes up the central concern of the Chartrians, the relationship of humanity to nature. Alan's poem renders a view of humanity that has fallen away from nature, and our excerpts give vent to this bifurcation more directly. The second poem excerpted here, the *Anticlaudianus*, is later than the *De planctu naturae*, dating from the early 1180s. Its topic is the moral quality of humanity, a focus suggested in the title,

ALAN OF LILLE

which derives from the poem *Against Rufinus* by the fourth-century poet
Claudian, who qualified much human activity in his poem in the context
of imperfection. Alan's poem is written against Claudian's view and seeks
the grounds on which moral improvement obtains. The poem is, properly
speaking, an epic, and its topic can be construed in epic terms, since Alan
sings of the perfection of humanity cultivated by the saving grace of nature's orderly care and God's sanctifying love.

The *De planctu naturae* has been edited by T. Wright (*Liber de planctu naturae*, in *The Anglo-Latin Satirical Poets and Epigrammatists of
the Twelfth Century*, vol. 2, pp. 429–522, Rolls Series, 59, London,
1872) and by N. M. Häring ("Alan of Lille, 'De Planctu Naturae,'" *Studi
Medievali*, ser. 3, 19.2 (1978), pp. 797–879). D. M. Moffat has translated
the poem into English for the Yale Studies in English series, vol. 36 (*The
Complaint of Nature*, New York, 1908), as has J. J. Sheridan for the Medieval Sources in Translation series of the Pontifical Institute of Mediaeval Studies, vol. 26 (*Alan of Lille, The Plaint of Nature*, New York,
1980). The *Anticlaudianus* has been edited by T. Wright (*Anticlaudianus*,
in *The Anglo-Latin Satirical Poets and Epigrammatists of the Twelfth
Century*, vol. 2, pp. 268–428, Roll Series, 59, London, 1872) and R. Bossuat (*Alain de Lille, Anticlaudianus*, Paris, 1955). J. J. Sheridan has translated the poem into English for the Pontifical Institute of Mediaeval Studies (*Alan of Lille, Anticlaudianus or the Good and Perfect Man*, Toronto,
1973). Wetherbee 1, 11ff. and 187ff. treats the wider context of twelfth-
century intellectual currents with respect to Chartrian humanism, Platonism, and the work of Alan specifically.

Häring's text of the *De planctu naturae* is reprinted without change;
Bossuat's text of the *Anticlaudianus* is followed, reading at 3.340 *Sic* for
Sir; and at 9.394–95 "i" for "j," as it is printed at 396 and elsewhere.
Throughout, consonantal and vocalic "u" are distinguished.

THE LAMENT OF NATURE

Illic forma rose picta fideliter
A vera facie devia paululum
Equabat proprio murice purpuram
Telluremque suo sanguine tinxerat.
5 Concludens sociis floribus affuit
Flos illic redolens gratus Adonidis

1. This metron is written in minor Asclepiads. **rose** = CL *rosae*. 3. **equabat** = CL
aequabat. 6. **Adonidis:** from *Adonis, Adonidis*, here = anemone (cf. Sheridan 1,
106, n. 3).

Argentoque suo nobile lilium
Preditabat agros imaque vallium.
Illic ore thimum dispare disputans
Certabat, reliquis floribus invidens,   10
Narcisi socio flore, iocantia.
Ridebant tacito murmure flumina.
Vultu florigero flos aquilegius
Florum prenituit lucifer omnium
Vernalisque loquens temporis ocia   15
Stellabat viole flosculus arbuta
Picture facies plena favoribus.
Hic floris speciem vivere iusserat
Que regalis erat cartula nominis,
Scribentisque tamen nescia pollicis.   20
Hee sunt veris opes et sua pallia,
Telluris species et sua sidera
Que pictura suis artibus edidit,
Flores effigians arte sophistica.
Hiis florum tunicis prata virentibus   25
Veris nobilitat gracia prodigi.
Hec bissum tribuunt illaque purpuram,
Que texit sapiens dextra Favonii.

—De Plan. Nat. met. 2.

Hec vestium ornamenta quamvis sue plenis splendititatis flammarent
ardoribus, eorundem tamen splendor sub puellaris decoris sidere pacieba-
tur eclipsim. In latericiis vero tabulis arundinei stili ministerio virgo varias

---

8. **preditabat:** from *praeditare* = "to enrich" (cf. Sheridan 1, 106). 9. **thimum** =
CL *thymum.* 11. **Narcisi:** the better spelling is *Narcissi,* from *Narcissus, i* = the
figure who fell in love with the reflection of his own form in a pool of water and,
though loved by Echo, pined away for himself. He was turned into a flower.
13. **aquilegius:** modifying *flos;* the phrase *flos aquilegius* = *aquilegia,* i.e., "the colum-
bine" (cf. Latham 27, Sheridan 1, 107). 14. **prenituit** = CL *praenituit.* 16. **viole** =
CL *violae.* 17. **picture** = CL *picturae.* 19. **que** = CL *quae.* 20. **pollicis:** from
pollex, icis; the description in these verses is a complicated periphrasis for the *basilisca*
(cf. Sheridan 1, 107, n. 6). 21. **hee** = CL *hae.* 27. **hec** = CL *haec,* modifying
prata, as does *illaque.* **bissum** = CL *byssum,* from *byssus, i* = "linen" (Latham 61).
    1. **sue** = CL *suae.* **splendititatis** = CL *splendoris* (cf. Sheridan 1, 108). 2. **pa-
ciebatur** = CL *patiebatur.* 3. **eclipsim:** from *eclipsis, is* = "eclipse"; this form is accusative singular (Latham 160). **arundinei** = CL *harundinei,* from *harundineus, a,
um,* modifying *stili.*

rerum picturaliter suscitabat imagines. Pictura tamen, subiacenti materie familiariter non coherens, velociter evanescendo moriens, nulla imaginum post se relinquebat vestigia. Quas cum sepe suscitando puella crebro vivere faciebat, tamen in scripture proposito imagines perseverare non
5   poterant. Virgo etiam, ut pretaxavimus, a celestis regie emergens confinio, in mundi passibilis tugurium curru vitreo ferebatur. Ipse vero Iunoniis alitibus nullius iugi magisterio disciplinatis sed sibi spontanea voluntate coniugis trahebatur. Homo vero, virginis capiti curruique supereminens, cuius vultus non terrenitatis vilitatem sed potius deitatis redolebat arch-
10   anum, inpotentiam sexus supplendo feminei, modesto directionis ordine currus aurigabat incessum. Ad cuius pulcritudinis dignitatem investigandam, dum tamquam manipulos oculorum radios legarem visibiles, ipsi tante non audentes maiestatis obviare decori, splendoris hebetati verberibus, nimis meticulosi ad palpebrarum contubernia refugerunt.
15   In prefate vero virginis adventu, quasi suas renovando naturas omnia sollempnizare crederes elementa. Firmamentum vero, quasi suis cereis virgineum iter illuminans, ut solito plenius radiarent suis imperabat sideribus. Unde et ipsa lux diurna tantam eorum mirari videbatur audaciam, que in eius conspectu quasi nimis insolenter viderat apparere. Phebus
20   etiam, solito vultum induens letiorem, in occursu virginis totas sui luminis effundebat divicias. Sororem etiam, quam sui splendoris depauperaverat ornamentis, ei veste iocunditatis reddita, regine venienti iubet occurrere.

                                  —*De Plan. Nat.* Prose 4.

2. **coherens** = CL *cohaerens*. **evanescendo:** the ablative gerund in ML often = present active participle, here with *moriens* describing *pictura*. 3. **sepe** = CL *saepe*.
4. **scripture** = CL *scripturae*. 5. **pretaxavimus:** from *praetaxare* = "to mention" (Blaise/Chirat 657). 6. **passibilis:** from *passabilis, is* = "passable" (Sheridan 1, 108). **Iunoniis:** from *Iunonius, a, um* = "Junonian," modifying *alitibus* (*ales, alitis*) (cf. LS 1018). 9. **terrenitatis:** from *terrenitas, atis* = "of an earthly character" (Blaise/Chirat 813). **archanum** = CL *arcanum*. 10. **inpotentiam** = CL *impotentiam*. 11. **pulcritudinis** = CL *pulchritudinis*. 13. **tante** = CL *tantae*.
15. **prefate** = CL *praefatae*, modifying *virginis*. 16. **sollempnizare:** the better ML spelling is *sollemnizare* = "to celebrate" (Blaise/Chirat 765). 19. **Phebus** = CL *Phoebus*. 21. **divicias** = CL *divitias*. **sororem:** i.e., the sister of Phoebus Apollo = Diana, the moon. **depauperaverat:** from *depauperare* = "to make poor" (Latham 139, s. v. *depauperatio—depaupero*). 22. **iocunditatis:** from *iocunditas, atis* = "delight" (Sheridan 1, 109). **regine** = CL *reginae*. **occurrere:** complement of *iubet*, with dative object.

Against Claudian

Pacis alumpna movet primos Concordia gressus,
Et pleno cuncta perfundens Copia cornu,
Et Favor, et multo perfusa favore Iuventus,
Et Risus nostre proscribens nubila mentis,
Et Pudor, et certo contenta Modestia fine,   5
Et Racio, mensura boni, quam semper adherens
Felici gressu felix comitatur Honestas,
Et Decus, et cuncta trutinans Prudentia libra,
Et Pietas, et vera Fides, que fraudis in umbra
Nobis ypocritum mentiri nescit amorem,   10
Et virtus que spargit opes, que munera fundit,
Quam penes ignorat ignavam gaza quietem
Nec dormire potest thesauri massa sepulti,
Sed mutat varios tociens peregrina magistros.
    Ultima Nobilitas, et forme laude secunda,   15
A longe sequitur harum vestigia; quamvis
Nescio quid presigne gerat, tamen huius ad unguem
Non poterat reliquis facies equare decorem;
Munere Fortune melior sed parcius ipsa
Gracia Nature dotes effundit in illa.   20

1. The lines excerpted here follow a lengthy prose prologue and 32 hexameters in which Nature, dismayed at the defects she spies in all of her creations, decides to form the perfect man. She therefore summons the Virtues to aid her in this undertaking, after which a description of her perfect habitat is offered. **alumpna** = CL *alumna*. **Concordia:** like the other figures named subsequently, Concord is a personification, one of the virtues whom Nature seeks out for assistance. 2. **Copia:** i.e., Plenty. 3. **Favor:** i.e., Favor; *Iuventus* is in apposition with it. 4. **Risus:** i.e., Laughter. **nostre** = CL *nostrae*. 5. **Pudor:** i.e., Temperance. **Modestia:** i.e., Moderation. 6. **Racio** = CL *Ratio*, i.e., Reason. 7. **Honestas:** i.e., Honesty. 8. **Decus:** i.e., Decorum. **Prudentia:** i.e., Prudence. 9. **Pietas:** i.e., Piety. **vera Fides:** lit., "true Faith," i.e., not a theological "faith," but a more general notion that is the opposite of deception or deceit, i.e., "Sincerity" (cf. Sheridan 2, 46 and n. 9). 10. **ypocritum:** this form is normally a substantive in ML (*hypocrita, ae* [cf. Blaise/Chirat 398]), but here Alan uses it adjectivally to modify *amorem*. 11. **virtus:** Alan describes in these lines *Largitas*, i.e., Generosity. 14. **tociens** = CL *totiens*. 15. **Nobilitas:** i.e., Nobility. **forme** = CL *formae*. 17. **presigne** = CL *praesigne*. 19. **Fortune** = CL *Fortunae*. 20. **Gracia:** or *Gratia*, from *Gratia, ae* = the Graces; though the form is singular here, the meaning is plural, as often in CL and ML poetry (cf. Ovid, *Met.* 6.429 and Sheridan 2, 46, n. 12). **Nature** = CL *Naturae*, dependent on *dotes*, the phrase is the object of *effundit*.

Hec superum soboles gressus maturat in arcem
Nature proprioque domum chorus afflat honore.
    Est locus a nostro secretus climate longo
Tractu, nostrorum ridens fermenta locorum:
25   Iste potest solus quicquid loca cetera possunt;
Quod minus in reliquis melius suppletur in uno;
Quid prelarga manus Nature possit et in quo
Gracius effundat dotes, exponit in isto,
In quo, pubescens tenera lanugine florum,
30   Sideribus stellata suis, succensa rosarum
Murice, terra novum contendit pingere celum.
Non ibi nascentis expirat gracia floris
Nascendo moriens; nec enim rosa mane puella
Vespere languet anus, sed vultu semper eodem
35   Gaudens, eterni iuvenescit munere veris.
Hunc florem non urit hyems, non decoquit estas.
Non ibi bacchantis Boree furit ira, nec illic
Fulminat aura Nothi, nec spicula grandinis instant.
Quicquid depascit oculos vel inhebriat aures,
40   Seducit gustum, nares suspendit odore,
Demulcet tactum, retinet locus iste locorum.
Iste parit, nullo vexatus vomere, quicquid
Militat adversum morbos nostramque renodat,
Instantis morbi proscripta peste, salutem.
45   Non vulgus verum, verum miracula gingnens
Sponte nec externo tellus adiuta colono,
Nature contenta manu Zephirique favore,
Parturit et tanta natorum prole superbit.
                                        —*Anticl.* 1.33–80.
    Unius vultus, uno contenta colore
50   Vestis in ornatum membrorum transit, eisdem

22. **afflat:** *afflare* + dative = "to breathe/blow on. . . ." 27. **prelarga** = CL *praelarga*. 31. **celum** = CL *caelum*. 35. **eterni** = CL *aeterni*. 36. **hyems** = CL *hiems*. **estas** = CL *aestas*. 37. **Boree** = CL *Boreae*, from *Boreas, ae* = North Wind. 38. **Nothi** = CL *Notus, i* (sometimes *Notos, i*) = South Wind (LS 1218). 39. **inhebriat** = CL *inebriat*. 45. **gingnens** = CL *gignens*, present active participle of *gignere*. 49. After summoning the Virtues, Nature asks them to work together to fashion her perfect man. Prudence notes that they can do everything but endow him with a soul— a task only God can accomplish. Reason suggests that Prudence be sent to God to ask for this soul, an assignment Prudence resists. Concord thus takes up the task of convincing her, and this excerpt describes Concord before she is set to address her sister Virtues.

Sic aptata foris quod eis inscripta putetur.
Illic arte sua vitam pictura secundam
Donat eis quos castus amor, concordia simplex,
Pura fides, vera pietas coniunxit et unum
Esse duos fecit purgati fedus amoris;   55
Nam David et Ionathas ibi sunt duo, sunt tamen unum;
Cum sint diversi, non sunt duo mente sed unus;
Dimidiant animas, sibi se partitur uterque.
Ut sibi Pyrithous se reddat, redditus orbi
Theseus inferni loca, monstra, pericula victat,   60
Vivere posse negat in se, nisi vivat in illo;
Tydeus arma rapit, ut regnet Thydeus alter,
In Polinice suo pugnat seseque secundum,
Dum regnare cupit sibi, poscere regna videtur.
Alter in Eurialo comparet Nisus et alter   65
Eurialus viget in Niso; sic alter utrumque
Reddit et ex uno comitum pensatur uterque.
Atride furit in furiis eiusque furorem
Iudicat esse suum Pilades patiturque Megeram,
Ne paciatur idem Pilades suus alter et idem.   70
Hec pictura suis loquitur misteria signis;
Non res ipsa magis, non lingua fidelius unquam
Talia depingit taliaque sophismate visum

---

55. **fedus** = CL *foedus*.   56. **David:** normally indeclinable, as here (cf. Sleumer 259).
Ionathas: from *Ionathas, ae;* in ML an indeclinable form, *Ionathan,* also exists; both =
Jonathan (cf. Sleumer 445).   58. The sentiment is owed to 1 Sam. 18.1ff.   59. **Pyri-**
thous . . . Theseus: in CL *Pyrithous* = *Pirithous,* the friend of Theseus, who traveled with
Pirithous to the underworld to claim Persephone as a bride for Pirithous after the death of
Pirithous's wife. Theseus was able to escape the capture they both suffered in their attempt
to rescue Persephone; Pirithous remained a prisoner of the underworld.   62. **Tydeus:** father of Diomedes and friend of Polynices, with whom he lost his life in battle.   63. **Poli-**
nice = CL *Polynice,* i.e., Polynices, who, when his brother Eteocles would not share his
rule over Thebes with him, attacked Thebes and was killed, along with his friend Tydeus.
65. **Eurialo . . . Nisus:** in CL, *Eurialo* = *Euryalo,* i.e., Euryalus, warrior-friend of Nisus,
both of whom died together in battle. Cf. Virgil, *Aen.* 9.176–445.   68. **Atride** = CL
Atrides, = "descendant of Atreus," i.e., Orestes, son of Agamemnon and Clytemnestra.
69. **Pilades** = CL *Pylades,* close friend of Orestes.   **Megeram** = CL *Megaeram,* one of
the Furies. When the Furies were threatening Orestes for avenging his father's murder at
the hands of his mother, Pylades attempted to protect his good friend from the anger of
Megaera.   71. **misteria** = CL *mysteria.*   73. **sophismate:** from *sophisma, atis* = "fal-
lacy"; the word in LL has a technical philosophical sense of "contentious syllogism" (cf.
Blaise/Chirat 766) but in ML it has the more general sense of something that is not true

Decipiens oculis, rerum concludit in umbra
75   Qui preco solet esse boni pacisque figura.
Virginis in dextra, foliorum crine comatus,
Flore tumens, fructus expectans, ramus olive
Pubescit nec matris humi solacia querit.
Quo mediante, vices, nexus et vincula rerum,
80   Fedus, amicitiam, pacem Concordia nectit.

—Anticl. 2.178–209.

Hoc igitur cultu virgo preculta laboris
Pondera non fugiens, ne pondere pondus honoris
Effugiat, dum vitat honus ne utiet honorem,
Robur virgineum cumulo virtutis et arte
85   Transgrediens, superat vir sensu, femina sexu:
Sic vir, sic mulier, animo non illa sed ille est.
Nec motu subito quod concipit exprimit actu,
Nec quod mens gignit subitos deducit in actus,
Nam, si conceptum pariat mens ipsa, priusquam
90   Formam suscipiat conceptus mentis in alvo,
Vel firmum capiat mentis matrice sigillum,
Nutritumque diu racionis fomite vivat,
Fetus abortivus subito decurret ad ortus,
Non vita dignus proprio morietur in ortu,
95   Vel vivens saltem lugebit crimina forme.
Ergo legitimo ne partus mentis ab ortu
Deviet et nullam ducat de matre querelam,
Mens gignit, nutrit racio, quod parturit actus
Fabricat in thalamo mentis mentale, priusquam
100   Materiale foras opus evocet. Ergo labore
Mentis et artificis animi studiique favore
Erigitur rota mentalis, post materiali
Effigie describit eam; sic mente priorem
Concipit ut pariat, actu parit illa secundam.

—Anticl. 3. 335–58.

---

or real (cf. Latham 445 and Sheridan 2, 74). 75. **preco** = CL *praeco.* 77. **olive** = CL *olivae.* 81. Eventually, Concord convinces Prudence to undertake the embassy to heaven, and a chariot is constructed specifically for this purpose. In the excerpt here, Arithmetica's excellent knowledge and skill are described in terms of gender and power. 91. **matrice:** from *matrix, icis* = "mother," though distinct from *mater* in the sense that *matrix* specifically denotes propagation (LS 1119). 92. **racionis** = CL *rationis.* 93. **fetus** = CL *foetus.*

Hec mirata diu Fronesis multumque retractans 105
Singula, que visus pregustat, freta sororum
Ducatu, summi regis conscendit in arcem
Qua residet rex ipse poli, qui cuncta cohercet
Legibus imperii, qui numine numina celi
Constringit, cuius nutu celestia nutant. 110
Hec igitur vicina Deo vix sustinet eius
Immortale iubar, ius magestatis inundans,
Expectat lumen, sed eam deffendit ab isto
Fulgure planicies speculi, quam visibus offert
Illa suis, lucem speculo mediante retardans. 115
Tunc virgo, genibus flexis et supplice vultu,
Submisse vocis modulo gestuque timentis
Supplicat eterno regi, verbumque salutis,
Prelibat, mixtaque tremunt formidine verba.
Sed superum genitor, reddens sua iura saluti, 120
Erigit hanc et stare iubet motusque timoris
Sistere, ne terror animum vocemque retardet.
Erigitur mentemque regit, partimque retardat
Virgo metum, stat mens cum corpore, corporis equat
Mens erecta situm. Sic mens submissa resumit 125
Vires, erectam mentem sua verba sequntur.

—Anticl. 6. 273–94.

Bella movet bellique novo iuvenescit in estu.
Debilitas, Morbi, Languores, Tedia, Lapsus

105. When the narrative picks up at this point, Prudence and Reason have traveled through the firmament, having enlisted Theology as their guide through some of the outer reaches of the heavens. They arrive, with Theology's help, at the conclusion of book 5, in Heaven. In the sixth book, then, from which this excerpt comes, Prudence visits Heaven but must view her surroundings in a mirror—for the intensity of divinity, so close at hand in Heaven, is too intense to be viewed without some sort of mediation. In these lines, she makes her way to God himself, in order to ask for the soul that she and her sisters need in order to fashion the perfect man. **Fronesis** = CL *Phronesis, is,* another name for Prudence. 110. **celestia** = CL *caelestia.* 113. **deffendit** = CL *defendit.* 124. **equat** = CL *aequat.* 127. By the point in the narrative excerpted here, Prudence has returned to her sisters with a soul, and they have succeeded in fashioning the perfect man. But the beauty and goodness of this creation has aroused Allecto, one of the three Furies, and she decides to wage a war against Nature's new creation, calling on the Vices to assist her. The excerpt here recounts the marshaling of the various evil cohorts of Allecto before the battle. 128. **Debilitas:** i.e., Weakness. **Morbi:** i.e., Disease. **Languores:** i.e., Weariness. **Tedia** = CL *Taedia,* i.e., Boredom. **Lapsus:** i.e., Failure.

Illius comittantur iter, qui Martis amore
130   Succensi, pugne cupiunt impendere vitam.
Ardet in arma furens, scisso velatus amictu
Luctus et, irrorans lacrimis, arat unguibus ora.
Tristicies, Lamenta, Dolor, Pressura, Ruine
Eius in obsequium fervent, dominique fatentur
135   Miliciam, belloque calent cum rege ministri.
Martis in ardorem nativos excitat ignes
Ignea Luxuries, multo comitata cliente.
Eius in auxilium iurant Periuria, spondet
Falsus Amor, Levitas animi, Lascivia mendax,
140   Insipidus Dulcor, sapidus Dolor, egra Voluptas,
Prosperitas adversa, Iocus lugubris, amara
Gaudia, Paupertas dives, Opulencia pauper.
Post alios in bella furens et promptus in arma,
Sublimi provectus equo gestuque superbus,
145   Excedens habitu verboque superfluus, actu
Degenerans Excessus adest, bellique furorem
Prevenit, et cunctis bellandi suggerit iras.
Quo duce signa gerit et bellum voce minatur
Hebrietas, Fastus, Iactancia, Crapula, Luxus.

—Anticl. 8.251–73.

150   Iam scelerum superata cohors in regna silenter
Arma refert, et se victam miratur, et illud
Quod patitur vix esse putat. Non creditur illi
Quod videt, et Stigias fugit indignata sub umbras.
Pugna cadit, cedit iuveni Victoria, surgit
155   Virtus, succumbit Vicium, Natura triumphat,

130. **pugne** = CL *pugnae.*   132. **Luctus:** i.e., Grief.   133. **Tristicies** = CL *Tristities,*
i.e., Sadness.   **Lamenta:** i.e., Lament.   **Dolor:** i.e., Sorrow.   **Pressura:** i.e., Depression
(cf. Blaise/Chirat 661).   **Ruine** = CL *Ruinae,* i.e., Disaster.   135. **Miliciam** = CL
Militiam.   136. **Martis:** from *Mars, Martis* = Mars, i.e., War.   137. **Luxuries:** i.e.,
Licentiousness.   138. **Periuria:** i.e., Perjury.   139. **Levitas animi:** lit., "lightness of
mind," i.e., Fickleness.   140. **egra** = CL *aegra.*   141. **Iocus:** i.e., "Joke," with *lugubris.*   142. **Opulencia** = CL *Opulentia.*   146. **Excessus:** i.e., Excess.   149. **Hebrietas** = CL *Ebrietas.*   **Fastus:** i.e., Arrogance.   **Iactancia:** i.e., Boasting.   **Crapula:**
i.e., Hangover. (For the names of all of these personified habits, cf. Sheridan 2, 198–
99).   150. In this excerpt, which comes just before the conclusion of the poem, the
battle has taken place and the new man has conquered his enemies. Alan describes
his victory and its consequences.   153. **Stigias** = CL *Stygias,* from *Stygius, a, um.*
155. **Vicium** = CL *Vitium.*

Regnat Amor, nusquam Discordia, Fedus ubique.
Nam regnum mundi legum moderatur habenis
Ille beatus homo, quem non lascivia frangit,
Non superat fastus, facinus non inquinat, urget
Luxurie stimulus, fraudis non inficit error.   160
In terris iam castra locant et regna merentur
Virtutes mundumque regunt, nec iam magis illis
Astra placent sedesque poli quam terrenus orbis.
Iam celo contendit humus, iam terra nitorem
Induit ethereum, iam terram vestit Olimpus.   165
Nec iam corrigitur rastro, nec vomere campus
Leditur, aut curvi deplorat vulnus aratri,
Ut tellus avido, quamvis invita, colono
Pareat, et semen multo cum fenore reddat.
Non arbor cultrum querit, non vinea falcem,   170
Sed fructus dat sponte novos et vota coloni
Fertilitate premit. Spes vincitur ubere fructu,
Gratis poma parit arbor, vitisque racemos,
Et sine se natas miratur pampinus uvas.
E tunicis egressa suis rosa purpurat ortos,   175
Nec spinam matrem redolet, sed sponte creata
Pullulat, atque novos sine semine prodit in ortus.
Sic flores alii rident varioque colore
Depingit terram florum primeva iuventus.

—Anticl. 9.380–409.

160. **Luxurie** = CL *Luxuriae.* 165. **ethereum** = CL *aethereum.* **Olimpus** = CL *Olympus.* 167. **Leditur** = CL *Laeditur.*

NIGEL WHITEACRE

The Mirror of Fools
(*Speculum stultorum;* c. 1180)

U nder the rubric of satire in the Latin Middle Ages, one finds two varieties: burlesque and invective. The latter is mainly a development of the Anglo-Latin writers of the twelfth century and includes two subgenres: the so-called "review of the religious orders" and the "general satire." The review consisted of a detailed accounting of the conventions of particular orders, often couched initially in praise but always including pointed analysis of contradictory or hypocritical activity. Walter Map (see pp. 637–41), among others, was a practitioner of this subgenre of satire. The general satire, by distinction, is comprehensive in the sweep of its scrutiny, leaving no figure or institution untouched. Burlesque developed at the same time, most notably as a form of beast poetry. In this immensely popular genre, which originated in the mid eleventh century with the *Ecbasis captivi,* and which was brought to maturer shape in the middle of the twelfth in Nivardus' *Ysengrimus* (see pp. 528–37), an array of animal figures was placed in incidents that set to worst advantage the foibles and idioms of medieval ecclesiastical culture.

Both burlesque and invective—as well as the sentiments of culture criticism found in Goliardic verse—are present also in the *Mirror of Fools,* a beast poem written in the late twelfth century by Nigel Whiteacre. Of all the satiric beast poems, however, the *Mirror of Fools* is perhaps the most complex in the amalgam of forms it includes. Like its counterparts, it relies on allegory for its fullest effects, especially satirizing monastic culture; for the ass Burnellus, one of the poem's main characters, represents, in Nigel's own words, an ambitious cleric or religious who seeks an abbacy or priorate "which he might proudly trail behind him like a tail." Burnellus seeks an education in Paris, therefore, in order to gain a new tail or, perhaps, grow a longer one. But within the complex narrative of the poem are subplots involving nearly twenty other characters and other literary subgenres common to Medieval Latin and vernacular literatures, including the exemplum, the homily, the bird parliament, the debate, and the complaint.

Several substantive portions of the *Mirror of Fools* are owed to earlier works—Avianus's *Ass and the Lion's Skin,* Nivardus's *Ysengrimus,* the

Ecbasis captivi, and popular and folk traditions deriving from the Celts. The poem's epilogue, in contrast, seems indebted to the Indian *Pantchatantra* and introduces into mainstream Western literature for the first time the story of the ungrateful man and the grateful animals, something Matthew Paris seems also to do at just about the same time. Most of the poem, however, is original to Nigel's imagination.

The broad literary aims of the *Mirror of Fools* ensured its reputation after it was written. The number of manuscripts that remain (nearly forty) attests to its wide circulation (especially in the fourteenth and fifteenth centuries, when most of the extant manuscripts were copied). Moreover, in the ways that he collates his material into coherent stories that move from one to the next topic, Nigel demonstrates his mastery of the narrative style of Ovid's *Metamorphoses,* itself a work of many stories stitched together like a patchwork, and an influential work in the literary firmament of the Latin Middle Ages. The extent that Nigel's poem was read in the thirteenth century—and beyond too, as for example by Boccaccio, Gower, or Chaucer (who mentions the *Mirror of Fools* in the *Nun's Priest's Tale,* which is itself a beast poem)—demonstrates the contemporary regard in which the poem was held, both for its comprehensive mastery of a panoply of literary forms, and for its satiric—its comedic—value (cf. Mozley/Raymo 5–8).

The life of Nigel Whiteacre is obscure. He was born around 1130 in Normandy. We know nothing of his activities until after 1170, when he had already been a monk of Christ Church, Canterbury, for some time— where he came into direct contact with Thomas Becket, and where he remained until his death some time around 1210. His patron was William of Longchamps, bishop of Ely, and an important figure in twelfth-century ecclesiastical politics. Nigel wrote a series of other poems: a hexametric accounting of the archbishops of Canterbury (down to 1184); the *Miracula Sanctae Dei Genetricis Virginis Mariae,* a collection of Mary legends; the *Passio Pauli Primi Heremitae;* the *Passio Sanctae Laurentii;* some shorter works; and his only prose work, the *Tractatus contra curiales et officiales clericos,* a criticism of the growing secularism of the monastic clergy in the late twelfth century.

The *Mirror of Fools* is written in elegiac couplets and is nearly 4,000 lines in length. Of the major beast poems in ML, it is perhaps the most difficult—though none are easy—owing mostly to periphrases, obscure uses of words, and constructions that tend to serve the aim of repetition rather than the accomplishment of plot.

The poem has been edited by J. H. Mozley and R. R. Raymo (*Nigel*

de Longchamps, Speculum Stultorum, Berkeley and Los Angeles, 1960),
with an excellent introduction, copious notes, and appendixes. It has
been translated into English by J. H. Mozley (*A Mirror for Fools: The
Book of Burnel the Ass,* Oxford, 1961; repr. Notre Dame, Ind., 1963). A
new translation by J. Mann is in preparation in the Cambridge Medieval
Classics series. See also Raby 2, vol. 2, 94ff. and 349ff.

The text of Mozley and Raymo is followed here, with "i" for "j," and
at v. 1598 reading *Venerunt* for *Neverunt.*

Burnellus Arrives in Paris and Joins the University

Talia cum pariter gradientes plura referrent,
    Parisius subeunt hospitiumque petunt.
Corpora fessa quies recreat, tenuisque diaetae
    Damna recompensat mensa calixque frequens.

5   Ossa, cutem, nervos, quae vel labor aut via longa
    Quassarat, refovent balnea, cura, quies;
Burnellusque sibi minuit crinesque totondit,
    Induit et tunica se meliore sua.
Pexus et ablutus tandem progressus in urbem

10   Intrat in ecclesiam, vota precesque facit.
Inde scholas adiens secum deliberat utrum
    Expediat potius ista vel illa sibi.
Et quia subtiles sensu considerat Anglos,
    Pluribus ex causis se sociavit eis.

15   Moribus egregii, verbo vultuque venusti,
    Ingenio pollent consilioque vigent.
Dona pluunt populis et detestantur avaros,
    Fercula multiplicant et sine lege bibunt.

1. **gradientes:** from *gradi,* the subject here of *referrent;* referring to Burnellus and a comrade named Arnoldus, whom Burnellus has picked up on his way to Paris. 2. **Parisius:** an indeclinable form of *Parisii, orum* = Paris (Sleumer 582), here in the accusative case. 4. **recompensat:** from *recompensare* = "to compensate for" (Niermeyer 890). 7. **minuit:** i.e., "Burnellus bled himself"; the practice of bloodletting was considered part of good health practices (cf. Mozley/Raymo 158). **totondit:** third person singular, perfect active indicative of *tondere.* 9. **pexus:** perfect passive participle of *pectere.* **ablutus:** perfect passive participle of *abluere.* 13. **Anglos:** from *Anglus, i* = English (Sleumer 110); at Paris the various students loosely arranged themselves by nationalities, a practice that was formalized in the thirteenth century (cf. Mozley/Raymo 158). 16. **pollent:** i.e., Englishmen. 18. **sine lege bibunt:** the English were notorious in continental Europe in the Middle Ages for their love of drink-

Washeyl et drinkheyl necnon persona secunda,
    Haec tria sunt vitia quae comitantur eis;   20
His tribus exceptis nihil est quod in his reprehendas;
    Haec tria si tollas, cetera cuncta placent.
Nec tamen haec ita sunt semper reprobanda, quod illis
    Esse locus nequeat tempore sive loco.
Nam duo praecipue sunt exclusiva dolorum,   25
    Laetitiaeque vias insinuare solent;
Tertia res cohibet, quo dicitur esse referta
    Gallia fermentum ne nocuisse queat.
Hinc comes Angligenis prudens desiderat esse,
    Possit ut illorum conditione frui.   30
Est in eis etiam quiddam (ceu publica fama
    Somniat) adiungi cur magis optet eis,
Si de convictu mores formantur eidem,
    Cur nihil accrescat si comes esse queat?
Si quid eis praeter sortem natura ministrat,   35
    Ante retrove bonum cur nihil inde ferat?
Accelerans igitur studio studiosus adhaesit,
    Ut discat lepide grammaticeque loqui.

---

ing (cf. Mozley/Raymo 158). 19. **washeyl:** lit., "be in good health" (= Old Norse *ves* or *ver heill;* cf. Anglo-Saxon *was hál,* Middle English *waes haeil* and, for more on these forms, see OED, s. v. *wassail*). There are numerous spellings for this word (cf. pp. 514–20 on Geoffrey of Monmouth's use). **drinkheyl:** "drink good health," or "good luck" (= Old Norse *drinc heill;* cf. Middle English *drinc hail* and on the forms, see OED, s. v. *Drinkhail*). **persona secunda:** the phrase is idiomatic, meaning something like "women" or even "lechery." (cf. Latham 345 and, on the idiom, Mozley/Raymo 159). 27. **referta:** perfect passive participle of *refercire,* with the sense here of "popular" (cf. Mozley/Raymo 159); the reference is to sexual intercourse. 28. **fermentum:** the object of *cohibet,* it means something like "heat," "passion" (Mozley/Raymo 159); the sense is playful and ironic, for normally the word refers to the rising of bread or yeast and can even refer to the Eucharist itself (cf. Niermeyer 418; Latham 189). 29. **Angligenis:** from *Angligenus, a, um* = Englishman (Latham 20, s. v. *Anglus—igena (igenus)*). 30. **frui:** complement of *possit,* it takes an ablative object. 34. **cur nihil accrescat si comes esse queat:** the specific reference is to Burnellus's aim to earn a new tail—or to make his current tail grow longer; the more general reference ties into the tradition in the Middle Ages of calling the English *caudati,* owing to a legend that claimed that Saint Augustine of Canterbury made the men of Dorset wear tails after they attacked him during a sermon. Cf. Mozley/Raymo 159. 36. **retrove:** *-ve* is an enclitic conjunction coordinating the phrase *ante retro.* 38. **grammaticeque:** adverb modifying *loqui* = "grammatically" (Mozley/Raymo 160).

Sed quia sensus hebes, cervix praedura, magistri
40   Dogmata non recipit, cura laborque perit.
Iam pertransierat Burnellus tempora multa,
          Et prope completus septimus annus erat,
Cum nihil ex toto, quodcunque docente magistro
          Aut socio, potuit discere praeter hy ha.
45   Quod natura dedit, quod secum detulit illuc,
          Hoc habet, hoc illi nemo tulisse potest.
Cura magistrorum multumque diuque laborans
          Demum defecit, victa labore gravi.
Dorso se baculus, lateri se virga frequenter
50   Applicat, et ferulam sustinuere manus.
Semper hy ha repetit, nihil est quod dicere possit
          Affectus quovis verbere praeter hy ha.
Vellicat hic aurem, nasum quatit ille recurvum,
          Excutit hic dentes, perforat ille cutem.
55   Hic secat, hic urit, hinc solvitur, inde ligatur
          Intonat iste minas, porrigit ille preces.
Sic in eo certant ars et natura vicissim,
          Ars rogat, illa iubet, haec abit, illa manet.
Quorum principia constant vitiosa fuisse,
60   Aut vix aut nunquam convaluisse valent.
A puero didicit Burnellus hy ha; nihil ultra
          Quam quod natura dat retinere potest.
Quod fuit innatum servat natura, quod artis
          Sic abit, ut vento pulvis abire solet.
65   Perdidit expensas, periit labor omnis et omne
          Quod fuit impensum conditione pari.
Spes quoque deperiit caudae superinstituendae,
          Sensit et Anglorum carmina falsa fore.

BURNELLUS BEMOANS HIS INABILITY TO LEARN

Ergo recordatus tandem Burnellus ineptae
          Damna iuventutis se reprehendit ita:
"Heu mihi, quid vixi? quis me furor egit, ut istas

---

44. **hy ha**: i.e., the sound of a donkey, used throughout the selection.   63. **innatum**: perfect participle of *innasci*.   66. **impensum**: perfect passive participle of *impendere*. 67. **superinstituendae**: from *superinstituere* = "to replace" (Latham 467); the aim of Burnellus's journey to and study in Paris is to increase or, if possible, to replace his tail, with which he is displeased.   68. **fore** = CL *esse*, as often in ML.

Aggrederer partes Parisiique scholas?
Quid mihi cum studio cunctoque labore petito?   5
  Nonne satis potuit esse Cremona mihi?
Alpibus emensis et post mea terga relictis
  Stultus in extremis partibus orbis agor.
Ut quid in has partes patriaque domoque relictis
  Trans Rodanum veni, regna videre nova?   10
Quae mihi cura fuit per tanta pericula mortis
  Cernere Francigenas Parisiique scholas;
Nosse vel Angligenas largos Gallosque tenaces,
  Hos calices, illos multiplicare minas?
Appulus huc veni, sed Gallicus ecce revertor;   15
  Burnellusque tamen qui fuit ante manet.
Hic nihil addidici, modicumque quod ante sciebam
  Hic ego me totum dedidicisse scio.
Gallica verba duo tantum retinere loquique
  Si possem, certe gratia magna foret.   20
Quod si forte tria vel multum quatuor essent
  Par Iovis aut maior crederer esse Iove;
Italiam facerem tanto trepidare timore,
  Quod mihi rex ipse certa tributa daret.
Tunc ego Parisius in vanum non adiissem,   25
  Si subiecta foret sic mea terra mihi.
Non modo vadit ita; longe mea stamina Parcae
  Venerunt aliter quam mea vota forent.
Dura mihi certe multum mea fata fuerunt,
  Quae mala multa mihi nilque dedere boni;   30
Quod satis apparet, quia toto peior in orbe
  Non est conditio conditione mea.

---

5. **petito:** perfect passive participle of *petere,* modifying *labore,* parallel with *cunctoque.* 6. **Cremona:** from *Cremona, ae* = Cremona (Sluemer 248); Burnellus's home. 7. **Alpibus:** from *Alpes, ium* = Alps (Sleumer 99). **emensis:** perfect participle of *emetiri.* 9. **ut quid:** often written in ML *utquid* = "to what end," "to what purpose" (Latham 502). 10. **Rodanum:** the better ML spelling is *Rhodanus, i* = Rhone river (Sleumer 675). 12. **Francigenas:** from *Francigenus, a, um* = French (Latham 200, s. v. *Francus—Francigena*). 13. **Gallosque:** from *Gallus, a, um* = French (Latham 207). 15. **Appulus:** the better spelling is *Apulus, a, um* = Apulian or, perhaps, Italian (Sleumer 120 and Mozley/Raymo 160). **Gallicus:** from *Gallicus, a, um* = French (Sleumer 350). 25. **Parisius:** indeclinable; here functioning as if in the accusative of place to which, without a preposition, as in CL. 26. **foret** = *esset.*

Sensus hebes meus est et saxo durior omni,
  Durius hoc pectus est adamante meum,
35 Cor, caput, et cerebrum sunt ponderis atque metalli
  Eiusdem, plumbo nam graviora magis.
Ferrea crura mihi, latus est quasi lamina ferri,
  Non est in toto corpore vena puto.
Aenea ceu pelvis cutis est mea, quae tamen ictus
40   Excipit incassum, nam nihil inde dolet.
Non ego verberibus, non per maledicta perire
  Possum, malleolis vix puto posse mori.
                    —*Spec. Stult.* 1503–1612.

JOHN OF HAUVILLE

The Arch-Weeper
(*Architrenius;* c. 1185)

The dazzling array of literary forms that inhabits the Latin Middle Ages is perhaps nowhere sustained in a more compelling way than in John of Hauville's mock epic poem, *Architrenius.* The poem indeed offers derision and sarcasm, for it is most broadly a satire, and it partakes of the regular poses assumed by the best exemplars of this genre, some of which have been reviewed above (cf. pp. 614–20). But the poem also draws on other traditions. It parlays epic meter, length (4,361 hexameters; 9 books), and diction into moments of seeming high seriousness. It describes nature, beauty, and the human longing for moral perfection and dignity in terms that affirm the traditions of personal poetry written in Latin since the age of Catullus. It draws on allegory, prophecy, burlesque, invective, moral exemplarism—the mainstays of satire. Yet its affirmation of a natural order, sanctioned by divine forces in harmony with nature and somehow reflected in the terrestrial world, highlights the poem's participation in the intellectual revolutions of twelfth-century thought, which included new approaches to viewing creation based on a fresh appreciation of Platonic cosmology and an increased tendency to harmonize ancient theogonies to the surer truths of Christianity.

These strains of twelfth-century influence are ballasted by the countervailing tendency in the *Architrenius* to view the world in harsh, even cynical terms and to worry about it and its inhabitants from the standpoint of imperfection and moral error. In particular, John frames his poem as an intellectual search for moral certitude, making the role and function of the intellect an important rubric of the poem. Indeed, one cannot escape the emphasis in the poem on the solitary figure of the Arch-Weeper, John's main character, who clearly is both example and product of the competing intellectual currents of the twelfth century—rich in new cosmologies, in scholastic methodologies, in reform movements, in secularism. At the same time, the quest for knowledge that takes the Arch-Weeper on his journey through a world fraught with change, difference, and diverse challenges itself speaks to the social context of the poem's composition. Much of the impetus for writing the poem must have come from a personal longing on the part of the poet for certitudes of a kind being challenged in his day, but also resulting from the fundamental changes in social and economic conditions, especially the rise of new money in the cities and the concomitant increase in the power of a newly enriched middle class. John's world was not the world of Saint Anselm. The cloister and the city were much more closely drawn together and the centers of power, formerly Church and state, now included new forces based on rising classes, new sources of revenue, and reformed or remodeled institutions.

The *Architrenius* is also exemplary in its own way of the diverse traditions informing ML literary culture. Not the least of its virtues is its simple blending of so many discrete literary elements into a coherent narrative. In this sense, especially, the *Architrenius* is culture criticism at its best, written squarely in the tradition of Nigel's *Mirror of Fools* or Nivardus's *Ysengrimus,* and even under the influences that inform Goliardic poetry. But John of Hauville cares deeply about the culture he criticizes; he pours out, after all, an extraordinary amount of learning in his epic, and the deftness of his final touch, especially given the amalgam of materials controlled by it, makes him, and his poem, without comparable partner in the Western literary tradition.

Of John of Hauville, very little is known. He was a *magister* at the cathedral school of Rouen and dedicated his poem to Walter of Coutances, bishop of Lincoln but archbishop-elect of Rouen at the time the poem was brought out, probably late in 1184 or early in 1185. John was probably a Norman by birth. His birth date is unknown; he died probably around 1210. The *Architrenius* is the only known work from John's hand. The plot of its lengthy verses is laid out in the headnotes to the various excerpts, but can be summarized briefly in the main. The Arch-Weeper, a young student, has become aware of the moral imperfection of his existence and seeks out the figure of Nature for severe questioning—she must, after all, be the source of his difficulties. The Arch-Weeper then undertakes a series of journeys, eventually meeting Nature in the paradisial Thylos, where she explains the (heretofore) incomprehensible (to him) order of the cosmos. She then offers him the personified figure of Moderation for his bride. Their marriage ends the poem—on a high note of moral, spiritual, and intellectual consonance. Yet never far from the affirmations of the poem's conclusions are its various dissonances—the lyric moments, the epic seriousness merged with comic and biting satire and culture criticism. This amalgam makes readers ever leery of false promises and easy endings. Moderation, it seems, is a path to pursue, but not the end of the Arch-Weeper's search, not the sure and best repose he seeks.

John of Hauville's Latin is classical in its formal features, except orthography, as the notes suggest. He was a careful student of the classical authors, as one would expect from a student trained in the cathedral schools of the twelfth century. At the same time, one finds expressions, idioms, vocabulary owed directly to ML; and though the syntax and grammar are typical of and in some cases better than what one normally finds in twelfth-century writing, the poem is not, and does not pretend to be, a classical pastiche. Like its topic, the poem's Latinity is manifold.

The *Architrenius* has been edited by T. Wright (*Architrenius*, in *The Anglo-Latin Satirical Poets and Epigrammatists of the Twelfth Century*, vol. 1, pp. 240–392, Rolls Series 59, London, 1872); and most recently by P. G. Schmidt (*Architrenius*, Munich, 1974). W. Wetherbee has translated the poem into English (*Johannes de Hauvilla, Architrenius*, in Cambridge Medieval Classics 3, Cambridge, 1994), which includes a substantive introduction, textual and explanatory notes, and Latin text facing the English translation. Wetherbee 1, 11ff. and 242ff., treats the wider context of John's poetry in detail. Raby 2, vol. 2, 100ff., also discusses the poem. Schmidt's text as reprinted in Wetherbee is followed here without change.

THE POWER OF NATURE

Illud enim supraque potest nullaque magistras
Non habet arte manus, nec summa potencia certo
Fine coartatur: astrorum flammeat orbes.
Igne rotat celos, discursibus aera rumpit,
Mollit aque speram, telluris pondera durat,   5
Flore coronat humum, gemmas inviscerat undis,
Phebificans auras, stellas intexit Olimpo.

In these lines, the main character of the poem, the "Arch-Weeper," is pondering the lowly state of his life. Especially ill at ease with the moral depravity that he feels controls all his appetites, he begins his tale by contrasting different paths that might be chosen, different postures that might be assumed (i.e., labor, sloth, arrogance, envy, etc.). The lines excerpted here follow closely on the beginning of the poem's narrative proper and describe the powers of Nature, that is, the larger context in which morality and human appetites subsist.   1. **potest:** the subject is Nature.   2. **potencia** = CL *potentia*.   4. **celos** = CL *caelos*.   **discursibus:** the more common meaning of *discursus* in ML is "argument," "conflict" (cf. Latham 150), but here it has the sense of "choppy motions."   7. **Phebificans:** from *phebificare*, "to shed light on" (Latham 349).   **Olimpo** = CL *Olympo*, metonymic

Natura est quodcumque vides, incudibus illa
Fabricat omniparis, quidvis operaria nutu
10   Construit, eventusque novi miracula spargit.
Ipsa potest rerum solitos avertere cursus,
Enormesque serit monstrorum prodiga formas,
Gignendique stilum variat, partuque timendo
Lineat anomalos larvosa puerpera vultus.

—*Archit.* 1.234–47.

A Description of the Girl

Verticis erecta moderatum circinat orbem
Sperula, nec temere sinuato deviat arcu.
Non obliqua means, ubi nec tumor advena surgit,
Nec vallis peregrina sedet; lascivit in auro
5   Indigena crinis, nec mendicatur alumpnus
Pixidis, exter honos, nec nubit adultera ficte
Lucis imago come: non exulat arte capilli
Umbra, nec aurifero ferrum sepelitur amictu.
    Hec capitis preciosa seges nec densior equo
10   Luxuriat, iuncto descensu prona, nec errat
Limite turbato, nec divertendo vagatur
Transfuga, nec cedit alio pulsante capillus.
    A frontis medio tractu directa superne
Verticis ad centrum via lactea surgit aranti
15   Pectine, cuius acu geminas discessit in alas,
Et tandem trifidum coma cancellatur in orbem
Divisoque prius iterum cohit agmine crinis.
    Liber apex frontis nitidum limante iuventa
Tenditur in planum: trito radiosa politu

---

of "the sky" here. **8. incudibus:** from *incus, udis.* **13. gignendique:** from *gignere.*
14. lineat: the normal sense in ML is "to measure," "to survey," but here it means something like "to give shape to . . ." (cf. Niermeyer 614; Wetherbee 3, 19). **larvosa:** from *larvosus, a, um* = "diabolical" (Latham 270).

Having decided to confront Nature, the Arch-Weeper journeys across the world to find her and eventually comes upon the palace of Venus, where he encounters one of the goddess's maiden-students, whose description is excerpted here. **2. sperula** = CL *sphaerula,* diminutive of *sphaera* = "little sphere" (LS 1741). **5. alumpnus** = CL *alumnus;* the use of the parasitic consonant is common in ML. **6. pixidis** = CL *pyxidis,* from *pyxis, idis.* **ficte** = CL *fictae.* **9. hec** = CL *haec.* **14. aranti:** present active participle of *arare* = "to plow" (LS 164).

Et bysso, quo prima cutem vestiverat etas,   20
Candida, nec macule nevo nubescit oloris
Emula, nec recipit vaccinia mixta ligustris.
  Ebriat aspectus, animum cibat; omne tuentis
Delicium facies et predo, cupidinis hamo
Piscatura viros; hec Nestoris esse timori   25
Iam gelidis annis, hec sollicitasse Catonem
Recia vel laquei vel pulmentaria possent.
  Hic color exultat placituro sedulus ori
Incola flamma rose, quam circumfusa coronant
Lilia, candentes vultus accendit et ignes   30
Temperat et parcit faculis et amicius urit
Blandior extremi fusa nive purpura limbi.
  Hec rosa sub senio nondum brumescit et oris
hic tener in teneris puerisque puellulus annis
Flosculus invitat oculos et cogit amorem   35
Mentibus illabi stupidis, Venerique ministrat
Arma suasque faces, lunatque Cupidinis arcum
Pectoris in vulnus. glacie contracta senecte
Non ibi languet hyemps, illuc inserpere ruga
Non presumit anus, subito circumvaga passu   40
Et faciem longo pede signatura viatrix.
                        —*Archit.* 1.364–85, 426–44.

THE WRETCHED LIFE OF THE SCHOLAR

  At diis paulo minor plebes Phebea secundos
Vix metit eventus, quicquid serat, undique tortis

20. **bysso:** from *byssus, i* = "linen" (Latham 61; LS 256). **etas** = CL *aetas*.
21. **macule** = CL *maculae*. **nevo** = CL *naevo*, from *naevus, i* = "wart," "blemish" (LS 1184). 22. **emula** = CL *aemula*. 25. **Nestoris:** from *Nestor, oris*, the sage and wiley figure in Homer, here metonymic of old age in general. 26. **Catonem:** from *Cato, onis*, the good Stoic sage of Lucan's *De bello civili*, here metonymic of moral chastity and purity. 27. **recia** = CL *retia*. 29. **rose** = CL *rosae*. **circumfusa:** perfect passive participle of *circumfundere*. 36. **Venerique:** from *Venus, eris*. 39. **hyemps** = CL *hiems*.
    After finishing his description of the maiden at the start of book 2, the Arch-Weeper spies Cupid and describes him in some detail, before turning to consider other topics—gluttony, food, Bacchus, drunkenness, moderation, and abstinence—before making his way to Paris. At the opening of book 3, excerpted here, the Arch-Weeper takes up a none-too-pleasant description of the life of the scholar, a life lived by many in the bustling intellectual center that Paris was in the twelfth century. 1. **Phebea** = CL *Phoebea*, from *Phoebeus, a, um*.

Vapulat adversis. gemit Architrenius agmen
Palladis a miseris vix respirare, beatos
5   Pectore philosophos, Fato pulsante, flagello
Asperiore premi, nulla virtute favori
Divitis annecti, studio sudante malorum
Continuare dies, senium prohibentibus annis
Precipitare malis, pubisque urgere senecte
10   Dampna rudimentis, dum vite abrumpit egestas
Gaudia, dum tenuem victum Fortuna ministrat
Ad modicum torpente manu. ruit omnis in illos
Omnibus adversis: vacui furit aspera ventris
Incola longa fames, forme populatur honorem
15   Exhauritque genas; macies pallore remittit,
Quam dederat Natura, nivem, ferrugine texit
Liventes oculos, facula splendoris adustam
Extinguit faciem; marcent excussa genarum
Lilia labrorumque rose, collique pruina
20   Deicitur livore luti; mestissima vultu
Mortis imago sedet; neglecto pectinis usu
Cesaries surgit, confusio crinis in altum
Devia turbat iter, digito non tersa colenti
Pulverulenta riget, secum luctamine crinis
25   Dimicat alterno; non hec discordia paci
Redditur, intortum digito solvente capillum.
     Cedere duriciem scopulis et in obvia flecti
Naturam hiis spero, quibus est immota potentum
Pectoris asperior rupes. non subsidet illis,
30   Quod veri extergunt tenebras rerumque retrusas
Altius effodiunt causas, nec preterit illos
Uncia totius orbis vel, si quid ab orbe
Cedit in immensos tractus, nec sufficit arto
Pectore diffusi clausisse volumina mundi,
35   Quin procul a superis acies admissa nec ullo
Limite fracta volet, surgatque relinquere mundi

---

4. **Palladis:** from *Pallas, adis.*   10. **dampna** = CL *damna.*   **vite** = CL *vitae.*
14. **forme** = CL *formae.*   20. **mestissima** = CL *maestissima.*   22. **cesaries** = CL
caesaries.   26. Subsequent to this description are nearly 300 lines that offer more
detail about the sorry life of scholars—their neediness, their lack of basic necessities,
their study habits, a discourse on the liberal arts—leading up to the following lines,
which describe some of the implications of being a scholar.

Ausa supercilium: nulla hec suffragia Musis
Subsidiique ferunt fomenta, sciencia nullo
Robore flectit opes; sed et hec novisse favorem
Divitis elidit et risu morsa sciendi   40
Gloria lesa iacet, laudisque sciencia dampnum
Ludibriosa dolet, et in aula maius habetur
Ignorasse magis; risu ledente notatur
Grandiloquis fame titulis incognita virtus.

—*Archit.* 3.1–26, 323–40.

THE MOUNT OF AMBITION

Mons surgente iugo Pelleam despicit urbem,
Astra supercilio libans, lunaque minorem
Miratur longe positam decrescere terram.
Sideribus vicinus apex, ut sepe meantem
Ocius offendat, cum cursu est infima, lunam   5
Augis in opposito, cum visu maxima pessum
Vergit in orbe brevi, mediumque aspectibus offert
Quadratura iubar; partem directior omnem
Vix aliqua vergit, facilemque admittere nescit
Arduus ascensum. sola hic latus omne pererrans   10
Ambicio reptat predilexitque colendum
Pro laribus montem, Zephiris ubi succuba Tellus
Veris alumpnat opes passimque intexit amara
Dulcibus: et fruticum nodis armantur olive
Et laurus cristata rubis suspectaque dumis   15
Quercus et horrenti crudescit coniuga rusco
Esculus et rigidis spine vallatur aristis

38. **sciencia** = CL *scientia.* 41. **lesa** = CL *laesa.* 42. **ludibriosa:** from *ludibriosus, a, um* = "mocking," "scornful" (Latham 282, s. v. *ludus—ludibriosus;* LS 1082). 43. **ledente** = CL *laedente.* 44. **fame** = CL *famae.*

After treating the topic of philosophy and philosophers at the conclusion to book 3, the Arch-Weeper turns at the beginning of book 4 to treat the theme of scholarly ambition. 1. **Pelleam** = CL *Pellaeam,* from *Pellaeus, a, um* = "Pellan," here modifying *urbem,* designating Pella, the birthplace of Alexander and a symbol of ambition. 4. **sepe** = CL *saepe.* 6. **augis:** from *aux, augis,* an astronomical term = "apogee" (Latham 39). **in opposito:** with *augis* = the reverse of the apogee (the perigee), the point when the moon is nearest to the earth. 8. **quadratura:** from *quadratura, ae* = "quarter" (Latham 385); the reference is to the moon's brightness based on the phase it is in. 11. **ambicio** = CL *ambitio.* 12. **succuba:** from *succuba, ae* = "concubine" (Latham 462; Blaise/Chirat 790), here in apposition to *Tellus.* 14. **olive** = CL *olivae.* 17. **esculus** = CL *aesculus.* **spine** = CL *spinae.*

Astra comis abies superum concivis inumbrans.
Hic, quecumque virum fit gloria crinibus arbor,
20   Gracia montis habet et, si qua audacius alto
Vertice diis certat; ibi nulla licencia presse
Arboris, ut surgat, montique assurgere nano
Crine mirica timet, steriles ibi verberat auras
Infecunda salix, riguisque libencior alnus
25   Ascendisse vadis, eternaque testis amorum
Populus Oenones, platanusque et, si qua neganti
Natura haut recipit partus ingloria fructum.

—Archit. 4.9–35.

PLATO'S ORATION ON ENVY

"Ecce furor livoris acus maiorque Megera
Invidie, fame cumulum raptura beatis.
Non pudet in mundos maculas iurasse, notatis
Adiecisse notas. Herebum fastidit Erinis
5   Maternamque Stygen, nostras peregrinat in edes
Hospita dente gravis, didicit revocasse favores,
Exacuisse dolos, clausos aperire reatus.
Ipsa scelus fictura nefas, tortura flagello
Pervigili mentes, successibus egra, sinistros
10   Ad casus lugubre canens, lacrimosa secundis,

18. **concivis:** from *concivis, is* = "fellow citizen" (LS 401).   19. **quecumque** = CL *quaecumque.*   21. **licencia** = CL *licentia.*   23. **mirica** = CL *myrica.*   24. **libencior** = CL *libentior.*   25. **eternaque** = CL *aeternaque,* with *testis,* in apposition to *populus.*   26. **Oenones:** from *Oenone, es* = Oenone, a Phrygian nymph once loved, then deserted, by Paris; cf. Ovid, *Her.* 5.25ff.

The remaining verses of book 4 attend further to the details of the geography and physical qualities of the Mount of Ambition, including attention to the sumptuous palace at its summit and the sorts of inhabitants who dwell in it. The fifth book begins with a description of the Hill of Presumption, which introduces longer narratives on various manifestations of presumption, pride, and cupidity, thence into a treatment of Arthurian material, which ends the book. At the beginning of book 6, then, the Arch-Weeper enters Thylos, a paradisial habitat where he receives lectures on various moral topics from important ancient and medieval thinkers. This excerpt is the first half of Plato's discourse on envy.   1. **Megera** = CL *Megaera,* here by metonymy = "fury."   2. **invidie** = CL *invidiae.*   3. **iurasse:** contracted perfect active infinitive of *iurare* = *iuravisse.*   4. **Herebum** = CL *Erebus, i.* **Erinis** = CL *Erinys, yos.*   5. **Stygen:** from *Styx, Stygis.* **edes** = CL *aedes, is.*   6. **revocasse:** contracted perfect active infinitive of *revocare* = *revocavisse.*   9. **egra** = CL *aegra.*

Gavisiva malis, ideo merore serenum
Et risu lacrimans fatum comitatur amaro.
    Livori assistunt Rabies animosa, Tumultus,
Pax armata dolis, suspectum Fedus, amoris
Umbra, latens Odium, gladio Mars igneus, "arma,   15
Arma, viri" Bellona tonans et pronuba belli
Sedicio, primumque ferens Discordia pilum."

—*Archit.* 6.78–94.

Boethius's Oration on the Harshness of Rulers

    "O meritos extrema pati, quos ardua tollit
Ala potestatis, quorum clemencia numquam
Hospita divertit, sed mortis larga tyrannis,
Iustorum risura neces, factura flagello
Quod pietatis erit. ha nulla potencia rebus   5
Oppressis tranquilla venit, non sumit ab illa
Pauper opes vel opem. gravis est flexisse favorem
Inferius, qui summa potest; aciesque laborat
Ardua, pressa videns. raro, qui surgit in aulam,
Respexisse casam placido dignatur ocello.   10
    Spernit hanelantis animi suspiria, surda
Preterit aure preces, lacrimis insultat easque
Ridet habere dolos, clamosaque pectora planctu
Exaudire vetat, gemitusque adversa loquentes
Vix recipit vultu, faciem pallore minantem   15
Horridiore fugit, domitas regnante repellit
Paupertate genas, fluidos merore tumenti
Nauseat ore sinus, senio rumpente solutos."

—*Archit.* 7. 10–27.

---

11. **merore** = CL *maerore*.   13. **Rabies . . . Tumultus:** i.e., Frenzy and Agitation (cf. Wetherbee 3, 149).   14. **Fedus** = CL *Foedus*, i.e., Covenant (cf. Wetherbee 3, 149). 17. **Sedicio** = CL *Seditio*, i.e., Sedition.
    The remainder of book 6 includes discourses by Cato, Diogenes, Socrates, Democritus, Cicero, Pliny, Crates, and Seneca, treating a variety of moral issues. The seventh book commences, after a brief statement of the Arch-Weeper's interest in philosophy, with a speech by Boethius on the severity of those in power, which is excerpted here.
2. **clemencia** = CL *clementia*.   5. **ha:** interjection.   11. **hanelantis** = CL *anhelantis*. 12. **preterit** = CL *praeterit*.   **aure** = CL *aurae*.

Nature's Speech on the Universe

"Omnigene partus homini famulantur, eique
Et domus et nutrix ancillaque, machina mundi,
Omne bonum fecunda parit, maiorque minori
Obsequitur mundus. tibi discors unio rerum
5   Eternum statura cohit, fractoque tumultu
Pax elementa ligat. gaude tibi sidera volvi
Defigique polos, mundique rotatilis aule
Artificem gratare Deum, dominumque ministro
Erexisse domum, cuius molicio summum
10   Actorem redolet. excelsi dextera tantis
Dotibus excoluit opifex opus, omnia posse
Disputat illud eam; nec enim decisa potestas
Est ea, qua numquam lapsurus volvitur orbis
Raptibus eternis, totusque volubilis axem
15   Circuit immotum, paribusque rotatibus actam
Precipitat speram, dum sola immobilis ima
Pondere vergit humus, nullo conamine surgens,
Se nulla levitate rotat, centroque coheret
Impaciens motus, medio pigrescit in axe
20   Infima, si veteres verum cecinere. moderne
At melior, famosa minus, sollercia pubis
Vel nichil est imum vel quelibet infima; mundus
Ne labet, immenso circummordetur inani.
    Terra vicem puncti recipit collata supremo,

The seventh book reports other discourses subsequent to Boethius's, including Xenocrates' lengthy statement on lust, Pythagoras on gluttony, Thales on fear of God, Bias on the importance of the love of God, and Periander on the importance of worshiping God. The first 300 or so verses of book 8 continue in this vein, before the Arch-Weeper finally spies Nature and offers a description of her. He is overjoyed in her presence, especially after she speaks on the attributes of creation over which she holds sway and about which the Arch-Weeper seeks knowledge. Her narrative is excerpted here. 1. **omnigene:** from *omnigena, ae* = "every kind" (cf. Blaise/Chirat 577) here in the genitive singular, dependent on *partus.* 7. **rotatilis:** from *rotatilis, e* = "rotating" (Blaise/Chirat 726). 19. **impaciens** = CL *impatiens.* 20. **moderne** = CL *modernae,* modifying *pubis.* 22. **nichil** = CL *nihil.* **quelibet** = CL *quaelibet.* 23. **circummordetur:** from *circummordere* = "to engulf" (Latham 88).

Unde modum terre visus punctum estimat, unde 25
Fraudari radios positis procul imputat astris."

—*Archit.* 8.324–49.

25. **terre** = CL *terrae.* **estimat** = CL *aestimat.* 26. Book 8 concludes with Nature's comments on the firmament, which includes much astrological detail, a narrative strategy John continues in book 9. At the conclusion of Nature's discourses, the Arch-Weeper clasps her knees and prays assiduously to her. Eventually, Nature insists that the Arch-Weeper take a wife, the maiden Moderation; and the details of their wedding conclude the ninth book and the poem as a whole. The Arch-Weeper thus finds fulfillment of the spirit in the knowledge granted him by Nature, and fulfillment of the flesh through his new bride under the guiding principle of moderation.

WALTER OF CHÂTILLON

The Alexandreis
(*Alexandreis;* c. 1185)

In the twelfth century, in addition to numerous experiments in literary art, there occurred a renewed interest in the Latin works of Roman antiquity. Interest in these works in general terms had never fallen away, to be sure, for the best examples of the Roman genres had formed the backbone of the medieval school curriculum for several centuries. But the bold forays into new literary terrain after the breakup of the Carolingian empire had the effect of diminishing the literary importance of Latin antiquity's best works. They were used, commented on, and memorized as pedagogical tools. But their careful integration into the literary activity of the Latin Middle Ages was less apparent in the centuries after Charlemagne.

By the middle of the twelfth century, however, a wave of secularism announced a renewed willingness to engage antique Roman works on their own terms. Secularism wielded a powerful influence throughout Western culture in the twelfth century, to be sure—in education, church politics, even in the basic ways Christians were now able to view themselves in relation to the cosmos. Literary artists found, therefore, that there were new lessons to be learned from antiquity, and the genres that had fallen from use—or had been transformed—since the fourth century found a fresh relevance.

Not the least of the genres that found yet another incarnation was epic. We have already seen earlier versions of epic, from the cento tradition of Proba (pp. 111–16) to Avitus' versions of the Pentateuch (pp. 143–48) to the *Waltharius* epic (pp. 310–18). But an engagement of Virgilian poetry on its own terms was something fundamentally new to the Latin Middle Ages when Walter of Châtillon produced his poem on Alexander, the *Alexandreis*.

Of Walter's life we know only a few details. The biographical accounts that are preserved report that he was born at Lille around 1135. He studied in France—at Paris and Reims—and became a teacher, though he eventually took up the study of the law at Bologna. Walter obtained an otherwise unspecified position at Reims after his legal studies were concluded, and wrote the *Alexandreis* there. We know that he died in 1204.

Walter was a prolific writer. In addition to his lengthy epic, there are theological tracts (*Tract against the Jews*) and a cohort of lyric poems of various meters, forms, and tones. In all his work, Walter evinces two qualities: an outstanding formal command of CL and a fluency in composing in a classicizing style. That style shows to best advantage in our excerpt from the *Alexandreis*. This poem, for which Walter (so he said) hoped to be remembered, is indeed memorable in several ways. Its Latinity is highly reminiscent of Virgilian hexameters; its vocabulary is thoroughly epical, the prosody of its lines is well crafted and in keeping with CL standards.

The *Alexandreis* is a lengthy work of some 5,464 lines. But its length serves thematic purposes, giving form to the life of a king who held the medieval imagination like few others—and a king, it should be noted, that no antique poet ever took as his topic. Its length also conforms to classical protocols of epic decorum. That decorum speaks ultimately to the esteem in which antiquity came to be held in many quarters of the Latin Middle Ages, as it speaks well of the abilities of Walter and of other poets like him to write a Virgilian epic that could—and still does—compete with Virgil's *Aeneid* for prominence, polish, and literary merit.

The *Alexandreis* has been edited by, among others, F. A. W. Mueldener (Leipzig, 1863) and M. L. Colker (*Galteri de Castellione Alexandreis,* in Thesaurus Mundi: Bibliotheca Scriptorum Latinorum Mediae et Recentioris Aetatis, vol. 17, Padua, 1978), which has an extensive bibliography and introduction. R. Telfryn Pritchard has translated the *Alexandreis* into English for the Mediaeval Sources in Translation series, vol. 29, of the Pontifical Institute of Mediaeval Studies (*Walter of Châtillon, The Alexandreis,* Toronto, 1986), with excellent introduction and notes; as has D. Townsend (*The "Alexandreis" of Walter of Châtillon, A Twelfth Century Epic,* Philadelphia, 1996). See also Raby 2, vol. 2, 79ff.

Colker's text is reprinted with "u" and "v" distinguished.

THE ALEXANDREIS

Iam fragor armorum, iam strages bellica vincit
Clangorem lituum, subtexunt astra sagittae,
Missiliumque frequens obnubilat aera nimbus.
Primus in oppositos pretenta cuspide Persas,

1. **vincit:** in the sense of "surpassed," rather than "conquered." 3. **obnubilat:** from *obnubilare* = "to darken" (Latham 318). 4. **primus:** anticipates and modifies *Macedo* two verses subsequent. **pretenta:** perfect passive participle of *praetendere,* modifying *cuspide* (*cuspis, idis*).

5   Ocius emisso tormenti turbine saxo,
       Torquet equum Macedo qua consertissima regum
       Auro scuta micant, ubi plurima gemma superbis
       Scintillat galeis, qua formidabile visu
       Aurivomis patulas absorbens faucibus auras
10   Igniti Dario prefertur forma draconis.
           Querentique ducem quem primo vulnere dignum
       Obruat obicitur Syriae prefectus Arethas,
       Cuius ab aurata volitans ac pendulus hasta
       Vendicat astra leo, galeam carbunculus urit.
15   Primus Alexandri tremebundo traicit ictu
       Chaldeus clipeum, sed fraxinus asseris artum
       Formidans aditum fracto crepat arida ligno.
       Gnaviter occurrens ferro Pelleus Arethae
       Dissipat umbonem qua barbara bulla diescit
20   Principis in clipeo, nec eo contenta trilicis
       Loricae dissartit opus, cordisque vagatur
       Per latebras animamque bibit letalis harundo.
       Occidit occisus, largoque foramine manans
       Purpurat arua cruor. regem clamore fatetur
25   Altisono vicisse suum primumque tulisse
       Primicias belli, faustum sibi predicat omen
       Greca phalanx letoque ferunt ad sydera plausu.
           Densantur cunei. Clytus et Tholomeus in armis
       Conspicui tanta levitate feruntur in hostes,

5. **emisso . . . saxo:** ablative of comparison with *Ocius*. 6. **Macedo:** from *Macedo, onis* = Alexander. **qua . . . ubi . . . qua:** coordinating adverbs. 8. **formidabile visu:** supine in the ablative expressing a parenthetical comment = "it is formidable to see" (cf. AG 510). 10. **Dario:** from *Darius, i* = the Persian general, king, and enemy of Alexander. **prefertur** = CL *praefertur*, from *praeferre* + dative object, *Dario*. 12. **prefectus** = CL *praefectus*. **Arethas:** Syrian satrap, as Walter explains; throughout declined as a masculine noun of the first declension. 16. **Chaldeus** = CL *Chaldaeus, a, um*, referring to Arethas. 18. **gnaviter** = CL *naviter*. **occurrens:** modifying *Pelleus* + dative object, *Arethae*. **Pelleus** = CL *Pellaeus*, from *Pellaeus, a, um*, lit., "of Pella," the birthplace of Alexander, hence metonymy for Alexander. 19. **diescit:** from *diescere* = "to gleam forth" (Latham 145). 20. **trilicis:** from *trilex, icis*. 24. **fatetur:** from *fateri*, the subject is *Greca phalanx*, three verses subsequent. 26. **predicat** = CL *praedicat*. 27. **Greca** = CL *Graeca*, modifies *phalanx*. **sydera** = CL *sidera*. 28. **Clytus** = CL *Clitus, i* = Clitus, a close friend of Alexander, eventually killed by him. **Tholomeus** = CL *Ptolomeus, i* = Ptolomey, son of Seleucus, who was killed in the battle described here (cf. Pritchard 79 and 95, n. 2).

In thauros quantum geminos rapit ira leones 30
Quos stimulat ieiuna fames, causamque furoris
Adiuvat excussae gravis obliquatio caudae.
Hic Tholomeus equo Parthum Dodonta supinat
Timpora transfixum cerebroque fluente gementem.
At conto Clytus Arthofilon evertere temptat, 35
Inque vicem sese feriunt, clipeisque retusa
Utraque dissiluit obtuso lancea ferro.
Quadrupedi quadrupes armoque opponitur armus,
Pectora pectoribus, orbisque retunditur orbe,
Torax torace, gemit obruta casside cassis. 40
Nec mora poblitibus ambo cecidere remissis
Vectores vectique simul, similesque peremptis
Exanimes iacuere diu. sed corpora postquam
Convaluere, prior reparato robore rectum
Inque pedes sese recipit Clytus Arthofiloque 45
Surgere conanti solo furialiter ictu
Demetit ense caput et terrae mandat humandum.
Preditus eloquio bello specieque sinistro
Fuerat in cornu Grecum Mazeus Yollam.
Ultor adest agilis stricto mucrone Phylotas, 50
Et quia Mazeum sonipes submoverat, Ochum
Cominus aggreditur, cuius latus ense bipertit.

—*Alex.* 3.1–52.

"Ad nova tendentes semper discrimina quis nos
Invictos tociens poterit prestare? secunde
Res ita se prebent ut nulli fas sit in uno 55
Semper stare gradu. sed quis spondere deorum

32. **obliquatio:** from *obliquatio, onis* = "a bending," "a winding" (LS 1236). 33. **Parthum Dodonta:** i.e., the "Parthian Dodontes"; *Parthum* is from *Parthus, a, um; Dodonta* is masculine, singular, accusative (cf. Pritchard 79). 34. **timpora** = CL *tempora*, used of the anatomy here. 35. **Arthofilon:** i.e., Ardophilus (cf. Pritchard 79). 40. **torax** = CL *thorax.* **torace** = CL *thorace.* **obruta:** perfect passive participle of *obruere.* 41. **poblitibus** = CL *poplitibus*, from *poples, poplitis.* 49. **Mazeus:** i.e., Mazaeus. **Yollam:** i.e., Iollas, modified by *Grecum*; CL has *Iolla, ae*, though not with reference to this figure. 50. **Phylotas:** i.e., Philotas, here in nominative singular masculine, modified by *agilis*, with *ultor* in apposition (cf. Pritchard 80). 51. **Ochum:** i.e., Ochus, here in the accusative singular masculine (cf. Pritchard 80). 53. Craterus is speaking to Alexander in the following lines. 54. **tociens** = CL *totiens.* **prestare** = CL *praestare.* 55. **prebent** = CL *praebent.*

Audeat hoc, Macedum diuturnum te fore sydus?
Quis te precipitem per mundi lubrica possit
Incolomem servare diu? cur te manifestis
60   Casibus obicis ut capias ignobile castrum?
Cum labor et merces equa sibi lance coherent
Et causis paribus respondent premia dampnis,
Dulcior esse solet fructus maiorque secundis
Rebus et adversis maius solamen haberi.
65   Esto tibi deinceps et nobis partior in te.
Obice nos cuivis portento. ignobile bellum,
Degeneres pugnas, obscura pericula vita.
Gloria quantalibet vili sordescit in hoste.
Indignum satis est ut consumatur in illis
70   Gloria vel virtus ubi multo parta labore
Ostendi nequeat." eadem Tholomeus et omnis
Concio cum lacrimis confusa voce perorat.

—*Alex.* 9.525–44.

57. **Macedum** = CL *Macetum*, genitive plural of *Macetae* = Macedonians (LS 1092, s. v. *Macetae*). **fore:** future active infinitive of *esse* = "to be about to be," here in an infinitive clause governed by *audeat.* **sydus** = CL *sidus.* 59. **incolomem** = CL *incolumem.* 61. **coherent** = CL *cohaerent.* 62. **premia** = CL *praemia.* **dampnis** = CL *damnis.* 72. **concio** = CL *contio.*

WALTER MAP

The Courtiers' Trifles
(*De nugis curialium;* c. 1190)

Walter Map was for many centuries famous as a poet of goliardic verse of a kind found in the *Carmina Burana* (see pp. 586–99) and in the collections of the Archpoet and Hugh Primas (see pp. 566–71); and for just as long he was equally famous as the author of a Latin version of the Arthur legend. There was only slight interest—in his day or down to our own—in his lengthy and important collection of short stories, the *De nugis curialium,* a prose amalgam of genres, traditions, and literary invention, incontrovertibly from Walter's hand. But now we know that most of the poems attributed to him are not of his own confection, and that the anonymous "translator" of the early twelfth century *Queste del saint Graal* had not—as he said he had in his preface—brought his story over from a Latin original written by Walter Map.

The *De nugis curialium* can hardly be less interesting than the poetry that has circulated for centuries under Walter Map's name, or, if he had written one, his version of the Arthur legend. In essence a collection of short stories written in strategically shifting prose styles (with occasional forays into poetic quotation (cf. 1.15 [Hildebert of Lavardin], 24, or 25 [Virgil]), the *De nugis* plays on the connotations of *nugae* in Latin ("trash," "junk," "baloney") for purposes of inclusion of material—for anything goes. But it relies on a host of compositional strategies that play to best advantage the long development of Latin as a literary language. Thus one finds a panoply of materials in the *De nugis* connected in ways one had not expected. The general topic is current events, gossip, the best reminiscences of this insider to power politics. But Walter never remains fixed on the contemporary scene. Instead, one finds all manner of variously crafted material: dialogues beholden to dramatic conventions, narratives written in the best traditions of medieval historical prose, flights of imaginative fancy written in a poetic style, engagement with literary, social, political, and religious traditions in a wide array of venues, embellishments of every sort, and, of course, as in the excerpts, more direct assessments of contemporary institutions and figures.

Of particular interest is Walter's engagement of literary convention, which often ends in parody. He ties in, for example, to the tradition of heroic prose expressed in Medieval Latin and, by Walter's day, in the vernaculars as well, by relating the story of Gado and Offa (2.17), but he also parodies Geoffrey of Monmouth in his presentation, making Gado and Offa sound like Geoffrey in the ways they, like he, relate national pedigree to genealogical, geographical, and personal detail (cf. above, pp. 514–20). Equally engaging in a more directly comical way is the lengthy 4.3, which appropriates many antique Latin sources—Cicero, Quintilian, Horace, Ovid, among others—to create an advice piece on marriage. Walter also engages the traditions of courtly romance and in so doing sheds light on the ways in which this genre developed. He works, again, in the antique sources, mostly Ovid and Terence, for the plot of the story of Sadius and Galo but shows that romance (even in the form he gives it, which is not entirely traditional) was not only a creation of Christian, Islamic, or Provençal influences (cf. C. Brooke, *The Twelfth Century Renaissance*, Norwich, 1969, pp. 170–74).

Walter Map was born around 1135, on the English–Welsh border. He was well educated and came from an important family, as the worlds recorded in the *De nugis* confirm, including as they do kings, nobles, churchmen, and the details of twelfth-century power and influence. He was particularly close to Henry II, the powerful king of England, husband of Eleanor of Aquitaine, and father of Richard the Lionhearted and John. Walter studied at Paris and seems to have lived there in the 1150s and 1160s. He was especially an intimate of Henry II from 1170 until the king's death in 1189, at which time he became a canon and then chancellor of Lincoln. In 1197 he became archdeacon of Oxford, a post he held until his death in 1209 or 1210.

The *De nugis curialium* has been edited by M. R. James (*Walter Map, De nugis curialium,* Oxford, 1914), who has also produced a translation into English (*Walter Map's De nugis curialium,* vol. 9 in the Record Series of the Honourable Society of Cymmrodorion, London, 1923). Both have been brought together and revised by C. N. L. Brooke and R. A. B. Mynors (*Walter Map, De Nugis Curialium, Courtiers' Trifles,* in Oxford Medieval Texts, Oxford, 1983), a bilingual edition of facing Latin and English with excellent introduction, notes, and appendixes.

The text of James, Brooke, and Mynors is reprinted here with "u" and "v" distinguished.

A Faithful Knight Templar

Circa tempus idem, clericus quidam a Sarracenis sagittabatur ut negaret. Quidam autem qui negaverat astans improperabat ei quod stulte crederet, et ad singulos ictus aiebat "Estne bonum?" Ille nichil contra. Cumque videret eius constanciam, uno sibi caput amputavit ictu, dicens "Estne bonum?" Caput autem resectum tamen proprio ore loquens intulit 5
"Nunc bonum est."

Hec et his similia primitivis contigerunt Templaribus, dum Dei caritas et mundi vilitas inerat. Ut autem caritas viluit et invaluit opulencia, prorsus alias audivimus, quas et subiciemus, fabulas; at et prius eorum primi a paupertate motus audiantur. 10

—*De Nug. Cur.* 1.19.

Royal Ways and Royal Sayings

Contigit ut cum rege moram facerem aliquamdiu Parisius, mecumque tractaret de regum diviciis inter sermones alios, dixitque: "Sicut diverse sunt regum opes, ita multis distincte sunt varietatibus. In lapidibus preciosis, leonibus et pardis et elephantis, divicie regis Indorum; in auro pannisque sericis imperator Bizancius et rex Siculus gloriantur; sed homines 5

1. **Sarracenis:** the better spelling is *Saracenis*, from *Saraceni, orum* = Saracens (Sleumer 696). **sagittabatur:** from *sagittare*, ML transitive form = "to shoot with a bow"; ML intransitive form, used here = "to riddle with arrows" (Niermeyer 929). **negaret:** i.e., "so that he would deny his faith," with the assumption that he would take up the faith of Islam. 2. **improperabat:** from *improperare* = "to reproach" (Niermeyer 516), with *ei* the indirect object and the *quod* clause the direct object. 3. **estne bonum?:** lit., "is it good," i.e., "do you like it?" **nichil** = CL *nihil*. **contra:** i.e., the Christian said nothing (*nihil*) against (*contra*) the faith. 4. **constanciam** = CL *constantiam.* 7. **hec** = CL *haec.* **Templaribus:** from *Templaris, aris* = Knights Templar (Latham 478, s. v. *templum—templaris*); the Knights Templar were one of several military-religious orders designed to protect the Crusader states established in the Holy Land. The Templars were established c. 1115 by Hugh de Payens, eventually earning the praise of none other than Bernard of Clairvaux (in the *De Laude Novae Militiae*), who wrote a monastic rule for them. Their energies were specifically leveled, as this passage suggests, against Islam. 8. **inerat:** from *inesse*, intransitive = "to be present"; the subjects are *vilitas* and *caritas.* **viluit:** from *vileo* = "to be held cheap" (Latham 512, s. v. *vilitudo—vileo*). **opulencia** = CL *opulentia.*

1. **rege:** i.e., Louis VII, King of France (d. 1180). **moram:** the year is probably 1178. **cum . . . facerem:** *cum* temporal + subjunctive. **Parisius:** an indeclinable form of *Parisii, orum* = Paris (Sleumer 582), here in the locative case. 2. **diverse** = CL *diversae.* 4. **divicie** = CL *divitiae.* 5. **sericis:** from *sericus, a, um*, in the plural = "silks." **Bizancius:** the better spelling is *Byzantius*, from *Byzantius, ia, ium* = Byzantine (Latham 61). **Siculus:** from *Siculus, a, um* = Sicilian (Sleumer 723, s. v. *Sicilia*).

non habent qui sciant aliud quam loqui; rebus enim bellicis inepti sunt. Imperator Romanus, quem dicunt Alemannorum, homines habet armis aptos et equos bellicos, non aurum, non sericum, non aliam opulenciam. Karolus enim magnus, cum terram illam a Sarracenis conquisisset, omnia
5   preter municiones et castella pro Christo dedit archiepiscopis et episcopis, quos per civitates conversas instituit. Dominus autem tuus, rex Anglie, cui nichil deest, homines, equos, aurum et sericum, gemmas, fructus, feras et omnia possidet. Nos in Francia nichil habemus nisi panem et vinum et gaudium." Hoc verbum notavi, quia comiter et vere dictum.
10   Circiter illud tempus, cum ad concilium Rome sub Alexandro papa tercio celebrandum precepto domini regis Anglie festinarem, suscepit me hospicio comes Campanie, Henricus filius Teobaldi, omnium largissimus, ita ut multis prodigus videretur, omni enim petenti tribuebat; et inter colloquendum laudabat Reginaldum de Muzun, nepotem suum, in omnibus
15   excepto quod supra modum largus erat. Ego vero sciens ipsum comitem tuam largum ut prodigus videretur, subridens quesivi si sciret ipse terminos largitatis. Respondit: "Ubi deficit quod dari potest, ibi terminus est; non enim est largitatis turpiter querere quod dari possit." Michi certe videtur hoc facete dictum; nam si male queris ut des, avarus es ut sis
20   largus.
    Huius predicti Lodovici patrisque sui multa fuit in factis sapiencia,

---

2. **Imperator Romanus:** i.e., the Holy Roman Emperor. **Alemannorum:** from *Alemanni, orum* = Germans (Latham 13). 4. **Karolus:** i.e., Charlemagne. **enim:** in this position, *enim* suggests sarcasm, i.e., that Charlemagne gave everything away, so that Charlemagne's successor, the Holy Roman Emperor, is now poor (cf. James 450, n. 2). 5. **preter** = CL *praeter*. **municiones** = CL *munitiones*. **archiepiscopis:** from *archiepiscopus, i* = "archbishop" (Sleumer 123). **episcopis:** from *episcopus, i* = "bishop" (Sleumer 306). 6. **Anglie:** the better spelling is *Angliae*, from *Anglia, ae* = England (Sleumer 110). 10. **circiter illud tempus:** in ML, *circiter* + accusative is common = "around that time." **concilium:** i.e., the Third Lateran Council of 1179. **Rome** = CL *Romae*. **Alexandro:** from *Alexandrum, i* = Alexander (Sleumer 95 ff.); with *papa* (*papa, ae*, cf. Latham 331) *tercio* = Pope Alexander III. 11. **precepto** = CL *praecepto*. 12. **hospicio** = CL *hospitio*. **Campanie:** the better spelling is *Campaniae*, from *Campania, ae* = Champagne (Sleumer 183–84). **Henricus:** from *Henricus, i* = Henry (Sleumer 379ff.), with *comes Campanie* = Henry I, count of Champagne, sometimes called Henry the Liberal (d. 1181). **Teobaldi:** from *Teobaldus, i* = Theobald IV, count of Blois and Champagne (cf. James 451, n. 4). 14. **Reginaldum de Muzun:** i.e., Reginald de Mouzon, the son of Reginald II, count of Bar (cf. James 452, n. 1). 16. **quesivi** = CL *quaesivi*. 19. **queris** = CL *quaeris*. 21. **predicti** = CL *praedicti*. **Lodovici:** from *Lodovicus, i* = Louis; the more common ML spelling is *Ludovicus, i* (Sleumer 483); Walter means here Louis VII. **sapiencia** = CL *sapientia*.

simplicitas in dictis. His tantam Deo reverenciam habebat, ut quociens aliquid emersisset cause, quod ipsum et ecclesiam contingeret, sicut unus canonicorum censura se capituli moderabatur et appellabat a gravamine.

Mos eius erat quod ubi sensisset sompnum obrepere quiesceret ibidem aut prope. Dormientem eum iuxta nemus in umbra, duobus tantum militibus comitatum (nam ceteri venabantur), invenit comes Theobaldus, cuius ipse sororem duxerat, et castigavit ne tam solus dormiret; non enim decebat regem. Ille respondit: "Dormio secure solus, quia nemo michi malum vult." Responsio simplex, pureque consciencie verbum. Quis hoc rex de se presumit alius?

Hic tam benigno favore clericos promovebat, ut ab omnibus Christianismi finibus sub ipso Parisius convenirent, et sub alarum eius umbra tam nutriti quam protecti perduraverunt in scolis in diem hunc.

—*De Nug. Cur. 5.5.*

1. **reverenciam** = CL *reverentiam.* **quociens** = CL *quotiens.* 2. **cause** = CL *causae.* 4. **sompnum** = CL *somnum;* the addition of a parasitic consonant in ML orthography is common. 8. **michi** = CL *mihi.* 9. **pureque consciencie** = CL *puraeque conscientiae.* 11. **Christianismi:** from *Christianismus* = Christendom (Niermeyer 178). 12. **sub ipso:** temporal construction; *ipso* = Louis VII. **Parisius:** here in the dative case. 13. **scolis** = CL *scholis.*

PLATE 30. A folio from a late fourteenth–century manuscript, showing Robert Grosseteste's *Computus*.

PLATE 30

Robert Grosseteste, *Computus*
Latin manuscript on paper, Italy, c. 1390, fol. 86 verso
Boethius, Grosseteste, Fibonacci Manuscript; J. G. Bergart Deposit
John Hay Library, Brown University

The work of scholars such as Roger Bacon (see pp. 662–66) had the effect of revolutionizing the study of mathematics, optics, physics, and what we would call the natural sciences. This revolution in natural knowledge was influenced by the rediscovery of the Greek philosophers, especially Aristotle, by the importation of Arabic scientific texts, and by a new approach to the physical world occasioned by the interface of Christianity with Muslim and Jewish philosophers of the Middle Ages. Robert Grosseteste was a leader in all these areas—he could read Latin, Greek, and Hebrew, digested much of Aristotle's work on physics, and wrote a compendium of scientific knowledge that adumbrated Bacon's emphases on experimentation and the scientific method.

The folio shown here is from a manuscript of Grosseteste's *Computus*, a mathematical treatise written by him in the early thirteenth century. The codex also includes a copy of Boethius's *De Arithmetica*. The two works were copied together for the sake of pedagogical convenience around 1390. They are written on paper, in dark brown ink. Both works are rubricated. The watermark on the paper—a crossbow in a circle—locates the manuscript to Italy. In the nineteenth century a third manuscript of several works of Fibonacci was bound to it, forming a unique compendium of medieval mathematical texts. The Fibonacci manuscript is discussed at plate 31.

MATTHEW PARIS

The Major Chronicle
(*Chronica maiora;* c. 1259)

One of the most durable genres of Medieval Latin literature, historical prose achieved yet another transformation in the thirteenth century, as aesthetic and literary aims began to assert their hegemony in the construction of national histories. No one better exemplifies the aim of remembering the past by giving it a finely rendered shape than Matthew Paris. Matthew aimed to record the past in his *Chronica maiora,* but in such a way that "what the ear hears the eyes may see." In his history, therefore, he attempts a balance between visual and textual material. It is a balance adumbrated by Hildegard in her illuminated works. But, in a larger sense, it is a balance that the Latin Middle Ages had accomplished hundreds of times before—in every devotional or psalter with a finely illuminated capital, in every commissioned manuscript with finely formed lettering, in any work adorned with the rich visual depictions that are so important a part of medieval text production. The systematic adjoining of illustration and text in the later Middle Ages, in works by important figures such as Hildegard and Matthew Paris, seems as much a natural development of the medieval literary scene as a novelty of individual confection. Matthew Paris's art work, therefore, reminds us that the literary culture of the Latin Middle Ages was as much a visual as a verbal construct.

Yet it is the quality of Matthew's words that place him on a par with his English counterparts—Bede, William of Malmesbury, Geoffrey of Monmouth. Like William and Geoffrey, Matthew lived a life involved in worldly affairs, for his historical works are peppered with the wit, sarcasm, and slyness of someone who, although a monk, was hardly a naive recluse. Like Bede, however, Matthew was a Benedictine monk who spent almost all his productive life at an important abbey, pursuing the life of the mind. St. Albans in Matthew's day had for some time been reaping the rewards of its illustrious pedigree. The abbey was old and large enough to have had for several centuries its own historian on the grounds—a post that Roger Wendover held before Matthew Paris himself. In the late twelfth century, moreover, St. Albans enlarged its already well-known scriptorium and began producing manuscripts at an even greater rate (behind it were such illustrious productions as the psalter for Christina of Markyate, brought out in the early twelfth century). St. Albans was in Matthew's time, then, an intellectually exciting place to be, given its large population, but it remained an important foundation for the production and dissemination of manuscripts.

This excitement is in evidence in Matthew's vast output. His greatest and largest work, excerpted here, is the *Chronica maiora,* a history of the world written in annalistic fashion, which is a revision of the *Flores historiarum* of Roger Wendover, Matthew's predecessor as historian of St. Albans, who himself had taken over the earlier annalistic work of John de Cella. Matthew's portion of the work covers only twenty-four years, running from 1235 (when Wendover left off) to 1259, the year of his death. Yet this part of the Chronicle accounts for over half the work's content.

Akin to his English predecessors in many ways, Matthew Paris is unlike Bede, Geoffrey, or William in that he worked from a foundation of annalistic history, which originated in monastic establishments in the chronological tables and calendars used to order the liturgical year. From the jumble of notes in the margins of such documents arose the earlier versions of Matthew's work which he inherited. He bettered that older tradition of historical accounting, however, by relying (as his English predecessors had, too) on documentary evidence. Matthew outdid all previous historians in this regard, however, and amassed so much material that he was forced to publish it in a separate volume, the *Liber additamentorum.* Then, too, the illustrations appealed, as Matthew Paris himself said, to two senses, both sight and sound. The "sound" accompanying the illustrations is, as the excerpts attest, anything but boringly annalistic. Matthew held firm views about the contemporary scene he chronicled, and he fashioned a Latin style to press home his points, which normally attended to the evils of the political world, especially where kings were concerned. His narratives are effective propaganda in his presentation of a corrupt world in need of the church and its mission, because he relies on short clauses, a consistent vocabulary, and much reporting of direct speech. He is not as novel as Geoffrey of Monmouth, who managed to merge history, romance, magic, prophecy, and national aspiration into one grand and workable collage. But Matthew Paris does take the raw data of history—facts, names, anecdote, and, often enough, seemingly unimportant events—and fashion them to a specific narrative point. He is not, in this regard, an annalist in spirit, even if the edifice of his history is, in the end, annalistic.

Matthew Paris's other works include the *Historia Anglorum,* an abridgment of the *Chronica maiora* for the years 1066–1253; the *Abbreviatio chronicorum Angliae* and the *Flores historiarum* (not to be confused with Roger Wendover's work of the same name), both of these works abridgments of various parts of the *Chronica maiora;* the *Gesta Abbatum,* on the lives of St. Albans's abbots; and a history of the origins of St. Albans.

The *Chronica maiora, Flores historiarum,* and *Liber additamentorum* have been edited by H. R. Luard (*Chronica Maiora,* 7 vols. Rolls Series, London, 1872–84; *Flores Historiarum,* 3 vols., Rolls Series, London, 1890; *Liber Additamentorum,* vol. 6 in the *Chronica Maiora,* Rolls Series, London 1882). The *Gesta Abbatum* has been edited by H. T. Riley (*Gesta Abbatum,* vol. 1, Rolls Series, 1867); the *Historia Anglorum* and *Abbreviatio chronicorum Angliae* by F. Madden (*Historia Anglorum,* 3 vols., Rolls Series, 1866–69; *Abbreviatio chronicorum Angliae,* vol. 3 of the *Historia Anglorum,* Rolls Series, London, 1869). The standard English translation of the *Chronicle* is by J. A. Giles (*Chronica Maiora: Matthew Paris's English History,* 3 vols., London, 1852–54). S. Lewis has written compellingly on the relationship of the art to the text of Matthew Paris (*The Art of Matthew Paris in the Chronica Majora,* Berkeley, 1987).

Luard's text, pp. 481–85, 706, is followed with "i" printed for "j," and some minor formatting changes.

A RIOT AT OXFORD

Tunc vero temporis dominus legatus cum Oxoniam adventasset, et honore summo, prout decuit, reciperetur, hospitatus est in domo canonicorum, scilicet abbatia de Oseneie. Clerici vero scholares eidem xenium

---

1. **tunc . . . temporis:** ML adverbial phrase = "at that time" (Latham 497). **dominus legatus:** from *legatus, i* = "papal legate" (*legatus* can designate several kinds of political positions, see Niermeyer 594–95). The phrase here designates Otto, who had arrived in England in 1238 to oversee the affairs of the Church during the reign of Henry III. The outcome of his arrival in Oxford constitutes the details of this and the subsequent passage. **Oxoniam:** from *Oxonia, ae* = Oxford (Sleumer 576); here in accusative of place to which without a preposition, as is common in ML (Blaise 75). **cum . . . adventasset:** *cum* temporal + subjunctive; *adventasset* is the syncopated pluperfect active subjunctive, third person singular, of *adventare* = *adventavisset.* 2. **canonicorum:** from *canonicus, i* = "canon" (Sleumer 185). 3. **abbatia:** this word has several dozen meanings in ML, from the concrete to the abstract; here it is used by Matthew concretely to designate the abbey of Oseney (on the various meanings see Niermeyer 1–3). **de Oseneie:** i.e., Oseney.

honorabile in poculentis et esculentis transmiserunt ante prandii tempus. Et post prandium, ut eum salutarent et reverenter visitarent, ad hospitium suum venerunt. Quibus advenientibus, ianitor quidam transalpinus, minus quam deceret aut expediret facetus, et more Romanorum vocem exaltans, et ianuam aliquantulum patefactam tenens, ait, "Quid quaeritis?" 5
Quibus clerici, "Dominum legatum, ut eum salutemus." Credebant enim confidenter, ut essent honorem pro honore recepturi. Sed ianitor, convitiando loquens, in superbia et abusione introitum omnibus procaciter denegavit. Quod videntes clerici, impetuose irruentes intrarunt; quos volentes Romani reprimere, pugnis et virgis caedebant; et dum obiurgantes 10
ictus et convitia geminarent, accidit quod quidam pauper capellanus Hyberniensis ad ostium coquinae staret, et ut quippiam boni pro Deo acciperet, instanter, more pauperis et famelici, postulaverat. Quem cum magister coquorum legati (frater legati erat ille, et ne procuraretur aliquid venenosum, quod nimis timebat legatus, ipsum ipsi officio praefecerat, 15
quasi hominum specialissimo) audivit, nec exaudivit, iratus in pauperem, proiecit ei scilicet in faciem aquam ferventem, haustam de lebete ubi carnes pingues coquebantur. Ad hanc iniuriam exclamavit quidam clericus de confinio Walliae oriundus, "Proh pudor! ut quid haec sustinemus?" Et arcum, quem portavit, tetendit, (dum enim tumultus accreverat 20
excitatus, clericorum aliqui arma, quae ad manus venerunt, arripuerant,) et ipse missa sagitta corpus coci, quem clerici satirice Nabuzardan, id est, principem coquorum, vocabant, transverberavit. Corruente igitur mortuo, clamor excitatur. Ad quem stupefactus legatus, et nimis perterritus timore qui posset in constantissimum virum cadere, in turrim 25
ecclesiae indutus capa canonicali se recepit, seratis post terga ostiis.

---

1. **poculentis:** in CL the form *poculentus* is an adjective of the first and second declensions (cf. LS 1390); in ML it is a noun, normally in the neuter plural only (Latham 357, s. v. *pocillator—poculenta*) = drinks." 7. **conviciando** = CL *conviciando* from *conviciari,* here in the form of a gerund. 11. **capellanus:** from *capellanus, i* = "chaplain" (Sleumer 186–87). 12. **Hyberniensis:** from *Hyberniensis, is* = "Irish" (Latham 226). **coquinae:** from *coquina, ae* = "kitchen" (Latham 115). 14. **coquorum:** from *coquus, i* = "cooks" (Latham 115). 17. **lebete:** from *lebes, lebetis* = "pot" (Habel/Gröbel 218). 19. **Walliae:** from *Wallia, ae* = Wales (Latham 519, s. v. *Wallensis* for the various forms of this place-name). The phrase *clericus de confinio Walliae oriundus* is a periphrastic way of saying "a Welsh cleric." **ut quid:** i.e., "why." 22. **coci:** from *cocus, i* = "cook," the form is equivalent to *coquus,* used above (cf. Latham 115, s. v. *coquina* for the various forms). **satirice:** adverb = "satirically" (Latham 420). **Nabuzardan:** indeclinable noun = Nabuzardan, one of the associates of Nebuchadnezzar, King of Babylon. 26. **capa:** from *capa, ae* = "hood" (Latham 68). **canonicali:** from *canonicalis, is* = "canonical" (Latham 67, s. v. 2 *canon—canonicalis*). **seratis:** from *seratus, a, um* = "locked" (Latham 434).

Ubi cum noctis opacae conticinium tumultum pugnae diremisset, legatus, vestimentis canonicalibus exutis, equum suum optimum ascendit expeditus, et ducatu eorum qui vada secretiora noverunt, amnem, qui proximus erat, licet cum periculo, transivit, ut ad protectionem alarum
5 regis ocius avolaret. Clerici enim furia invecti legatum etiam in abditis secretorum latebris quaerere non cessabant, clamantes et dicentes: "Ubi est ille usurarius, simonialis, raptor reddituum, et sititor pecuniae, qui, regem pervertens et regnum subvertens, de spoliis nostris ditat alienos?" Insequentium autem adhuc clamores cum fugiens legatus audiret, dixit
10 intra se,
"Cum furor in cursu est, currenti cede furori."
Et patienter omnia tolerans, factus est sicut homo non audiens, et non habens in ore suo redargutiones.
Cum autem, ut praedictum est, amnem vix pertransisset, paucis, pro
15 difficultate transitus, comitantibus, caeteris in abbatia latitantibus, ad regem anhelus et turbidus usque pervenit; et lacrimabiliter, singultibus sermones suos interrumpentibus, rei gestae ordinem, gravem super hoc reponens querimoniam, tam regi quam suis collateralibus explicavit. Cuius querulis sermonibus cum rex attonitus nimis compateretur, misit prop-
20 eranter comitem Waranniae cum armata manu Oxoniam, eos qui latuerant Romanos eripere et scholares arripere. Inter quos captus est truculenter magister Odo legista, et ipse cum aliis triginta vinculis et carceri in castro de Waligeford, quod non multum distat ab Oxonia, ignominiose mancipatus. Legatus vero contrito laqueo liberatus, episcopis convocatis
25 nonnullis, Oxoniam supposuit interdicto, et omnes illi enormi facto consentaneos excommunicavit. Postea in bigis, more latronum, ad arbitrium

---

3. **ducatu:** from *ducatus, us,* the sense here is "guidance," "advice," rather than the more usual connotation of "military leadership." 7. **usurarius:** from *usurarius, ii* = "usurer" (Latham 502, s. v. *usuria—usurarius*). **simonialis:** from *simonialis, is* = "simoniacal," i.e., a practitioner of simony, or the buying and selling of church offices (Latham 440, s. v. *simonia—simonialis*). 11. The quotation comes from Ovid, *Rem. Am.* 119. 15. **caeteris** = CL *ceteris*. **latitantibus:** from *latitare,* predicative here. 18. **collateralibus:** from *collateralis, is* = "companions" (Latham 96). 19. **compateretur:** imperfect subjunctive, third person singular of *compati* = "to commiserate" (Blaise/Chirat 180); construe with *cum* in a temporal construction. 20. **comitem:** *comes, itis* = "count," "earl" (Latham 98). **Waranniae:** i.e., Warenne; in the genitive here, dependent on *comitem.* 22. **legista:** from *legista, ae* = "legist," "lawyer" (Niermeyer 595); Odo is his name. 23. **Waligeford:** i.e., Wallingford. **ignominiose:** adverb = "disgracefully" (Niermeyer 509). 26. **bigis:** in ML the form is *biga, ae* = "cart" (Niermeyer 50).

legati Londonias sunt transvecti, et ibidem carceri et vinculis arctaeque
custodiae redditibus spoliati et anathemate innodati mancipantur.

—*Chron. Mai.* 3 (excerpts).

THE AFTERMATH OF THE RIOT

Legatus vero, qui versus partes Angliae aquilonares tetenderat, flexo
loro, Londonias reversus est. Et vix auso in regali hospitio episcopi Dunelmensis, ubi solito hospitabatur, commorari, significavit rex civitati
Londoniarum, ut eundem legatum diligentibus excubiis cum armata
manu ut pupillam oculi, custodiret maior civitatis cum civium univer-   5
sitate.

Legatus igitur archiepiscopum Eboracensem et omnes episcopos Angliae, auctoritate qua fungebatur, ut Londonias convenirent, districte con-
vocavit, de statu ecclesiae et cleri periclitantis decimo sexto kalendas Iunii
communiter tractaturi. Quo cum die praefixo pervenissent, tractatum est   10
diligenter per episcopos, ut salvaretur status clericalis universitatis, veluti
secundae ecclesiae; quibus et legatus condescendit, salvo tamen honore
ecclesiae Romanae, ne improperando diceretur, ut qui venerat clerum
cum ecclesia reformare, potius deformaret. Tandem suggestum est legato
ab episcopis et universitate cleri, quae ibidem in praesenti fuit, quod cer-   15
taminis discrimen a familia sua sumpsit exordium, et in fine certaminis

---

1. **Londonias:** i.e., London; the common ML form for London is *Londinium* (cf.
Sleumer 479).   2. **redditibus:** from *redditus, us* = "revenues," "incomes" (Latham
396, s. v. *redditio—redditus*).   **anathemate:** from *anathema, atis* = "anathema"
(Sleumer 107).   **innodati:** perfect passive participle of *innodare* = "placed under"; in
EL/ML the phrases *anathemate innodati* or *innodatio anathematis* are common for
"to be excommunicated or anathematized" (cf. Latham 251, s. v. *innodatio*).

1. **aquilonares:** from *aquilonaris, is* = "northern" (Latham 27, s. v. *aquilonalis—
aquilonaris*).   2. **Dunelmensis:** i.e., "of Durham"; the substantive for Durham is
Dunclinum (Sleumer 288).   5. **pupillam** = CL *pupulam*.   **maior:** this word has various forms and meanings, both adjectival and substantive, in ML; here, with *civitatis* =
"mayor" (Latham 286 gives a complete list).   7. **archiepiscopum:** from *archiepiscopus, i* = "archbishop" (Latham 28).   **Eboracensem:** from *Eboracensis, e* = York
(Sleumer 290, s. v. *Eboracum*).   **episcopos:** from *episcopus, i* = "bishop" (Sleumer
306).   **Angliae:** from *Anglia, ae* = England (Sleumer 110).   8. **districte:** adverb =
"rigorously" (Blaise/Chirat 286).   11. **clericalis:** from *clericalis, is* = "clerics,"
"monks" (Niermeyer 190), but with *universitatis* = "the whole body of clerics," i.e.,
all the Oxford scholars.   13. **improperando:** from *improperare* = "to cast reproach"
(Niermeyer 516).   14. **reformare:** as often in ML, the infinitive is used to express
purpose (cf. Blaise 331).

clerus deteriorem calculum reportavit; insuper iam de clero pars magna
ad nutum suum carceri mancipatur, et pars reliqua, mandato suo parens,
parata fuit humiliter subire, in loco ab Oxonia circiter tribus distante dietis; ad petitionem tot et tantorum virorum, ad misericordiam inclinare
5   debere. Tandem elaboratum est, quod hanc faceret legatus misericordiam,
quod, comitantibus episcopis pedes euntibus, scholares omnes ibidem
congregati ab ecclesia Sancti Pauli, quae fere per unum miliare ab hospitio
legati distabat, pedes irent; ita tamen, quod, cum venirent ad hospitium
episcopi Carleolensis, illinc sine capis et mantellis discincti et discalciati,
10   usque ad hospitium legati procederent, humiliter veniam postulantes, misericordiam et veniam consequendo conciliarentur; quod et factum est.
Videns autem dominus legatus hanc humiliationem, recepit eos in gratiam suam, restituens universitatem loco suo ipsius municipii, interdictum
cum sententia misericorditer ac benigne relaxando, literasque eis confi-
15   ciendo, ne illis proinde nota infamiae aliquando procaciter obiceretur.

—*Chron. Mai.* 3 (excerpts).

THE KING SPEAKS HARSHLY TO LEICESTER

Augebat insuper baronum pavorem et sollicitudinem tempus Iulii,
cum suo leone pestifero et rapida canicula, quae latratu letifero temperiem consuevit aeris perturbare. Terrueruntque eos plus omnibus aliis
regis mutabilitas et investigabilis duplicitas, quam in quodam verbo illius
5   terribili perceperunt. Cum enim una dierum extra palatium suum prandere descendisset per navem in Tamisiam a Westmonasterio, obiter aere

---

1. **deteriorem calculum reportavit:** this idiomatic phrase means something like "got
the worst of it." 3. **dietis:** from *dieta, ae* = "day's journey" (Latham 145). 6. **pedes:** adverb = "by foot" (Latham 347). 7. **Pauli:** from *Paulus, i* = Paul (Sleumer
587). **per unum miliare:** *miliare* = "mile" (Latham 299, s. v. *millena—miliare*); with
per unum = "one mile." 9. **Carleolensis:** i.e., "of Carlisle"; modifies *episcopi*.
capis: from *capa, ae* = "cloak" (Latham 68). **mantellis:** from *mantellum, i* = "mantle" (Latham 289). **discalciati:** perfect passive participle of *discalciare* = "shoeless"
(Niermeyer 336). 13. **universitatem:** the term *universitas* in ML designates several
collective bodies, and here = "university" (cf. Niermeyer 1051 on the various meanings). 14. **misericorditer:** adverb = "mercifully" (Habel/Gröbel 243).

    1. **baronum:** from *baro, onis* = "barons" (Niermeyer 85–86). In England, the
barons constituted a large group of important landowners who, with their successes
with King John, were increasingly hostile to the rights claimed by his son, Henry III,
the monarch remembered in this passage. The events it recounts took place in 1258,
making it one of the last narratives recorded by Matthew in the *Chronica maiora*,
since he died in 1259. 4. **investigabilis:** from *investigabilis, is,* "untraceable."
6. **Tamisiam:** i.e., the River Thames; the better form is *Tamesis, is;* the form Matthew
uses must come from *Tamesa, ae* (cf. Sleumer 767). **Westmonasterio:** from *Westmo-*

denigrato, tonitrus inhorruit cum choruscatione et imbrium inundatione.
Rex autem huiusmodi tempestatem plus omnibus formidans, iussit ilico
se poni ad terram. Erat autem navicula ante nobile palatium episcopi Dunelmensis, quod tunc erat hospitium comitis Legrecestriae. Quod cum
sciret comes, laetus occurrit et serenus, salutans eum reverenter, ut decuit;　5
consolansque ait, "Quid est quod timetis? iam tempestas pertransiit." Cui
rex non iocose sed serio respondit, vultuque severo: "Supra modum tonitrum et fulgur formido, sed per caput Dei, plus te quam totius mundi
tonitrum et fulgur contremisco." Cui comes benigne respondit: "Domine
mi, iniustum est et incredibile, ut me amicum vestrum stabilem, et semper　10
vobis et vestris et regno Angliae fidelem, paveatis; sed inimicos vestros,
destructores et falsidicos, timere debetis." Haec autem verba stupenda
suspicabantur omnes inde erupisse, quod scilicet comes Legrecestriae virilius perstitit et ferventius in prosequenda provisione, ut scilicet regem et
omnes adversantes suis astare consiliis cogerent, et eius fratres totum reg-　15
num corrumpentes funditus exterminarent.

—Chron. Mai. 5 (excerpts).

---

nasterium, ii = Westminster (Sleumer 832).   1. **denigrato:** perfect passive participle
from *denigrare* (Latham 138, s. v. *denigratio—denigro*).   **choruscatione** = CL *corus-*
catione = "flashing light" (LS 475; cf. Latham 118); the accretion of aspirates in ML
orthography, as here, is common.   4. **Legrecestriae:** i.e., Leicester; the form derives
from *Legionis castra.* The Earl of Leicester at this time was Simon de Montfort, who
had long supported King Henry III, but who ultimately went over to the barons. He
was killed at the battle of Evesham.   12. **stupenda:** gerundive of *stupere,* modifying
haec . . . verba.   16. **funditus:** adverb.   **exterminarent:** from *exterminare* = "to destroy," "to ruin" (Niermeyer 400).

Saint Bonaventure

Commentary on the Gospel of Luke;
The Life of Saint Francis of Assisi
(*Commentarius in Evangelium Lucae, c. 1255;*
Legenda Maior Sancti Francisci, 1263)

The earnest Latinity of Gregory VII (pp. 437–43) and the descriptive ecclesiology of Bernard of Clairvaux (pp. 554–62) evince two of the more important strains of ML writing—the ecclesiastical prose of the church bureaucracy; and the commentaries, glosses and sermons that arose both in monastic and scholastic settings, especially in the twelfth century. Both forms evolved in discrete social and political contexts, as we have seen; both were practiced by the elites of the church hierarchy; and both forms were at once a cause and an effect of the monastic and ecclesiastical reform movements of the eleventh and twelfth centuries. Left out of this amalgam of politics, reform, and spiritual nourishment, however, were the non-elites, the lay persons who, needing spiritual sustenance no less than did a crusading pope or an enthusiastic monk, often turned in the late twelfth and early thirteenth centuries to heretical movements that were preached directly to them in simple and appealing terms. This tendency has a literary analogue in the profusion in the thirteenth century of a simple Latin style whose main task was to bring uneducated listeners over to a particular side. Perhaps at no time since the days of the earliest Church Fathers, in the second and third centuries, did Latin feel the full pressure of vulgar expressiveness, only now it was vernacular as well as Latinate pressures that were brought to bear.

The movement known as Franciscan Christianity arose in this mingling of popular expressiveness and spiritual longing; and, in direct competition with heretical movements—Waldensianism, Catharism, Joachimism—it preached a simplicity of life, reaching into the whole of Christianity's adherents for support. Francis of Assisi (1182–1226), the founder of the movement that bears his name, was surely thinking of Catharism in his insistence that the material world did matter—hence his concern in his preaching for the unity of all creation, including the lower forms of life, whose existence demonstrated divine order and love. But his general concern for charity, poverty, human love, and fellowship struck a wellspring of feeling in the West. The order that arose from his work spread throughout all of western Europe in Francis's lifetime and initiated a large body of Latin writing in its service, one of the lasting—and final—monuments of Medieval Latinity.

One of the chief leaders of the Franciscans—and of Franciscan spirituality—in the generation after Francis was John of Fidanza, more famously known as Bonaventure (a name supposedly given to him by Francis himself). Bonaventure was born at Balneoregio in 1217 and joined the Franciscan order when he was twenty-two. He was a prodigious intellect and studied under Alexander of Hales at Paris, becoming in 1253 the master of the Franciscan school in Paris and, in 1257, minister-general of the Franciscan order.

In his role as the leader of a large and fractious spiritual movement, Bonaventure applied the rule of moderation. A minority within the Franciscan order, the Spiritualists, preached a severe adherence to the strictest interpretation of Saint Francis's preachings about poverty, chastity, and the simplicity of life. A severe distrust of learning was one of the fundaments of this view. Bonaventure steered a middle path between rejection of learning, on the one hand, and, on the other, acceptance of the equally severe scholasticism of the twelfth and thirteenth centuries, in which theology and divinity were exposed to the blade of rational scrutiny—a methodology perfected by Bonaventure's contemporary, Thomas Aquinas. His moderate stand, the Conventualist view, held the day, though only as long as he lived. His predecessor as minister-general, John of Parma, had been a Spiritualist and verged close to heresy in his avowal of Saint Francis as a harbinger of a new kingdom of the spirit. His resignation brought about the immediate elevation of Bonaventure to the minister-generalship.

Though he was more moderate in his understanding of Francis's ministry, Bonaventure lived in conscious imitation of Christ's life. In particular, Bonaventure emphasized Christ as a figure reflective of both humanity and the individual Christian, hearkening back to earlier days of Christianity—to Augustine's *Confessions*, or Ambrose's *Hymns*. In much of Bonaventure's writing, therefore, one finds a strategic emphasis on the details of Christ's life and its manifold meanings related to contemporary figures and events. In the *Commentary on Luke*, for example, excerpted here, there is an emphasis on the moral perfection of Christ, on the harmony of scriptural teaching, and on the currency of Christ's ancient witness to the modern task of preaching to diverse audiences. Indeed, this more modern task is presumably the reason for which the commentary was written (it was not written, as so many commentaries were, for instruction). In a much more exalted and intensive way, Bonaventure focuses on the figure of Christ and his relationship to Saint Francis in the *Life of Saint Francis,* excerpted below (there is also a second, shorter life of Saint Francis, written for liturgical purposes). Here, the operating principle is love, the hope is for understanding, while the goal remains mystical ascent. In keeping with the aims of Bonaventure's output, one finds a Latinity that is never bombastic or scholastic, though the style of the *Life of Saint Francis* is much simpler than the more didactic lines of the *Commentary on Luke.* At the same time, as the earliest Church Fathers had proven, especially in Jerome's magisterial rendition of the Latin, Greek, and Hebrew versions of the Bible into what became the Vulgate, syntactic simplicity often enough ratified the grand majesties of a shared love of learning and a common desire for Christian community.

The works of Bonaventure have been collectively edited at the Collegio S. Bonaventura (*Doctoris Seraphici S. Bonaventurae Opera Omnia,* 10 vols., Quaracchi, 1882–1902). The *Legenda maior Sancti Francisci* has been separately edited (*Analecta Franciscana,* Quaracchi, 1926–46, vol. 10, pp. 555–652). The *Commentarium in Evangelium Lucae* is in vol. 7, pp. 1–604, of the collected works. A lexicon of Bonaventure's Latinity has been prepared by J. G. Bougerol (*Lexique saint Bonaventure,* Paris, 1969). There are numerous English translations of Bonaventure's work; a useful sampling is by E. Cousins (*Bonaventure: The Soul's Journey to God, The Tree of Life, The Life of St. Francis,* in The Classics of Western Spirituality, Ramsey, N.J., 1978). This work has an excellent introduction and bibliography. T. F. Reist has translated Bonaventure's comments on Luke 18.34–19.42 (*Saint Bonaventure as a Biblical Commentator: A Translation and Analysis of his Commentary on Luke, XVIII, 34–XIX, 42,* Lanham, 1985), which contains a complete introduction, bibliography and helpful comments on the exegetical side of Bonaventure's work. See also Raby 1, 421ff.

The *Legenda maior* is reprinted from the Quaracchi edition without change; the *Evangelium Lucae* from Reist's reprint of the Quaracchi text has *fuit* for *vit* at line 17.

COMMENTARY ON LUKE 19:28

Secundo quantum ad rebellium personam insinuandam subdit: "Et his dictis, praecedebat ascendens Ierosolymam," quasi ex ipso facto ostendat, se dicere praedicta propter Ierosolymitas, qui erant eum negaturi non esse suum regem. Propter quam etiam causam statim consequenter agitur, quomodo ut rex venit in Ierusalem, sedens super asinam. Sed post illam 5 magnam gloriam sustinere debebat contumeliam. Et quia ad illam non ibat compulsus, sed voluntarius, ideo signanter dicitur, quod praecedebat, ut animaret ceteros ad tolerantiam passionum, secundum illud primae Petri secundo: "Christus passus est pro nobis, vobis relinquens exemplum, ut sequamini vestigia eius"; et ad Hebraeos duodecimo: "Cur- 10 ramus ad propositum nobis certamen, aspicientes in auctorem fidei et consummatorem Iesum" etc. Ideo etiam praecedebat, ut formam daret praelatis praecedendi oves, contra ferocitatem lupinam; Ioannis decimo: "Bonus pastor, cum proprias oves emiserit, ante eas vadit, et oves illum sequuntur, quia noverunt vocem eius." In huius figuram dicitur de Iuda 15 primi Machabaeorum quinto, quod, "cum videret populum trepidantem ad transfretandum torrentem, transfretavit primus." Huius nobilis imita-

1. **quantum ad:** ML idiom = "with regard to," "concerning" (Latham 386), governing the accusative. **subdit:** in ML one of the senses of this verb, used by Bonaventure here, is "to continue speaking" (cf. Blaise/Chirat 780, s. v. *subdo* 4, 5). The subject is the verse of the gospel of Luke being analyzed (19.28). 2. **Ierosolymam:** from *Ierosolyma, ae* = Jerusalem (Sleumer 404); this quotation comes directly from Luke 19.28. 3. **dicere praedicta:** infinitive clause with *ostendat; se* is the subject accusative; *praedicta* has the sense of "warnings" here, rather than a more literal meaning of "things already mentioned." **Ierosolymitas:** from *Ierosolymita, ae* = "inhabitants of Jerusalem" (cf. Sleumer 386, s. v. *Hierosolymita*). **non:** lit., "who were about to deny that he was not their king . . .," *non* is an example of pleonastic strengthening with *negaturi*, which reinforces the denial implicit in *negaturi*, i.e., "who were about to deny that he was their king. . . ." 4. **propter quam etiam causam:** i.e., "for this reason. . . ." **agitur:** "it is shown . . . "; the object is the clause introduced by *quomodo*. 8. **primae Petri secundo:** this phrase identifies the location of the passage about to be quoted at 1 Peter 2 = 1 Pet. 2.21. 10. **Hebraeos duodecimo:** i.e., Hebrews 12 = Heb. 12.1–2. *Hebraeos* is from *Hebraeus, a, um* (Sleumer 377). 12. **consummatorem:** from *consummator, oris* = "one who brings to perfect fruition" (on shades of meaning Blaise/Chirat 211); the nouns *auctorem* and *consummatorem* are in apposition to *Iesum*. 13. **praelatis:** from *praelatus, i* = "prelates" (Blaise/Chirat 649, s. v. I *praelatus*). **praecedendi:** modifies *praelatis;* the whole phrase means something like "so that he might give an example (*formam*) to the prelates in order that they might go before the sheep, and oppose the wolfish ferocity." **Ioannis decimo:** i.e., John 10 = John 10.4. *Ioannis* is from *Ioannes, is* (Sleumer 438 ff.). 15. **Iuda:** from *Iuda, ae* = Judas Maccabeus (Sleumer 451). 16. **primi Machabaeorum quinto:** i.e., 1 Maccabees 5 = 1 Macc. 5.43. *Machabaeorum* is from *Machabaeus, i* (Sleumer 488).

tor fuit Paulus, qui, licet sciret, quod multa a Iudaeis deberet pati in Ierusalem, secure ascendit ad subditorum salutem; Actuum vigesimo: "Spiritus sanctus per omnes civitates protestatur mihi, quod vincula et
tribulationes Ierosolymis me manent. Sed non facio animam meam preti-
5   osiorem quam me, dummodo consummem cursum meum et ministerium
verbi, quod accepi." Sic et Christus faciebat; unde licet ad tempus Iudaeam declinasset, quia nondum venerat hora eius; nunc ibat tradere animam suam propter nos in manus inimicorum, secundum illud Ieremiae
duodecimo: "Dedi dilectam animam meam in manus inimicorum eius."
10   Ideo igitur ascendebat Ierusalem, "quia," sicut supra decimo tertio dictum est, "non capit, Prophetam perire extra Ierusalem." —Quare autem
hoc? Ratio supra reddita est, quia hoc exigit excellentia pontificalis, magistralis et regiae dignitatis. Unde Glossa: "Finita parabola, vadit Ierosolymam, ut ostendat, de eiusdem maxime civitatis eventu parabolam fuisse
15   praemissam."

—*Com. Luc.* 2.42.

The Life of Saint Francis

Caritatem ferventem, qua Sponsi amicus Franciscus ardebat, quis enarrare sufficiat? Totus namque quasi quidam carbo ignitus divini amoris
flamma videbatur absorptus. Subito enim ad auditum amoris Domini ex-
citabatur, afficiebatur, inflammabatur, quasi plectro vocis extrinsecae
5   chorda cordis interior tangeretur. Talem pro eleemosynis censum offerre
nobilem prodigalitatem dicebat, et eos qui minus ipsum quam denarios

1. **Iudaeis:** from *Iudaei, orum* = Jews (Sleumer 451).   **Ierusalem:** from *Hierosolyma,*
ae = Jerusalem (Sleumer 404).   2. **subditorum:** from *subditus, i* = "subjects," sometimes in ML with social implications also, i.e., "vassal" (cf. Niermeyer 996).   **Actuum**
vigesimo: i.e., Acts 20 = Acts 20.23–24. *Actuum* is from *Actus, us* (Sleumer 75).
4. **Ierosolymis:** from *Hierosolyma, ae* = Jerusalem (Sleumer 404); here in the locative
case.   6. **Iudaeam:** from *Iudaea, ae* = Judea (Sleumer 451).   8. **Ieremiae duodec-**
imo: i.e., Jeremiah 12 = Jer. 12.7. *Ieremiae* is from *Ieremias, ae* (Sleumer 403).
10. **decimo tertio:** i.e., Luke 13.33.   12. **pontificalis:** from *pontificalis, is* =
"priestly," "episcopal" (cf. Niermeyer 812).   **magistralis:** from *magistralis, is* = "magisterial," "teacherly" (Latham 285, s. v. *magister—magistralis*).   13. **Glossa:** Bonaventure means the *Glossa Ordinaria,* the standard commentary on the Vulgate in the
Latin Middle Ages.   **parabola:** from *parabola, ae* = "parable" (Latham 331).

1. **qua:** the antecedent is *caritatem,* the object of the main clause, *quis enarrare*
sufficiat.   **Sponsi amicus:** this description is in apposition to *Franciscus,* and is a tag
from John 3.29. *Franciscus* is from *Franciscus, i* = Saint Francis (cf. Sleumer 346ff.).
3. **flamma:** ablative of means or specification   5. **eleemosynis:** from *eleemosyna,*
ae = "alms" (Niermeyer 368).   6. **prodigalitatem:** from *prodigalitas, atis* = "prodi-
gality" (Blaise/Chirat 667).

reputarent, esse stultissimos, pro eo quod solius divini amoris impretiabile pretium ad regnum caelorum sufficiat comparandum, et eius qui nos
multum amavit, multum sit amor amandus. —Ut autem ex omnibus exci-
taretur ad amorem divinum, exsultabat in cunctis operibus manuum Domini et per iucunditatis spectacula in vivificam consurgebat rationem et   5
causam. Contuebatur in pulcris pulcherrimum et per impressa rebus vestigia prosequebatur ubique dilectum, de omnibus sibi scalam faciens, per
quam conscenderet ad apprehendendum eum qui est desiderabilis totus.
Inauditae namque devotionis affectu fontalem illam bonitatem in creaturis singulis tamquam in rivulis degustabat, et quasi caelestem concentum   10
perciperet in consonantia virtutum et actuum eis datorum a Deo, ipsas
ad laudem Domini more Prophetae David dulciter hortabatur.

Christus Iesus crucifixus intra suae mentis ubera ut myrrhae fascicu-
lus iugiter morabatur, in quem optabat per excessivi amoris incendium
totaliter transformari. Praerogativa quoque peculiaris devotionis ad ip-   15
sum ab Epiphaniae festo usque ad continuos quadraginta dies, eo scilicet
tempore, quo Christus latuit in deserto, ad solitudinis loca declinans cel-
laque reclusus, quanta poterat arctitudine cibi et potus, ieiuniis, orationibus et laudibus Dei sine intermissione vacabat. Tam fervido quidem in
Christum ferebatur affectu, sed et dilectus illi tam familiarem rependebat   20
amorem, ut videretur ipsi famulo Dei quasi iugem prae oculis ipsius
Salvatoris sentire praesentiam, sicut aliquando sociis familiariter revela-
vit. —Flagrabat erga Sacramentum dominici corporis fervore omnium
medullarum, stupore admirans permaximo illam carissimam dignationem et dignantissimam caritatem. Saepe communicabat et tam devote, ut   25
alios devotos efficeret, dum ad immaculati Agni degustationem suavem,
quasi spiritu ebrius, in mentis ut plurimum rapiebatur excessum.

Matrem Domini Iesu Christi indicibili complectebatur amore, eo
quod Dominum maiestatis fratrem nobis effecerit, et per eam simus misericordiam consecuti. In ipsa post Christum praecipue fidens, eum sui ac   30
suorum advocatam constituit et ad honorem ipsius a festo Apostolorum

---

1. **pro eo quod** = ML *eo quod*, "because" (Latham 373).   **impretiabile:** from *impre-
tiabilis, is* = "inestimable," "priceless" (Niermeyer 515).   6. **pulcris** = CL *pulchris*.
9. **fontalem:** from *fontalis, is* = "baptismal" (Blaise/Chirat 358).   12. **David:** indeclinable noun (Sleumer 259).   14. **excessivi:** from *excessivus, a, um* = "excessive"
(Niermeyer 388, who dates it to the thirteenth century).   16. **Epiphaniae:** from *Epi-
phania, ae* = Epiphany (Sleumer 305); with *festo* = "feast of the Epiphany."   18. **arctitudine:** from *arctitudo, inis* = "narrowness" (Latham 29; cf. Niermeyer 58), here
with *cibi et potus*, having the sense of "lack."   26. **degustationem:** from *degustatio,
onis* = "taste" (Blaise/Chirat 249).   28. **indicibili:** from *indicibilis, is* = "indescrib-
able," "unspeakable" (Niermeyer 525).

Petri et Pauli usque ad festum Assumtionis devotissime ieiunabat. Angel-
icis spiritibus ardentibus igne mirifico ad excedendum in Deum et elec-
torum animas inflammandas inseparabilis erat amoris vinculo copulatus
et ob devotionem ipsorum ab Assumtione Virginis gloriosae quadraginta
5 diebus ieiunans orationi iugiter insistebat. Beato autem Michaeli Archangelo, eo, quod animarum repraesentandarum haberet officium, speciali
erat amore devotior propter fervidum quem habebat zelum ad salutem
omnium salvandorum. Ex recordatione Sanctorum omnium tanquam
lapidum ignitorum in deificum recalescebat incendium, Apostolos omnes,
10 et praecipue Petrum et Paulum, propter fervidam caritatem, quam habuerunt ad Christum, summa devotione complexans; ob quorum reverentiam et amorem Quadragesimae specialis ieiunium Domino dedicabat.
Non habebat aliud Christi pauper nisi duo minuta, corpus scilicet et animam quae posset liberali caritate largiri. Sed haec per amorem Christi
15 sic offerebat continue, ut quasi omni tempore per rigorem ieiunii corpus
et per ardorem desiderii spiritum immolaret, exterius in atrio sacrificans
holocaustum et interius in templo concremans thymiama.

Sic autem eum caritatis excessiva devotio sursum in divina ferebat, ut
eiusdem affectuosa benignitas ad naturae consortes et gratiae dilataret.
20 Quem enim creaturis ceteris germanum pietas cordis effecerat, mirum
non est, si Creatoris insignitis imagine et sanguine redemptis Auctoris
germaniorem Christi caritas faciebat. Non se Christi reputabat amicum,
nisi animas foveret, quas ille redemit. Saluti animarum nihil praeferen-
dum esse dicebat, eo maxime probans, quod Unigenitus Dei pro anim-
25 abus dignatus fuerit in cruce pendere. Hinc sibi in oratione luctamen, in
praedicatione discursus et in exemplis dandis excessus. Unde quoties
austeritas nimia reprehenderetur in ipso, respondebat, se datum aliis in
exemplum. Licet enim innocens eius caro, quae iam se sponte subdebat
spiritui, nullo propter offensas egeret flagello; tamen exempli causa reno-
30 vabat illi poenas et onera, custodiens propter alios vias duras. Dicebat

1. **Petri:** from *Petrus, i* = Peter (cf. Sleumer 600ff.). **Pauli:** from *Paulus, i* = Paul (cf.
Sleumer 587ff.). **Assumtionis:** the better spelling is *Assumptionis*, from *Assumptio,
onis* = Assumption (Sleumer 133). 5. **Michaeli:** from *Michael, elis* = Michael
(Sleumer 519). **Archangelo:** from *Archangelus, i* = Archangel (Sleumer 123).
8. **tanquam** = CL *tamquam.* 9. **deificum:** from *deificus, a, um* = "holy," "divine"
(Niermeyer 315). 13. **minuta:** from *minutum, i* = "coin" (Niermeyer 691); this line
comes from Mark 12.42. 17. **holocaustum:** from *holocaustum, i* = "holocaust"
(Niermeyer 491). **thymiama:** from *thymiama, atis* = "incense" (Blaise/Chirat 817).
19. **affectuosa:** from *affectuosus, a, um* = "agreeable" (Blaise/Chirat 49). 24. **Unigenitus:** from *Unigenitus, i* = "only-begotten" (Latham 501). **animabus:** ablative
plural of *anima.*

enim: "Si linguis hominum loquar et Angelorum, caritatem autem in me ipso non habeam et proximis virtutum exempla non monstrem, parum prosum aliis, mihi nihil."

—*Leg. S. Fran.* 9.1–4.

1. **Angelorum:** from *angelus, i* = "angel" (Sleumer 109); the reference comes from 1 Cor. 13.1–3.

PLATE 31. A folio from a late fourteenth–century manuscript, showing
Leonardo Fibonacci da Pisa's *Liber flos*.

PLATE 31

Leonardo Fibonacci da Pisa, *Liber flos*
Latin manuscript on paper, Italy, c. 1390, fol. 145 verso
Boethius, Grosseteste, Fibonacci Manuscript; J. G. Bergart Deposit
John Hay Library, Brown University

The revolution in scientific thinking and the production of new scientific works, not the least by Roger Bacon, helped to situate much of the knowledge gleaned in the high Middle Ages in a new perspective. Some of that knowledge attended to mathematics and helped in the formulation of Leonardo Fibonacci da Pisa's mathematical output, which included the *Liber flos,* a folio from a copy of which is reproduced here. Fibonacci is considered one of the great mathematicians of the Latin Middle Ages, and his work brought about a mathematical renaissance of sorts in the thirteenth century. The *Liber abbaci,* his most important work, written in 1202, is the first complete and systematic explanation of the Hindu numerals. The *Liber flos,* from which this folio comes, forms chapters 14 and 15 of the *Liber abbaci,* the most advanced chapters of the work.

This manuscript of the *Liber flos* is written in a dark brown ink, in an Italian humanistic cursive. The initials and chapter headings were left blank, for rubrication. The watermark on the paper of the manuscript proves an Italian provenance (Venice). In the nineteenth century this manuscript was bound to a manuscript preserving the *Computus* of Robert Grosseteste and Boethius' *De arithmetica,* forming a unique compendium of medieval mathematical texts (on these other manuscripts, see plate 30).

ROGER BACON

The Greater Work
(*Opus maius;* c. 1267)

When Cicero had championed a Latin purified of its Greek luxuriance in the first century B.C.E., he had in mind to make it difficult for Latin to support philosophical speculation or poetic expressiveness. Horace, Virgil, Ovid, Lucan, and Cicero's enemy, Catullus, did their best to make Latin available for poetry. It would take three centuries and the importation of a new wave of Greek rhetorical principles before Latin could even begin to be used for serious philosophical or, by this time, better to say, theological speculation. Tertullian especially expanded the language, manipulating it in order to say new things through old means, importing terms from Greek, and making possible a serious discussion of Christian theology in a language that had not been deployed in centuries—if at all—for the tasks of abstract discourse. After this point, Latin was made to fit the intellectual needs of succeeding generations with increasing ease.

By the thirteenth century, those needs had become universal in scope, including a large body of philosophical, theological, speculative, and systematic writing on virtually all aspects of human knowledge. The theological arts had experienced an explosion of writing in the twelfth century, and scholasticism, the rise of law, and the changes in educational patterns as cathedral schools gave way to organized "university" faculties each had an effect on the kinds of writings produced in Latin. An increase in the student population, in lay devotion, in popular spirituality, in book production and, generally, in literacy meant that practically any and every genre imaginable was well represented in Latin by the year 1200. In particular, scientific inquiry, spurred on by fruitful exchanges with Islamic intellectuals and Eastern scholars, and by the reintroduction of Greek into the Western mainstream, had the effect of stimulating scientific writing. Robert Grosseteste, for example, wrote commentaries on Aristotle's work on physics and produced a compendium of scientific knowledge that featured prominently experimentation and an emphasis on scientific method, anticipating in this regard his younger contemporary, Roger Bacon.

Roger Bacon was an experimental scientist and shared with Grosseteste an interest in vision, light, and optics. But he was a student of his age and had been raised with the idea that all knowledge was part of an ordered structure reflective of an even higher, divine order. Feeling that much of what interested him was ignored by the university faculties and cathedral schools of his day, Bacon's main thrust for much of his career was organizational, viz., he hoped to revise the educational system he found in place. His work, the *Opus maius,* excerpted here, lays out his plan for such a revision. It may have been written for, but in any case was sent to, Bacon's mentor, Clement IV, in the hope that he might be able to energize the reforms called for in the work. In 1292 a revision of this plan was published, the *Compendium studii theologiae.*

Bacon was born in England around 1215, of lower nobility. At the nascent University of Oxford he studied the seven liberal arts and gained mastery also of Greek, eventually adding Hebrew and Arabic to his linguistic arsenal. He went to Paris, to teach at the University, in 1245, and set about a long career of thinking, writing, and lecturing. His work at Paris was crucial in Bacon's determination to reform the curriculum of education in the West, and this emphasis in his writing became especially acute after concentrated study of Aristotle's works during his Paris years. When he returned to Oxford around 1250, Bacon had already taken up his scientific inquiries in full force and also decided to become a Franciscan (a common choice for thirteenth-century intellectuals, the anti-intellectualism of the Spiritualists notwithstanding). His enthusiasm and, one gathers, his zealous pursuit of his research and his goals for integrating it into the curriculum seem to have gotten him banned from Oxford for the decade beginning around 1255, and for the intervening years Bacon was back in Paris, not returning to Oxford until 1267. But the disputes of the latter half of the thirteenth century—over the notion of monastic poverty, over the relative positions of the Dominican and Franciscan orders, over popular religious movements—had their effect on Bacon. He was sent back to Paris by the Oxford authorities in the 1280s, perhaps owing to an inclination on his part to Joachimism, not to return to Oxford again until the early 1290s, just before his death in 1292.

The Latin of Roger Bacon reflects the innovations in intellectual inquiry of the eleventh and twelfth centuries, including the rise of the scholastic methodology, but also the inculcation of a new style of ecclesiastical prose into the mainstream of Western writing through the advent of the Church's powerful bureaucracy. In the excerpts, for example, the grammar and syntax are clear, the vocabulary typical for the age; there is, on the model of scholastic discourse, quotation of authoritative sources, and a firm logic of presentation. The specific topics treated here—the four causes of error and the importance of language study—were at the center of Bacon's efforts to revivify education in the West and to integrate all of knowledge, especially scientific knowledge, into the mainstream curriculum.

The *Opus maius* has been edited by J. H. Bridges (*The Opus Maius of Roger Bacon*, 2 vols., London, 1897–1900; repr. Frankfurt-am-Main, 1964). Part 7 of the *Opus maius* has been edited separately by E. Massa (*Rogeri Baconis Moralis Philosophia*, Zurich, 1953). R. B. Burke has translated the *Opus maius* into English (*The Opus Maius of Roger Bacon*, 2 vols., Philadelphia, 1928).

Bridges's text is reprinted with "j" changed to "i.".

THE FOUR GROUNDS OF ERROR

Quatuor vero sunt maxima comprehendendae veritatis offendicula, quae omnem quemcumque sapientem impediunt, et vix aliquem permittunt ad verum titulum sapientiae pervenire, videlicet fragilis et indignae auctoritatis exemplum, consuetudinis diuturnitas, vulgi sensus im-
5 periti, et propriae ignorantiae occultatio cum ostentatione sapientiae apparentis. His omnis homo involvitur, omnis status occupatur. Nam quilibet in singulis artibus vitae et studii et omnis negotii tribus pessimis ad eandem conclusionem utitur argumentis, scilicet, hoc exemplificatum est per maiores, hoc consuetum est, hoc vulgatum est; ergo tenendum. Sed
10 oppositum conclusionis longe melius sequitur ex praemissis, sicut per auctoritatem et experientiam et rationem multipliciter probabo.

Si vero haec tria refellantur aliquando magnifica rationis potentia, quartum semper in promptu est et in ore cuiuslibet, ut quilibet suam ignorantiam excuset; et licit nihil dignum sciat, illud tamen magnificet impru-
15 denter, ut sic saltem suae stultitiae infelici solatio veritatem opprimat et elidat. Ex his autem pestibus mortiferis accidunt omnia mala humano generi; nam ignorantur utilissima et maxima et pulcherrima sapientiae documenta, et omnium scientiarum et artium secreta; sed peius est quod homines horum quatuor caligine excaecati non percipiunt suam ignoran-
20 tiam, sed cum omni cautela palliant et defendunt, quatenus remedium non inveniant; et quod pessimum est, cum sint in tenebris errorum densissimis, aestimant se esse in plena luce veritatis; propter quod verissima

1. **offendicula:** from *offendiculum, i* = "hindrances" (Blaise/Chirat 574).   4. **diuturnitas:** from *diuturnitas, atis* = "long period of time" (Blaise/Chirat 288).   8. **exemplificatum est:** from *exemplificare* = "to exemplify" (Latham 177).   15. **solatio** = CL *solacio*.   20. **palliant:** from *palliare* = "to cover," "to hide" (Niermeyer 755).

reputant esse in fine falsitatis, optima nullius valoris, maxima nec pondus
nec pretium obtinere et e contrario falsissima celebrant, pessima laudant,
extollunt vilissima, caecutientes, aliud esse omnem sapientiae fulgorem,
fastidientes quae magna facilitate possunt adipisci. Et propter stultitiae
magnitudinem ponunt summos labores, consumunt tempora multa, mag-   5
nas expensas effundunt in iis, quae nullius utilitatis vel parvae sunt, nec
dignitatis alicuius secundum iudicium sapientis. Et ideo necesse est ut violentia et malitia harum quatuor causarum omnis mali cognoscantur in
principio, et reprobentur, et longe a consideratione sapientiae relegentur.
Nam ubi haec tria dominantur, nulla ratio movet, nullum ius iudicat,   10
nulla lex ligat, fas locum non habet, naturae dictamen perit, facies rerum
mutatur, ordo confunditur, praevalet vitium, virtus extinguitur, falsitas
regnat, veritas exsufflatur. Et ideo nihil magis necessarium est consider-
ationi, quam certa damnatio istorum quatuor per sententias sapientum
electas, quibus non poterit contradici.   15

—*Op. Mai.* 1.1.

THE IMPORTANCE OF LANGUAGE STUDY

Declarato igitur, quod una est sapientia perfecta, quae sacris literis
continetur per ius canonicum et philosophiam, qua mundus habet regi,
nec alia requiritur scientia pro utilitate generis humani, nunc volo descendere ad ea huius sapientiae magnifica, quae maxime valent exponi. Et
sunt quinque, sine quibus nec divina nec humana sciri possunt, quorum   5
certa cognitio reddit nos faciles ad omnia cognoscenda. Et primum est
Grammatica in linguis alienis exposita, ex quibus emanavit sapientia Latinorum. Impossibile enim est, quod Latini perveniant ad ea quae necessaria sunt in divinis et humanis, nisi notitiam habeant aliarum linguarum,
nec perficietur eis sapientia absolute, nec relate ad ecclesiam Dei et reliqua 10
tria praenominata. Quod volo nunc declarare, et primo respectu scientiae
absolutae. Nam totus textus sacer a Graeco et Hebraeo transfusus est, et
philosophia ab his et Arabico deducta est; sed impossibile est quod pro-

---

9. **reprobentur:** from *reprobare* = "to be condemned" (Niermeyer 910).   11. **dictamen:** from *dictamen, inis* = "precept" (Latham 144).   12. **falsitas:** from *falsitas,
atis* = "falsity" (Niermeyer 407).   13. **exsufflatur:** from *exsufflare* = "to blow away"
(Latham 400).

2. **canonicum:** from *canonicus, a, um* = "canon" (Niermeyer 127).   7. **Grammatica:** i.e., Philology.   10. **relate:** adverb = "relatively" (Sleumer 665).   **reliqua
tria:** i.e., Scripture, canon law, and philosophy.   12. **Hebraeo:** from *Hebraeus, i* =
Hebrew (Sleumer 377).   13. **Arabico:** from *Arabicus, a, um* = Arabic (Sleumer 121).

prietas unius linguae servetur in alia. Nam et idiomata eiusdem linguae variantur apud diversos, sicut patet de lingua Gallicana, quae apud Gallicos et Picardos et Normannos et Burgundos multiplici variatur idiomate. Et quod proprie dicitur in idiomate Picardorum horrescit apud
5   Burgundos, immo apud Gallicos viciniores: quanto igitur magis accidet hoc apud linguas diversas? Quapropter, quod bene factum est in una lingua, non est possibile ut transferatur in aliam secundum eius proprietatem quam habuerit in priori.

Unde Hieronymus, in epistola de optimo genere interpretandi, sic di-
10   cit, "Si ad verbum interpretor, absurdum resonat." Quod si cuiquam videatur linguae gratiam interpretatione non mutari, Homerum exprimat in Latinum ad verbum. Si quis autem eundem in sua lingua per se interpretetur, videbit ordinem ridiculosum, et poetam eloquentissimum vix loquentem. Quicunque enim aliquam scientiam ut logicam vel aliam quam-
15   cunque bene sciat, eam, etsi nitatur in linguam convertere maternam, videbit non solum in sententiis sed in verbis deficere. Et ideo nullus Latinus sapientiam sacrae scripturae et philosophiae poterit ut oportet intelligere, nisi intelligat linguas a quibus sunt translatae.

—*Op. Mai.* 3.1.

2. **Gallicana:** from *Gallicanus, a, um* = French (Sleumer 350), modifies *lingua*.   **Gallicos:** from *Gallicus, a, um* = French (Sleumer 350), modifies an understood *populos*.
3. **Picardos:** from *Picardus, a, um* = Picards (Latham 350).   **Normannos:** from *Normanni, orum* = Normans (Sleumer 551).   **Burgundos:** from *Burgundii, orum* = Burgundians (Sleumer 176).   **idiomate:** from *idioma, atis* = "language" (Niermeyer 508).
9. **Hieronymus:** from *Hieronymus, i* = Saint Jerome, the translator of the Vulgate (d. 419).

PLATE 32. A hornbook insert from the fifteenth century, one the oldest in the world.

PLATE 32

Loose Hornbook Insert; Paper, fifteenth century
AMB ms. 1a; Annmary Brown Memorial Collection
John Hay Library, Brown University

In the Middle Ages, learning began in school with the alphabet, set down in an almost formulaic way by the late thirteenth century, as shown here. After a cross (not included here), there came a capital "A" followed by the Latin alphabet in minuscule (as shown here), with alternate forms for "r," "s," and "u" (as here). Therefollowed the abbreviations for *et* and *con* and then the words *est amen* (here just *est*). The *Pater noster* would then be copied out, as here.

This loose insert has 12 ink-ruled lines and margins. There are four lines of letters and abbreviations, followed by 8 lines of the *Pater noster*, which ends abruptly in mid-line, perhaps because of the errors apparent in the line. One can also see here the lettering, written in dark black ink, of the reverse side, where only practice letters are found, bleeding through. The insert is 12.5 cm. × 8.5 cm., with a dark red stain at the left top, perhaps suggesting its later use as a bookmark. This is one of the oldest horn inserts in the world.

INDEX